# AdvancED Flex 3

Shashank Tiwari, Jack Herrington,
Elad Elrom, and Joshua Mostafa

friendsof

DESIGNER TO DESIGNER™

an Apress® company

# AdvancED Flex 3

## Credits

*My efforts on this book are dedicated to my wife, Caren, and sons, Ayaan and Ezra. The credit for everything that I do successfully goes to them.*
*—Shashank Tiwari*

*I would like to dedicate my work on this book to my best friend, Mel Pleasant.*
*—Jack Herrington*

*I would like to dedicate this book to my wife, Jordana, and my baby girl, Romi Scarlett.*
*—Elad Elrom*

# CONTENTS AT A GLANCE

## PART ONE HARNESSING THE POWER OF FLEX 3

## PART TWO INTEGRATING WITH CLIENT- AND SERVER-SIDE TECHNOLOGIES

# CONTENTS

## PART ONE  HARNESSING THE POWER OF FLEX 3

## PART THREE **GAINING REAL ADVANTAGE IN THE NEW WEB**

# FOREWORD

One of Flex's greatest assets is its approachability. A developer new to the platform can quickly get up to speed on the tools and APIs to create functional and visually appealing applications. Components, data, networking, charting, graphics, animation, and much more are available for use even by programmers who are just starting out with Flex.

Much of Flex's power and robustness for novice users comes from its built-in use of its own capabilities. For example, someone starting out may not manually insert animations into his application, but the base Flex components come with some amount of animation built in so that even the simplest of applications demonstrates dynamic behavior, contributing to a rich experience for the application's users.

The Flex framework also provides many powerful features so that developers, when they are ready, can add more and more of these features to their applications. For example, states and transitions offer a rich way to declaratively describe different screens of an application and animate between those states. This is probably not something that beginning programmers would even think to ask for, but when they are ready for states and transitions, they have immediate access to these capabilities, which is far more convenient than if they had to build states and transitions themselves.

In some sense, Flex is like an onion, with each layer complete in and of itself, but which, when pulled back, exposes another deeper layer that the developer can enjoy. Except that an onion smells bad, and Flex certainly doesn't make you cry, nor do you risk slicing your thumb off when programming it. So maybe the simile doesn't work entirely, but hopefully you see what I'm getting at.

With Flex, as with any development platform, developers will grow beyond simple applications to ones of great complexity or with ambitious goals. At this stage, it is useful to know how to attack particular problems in tried-and-true ways, and in ways that are compatible with the architecture of Flex. Of course, we're all engineers and therefore prefer to reinvent things when we can, but there's a limit to what we can do on our own (at least I've heard rumors that such a limit exists). Moreover, isn't it nice to depend on existing solutions for some problems so that we can get to the issues that aren't solved yet, and thus finish our work and get our products out there?

That's what this book is about: providing techniques and code for implementing common features. The book is rife with architectural discussions, design patterns, and canonical approaches that are used by Flex developers to solve real-world problems that they encounter in Flex applications. There are sections on web application solutions, covering topics from database streaming to web service integration to talking to different-language back ends. There are sections on the client interface, exploring custom components, desktop AIR applications, business data visualization, and 3D rendering. There are architectural discussions, ranging from existing and new frameworks to performance tuning to common design patterns. There are sections on creating modern consumer web applications like mashups, Web 2.0 applications, and streaming video and audio, and talking to web services from providers like Amazon and YouTube. And throughout the book, there is a lot of Flex code to show exactly how to implement various features.

With lots of demo code to illustrate the points, this book helps Flex developers who are familiar with the language and APIs understand how to apply Flex in various different situations that they will encounter. And it serves as a handy book-sized reference when you hit these problems in your real-world projects.

So OK, Flex may not be like an onion after all. But you have to admit it does have a-peel.

Chet Haase
*Senior Computer Scientist and Graphics Geek*
*Flex SDK team at Adobe Systems*

# ABOUT THE AUTHORS

 **Shashank Tiwari** is chief technologist at Saven Technologies (http://www.saventech.com), a technology-driven business solutions company headquartered in Chicago, Illinois. As an experienced software developer, enterprise architect, and computational mathematician, he is adept in a multitude of technologies and a host of programming languages. He is an expert group member on a number of Java Community Process (JCP) specifications and is an Adobe Flex Champion. Currently, he passionately builds rich high-performance applications and advises many on RIA and SOA adoption. Many of his clients are banking, money management, and financial service companies for which he has helped build robust, quantitative, data-intensive, highly interactive, and scalable high-performance applications. He writes regularly in many technical magazines, presents in seminars, and mentors developers and architects. He is an ardent supporter of and contributor to open source software. He lives with his wife and two sons in New York. More information about Shashank can be accessed at his web site (http://www.shanky.org).

**Jack Herrington** is an engineer, author, and presenter who lives and works in the Bay Area. His mission is to expose his fellow engineers to new technologies. That covers a broad spectrum: from demonstrating programs that write other programs in *Code Generation in Action* (Manning, 2003); providing techniques for building customer-centered web sites in *PHP Hacks* (O'Reilly, 2005) and *Getting Started with Flex 3* (Adobe Developer Library, 2008); all the way to writing a how-to on audio blogging called *Podcasting Hacks* (O'Reilly, 2005)—all of which make great holiday gifts and are available online and at your local bookstore. Jack also writes articles for O'Reilly, DevX, and IBM developerWorks.

Jack lives with his wife, daughter, and two adopted dogs. When he is not writing software, books, or articles, you can find him on his bike, running, or in the pool training for triathlons. You can keep up with Jack's work and his writing at http://jackherrington.com.

 **Elad Elrom** is the CEO of Elrom LLC, a Rich Internet Application firm. He has been managing and developing Internet-based applications since 2000 and has consulted for sophisticated clients including MTV Networks, Vitamin Water, Weight Watchers, Davidoff, and many more. He has been developing Flash applications since the release of Flash 5 and has been developing Flex applications since the release of Flex 2. His deep understanding of the full project cycle, as well as development in numerous programming languages, contributes to his understanding of the "big picture." In the past, Elad served in the Israeli Navy Defense Forces as part of an elite group of engineers assisting the Israeli Navy Seals.

Visit Elad's blog at http://www.elromdesign.com/blog/.

**Joshua Mostafa** grew up in the UK. Now he lives in the Blue Mountains region of Australia with his beautiful wife and their various offspring and rodents. He codes for a living, writes stories and essays on the train ride to Sydney, and sometimes tries to make music.

Josh rambles, rants, and raves about technology and miscellanea on his blog at http://joshua.almirun.com/.

# ABOUT THE TECHNICAL REVIEWER

 **Peter Elst** is an Adobe Community Expert, a certified instructor, and an active member in Adobe User Group Belgium.

As a freelance Flash platform consultant and respected member of the online community, Peter has spoken at various international industry events and published his work in leading journals. Most recently Peter was lead author of *Object-Oriented ActionScript 3.0* (friends of ED, 2007). Visit his web site: http://www.peterelst.com.

# ABOUT THE COVER IMAGE DESIGNER

**Bruce Tang** is a freelance web designer, visual programmer, and author from Hong Kong. His main creative interest is generating stunning visual effects using Flash or Processing.

Bruce has been an avid Flash user since Flash 4, when he began using Flash to create games, web sites, and other multimedia content. After several years of ActionScripting, he found himself increasingly drawn toward visual programming and computational art. He likes to integrate math and physics into his work, simulating 3D and other real-life experiences onscreen. His first Flash book was published in October 2005. Bruce's folio, featuring Flash and Processing pieces, can be found at http://www.betaruce.com, and his blog at http://www.betaruce.com/blog.

The cover image uses a high-resolution Henon phase diagram generated by Bruce with Processing, which he feels is an ideal tool for such experiments. Henon is a strange attractor created by iterating through some equations to calculate the coordinates of millions of points. The points are then plotted with an assigned color.

$$x_{n+1} = x_n \cos(a) - (y_n - x_n^p) \sin(a)$$

$$y_{n+1} = x_n \sin(a) + (y_n - x_n^p) \cos(a)$$

# ACKNOWLEDGMENTS

This book represents the efforts of many people, and I sincerely thank them for their contribution.

Thanks to Elad, Jack, and Joshua for contributing their expertise, time, and sweat as coauthor(s) of this book.

Many thanks to the entire team at friends of ED (an Apress company). You made this book possible! Clay Andres took this book from a proposal to a real project. Peter Elst, Tom Welsh, and Ami Knox diligently and patiently reviewed and edited the manuscript. Kylie Johnston managed the team's efforts effectively, thereby ensuring that the job was done on time. Ellie Fountain effectively coordinated the production process.

Special thanks to the folks at Adobe. James Ward's efforts toward migrating a JSP-based Pentaho Dashboard to Flex is included in Chapter 11. Thanks, James, for generously helping out and contributing code. Mike Potter extended help throughout the book writing process. Thanks for the continued support. Ely Greenfield, creator of the wonderful FlexBook component, was kind enough to allow us to publish part of the component code in Chapter 2. Similarly, Renaun Erickson permitted us to reproduce the code from his AdvancedForm component. Chet Haase, a valued member of the Flex SDK team, was gracious to accept the invitation to write a foreword to the book. Many others from Adobe have inspired and helped. I sincerely value your inputs.

Ben Stucki and Doug McCune also let us reproduce the code for the custom components they had created. Thank you, I sincerely appreciate your letting us do so.

Thanks to my colleagues at Saven Technologies for the excellent work they continue to do using Flex. Sridhar Chelikani, President, Saven Technologies Incorporated, has been championing RIA with patience and perseverance. Thanks for the ongoing commitment.

Moreover, thanks to my friends and family for their assistance and encouragement. My wife, Caren, and sons, Ayaan and Ezra, were extremely loving and accommodating while I culled time on many evenings and early mornings in the last five or so months to get through with the book. Without their countenance and affection, I would have never been able to write this book.

Thanks also to my parents, in-laws, and all other near and dear ones for accommodating my writing activities during vacation in their company and at their homes.

Thanks to Kunal and Anila for unconditionally helping always. Also, thanks for taking the picture that forms part of my profile in this book.

It's not possible to list every single person who has directly or indirectly contributed to my writing this book. That may fill up quite a few pages! However, I recognize that you have influenced me immensely.

Shashank Tiwari

## ACKNOWLEDGMENTS

Thanks to Douglas Thompson and the Papervision3D mailing list folks.

Joshua Mostafa

# INTRODUCTION

The idea of this book emerged as a result of the many questions that attendees posed at my Flex-related speaking events in the last 12 months. It was continuously reinforced that while many books covered the fundamentals of Flex very well, few ventured into advanced topics. There was plenty of material to be dug up online that dealt with the advanced stuff, but there was little organized writing, especially in the form of a book, that helped a beginning Flex developer graduate to a real-world rich application developer.

I was keen to fill this gap and satiate the enthusiastic developer's appetite. Luckily, I found Elad, Jack, Joshua, and Clay, who bolstered my quest to write such a book and helped shape ideas into reality. The result is the book you now have in your hands!

This book is pegged on the assumption that you know a few elementary things about Flex. It assumes you know some bits of ActionScript 3.0 (AS3), MXML, and the Flex compiler, at least to the extent that you can write a "Hello World" application without help. From these simple expectations, it attempts to present enough information to transform you into an expert RIA developer.

Flex 3 truly is a promising enterprise-grade framework that provides effective hooks for server-side integration, advanced data binding, high-capability rendering, media streaming, mashups, desktop-based delivery, and more. It involves a healthy mix of object-oriented programming with AS3 and declarative development with MXML. In this book, the attempt is to illustrate many of these capabilities. Two out of the three parts of this book attempt to describe all advanced features and integration scenarios.

While leveraging the advanced features is a challenge for a novice, building a well-designed and maintainable application is as much of a puzzle. Therefore, the first part of this book concentrates on effective architecture and design. In the very first chapter, you learn about good architectural and design patterns and how they apply to Flex application development. The discussion builds to explain Flex internals, data-binding issues, and framework-extension and performance-tuning recommendations in the remaining chapters in this part of the book.

After you read this book, you will be well enriched to confidently build high-quality, engaging, and interactive scalable applications. I hope you enjoy your journey through the content in this book.

# Who this book is for

Every web developer interested in building rich interactive applications should be able to leverage and use this book. This includes developers who are familiar with the Flash platform and those who are completely new to it.

However, those with some existing knowledge of Flex may be able to traverse the book nonlinearly. For example, they could pick up the portions on integration, advanced visualization, media streaming, application architecture, or performance tuning, as many of these could be approached independent of the rest of the content in this book.

Bare essential knowledge of Flex is assumed of the readers.

# How this book is structured

Advanced Flex 3 is divided into 3 parts that include 15 chapters in all.

### Part One: Harnessing the Power of Flex 3

Part 1 explains how to extend Flex to achieve more than what is offered off the shelf to create superior applications.

### Chapter 1: Leveraging Architectural and Design Patterns

This chapter is the 101 of how to design and architect a robust enterprise-grade Flex application. A few advanced frameworks, design patterns, and architectural principles are discussed as illustrations and prescriptions.

### Chapter 2: Constructing Advanced Components

This chapter starts with lessons on extending the existing components and progresses on to explain the essentials of creating custom advanced components. A few custom advanced components are discussed in detail to explain the primary ways of creating components that have the appeal of high-definition desktop applications.

### Chapter 3: Turbo-Charging Data Binding

Flex provides numerous standards-based options to bind with external data. It lets the application integrate via RESTful services, web services, or remoting, and it provides a binary protocol for faster data transmission. This chapter explains how some of these can be combined and enhanced with concepts like streaming, buffering, compressing, and multicasting to create high-performance applications that can manage high-frequency data updates. Data-aware controls, data access templates, and implicit data binding (to achieve CRUD application generation–like effectiveness) are also discussed.

### Chapter 4: Tuning Applications for Superior Performance

In software development, despite all efforts, there is always room for some performance tuning. However, a fine balance has to be maintained between getting efficiency out of tuning and adding overhead due to tuning. Techniques for performance evaluation and subsequent tuning are detailed here. Also, no tuning makes sense without measuring the application performance metrics, so this topic is blended in with the topic of tuning.

### Chapter 5: Flex and AIR: Taking Applications to the Desktop

AIR now makes it possible to take the interactive RIA to the desktop and have it interact with the file system and the document management technologies. It also makes it possible to include HTML technologies and Flash platform technologies under one umbrella. In this chapter, you learn all about AIR.

### Part Two: Integrating with Client- and Server-Side Technologies

Part 2 focuses on how to integrate Flex with other technologies, both on the client and the server side.

### Chapter 6: Integrating with Java Using Services

This chapter is about loosely coupled integration with Java back ends using a service-oriented approach. RESTful patterns, JSON transmission, and web services are explored.

### Chapter 7: Integrating via Data and Media Services

In this chapter, integration between Flex and Java is explored using remoting and messaging-based infrastructure. Most of the discussion hovers around BlazeDS, its alternatives and its possible extensions. Streaming is also touched upon.

### Chapter 8: PHP and Flex

PHP is the most popular open source language for building web applications. AMFPHP is an open source remoting library that connects to PHP from Flex. In this chapter, you get a chance to see Flex working with a few popular PHP tools, frameworks, and libraries.

### Chapter 9: Talking with JavaScript and HTML: Web Page Integration

Flex can also integrate well with client-side technologies and help users retain browsers with their typical behavior intact while they experience rich interfaces. This chapter explains the available options, which span from parameter passing to comprehensive bridging. It also includes a discussion on widgets.

### Part Three: Gaining Real Advantage in the New Web

Part 3 explains how Flex could be leveraged to implement Web 2.0 ideas in practice.

### Chapter 10: Flex Mashups

Mashups are the new-generation style of dynamically creating composite applications. Mashups are popular in the browser-based Ajax world, but they can also be as pertinent in the world of Flex. This chapter explains ways to create mashups with Flex and analyzes the advantages and pitfalls in creating mashups using this technology.

### Chapter 11: Migrating Web 1.0 Interfaces to RIA

Enterprises have a lot invested in current-generation web applications and so reinventing the wheel is not an option for many of them. This chapter provides guidelines for migration with the help of two fully functional case studies that include Apache Struts and Ruby on Rails applications, respectively.

### Chapter 12: Sculpting Interactive Business Intelligence Interfaces

Business intelligence and advanced analytics need advanced and configurable visual representation of manipulated data. Flex is a good choice to create rich interfaces for these. The involved concepts are explained with the help of detailed use cases in this chapter.

### Chapter 13: Working with Web 2.0 APIs

Social and professional networking is a major force in the Web 2.0 evolution. This chapter will show how to create Twitter applications, integrate with Salesforce, and more. It will also discuss the challenges related to managing large volumes of networked data or lazy loading that becomes important in these scenarios.

### Chapter 14: Facilitating Audio and Video Streaming

Rich Web 2.0 applications involve as much audio and video as text. Here you see how to create your own video player, jukebox, and online TV program using Flex.

### Chapter 15: Using 3D in Flex

Users desire more than the regular applications when it comes to gaming. They need 3D applications. I believe that 3D will become popular with regular application development once it gets easier to build such applications. In this chapter, you get the initial lessons on how to build a 3D UI.

# Layout conventions

To keep this book as clear and easy to follow as possible, the following text conventions are used throughout:

Important words or concepts are normally highlighted on the first appearance in **bold type**.

Code is presented in `fixed-width` font.

New or changed code is normally presented in **`bold fixed-width font`**.

Menu commands are written in the form Menu ➤ Submenu➤ Submenu.

To draw your attention to something, text is highlighted like this:

> *Ahem, don't say I didn't warn you.*

Sometimes code won't fit on a single line in a book. Where this happens, sometimes an arrow like this is used: ➥.

```
This is a very, very long section of code that should be written all on the same ➥
line without a break.
```

# Prerequisites

For most part, the only thing you need is the free Flex 3 SDK and a text editor. For some parts of the book, access to Flex Builder 3 Professional Edition is necessary. If you don't have licensed copies of Flex Builder, consider downloading the evaluation version of the software. In the chapters on integration and migration, you will benefit from having a Java, a PHP, and a Ruby on Rails server-side environment. A few open source libraries and components, including BlazeDS, will also be required in specific chapters. Links to external libraries and details about them are included in the text.

# Downloading the code

The source code for this book is available to readers at http://www.friendsofed.com in the Downloads section of this book's home page. Please feel free to visit the friends of ED web site and download all the code there. You can also check for errata and find related titles from friends of ED and Apress.

# Contacting the authors

Shashank Tiwari:

E-mail: tshanky@gmail.com or stiwari@saventech.com

Home page: http://www.shanky.org or http://www.shashanktiwari.com

Part One

# HARNESSING THE POWER
# OF FLEX 3

# Chapter 1

# LEVERAGING ARCHITECTURAL AND DESIGN PATTERNS

By Shashank Tiwari

Adobe Flex 3, with its framework, underlying technologies (the Flash Platform), associated tools (compiler and debugger), IDE (Flex Builder 3), and server-side gateways (BlazeDS and LifeCycle Data Services) makes it easy for you to build sophisticated Rich Internet Applications (RIAs) effectively. It helps you get your interactive and engaging rich, and sometimes revolutionary, application to your users on time and within budget. What it does not do is write your business logic or application flow. You need to take care of that.

For applications that are limited in scope and complexity, you know the additional effort of implementing business logic and application flow is manageable. However, when the scope and complexity increase, things typically begin to get out of hand. The code gets distributed across numerous files, and it soon tends to lose proper structure. The business logic implementation, if not well planned and designed in advance, begins to make the codebase inflexible. With this growing rigidity, it becomes increasingly difficult to change the implementation or add newer functionality. On top of this, the application flow and control keeps evolving with changing requirements, making it extremely difficult to manage and maintain the application. Therefore, by the time the application is ready for deployment, it often becomes unmaintainable spaghetti. This is a situation you want to avoid—which can only be done by planning properly in advance and using simple and clean design principles throughout.

Making a maintainable and flexible application tests your desire to bring good programming principles to life, through multiple iterations, throughout the application development life cycle. Your endeavor to write robust applications is a journey that will continuously evolve you into a better programmer and a perseverant human being. If you already possess some or all of these virtues, your endeavor will only make you better at leveraging them.

In this arduous, though enriching, task of building robust applications, you may want a companion that will make things interesting, provide a few tips, and vicariously add to your experiences as you sharpen your skills with patience and perseverance. This book is that companion. This book includes plenty of actionable advice and useful source code to accompany you on your journey. All along, it remains honest and makes its best effort.

Let's get started.

In this chapter, the focus is on how to design and architect a Rich Internet Application so that it's flexible, maintainable, and scalable (and in line with your user's expectations). The discussion and recommendation is practical, though we touch upon theory as required. Abundant examples are used to illustrate the prescriptions.

From a structural perspective, the discussion in this chapter is divided into four parts:

- Understanding the usage of architectural and design principles in a practical context
- Summarizing the key benefits and challenges of adopting architectural and design principles
- Surveying the available architectural frameworks
- Choosing between the available frameworks vs. starting from scratch

It is my assumption and belief that a good understanding of architectural and design patterns, without any reference to their aggregation in a specific reference architecture or micro-architecture, will establish an unbiased ground to compare the existing frameworks. Once through with the fundamentals, you will be able to evaluate and choose among frameworks judiciously.

In my discussion and recommendations, I won't distinguish between architectural patterns and design patterns, because I don't need to in the context of this book.

# Adopting architectural and design patterns

This section is about the well-known solutions to well-known problems, commonly known as **design patterns** or simply **patterns**, as sometimes they go beyond design to architectural considerations. Formal classification likes to go a step further and categorizes architectural pattern artifacts as meta-pattern, reference architecture, micro-architecture, and conceptual architecture. In this book, however, my coauthors and I are only interested in helping you apply patterns to help make your next project a success. Your goal is to build robust, maintainable applications, and a practical knowledge of patterns is all you need for that.

To start with, you may wonder why these problems are repeated if they are so well known. If we as developers have the foresight to catalog solutions to these problems, why don't we start each application development task with them? Why do we first make the mistakes and then go back to correct them? Like many other things in the world of patterns, the answer to these questions is neither uniform nor well understood. Starting with the famous Gang of Four book, *Design Patterns: Elements of*

*Reusable Object-Oriented Software* by Erich Gamma, Richard Helm, Ralph Johnson, and John Vlissides (Addison-Wesley Professional, 1994), which talked about design patterns in the context of C++ and Smalltalk, there has been a rush to document and classify solutions to repeated problems. This has led to proliferation in the number of patterns, which has grown from 23 to several hundred at least. It has also led to classification of patterns as being pertinent to specific technologies, as an example, J2EE patterns; or relevant for specific use cases, for example, Ajax patterns. The abundance of patterns has inspired many developers to overdesign and overarchitect when simpler solutions have existed. Sometimes, it has misguided many of us to force-fit them into our applications without understanding the problem fully. However, this does not imply that they are useless or add no value. What it means is that using patterns effectively requires practice and experience and not a mere knowledge of what patterns are.

It is always good to start from first principles—understand the requirements and build a simple and straightforward solution to satisfy them. If you do this, you will start using some of the patterns without realizing that you are doing so. At the same time, it's good to be cognizant of some of the essential architectural and design patterns. That way, you may be able to quickly identify a solution in a pattern and avoid reinventing the wheel. Easier said than done, as this process is an iterative one and often involves patience, commitment, courage, and willingness to continuously learn.

Through practical explanations, this section will help get you started with this process.

## Going back to the basics

MVC is the single most important and relevant design pattern when it comes to user interfaces, so let's start with it.

There are three elements in an MVC pattern—model, view, and controller. The model is what holds the data and its state, the view is what you see and interact with, and the controller is what helps update the model and view based on user input.

Every pattern is an effective known way to solve a recurring problem. MVC solves the problems that arise if you keep the model and view in a tightly coupled unit. If the model and the view reside together in the same class, they create a rigid structure. In such a situation, minor changes in the model force modification of the way the model is bound with the view elements. If two or more views use the same model, the tight coupling leads to repetition of the model definition as many times. This causes inconsistencies and maintenance problems as the application evolves. It creates barriers to adding newer views on the same model.

Therefore, the first principle of MVC is to keep the model and view independent of each other. In fact, let the model be totally unaware of the view. The model provides access to its data (state) and publishes changes to it but knows nothing about the views that consume it. To achieve this, the model defines an application programming interface (API) that remains unchanged in the event of changes to the model's elements, its state, or the logic that manages the state. This does not mean that the API remains static through its existence. It means that modifications translate to addition of overloaded or newer functions to support newer parameters and data types. It means that your existing interfaces are kept intact. The view knows about the model, but you will learn a little later how it could use an intermediary to get hold of a model instance.

A typical view allows a user to create, read, update, and delete (the so-called CRUD operations) model elements. Read is the easiest of the operations, and access to the model is all that is required for this operation. For create, update, and delete, the view needs to modify model elements, and in most cases it impacts the model state. This is where the controller comes in. A controller is the mediator that updates the model (and subsequently the view) on the basis of the user input. A controller also acts as the third party that manages switching between the multiple views that bind to a model.

The controller and the view can be together in one class or in separate classes. As a rule of thumb, except for the simplest of situations, it is best to keep them in separate classes. In simple situations when the controller and view are together in one class, the pattern is often called a **Document View** pattern.

## A simple example

Let's take a simple example so you can see MVC in practice. Our model is the list of top five medal-winning countries at the Athens 2004 Olympic Games. We build three alternative views of this model. In one view, we show the data in a table, and in the other two, we represent it pictorially in a column and a bar chart.

In Flex, a data model can be declared and compiled into a tree of ActionScript objects, using the MXML Model tag. To focus on MVC, we utilize this mechanism and keep our model in a simple XML file, which we bind as the source of a Model tag. At a later stage, we explore architectural and design considerations around model management. The Model tag and a snippet of the XML file are as follows:

```
<mx:Model source="/com/riarevolution/advancedflex3/examples/
athens2004/model/medal_tally_top_5.xml" id="medalTally" />
<!-- Snippet from medal_tally_top_5.xml, -- >
<!-- the xml file that stores the data -->
<MedalTally>
    <MedalWinner>
        <ThreeLetterCode>USA</ThreeLetterCode>
        <Name>United States</Name>
        <GoldMedalCount>35</GoldMedalCount>
        <SilverMedalCount>39</SilverMedalCount>
        <BronzeMedalCount>29</BronzeMedalCount>
    </MedalWinner>
    <MedalWinner>
</MedalTally>
```

This model is bound simultaneously to three different views, put next to each other in a single MXML file. Flex provides a convenient and effective mechanism for data binding using curly braces. Any appropriate value can be assigned to a variable by reference. The reference or pointer, also called the binding source, is bound to the variable using curly braces. On evaluation, the actual value is assigned to the variable. The assignment is carried out by copying property values from the source to the destination. The value of the source property, which is referenced within the curly braces, is copied to the destination property, the variable to which the reference is assigned. This allows for dynamic binding of values to variables and keeps the source of the value and the consumption point loosely coupled.

The curly braces mechanism for data binding allows the following:

- Usage of ActionScript expressions within the curly braces
- Usage of E4X expressions within the curly braces
- Usage of ActionScript functions within the curly braces

Any ActionScript expression that returns a value can be used as the binding source within the curly braces. It could be a single bindable property or a concatenation of strings that includes a bindable property. It could be a calculation on a bindable property or a conditional expression that evaluates a bindable property. As mentioned previously, it could also be an E4X expression or an ActionScript function. The focus here is on your understanding MVC, so I will refrain from getting carried away into a discussion of data binding for now. Chapter 3 will pick up this topic again and analyze the different methods of data binding, including, but not restricted to, the curly braces, and analyze the application performance under these different alternatives.

Most Flex view controls have a dataProvider attribute to define the data model source. This attribute accepts references using the curly braces style just discussed. Therefore a simple, yet elegant, way to bind a model value to multiple views is available out of the box in Flex. A practical example of a Panel with three views (one of which is a DataGrid, and the other two charts) that bind to the same model is as follows:

```
<mx:Panel title="Athens 2004: Top 5 Medal Winners">
    <mx:Panel id="dataGridPanel" title="Medal Tally: DataGrid Panel"
        height="35%" width="100%" >
        <mx:DataGrid
        dataProvider="{medalTally.MedalWinner}"
        height="100%"
        width="100%">
        <mx:columns>
            <mx:DataGridColumn dataField="ThreeLetterCode"
            headerText="Country Code"
            headerRenderer="mx.controls.Label" />
            <mx:DataGridColumn dataField="Name"
            headerText="Country Name"
            headerRenderer="mx.controls.Label" />
            <mx:DataGridColumn dataField="GoldMedalCount"
            headerText="Gold"
            headerRenderer="mx.controls.Label" />
            <mx:DataGridColumn dataField="SilverMedalCount"
            headerText="Silver"
            headerRenderer="mx.controls.Label" />
            <mx:DataGridColumn dataField="BronzeMedalCount"
            headerText="Bronze"
            headerRenderer="mx.controls.Label" />
        </mx:columns>
        </mx:DataGrid>
    </mx:Panel>

    <mx:Panel id="chartPanel" title="Medal Tally: Charts Panel"
        height="65%" width="100%" layout="horizontal" >

        <mx:ColumnChart id="column" height="100%" width="45%"
            paddingLeft="5" paddingRight="5"
            showDataTips="true"
            dataProvider="{medalTally.MedalWinner}">
```

```
                      <mx:horizontalAxis>
                          <mx:CategoryAxis categoryField="Name"/>
                      </mx:horizontalAxis>

                  <mx:series>
                      <mx:ColumnSeries
                      xField="Name"
                      yField="GoldMedalCount"
                      displayName="Gold"/>
                      <mx:ColumnSeries
                       xField="Name"
                       yField="SilverMedalCount"
                       displayName="Silver"/>
                      <mx:ColumnSeries
                      xField="Name"
                      yField="BronzeMedalCount"
                      displayName="Bronze"/>
                  </mx:series>
              </mx:ColumnChart>

              <mx:Legend dataProvider="{column}"/>

              <mx:BarChart id="bar" height="100%" width="45%"
                  paddingLeft="5" paddingRight="5"
                  showDataTips="true"
                  dataProvider="{medalTally.MedalWinner}">

                  <mx:verticalAxis>
                      <mx:CategoryAxis categoryField="Name"/>
                  </mx:verticalAxis>

                  <mx:series>
                      <mx:BarSeries
                      yField="Name"
                      xField="GoldMedalCount"
                      displayName="Gold"/>
                      <mx:BarSeries
                      yField="Name"
                      xField="SilverMedalCount"
                      displayName="Silver"/>
                      <mx:BarSeries
                       yField="Name"
                       xField="BronzeMedalCount"
                       displayName="Bronze"/>
                  </mx:series>
              </mx:BarChart>
              <mx:Legend dataProvider="{bar}"/>
          </mx:Panel>
      </mx:Panel>
```

This simple example does not include updates or modifications to the model and so leaves the controller out of scope. The output of this code is depicted in Figure 1-1.

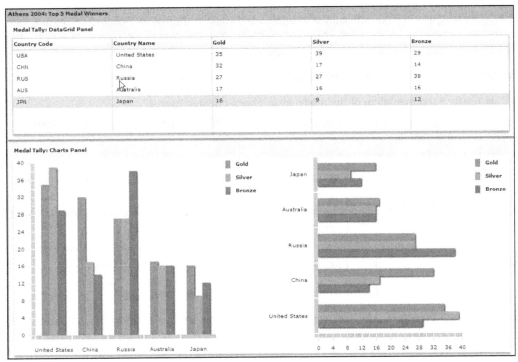

**Figure 1-1.** The application with three views of the winner tally data. One view is a data grid, and the other two are graphical representations of the same data.

While our example is elementary so far, it has shown the simplest case of an MVC, which involves model-view separation and loose coupling. To make things a bit more interesting, let's make the model closer to a real-life scenario. More precisely, we now assume that the model could exist in any of the following five ways:

- Stored locally in an XML file and bound to an MXML model tag—we already covered this scenario in our elementary example.
- Published as an XML file online and accessed through a URL.
- Available in a relational database and fetched through an application tier.
- Accessible via a web service.
- Callable via Remote Procedure Call (RPC) from an existing model in a different language—say Java, Python, or PHP. RPC allows invocation of functions on remote objects.

## Adding reality (and some complexity) to our simple example

The preceding assumption implies support for five possible alternative model implementations for a single view. To achieve this, you would need to abstract the model into a structure wherein the data from each of these alternative sources could be bound to it and consumed by the application from within this structure. Typically, creation of such a structure means creating an object-oriented (OO) representation of the model and possibly implementing proxies for remote sources.

Instead of merely making these changes to the model, this may be an opportune moment to replace the simple MVC architecture with a loosely coupled and scalable alternative. Doing so will ensure that increasing complexity in the view, controller, services, and the overall interaction model is also addressed.

To achieve this, we need to do the following:

- Create a representation of the model in an object-oriented format.
- Create a proxy for the model so that it can be accessed and manipulated uniformly, whether it is local or remote.
- Wrap external data access within services.
- Create a registry of all services that help the Flex application interface with external and internal sources of data.
- Provide a mechanism to look up the service registry and invoke a service (a possible alternative could be to have the service implementations injected when required).
- Create a command to call the service and invoke the command on a user or system event.
- Create a mechanism for the model and the view to send notifications to each other.

To scale this model to complex scenarios, we need to do a few additional things:

- Create a loosely coupled (i.e., with minimal rigid dependencies) event bus to propagate and consume events as they get generated during the application interaction life cycle. This would be an extension of the existing event system in Flex.
- Create a model registry and have a mechanism to store and retrieve models using the registry.
- Allow for generation of entire applications on the basis of model definition, especially for CRUD applications.
- Create a namespace-separated model registry if sharing data involves multiple Flex applications and involves multiple access control levels.
- Create a command registry and have a mechanism to store and retrieve commands using this registry.

If you are intimidated by this list, don't worry. As I walk you through the rationale behind each of these steps and elucidate them, soon it will all appear intuitive and straightforward. Further, for your benefit, all these concepts have been aggregated into a framework called **Fireclay**, which can be easily and readily used within your application. Fireclay is hosted on Google Code and can be accessed at http://code.google.com/p/fireclay/.

Let's start by studying the principles and steps involved at a high level and then drill down until it becomes clear enough to be applied fruitfully. Our initial discussion here is in the context of fetching the model from multiple alternative sources, but soon we will focus on artifacts like service abstraction, the command, the proxy, and the event bus, which will come in handy for all types of model manipulations and controller interactions. Some of these ideas, like the event bus, will be relevant even when you try to loosely assemble multiple Flex applications under one umbrella, as in a portal.

At a high level, there are the three usual parts of the pattern, model, view, and controller, and two additional parts, service and event bus. The view has a few components, usually called **helpers** and **utilities**, which help it render and manage its constituents effectively and apply transitions and effects to these constituents. The model can be local or remote and therefore abstracts this complexity with the help of proxies. The controller seeks event propagation and notification help from the event bus and indirectly invokes commands through event listeners to call a service or implement business logic. All the ideas support loose coupling and event-driven architecture. I also suggest you actively shun a few ideas, which are listed here as antipatterns:

■ Rampant use of data binding for model change propagation is discouraged. Binding is based on the event model, but excessive usage of binding essentially leads to creation and propagation of many events that are never handled or utilized. Often you are only trying to capture the changed property value of a specific model element at certain points of interaction.

■ Use of a singleton model locator, as advocated by Cairngorm, is both redundant and a performance inhibitor. Cairngorm is a popular open source Flex application development framework, and we'll take a closer look at it later in this chapter.

■ The use of Front Controller, typically popular in request-response web applications, is redundant in a Flex application.

■ The use of singletons, except in the case of registry instances or the event bus instance, is considered unnecessary because it usually restricts extension and reuse and makes it difficult to unit test code.

I will discuss some of these antipatterns in the context of the proposed and recommended architectural and design considerations. These details start with the following section. However, before you go there, it may be worthwhile to take a look at the critical elements of our new and revised MVC architecture in the diagram in Figure 1-2.

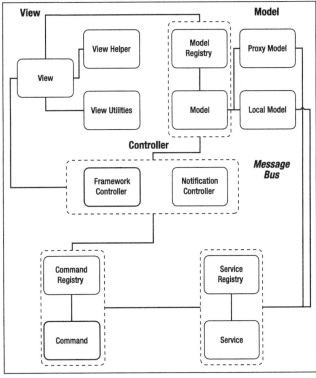

**Figure 1-2.** Conceptual representation of the model and services and modules that invoke these services

# Representing the model the object-oriented way

ActionScript 3 (AS3) is an object-oriented language, so we should represent our domain model in terms of objects. Essentially, in our example, we create a MedalWinner object with properties like ThreeLetterCode, Name, GoldMedalCount, SilverMedalCount, and BronzeMedalCount. Then we create a MedalTally class as a collection of multiple MedalWinners. Using objects with properties, and properties with logical names, makes it easy for everyone to understand the model entities and their behavior. In some cases of remote procedure calls, especially when the language across the wire is also object oriented (as in Java), these same objects or derivatives of them could get serialized and deserialized across the wire. These objects are often called data transfer objects (DTOs). DTOs serve the purpose of holding together the entire data in a call, which traverses multiple application tiers. If you are not familiar with the concept, then you can learn about this pattern at the following web sites:

- **Patterns of Enterprise Application Architecture**: http://www.martinfowler.com/eaaCatalog/dataTransferObject.html
- **Core J2EE Patterns—Transfer Object**: http://java.sun.com/blueprints/corej2eepatterns/Patterns/TransferObject.html

The code listings that follow show the model from our earlier example as a related set of objects. The source code listing shows the MedalTally object but does not show how its collection of MedalWinners is populated. There is no restriction in the way this collection could be populated. It could be hardwired or if the situation demands, the collection could be injected into the MedalTally array based on loosely coupled configurations.

MedalWinner.as defines a MedalWinner class with its attributes and operations:

```
package com.riarevolution.advancedflex3.examples.athens2004.model
{
    public class MedalWinner
    {
        public function MedalWinner() {
            super();
        }
        private var _threeLetterCode:String;
        private var _name:String;
        private var _goldMedalCount:int;
        private var _silverMedalCount:int;
        private var _bronzeMedalCount:int;

        /**
         * threeLetterCode uniquely identifies a medal-winning country
         */
        public function get threeLetterCode(): String {
            return _threeLetterCode;
        }

        /**
         * @private
         */
        public function set threeLetterCode(value:String):void {
```

```
        _threeLetterCode = value;
}

/**
 * The medal-winning country name
 *   thats maps 1 to 1 with the threeLetterCode
 */
public function get name(): String {
    return _name;
}

/**
 * @private
 */
public function set name(value:String):void {
    _name = value;
}

/**
 * goldMedalCount is the total number of
 * gold medals won by the medal-winning country
 */
public function get goldMedalCount(): int {
    return _goldMedalCount;
}

/**
 * @private
 */
public function set goldMedalCount(value:int):void {
    _goldMedalCount = value;
}

/**
 * silverMedalCount is the total number of
 * silver medals won by the medal-winning country
 */
public function get silverMedalCount(): int {
    return _silverMedalCount;
}

/**
 * @private
 */
public function set silverMedalCount(value:int):void {
    _silverMedalCount = value;
}

/**
```

```
    * bronzeMedalCount is the total number of
    * bronze medals won by the medal-winning country
    */
   public function get bronzeMedalCount(): int {
       return _bronzeMedalCount;
   }

   /**
    * @private
    */
   public function set bronzeMedalCount(value:int):void {
       _bronzeMedalCount = value;
   }
   }
}
```

MedalTally.as is a collection of MedalWinners. The following code snippet shows this collection class.

```
package com.riarevolution.advancedflex3.examples.athens2004.model
{
    public class MedalTally
    {
        public function MedalTally() {
            super();
        }

        private var _medalWinners:Array;

        /**
         * medalWinners is the collection of winners.
         * Medal count for each type of medal is
         * a property of the MedalWinner class.
         */
        public function get medalWinners():Array {
            return _medalWinners;
        }

        /**
         * @private
         */
        public function set medalWinners(value:Array):void {
            _medalWinners = value;
        }

    }
}
```

Next, the MedalWinner and MedalTally classes are depicted in terms of UML class diagrams (see Figure 1-3).

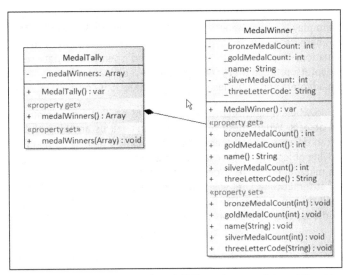

**Figure 1-3.** MedalWinner.as and MedalTally.as classes and the relationship between the two represented in a UML diagram

The object-oriented representation moves away from manipulation of the model in terms of result sets, data sets, or raw data types to meaningful objects. Therefore, the overhead of marshalling and unmarshalling between formats is reduced, and the task of attaching semantics to data is simplified.

In our example, the model is simple. In real life, model elements could have complex interrelationships, dependencies, and referenced constraints. For example, our sample application may want to drill down into the medal winner records. That is, you may select a MedalWinner (a medal-winning country) and list all the sports in which the medals were won. For each sport in which a medal-winning country won a medal, you could list the event, the medal type, and the athlete who won the medal. For example, one of the gold medals won by the United States at the Athens 2004 Olympic Games would map to "Track and Field," wherein Justin Gatlin (the athlete) won the medal in the Men's 100m event. Metrics related to the event, as in Justin Gatlin completing the Men's 100m event in 9.85 seconds, could also be stored and referenced. With the availability of this kind of detailed and referenced data, it would be possible to query by athlete, event, sport, winning country, metric range, and medal type. Therefore, the interrelationships among objects that hold this data needs to be traversed to get the accurate result set. Now if the data is stored as the same set of objects, the problem of managing these relationships isn't that difficult. However, this is rarely the case. More often than not, data resides in relational stores and tabular forms. This brings forth the challenge of mapping objects to their relational counterparts. This is popularly called Object Relational Mapping (ORM). It becomes necessary if your services that fetch external data bring in result sets in relational form.

A Flex application could get data in one of the following ways:

- Fetch data from a remote server, which can serialize objects through to the Flash Player.
- Fetch data from some remote source in terms of record sets (this could be returned via an HTTPService, WebService, or some other form of remote service).

When objects are serialized to the application, we are not really concerned with the ORM issues. The only time it comes into play is when the Flex application tries to work directly with persistence layers, for example, JPA or Hibernate in Java. In such situations, a Hibernate adapter with data services usually takes care of the situation. There are both commercial and open source data services for Hibernate out there. The dsadapters project (http://code.google.com/p/dsadapters/) is getting an entire repertoire of custom adapters and factories in place for BlazeDS. I cover BlazeDS in Chapter 7.

So ORM issues crop up when we get record sets instead of objects, and we need to reconcile them with our application objects. When these record sets don't tell us anything about the object types, there is nothing we can do except map them to our application objects by hand. However, if we can figure out the underlying object types, for example, if we have control over the SQL commands fetching the data and the metadata or have strongly typed data returns from web services, we can try to map these to objects automatically. LifeCycle Data Services (the commercial robust data services from Adobe, which are built on top of BlazeDS) has a SQL adapter as a part of the data management service feature, and the dsadapters project has a few adapters and client-side libraries for SQL and web services.

To keep the focus on the elements of MVC implementation and good application architecture and design, I will forgo any additional discussion on ORM and its usage within Flex applications.

A more immediate concern is to allow manipulation of models, consisting of local or remote data, in a uniform manner. A pattern that usually provides a good solution to this requirement and also allows for lazy loading of model elements is the Proxy pattern, which is the next topic.

## Creating a model proxy for uniform access to local and remote entities

A proxy takes the place of a real object when the real object is not available or is not present locally. If the real object performs expensive operations or takes a while to load, the proxy sits in place of the real object, until the real object is ready for use. A proxy's API is identical to that of the real object, so it allows you to make calls on it while this real object is getting loaded or initialized. When the real object is available, the calls are passed to it, and it responds to the calls.

Proxies can be of two types, a virtual proxy or a remote proxy. A **virtual proxy** corresponds entirely to the definition of a proxy as per the preceding paragraph. A **remote proxy** is slightly different in that it sits in place of an object that is not available locally.

In the case of a remote object, a proxy serves as a local stub or handle for it. Calls are made to the proxy object and in turn relayed to the real remote object. Responses when received from the remote object are sent to the caller. A remote proxy is commonly used in almost all languages that allow invocation of RPCs on distributed remote objects. In such situations, it's usually called the **stub** and its real counterpart is called the **skeleton**.

In order to create a uniform model access mechanism for external and internal data, we need to implement a remote proxy for the external data sources. At the same time, in sophisticated applications, some of the data may involve expensive operations. Often these expensive operations occur in conjunction with remote calls. Therefore, we create a proxy that has features of both a virtual and a remote proxy.

From a caller's standpoint, the calls to local and remote, lightweight and expensive resources look identical.

The model can vary in its type and characteristics, so the implementation of the proxy would vary from object to object. We define an IModelProxy marker interface to specify the model class as a proxy type. The proxy class also implements the flash.events.IEventDispatcher interface and defines methods for adding and removing event listeners and dispatching events. When a remote operation returns successfully, an appropriate event is fired. Event handlers are defined to handle these events and complete the call as desired.

In our example, we would like the MedalWinner and MedalTally objects to behave the same way, whether data is in a local file or it is accessed from an external Uniform Resource Identifier (URI). Therefore, we would implement both of these as model proxies.

In a few situations, your model may manifest in separate entities in the source code. In such a case, you may want to compose them into a desired preferred object before making that object available in the application. In such a case, you may want a façade and not a proxy. You may still expect your façade to lazily load the data and demonstrate a few of the proxy's behaviors. A façade sometimes could also simplify the complexity of ORM, as joins between related data are already made before the composed object is available in the application.

In another situation, you may not need any composition but may need to alter the API of the original model. This is typically when you need to shape the external data to fit your application model. In such a case, you may want an adapter and not a proxy or a façade. Again, you may want your adapter to support lazy loading and sit in place of the original data as in a proxy.

Let's reshape our simple model as a proxy to understand what it looks like under the new structure. For simplicity, we only implement MedalTally as the object holding the collection that resides in the XML file. In a real-life situation, you would have MedalWinner objects and then MedalTally as a collection of these objects. The UML diagram in Figure 1-4 shows how we structure our interfaces and classes to implement our proxy.

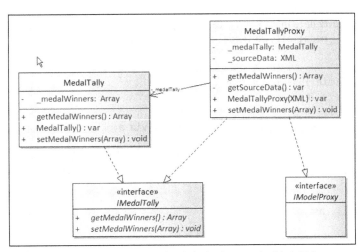

**Figure 1-4.** Classes and interfaces that help implement the MedalTally proxy, represented in a UML diagram

The source code for the MedalTally.as and MedalTallyProxy.as implementation classes to include the characteristics of a proxy is as shown here. First, the code for MedalTallyProxy.as:

```
package com.riarevolution.advancedflex3.examples.athens2004.model.proxy
{
    public class MedalTallyProxy implements IMedalTally, IModelProxy
    {
        private var _sourceData:XML;
        private var _medalTally:MedalTally;

        public function MedalTallyProxy(_sourceData:XML)
        {
            _sourceData = getSourceData();
            _medalTally = new MedalTally();
            //TODO: implement function
        }

        public function getMedalWinners():Array
        {
            if(_medalTally.getMedalWinners() == null) {
                _medalTally.setMedalWinners➥
(mx.utils.ArrayUtil.toArray(_sourceData.MedalWinner));
            }
            return _medalTally.getMedalWinners();
        }

        public function setMedalWinners(value:Array):void
        {
            mx.utils.ArrayUtil.toArray➥
(_sourceData.MedalWinner) = value;
            _medalTally.setMedalWinners(value);
        }

        private function getSourceData() {
            // Implements the remote proxy
            // to get the data from the
            // external XML file accessible via a URL
        }

    }
}
```

And now, MedalTally.as:

```
package com.riarevolution.advancedflex3.examples.athens2004.model.proxy
{
    public class MedalTally implements IMedalTally
    {
        private var _medalWinners:Array;
```

```
public function MedalTally()
{
    super();
}

public function getMedalWinners():Array
{
    return _medalWinners;
}

public function setMedalWinners(value:Array):void
{
    _medalWinners = value;
}

    }
}
```

Observe that in the MedalTallyProxy.as class, the actual method that fetches the external data is not implemented. You could use the URLLoader class to load data from the external XML file and implement it as a remote proxy, especially if it's a large XML file and you would like to load it on demand.

Having taken care of the model side of the story, it's time to look at the external source that a model or a model proxy accesses.

## Wrapping external data access within services

External data may be available in a database or through an application layer. The application layer may expose itself as an API or set of methods in the programming language that it is written in, or may expose itself as a set of platform-independent interfaces as in a web service or an HTTP endpoint.

A Flex application can make direct calls to a database, provided the database exposes its connections over a host name or an IP address so that a socket connection can be established to it, and it defines a crossdomain.xml file with the required security permissions at the root of this access point. It cannot make a call directly to a data store in the traditional sense. Making a direct call means writing your own database drivers in ActionScript for the purpose. This is not a trivial task and may possibly keep you away from using it. Also, direct database access makes the Flex application tightly coupled with it, which could pose problems. Therefore, an application layer is necessary to fetch the data. Whether in a platform-independent or a language-dependent manner, it's recommended that this application layer interface act like a service. This may raise an obvious question in your mind—what exactly is a service? It is an abstraction that provides business functionality and has the following characteristics:

- Is a simple and independent well-defined interface that often accomplishes a unit of work
- Has clear separation of concerns between those who produce and those who consume this functionality
- Defines the interface independent of the underlying implementation
- Is often stateless, reusable, and extensible

Therefore, external data in a Flex application as far as possible should be defined in a way that it respects this definition.

If the volume and frequency of external data access is minimal, exposing the application layer as a standard HTTP or web service endpoint may be prudent. This has two advantages: it provides for easy reuse, and it alleviates the usage of a server-side data service for the Flex application. The only requirement for accessing these services in non-data-service scenarios is that they should be served from a trusted domain, for example, the same domain from where the Flex application SWF is served or a domain that defines the `crossdomain.xml` security policy file.

If the data calls are more fine-grained and frequent or involve access to many remote procedures, it may be worthwhile to use server-side data services and use the remoting infrastructure. In such cases as well, service-oriented exposition of application layer functionality is beneficial.

If you come from the world of web applications, you may be concerned about state management and may question the use of stateless services. In the context of Flex, the application runs within the Flash Virtual Machine (VM) and maintains state within the client. Flex applications almost never need to keep state on the server. The only exceptions may be scenarios where multiple Flex applications collaborate on the same data set or situations where Flex applications tightly integrate with the server-side persistence layers. So, stateless services are appropriate for most situations. They scale better and are easy to reuse and pool.

Often the data resides in existing legacy systems that are not service oriented. In such situations, creation of server-side application layer service abstractions is usually wiser than consuming data as is. By doing so, it also ensures that legacy consumers are unaffected and the Flex application talks with a service layer that is built just for its purpose. The only thing to remember is to keep this service layer simple and clean. Avoid burdening it with business algorithms or complex data manipulation logic.

Our existing model data resides in an XML file. At the simplest level, this XML file could be deployed as it is onto a web server and made accessible via an HTTP endpoint. More specifically, it could be accessible with a URL, say http://www.riarevolution.com/AdvancedFlex3/Athens2004/ medal_tally_top_5.xml. This is what we have done so far. This makes it accessible in a REST-style HTTP GET method call but does not necessarily make it a service. (Read more about REST, or Representational State Transfer, online, at http://www.ics.uci.edu/~fielding/pubs/dissertation/ top.htm.) The MedalTally collection of top five winners may not be the only way to get the data. It's possible you may want to fetch data for a single MedalWinner or get a collection different from the set of top five winners. Therefore, our XML over the URL does not provide for clear, well-defined calls and is not fine-grained enough. Now, if we put our data behind a simple web application that serves the data appropriately based on an input parameter, we effectively create a simple service. Let's say such a web application would be accessible via a URL, say http://www.riarevolution.com/ AdvancedFlex3/Athens2004/getMedalWinners?set=top5. In this service, the value of the query string parameter set would be the input parameter and would help return different appropriate data sets. This creates our simplest RESTful HTTPService. For simplicity, a web application to implement this service is built using Python. You can download the code at http://www.riarevolution.com/ advancedflex3/examples/Athens2004.

You will see more about how our existing example application could be modified within the realm of data access using external services, but before we get to that, let me show you some more on how to store and retrieve references to these services. Chapter 11 describes the process of service abstracting legacy in detail.

## Creating a service registry and invoking services after looking them up

I mentioned that our domain model may fetch the data from an external source, and I recommended that in such a situation we abstract the external interfacing part of the program in a service. Now we walk through the detailed mechanisms of the service registry and its interaction with the model elements.

Let's assume the data is accessible as a RESTful web service. In most scenarios, this type of a web service is barely any different from a regular HTTP call. Therefore, we use the HTTPService component to make such a service call. The source code that follows shows what it could look like.

First, the MXML for the HTTPService Flex component to fetch the external data accessible via a URL:

```
<mx:HTTPService
        id="medalTallyDS"
        url="http://www.riarevolution.com➡
/AdvancedFlex3/Athens2004/getMedalWinners?set=top5"
        useProxy="false"
        result="httpResult()"
        fault="httpFault()" />
```

And now the ActionScript for the component:

```
import mx.controls.Alert;
import mx.rpc.http.HTTPService;
import mx.rpc.events.ResultEvent;
import mx.rpc.events.FaultEvent;

private var service:HTTPService

public function useHttpService(parameters:Object):void {
        service = new HTTPService();
        service.destination = "http://www.riarevolution.com➡
/AdvancedFlex3/Athens2004/getMedalWinners?set=top5";
        service.method = "GET";
        service.addEventListener("result", httpResult);
        service.addEventListener("fault", httpFault);
        service.send(parameters);
}
public function httpResult(event:ResultEvent):void {
        var result:Object = event.result;

        //Do something with the result.
}

public function httpFault(event:FaultEvent):void {
        var faultstring:String = event.fault.faultString;
        Alert.show(faultstring);
}
```

21

Although not relevant in our simple example, REST-style web services also often need header manipulation, and this is where HTTPService off the shelf falls short. One way is to use the Socket class and make a connection to the resource on port 80, the default HTTP port, and communicate with it using HTTP. To keep our discussion focused on services and service registry, details of these possible workarounds will not be discussed here.

Before we do anything more with the service, we create a service registry and make sure that at any given time we have at most one instance of this registry per named reference. In other words, we implement service registry as a multiton. The Singleton pattern specifies the creation of a single instance of a class. In the same lines, the Multiton pattern specifies the creation of a finite predetermined number of instances of a class, where each of these instances can be accessed with a unique identifier. Then we create a way to store a list of services within this registry and provide a mechanism to look up this store. We define a service manager to keep and find services and associate this with our service registry. To make things more flexible and allow for more than one service manager implementation to be plugged in if desired, we create a service manager interface and move the concrete implementation to an implementation class. In addition to this, we define a service assembler, which as the name suggests assembles the desired service manager implementation to the service registry. **Service manager implementation** is a composition that implements the two important behaviors of keeping and finding services. A service finder and a service keeper are the delegates that carry out the job of service finding and storing, respectively. These are the two functions that get together in a service manager implementation.

The concept of a registry with an assembler that binds a manager to help look up and store entities has relevance beyond services to models, commands, and logic execution components. Therefore, it may be worthwhile to create generic versions of these and then extend them for each of the specific use cases. If all this is beginning to sound a bit hazy, it's time to look at Figure 1-5, which shows the generic registry, assembler, and manager, and relates them to our case of services.

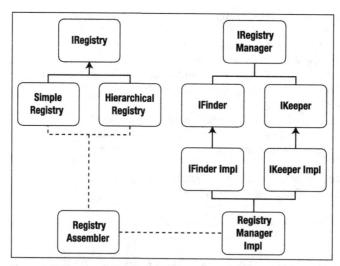

**Figure 1-5.** The generic registry model, with its finder and keeper (managers) and the assembler

Now we get back to the task of registering our instance of the HTTPService in the registry. This service could then be looked up when you need to use it using the simple mechanism of saving a service reference with a unique name in the registry. This unique name could be used as the handle to retrieve the service at a later time. For simple applications, the registry could be flat and may keep references in a simple dictionary or map. For more complex scenarios, you could use a hierarchical and namespace-separated registry. A little later, in a section titled "A few additional tips on registries," I will briefly discuss the case of these complex registries.

The next big question is, who calls this service and when? From a naive standpoint, we could call the service from within the user or system event handler, but this is one antipattern you want to avoid as much as possible. If not, you will soon end up with a rigid structure. Services are often reusable, and I have already suggested collating them together in a registry. User or system events act on a model element and expect to alter the state and behavior. So event handlers should act like command executors. These command executors should call services as and when they need to. The model elements should also use these commands as the delegates for invoking services during initialization. We will remodel our example using such a pattern in the next section. Before that, though, you need to understand the command executors a bit better.

## Creating the command workhorses

The Command pattern is a design pattern that provides the ability to call any of the different command executors, as far as they implement a common interface. It decouples the command executor from the initiator. Both these reasons make it an ideal pattern for creation of the command workhorses that are invoked when an event occurs.

The first important definer of this pattern is the command interface. This interface has one essential function, which is the execute function. The interface could also have a couple of optional functions, namely undo and redo, to support undoable and redoable commands. The undo and redo features usually come handy, and so it's advisable to include them. A typical ICommand interface could look like this:

```
package com.riarevolution.➥
advancedflex3.examples.athens2004.➥
logicexecution
{
    public interface ICommand
    {
        function execute();

        function undo();

        function redo();
    }
}
```

A concrete command implements the ICommand interface. The execution logic is defined in the execute function, and the undo and redo logic is defined in the undo and redo functions. A command is invoked by an entity, called an **invoker**, and a command targets an entity, called a **target**. The concrete implementation class often references the target because often the execute operation impacts the target directly. The invoker is usually the component or artifact that triggers the user or system event that invokes the command. Apart from these there is usually an entity that instantiates the command so that it can be used.

Service calls should be made from within the execute, undo, and redo functions of the command, as required. We could refactor our example to include a command. In the simplest form, it may look like this:

```
//Modify this source code
package com.riarevolution.➥
advancedflex3.examples.athens2004.logicexecution
{
    import com.riarevolution.➥
advancedflex3.examples.athens2004.model.proxy.*;

    public class CollectionAccessor implements ISimpleCommand
    {
        private var medalTallyProxy = new MedalTallyProxy();
        private var _myArray;

        public function CollectionAccessor()
        {
            //do nothing
        }

        public function execute()
        {
            _myArray = medalTallyProxy.getMedalWinners();

        }

    }
}
```

If the situation is overly complex, there might be a case for including a delegate to avoid direct exposure to services from within a command. In most cases, though, it is better to avoid them.

The delegate in this case in inspired by a J2EE pattern of the same name. If you need to read about it, just browse to the following link: http://java.sun.com/blueprints/corej2eepatterns/Patterns/BusinessDelegate.html.

## The case for business delegates

Business delegates have their place in multitiered Java EE applications where they shield the presentation layers from the details of the business services. In Flex, the Cairngorm framework supports usage of business delegates because the framework creators believe that a service call could be invoked several times in an application and desire different result handling during these numerous calls. In our framework, Fireclay, we don't see huge benefits in the usage of a business delegate. A Flex application resides within a single VM, and there seems to be no need for business delegates. The service in our case is abstracted through the presence of a registry. This abstraction is purely for storage and retrieval in an organized fashion. In most cases, a service can be invoked directly from a command. It's possible to include a nested set of commands where a command later in the chain could act as the service invoker but disintermediation through a true Java EE–style delegate does not seem to provide additional benefits. This is possibly because the service invoker already assumes many of the responsibilities of the delegate.

Our next discussion is again centered around the fundamental tenets in Flex—for example, event-driven interactions. Events are at the heart of Flex, and if there is only one thing you need to remember while architecting your solution, it should be to make sure you facilitate loosely coupled event-driven interactions.

## Notifications between the view and the model

We started our MVC discussion by saying that the model and the view need to be separated. I mentioned that views could be aware of the model and directly read off the values, but models should be unaware of the views or any other entities that consume them or interact with them. This would mean models should also be unaware of the controllers that help them interact with the views.

In the simplest form, a bindable model could be consumed in a view, especially by binding a destination to bindable sources using curly braces. In such a case, changes to the model would be propagated to the view automatically. Some frameworks like Cairngorm advocate this as a preferred form of data binding. However, from a performance and scalability standpoint, it is not the best solution. When data binding is used, the Flex framework continues to send source modification updates to the destination components even if the components are alive but not visible anymore. This means you may be doing some unnecessary binding when you don't even need it.

A better way to do data binding is to use the mx.binding.utils.BindingUtils class and to explicitly bind properties and setters. Both the bindProperty and the bindSetter methods return a ChangeWatcher instance. A ChangeWatcher has methods that help you define event handlers, which are executed whenever a bindable property is updated. It's possible to call unwatch on a ChangeWatcher and turn data binding off when a component does not listen to changes any more, even if it's alive. This may be a better idea from a performance standpoint, but it could involve more work than the standard curly braces–based data binding alternative. So what should be done then? The answer, as always, lies in striking the balance. Simple text labels and similar fields could utilize the curly braces–based data binding, as the explicit BindingUtils-based alternative does not provide substantial benefits to these situations. However, for most complex scenarios, it may be wise to use BindingUtils and explicitly bind the required properties. Also, remember that making properties bindable has its overhead, and sometimes you may want to trigger property change events explicitly instead of making them bindable. Using the "event triggers on data change" approach, you could control when to trigger these events and how best to handle them.

Finally, everything in Flex is based on events that get fired based on user or system triggers, so why not implement an event bus, where you propagate events and listen to them? This way, the entire application becomes loosely coupled and flexible. The advantage is that interdependencies are reduced, and it becomes easy to add newer events and have newer listeners for those events, without the need to reorganize what's already there. Benefits of an event bus have been realized in service-oriented event-driven scenarios and Flex applications make a good use case for it as well. Let's try and understand the event bus conceptually a bit and see how it's implemented in the Fireclay framework.

## Leveraging an event bus

An event bus is a pattern and a piece of software that implements a publish-subscribe mechanism to broadcast events and listen to them. An event bus could also be thought of as a manifestation of the Event Collaboration pattern. An Event Collaboration pattern recommends that multiple components communicate and collaborate by sending events to each other when their internal state changes. More about event collaboration can be read at http://martinfowler.com/eaaDev/EventCollaboration.html.

We will start with defining a generic event bus and then see how it would work in a single-threaded Flash VM environment. To begin with, a typical event bus API may act like a queue. Event-target (event listener) pairs would be put on this queue, and they would be picked up and processed one after the other. In Flex, this would be redundant because such a one-to-one pairing mechanism already exists, where most controls and components allow definition of an event handler function with the event. As an example, a Button control click event could have a clickHandler function associated with the event by simply assigning the listener function as the click property value. I said earlier that an event bus facilitates broadcasting events in a publish-subscribe mechanism, so this point-to-point communication in any case seems redundant. Therefore, we define our event bus with publish-subscribe in mind. We could draw inspiration from the world of messaging and define topics as our initial artifacts. Then multiple events could be associated with a topic. Consumers, or in this case event listeners, could subscribe to topics. When an event is fired related to a topic, it would be dispatched to all its subscribed listeners. Now if we have a special case where one event maps to one topic and it has only one listener, then we could also include the point-to-point scenario.

So the first thing our event bus needs is a helper class that would maintain the topic-to-subscribers (event listeners) mapping. This could be a dictionary or map type of data structure and may allow for dynamic subscription. The next helper it needs is an event-to-topic mapping class. This again could be a dictionary or a map-type data structure. Now our event bus could be again somewhat like a queue that would receive a stream of events and in a sequential manner pick up events and dispatch them to all the event listeners associated with the event topic. In a multithreaded situation, you may allow parallel processing of events, but in the case of the Flash VM, this may be irrelevant because the Flash VM is single threaded. Also, the Flash API defines an EventDispatcher class and an IEventDispatcher interface to help dispatch events. The class or the interface could be used to implement the event bus. The default event bus in Fireclay extends the EventDispatcher class for now. In the future, this may change if a superior event-dispatching infrastructure emerges or multithreading is introduced in the Flash VM. To get a better idea of what I have said so far, let's view all of this in a simplified diagram (see Figure 1-6).

This simplified event bus could have an API as follows:

```
package fireclay.core.event
{
import flash.events.Event;

public interface IEventBus
{
    function initialize():void;

    function isInitialized():Boolean;

    function getEventBus():IEventBus;

    function queue(event:Event):void;

    function dequeue():Event;
```

```
function bindEventToTopic(event:Event, topic:String):void;

function transmit(event:Event, topic:String):void;

function broadcast(topic:String, listeners:Array): void;

    }
}
```

The event bus is extremely useful in event broadcasting and even extends to cases where multiple Flex components and modules need to communicate with each other. I do not recommend morphing events under a certain common type and propagating them. You should keep them unaltered.

This completes some of the most important aspects of this discussion on architectural and design patterns that you may want to adopt. By no means is this discussion comprehensive or universally applicable. You have to use your discretion and judgment in their correct usage. Looking at examples and implementation guidelines will help, but as with all frameworks, if you have doubts about a pattern's usefulness, then just avoid using it. Always favor simplicity and lucidity over unnecessary complexity.

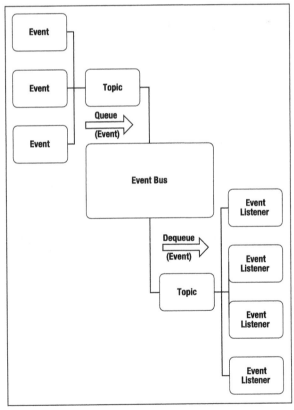

**Figure 1-6.** A high-level view of the event bus and its consitutent elements

## A few additional tips on registries

The next couple of sections briefly touch on the topics of model and command registries and namespaces.

### Creating model and command registries

We looked at a registry and its structure in the context of services. Almost identical concepts could be applied to implement a registry for models and commands. The Fireclay framework implements a generic set of registry-related classes, which are in the util package of its distribution. These classes could be used to create registry for services, models, and commands, as well as be utilized for any other situation where such an implementation makes sense.

The basic idea of a registry is to facilitate storage and retrieval and provide a simple and uniform mechanism for these operations. If your application is limited in scope and has only a few services, models, or commands, then the usage of a registry should be restricted to a simple dictionary or a list. However, if the application is complex and needs to implement access policies on these artifacts and expose them in shared contexts, a registry could be quite sophisticated and may even involve hierarchical partitions and namespaces.

### Using a namespace-based partition in a registry

Namespaces are commonly used to partition programs into logical areas. As an example, the package structure used in ActionScript is a namespace. Similarly, XML namespaces classify XML schemas into different logical groupings. The concept of a namespace, or in simple words, hierarchical classification to create partitions in the registry, seems like a viable idea, especially when the numbers of registry entries are huge. Oftentimes entries need to be made accessible according to certain privileges or access control criteria and may involve multiple entries against a single variable, each relevant to a particular context. I do not recommend any specific implementation strategy. The hierarchical registry is defined with a namespace as the highest level of separation, and that is the closest you get to an implementation. You can always implement a custom registry by extending the IRegistry interface.

Now we are ready to go to our next topic: the benefits and challenges of adopting architectural and design patterns.

# Benefits and challenges of adopting patterns

This section starts to evaluate pattern adoption. It begins by enumerating some of the main benefits and challenges. The next few sections view examples in the light of specific patterns and micro-architectures. Finally, our evaluation concludes with a few guidelines to assist decision making when moving forward with patterns.

Good things come first, and so I'll start by listing the benefits!

## Benefits

Now you know, if you didn't already, that design patterns are common ways of avoiding known problems. In other words, they are guides to "best practices" for building applications.

- **Avoids common problems**: The very definition of a pattern is a solution to a common problem. By understanding a pattern, we can effectively avoid the corresponding problem. Interestingly, in software development, people continue to make common mistakes and often spend enormous amounts of time struggling to solve them. This is true even today, when many of these problems (and their solutions) are well documented. By being ready to learn and look at patterns, you make the first commitment to avoid wasting time and effort on issues that have already been solved. This alone is reason enough to consider patterns.

- **Promotes reuse**: In most cases, theoretical ideas of solution patterns are accompanied with corresponding implementations. These implementations are available as libraries and frameworks. Therefore, patterns promote reuse at multiple levels: at the level of ideas and at that of code reuse. As an example, the Fireclay project could be thought of as a pattern implementation library and a starting point for Flex and AIR application development.

- **Promotes rapid development**: Many frameworks promote agility and also generate code that cuts application development time and effort. Some may even provide implementations that you would otherwise need to write yourself. Moreover, frameworks also take care of the root-level plumbing. Therefore, application development is usually quicker with an effective framework than without one.

- **Enables community support**: Frameworks, especially the popular open source ones, have a vibrant community that helps troubleshoot and extend the framework. This provides for continuous improvement and better functionality.

- **Facilitates uniform communication**: Frameworks also standardize vocabulary. The patterns themselves give standard names to complex concepts. Frameworks build on that and provide additional vocabulary to effectively communicate ideas among team members and external participants.

## Challenges

Adopting frameworks isn't all that easy and can lead to its own troubles:

- **Brings the perils of over architecting**: It is a common misunderstanding that complex situations demand complex solutions. Often this misunderstanding inspires architects and developers to adopt the complex and most comprehensive frameworks when the situation could often have a much simpler and cleaner solution.

- **Impedes clear thinking**: If you give somebody a solution to a puzzle, you frustrate that person's ability to derive the solution by logically thinking through the problem and the possible solutions. The presence of a framework often seduces developers into forcing their application to fit it. Developers and architects may then stop thinking clearly about the problem.

- **Prevents easy testing and debugging**: Testing and debugging a framework-based application can be very difficult, especially if the framework code is intractably obfuscated or involves many singletons and statics.

- **Introduces infrastructural complexity**: Frameworks create an infrastructure for an application. Sometimes, their container features pose complexity when they are deployed in a shared or clustered infrastructure.

# Surveying the available architectural frameworks

So far we have indulged in discussions on individual patterns, their combinations, and the benefits and challenges involved in adopting them. Now we walk through simple example applications built using two of the best-known Flex frameworks and discuss them in the light of one new framework to see what it really means to adopt them. The two well-established players are Cairngorm and PureMVC. The new framework is Fireclay. Shortcomings in the established players inspired me to create this cleaner, easier, robust, and scalable alternative. Later in the chapter, in the section "Choosing what's there vs. creating your own," I will outline the rationale for creating Fireclay. You should be able to reuse some of those thought processes in your own quest to decide on the preferred option.

For now, let's walk through the example applications. In each case, it's the same example: a flight status enquiry application. It's a simple application that has a text box to specify the flight number, a text area to display the flight status, and a button to submit the request for information. If no matching flights are found, a "Can't locate flight" message with the flight number input is returned. It's an elementary application that is only meant to show the use of the frameworks. The example is too elementary to judge the viability or appropriateness of a particular framework for real-life situations. In fact, this chapter doesn't get into serious comparisons at all. It only provides a set of parameters to use for comparison and leaves the actual job of comparison to you. You know your requirements best, and you are always the best judge in choosing the right thing for yourself. My intent is only to arm you with all the information you need so that you make a well-informed choice.

## Cairngorm

Cairngorm is the best-known brand in the Flex framework world. It emerged from a niche consulting outfit called Iteration Two, which was later bought out by Adobe. Most of Iteration Two transformed into the EMEA team of Adobe Consulting. Being the creators of the frameworks, the members of this team continued to maintain and evolve the framework. Today Cairngorm is actively used and evangelized by Adobe Consulting.

The Cairngorm framework developers were inspired by what they learned in their Java (especially J2EE) days, and therefore Cairngorm is a J2EE design patterns–inspired framework. It also takes a lot of ideas from Apache Struts, a one-time leading Java web application framework. While J2EE patterns and Struts work very well for J2EE problems and request-response Java web applications, I believe some of those concepts have been force-fit into the radically different (from J2EE) world of RIA. In any case, different people have different needs, and for many large enterprises, the distributed J2EE-style development appears fit for RIA as well. Whether effective or not, Cairngorm enjoys a healthy following. In this section, I show a simple step-by-step RIA example application development using Cairngorm.

We use Flex Builder 3 as the IDE. For starters, we create a new Flex project and then add the Cairngorm library to the project library path. Obviously, this assumes we first get a copy of the latest stable release of the Cairngorm binary distribution. At the time of this writing, Cairngorm version 2.2 is the latest stable release version. Figure 1-7 shows the Cairngorm SWC file added to our library path.

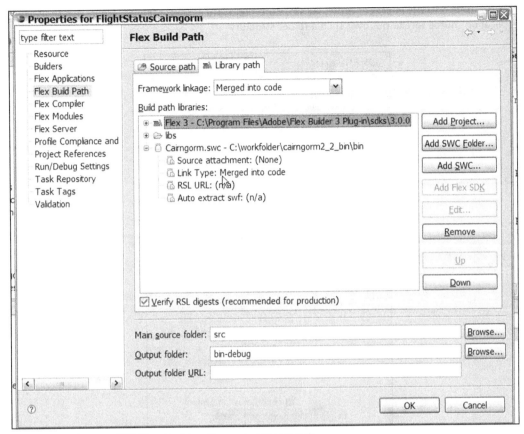

**Figure 1-7.** Cairngorm SWC file added to a Flex project library path

Any Cairngorm application includes a few key artifacts:

- **Views**: These are what you see. They are the interaction interface for a user.

- **Commands**: These implement a particular function or get a particular job done and are activated by a user or system event.

- **Front controller**: All user interactions at the view are routed through this front controller to the commands. The controller maps commands to events.

- **Cairngorm event**: This is a wrapper event that wraps up all other events and gets propagated up to the event handlers. Custom events in Cairngorm extend the Cairngorm event.

- **Model**: This is the part that stores data and its state. Model elements in a Cairngorm application are recommended to be bound to a singleton model instance, which implements the Model marker interface.

- **Services**: These invoke remote services and interact with remote sources of data.

- **Delegates**: These come in the middle of commands and services. Business layer functionality is delegated to them.

To keep these artifacts in proper order, we structure them into separate folders. Figure 1-8 shows the application source spread out over such a folder structure.

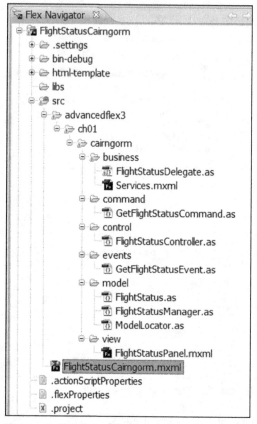

**Figure 1-8.** FlightStatusCairngorm project file structure

This example implementation is intentionally modeled on existing Cairngorm examples. I thought that was the best way to stick to what the framework team recommends. Further, this has another advantage: if you wanted to read the Cairngorm documentation to understand the details, you wouldn't feel lost.

The entry point of the application is FlightStatusCairngorm.mxml, which hosts an <mx:Application/> tag. This component includes the view component, FlightStatusPanel.mxml. Here is the source for FlightStatusCairngorm.mxml:

```
<?xml version="1.0" encoding="utf-8"?>
<mx:Application xmlns:mx="http://www.adobe.com/2006/mxml"
    layout="absolute"
    xmlns:view="advancedflex3.ch01.cairngorm.view.*">
    <view:FlightStatusPanel/>
</mx:Application>
```

FlightStatusPanel.mxml has all the view code in it. Here is the source:

```
<?xml version="1.0" encoding="utf-8"?>
<mx:Panel xmlns:mx="http://www.adobe.com/2006/mxml"
creationComplete="initFlightStatus();" >

<mx:Script>
    <![CDATA[
        import com.adobe.cairngorm.control.CairngormEventDispatcher;
        import advancedflex3.ch01.➥
cairngorm.events.GetFlightStatusEvent;
        import advancedflex3.ch01.cairngorm.model.FlightStatus;
        import advancedflex3.ch01.cairngorm.model.ModelLocator;

        public var statusId : String;
        [Bindable]
        private var flightStatus : FlightStatus;
        private var model : ModelLocator = ModelLocator.getInstance();

        private function initFlightStatus() : void
        {
            flightStatus = ➥
model.flightStatusManager.➥
getFlightStatus(statusId);
        }

        private function getStatusForFlight() : void
        {
            var event : GetFlightStatusEvent =
new GetFlightStatusEvent➥
( statusId, flightIdTextInput.text );
            CairngormEventDispatcher.➥
getInstance().dispatchEvent( event );
        }
    ]]>
</mx:Script>
<mx:Form>
    <mx:FormItem label="Flight Id (Number)">
        <mx:TextInput id="flightIdTextInput"/>
        <mx:Button
        label="Get Flight Status"
        click="getStatusForFlight();"/>
    </mx:FormItem>
    <mx:FormItem label="Flight Id (Number)">
        <mx:Label text="{ flightStatus.lastFlightStatus }"/>
    </mx:FormItem>
    <mx:FormItem>
        <mx:Label text="{ flightStatus.flightStatusError }"/>
    </mx:FormItem>
```

```
            </mx:Form>
          </mx:Panel>
```

The <mx:Form /> block includes a label with a text input and a button to get the user input and submit the request, respectively. It also includes form elements that show the returned result. When the button is clicked, a function called getStatusForFlight is invoked. The getStatusForFlight function does two things:

- Creates a custom event
- Dispatches the custom event with the help of an event dispatcher

The mechanism conceptually is no different from a regular event-driven interaction in Flex, where user events like a button click translate to event activation and propagation. However, there are differences in the way it is implemented in Cairngorm. The Cairngorm framework believes in generating custom events on the basis of every user or system interaction. Each such custom event inherits from a framework event called CairngormEvent, which resides in the com.adobe.cairngorm.control package. GetFlightStatusEvent looks like this:

```
package advancedflex3.ch01.cairngorm.events
{
import com.adobe.cairngorm.control.CairngormEvent;
import advancedflex3.ch01.cairngorm.control.FlightStatusController;

public class GetFlightStatusEvent extends CairngormEvent
{
    public var statusId : String;
    public var flightId : String;

    public function
    GetFlightStatusEvent(statusId:String, flightId:String)
    {
        super( FlightStatusController.EVENT_GET_FLIGHT_STATUS );
        this.statusId = statusId;
        this.flightId = flightId;
    }


}
}
```

You will notice that apart from extending CairngormEvent, this class also passes a static variable bound to the controller class, in this case FlightStatusController, to the constructor of its super class. This may look fuzzy now, but soon it will all appear clear. A controller acts as a gateway and a router of all interaction-generated events in Cairngorm. That's why it is also called the "front controller," which is the name of the pattern that encapsulates these concepts. In the interaction flow, events are passed on to the commands, which are mapped to them. Commands are essentially the event listeners. The controller is the critical element that manages this mapping and event dispatch. This part of Cairngorm is inspired by Apache Struts, which also happens to define a front controller. In the case of Struts, it's the traditional web application style request-response interactions. Therefore, requests in that case are mapped to commands via the front controller.

A look at FlightStatusController may shed more light, and here is what that class is like:

```
package advancedflex3.ch01.cairngorm.control
{
    import com.adobe.cairngorm.control.FrontController;
    import advancedflex3.ch01.cairngorm.command.*;

    public class FlightStatusController extends FrontController
    {
        public function FlightStatusController()
        {
            addCommand( FlightStatusController.➥
EVENT_GET_FLIGHT_STATUS, GetFlightStatusCommand );
        }

        public static const ➥
EVENT_GET_FLIGHT_STATUS : String = ➥
"EVENT_GET_FLIGHT_STATUS";

    }
}
```

This class has a static constant called EVENT_GET_FLIGHT_STATUS, which assigns a name to the event and allows static access to the event handler. This event and a command, which in our simple application is called GetFlightStatusCommand, are paired together in the controller in the addCommand method. The command implements the Command pattern. Our example is elementary, so we have only one command that calls the business and service layer to get the flight status. GetFlightStatusCommand is as follows:

```
package advancedflex3.ch01.cairngorm.command
{
    import com.adobe.cairngorm.commands.Command;
    import com.adobe.cairngorm.control.CairngormEvent;
    import com.adobe.cairngorm.business.Responder;
    import advancedflex3.ch01.cairngorm.business.FlightStatusDelegate;
    import advancedflex3.ch01.cairngorm.events.GetFlightStatusEvent;
    import advancedflex3.ch01.cairngorm.model.ModelLocator;
    import advancedflex3.ch01.cairngorm.model.FlightStatus;

    public class GetFlightStatusCommand implements Command, Responder
    {
        private var model : ModelLocator = ModelLocator.getInstance();
        private var statusId : String;

        public function GetFlightStatusCommand()
        {
            //TODO: implement function
        }

        public function execute(event:CairngormEvent):void
```

```
        {
                var flightStatusEvent : GetFlightStatusEvent = ➥
GetFlightStatusEvent( event );
                var flightId : String = flightStatusEvent.flightId;
                statusId = flightStatusEvent.statusId;
                var delegate : FlightStatusDelegate = ➥
new FlightStatusDelegate( this );
                delegate.getStatusForFlight( flightId );
        }

        public function onResult(event:* = null):void
        {
                var lastFlightStatus : String = event;
                var flightStatus : FlightStatus = ➥
model.flightStatusManager.getFlightStatus(statusId);
                flightStatus.lastFlightStatus = lastFlightStatus;
                flightStatus.flightStatusError = "";
        }

        public function onFault(event:* = null):void
        {
                var flightStatus : FlightStatus = ➥
model.flightStatusManager.getFlightStatus(statusId);
                flightStatus.lastFlightStatus = null;
                flightStatus.flightStatusError = "An error occured.";
        }
    }
}
```

The execute method of the command contains the core logic used to get the job done. In this case, the command invokes the remote getStatusForFlight method via a business delegate. A command can also call a service directly.

All services are defined in Cairngorm in an MXML file, conventionally called Services.mxml. We use a RemoteObject to connect to server-side counterparts. We could have used HTTPService or WebService, too. The services and the delegates are put together in the business folder (refer back to Figure 1-8). Our delegate class is called FlightStatusDelegate. For reference, the source code of that class is listed here:

```
package advancedflex3.ch01.cairngorm.business
{
    import mx.rpc.AsyncToken
    import com.adobe.cairngorm.business.Responder;
    import com.adobe.cairngorm.business.ServiceLocator;

    public class FlightStatusDelegate
    {
        private var responder : Responder;
        private var service : Object;
```

```
        public function FlightStatusDelegate(responder:Responder)
        {
            this.service =
ServiceLocator.getInstance().➥
getService( "flightStatusService" );
            this.responder = responder;
        }

        public function getStatusForFlight( flightId : String ) : void
{

            var token : AsyncToken = ➥
service.getStatusForFlight( flightId );
            token.resultHandler = responder.onResult;
            token.faultHandler = responder.onFault;
            if( flightId == "fail" )
            {
                responder.onFault();
            }
            else
            {
                var flightStatus : String = "A sample status string";
                responder.onResult( flightStatus );
            }
        }


    }
}
```

There is one more piece to the Cairngorm puzzle, and that is the model. Cairngorm defines a ModelLocator marker interface and recommends that the implementation of this interface be a singleton. All model elements are organized in an object-oriented manner and are bound to this singleton instance. These object-oriented representations are also called DTOs. Historically, these DTOs were called value objects (VO). VO is now used to connote something else. Cairngorm likes to refer to these object-oriented representations as VOs.

Listed in order are the ModelLocator, FlightStatus, and FlightStatusManager classes:

```
/*ModelLocator.as*/
package advancedflex3.ch01.cairngorm.model
{
    import com.adobe.cairngorm.model.ModelLocator;

    public class ModelLocator implements
com.adobe.cairngorm.model.ModelLocator
    {
        public static function
getInstance() :
advancedflex3.ch01.cairngorm.model.ModelLocator
    {
```

```
                if ( modelLocator == null )
                    modelLocator =
new advancedflex3.ch01.➡
cairngorm.model.ModelLocator();


                return modelLocator;
            }

        public function ModelLocator()
        {
            //TODO: implement function
            if ( advancedflex3.ch01.➡
cairngorm.model.ModelLocator.modelLocator != null )
            throw new Error➡
( "Only one ModelLocator instance should be instantiated" );
        }

        private static var modelLocator : ➡
advancedflex3.ch01.cairngorm.model.ModelLocator;

        public var flightStatusManager : ➡
FlightStatusManager = new FlightStatusManager();

    }

}


/*FlightStatus.as*/
package advancedflex3.ch01.cairngorm.model
{
    public class FlightStatus
    {
        public function FlightStatus()
        {
            //TODO: implement function
        }

        [Bindable]
        public var lastFlightStatus : String;
        [Bindable]
        public var flightStatusError : String;

    }
}

/*FlightStatusManager.as*/
package advancedflex3.ch01.cairngorm.model
{
```

```
import flash.utils.Dictionary;

public class FlightStatusManager
{
    private var flightStatusCollection : Dictionary;

    public function FlightStatusManager()
    {
        flightStatusCollection = new Dictionary();
    }

    public function ➥
getFlightStatus( statusId : String ) : FlightStatus
    {
        var key : String = statusId;
        if( flightStatusCollection[ key ] == null )
        {
            var flightStatus : FlightStatus = ➥
new FlightStatus();
            flightStatusCollection[ key ] = flightStatus;
        }
        return FlightStatus( flightStatusCollection[ key ] );
    }

}
}
```

Although a discussion on Cairngorm can go on longer, our simple example application is covered, so I will stop right here. Next, we take our simple sample application and build it using PureMVC, an alternative to Cairngorm.

## PureMVC

PureMVC is an alternative framework to Cairngorm, as far as MVC goes. More accurately, the ActionScript 3.0 implementations of the platform-independent PureMVC framework compete with Cairngorm. As the name suggests, the framework focuses exclusively on MVC. PureMVC has four core artifacts:

- **Model**: A singleton that keeps named references to proxies that interact with the data model and the underlying services
- **View**: A singleton that keeps named references to mediators that facilitate view-level manipulation and interaction capabilities
- **Controller**: A singleton that keeps named references to stateless commands that as always help in getting the job done
- **Façade**: A singleton that keeps references to the other three singletons (Model, View, and Controller) and provides access to all the public functions of these singletons

In the standard configuration, the core of the framework, which is the four elements, Model, View, Controller, and Façade, is composed of all singletons. In the multicore configuration, each of these four elements are multitons. The Multiton pattern, unlike the Singleton pattern, keeps one instance per named reference in a dictionary. Therefore, there can be multiple instances, but each name (reference) maps to a unique object. In this example, we consider the standard configuration.

In PureMVC, proxies, mediators, and commands are the primary objects. These objects, as mentioned previously, are accessed through Model, View, and Control elements, respectively.

Let's build our sample application that gets the flight status using PureMVC. As we build out, I will also annotate our actions, and that should help you understand the mechanics of the framework.

We start by creating a Flex Project in Flex Builder 3. We call our Flex Project FlightStatusPureMVC. The current stable release of PureMVC for AS3 (Standard) is version 2.0.3. You can download the distribution in ZIP archive format from http://www.puremvc.org. When you extract the archive, you will find three folders within the distribution: asdoc, bin, and src. What you need is the SWC file in the bin folder. Add this to your library path in your Flex project in the same style that you added the Cairngorm SWC file. Figure 1-9 shows this.

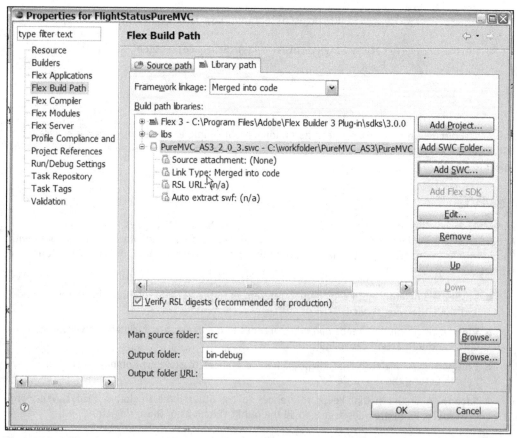

**Figure 1-9.** Adding the PureMVC SWC file to the library path

Now create the folder structure that will be appropriate for a PureMVC project. Figure 1-10 shows the folder structure.

**Figure 1-10.** Folder structure for a simple PureMVC-based Flex project

The code is divided into three main parts: model, view, and controller. In our case, the view is quite simple and includes only one MXML component. Views in PureMVC are supported by mediators, which are view helpers. Our view and mediator are as follows:

```
/*FlightStatusPanel.mxml */
<?xml version="1.0" encoding="utf-8"?>
<mx:Panel xmlns:mx="http://www.adobe.com/2006/mxml" >
<mx:Script>
    <![CDATA[
        import advancedflex3.ch01.puremvc.*;

        private static const
GET_FLIGHT_STATUS:String =
"getFlightStatus";

        private function getStatusForFlight() : void
        {
            dispatchEvent(new Event(GET_FLIGHT_STATUS));
        }
```

```
        ]]>
    </mx:Script>
    <mx:Form>
        <mx:FormItem label="Flight Id (Number)">
            <mx:TextInput id="flightIdTextInput"/>
            <mx:Button label="Get Flight Status"
click="getStatusForFlight();"/>
        </mx:FormItem>
        <mx:FormItem label="Flight Id (Number)">
            <mx:TextInput id="lastFlightStatus"/>
        </mx:FormItem>
        <mx:FormItem>
            <mx:TextInput id="flightStatusError"/>
        </mx:FormItem>
    </mx:Form>
</mx:Panel>


/*FlightStatusMediator*/
package advancedflex3.ch01.puremvc.view
{
    import advancedflex3.ch01.puremvc.model.FlightStatusProxy;

    import org.puremvc.as3.interfaces.IMediator;
    import org.puremvc.as3.interfaces.INotification;
    import org.puremvc.as3.patterns.mediator.Mediator;

    public class FlightStatusMediator
extends Mediator implements IMediator
    {
        /* Canonical name of the mediator */
        public static const NAME:String = "FlightStatusMediator";

        public function
FlightStatusMediator(viewComponent:Object=null)
        {
            super(NAME, viewComponent);
            flightStatusProxy =
FlightStatusProxy( facade.➥
retrieveProxy( FlightStatusProxy.NAME ) );
            flightStatusPanel.➥
addEventListener( FlightStatusPanel.➥
GET_FLIGHT_STATUS, getFlightStatus);

        }


        public function listNotificationInterests():Array
        {
            //TODO: implement function
            return null;
```

```
        }

        public function➡
handleNotification(notification:INotification):void
        {
            //TODO: implement function
        }

        protected function get flightStatusPanel():FlightStatusPanel
        {
            return viewComponent as FlightStatusPanel;
        }

        private function getFlightStatus( event:Event = null ) : void
        {
            //method that passes the flight status
            //request down the chain
        }

        private var flightStatusProxy:FlightStatusProxy;

    }
}
```

In PureMVC, the data and the state are captured in the model. The model has three parts: the object representation of the entities (also called value objects), the delegates for external service invocation and other business-layer functionality, and the proxies of the value objects. The proxies provide a handle to the value object and the business delegates. The simple FlightStatus value object is as follows:

```
package advancedflex3.ch01.puremvc.model.vo
{
    public class FlightStatus
    {
        public function
FlightStatus(lastFlightStatus:String,
flightStatusError:String)
        {
            this.lastFlightStatus = lastFlightStatus;
            this.flightStatusError = flightStatusError;
        }

        public var lastFlightStatus : String;
        public var flightStatusError : String;

    }
}
```

The controller contains the commands, which as always conduct some desired action. I am going to skip listing all those details. All of this source code is available for download from the book's web site.

PureMVC is a small but scalable framework and works well for simple and complex scenarios alike.

## Fireclay

The last of the frameworks is Fireclay, which I created. Many of the best practices–related discussion earlier are about patterns and frameworks that are implemented in Fireclay. I will avoid walking you through details here because I have already done that previously. However, I will summarize the key concepts for completeness. To build our simple example, this is what you would do:

- You start by building a simple view with the form elements.
- Then you have a view helper do the event propagation based on user button click.
- The event dispatcher posts the event to the event bus.
- The event bus looks up the mapping dictionary to identify the event listeners.
- Explicit event listeners can be specified at the time of posting.
- Commands are defined as event listeners.
- On the event firing, the execute method of commands are invoked.
- The commands could be classified in a registry and bound to namespaces, if there are enough of these and such a structure is required.
- The model elements are accessed via proxies.
- Services are invoked to get external data and business functionality.

All registries and the event bus in Fireclay implement the Multiton pattern. The event bus itself is unique to Fireclay. An event bus can handle events in a sequenced queue or could work in publish-subscribe mode. A default event bus comes with the framework. However, you could implement one of your own by implementing the IEventBus interface.

# Choosing what's there vs. creating your own

Reinventing the wheel is never advisable; therefore, you should try and leverage an existing framework as far as possible. However, when the discipline is young and the field is evolving, it's difficult to judge the stability of the current innovation. In this section, I attempt to bring forth a few perspectives that may help you choose a framework.

## It's an emerging discipline

RIA is still a new technology. Flex is an evolving application framework, where a newer release is typically a substantial change from the existing one. Web technologies are being stretched every day to become and behave like the desktop. Newer types of collaborative and highly scalable applications are becoming common. In short, the world is changing every day. So, best practices and recommendations of yesterday sometimes are outdated or less relevant today. That is precisely the state of the existing Flex metapatterns or frameworks. Cairngorm is too deeply tied to the J2EE world, which is losing strength today. It does not address many of the desired features in today's RIA. It involves artifacts that look redundant (and at times serve as antipatterns). PureMVC is a better choice than Cairngorm, but it focuses exclusively on MVC. It does not address all the features you would expect of a micro-architecture.

## A way to decide

One way to choose a framework is to see whether the framework in question addresses everything that you need in building your application successfully. If there are many gaps, it's probably wise to start from the ground up. This is precisely what I did. I wanted an event bus to loosely plug in listeners for the user events and have the components in multiple containers interact with each other based on these events. None of the existing frameworks could do it, so I created one of my known. It's quite likely that more frameworks will emerge before a few prominent ones become the standard choice.

# Summary

In this chapter, I started with the Model-View-Controller metapattern, which is the most important design pattern by far when it comes to user interfaces. Then I surveyed and analyzed some of the key ideas that could help create robust enterprise-grade applications. Subsequently, we ventured briefly into application development with the two popular frameworks—Cairngorm and PureMVC. I also touched upon Fireclay. I enlisted a few recommendations and left you with enough food for thought. At all times, I maintained the opinion that there is no universally applicable idea and recommended using these as you see them fitting into your specific case.

All along, the chapter stuck to simple examples to keep the focus on clarifying the concepts. However, these ideas and its implementation in the form of the Fireclay framework will work smoothly even in complex applications.

The gain of adopting a framework like Fireclay or even adopting some of these architectural and design patterns piecemeal is that you will be able to create scalable, flexible, and extensible applications with ease. The challenge is that you may end up overrelying on these patterns or the framework and expect them to solve all your application-wide problems. In such situations, there is the potential of your getting disillusioned and abandoning the good ideas altogether. Therefore, as mentioned before, it is always wise to first understand the requirements and build a simple solution that meets them and then subsequently refactor the application using ideas from here.

The next chapter onward picks up one advanced Flex/AIR topic and drills deeper into it. In each of these chapters and beyond this book, this architectural and pattern discussion should still be relevant.

## Chapter 2

# CONSTRUCTING ADVANCED COMPONENTS

By Shashank Tiwari

Flex is a component-based application development framework. It comes with a set of prebuilt visual and nonvisual components. These components are available through the framework API in both ActionScript 3.0 (which from here on will be referred to as AS3) and MXML form. AS3 is the latest version of ActionScript, the ECMA (third edition: ECMA-262) standard–compliant language that compiles to byte-code for the Flash Virtual Machine (VM). AS3 runs on ActionScript Virtual Machine 2 (AVM2), which is available with Flash Player 9. AVM2 improves the application run-time performance over ten times as compared to ActionScript Virtual Machine 1 (AVM1). AS3 is a statically and strongly typed object-oriented language. MXML is an XML-based user interface markup language that translates to AS3 code before being compiled to run on the Flash VM. This rich set of components, exposed via AS3 and MXML APIs, helps you rapidly build your applications and provides you a starting point to extend the framework to implement advanced controls, containers, and service components. Components can be extended using AS3 or MXML. Either of the approaches has its advantages and disadvantages, and the choice should be driven by the specific use case at hand.

Let's start by extending MXML components.

# Extending components using MXML

Flex exposes its controls and containers in MXML. This makes it possible for you to build rich interactive applications using declarative XML markups. As mentioned earlier, MXML code translates to AS3 classes. Snippets of AS3 code can be embedded in an MXML file within the Script begin and end tags, and this code becomes part of the AS3 class that maps to the MXML component. This technique is useful because often XML markups alone are not sufficient to manipulate data and implement behavior. Another advantage of this technique is that it lets you abstract out reusable pieces as custom components.

Therefore it's possible to extend the available set of framework components and package those components up as reusable pieces without much trouble. This is exactly what we do when creating custom components using MXML. The best way to learn the details of this process is to walk through a few examples.

## Walking through a simple example

As a first example, let's create a custom radio button group with five buttons, labeled as follows:

- Strongly Agree

- Agree

- Indifferent

- Disagree

- Strongly Disagree

Such a radio button group can be reused in a questionnaire application, which records responses to various questions on a scale that varies from strong agreement to strong disagreement. Such questions are common when measuring personality tests or invoking responses to political or economic issues. The code for such a button group could be as follows:

```
<?xml version="1.0" encoding="utf-8"?>
<mx:VBox
xmlns:mx="http://www.adobe.com/2006/mxml"
width="400" height="300">
    <mx:RadioButton groupName="responseType"
        id="stronglyAgree"
        label="Strongly Agree"
        width="150"/>
    <mx:RadioButton groupName="responseType"
        id="agree"
        label="Agree"
        width="150"/>
    <mx:RadioButton groupName="responseType"
        id="indifferent"
        label="Indifferent"
        width="150"/>
    <mx:RadioButton groupName="responseType"
        id="disagree"
```

```
                label="Disagree"
                width="150"/>
        <mx:RadioButton groupName="responseType"
            id="stronglyDisagree"
            label="Strongly Disagree"
            width="150"/>
    </mx:VBox>
```

This custom button can reside in a file called CustomRadioGroup.mxml. By doing this, you create a custom component called CustomRadioGroup. There is no restriction on the name of the MXML file. Just remember that whatever name you give it becomes the name of your custom component. In AS3 though, the name of the file needs to correspond to the public class contained in the file. In AS3, you can have more than one class in a file but only one of them can be public.

Now you can use this custom component in your application. You first have to define a namespace for the custom component location and give the namespace a handle. Next, you include the custom component by simply appending the custom component name to the namespace handle. Here is the code for it:

```
<?xml version="1.0" encoding="utf-8"?>
<mx:Application xmlns:mx="http://www.adobe.com/2006/mxml"
    xmlns:custom="*">
    <custom:CustomRadioGroup/>
</mx:Application>
```

This simple application, which contains just the custom component we built, is as shown in Figure 2-1.

In every Flex application, the framework components are aliased with a handle as well. Most often mx is the name of this handle. The handle can be renamed as desired simply by modifying the namespace declaration, which in its usual form is as follows: xmlns:mx="http://www.adobe.com/2006/mxml".Therefore, binding a handle to the custom component namespace and accessing custom components using the handle is identical in approach to the mechanism used to get hold of the standard framework components. This consistency makes it effortless to use custom components.

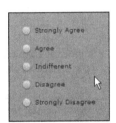

**Figure 2-1.** Radio Button Group custom component

In our example of the radio button group, we merely bundled a specific implementation of a set of radio buttons (laid out in a VBox) as a custom component. This exercise could be classified as aggregating and extending the built-in components. It's also possible to start from scratch, but remember not to reinvent the wheel if you don't need to. The Flex framework has a rich and exhaustive set of components, and extending and combining them satisfies most custom component development use cases. Therefore, building a custom component in Flex often is not only about future reuse, but also about immediate reuse of the framework components. Extending components has other advantages as well. It puts components in a component hierarchy and brings the benefits of inheritance and polymorphism. Custom components can substitute for their parents by providing the additional functionality without breaking the intercomponent and intraframework contracts.

Components can be customized through a set of public properties, styles, and effects that they expose via the API. Such manipulation does not require creation of custom components. It only amounts to setting appropriate values for these publicly exposed attributes. This type of customization satisfies a large number of requirements. It's possible to save a specific configuration of these attribute values as a reusable components, if need be. Sometimes, though, attribute setting is not enough because the components need to include newer attributes and implement additional behavior. Such cases that require us to add newer properties and behavior or aggregate a set of the available components are the ones for which we usually need to create custom components.

# Extending our example

Let's go back to our initial example and add more features to get a sense of custom component creation nuances and complexity. To our initial radio group example, we add a simple method to capture the user choice and bind it to a label. The initial value of the label is set to No Selection because that is exactly the case. The modifications to the code involves inclusion of an <mx:Script> </mx:Script> block with the following code:

```
<mx:Script>
    <![CDATA[
        [Bindable]
        private var selection:String = "No Selection";

        private function rb_selection(evt:Event):void {
            var rb:RadioButton = evt.currentTarget as RadioButton;
            this.selection = rb.label;
        }
    ]]>
</mx:Script>
```

The code in the Script block can reside in an external AS3 class file. This class file can be assigned as the source of an <mx:Script> block.

Each of the radio buttons in our MXML component needs to set the rb_selection function as the event listener for the change event. In our case, it means we set the event listener for all five instances of the radio button. To define an event handler for the change event, each of the radio button components needs to include an additional property as follows:

```
change="rb_selection(event)"
```

A change event is fired by a radio button when it is selected. On the event firing, a registered event listener is invoked. An Event object is passed to the event listener. The Event object contains all the information about the event target that dispatches the event. Information about the event target is culled out in the event listener and acted upon as desired.

To show the listener in action, we also include a Label component to display the selection. The Label code is as shown:

```
<mx:Label text="{selection}"/>
```

Now every selection you make on the custom radio button group component gets reflected on the Label available as a part of the component.

You may have noticed that data binding was used to bind the value of the selection variable to the text of the Label. In our example, the variable that holds the selection is private, and we have no trouble consuming it internally. Things will be slightly different though, if we want to consume this value from outside the component. For a start, the value needs to be accessible publicly. This can be done by either defining the variable as public or defining a combination of public getter and setter for this variable. Although the two ways achieve pretty much the same result, I prefer using and a getter and a setter as it allows me to manipulate or process the set value before it's used. Normally the variable declaration is done using AS3 (within the script block) in MXML components. You can also use MXML only to include public properties. For example, an alternative way of declaring the variable called selection is as follows:

```
<mx:String id="selection">No Selection</mx:String>
```

Once the variable is accessible from outside, we wire it up so that external components can listen to the changes in our custom component.

## Events and loose coupling

If you want to include this component in an application, you may want to extract the radio button selection information easily within this new context. In order to do that, it may be best to redispatch the change event. The new application context can listen to the redispatched event and take appropriate action on its occurrence. This makes a loosely coupled arrangement between the custom component and the application that uses it.

With this modification, the <mx:Script> block appears as follows:

```
<mx:Script>
    <![CDATA[
        private function rb_selection(evt:Event):void {
                dispatchEvent(evt);
        }
    ]]>
</mx:Script>
```

To make this event available in a calling MXML file, we also need to define the event within a metadata tag. Here is what the code looks like:

```
<mx:Metadata>
        [Event(name="change", type="flash.events.Event")]
</mx:Metadata>
```

Failing to declare the event metadata tag throws errors and makes the event inaccessible.

Once all the required modifications are made, the application is ready to include our custom component. The calling application gets modified as follows:

```
<?xml version="1.0" encoding="utf-8"?>
<mx:Application xmlns:mx="http://www.adobe.com/2006/mxml"
    xmlns:custom="*">
    <mx:Script>
        <![CDATA[
```

```
                import mx.controls.RadioButton;
                import flash.events.Event;

                [Bindable]
                private var selection:String = "No Selection";

                private function
        rb_selection_handler➥
      (eventObj:Event):void {
                    var rb:RadioButton =➥
        eventObj.currentTarget as RadioButton;
                    this.selection = rb.label;
                }
            ]]>
        </mx:Script>
        <custom:CustomRadioGroup change="rb_selection_handler(event)"/>
        <mx:Label text="{selection}"/>
    </mx:Application>
```

You are now ready to compile and use this application.

In a real-life situation it's also advisable to create custom event types where required and utilize static constants to enable compile-time checking for the new event type. Here is a possible example snippet:

```
    package
    {
        import flash.events.Event;

        public class CustomEvent extends Event
        {
            // Define static constant for event type.
            public static const CUSTOM_EVENT:String = "customEvent";
```

When you create an instance of the custom event using new Event(CustomEvent.CUSTOM_EVENT), you also do compile-time checking for the event type. This means errors will be thrown if you try to create the custom event using an incorrect value for the static constant. For example, new Event(CustomEvent.MY_CUSTOM_EVENT) will not work. In ordinary cases, where we use instance variables and not constants, these types of incorrect name passing go undetected at compile time.

So far you have seen the creation of custom events and addition of properties and methods to a component. Now I will show you how to create custom components by combining two or more of the standard ones.

# Aggregating components

With MXML, it's easy to aggregate components into a container, and this is often an inspiration for creation of custom components. Say you need a form with username and password text entry fields and a button with a Submit label to be used in many of your applications. Wouldn't it be better to create it once and use it many times? You often need such a form to get users to input their login credentials.

In MXML, this would imply putting the code together as follows:

```
<?xml version="1.0" encoding="utf-8"?>
<mx:Form
xmlns:mx="http://www.adobe.com/2006/mxml"
width="400" height="300">
    <mx:FormHeading label="Login Form" />
    <mx:FormItem label="User Name:">
        <mx:TextInput id="userName" />
    </mx:FormItem>
    <mx:FormItem label="Password:">
        <mx:TextInput id="password" />
    </mx:FormItem>
    <mx:FormItem>
        <mx:Button id="submit" label="Submit" />
    </mx:FormItem>
</mx:Form>
```

The output of this aggregation is as shown in Figure 2-2.

With MXML, you can create almost all types of components, except those that involve logging or require the creation of a new layout scheme, different from the ones that come in the standard distribution. The script block lets you write almost any sort of AS3 code, so you can do almost all the custom things in your MXML component that you would do in your AS3 component, except for the ones I just mentioned. MXML components map to an AS3 class when parsed. All the additional properties and methods defined in the script block of the MXML file become part of the relevant AS3 class.

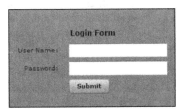

**Figure 2-2.** Reusable login form component

# Component context

A Flex application often uses the MXML Application tag as the entry point and the primary container for the application. When you include a control or a container within an Application tag, you scope these components within the same Application. In other words, a reference to the this keyword from anywhere in the application resolves to the Application context. However, the use of this from within a custom component, included in the Application, does not show the same behavior. In other words, using this in a radio button group example like the one shown earlier would resolve to VBox and not to the containing Application. Using the mx.core.Application.application static variable would be an appropriate way to get hold of the application context.

Access to the application context becomes especially important when a custom component needs to refer to something that lies outside of it but within the same application. It is also handy if the custom component needs to get application-wide control. An example of this might be changing the keyboard focus to the application stage instead of the component, when using hidden components.

Before we move on to constructing custom components using ActionScript, let me emphasize once again that, if you like the declarative MXML-style programming model, you will be able to leverage that to create interesting advanced components. Other than with nonvisual components, there is little restriction in what you can do with MXML. Next, let's get into custom component creation with ActionScript.

# Extending components using ActionScript

Our next endeavor is to create custom components using ActionScript (actually AS3 because Flex is an AS3 framework). We can create both visual and nonvisual (Formatters, Validators, and Effects) components with AS3. We will start with visual components and then move on to nonvisual components.

## Creating custom visual components

Creating visual components in AS3 is similar to creating them in MXML, except that now we use an object-oriented programming language throughout instead of a mixture of XML and an object-oriented language.

The best starting point is to understand the object hierarchy of the user interface components in Flex. All visual components in the Flex framework inherit from the UIComponent class. The UIComponent class is the parent of both interactive and noninteractive components. Interactive components let a user interact through keyboard and mouse events, whereas a noninteractive component is a display component. For example, a MenuBar is an interactive component, while a Label is a noninteractive component. Although the UIComponent is the base class for all visual component classes, it is never used directly in MXML, and therefore there are no corresponding MXML tags. At the first level of inheritance from UIComponent stand Container, Button, NumericStepper, and ComboBase.

Container is the base class for all layout components, which control the layout of its child components. Container itself is an abstract class. One of its subclasses (i.e., Box, Canvas, Accordion, Form, Panel, Tile, or ViewStack) is used as a layout container. Container or one of its subclasses is the appropriate class to extend from when creating custom layouts. As an example, you extend Container or Canvas to create a card layout, which stacks its children as a pack of cards.

Button, by means of pressing or clicking, enables a user to trigger an action. Its form and appearance can be customized, but most often it is rectangular in shape. Its subclasses allow it to manifest in many forms, including LinkButton, PopUpButton, RadioButton, or CheckBox.

NumericStepper lets a user select a value from an ordered set. Visually the component has a text input field and a pair of up and down arrows to step through the numeric values. NumericStepper is fairly unique in its functionality and branches out as a separate stream from the UIComponent class. You can extend a numeric stepper to render an ordered set as a dial or another such option.

ComboBase is a combination of two features, a display and a chooser. What is displayed is what you choose. ComboBox, ColorPicker, and DateField are subclasses of the abstract ComboBase class.

It's important to familiarize yourself with this API structure, because every time you create a custom component in AS3, you extend an existing class from this hierarchy. Our very first example will confirm this statement. Details of all AS3 classes in Flex are listed with all their public properties, methods, styles, and events in the language reference, which is accessible through the online Flex 3 LiveDocs.

### Custom AS3 component example

To keep things consistent and comparable, we implement our first MXML custom component, a radio button group component, using AS3. Here is the code:

```
package
{
```

```
      import mx.containers.VBox;
      import mx.controls.RadioButton;

      public class CustomRadioGroupAS extends VBox
      {
          public function CustomRadioGroupAS()
          {
              super();
              createMembers();
          }


          private function createMembers():void {
              var stronglyAgree:RadioButton =➡
createRadioButton➡
("Strongly Agree", "150", "responseType");
              var agree:RadioButton = ➡
createRadioButton➡
("Agree", "150", "responseType");
              var indifferent:RadioButton = ➡
createRadioButton➡
("Indifferent", "150", "responseType");
              var disagree:RadioButton = ➡
createRadioButton➡
("Disagree", "150", "responseType");
              var stronglyDisagree:RadioButton = ➡
createRadioButton➡
("Strongly Disagree", "150", "responseType");
              this.addChild(stronglyAgree);
              this.addChild(agree);
              this.addChild(indifferent);
              this.addChild(disagree);
              this.addChild(stronglyDisagree);
          }

          private function ➡
createRadioButton➡
(labelValue:String, widthValue:String, ➡
groupNameValue:String):RadioButton {
              var rb:RadioButton = new RadioButton();
              rb.label = labelValue;
              rb.width= new Number(widthValue);
              rb.groupName = groupNameValue;
              return rb;
          }
      }
  }
```

The output of this AS3 component is identical to what you see in Figure 2-1.

This was a trivial example. Nonetheless, it shows that creating custom components in AS3 is fairly straightforward, especially if you know object-oriented programming. Even if you are new to object-oriented programming, there isn't anything to fret about. Object-oriented programming is intuitive, and with moderate effort developers can learn to leverage it.

In any case, to use and leverage Flex, you need to know AS3. Knowledge of fundamental AS3 goes a long way when creating advanced custom components.

Let's go back to our example and continue adding new features to it. This will help us analyze the issues and advantages of creating custom components with AS3. Once more, we will try and reimplement the features in our MXML custom component example using AS3.

In the MXML example, we added an event listener to handle the change events triggered by our custom component radio buttons. The listener function was assigned as the value of the change event property in the component tags. To do the same in AS3, we use code like this:

```
rb.addEventListener(Event.CHANGE, rb_selection(event));
```

The event listener function in MXML was written in AS3 within the script block, and that will not need any modification to be used in the AS3 code. Just copy and paste it in. Our radio button group with the listener using AS3 is now ready.

Public properties can be added to custom AS3 components using public variables or a set of getters and setters. This is no different from what you saw in MXML script blocks. It's also no different from how you always define and access attributes and properties in AS3.

For clarity and to bolster what you have learned so far, let's look at one more complete example of a custom component in AS3. This custom component is a custom item renderer for the Tree component. It extends TreeItemRenderer and can be assigned as the item renderer for a Tree component. When assigned as the item renderer for a tree component, the custom item renderer displays different images for different tree levels. To restrict complexity, we only differentiate a tree element as a branch or a leaf. In the custom tree, different images are shown for the branch level and the leaf levels of this tree. Here is a snippet of that code:

```
package advancedFlex3.ch02 {
public class MyTreeItemRenderer extends TreeItemRenderer {
    protected var myImage:Image;
    private var imageWidth:Number = 30;
    private var imageHeight:Number = 20;
    private var imageToLabelMargin:Number = 2;
    private var showDefaultBranchIcon:Boolean = false;
    private var showDefaultLeafIcon:Boolean = false;

    private var branchImage:String = "../assets/branch_image.PNG";
    private var leafImage:String = "../assets/leaf_image.PNG";

    public function MyTreeItemRenderer() {
        super();
        mouseEnabled = false;
    }
```

```
....
override protected function createChildren():void {
    myImage = new Image();
    myImage.width = imageWidth;
    myImage.height = imageHeight;
    myImage.setStyle( "verticalAlign", "middle" );
    addChild(myImage);
    addEventListener( MouseEvent.CLICK, openBranch  );
    super.createChildren();
}

override public function set data(value:Object):void {
    super.data = value;
    var _tree:Tree = Tree(this.parent.parent);
    if(TreeListData(super.listData).hasChildren) {
        setStyle("color", 0xff0000);
        setStyle("fontWeight", 'bold');
        if( !showDefaultBranchIcon ) {
            _tree.setStyle("folderClosedIcon", null);
            _tree.setStyle("folderOpenIcon", null);
        }
    } else {
        setStyle("color", 0x000000);
        setStyle("fontWeight", 'normal');
        if( !showDefaultLeafIcon ) {
            _tree.setStyle("defaultLeafIcon", null);
        }
    }
}

override protected function➥
updateDisplayList(unscaledWidth:Number, ➥
unscaledHeight:Number):void {
        super.updateDisplayList(unscaledWidth, unscaledHeight);
            if(super.data) {
                if(TreeListData(super.listData).hasChildren) {
                    var currentNodeXMLList:XMLList = ➥
new XMLList(TreeListData(super.listData).node);
                    var numOfImmediateChildren:int = ➥
currentNodeXMLList[0].children().length();
                    myImage.source = branchImage;
                    super.label.text = ➥
TreeListData(super.listData).text + ➥
"(" + numOfImmediateChildren + ")";
    } else {
            myImage.source = leafImage;
        }
        myImage.x = super.label.x;
        super.label.x = myImage.x + ➥
```

```
imageWidth + imageToLabelMargin;
                }
            }
    }
    }
    }
```

Please don't get lost in the details of the implementation. The purpose is to show creation of a custom component in AS3, and let's stick to that. The specifics of the custom logic will always depend on what you want to build and how you want to use the component.

## Beyond the very basics

Next, I discuss a couple of small but interesting aspects that are useful when creating custom components in AS3.

When used within MXML, a Flex component sometimes allows you to specify values within its begin and end tags without actually specifying the property name. The value you specify gets allocated to a component property. Such a property is the default property of the component. As with built-ins, you can define a default property in your custom AS3 component as well. A class that implements the component needs to be annotated with [DefaultProperty("defaultProperty")] if defaultProperty is the default property for the class. A small code sample follows:

```
package advancedflex3.ch02.as3components {
    import mx.controls.Button;

    [DefaultProperty("defaultLabel")]

    public class ButtonDefaultProperty extends Button {

        public function ButtonDefaultProperty() {
            super();
        }

        public function set defaultLabel(value:String):void {
            if (value!=null)
            label=value;
        }

        public function get defaultLabel():String {
            return label;
        }
    }
}
```

The preceding code creates a custom button that accepts a default property. An application using this custom button component could easily set a value, say Submit, to the custom button simply by passing it between the begin and end tags of the custom components, as follows:

```
<custom: ButtonDefaultProperty >Submit</custom: ButtonDefaultProperty>
```

Another interesting annotation with respect to added properties is to make them user editable or inspectable by Flex Builder. In this case, the property needs to be annotated as [Inspectable]. Here is a small example:

```
[Inspectable]
var propName:SomeActionScriptType;
```

This completes the essentials of custom visual component creation using AS3. However, the possibilities of adding advanced features are limitless. AS3 is a powerful programming language, and you are hardly restricted because of the language or the Flex framework capabilities.

Before we move on to nonvisual classes and advanced topics on custom components with AS3, it may be beneficial to quickly revisit the obvious but important concepts around data binding and method override. Data binding and method override are not directly related to each other, but they both show up frequently in all types of applications.

Values can be assigned to properties via all the standard mechanisms that you use in Flex applications. One of the popular ways is to use data binding, which works the same here as anywhere else. Use curly braces to specify the expression or the source and make the source [Bindable] so that changes to it can be propagated to the destination. Remember that making a class bindable makes all its public properties bindable. When a source value changes, a propertyChange event is dispatched, and this is what carries the value through to the destination. Sometimes making a variable bindable imposes overheads. In such cases, you could explicitly dispatch the value change events and handle them to receive the new value. When using getter and setter accessor methods for properties, dispatching the event from within a setter is a good choice because that is where the changed value is set.

When we spoke of data binding, we also mentioned overriding methods. You know that you can define methods in your AS3 custom components. However, you don't need to create new methods every time. It's also possible to override the existing methods of your superclass. Just keep the same method signature as that of the superclass, and make sure to append that definition with the override keyword. Also, remember to provide your own custom implementation to override the existing logic. This is all standard AS3 and demonstrates the power of object orientation. Here is a small example (which appeared earlier in the custom item renderer example):

```
override public function set data(value:Object):void {
        super.data = value;
        var _tree:Tree = Tree(this.parent.parent);
         if(TreeListData(super.listData).hasChildren) {
            setStyle("color", 0xff0000);
            setStyle("fontWeight", 'bold');
            if( !showDefaultBranchIcon ) {
                _tree.setStyle("folderClosedIcon", null);
                _tree.setStyle("folderOpenIcon", null);
            }
        } else {
            setStyle("color", 0x000000);
            setStyle("fontWeight", 'normal');
            if( !showDefaultLeafIcon ) {
                _tree.setStyle("defaultLeafIcon", null);
            }
```

```
        }
    }
```

Apart from property and behavior attributes, visual components have another set of important characteristics, namely styles and skins. Styles and skins affect the appearance of the visual components. They provide a way to customize the look and feel of those components. Specific configurations of styles and skins can be bundled with standard and custom components, and such bundles can be reused.

## Styles and skins

A Flex application's look and feel is defined and impacted by styles that affect the font type, font size, background color, relative positioning, and other such parameters. In Flex, such style configurations can be done in more than one way, by

- Including styles in an external CSS file
- Specifying styles inline
- Using an instance style attribute
- Programmatically using the StyleManager
- Using AS3 style getter and setter methods
- Defining styles via themes

Let's quickly describe and analyze each of these techniques.

**Including styles in an external CSS file** CSS allows a standard, flexible, and reusable way of defining styles in an external file. This external file can be included as the source attribute of a Style tag. For example:

```
<mx:Style source="externalCSSStyle.CSS" />
```

The external file contains all the style attributes. Style attributes can be defined at a type selector level, for example, for type Button, or at a global level. Here is what the style definition for a Button can be like:

```
Button {
        fontSize: 11;
        color: #99CCFF;
    }
```

Application, which is the root type of a Flex application, also qualifies as a type for style specification. Style attributes can be defined for the Application type level. Styles at this level would apply, in most cases, to all the components contained in the application. However, not all styles inherit in this fashion. To assure uniform style definitions for all components in an application, it is better to use the global style level. Global styles apply to all application components in a consistent manner.

The Flex framework components are bundled in a SWC called framework.swc. This framework archive distribution file contains default style specifications in a file called defaults.css. These default styles along with skins form the default Halo theme in Flex applications. Themes, which we will peek into a little later, are combinations of styles and skins that determine an application look and feel. It's possible to define an alternative default CSS file by explicitly passing the path to the alternative CSS file using the default-css-url parameter of the Flex compiler during compilation. If the intention is to merely remove the defaults, one could also resort to the crude method of renaming or deleting defaults.css from the /framework/libs directory to get rid of it.

Similar style definitions can also be placed inline with your application code.

**Specifying styles inline** Although styles in an external file are most flexible, sometimes it is convenient to define them within the application code. The style CSS structure itself won't be different but will now reside in an application, within the Style begin and end tags. Here is the Button style, defined inline:

```
<mx:Style>
Button {
        fontSize: 11;
        color: #99CCFF;
    }
</mx:Style>
```

An application can have both external CSS and inline CSS at the same time, but they cannot reside in the same Style tag.

**Using an instance style attribute** Simpler than inline styles is style specification at an instance level. Our Button example could then become

```
<mx:Button id="myButton" fontSize="11" color="#99CCFF" />
```

Components expose style attributes as they expose properties. Such a style is applied to the component instance and not to the component type as you saw in the previous two techniques of applying styles. This provides fine-grained control but can be cumbersome when applying styles at application-wide levels.

All the three style definition techniques mentioned so far are declarative in approach. Next we look at doing the same thing programmatically.

**Programmatically using StyleManager** The StyleManager class in the mx.styles package enables style to be set at the class, type, and global levels. It's the AS3 way of managing styles. It defines new CSS-based styles programmatically. Using StyleManager, the style in our Button class (in the preceding example) could be set as follows:

```
StyleManager.getStyleDeclaration("Button").setStyle("fontSize",11);
StyleManager.getStyleDeclaration("Button").setStyle("color","#99CCFF");
```

A call to the getStyleDeclaration method returns an object-oriented representation of CSS rules, as an object of type mx.styles.CSSStyleDeclaration. CSS declaration in MXML translates to an object of type CSSStyleDeclaration for each selector type. Therefore, CSS rules for a type Button are all encapsulated in such an object. The preceding code in other words adds a few CSS rules for a Button type just as the MXML Style tags do.

It's also possible to create a style declaration and then assign it to a selector type. Therefore, as an alternative to the getStyleDeclaration and the setStyle calls, to implement the style for our

Button, we could first create a style declaration and assign it to a Button type selector. Here is the code for the alternative implementation:

```
buttonStyle = new CSSStyleDeclaration('buttonStyle');
buttonStyle.setStyle('fontSize', 11);
buttonStyle.setStyle('color','#99CCFF');
StyleManager.setStyleDeclaration("Button", buttonStyle, true);
```

We use the setStyle method with the StyleManager class to set a style. However, such methods to get and set style can be called to access and manipulate the component instance styles or the style sheets directly at runtime.

**Using AS3 style getter setter methods** setStyle can be called on a component instance to set style. Once more we style our Button. This time we use the setStyle call on an instance of the button. Here is the code:

```
<mx:Script>
....
b1.setStyle("fontSize", 11);
b1.setStyle("color", #99CCFF);
....
</mx:Script>
<mx:Button id="b1" />
```

This way of setting style is flexible and allows for style configuration at runtime. However, with flexibility often comes performance overhead. So don't use this method unless you really need runtime style setting. Better still, don't use this technique for new style setting at all. Use one of the methods listed previously to set style the first time. Use the setStyle call to modify styles at runtime.

getStyle gets hold of a style. Make sure to cast the return type appropriately to retrieve the style information correctly.

Now we move to the last of the techniques on our list of ways to set style for Flex components and the application.

**Defining styles via themes** Themes are abstractions that contain style and skinning information to define the look and feel of Flex components and the application. They usually combine programmatic and graphical assets. A theme often exists in a separate SWC archive file, which can be passed to an application as command-line parameters during compilation. As an example, the default Halo theme exists in the Flex framework.swc. Being packaged as SWC, it is easy to reuse and distribute themes. Themes make an interesting topic to understand and leverage, but in our current context we will not explore it further. My purpose was to list it as a styling alternative, and I have already done that.

When we make custom components, styling these components can be seen as both

- A customization itself
- A way to provide the essential look-and-feel definition of the custom components

We have now seen a few ways to set styles on Flex components. Each of these style-setting mechanisms is relevant and comes in handy in the context of custom components as well. Before discussing styles, we created additional properties, methods, and events in custom components and exposed these newer additions via an API (often the component tag attributes) for component users. In the next few paragraphs, you learn to expose style parameters in a similar manner—as a set of public component tag attributes that can be set by the user.

To create style attributes, do the following:

1. Annotate the custom component class with the Style metadata tag.
2. Override the styleChanged method to detect changes to the property.
3. Override updateDisplayList to update the component display with the new style.
4. Set default styles via static initializers.

Instead of theoretically explaining these involved steps, let's create a custom component and expose style attributes of that component using the process. We create a simple circle and set its color. The color is the style attribute, and that is what we expose via our custom circle MXML tag attribute. Following is the code for the custom circle:

```
package advancedflex3.ch02
{
    import mx.core.UIComponent;
    import mx.styles.CSSStyleDeclaration;
    import mx.styles.StyleManager;
    import flash.display.GradientType;

    [Style(name="color",type="String",format="Color",inherit="no")]
    public class CustomCircle extends UIComponent
    {
        private static var classConstructed:Boolean = classConstruct();

        private static function classConstruct():Boolean {
            if (!StyleManager.getStyleDeclaration("CustomCircle"))
            {
                var myCircleStyle:CSSStyleDeclaration = ➡
new CSSStyleDeclaration();
                myCircleStyle.defaultFactory = function():void
                {
                    this.color = "0xFF0000";
                }
                StyleManager.setStyleDeclaration➡
("customCircle", myCircleStyle, true);

            }
            return true;
        }

        // Constructor
        public function CustomCircle() {
            super();
        }
```

```
        override protected function measure():void {
            super.measure();

            measuredWidth = measuredMinWidth = 100;
            measuredHeight = measuredMinHeight = 100;
        }

        private var bStypePropChanged:Boolean = true;
        private var colorData:String;

        override public function styleChanged(styleProp:String):void {

            super.styleChanged(styleProp);
            if (styleProp=="color")
            {
                bStypePropChanged=true;
                invalidateDisplayList();
                return;
            }
        }

        override protected function ➥
updateDisplayList(unscaledWidth:Number,
                unscaledHeight:Number):void {
            super.updateDisplayList(unscaledWidth, unscaledHeight);

            if (bStypePropChanged==true)
            {
                colorData=getStyle("color");
                graphics.drawRoundRect➥
(0,0, unscaledWidth, unscaledHeight, ➥
color="colorData");

                bStypePropChanged=false;
            }
        }
    }
}
```

This custom circle can be used in an application, and its color can be set as follows:

```
<?xml version="1.0"?>
<mx:Application xmlns:mx="http://www.adobe.com/2006/mxml"
    xmlns:custom="advancedflex3.ch02.*">
    <mx:Style>
        CustomCircle {color: #FF00FF}
    </mx:Style>
    <custom:CustomCircle/>
</mx:Application>
```

Although the example is simple, it arms you with the knowledge of styles in custom components. Let's now carry on with our task of creating custom components with AS3 and see what other customizations we can accomplish with the available language and framework features.

I mentioned earlier that AS3 could create nonvisual components as well. Let's see what these nonvisual components are and how we create custom versions of them.

# Creating custom nonvisual components

Formatters, validators, and effects are the nonvisual components that can be extended to include new properties and behavior. The best way to learn to extend these three may be to treat them separately. The next three sections deal with creating custom formatters, validators, and effects, respectively.

## Custom formatters

This book has not covered the topic of formatters at all. Since this is an advanced book, the other authors and I assume that you are familiar with formatters. However, in case you are not, here is a very brief explanation.

Formatters take raw data as input and transform it into a desired string format. Formatters can be configured via properties. Flex includes a few formatters for ready use:

- CurrencyFormatter
- DateFormatter
- NumberFormatter
- PhoneFormatter
- ZipCodeFormatter

The names of the built-in formatters are intuitive and suggest what they format. Let's see a couple of quick examples of a CurrencyFormatter and a DateFormatter. The CurrencyFormatter code is as follows:

```
<?xml version="1.0"?>
<!-- formatters\ExampleCurrencyFormatter.mxml -->
<mx:Application xmlns:mx="http://www.adobe.com/2006/mxml">

    <mx:Script>
        <![CDATA[
            // Define variable to hold the price.
            [Bindable]
            private var dollarValue:Number=5229;
        ]]>
    </mx:Script>
    <mx:CurrencyFormatter id="Price" precision="2"
        rounding="none"
        decimalSeparatorTo="."
        thousandsSeparatorTo=","
        useThousandsSeparator="true"
        useNegativeSign="true"
```

```
            currencySymbol="$"
            alignSymbol="left"/>
        <mx:TextInput text="The price is {Price.format(dollarValue)}."/>
    </mx:Application>
```

The CurrencyFormatter, like all other formatters, inherits from the mx.formatters.Formatter class. CurrencyFormatter works like a number formatter, except that it also prefixes a symbol to the formatted numbers. CurrencyFormatter and NumberFormatter are easily configurable. The preceding example sets only a small set of properties out of the many that the component provides.

Our next example involves a date formatter. Date values often have complex rules around formats, which depend on the context, the geographical location, and the usage styles. The built-in date formatter is quite capable of handling these complex conditions. The example shows a little of its capability. The code is as follows:

```
    <?xml version="1.0"?>
    <!-- formatters\ExampleDateFormatter.mxml -->
    <mx:Application xmlns:mx="http://www.adobe.com/2006/mxml">
        <mx:Script>
            <![CDATA[
                // Define variable to hold the date.
                [Bindable]
                private var todaysDate:Date = new Date();
            ]]>
        </mx:Script>
        <!-- Declare a DateFormatter and define parameters.-->
        <mx:DateFormatter id="DateF"
            formatString="MMMM D, YYYY"/>
        <!-- Display the date in a TextArea control.-->
        <mx:TextArea id="myTA" text="{DateF.format(todaysDate)}"/>
    </mx:Application>
```

If you knew nothing about formatters earlier, the brief introduction here should have bridged that gap, and now you will be ready to create custom formatters.

Many situations in real life, including national IDs, stock prices, game scores, and corporate memos, define their own formats. Using Flex, you can create a custom format to meet such a requirement, if the built-in formatters fall short.

You can create a custom formatter by extending mx.formatters.Formatter or any of the other formatter classes. All formatter classes subclass the Formatter class, so one way or the other every formatter extends from the Formatter class. If you go back to the preceding examples, you will notice that both our formatters had a format method, which took one argument and returned a string, which contained the formatted value. This is characteristic of all formatters. So include a format method similarly in your custom formatter. If you are extending from an existing formatter, override the method if required. Most formatters also provide a set of properties to specify the expected format type. Remember to include properties for configuration in your custom formatter as well. Let's create a custom formatter to change a regular number format to an exponential notation or a fixed-point notation with two fractional digits. Here is what the code looks like:

```
package advancedflex3.ch02
{
    import mx.formatters.Formatter

    public class NewNumberFormatter extends Formatter
    {
        public var exponentialFormatString:String = "exponential";

        public function NewNumberFormatter() {
            super();
        }

        override public function format(value:Object):String {
            // 1. Validate value - must be a nonzero length string.
            if( value.length == 0)
                {   error="0 Length String";
                    return ""
                }

            // 2. If the value is valid, format the string.
            switch (exponentialFormatString) {
                case "exponential" :
                    var exponentialString:String = ➡
value.toExponential(2);
                    return exponentialString;
                    break;
                case "fixedPoint" :
                    var fixedPointString:String = ➡
value.toFixed(2);
                    return fixedPointString;
                    break;
                default :
                    error="Invalid Format String";
                    return ""
            }
        }
    }
}
```

Custom formatters are useful components that can save you a lot of time and energy because you define them once and use them as many times as you want. In large enterprise scenarios, it's common to require special formats for official documents, data fields, reports, and numbers. These formatters can come to your rescue in such situations.

## Custom validators

While formatters are concerned with desired display formats, validators are the constraints and rules evaluators that check for input data validity or appropriateness. All basic validators extend from the class mx.validators.Validator. As with formatters, a brief presentation on validators is included here to get you up to speed with the concept.

User input needs to be validated before it is processed. Doing this ensures that you catch any data entry errors early on. Typical HTML-based web applications validate user input at the server and possibly supplement it with some JavaScript-based client-side validation. On the contrary, Flex provides a robust infrastructure to conduct fairly exhaustive client-side validations. This improves application interactivity and responsiveness.

Flex has a bunch of built-in validators to check for many frequently occurring cases like currency, credit card numbers, e-mail addresses, dates, phone numbers, and ZIP codes. Flex also allows for validation rule definition using regular expressions.

A validator is bound to an input field by

- Specifying the instance of the input component as the source of the validator,
- Specifying the property of the input component, whose value needs to be validated, as the property of the source.

Depending on MXML or AS3, this specification of source and property varies a little. In MXML, the source and property of a validator are specified as follows:

```
<?xml version="1.0"?>
<mx:Application xmlns:mx="http://www.adobe.com/2006/mxml">
    <mx:ZipCodeValidator id="zipCodeValidator"
        source="{zipCodeInput}" property="text"/>
    <mx:TextInput id="zipCodeInput"/>
</mx:Application>
```

In AS3, the same specification of source and property for a ZIP code validator is done as follows:

```
<?xml version="1.0"?>
<mx:Application xmlns:mx="http://www.adobe.com/2006/mxml">
    <mx:Script>
        <![CDATA[
            import mx.validators.ZipCodeValidator;

            private var zcv:ZipCodeValidator = new ZipCodeValidator();

            private function createValidator():void {
                zcv.source = zipCodeInput;
                zcv.property = "text";
            }
        ]]>
    </mx:Script>
    <mx:TextInput id="zipCodeInput"
creationComplete="createValidator();"/>
</mx:Application>
```

A validator is usually triggered on an event. Such events could be button click events, mouse out events, or value commit events. Most often this process of validation triggering is automatic. However, you are not restricted to rely on automatic triggering alone. You can explicitly call the validate method of the validator to trigger validation.

When a validation process completes, events are fired by the validator. Two types of events are possible: valid and invalid. Under default scenarios, invalid events are handled by the framework. The invalid data input field is encapsulated in a red-colored box, and the error is displayed when a mouse is hovered over the invalid data entry field. Figure 2-3 shows an error display on invalid data for a ZIP code validator, the type we created previously. Most often, a valid event is ignored and no special action is triggered on such an event. However, if required, event listeners for both these types of events can be defined.

**Figure 2-3.** Error display on invalid ZIP code entry

Examples in the preceding paragraphs describe the fundamentals of validators. Now let's create a custom validator.

You extend mx.validators.Validator or one of the existing validator classes to create a custom validator. All validators extend mx.validators.Validator, so one way or the other you extend this class. The doValidation method of the validator contains the core logic for validation. In order to define custom validation logic, override the protected doValidation method and return an array of ValidationResult objects. A ValidationResult object encapsulates a validation error and has the following properties:

- errorCode: The error code, which you can set
- errorMessage: The message that is displayed
- isError: A Boolean flag that is set to true for an error
- subfield: The subfield associated with the ValidationResult object

ValidationResult is not sent for cases that pass the validation. Also, it's advisable to call the doValidation method on the super class, so that inherited validations like the one that checks the required value for a field is also included. The custom validator itself is triggered using events or an explicit call to the validate method.

Here is example code for a simple custom validator:

```
package advancedflex3.ch02
{
    import mx.validators.Validator;
    import mx.validators.ValidationResult;

    public class CustomValidator extends Validator {

        private var results:Array;

        public function CustomValidator() {
            super();
        }
```

```
override protected function doValidation(value:Object):Array {

    //Custom Validation Logic
    results = [];

    results = super.doValidation(value);
    if (results.length > 0)
        return results;

    //Additional Custom Validation Logic
    return results;

    }
  }
}
```

We can now use this custom validator in our application in the same way that we use the built-in validators.

Next, we pick up the last of the nonvisual components: effects.

## Custom effects

Like formatters and validators, you may need a little background information on effects. Therefore, I'll first explain the basic concepts, and then illustrate how to create custom effects.

Effects are dynamic behavior that is applied to target components on effect triggers. Therefore, there are two aspects of an effect:

- **Trigger**: Effect triggers are activated in a manner similar to the events. The effect triggers are analogous but distinct from the events themselves. For example, there is a MouseDownEffect and a MouseDownEvent, and both are triggered at the same time and under the same circumstances.

- **Target**: On effect triggers, a specified behavior is applied to a target. For example, you may want a text input field to glow on mouse out. In such a case, glow is the applied behavior, the mouse out effect is what triggers application of this behavior, and the text input is the target component that glows.

Every effect is defined using a factory method. The factory method can accept parameters for custom configuration. When you specify an effect and configure it, you configure an **effect factory**. When Flex plays an effect, it creates an instance of the factory and uses it to play the effect. Once the effect is played, the instance is deleted.

A few common effects, behaviors that play on a target for a certain specified duration, are as follows:

- AnimateProperty
- Blur
- Dissolve
- Fade

- Glow
- Iris
- Move
- Pause
- Resize
- Rotate
- SoundEffect
- WipeLeft
- WipeRight
- WipeUp
- WipeDown
- Zoom

Descriptions for these are not provided here, but you can easily look that info up on the Flex 3 LiveDocs. Similarly, to trigger these effects, Flex defines a few built-in effect triggers. Following are some of the common effect triggers:

- addedEffect
- creationCompleteEffect
- focusInEffect
- focusOutEffect
- hideEffect
- mouseDownEffect
- mouseUpEffect
- moveEffect
- removedEffect
- resizeEffect
- rollOutEffect
- rollOverEffect
- showEffect

Using MXML, an effect trigger and an effect can be defined as follows:

```
<?xml version="1.0"?>
<mx:Application xmlns:mx="http://www.adobe.com/2006/mxml">
    <mx:Fade id="fadeEffect" duration="1000"/>
    <mx:Button id="myButton"
label="Fade Me Out"
mouseDownEffect="{fadeEffect}"/>
</mx:Application>
```

The same can alternatively be defined using AS3, as follows:

```
<?xml version="1.0"?>
<mx:Application xmlns:mx="http://www.adobe.com/2006/mxml"
    creationComplete="createEffect(event);" >
    <mx:Script>
        <![CDATA[
            import mx.effects.*;
            private var fadeEffect:Fade;

            private function createEffect(eventObj:Event):void {
                fadeEffect=new Fade();
                fadeEffect.duration=1000;
                myButton.setStyle('mouseDownEffect', fadeEffect);
            }
        ]]>
    </mx:Script>
    <mx:Button id="myButton"  label="Fade Me Out"/>
</mx:Application>
```

You may have noticed that we use the setStyle method to set an effect for an effect trigger. getStyle and setStyle are the method pairs that act as the getter and setter for accessing and setting effect triggers and effect pairs, using AS3.

Now that you know the essentials of effects, let's see how you can create custom effects if need be. To create a custom effect, we create two classes, a factory class and an instance class, for each effect. The Flex factory extends the mx.effects.Effect class or one of its subclasses (long-playing animations should be extended from the TweenEffect class because the TweenEffect class defines methods and properties that take better care of long-playing animation scenarios) and a factory instance extends mx.effects.FactoryInstance or one of its subclasses. Unlike the formatters and the validators, custom effects need you to do more than override a single method. Often multiple methods need to be overridden to create a factory and a factory instance class. A factory class often defines the following methods and properties:

- constructor: Instantiates and initializes a factory. A constructor should accept at least one argument of type Object to specify the target.
- Effect.initInstance: Method that copies properties from the factory to the factory instance. This method is called by the framework from within the Effect.createInstance method.
- Effect.getAffectedProperties: Array of properties that are affected by the effect.
- Effect.instanceClass: An important parameter that wires a factory instance class to a factory class.
- Effect.effectEndHandler: Called at the end of the effect play.
- Effect.effectStartHandler: Called at the beginning of the effect play.

Similarly, a factory instance defines a set of methods and properties; following are a few common ones:

- constructor: The class constructor
- EffectInstance.play: Invokes the effect
- EffectInstance.end: Interrupts an effect play
- EffectInstance.initEffect: Called if effect was triggered by an EffectManager

Let's see a simple example of a custom effect. Following is the code for the custom effect factory class:

```
package advancedflex3.ch02.effects
{
    import mx.effects.Effect;
    import mx.effects.EffectInstance;
    import mx.effects.IEffectInstance;

    public class CustomEffect extends Effect
    {
        public function CustomEffect(targetObj:Object = null) {
            super(targetObj);
            instanceClass= CustomEffectInstance;
        }

        override public function getAffectedProperties():Array {
            return [];
        }

        override protected function ➥
initInstance(inst:IEffectInstance):void {
            super.initInstance(inst);
        }
    }
}
```

A factory instance, which we have already specified in the instanceClass property, needs to be created for this factory. Snippets of such a factory instance class are as follows:

```
package advancedflex3.ch02.effects
{
    import mx.effects.EffectInstance;

    public class CustomEffectInstance extends EffectInstance
    {
        ....

        public function CustomEffectInstance(targetObj:Object) {
            super(targetObj);
        }

        override public function play():void {
```

```
                    //Implement the effect play logic here
                }

                override public function end():void {
                    //Implement the interruption logic here
                }
            }
        }
```

Although our effect factory and factory instance example was only a shell, a real-life effect would not differ from this example in its approach to implementing its custom effects.

So far we have created a custom effect for existing effect triggers. We can also create custom effect triggers themselves. As mentioned earlier, effect triggers are paired with events. Effect triggers can be defined where we define our custom events. Like events, effect triggers will need to be annotated with metadata tags. Here is a short snippet of the metadata declaration:

```
<mx:Metadata>
    [Event(name="customEvent", type="flash.events.Event")]
    [Effect(name="customEffect", event="customEvent")]
</mx:Metadata>
```

Custom effects can be as complex as required and could work in association with transitions as regular effects do.

At this stage, I can confidentially say I have demonstrated a lot of theory and small examples of custom component creation. You have learned how to create visual and nonvisual components using AS3. You have also seen how MXML can be used alone to create visual custom components. Now, so you can appreciate the topic further and realize the unlimited potential custom components hold, let's quickly survey four open source custom components. The choice of these four components is arbitrary, except that all four are well established, freely available, and well documented.

# Advanced component examples

Our four open source custom components that we survey are as follows:

- AdvancedForm: Part of the famous FlexLib project (component contributed by Renaun Erickson)
- ReflectionExplorer: Famous reflection custom container created by Ben Stucki
- Flipbook: Famous book component from Ely Greenfield
- CoverFlow: Carousel-like 3D component from Doug McCune

## AdvancedForm

AdvancedForm is a component that adds reset, undo, and redo functionality to a form. The undo and redo functions are accessible via keyboard shortcuts, namely Ctrl+Z and Ctrl+Y. Figure 2-4 is a snapshot of the component at initialization.

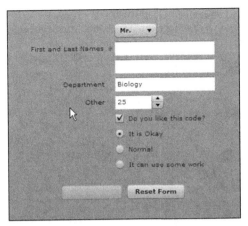

**Figure 2-4.** AdvancedForm from the FlexLib project

AdvancedForm is part of the FlexLib project. The FlexLib project is hosted on Google Code and is accessible online at http://code.google.com/p/flexlib/. There are numerous contributors to this open source components initiative. This particular component is contributed by Renaun Erickson.

The component itself is quite simple and enhances the Form component only marginally. Because of its simplicity, it provides a gentle view into the complex world of custom components in real life. Following is a portion of the source file, AdvancedForm.as, that shows the implementation of reset, undo, and redo methods:

```
public class AdvancedForm extends Form
{
....
    public function resetForm():void {
                var children:Array = this.getChildren();
                resetValues( children, resetSnapshotKey );
                undoCounter = 0;
                undoCurrentIndex = -1;
                modelStack = new Object();
                snapshotValues( this.getChildren(), resetSnapshotKey );
    }
....
      /**
        *       @private
        */
        private function doUndo():void {
                //debug += "\ndoUndo: undoCurrentIndex: " + ➥
undoCurrentIndex + " undoCounter: " + undoCounter;
                noSnapshotFlag = true;
                var index:int = undoCurrentIndex - 1;
                if( index >= ( undoCounter - 1 - undoHistorySize ) ➥
&& index > -2 ) {
```

```
                                    undoCurrentIndex--;
                                    //debug += "\ndoUndo: resetValues: " ➥
                    + undoCurrentIndex;
                                    resetValues( this.getChildren(), ➥
                    getSnapshotKey( undoCurrentIndex ) );

                            }
                            noSnapshotFlag = false;
                    }

                    /**
                     *      @private
                     */
                    private function doRedo():void {
                            //debug += "\ndoRedo: undoCurrentIndex: " ➥
                    + undoCurrentIndex + " undoCounter: " + undoCounter;
                            noSnapshotFlag = true;
                            var index:int = undoCurrentIndex + 1;
                            if( index < undoCounter ) {
                                    undoCurrentIndex++;
                                    resetValues( this.getChildren(), ➥
                    getSnapshotKey( undoCurrentIndex ) );
                            }
                            noSnapshotFlag = false;
                    }

            ....
            }
            }
```

The central idea in this implementation is to save the current state in a model stack. On an undo or a redo request, the logic navigates through the stack elements appropriately. On reset, the custom class gets rid of the relevant state snapshot. The additional features are implemented by adding newer properties and methods to a custom class that extends the Form class.

This was a simple component. Next, let's analyze a slightly more complex case.

## ReflectionExplorer

ReflectionExplorer is a custom component that creates a reflection of a container and allows for numerous parameter-driven settings to govern the way the container is reflected. Ben Stucki is the creator of this custom component. Details about the component and links to the source download are at http://blog.benstucki.net/?p=20. Although the component was built for Flex 2, it works just fine in Flex 3 as well. The best way to get familiar with the component is to see it in action. Figure 2-5 captures a snapshot of the component at startup to give a flavor of what it's like.

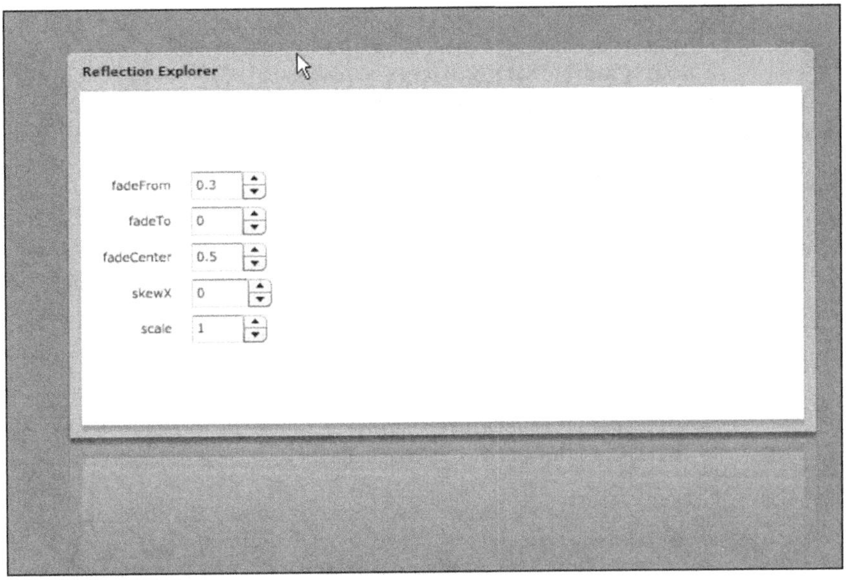

**Figure 2-5.** Ben Stucki's ReflectionExplorer

ReflectionExplorer.mxml is the application file. The core features of the custom component are implemented in AS3. The AS3 file is called Reflection.as. The Reflection class implements a majority of features from the ground up and therefore extends the UIComponent class. I won't get into the details of the reflection logic and the math behind it. My focus is to help you experience custom components, and I will only show you a glimpse of the implementation. For details, you can always download and analyze the available source code.

Most of the functionality is implemented in a single method of the Reflection class. The name of the method is drawReflection and is as follows:

```
public function drawReflection( e:Event = null ):void {
    if( this.width>0 && this.height>0 ) {

        //draw reflection
        var bitmapData:BitmapData = ➥
new BitmapData(this.width, this.height, true, 0);
        var matrix:Matrix = ➥
new Matrix( 1, 0, skewX, -1*scale, 0, target.height );
        var rectangle:Rectangle = ➥
new Rectangle(0,0,this.width,this.height*(2-scale));
        var delta:Point = ➥
matrix.transformPoint(new Point(0,target.height));
        matrix.tx = delta.x*-1;
        matrix.ty = (delta.y-target.height)*-1;
        bitmapData.draw➥
(target, matrix, null, null, rectangle, true);
```

```
                //add fade
                var shape:Shape = new Shape();
                var gradientMatrix:Matrix = new Matrix();
                gradientMatrix.createGradientBox➥
(this.width,this.height, 0.5*Math.PI);
                shape.graphics.beginGradientFill➥
(GradientType.LINEAR, new Array(0,0,0), ➥
new Array(fadeFrom,(fadeFrom-fadeTo)/2,fadeTo), ➥
new Array(0,0xFF*fadeCenter,0xFF), gradientMatrix)
                shape.graphics.drawRect(0, 0, this.width, this.height);
                shape.graphics.endFill();
                bitmapData.draw(shape, null, null, BlendMode.ALPHA);

                //apply result
                bitmap.bitmapData.dispose();
                bitmap.bitmapData = bitmapData;

        }
    }
```

The application MXML file itself is quite simple. It creates an instance of the Reflection component and allows users to select a bunch of parameters that affect the component behavior, which are displayed in a panel. The application MXML code is as follows:

```
<?xml version="1.0" encoding="utf-8"?>
<mx:Application
xmlns:mx="http://www.adobe.com/2006/mxml"
xmlns:fx="com.fusiox.ui.*"
xmlns="*" layout="absolute">
    <mx:Style>
        @font-face {
            src:url("verdana.ttf");
            font-family: myFont;
        }

        FormItem, TextArea {
            font-family: myFont;
            font-weight: normal;
        }
    </mx:Style>
    <mx:VBox width="100%" height="100%">
        <mx:VBox id="myStage"
width="100%" height="80%"
verticalAlign="bottom" horizontalAlign="center">

            <mx:Panel
id="explorer"
title="Reflection Explorer"
width="600" height="300"
```

```
horizontalAlign="center"
verticalAlign="middle"
horizontalCenter="0"
verticalCenter="0">
                <mx:HBox
width="100%"
height="100%"
verticalAlign="middle"
horizontalAlign="left">
                    <mx:Form>
                        <mx:FormItem
label="fadeFrom"
direction="horizontal">
                            <mx:NumericStepper
stepSize="0.1"
minimum="0"
maximum="1"
value="0.3"
change="reflection.fadeFrom=event.target.value" />
                        </mx:FormItem>
                        <mx:FormItem
label="fadeTo"
direction="horizontal">
                            <mx:NumericStepper
stepSize="0.1"
minimum="0"
maximum="1"
value="0"
change="reflection.fadeTo=event.target.value" />
                        </mx:FormItem>
                        <mx:FormItem
label="fadeCenter"
direction="horizontal">
                            <mx:NumericStepper
stepSize="0.1"
minimum="0"
maximum="1"
value="0.5"
change="reflection.fadeCenter=event.target.value" />
                        </mx:FormItem>
                        <mx:FormItem
label="skewX"
direction="horizontal">
                            <mx:NumericStepper
stepSize="0.1"
minimum="-5"
maximum="5"
value="0"
change="reflection.skewX=event.target.value" />
```

```
                        </mx:FormItem>
                        <mx:FormItem
label="scale"
direction="horizontal">
                                    <mx:NumericStepper
stepSize="0.1"
minimum="0"
maximum="1"
value="1"
change="reflection.scale=event.target.value" />
                        </mx:FormItem>
                    </mx:Form>
                </mx:HBox>
            </mx:Panel>

        </mx:VBox>
        <fx:Reflection
id="reflection"
target="{myStage}"
enterFrame="event.target.drawReflection()"
width="100%"
height="20%" />
        </mx:VBox>
</mx:Application>
```

ReflectionExplorer is a very impressive component that implements complex functionality in a few lines of code. It shows how custom components can be quite nifty without being too complex. To continue our exploration of custom components, let's move on to the next one: FlexBook.

## FlexBook

FlexBook is a very sophisticated and versatile custom component, the fruit of Ely Greenfield's genius. Information about the component, as well as the source for download, is available at http://www.quietlyscheming.com/blog/components/flexbook/. FlexBook is a configurable component that acts as a container and can be set with numerous styles and properties to behave as an image browser, a softcover book, or a hard-bound book. Figure 2-6 shows a snapshot of the component when used as a container.

The source for this component does not reside in a couple of files as you have seen in the last couple of cases. Because this component tries to achieve many things at the same time and comes with a set of example implementations, the source is spread across multiple files and folders.

FlexBook visual components directly inherit from the UIComponent. The features of this component are quite unique compared to the standard set of controls and containers in the Flex framework. So starting from scratch is advisable in this case.

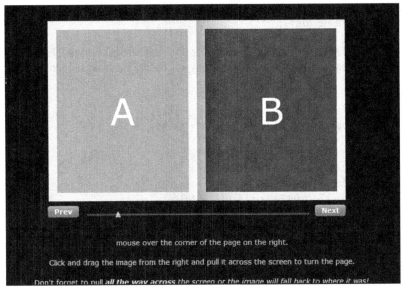

**Figure 2-6.** FlexBook as a container

FlexBook.as in the qs.controls folder is one of the main source files. FlexBook extends DataDrivenControl, another custom class that extends UIComponent. The FlexBook class implements the mathematics and logic involved in turning pages and animating the same. It's beyond the scope of this chapter to get into the details of this component, but for the sake of samples, I show the constructor and one of the flip animation setup method implementations. Here it is:

```
....
//Constructor
public function FlexBook():void
        {
            _timer = new Timer(10);
            _timer.addEventListener(TimerEvent.TIMER,timerHandler);
        }

        override protected function createChildren():void
        {
            _flipLayer= new Shape();
            _interactionLayer = new Sprite();

            _frontTurningPage = new FlexBookPage();
            _backTurningPage = new FlexBookPage();

            _backTurningPage.addEventListener➡
(FlexEvent.UPDATE_COMPLETE,➡
bitmapSourceDrawHandler);

            _frontTurningPage.addEventListener➡
```

```
(FlexEvent.UPDATE_COMPLETE,➥
bitmapSourceDrawHandler);

            _frontTurningPage.cachePolicy = _cachePagesAsBitmapPolicy;
            _backTurningPage.cachePolicy = _cachePagesAsBitmapPolicy;


            _frontTurningPage.styleName = this;
            _backTurningPage.styleName = this;

            addChild(_frontTurningPage);
            addChild(_backTurningPage);
            _frontTurningPage.visible = false;
            _backTurningPage.visible = false;

            _leftPageStackBitmap = new Bitmap();
            addChild(_leftPageStackBitmap);
            _rightPageStackBitmap = new Bitmap();
            addChild(_rightPageStackBitmap);

            _currentPage = new FlexBookPage();
            _currentPage.cacheAsBitmap = ➥
true;//cachePolicy = _➥
cachePagesAsBitmapPolicy;
            _currentPage.styleName = this;
            addChild(_currentPage);

            addChild(_flipLayer);
            addChild(_interactionLayer);

            _interactionLayer.➥
addEventListener(MouseEvent.MOUSE_DOWN,➥
mouseDownHandler);

            _interactionLayer.➥
addEventListener(MouseEvent.MOUSE_MOVE,➥
trackCornerHandler);

            _interactionLayer.➥
addEventListener(MouseEvent.ROLL_OVER,➥
trackCornerHandler);

            _interactionLayer.➥
addEventListener(MouseEvent.ROLL_OUT,➥
trackCornerHandler);
}
....
//Setup for flip effect
private function ➥
```

```
setupForFlip(x:Number,y:Number,➥
targetPageIndex:Number = NaN):void
{
        var code:Number = getCornerCode(x,y);
        var delta:Vector;

        switch(code)
        {
            case TOP_LEFT:
                _pointOfOriginalGrab = new Point(_pageLeft,_pageTop);
                break;
            case TOP_RIGHT:
                _pointOfOriginalGrab = new Point(_pageRight,_pageTop);
                break;
            case BOTTOM_LEFT:
                _pointOfOriginalGrab = ➥
new Point(_pageLeft,_pageBottom);
                break;
            case BOTTOM_RIGHT:
                _pointOfOriginalGrab = ➥
new Point(_pageRight,_pageBottom);
                break;
            default:
                _pointOfOriginalGrab = new Point(x,y);
                break;
        }

        if (!isNaN(targetPageIndex))
        {
            _targetPageIndex = targetPageIndex;
        }
        else
        {
            if (_pointOfOriginalGrab.x < unscaledWidth/2)
            {
                _targetPageIndex = _currentPageIndex - 1;
            }
            else
            {
                _targetPageIndex = _currentPageIndex + 1;
            }
        }
        if (_targetPageIndex < _currentPageIndex)
        {
            if(canTurnBackward() == false)
                return;
            _displayedPageIndex = _currentPageIndex;
            _turnDirection = TURN_DIRECTION_BACKWARDS;
        }
```

```
            else
            {
                if(canTurnForward() == false)
                    return;
                _turnDirection = TURN_DIRECTION_FORWARD;
                _displayedPageIndex = _currentPageIndex;
            }

            _targetPoint = new Point(x,y);

            if (_pointOfOriginalGrab.x > _hCenter)
            {
                _pointOfOriginalGrab.x = _pageRight;
            }
            else
            {
                _pointOfOriginalGrab.x = _pageLeft;
            }
            if(_pointOfOriginalGrab.y > (_pageTop + _pageBottom)/2)
            {
                if (_pointOfOriginalGrab.x > _hCenter)
                {
                    delta = new ➡
Vector(new Point(x,_pointOfOriginalGrab.y),➡
new Point(x+10,_pointOfOriginalGrab.y+1));
                }
                else
                {
                    delta = new Vector(new ➡
Point(x,_pointOfOriginalGrab.y),➡
new Point(x-10,_pointOfOriginalGrab.y+1));
                }
                _pointOfOriginalGrab.y = ➡
Math.min(_pageBottom,➡
delta.yForX(_pointOfOriginalGrab.x));
            }
            else
            {
                if (_pointOfOriginalGrab.x > _hCenter)
                {
                    delta = new ➡
Vector(new Point(x,_pointOfOriginalGrab.y),➡
new Point(x+10,_pointOfOriginalGrab.y-1));
                }
                else
                {
                    delta = new ➡
Vector(new Point(x,_pointOfOriginalGrab.y),➡
new Point(x-10,_pointOfOriginalGrab.y-1));
```

```
            }
                _pointOfOriginalGrab.y = ➡
Math.max(_pageTop,➡
delta.yForX(_pointOfOriginalGrab.x));
            }
            _currentDragTarget = _pointOfOriginalGrab.clone();

            _timer.start();
        }
```

This component is fairly complex compared to our earlier examples. Custom components can be of all degrees of complexity and can vary from a few lines of code to multiple source files. The last three files show that.

Our last example is a great 3D container. Flex does not include 3D manipulations in the framework as such, but there are plenty of open source packages that fill this gap.

## CoverFlow

CoverFlow is a brilliant 3D container created by Doug McCune. It can behave as a carousel and can be laid out both horizontally and vertically. In one of his recent blog posts at http://dougmccune.com/blog/2007/11/19/flex-coverflow-performance-improvement-flex-carousel-component-and-vertical-coverflow/, Doug McCune talks about improvements to the cover flow component. He also provides source code download links at the site.

This component again, like the last one, is fairly complex, and because of its multiple implementations and exhaustive set of features, it is spread over a bunch of source code files. We look at only one of the files called CarouselContainer.as.

CarouselContainer extends from a custom class called BasePV3DContainer, which extends the ViewStack component. BasePV3DContainer uses the Papervision3D library to lay out its child components. Papervision3D and Away3D are the two best-known open source 3D libraries for Flex and the Flash platform. Details about Papervision3D can be obtained at http://blog.papervision3d.org/. Information about Away3D is available at http://away3d.com/. Chapter 15 discusses creating 3D applications with Flex.

Like with the earlier three components, we will not delve into the details of the implementation, but I will provide a snippet of the source so you can get a feel of the complexity. CarouselContainer source is as follows:

```
package com.dougmccune.containers
{
import caurina.transitions.Tweener;

import flash.display.DisplayObject;
import flash.events.Event;

import mx.core.EdgeMetrics;

import org.papervision3d.objects.DisplayObject3D;
```

```
public class CarouselContainer extends BasePV3DContainer
{
    override public function ➡
addChild(child:DisplayObject):DisplayObject {
        var child:DisplayObject = super.addChild(child);

        var plane:DisplayObject3D = lookupPlane(child);
        plane.material.doubleSided = true;

        var reflection:DisplayObject3D = lookupReflection(child);
        reflection.material.doubleSided = true;

        return child;
    }


    private var _angle:Number;

    public function set angle(value:Number):void {
        _angle = value;

        moveCamera();
        scene.renderCamera(camera);
    }

    public function get angle():Number {
        return _angle;
    }

    private function moveCamera():void {
        camera.x =  Math.cos(_angle) *(width);
        camera.z =  Math.sin(_angle) *(width);
    }

    override protected function ➡
layoutChildren(unscaledWidth:Number, ➡
unscaledHeight:Number):void {
        super.layoutChildren(unscaledWidth, unscaledHeight);

        var numOfItems:int = this.numChildren;

        if(numOfItems == 0) return;

        var radius:Number = unscaledWidth-10;
        var anglePer:Number = (Math.PI*2) / numOfItems;

        for(var i:uint=0; i<numOfItems; i++)
        {
            //var childIndex:int = (selectedIndex + i) % numOfItems;
```

```
        var child:DisplayObject = getChildAt(i);

        var p:DisplayObject3D = lookupPlane(child);
        p.container.visible = true;

        var zPosition:Number = Math.sin(i*anglePer) * radius;
        var xPosition:Number = Math.cos(i*anglePer) * radius;
        var yRotation:Number = (-i*anglePer) * (180/Math.PI) + 270;

        p.x = xPosition;
        p.z = zPosition;
        p.rotationY = yRotation;

        if(reflectionEnabled) {
            var reflection:DisplayObject3D = ➥
lookupReflection(child);
            reflection.x = xPosition;
            reflection.z = zPosition;
            reflection.y = -child.height - 2;
            reflection.rotationY = yRotation;
        }
    }


    if(selectedChild) {
        var bm:EdgeMetrics = borderMetrics;

        selectedChild.x = unscaledWidth/2 ? ➥
selectedChild.width/2 - bm.top;
        selectedChild.y = unscaledHeight/2 ? ➥
selectedChild.height/2 - bm.left;

        selectedChild.visible = false;
    }

    var cameraAngle:Number = anglePer*selectedIndex;

    if(cameraAngle - _angle > Math.PI) {
        _angle += Math.PI*2;
        moveCamera();
    }
    else if(_angle - cameraAngle > Math.PI) {
        _angle -= Math.PI*2;
        moveCamera();
    }

    camera.zoom = 1 + 20/unscaledWidth;
    camera.focus = unscaledWidth/2;
```

```
            Tweener.➡
addTween(this, ➡
{angle:cameraAngle, time:tweenDuration});

    }

    override protected function enterFrameHandler(event:Event):void {
        try {
            if(Tweener.isTweening(camera)){
                scene.renderCamera(camera);
            }
        }
        catch(e:Error) { }
    }
}
}
```

The container itself as a carousel looks as shown in Figure 2-7.

**Figure 2-7.** Doug McCune's 3D carousel custom component, as shown on his blog

With this last advanced custom component example, we are ready to wrap up.

# Summary

This chapter on custom components started with an introduction to creating custom components using MXML, graduated to custom component creation using AS3, and finally went on to describe a few advanced custom components. Now at the end of it, I am hopeful that you realize the power of the framework, its flexibility, and its extensibility. Reusable custom components can be essential building blocks for creating agile and robust applications. From now on, always break your Flex application development task into two parts:

- Creation of custom components
- Assembly of custom components in the particular application

Adopting this simple idea will go a long way in helping you create clean and reusable code.

One topic we did not speak about was packaging components and distributing them as archive files, most often as SWC files. Using SWC files in applications has its benefits and challenges. Chapter 4 analyzes this in great detail. Read that chapter to see how your custom components will fare in your own applications and those of others.

Chapter 3

# TURBO-CHARGING DATA BINDING

By Elad Elrom

The Web is a network system composed of a client-server software architecture model. The Web architecture describes the relationship between the client, which makes service requests, and the server, which responds back.

Let's take an example. When you use your web-based e-mail account, you open up a web browser, which is the client. You then navigate to the login URL. At that point, the client forwards your request to a web application, which displays the login page. The login page is a client-side scripting page (HTML). Once you fill in your information and submit the form, the request is forwarded to a server-side script (such as ASP, JSP, or PHP) that creates a request/response communicating with the database. The server-side script finally redirects your client to another web page that requests your e-mails, and so on. See the diagram on the left side of Figure 3-1 for an illustration.

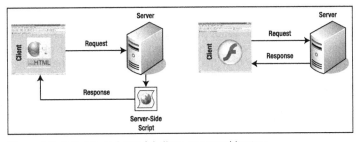

**Figure 3-1.** Stateless and stateful client-server architecture

Traditionally, web applications performed activities such as computing, storing data, and processing without storing the state. The **state**, also known as the **model**, stands for storing data through the life cycle of the web application.

Under the traditional architecture, request and response activities are performed, and the client is not responsible for storing the state, only for displaying the content on a static HTML page. Cookies and sessions are often used to store information; however, they usually store small pieces of information, such as the user's personal information, and not the model. The data is stored on the server, and each request updates the model on the server. Traditional web applications are referred to as **stateless client-server architecture**.

RIA in general, and Flex in particular, offers a new paradigm for web development of applications: **stateful client-server architecture**. The client includes the Flash Player plug-in that plays the SWF movie clip. Once data is retrieved from the server to the client, you can store the state on the client side (the Flash Player), as the user interacts with the application. The client can now handle activities such as storing data, computing, and processing. When needed, request/response calls are made to synchronize the information between the client and the server. See the diagram on the right side of Figure 3-1 for an illustration.

This new paradigm of storing the state is one of the main reasons why Flex is so powerful. It lets you finally break free from the traditional **stateless** approach and start building **stateful** client applications.

The advantages are significant:

- It allows you to create richer and more responsive applications rather than traditionally limited static HTML pages, without the need to turn to the server every time you need to compute or process information.
- You are freeing server overhead, allowing the server to process more clients at the same time.
- The application is consistent across different types of browsers.

When developing data-driven Flex applications, you should aim at achieving a well-balanced stateful client-server architecture by computing and processing your data in Flex and sending/receiving requests to the server. Transfer data only when changes are made, thereby making fewer requests than in traditional client-server architecture.

Flex data binding is a key ingredient in altering the user interface when changes are made to the client model. This chapter explores advanced techniques of data binding, as well as transferring data between the client and the server and creating an effective CRUD application.

Let's get started.

Flex data binding is all about mapping the value of a property in one object to a property in another object. For instance, let's say that we want to bind the text property of an <mx:label /> component to a variable, so every time the data changes, we will see the changes in the component.

To map the text property of a Label component, you can use the curly braces syntax and bind the values into components, keeping the components loosely coupled from the data. Once we make changes in the data, the components change accordingly.

```
<?xml version="1.0" encoding="utf-8"?>
<mx:Application xmlns:mx="http://www.adobe.com/2006/mxml"
    layout="absolute">

  <mx:Script>
    <![CDATA[

      [Bindable]
      public var value:String;
    ]]>
  </mx:Script>

  <mx:Label text="{value}"/>

</mx:Application>
```

Behind the scenes, the Flex compiler automatically generates an event named propertyChange as a default for every [Bindable] tag. The compiler sees every tag as [Bindable(event="propertyChange")]. It is common practice in component development to specify a custom event to the [Bindable] tag instead of propertyChange.

In addition to mapping values in your own application (client), binding is also used to synchronize the client layer with the server layer so data is consistent and the data layer can be updated upon change.

# Implicit and explicit data binding

There are two types of data binding that are used when binding your data: implicit and explicit. The value of data is transformed from one data type into another. Why is this necessary?

The reason is that when we communicate with the server, the business layer is not ActionScript, and we cannot just map a value of, say, a date object to a Java date object.

> *The main difference between implicit and explicit data binding is that implicit data binding is done at run time, while explicit data binding is done at compile time.*

## Implicit data binding

Implicit data binding is used in the following cases:

- In functions when values are passed as arguments and when values are returned from functions. Example: private function SomeMethod(value:Number):String.
- In assignment statements.
- In expressions when using some operators and the values are not yet set.

As an example of implicit data binding, we will be using an implicit getter and setter. First, create a new class and call it ClassA. Create the setter and getter and add the [Bindable] tag.

The [Bindable] metadata tag is compiled as [Bindable(event="propertyChange")]. The setter dispatches an event that will be added automatically.

```
package
{
    import flash.events.Event;

    import mx.core.UIComponent;

    public class ClassA extends UIComponent
    {
        private var _value:Number;

        [Bindable]
        public function get value():Number
        {
            return _value;
        }

        public function set value(num:Number):void
        {
            _value = num;
        }
    }
}
```

Create an MXML entry point (see the following code). Once the application starts, the init method is called and changes the property value to 1. However, since we didn't set the event listener, the event will not be recognized. Next, we set the listener and change the property again to 5, which dispatches the event and calls the handler. The handler displays the message in the console: New value: 5, Old value: 1.

```
<?xml version="1.0" encoding="utf-8"?>
<mx:Application xmlns:mx="http://www.adobe.com/2006/mxml"
    layout="absolute" initialize="init(5)">

  <mx:Script>
    <![CDATA[

      private var classA:ClassA = new ClassA();

      private function init(num:Number):void
      {
          classA.addEventListener("propertyChange", handler);
          classA.value = num;
      }

      private function handler(event:PropertyChangeEvent):void
      {
          trace("New value: "+event.newValue + ➥
```

```
      ", Old value: "+event.oldValue);
            }
         ]]>
      </mx:Script>

   </mx:Application>
```

To see what's going on behind the scenes, place a line breakpoint where the trace command is located, and you can click the Step Into icon and follow the code. UIComponent is calling dispatchEvent with a PropertyChangeEvent event that includes properties to store the old value and the new value.

You can also create your own custom event by changing the ClassA bindable tag to include a specific name, as well as dispatching an event once the setter is called.

```
[Bindable(event="valueWasChanged")]
public function get value():Number
{
    return _value;
}

public function set value(num:Number):void
{
    _value = num;

    var eventObj:Event = new Event("valueWasChanged");
    dispatchEvent(eventObj);
}
```

Don't forget to also change the MXML event name to the new event name:

```
classA.addEventListener("valueWasChanged", handler);
```

# Explicit data binding

Explicit data binding, also called casting, is often used in the following cases:

- You want to cast an object type with another object type.
- You want to avoid compile-time errors in a mismatch between objects.
- You are dealing with forms where all the properties are of type String, but they need to be converted to another format.

An example of explicit data binding is trace(Number("2"));. Another example is to cast an object to a UIComponent type: var com:UIComponent = object as UIComponent.

To try explicit data binding yourself, create the following MXML component:

```
<?xml version="1.0" encoding="utf-8"?>
<mx:Application
    xmlns:mx="http://www.adobe.com/2006/mxml"
```

```
          layout="absolute">

    <mx:Script>
      <![CDATA[

        [Bindable]
        private var num:Number = 5;

        private function init(num:Number):void
        {
            this.num = num;
        }

      ]]>
    </mx:Script>

    <mx:Label id="lbl" width="50"
        text="{num.toString()}"
        click="num++" />

</mx:Application>
```

The component assigns a bindable primitive Number type; however, the text property expects a primitive value of a String. Once you compile the application, you will get an error message in the console: Implicit coercion of a value of type Number to an unrelated type String.

The error occurs at compile time since the compiler tried to assign a Number to a String type. What we need to do is cast the Number as a String.

```
    <mx:Label id="lbl" width="50" text="{num.toString()}" click="num++" />
```

You can also use one of the following methods to cast as a String:

```
    num as String;
    String(num);
```

# MVC framework

Model-View-Controller (MVC) frameworks such as PureMVC (http://puremvc.org/) and Cairngorm (http://labs.adobe.com/wiki/index.php/Cairngorm) offer an elegant way of maintaining your state, by keeping a class that stores data through the life cycle of the application. Once you make changes to the data, the model changes, which changes the view accordingly.

What is the MVC pattern? To answer that quickly, think about separating the three major parts of your application: state/data, processing, and presentation.

- **Model**: Model and state are the same thing; they both store the data through the life cycle of the application.
- **View**: The view holds the presentation layer; this is the user interface (UI).
- **Controller**: The controller is the glue between the view and the model. It handles events from the user interaction and notifies the model.

Data binding in your application is not enough; you also need to bind the data to the server. This chapter will explore different data objects, demonstrating how to transmit them over different types of connections in order to achieve data binding of your client state with server state. The connections we will be using are traditional RESTful methods as well as Flash Remoting (AMF) connections.

# Value object model

The core of data binding and maintaining client state is the data, and when dealing with an application that involves data transfer between a server and client, it is highly recommended to separate the data from the UI and keep track of the state.

As I mentioned before, separation of the data model is common practice in MVC architecture and used often in application development.

To achieve separation, you use a value object (VO), which contains all the properties of the data. The VO was borrowed from J2EE, which uses an object called a data transfer object (DTO).

Think of a VO as an entity in a database, for instance, take a look at a data object to store customers' information, as shown in Figure 3-2.

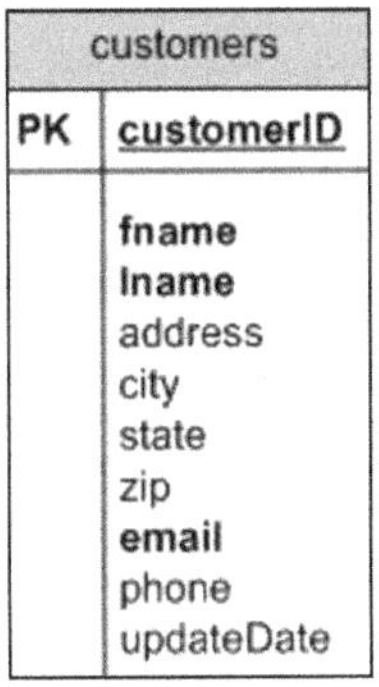

Let's translate the object entity into a VO. See the following class, which is a collection of properties that describes the customer:

| customers | |
|---|---|
| PK | **customerID** |
| | **fname** |
| | **lname** |
| | address |
| | city |
| | state |
| | zip |
| | **email** |
| | phone |
| | updateDate |

**Figure 3-2.**
Customers' entity

```
package com.vo
{
        [Bindable]
        public class CustomerVO
        {
                public var customerID:int;
                public var fname:String;
                public var lname:String;
                public var address:String;
                public var city:String;
                public var state:String;
                public var zip:String;
                public var phone:String;
                public var email:Date;
                public var updateDate:Date;
        }
}
```

Notice that we assigned a [Bindable] tag at the class declaration. The tag makes every property in the customerVO class binding, so there's no need to add the [Bindable] tag to any other property.

Using a VO has the following advantages:

- It provides a clean, readable way to transfer data between the server and your Flex application.
- When creating an instance of the class, we can get code hinting of all the properties of the data (see Figure 3-4 a little later in this chapter).

- It allows us to attach these VOs to one central location, making them accessible from every part of the Flex application.

- It allows maintenance of a consistent object model on the client and the server.

To demonstrate the power of VOs, let's create an application that launches a `TitleWindow` pop-up, which prompts the user to enter her personal information, validate the information, place it in a VO, and then keep the information available throughout the cycle of the application (see Figure 3-3).

**Figure 3-3.** Insert customer information application

1. Create a new Flex project. Next, create a new MXML application by selecting File ➤ New ➤ MXML Application and save the file as `RegistrationForm.mxml`.

   The stateDP will be used to store all the different states in the USA. I used only a few, but you can complete the rest on your own. Notice that the variable is bindable, which allows the ComboBox component to display the states.

```
[Bindable]
private var statesDP: Array = [ {label: "Alabama"   , data: "AL"},
                               {label: "Alaska"    , data: "AK"},
                               {label: "Arizona"   , data: "AZ"},
                               {label: "Arkansas"  , data: "AR"},
                               {label: "California" , data: "CA"}];
```

2. We also need to validate the form. There are different ways to do so. I chose to create an individual Validator for each input box. However, you can also create a custom Validator that extends the base class `mx.validators.Validator`.

   To invalidate the form, I created a flag called validateFlag. Initially, the flag needs to be set to false, as follows: `private var validateFlag:Boolean = false;`.

   Then each validator will change validateFlag to true when the form is invalidated, and the last validator will switch validateFlag to true. So next time, the onSubmit() method will be dispatched if the validator is valid.

```
<mx:ZipCodeValidator source="{zip}" property="text"
    trigger="{submitButton}" triggerEvent="click"
```

```
                    invalid="validateFlag=false;" />

    <mx:PhoneNumberValidator source="{phone}" property="text"
        trigger="{submitButton}" triggerEvent="click"
        invalid="validateFlag=false;" />

    <mx:EmailValidator source="{email}" property="text"
        trigger="{submitButton}" triggerEvent="click"
        invalid="validateFlag=false;" />

    <mx:StringValidator source="{fname}" property="text"
        tooLongError="250"
        trigger="{submitButton}" triggerEvent="click"
        invalid="validateFlag=false;" />

    <mx:StringValidator source="{lname}" property="text"
        tooLongError="250" invalid="validateFlag=false;"
        trigger="{submitButton}" triggerEvent="click"  />

    <mx:StringValidator source="{address}" property="text"
        tooLongError="250" invalid="validateFlag=false;"
        trigger="{submitButton}" triggerEvent="click"  />

    <mx:StringValidator source="{city}" property="text"
        tooLongError="250" invalid="validateFlag=true;" valid="onSubmit()"
        trigger="{submitButton}" triggerEvent="click"  />
```

**3.** Use a Formatter tag to format the phone number to the following format: (###)###-####:

```
    <mx:PhoneFormatter id="phoneFormatter"
        formatString="(###)###-####" validPatternChars="#-(), "/>
```

Following is the form that will be used:

```
        <mx:Form width="307" height="279">
            <mx:FormItem label="First Name:" required="true">
                <mx:TextInput id="fname"/>
            </mx:FormItem>
            <mx:FormItem label="Last Name:" required="true">
                <mx:TextInput id="lname"/>
            </mx:FormItem>
            <mx:FormItem label="Address:" required="true">
                <mx:TextInput id="address"/>
            </mx:FormItem>
            <mx:FormItem label="City:" required="true">
                <mx:TextInput id="city"/>
            </mx:FormItem>
            <mx:FormItem label="State:" required="true">
                <mx:ComboBox id="state"
                    dataProvider="{statesDP}" />
            </mx:FormItem>
```

```
                    <mx:FormItem label="Zip Code:" required="true">
                            <mx:TextInput id="zip"/>
                    </mx:FormItem>
                    <mx:FormItem label="Phone Number:" required="true">
                            <mx:TextInput id="phone"/>
                    </mx:FormItem>
                    <mx:FormItem label="Email Address" required="true">
                            <mx:TextInput id="email"/>
                    </mx:FormItem>
                    <mx:FormItem>
                            <mx:Button id="submitButton" label="Submit"/>
                    </mx:FormItem>
        </mx:Form>
```

4. Once the onSubmit method is called, we need to have the method check whether the fields are validated and assign the values to the customerVO.

```
protected function onSubmit():void
{
        if (validateAll)
        {
            var customer:customerVO = new customerVO;
            customer.fname       = fname.text;
            customer.lname       = lname.text;
            customer.address     = address.text;
            customer.city        = city.text;
            customer.state       = state.selectedItem.data;
            customer.zip         = Number(zip.text);
            customer.phone       = phoneFormatter.format(phone.text);
            customer.email       = email.text;
            customer.updateDate = new Date();
        }
}
```

5. Notice that once we create an instance of the VO, we can easily see the properties of the VO through code hinting. Just type customer once, add a dot, and you will be able to choose the properties you need, as shown in Figure 3-4.

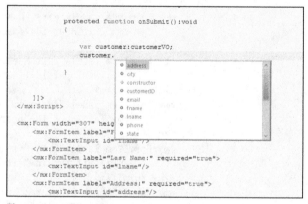

**Figure 3-4.** VO code hinting

Following is the complete component code:

```xml
<?xml version="1.0" encoding="utf-8"?>
<mx:TitleWindow xmlns:mx="http://www.adobe.com/2006/mxml"
    layout="absolute" width="348"
    height="330" showCloseButton="true"
    close="closePopup()">

    <mx:Script>
        <![CDATA[
            import mx.managers.PopUpManager;
            import com.vo.customerVO;

            [Bindable]
            private var statesDP: Array = [
                        {label: "Alabama", data: "AL"},
                        {label: "Alaska", data: "AK"},
                        {label: "Arizona", data: "AZ"},
                        {label: "Arkansas", data: "AR"},
                        {label: "California", data: "CA"}];

            protected var validateFlag:Boolean = true;

            protected function onSubmit():void
            {
                if (validateFlag)
                {
                    var customer:customerVO = new customerVO;
                    customer.fname      = fname.text;
                    customer.lname      = lname.text;
                    customer.address    = address.text;
                    customer.city       = city.text;
                    customer.state      = state.selectedItem.data;
                    customer.zip        = Number(zip.text);
                    customer.phone      = phoneFormatter. ➥
format(phone.text);
                    customer.email      = email.text;
                    customer.updateDate = new Date();

                    closePopup();
                }
            }

            protected function closePopup():void
            {
                PopUpManager.removePopUp(this);
            }
        ]]>
    </mx:Script>
```

**101**

```
<mx:ZipCodeValidator source="{zip}" property="text"
trigger="{submitButton}" triggerEvent="click"
invalid="validateFlag=false;" />

<mx:PhoneNumberValidator source="{phone}" property="text"
trigger="{submitButton}" triggerEvent="click"
invalid="validateFlag=false;" />

<mx:EmailValidator source="{email}" property="text"
trigger="{submitButton}" triggerEvent="click"
invalid="validateFlag=false;" />

<mx:StringValidator source="{fname}" property="text"
    tooLongError="250"
trigger="{submitButton}" triggerEvent="click"
invalid="validateFlag=false;" />

<mx:StringValidator source="{lname}" property="text"
    tooLongError="250" invalid="validateFlag=false;"
trigger="{submitButton}" triggerEvent="click"  />

<mx:StringValidator source="{address}" property="text"
    tooLongError="250" invalid="validateFlag=false;"
trigger="{submitButton}" triggerEvent="click"  />

<mx:StringValidator source="{city}" property="text"
tooLongError="250" invalid="validateFlag=true;"
valid="onSubmit()"
trigger="{submitButton}" triggerEvent="click"  />

<mx:PhoneFormatter id="phoneFormatter"
formatString="(###)###-####" validPatternChars="#-(), "/>

<mx:Form width="307" height="279">
    <mx:FormItem label="First Name:" required="true">
        <mx:TextInput id="fname"/>
    </mx:FormItem>
    <mx:FormItem label="Last Name:" required="true">
        <mx:TextInput id="lname"/>
    </mx:FormItem>
    <mx:FormItem label="Address:" required="true">
        <mx:TextInput id="address"/>
    </mx:FormItem>
    <mx:FormItem label="City:" required="true">
        <mx:TextInput id="city"/>
    </mx:FormItem>
    <mx:FormItem label="State:" required="true">
        <mx:ComboBox id="state"
            dataProvider="{statesDP}" />
```

```
        </mx:FormItem>
        <mx:FormItem label="Zip Code:" required="true">
            <mx:TextInput id="zip"/>
        </mx:FormItem>
        <mx:FormItem label="Phone Number:" required="true">
            <mx:TextInput id="phone"/>
        </mx:FormItem>
        <mx:FormItem label="Email Address" required="true">
            <mx:TextInput id="email"/>
        </mx:FormItem>
        <mx:FormItem>
            <mx:Button id="submitButton" label="Submit"/>
        </mx:FormItem>
    </mx:Form>

</mx:TitleWindow>
```

6. Now that we have created the TitleWindow component, we want to create another application that launches the pop-up. Choose File ➤ New ➤ MXML Application and call the MXML application CustomerForm.mxml.

7. Add a button that triggers the following method:

```
        private function showForm():void {
            var registrationWindow:IFlexDisplayObject =
            PopUpManager.createPopUp(this, RegistrationForm);
        }
        <mx:Button label="Register" click="showForm()" />
```

8. Place a line breakpoint after the form is submitted inside the onSubmit() method, and you will be able to view the customerVO object. Notice that all the properties are stored correctly, as can be seen in Figure 3-5.

9. The only problem with this application is that once the instance of the TitleWindow is closed, the VO class will be erased. To solve that problem, we need to keep track of the state so we will be able to access the VO throughout the application. A good solution is to use the Cairngorm architecture where the state is kept in a class called Model.

   Download Cairngorm 2.2 Binary from here: http://labs.adobe.com/wiki/index.php/Cairngorm:Cairngorm2.2:Download. Place Cairngorm.swc in the libs directory, and you are all set to go.

10. We can now create the model/state class. In Chapter 1, you first learned about creating the model, view, controller, and VO. So now it all starts to make sense! The model is a class that follows the **Singleton** design pattern. The class can be created only once, and it will keep the data throughout the life span of the application.

```
package com.model {
    public class ModelLocator {

        private static var instance:ModelLocator;
        private static var allowInstantiation:Boolean;
```

**Figure 3-5.** Line breakpoint inside of the onSubmit method

**103**

```
    public static function getInstance():ModelLocator {
        if (instance == null) {
            allowInstantiation = true;
            instance = new ModelLocator();
            allowInstantiation = false;
        }
        return instance;
    }

    public var customer:CustomerVO;

    public function ModelLocator():void {
        if (!allowInstantiation) {
            throw new Error("Error: Instantiation failed: ➥
Use ModelLocator.getInstance() instead of new.");
        }
    }
}
}
```

11. Placing our data on the model allows us to access our VO at any time by creating an instance of the Singleton class as follows:

```
        [Bindable]
        private var model:ModelLocator = ModelLocator. ➥
getInstance();
```

We are able to read or change the value of customer properties consistently across the application.

```
        protected function onSubmit():void
        {
            if (validateFlag)
            {
                var customer:customerVO = new customerVO;
                customer.fname = fname.text;
                model.customer = customer;

                closePopup();
            }
        }
```

12. Place the following Label in RegistrationForm.mxml so you will be able to view the customer name once the user closes the pop-up. Run the application, and once you close the pop-up, you will see the customer name that was entered.

`<mx:Label text="{model.customer.fname}" y="30"/>`

Although the application is working correctly, we are not done yet. Notice that we are accessing the ModelLocator class directly; however, it is not recommended that you make changes to the ModelLocator class directly.

Here we have only two classes, but when building a large application, we may have hundreds of classes, all accessing the same model, and we may find our data changes without knowing who changed it. Additionally, we will have a hard time debugging and finding the view component that changed our model.

The process is as shown in Figure 3-6. The view, which in our case is CustomerForm.mxml, will dispatch and pass the CustomerVO. The controller will process the event and send it to the appropriate command, which will update the model. Once the model is updated, RegistrationForm.mxml will get updated since the label property is bindable. It may seem complex, but it starts to make sense when you come to deal with a large-scale application.

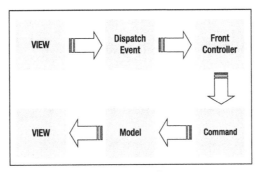

**Figure 3-6.** Cairngorm process diagram

13. Create an event called UpdateCustomerVOEvent that will pass the CustomerVO:

```
package com.store.event
{
    import com.adobe.cairngorm.control.CairngormEvent;
    import com.vo.CustomerVO;

    import flash.events.Event;

    public final class UpdateCustomerVOEvent extends CairngormEvent
    {
        public static const EVENT:String = "CustomerState";

    public var customer:CustomerVO;

        public function UpdateCustomerVOEvent(customer:CustomerVO)
        {
            super( EVENT );
            this.customer = customer;
        }

        public override function clone() : Event
        {
            return new UpdateCustomerVOEvent(customer);
        }
    }
}
```

**14.** Create a controller that will process the event and trigger the appropriate command:

```
package com.store.control
{
    import com.adobe.cairngorm.control.FrontController;
    import com.store.event.*;

    public final class StoreController extends FrontController
    {
    public function StoreController() {
        this.initialize();
    }

        protected function initialize() : void
        {
            this.addCommand( UpdateCustomerVOEvent.EVENT, ➥
DeleteWeightEntryCommand );
        }
    }
}
```

**15.** We also need the command that will update the model:

```
package com.weightwatchers.weightTracker.commands
{
    import com.adobe.cairngorm.commands.ICommand;
    import com.adobe.cairngorm.control.CairngormEvent;
    import com.model.ModelLocator;
    import com.store.event.UpdateCustomerVOEvent;

    public final class UpdateCustomerVOEventCommand implements ICommand
    {
        private var model:ModelLocator = ModelLocator.getInstance();

        public function execute(event:CairngormEvent) : void
        {
            var evt:UpdateCustomerVOEvent = event ➥
as UpdateCustomerVOEvent;
            model.customer = evt.customerVO;
        }
    }
}
```

**16.** You are all set. All you have to do is place the controller in your main view, which is the component that launches the window CustomerForm.mxml:

```
<control:StoreController id="control"/>
```

And instead change onSubmit to dispatch the event:

```
protected function onSubmit():void
{
```

```
        if (validateFlag)
        {
            var customer:CustomerVO = new CustomerVO;
            customer.fname      = fname.text;
            customer.lname      = lname.text;
            customer.address    = address.text;
            customer.city       = city.text;
            customer.state      = state.selectedItem.data;
            customer.zip        = zip.text;
            customer.phone      = phoneFormatter.format(phone.text);
            customer.email      = email.text;
            customer.updateDate = new Date();

            var event:UpdateCustomerVOEvent = ➡
new UpdateCustomerVOEvent(customer);
            event.dispatch();
            closePopup();
        }
    }
```

**17.** Run the application, and once you submit the form and close the window, you should see the name on the UI, since the Label component is binding to the model:

```
<mx:Label text="{model.customer.fname}" y="30"/>
```

# Synchronizing client and server

Now that we have created a data object and we are storing the state (or model) across the Flex application, the next challenge is to synchronize the client and server models.

Traditionally, as I mentioned before, in client-server architecture, all the computing and processing as well as storing of the state is done in the middle layer, also known as the business layer, and the client is stateless. In the new RIA paradigm, stateful client-server architecture, Flex is used to process and compute information as well as store the state (see Figure 3-7).

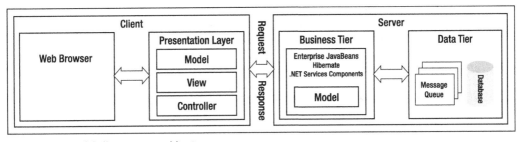

**Figure 3-7.** Stateful client-server architecture

The business layer can be services, components, or any other server-side technology such as PHP, Enterprise JavaBeans (EJB), Hibernate, ColdFusion, or .NET. The last layer is the data layer, where the information is stored.

There are different ways to synchronize between the client model and the business model in order to keep the data consistent.

Synchronizing depends on the server you are working on. Working on an existing project, you may not get the luxury of choosing the business layer technology. The business layer technology that is in use will dictate what you will be using. It is preferable to transmit your VO using binary objects rather than XML type objects.

> *Transmitting binary objects has advantages: the speed of communicating across the wire is much faster, it needs less memory from the client computer, and it reduces processing time compared to XML data type transmitting.*

When synchronizing the client and server, be careful of making the same service calls several times. It is recommended to create one central place to send and receive your requests and responses.

# Converting between XML and value objects

The Remote Procedure Call (RPC) component is a popular way to synchronize your client model with the server model. You will send a request and receive a response, all in XML format.

To convert your VO object to an XML object, you can use either ActionScript or MXML.

1. You can create an XML object using an MXML tag as shown here:

```
<mx:XML id="customer" format="e4x">
    <root label="customer">
        <name>
            <first>{model.customer.fname}</first>
            <last>{model.customer.lname}</last>
        </name>
            <address>{model.customer.address}</address>
            <city>{model.customer.city}</city>
            <state>{model.customer.state}</state>
            <zip>{model.customer.zip}</zip>
            <phone>{model.customer.phone}</phone>
            <email>{model.customer.email}</email>
            <updateDate>{model.customer.updateDate}</updateDate>
    </root>
</mx:XML>
```

Or you can create the same XML object using ActionScript as shown here:

```
var customerXML:XML =
 <root label="customer">
    <name>
        <first>{model.customer.fname}</first>
        <last>{model.customer.lname}</last>
    </name>
```

```
        <address>{model.customer.address}</address>
        <city>{model.customer.city}</city>
        <state>{model.customer.state}</state>
        <zip>{model.customer.zip}</zip>
        <phone>{model.customer.phone}</phone>
        <email>{model.customer.email}</email>
        <updateDate>{model.customer.updateDate}</updateDate>
    </root>;
```

2. Once the object is created, you will be able to bind the VO to the XML object:

```
<?xml version="1.0" encoding="utf-8"?>
<mx:Canvas xmlns:mx="http://www.adobe.com/2006/mxml"
    width="400" height="300"
    creationComplete="completed()">

    <mx:Script>
      <![CDATA[

        import com.model.ModelLocator;

        [Bindable]
        private var model:ModelLocator = ModelLocator.getInstance();

        private function completed():void
        {
            var customerXML:XML =
                <root label="customer">
                  <name>
                     <first>{model.customer.fname}</first>
                     <last>{model.customer.lname}</last>
                  </name>
                  <address>{model.customer.address}</address>
                  <city>{model.customer.city}</city>
                  <state>{model.customer.state}</state>
                  <zip>{model.customer.zip}</zip>
                  <phone>{model.customer.phone}</phone>
                  <email>{model.customer.email}</email>
                  <updateDate>{model.customer.updateDate}</updateDate>
                </root>;
        }

      ]]>
    </mx:Script>
</mx:Canvas>
```

3. Now let's do it the other way around: convert an XML object into a VO. Once a response is returned from the server, you can convert it back to a VO by utilizing the E4X format. The following example takes an XML object and formats it back into a VO. We are using object-style notation to call the different properties in the XML.

```
<?xml version="1.0" encoding="utf-8"?>
<mx:Canvas xmlns:mx="http://www.adobe.com/2006/mxml"
    width="400" height="300"
    creationComplete="completed()">

  <mx:Script>
    <![CDATA[
        import com.vo.CustomerVO;

        import com.model.ModelLocator;

        [Bindable]
        private var model:ModelLocator = ModelLocator.getInstance();

        private function completed():void
        {
            var customerXML:XML =
                <root label="customer">
                    <name>
                        <first>{model.customer.fname}</first>
                        <last>{model.customer.lname}</last>
                    </name>
                    <address>{model.customer.address}</address>
                    <city>{model.customer.city}</city>
                    <state>{model.customer.state}</state>
                    <zip>{model.customer.zip}</zip>
                    <phone>{model.customer.phone}</phone>
                    <email>{model.customer.email}</email>
                    <updateDate>{model.customer.updateDate}</updateDate>
                </root>;

            var customer:CustomerVO = new CustomerVO();
            customer.fname  = customerXML.name.first;
            customer.lname = customerXML.name.last;
            customer.address = customerXML.address;
            customer.city = customerXML.city;
            customer.state = customerXML.state;
            customer.zip = customerXML.zip;
            customer.phone = customerXML.phone;
            customer.email = customerXML.email;

            var milliseconds:Number = ➥
Date.parse(String(customerXML.updateDate));
            var date:Date = new Date();
            date.setTime(milliseconds);
            customer.updateDate = date;
        }

    ]]>
```

```
      </mx:Script>
   </mx:Canvas>
```

4. We need to convert the date from a String format into a Date object; here let's use the method called parse. This method takes a String and returns a Number with the amount of milliseconds passed since January 1, 1970. Then we use the setTime method, which converts a millisecond number to a Date object.

```
var milliseconds:Number = Date.parse(String(customerXML.updateDate));
var date:Date = new Date();

date.setTime(milliseconds);
customer.updateDate = date;
```

# Synchronizing XML data objects

Now that you know how to convert a VO into an XML object and an XML object back into a VO, you are ready to send and receive XML requests from the server middle layer.

HTTPService is usually used for RESTful services, and WebService is usually used for SOAP. We will show you how to use both of these RPC components through the HTTP protocol.

> SOAP once stood for Simple Object Access Protocol, but the acronym has been dropped, since calling an object simple is considered by many to be false. SOAP is a common protocol for exchanging XML objects over networks. SOAP sends requests using the HTTP/HTTPS protocols and provides a messaging framework. RPC is the most common messaging pattern used in which the client sends an XML request object to the server, and the server replies with an XML response object. SOAP is often very verbose for handling communication behind proxies and firewalls. Also, SOAP is often heavy across the wire, which can result in higher client memory usage and processing time. To learn more about SOAP, visit the official web page located at http://www.w3.org/TR/soap/.

To receive an XML object from the HTTPService component, let's use the same XML structure, and call the XML file assets/xml/customer.xml:

```
<customer>
   <name>
      <first>John</first>
      <last>Do</last>
   </name>
   <address>111 14th street</address>
   <city>Los Angeles</city>
   <state>CA</state>
   <zip>90010</zip>
   <phone>(213)111-1111</phone>
   <email>John@gmail.com</email>
   <updateDate>Sun Nov 30 01:20:00 GMT-0800 2008</updateDate>
</customer>
```

**111**

We can create the HTTP component using the HTTPService MXML tag. The method resultFormat allows us to specify how we want the result to be formatted. We will be using E4X, so we can use object-style notation.

```
<mx:HTTPService id="hs"
    url="assets/xml/customer.xml"
    resultFormat="e4x"
    result="resultHandler(event)"
</mx:HTTPService>
```

We will be using the same technique as before to convert the XML object into a VO. The object will be formatted as E4X, so we use explicit data binding and cast the event.result object as an XML object, and thus be able to read the object as E4X.

```
private function resultHandler(event:ResultEvent):void
{
    var customer:CustomerVO = new CustomerVO();
    var customerXML:XML = event.result as XML;

    customer.fname  =  customerXML.name.first;
    customer.lname = customerXML.name.last;
    customer.address = customerXML.address;
    customer.city = customerXML.city;
    customer.state = customerXML.state;
    customer.zip = customerXML.zip;
    customer.phone = customerXML.phone;
    customer.email = customerXML.email;

    var milliseconds:Number = Date. ➥
parse(String(customerXML.updateDate));
    var date:Date = new Date();
    date.setTime(milliseconds);
    customer.updateDate = date;

    cleanListeners();
}
```

The complete code is listed here:

```
<?xml version="1.0" encoding="utf-8"?>
<mx:Application
    xmlns:mx="http://www.adobe.com/2006/mxml"
    layout="absolute"
    creationComplete="hs.send();">

    <mx:Script>
      <![CDATA[
          import com.vo.CustomerVO;
          import mx.controls.Alert;
          import mx.rpc.events.FaultEvent;
```

```
            import mx.rpc.events.ResultEvent;

            private function resultHandler(event:ResultEvent):void
            {
                var customer:CustomerVO = new CustomerVO();
                var customerXML:XML = event.result as XML;

                customer.fname  =  customerXML.name.first;
                customer.lname = customerXML.name.last;
                customer.address = customerXML.address;
                customer.city = customerXML.city;
                customer.state = customerXML.state;
                customer.zip = customerXML.zip;
                customer.phone = customerXML.phone;
                customer.email = customerXML.email;

                var milliseconds:Number = Date.parse ➥
(String(customerXML.updateDate));
                var date:Date = new Date();
                date.setTime(milliseconds);
                customer.updateDate = date;

                cleanListeners();
            }

            private function faultHandler(event:FaultEvent):void
            {
                Alert.show(event.fault.message, "Error connecting");
                cleanListeners();
            }

            private function cleanListeners():void
            {
                hs.removeEventListener(ResultEvent.RESULT, resultHandler);
                hs.removeEventListener(FaultEvent.FAULT, faultHandler);
            }

        ]]>
    </mx:Script>

    <mx:HTTPService id="hs"
        url="assets/xml/customer.xml"
        resultFormat="e4x"
        result="resultHandler(event)"
        fault="faultHandler(event)" />

</mx:Application>
```

**113**

To update the server, we need to be able to send the VO back to the server so that the client model will sync with the server model, as discussed before. In sending an XML object using HTTPService components, there are two ways to send the request:

- You can send the XML as a request parameter using send(parameters:Object).
- You can send the XML as an application/xml request using the <mx:request> tag.

Create the HTTPService component that you will be using as follows:

```
<mx:HTTPService id="hs"
    url="http://www.YourDomain.com/UpdateModel.php"
    resultFormat="e4x">
```

Convert the VO into an XML object, just as you did in an earlier section of this chapter.

```
var customerXML:XML =
    <root label="customer">
        <name>
            <first>{model.customer.fname}</first>
            <last>{model.customer.lname}</last>
        </name>
            <address>{model.customer.address}</address>
            <city>{model.customer.city}</city>
            <state>{model.customer.state}</state>
            <zip>{model.customer.zip}</zip>
            <phone>{model.customer.phone}</phone>
            <email>{model.customer.email}</email>
            <updateDate>{model.customer.updateDate}</updateDate>
    </root>;
```

And now you can pass the XML object as a parameter by triggering the HTTPService component from an ActionScript code block or MXML tag:

```
<mx:Script>
  <![CDATA[

  private function init():void
  {
        hs.send(customerXML);
  }

  ]]>
</mx:Script>
```

To send the XML object as an application/xml request, we use the <mx:request> tag inside of the HTTPService component:

```
<mx:HTTPService id="hs"
    url="http://www.yourdomain.com/UpdateModel.php"
    resultFormat="e4x"
```

```
            result="resultHandler(event)"
            fault="faultHandler(event)">

    <mx:request>
        <root label="customer">
            <name>
                <first>{model.customer.fname}</first>
                <last>{model.customer.lname}</last>
            </name>
            <address>{model.customer.address}</address>
            <city>{model.customer.city}</city>
            <state>{model.customer.state}</state>
            <zip>{model.customer.zip}</zip>
            <phone>{model.customer.phone}</phone>
            <email>{model.customer.email}</email>
            <updateDate>{model.customer.updateDate}</updateDate>
        </root>
    </mx:request>

</mx:HTTPService>
```

The process of using the WebService component is the same as that for HTTPService.

WebService allows you to send and receive XML objects to SOAP-compliant web services.

Here's an example for connecting to the Amazon SOAP API, which I will discuss in more detail in Chapter 10 when I talk about mashups:

```
<mx:WebService id="AmazonSearch"
    wsdl="http://SomeServer.com/Service.wsdl"
    showBusyCursor="true"
    fault="Alert.show(event.fault.faultString)">

    <mx:operation name="ItemSearch" resultFormat="object"
        result="searchResultHandler(event)">
        <mx:request>
            <root label="customer">
                <name>
                    <first>{model.customer.fname}</first>
                    <last>{model.customer.lname}</last>
                </name>
                <address>{model.customer.address}</address>
                <city>{model.customer.city}</city>
                <state>{model.customer.state}</state>
                <zip>{model.customer.zip}</zip>
                <phone>{model.customer.phone}</phone>
                <email>{model.customer.email}</email>
                <updateDate>
                    {model.customer.updateDate}
                </updateDate>
```

```
                        </root>
                    </mx:request>
                </mx:operation>

            </mx:WebService>
```

You can see why using XML objects is such a popular method to transmit information across the wire; it's easy to use, intuitive, and requires very little work.

# Converting between a value object and binary data

Another way to communicate and sync between the client model and the server model is by working with unformatted binary data; as mentioned earlier, it has the advantage of speed of communication across the wire compared to XML objects.

> The process of converting binary data to text is called **deserialization**, and the process of converting text into a binary format is called **serialization**.

Flash provides an API called ByteArray that allows you to both serialize and deserialize data. The data is stored in an array collection of bytes.

> As a reminder, a **byte** is a basic unit of data and consists of 8 binary digits (bits), each 0 or 1.

Once the data ArrayCollection is created, it can be stored in the following ways:

- In an in-memory file
- Via zlib compression and decompression
- Via Flash remoting (AMF0/AMF3)

Let's look again at our VO class CustomerVO:

```
package com.vo
{
        [Bindable]
        public class CustomerVO
        {
                public var customerID:int;
                public var fname:String;
                public var lname:String;
                public var address:String;
                public var city:String;
                public var state:String;
                public var zip:Number;
```

```
            public var phone:String;
            public var email:Date;
            public var updateDate:Date;
        }
    }
```

Here's how we create a binary type object and serialize as well as deserialize the object:

```
<?xml version="1.0" encoding="utf-8"?>
<mx:Application xmlns:mx="http://www.adobe.com/2006/mxml"
    layout="absolute" initialize="createVO()">


  <mx:Script>
    <![CDATA[
        import com.vo.CustomerVO;
        import com.model.ModelLocator;

        import mx.collections.ArrayCollection;
        import flash.utils.ByteArray;

        [Bindable]
        private var model:ModelLocator = ModelLocator.getInstance();

        private function serialize(object:Object):ByteArray
        {
           var bytes:ByteArray = new ByteArray();
           bytes.writeObject(object);
           return bytes
        }

        private function deserialize(bytes:ByteArray):Object
        {
         var ob:Object = new Object
         bytes.position = 0;

         try {
        ob = bytes.readObject();
         }
         catch(e:EOFError) {
        trace(e);
         }

            return ob;
        }

        private function createVO():void
        {
           var customer:CustomerVO = new CustomerVO();
```

```
        customer.fname = "John";
        customer.lname = "Doe";
        customer.address = "111 14th Street";
        customer.city = "Los Angeles";
        customer.state = "CA";
        customer.zip = "90010";
        customer.phone = "(213)111-1111";
        customer.email = "john@gmail.com";
        customer.updateDate = new Date();

        model.customer = customer;

        init();
    }

    private function init():void
    {
        var bytes:ByteArray;
        var receivedCollection:Object;
        var collection:Object = ({fname: model.customer.fname,
                        lname: model.customer.lname,
                        address: model.customer.address,
                        city: model.customer.city,
                        state: model.customer.state,
                        zip: model.customer.zip,
                        phone: model.customer.phone,
                        email: model.customer.email,
                        updateDate: model.customer.updateDate. ➥
toString()});

        bytes = serialize(collection);
        receivedCollection = deserialize(bytes);
    }

    ]]>
  </mx:Script>

</mx:Application>
```

Using the same process, we can serialize and deserialize other types of binary data:

```
bytes.writeBoolean(false);
bytes.writeDouble(1.99);

catch(e:EOFError) {
    trace(e);
}

try {
```

```
    trace(bytes.readBoolean());
}
catch(e:EOFError) {
    trace(e);
}

try {
    trace(bytes.readDouble());
}
catch(e:EOFError) {
    trace(e);
}

try {
    bytes.position = 0;
    trace(bytes.readDouble());
}
catch(e:EOFError) {
    trace(e);
}
```

# Synchronizing binary data objects

Once the binary object is serialized, we can transmit it over the network or write it to a file for future usage.

It is possible to send and receive binary data in all three RPC connections. However, keep in mind that you cannot send or receive binary data through WebService or HttpService in its native format, and you will need to first convert it to a text string or convert it from a text string into a binary format.

Any connection that allows transmitting of Action Message Format (AMF) will let you transmit data in its binary native format. ActionScript offers the following APIs to send and receive binary data in its native format:

- RemoteObject
- NetConnection
- LocalConnection
- Shared Objects

> *AMF is a message protocol originally created by Macromedia (now Adobe) and used in different ActionScript 3.0 APIs.*

The AMF file format is a binary file format representing a serialized ActionScript object. This file type is used in many places within the Flash Player and AIR for data storage and data exchange. There are two versions of AMF available: AMF0 and AMF3. It's preferable to use AMF3. AMF3 improves AMF0 by sending object traits and strings by reference, in addition to object references, and supporting new data types that were introduced in ActionScript 3.0.

The benefits of using the AMF format are significant:

- AMF objects are the fastest way to send and receive data between Flash and a server.
- AMF objects are compressed using zlib, and the size of the file is small.
- AMF is transformed to ActionScript bytecode; there is no interpretation or parsing of the AMF object.
- There is no overhead text, such as SOAP XML objects, sent over the wire.

The complete specification for AMF0 can be downloaded from here: http://opensource.adobe.com/wiki/download/attachments/1114283/amf0_spec_121207.pdf?version=1.

And the specification for AMF3 can be found here: http://opensource.adobe.com/wiki/download/attachments/1114283/amf3_spec_05_05_08.pdf?version=1.

The most common component used to transmit the AMF object format to the business layer is RemoteObject. Using RemoteObject, you can call class methods on ColdFusion or Java directly. Additionally, you can use third-party solutions to connect with many other middle-layer technologies such as the following:

- AMFPHP allows access of PHP classes.
- RubyAMF allows access of Ruby classes.
- AMF.NET allows access of .NET classes.

Using RemoteObject to transmit AMF objects allows you to easily create an application that interacts with the server business layer in order to sync the model between your client and server. Once your server model is updated, it can communicate with elements in the server data layer, such as a MySQL database.

1. Let's create a Hello World application using AMFPHP. Download AMFPHP from here: http://www.amfphp.org/. The download is available under the Download link. The latest version at the time of this writing is 1.9.

2. Next, install a PHP and MySQL database on your local machine. You can install a PHP/MySQL database on your local machine with open source products such as XAMPP for PC (http://www.apachefriends.org/en/xampp.html) or MAMP for Mac (http://www.mamp.info/en/index.php).

In Figure 3-8, you can see the XAMPP control panel. You can open the XAMPP control panel and click the Explore link to navigate to where your localhost directory is located. Place the AMFPHP directory in the htdocs directory and test that it is working correctly by navigating to the following URL using your browser: http://localhost/amfphp/browser/.

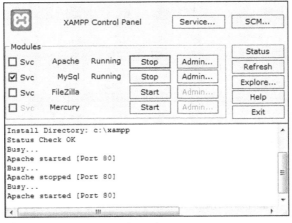

**Figure 3-8.** XAMPP control panel

3. In XAMPP, all the services you will be creating are going to reside in a directory called services. Under that directory you can keep creating subdirectories and place classes inside of these directories.

Next, we create a PHP class and name it HelloWorld.php. See the following method, which will return "Hello World":

```php
<?php
/**
 * Hello world class
 */
class HelloWorld
{
    /**
     * Method to demonstrate Hello World
     * @returns a string saying 'Hello World!'
     */
    function hello()
    {
        return "Hello World!";
    }
}
?>
```

**4.** Place the PHP file in a new directory and name the directory test (see Figure 3-9). It's crucial, just as in ActionScript packages, to name the class the same as the file name; otherwise, you will get an error message.

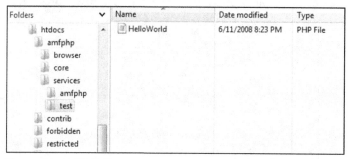

**Figure 3-9.** AMFPHP directory structure

**5.** AMFPHP version 1.9 contains an easy-to-use Flex application called Services browser, which lists all the services available. You can open the Services browser by navigating to http://localhost/amfphp/browser/ (see Figure 3-10). The Services browser application includes all the classes available for usage. When the application starts, the welcome panel will ask for information:

**a.** Gateway location should stay as the default: http://localhost/amfphp/gateway.php.

**b.** Choose AMF3 encoding over AMF0, set the results as Set tab after call, and click Save.

Once completed, you will be able to view your classes and call the methods on each class (see Figure 3-10).

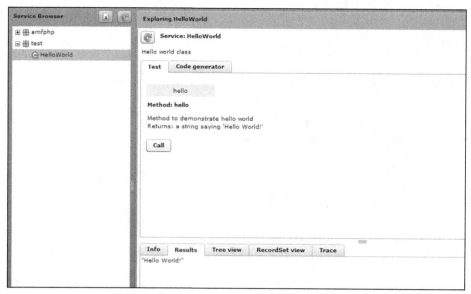

**Figure 3-10.** AMFPHP Services browser

**6.** To complete the application, call the hello method in the HelloWorld class from ActionScript:

```
<mx:RemoteObject
    id="myservice"
    endpoint="http://localhost/amfphp/gateway.php"
    source="test.HelloWorld"
    destination="amfphp"
    fault="fault(event)"
    showBusyCursor="true">
    <mx:method name="hello" result="result(event)" />
</mx:RemoteObject>
```

**7.** Initiate the service call, myservice.getOperation("hello").send();, and set the fault and result event handlers:

```
<?xml version="1.0" encoding="utf-8"?>
<mx:Application xmlns:mx="http://www.adobe.com/2006/mxml"
    layout="absolute" creationComplete="init()">

    <mx:Script>
        <![CDATA[
            import mx.rpc.events.FaultEvent;
            import mx.rpc.events.ResultEvent;

            private function init():void
            {
                service.getOperation("hello").send();
            }

            private function result(event: ResultEvent): void
            {
                trace(event.result);
            }

            private function fault(event: FaultEvent): void
            {
                trace("fault");
            }
        ]]>
    </mx:Script>

    <mx:RemoteObject
        id="service"
        endpoint="http://localhost/amfphp/gateway.php"
        source="test.HelloWorld"
        destination="amfphp"
        fault="fault(event)"
        showBusyCursor="true">
        <mx:method name="hello" result="result(event)" />
    </mx:RemoteObject>

</mx:Application>
```

**123**

**8.** Notice the endpoint property in the RemoteObject component that points to the production server. It is a good practice to include a property called PRODUCTION so you can switch between a production URL and a live URL:

```
private const PRODUCTION:Boolean = false;

private function init():void
{
    var endpoint:String;

    if (this.PRODUCTION)
        endpoint = "http://localhost/amfphp/gateway.php";
    else
        endpoint = "http://www.YourServer.com/gateway.php";

    service.endpoint = endpoint;
    service.getOperation("hello").send();

}
```

**9.** If you are running into trouble connecting, try using a web debugging proxy such as Charles (http://www.charlesproxy.com/) for PCs or ServiceCapture (http://kevinlangdon.com/serviceCapture/), which works on both PCs and Macs. Charles and ServiceCapture have native support for AMF. You will be able to keep track of all the services you are using (see Figure 3-11).

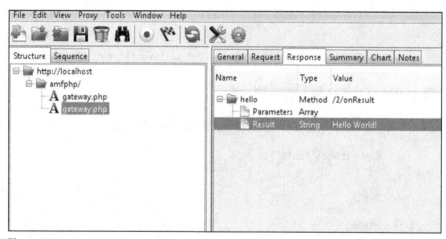

**Figure 3-11.** Charles debugging proxy

We have successfully created our Hello World application, and at this point we can utilize PHP to communicate with the server, serialize and deserialize different data types, and synchronize our VO with the server.

To sync your VO is quite simple. Here is an example. We will create a class in PHP that includes two methods: one that returns the CustomerVO object and one that receives a property in the CustomerVO and updates the class.

Create the following class in PHP. Save the file in the following directory: C:\xampp\htdocs\ amfphp\services\CustomerVOService.php.

```php
<?php
/**
 * Service to map between client model and server model.
 */
class CustomerVOService
{
    var $customerVO = array();

    /**
     * Method to return the array containing customerVO
     * @returns customerVO array
     */
    function getCustomerVO()
    {
        $this->customerVO['fname'] = "John";
        $this->customerVO['lname'] = "Doe";
        $this->customerVO['address'] = "111 14th Street";
        $this->customerVO['city'] = "Los Angeles";
        $this->customerVO['state'] = "CA";
        $this->customerVO['zip'] = "90010";
        $this->customerVO['phone'] = "(213)111-1111";
        $this->customerVO['email'] = "john@gmail.com";
        $this->customerVO['updateDate'] = ➥
"Sat Nov 29 00:00:00 GMT-0800 2008";

        return $this->customerVO;
    }

    /**
     * Method to receive the customer name
     * @returns success or failure message
     */
    function setCustomerName($name)
    {
        $this->customerVO['fname'] = $name;
        return "Customer name: ".$this->customerVO['fname'];
    }
}
?>
```

Test that the PHP class is working as intended by going to the AMFPHP browser application:
http://localhost/amfphp/browser/ (see Figure 3-12).

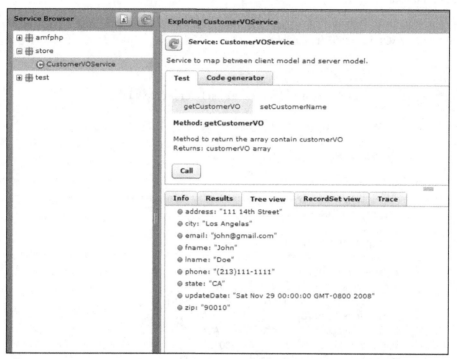

**Figure 3-12.** CustomerVOService displayed in the AMFPHP Services browser

Now we can create the Flex application, which will retrieve the CustomerVO from the server and
update our client model.

```
<?xml version="1.0" encoding="utf-8"?>
<mx:Application xmlns:mx="http://www.adobe.com/2006/mxml"
    layout="absolute" creationComplete="init()">

    <mx:Script>
        <![CDATA[
            import mx.rpc.events.FaultEvent;
            import mx.rpc.events.ResultEvent;

            private function init():void
            {
                myservice.getOperation("getCustomerVO").send();
            }

            private function result(event: ResultEvent): void
            {
                trace(event.result);
```

```
            }

            private function fault(event: FaultEvent): void
            {
                trace(event.fault.faultString);
            }
        ]]>
    </mx:Script>

    <mx:RemoteObject
        id="myservice"
        endpoint="http://localhost/amfphp/gateway.php"
        source="store.CustomerVOService"
        destination="amfphp"
        fault="fault(event)"
        showBusyCursor="true">
        <mx:method name="getCustomerVO" result="result(event)" />
    </mx:RemoteObject>

</mx:Application>
```

Place a line breakpoint in the result method; you will notice that you have received the arrays containing the VO information from AMFPHP (see Figure 3-13). You can now update the model on the client side via an event that will update the model just as you did before.

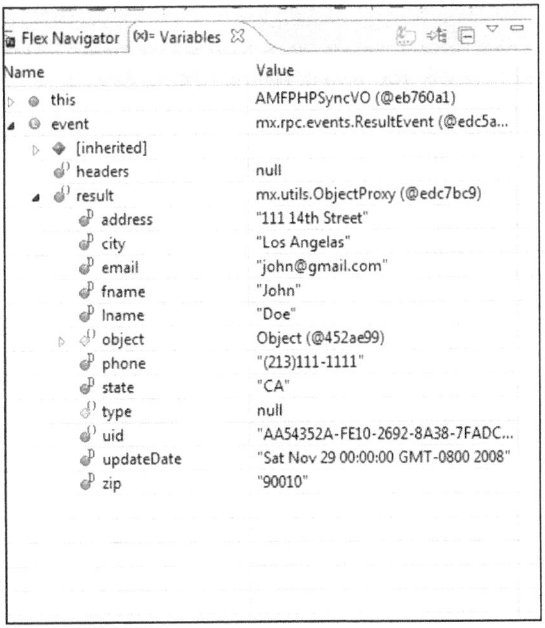

**Figure 3-13.** Adding a line breakpoint after the event handler displays CustomerVO

# Creating effective CRUD applications

So far, we synchronized our client model with the server model. However, in order to create a complete application with the ability to run Create, Retrieve, Update, and Delete (CRUD) statements, we will have to put in a lot of effort. This includes mapping the data attributes and creating all the middle layer scripts to communicate with Flex and the database, not to mention dealing with data-aware controls, serializing and deserializing the data, and synchronizing updates between the client and the server. We also have to take into consideration that a few other people might be working on the same application.

Flex Builder 3 has a new feature built into Eclipse, the Create Application from Database Wizard, that enables us to generate the server services automatically without writing a single line of code. This wizard supports ASP.NET, PHP, ColdFusion, J2EE, and other server-side technologies to easily create full CRUD applications. This can be the foundation of new applications or added services to an existing application.

As an example, we will create a Flex application that utilizes PHP as the business layer, Flex as the UI layer, and MySQL as the data layer technology. Once the CRUD scripts are created, we will be able to sync the model on the server with the model on the client.

We will be working locally using XAMPP. If you didn't install XAMPP previously, please see the instructions earlier in this chapter in the section "Synchronizing binary data objects" or go directly to the XAMPP site: http://www.apachefriends.org/en/xampp.html/. Make sure the Apache and MySQL service are running by navigating to http://localhost and then clicking Tools ➤ phpMyAdmin to open the MySQL admin tool. If you can view the pages, you are running PHP and MySQL correctly; otherwise, open the XAMPP control panel and start the services.

First, we need to create a new project. Select File ➤ New ➤ Flex Project. Name the project Store, and select PHP as the server technology, as shown in Figure 3-14.

Click the Next button. In the next window, set Web root to the XAMPP location. If you select default values during installation of XAMPP, specify C:/xampp/htdocs and set Root URL to http://localhost/. Click Validate configuration to ensure the URL is valid. Make sure you set your compiled project under the XMAPP directory; otherwise, you will not be able to run PHP scripts (see Figure 3-15). Click Finish, and the project is created.

Our next task is to create the database. Open phpMyAdmin by navigating to http://localhost/phpmyadmin/.

phpMyAdmin is an open source administration script written in PHP that allows you to manage a MySQL database over the Web.

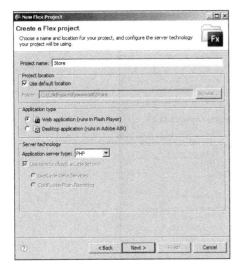

**Figure 3-14.** Create a Flex project window

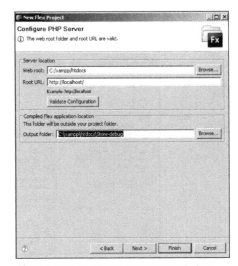

**Figure 3-15.** Configure PHP Server window

We will be using a simple database that includes products, categories, customers, and productcategoriesint entities. The intersection entity, productcategoriesint, is used so we can store many products that relate to many categories. See the Unified Modeling Language (UML) graphical notation for the database design in Figure 3-16.

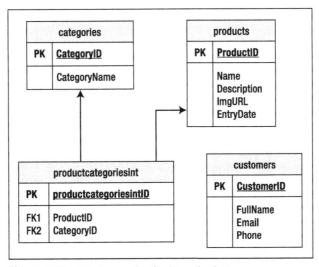

**Figure 3-16.** UML diagram for the Store database

In phpMyAdmin, under Create new Database, enter the name Store and click Create, as shown in Figure 3-17.

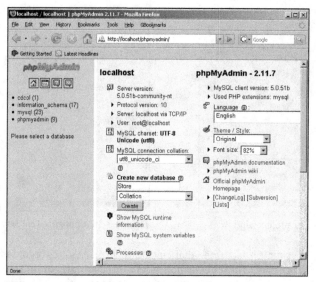

**Figure 3-17.** phpMyAdmin adminstrator script

Choose the store database from the left navigation menu, and then select SQL from the top navigation tabs. Enter and execute the following SQL command to create the database, as shown in Figure 3-18.

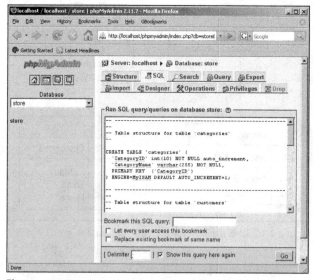

**Figure 3-18.** Running a SQL command in phpMyAdmin

```
-- ---------------------------------------------------------
--
-- Table structure for table `categories`
--

CREATE TABLE `categories` (
  `CategoryID` int(10) NOT NULL auto_increment,
  `CategoryName` varchar(255) NOT NULL,
  PRIMARY KEY  (`CategoryID`)
) ENGINE=MyISAM DEFAULT AUTO_INCREMENT=1;


-- ---------------------------------------------------------
--
-- Table structure for table `customers`
--

CREATE TABLE `customers` (
  `CustomerID` int(10) NOT NULL auto_increment,
  `FullName` varchar(255) NOT NULL,
  `Email` varchar(255) NOT NULL,
  `Phone` varchar(255) NOT NULL,
  PRIMARY KEY  (`CustomerID`)
) ENGINE=MyISAM DEFAULT AUTO_INCREMENT=1;


-- ---------------------------------------------------------
--
-- Table structure for table `products`
--

CREATE TABLE `products` (
  `ProductID` int(11) NOT NULL auto_increment,
  `Name` varchar(255) default NULL,
  `Description` varchar(255) default NULL,
  `ImgURL` varchar(255) default NULL,
  `EntryDate` varchar(255) default NULL,
  PRIMARY KEY  (`ProductID`)
) ENGINE=MyISAM DEFAULT AUTO_INCREMENT=1;



-- ---------------------------------------------------------
--
-- Table structure for table `productcategoriesint`
--

CREATE TABLE `productcategoriesint` (
  `productcategoriesintID` int(10) NOT NULL auto_increment,
  `ProductID` varchar(255) NOT NULL,
  `CategoryID` varchar(255) NOT NULL,
```

```
        PRIMARY KEY  (`productcategoriesintID`)
) ENGINE=MyISAM DEFAULT CHARSET=latin1 AUTO_INCREMENT=1 ;


--
-- Dumping data for table `productcategoriesint`
--
```

We are ready to create a connection profile so we will be able to view the entities as well as create CRUD statements for each entity (table). Open the connectivity view by selecting Window ➤ Show View ➤ Connectivity ➤ Data Source Explorer.

Under database, right-click and select new. You can see the list of possible databases that are available, as shown in Figure 3-19. Select Simple MySQL Connection since we are using a MySQL database.

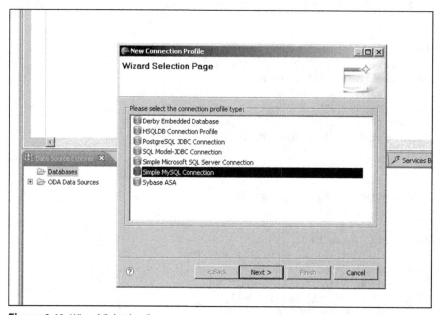

**Figure 3-19.** Wizard Selection Page

After selecting the MySQL database, click Next.

In this next window, you can select a name for the profile. Enter Store as the name. In the next window, fill in the following information:

- Host URL: localhost
- Database Name: Store
- User name: root (This is the default for the MySQL username.)
- Password: (Leave this field empty since there are no default values for the MySQL password.)

Complete creating the profile by clicking Next and then Finish, and you can see the profile as well as a list of tables available, as shown in Figure 3-20.

**Figure 3-20.** Data Source Explorer tables

To create the server services, select the products table, right-click, and select Create application from database. In the window that appears, you'll find the table, connection, and primary key defaults have been supplied, as shown in Figure 3-21, so we can move to the next window.

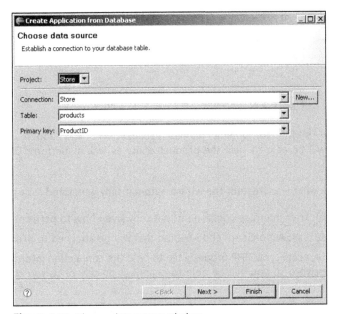

**Figure 3-21.** Choose data source window

In the next window, confirm the following settings:

- User default settings: PHP
- Source folder: `bin-debug`
- PHP file name: `Products.php`

Click Next. In the next window (see Figure 3-22), you can specify the data object properties and how to filter the request if needed. Once you complete setting up the properties, click Finish.

**Figure 3-22.** Generate client-side code window

Notice that a new MXML component named `product.mxml` was added. Compile and run `product.mxml`. You will be able to view the product entity as well as perform CRUD operations, as shown in Figure 3-23.

Now let's take a look what was created. The wizard automatically generated for us the following files:

- `products.mxml`: User interface component that shows you how to perform CRUD operations.
- `productsScript.as`: ActionScript code-behind that will be attached to `products.mxml`.
- `bin-debug/Storeconn.php`: PHP property file to hold the connection information such as username and password so you will be able to change it quickly once you change the database information.
- `bin-debug/XmlSerializer.class.php`: File that uses the PEAR XML parser to generate a server XML object response.
- `bin-debug/PEAR/*`: PEAR framework, which is a PHP extension and includes components to easily handle the XML object. Visit PEAR at `http://pear.php.net/`.

**Figure 3-23.** The products.mxml component

The wizard serializes and deserializes the XML object. It also created the services, database, CRUD statements, and VO. The VO is stored in an object called fields:

```
private var fields:Object = {'ProductID':Number, 'Name':String, ➥
'Description':String, 'ImgURL':String, 'EntryDate':Date};
```

From here, you can create CRUD services for other entities as well as start building your application. Keep in mind that we built services for PHP and MySQL, but you can create services for other technologies using the same techniques.

# Creating a ColdFusion CRUD application

Most of the time, you will probably not have a chance to choose which server technology to use for the business layer; however, when you do get a chance to choose, there is an advantage to choosing ColdFusion as your business layer. Adobe has created the ColdFusion/Flex Application Wizard to go one step beyond the Create Application from Database Wizard: the ColdFusion/Flex Application Wizard generates the client VO as well as custom CRUD statements.

The ColdFusion/Flex Application Wizard is a plug-in that enables you to create complete CRUD database applications by using ColdFusion as the business layer and Flex as the UI layer. The code creates MXML and ColdFusion files that conform to best practices.

The application we will build in this section can serve as

- A content management system (CMS) for an existing application
- The foundation for an application

The connection is made using RemoteObject. Once the code is created, we can modify it to create a user-protected page and utilize it as a CMS system. In addition, we can use the model, VO, and other code as the base for the model layer in an MVC structured application.

1. Install ColdFusion version 7.0.2 or above, which can be downloaded from here: http://www.adobe.com/support/coldfusion/downloads.html.

2. We will be using the same store database as we did earlier in this chapter, so please make sure you have MySQL installed and execute the SQL command line, as shown earlier in this chapter.

3. We need to configure the ColdFusion data source to point to the Store database we created. Open ColdFusion Administrator by navigating to http://127.0.0.1:8500/CFIDE/administrator/ in your browser.

   Click the DataSources link under Data & Services and create a data source, as shown in Figure 3-24. Name the data source Store, same as the database. Choose the MySQL driver and click Add.

> We are creating a MySQL database, but you can create any database as long as ColdFusion has a driver for that database.

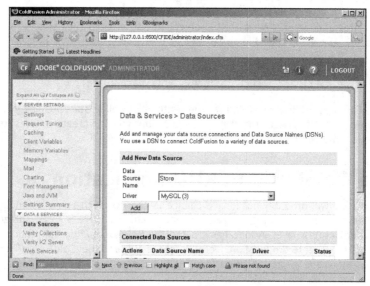

**Figure 3-24.** Creating ColdFusion data sources

4. In the next window, we will be setting the database information. Since we are using our local machine, specify localhost as the server, with the database username and password as shown in Figure 3-25. Notice that MySQL is using port 3306 by default; if you change the port, make sure to change this setting. Click Submit, and you should get a success message: # datasource updated successfully. We are done with configuration, and both ColdFusion and the MySQL database are ready.

**136**

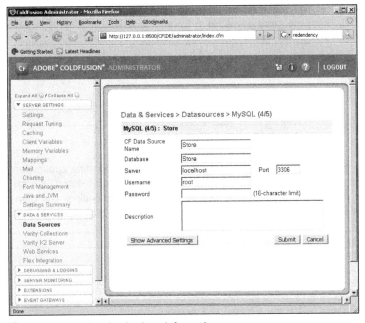

**Figure 3-25.** Setting the database information

**5.** Open Eclipse and start the ColdFusion/Flex Application Wizard: File ➤ New ➤ Other ➤ ColdFusion Wizard. The wizard window will appear, as shown in Figure 3-26.

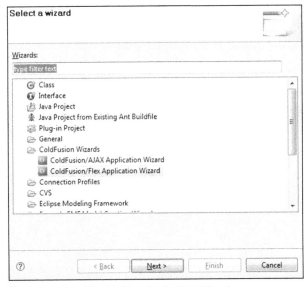

**Figure 3-26.** ColdFusion/Flex Application Wizard

**137**

**6.** Click Next twice. You will then be asked to enter your RDS localhost server password (see Figure 3-27). That's the same password as for your ColdFusion administration login page.

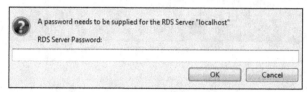

**Figure 3-27.** RDS server password request

**7.** Next, you get a settings page, and here you can choose an existing application or create a new application (see Figure 3-28). Once your application has been created, you can always go back and make changes in the application by clicking Load Wizard Settings and then clicking Next. Or you can keep the Previous Wizard Setting File field empty and click Next to start a new application.

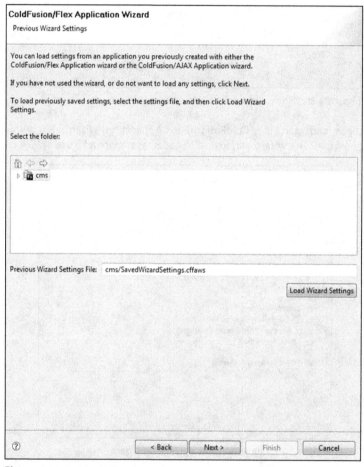

**Figure 3-28.** Previous Wizard Settings page

**8.** You will be given an option to choose your data source (see Figure 3-29). Choose the data source we created named Store.

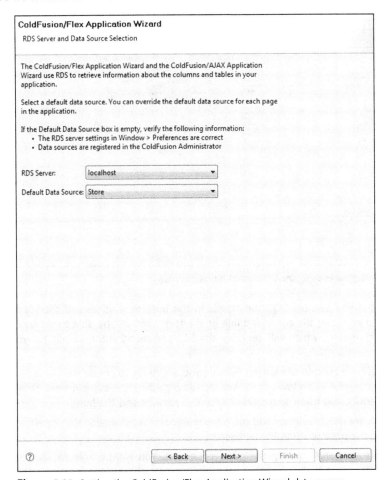

**Figure 3-29.** Setting the ColdFusion/Flex Application Wizard data source

**9.** In the next window, you have the option to create different types of pages: Master, Detail, Master/Detail.

Click + to create a new page. Name the page Products and choose Master/Detail for the page type. Once you click Edit Master Section, you will be able to configure the page, as shown in Figure 3-30.

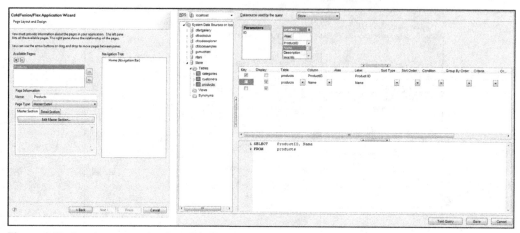

**Figure 3-30.** Creating pages using the ColdFusion templates plug-in

**10.** Notice that you can see SQL commands in the bottom window and modify the statements directly using either the command line or the form. You will be able to set sort, condition, and criteria parameters, which will generate the SQL command automatically for you. Once done, click the Save button.

**11.** Once you have created the Master Section, you are ready to create the Detail Section page. The Edit Detail Section will allow you to see details regarding the current field. Drag and drop the Product entity, and make specifications for the Validator and the Mask.

**12.** Once you are done, you can add the page under Home (Navigation Bar) by either dragging and dropping the page or using the arrow icon.

**13.** Once you are done creating the page, click Next. You will be able to save the project (see Figure 3-31). Note that you cannot have two projects at the same location; otherwise, you will get an error message.

**14.** Once the page is ready, you can launch the application and modify, insert, and delete fields, as you can see in Figure 3-32.

**Figure 3-31.** Completing the ColdFusion/Flex Application Wizard process

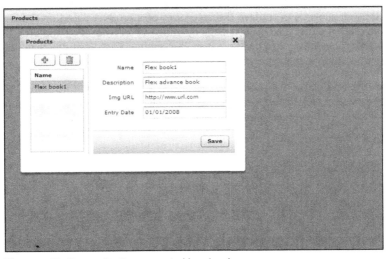

**Figure 3-32.** Flex application generated by wizard

15. Let's continue by creating the following pages: Categories, Customers, ProductsCategoriesINT. In Eclipse, choose File ➤ New ➤ Other ➤ ColdFusion Wizard. Choose the project Store and then select Load Wizard Settings. Click Next twice.

16. We are back at the wizard plug-in section. To create the Categories page, add a page using the + sign, and choose Master/Detail ➤ Edit Master Section.

    In the user interface, we want to be able to display the category names and show them in ascending order. To do that, click Display checkbox and choose Sort Type Ascending and Sort Order 1. Then save the page.

17. For the Detail Section, drag and drop the Categories entity to the top screen and display the category name while the CategoryID is auto-created. Click Save to commit your changes.

18. Continue by creating a template for the Customers page: add a page using the + sign, choose Master/Detail ➤ Edit Master Section, choose the fields you would like to display, and click Save once done.

19. Create the Detail Section: drag and drop the Customers entity. For validation, choose e-mail for the Email field and Phone Number for the Phone field. Note that you can also mask the phone to fit the following format: (999) 999-9999. Once done, click Save.

20. The next step is to set the intersection page. Following the normalization process, we have created an entity of many-to-many relationships, so we can associate a few of the same products to many categories. Create a new page template and call it ProductsCategoriesINT, and then create the Master/Detail page just as you did before.

21. In the Detail page, we have two fields, ProductID and CategoryID, which have a foreign key in the ProductsCategoriesINT entity. You can create an input lookup query, which is essentially a SQL command that will execute a lookup for all ProductIDs and CategoryIDs. Choose Combobox as the input control, click input lookup query, and display ProductID for the ProductID field and CategoryID for the CategoryID field.

22. The last page we will create is a ProductsCategories page, which will hold the products that are associated with a category. Choose Master ➤ Edit Master Page. Next, drop the ProductsCategoriesINT entity and associate ProductID to the ID in the Parameters window. Doing this will allow us to retrieve the categories of a product based on ProductID. Save the page and place it under the Products page by using the arrow or drag and drop the page from the Available pages window to the Navigation Tree window. Click Finish to create the application. You can now compile the application (see Figure 3-33).

As you can see, the possibilities are endless. We have created a complete CRUD application in a very short time. We can start using the application to add, delete, and update fields. In Chapter 14, we will revisit the ColdFusion wizards to generate a custom application similar to YouTube.

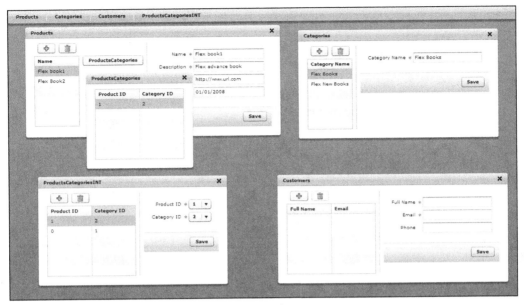

**Figure 3-33.** Complete Flex application generated by wizard

# Summary

This chapter talked about the new paradigm for web development of stateful applications. Data binding of the client model and the server model allows us to create stateful applications. Storing the client state is the key to building a data-driven Flex application.

I showed you how to use explicit and implicit data binding as well as create a value object model. I also showed you how to synchronize the client model with the server model. You used XML objects to sync the data as well as binary data objects for faster transmission.

You utilized existing plug-ins to create a powerful CRUD application that can handle processing data and presentation as well as provide fast transmission to the server without writing a single line of code. The application included complete CRUD operations using PHP, ColdFusion as the business layer, and MySQL as the data layer.

By storing and binding the model and sync only when needed, you reduced overhead from the server, allowing the server to increase available memory and the number of clients it serves at the same time. In the next chapter, you will see how to leverage this even further by fine-tuning your Flex applications to deliver superior performance.

Chapter 4

# TUNING APPLICATIONS FOR SUPERIOR PERFORMANCE

By Shashank Tiwari

Tuning an application is an art rather than a science. So, the more you put performance-tuning ideas into practice, the more familiar you become with the power and limitations of these ideas. However, nothing can be as fruitless as applying a performance-tuning principle without understanding the underlying mechanics. Therefore, this chapter starts by looking under the hood of Flex and related player features that impact performance. Once the foundational matters have been established, we progress to fine-tuning applications for better performance.

Before we go further, you need to be clear about what I mean when I use the word "performance." Although there is no universal definition of performance, it's usually measured in terms of the following:

- **Latency**: Measures the immediacy characteristics of the application. Also known as responsiveness. A low value implies quicker response time during interaction, lesser time taken during initialization, and faster responses during invocation.

- **Scalability**: Measures how the application matches up to expectations in the wake of more users, higher throughput, faster communication, and larger amounts of data.

- **Reliability**: Measures the consistency with which an application delivers to promise.

- **Availability**: Measures the accessibility of the application. Higher availability implies a higher application uptime and greater support for failover.

Let's start our journey by exploring a typical Flex application run-time life cycle.

# Run-time life cycle

Flex applications are created using ActionScript and MXML (which in turn corresponds to ActionScript or compiler directives). On compilation, they generate bytecode that runs on the Flash Player. A Flex application at its core is a Flash MovieClip. This means it runs along a temporal dimension. Units of this temporal dimension, which represent the current state of the running application at any point in time, are called **frames**. Traditionally, Flash applications, which also compile to the bytecode that runs on the Flash Player, allow developers to program along a timeline that defines multiple frames. However, Flex moves away from the timeline-based model and defines only two frames in any application, listed here:

- **Preloader frame**: This is the first of the two frames that all Flex applications have. When you access a Flex application and see the download progress, you are in this frame. Flex comes with a default preloader. If required, you can define your own preloader instead.
- **Application frame**: This is the main application frame. This is where the entire application is downloaded, instantiated, initialized, and set up.

The preloader frame is extremely lightweight and includes nothing of the Flex framework. All the application code, with the Flex framework, forms part of the application frame. As a Flex application downloads, instantiates, initializes, and sets itself up, it dispatches events at every milestone. I will illustrate these events a little later in the section "Typical life-cycle events."

I started by saying that every Flex application is a MovieClip. What I meant was that every Flex application has mx.managers.SystemManager at its kernel, which in turn extends from flash.display.MovieClip and has the properties and behavior of a MovieClip.

The entry point for a Flex application is an instance of an mx.core.Application layout container. Application, being a LayoutContainer, inherits indirectly from the UIComponent class, which is at the base of all visual components in Flex. The entry point for AIR applications is an instance of WindowedApplication, a subclass of the Application class. Figure 4-1 illustrates this hierarchy in a diagram.

Each Application is associated with a SystemManager and interacts via events with the SystemManager during instantiation and initialization. The Application is in the second of the two frames of a Flex application. Every UIComponent has a systemManager property that holds the value of the associated SystemManager object. So a reference to a Flex application's underlying SystemManager can be obtained easily using the systemManager property of the Application.

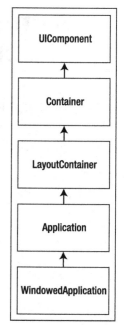

**Figure 4-1.** Application, WindowedApplication, and its relationship with the UIComponent

## Typical life-cycle events

Now that you know the roles of the Application and the SystemManager class, we are ready to walk through the life cycle of a Flex application. Figure 4-2 shows the milestones and the events in a typical life cycle of a Flex application.

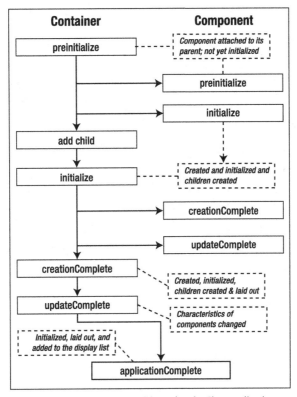

**Figure 4-2.** Events during the life cycle of a Flex application

The annotations in the diagram explain when the events are dispatched. I'll recap a few of the salient points here:

- preinitialize is the first event in the life cycle. It's so early in the process that a container at this point is not even initialized, and its components are not even created.

- Initialization functions are often called in the creationComplete event handler.

- If a container is within another container, the internal container goes through the same life cycle as the outer one. From the outer container's standpoint, the inner container is treated the same as any other component.

- The last event fired before the application is ready to be used is the applicationComplete event.

- The preloader is removed by the time the applicationComplete event is fired.

The Flex application life cycle just discussed is applicable to single-view containers like Box, Canvas, and Panel but does not hold for multiple-view containers like TabNavigator, Accordion, and ViewStack. Multiple-view containers delay or defer the creation and layout of their children components in their views, until a user accesses a particular view. This means only the default view of these multiple-view containers is fully created and initialized at application startup. In the following section, you will see how you could leverage explicit mechanisms and defer the creation of components, where applicable.

# Creation policy

By default, Flex creates, initializes, and lays out all containers that users can see and their child components. As mentioned earlier, this means all single-view containers' children are created right away, whereas only the visible tabs of the navigator components are fully created. This is the default behavior, but it can be altered if required. Every container has a property called creationPolicy, which can be set appropriately to affect the way components are created in the container.

The creationPolicy property can take four valid values:

- all: Create all components, child containers, and controls immediately.
- auto: Create components automatically, which means implement default behavior.
- none: Don't create any components up front. Create them when the createComponentsFromDescriptors method is called.
- queued: Create all containers first and then fill their children in one by one.

The creationPolicy property affects single-view and navigator components differently because the default creation priorities in the two types of containers are different.

Let's now see an example of a single-view container with the creationPolicy property set to none for an inner container. Here is the code:

```
<?xml version="1.0"?>
<!-- CreationPolicySingleView.mxml -->
<mx:Application xmlns:mx="http://www.adobe.com/2006/mxml">
<mx:Panel title="Creation Policy in a Single View container" >
    <mx:VBox id="outerVBox" creationPolicy="auto">
        <mx:Label id="lb1"
            text="VBox creation policy set to➡
            {innerVBox.creationPolicy}" />
        <mx:VBox id="innerVBox" creationPolicy="none">
            <mx:Label id="lb2" text="Label in inner VBox" />
            <mx:Button id="b1" label="Button in the inner VBox" />
            <mx:VBox id="secondLevelInnerVBox" creationPolicy="all">
                <mx:Button id="b2"
                label="Button in the second level inner VBox" />
            </mx:VBox>
        </mx:VBox>
    </mx:VBox>
</mx:Panel>
</mx:Application>
```

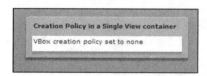

The result as expected is just a label with the text VBox creation policy set to none. Figure 4-3 shows what it looks like.

**Figure 4-3.** Only a label can be seen, as the creationPolicy is set to none on the peer container.

If we change the creationPolicy of the VBox with ID, innerVBox, to auto, all controls in the example are created and visible. Figure 4-4 shows a snapshot of the example. All components and their children are created and laid out in this picture.

**Figure 4-4.** Example application when the creation policy is set to auto

The creation policy can directly impact the time taken to create and initialize components. Too much eager initialization of components can consume a large amount of time. This means a user waits for a long time between the beginning of an application download and the time when it is ready for use. Such long wait times are a typical symptom of lower-than-expected performance.

This brings us to the following question: is there a way to reliably measure the elapsed time within the application, or do we have to rely on our gut feel or external time recorders? If we can't measure something, we often find we can't change it. Therefore, the question is of paramount importance. The answer is encouraging and positive, because there are ways to measure latency and related performance metrics in a Flex application. Moreover, these options are easy to use and reliable.

Next, I will introduce the measuring tools and the recommended ways of using them. Once you are familiar with them, we will come back to the topic of creation policy and fine-tune the performance during initialization and startup.

## Measuring latency at startup

One of the accepted approaches to recording elapsed time between two events is to measure the time at the beginning and at the end of the event and then calculate the difference between the two. An alternative way to record the time elapsed is to use a profiling tool like Flex Profiler. The Flash Player includes a utility that can be accessed via the getTimer method to record elapsed time using this technique. On invocation, the getTimer method provides the time in milliseconds elapsed since the player started playing. Here is an example that uses getTimer to record a set of time metrics around the time taken to create containers and their child components. The code is as follows:

```
<?xml version="1.0" encoding="iso-8859-1"?>
<!-- optimize/ShowElapsedTime.mxml -->
<mx:Application xmlns:mx="http://www.adobe.com/2006/mxml"
preinitialize="callLater(init)" height="1100">
    <mx:Script><![CDATA[
        import mx.collections.ArrayCollection;
    [Bindable]
    public var topFourIMF:ArrayCollection = new ArrayCollection([
        {Country:"United States", GDP:13843825},
        {Country:"China (PRC)", GDP:6991036},
        {Country:"Japan", GDP:4289809},
        {Country:"India", GDP:2988867}
    ]);

        [Bindable]
        private var recordedTimeArray:ArrayCollection =
            new ArrayCollection();
```

```
private function init():void {
    hbox1.addEventListener➥
    ("preinitialize", logRecorderTime, true);
    hbox1.addEventListener➥
    ("initialize", logRecorderTime, true);
    hbox1.addEventListener➥
    ("creationComplete", logRecorderTime, true);
    hbox1.addEventListener➥
    ("updateComplete", logRecorderTime, true);

    this.addEventListener("applicationComplete",
        logRecorderTime, true);

}

private var isFirst:Boolean = true;

private function logRecorderTime(e:Event):void {
    // Get the time when the preinitialize event is dispatched.
    var targetCompId:String = e.target.id;
    if(targetCompId != null) {
    var recordedTime:Number = getTimer();

    var eventType:String = e.type;
    var recorderObj:Object = new Object();
    recorderObj.compId = targetCompId;
    recorderObj.eventT = eventType;
    recorderObj.time = recordedTime;
    recordedTimeArray.addItem(recorderObj);
    }

}

]]></mx:Script>
<mx:VBox id="vbox2" width="100%" height="100%">
    <mx:HBox id="hbox4" width="100%" height="100%">
        <mx:DataGrid
        id="dataGrid2"
        dataProvider="{recordedTimeArray}"
        width="100%"
        height="100%">
            <mx:columns>
                <mx:DataGridColumn
```

```
                        dataField="compId"
                        headerText="Component Id"/>
                    <mx:DataGridColumn
                        dataField="eventT"
                        headerText="Event Type"/>
                    <mx:DataGridColumn
                        dataField="time"
                        headerText="Milliseconds Elapsed"/>
                </mx:columns>
            </mx:DataGrid>
        </mx:HBox>
    </mx:VBox>
    <mx:HBox id="hbox1">
        <mx:HBox id="hbox2">
            <mx:Form id="form1">
                <mx:FormHeading label="A Form" id="formHeading1"/>
                <mx:FormItem label="A List Control" id="formItem1">
                    <mx:List dataProvider="{topFourIMF}"
                    labelField="Country"
                    id="list1"/>
                </mx:FormItem>
                <mx:FormItem label="Date controls" id="formItem2">
                    <mx:DateChooser id="dateChooser1"/>
                    <mx:DateField id="dateField1"/>
                </mx:FormItem>
            </mx:Form>
        </mx:HBox>
        <mx:HBox id="hbox3">
            <mx:PieChart id="myChart1"
            dataProvider="{topFourIMF}"
            showDataTips="true">
                <mx:series>
                    <mx:PieSeries id="pieSeries1"
                    field="GDP"
                    nameField="Country"
                    labelPosition="callout"/>
                </mx:series>
            </mx:PieChart>
            <mx:Legend dataProvider="{myChart1}" id="legend1"/>
        </mx:HBox>
    </mx:HBox>
</mx:Application>
```

**151**

The container and components are shown in Figure 4-5. The getTimer results are added to an ArrayCollection, and this ArrayCollection is bound to a DataGrid. Figure 4-5 shows this time record data grid.

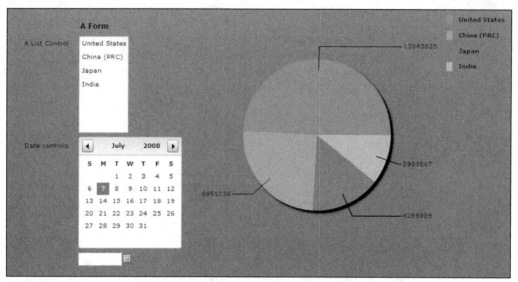

**Figure 4-5.** A set of containers and components

The init method in this example registers event listeners for life-cycle events for the top-level containers. Creation, initialization, and layout of each container in turn invokes the creation, initialization, and layout of its child components. Therefore, the child component life-cycle events also get registered in the getTimer calls. The first of the life-cycle events records an elapsed time of 1366 milliseconds. This is the amount of time elapsed since the Flex application, i.e., the SystemManager and not the Application, started playing. Think of it as a movie and the length of time since the beginning of the movie.

Notice the init function is called at the Application preinitialize event. The init function is wrapped in a callLater method when assigned as the event handler of the preinitialize event. It's logical that functions are called only on objects that are created and are available. However, because applications are event driven and asynchronous in nature, you can often not guarantee the exact time when a function would be executed or ensure that the component is available. Possibly the only exception may be to wait until everything is created, initialized, laid out, and ready, essentially after the applicationComplete event is dispatched. You can't wait that long in every situation. So wouldn't it be convenient to have a mechanism where a function is called on an object only if it's available, or else skipped and recalled at a later time on a second pass? This is exactly what the callLater function does. It essentially queues a request for the next container update instead of the current one, so that you don't try and access a property that is not yet available. The callLater method signature allows arguments to be passed in an Array to the function that is called.

Our approach of measuring time using the getTimer method is useful but fairly crude and involves manual manipulation of the timer data to get meaningful results. Figure 4-6 shows the time elapsed data recorded using the getTimer method for a particular example. An alternative to this is to use the Flex Profiler. The Flex Profiler comes with the Adobe Flex Builder 3 Professional Edition. It's a full-featured application profiler that can help capture latency, memory usage, and other performance-related metrics.

Flex Profiler and its features are discussed later in this chapter.

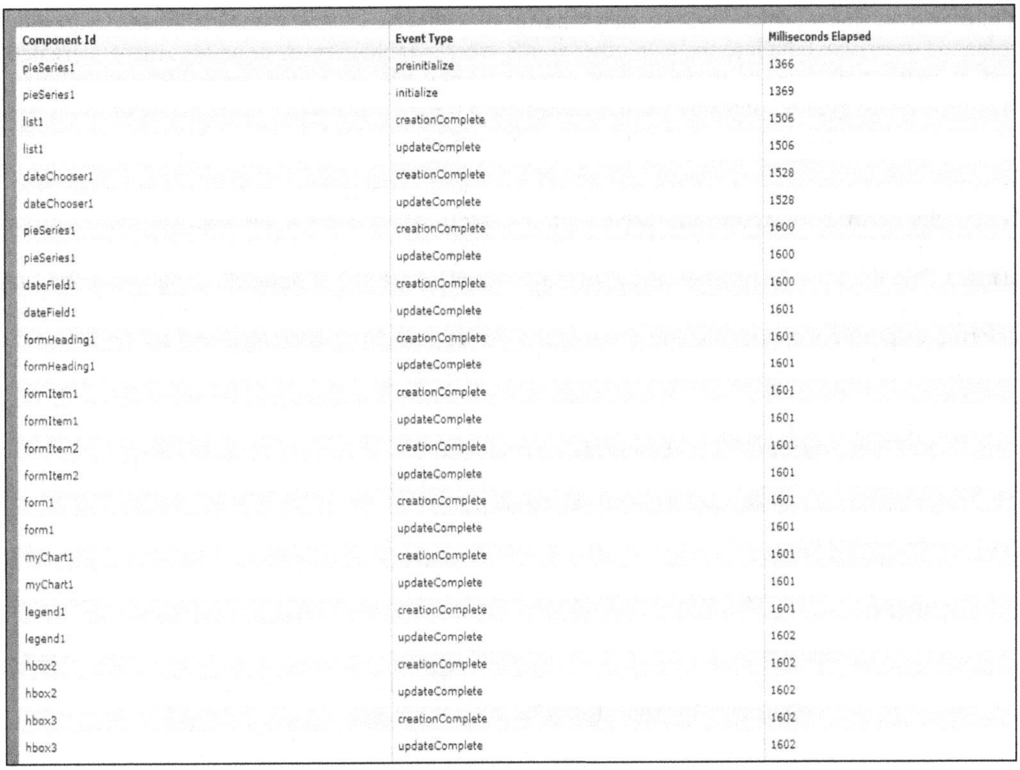

| Component Id | Event Type | Milliseconds Elapsed |
|---|---|---|
| pieSeries1 | preinitialize | 1366 |
| pieSeries1 | initialize | 1369 |
| list1 | creationComplete | 1506 |
| list1 | updateComplete | 1506 |
| dateChooser1 | creationComplete | 1528 |
| dateChooser1 | updateComplete | 1528 |
| pieSeries1 | creationComplete | 1600 |
| pieSeries1 | updateComplete | 1600 |
| dateField1 | creationComplete | 1600 |
| dateField1 | updateComplete | 1601 |
| formHeading1 | creationComplete | 1601 |
| formHeading1 | updateComplete | 1601 |
| formItem1 | creationComplete | 1601 |
| formItem1 | updateComplete | 1601 |
| formItem2 | creationComplete | 1601 |
| formItem2 | updateComplete | 1601 |
| form1 | creationComplete | 1601 |
| form1 | updateComplete | 1601 |
| myChart1 | creationComplete | 1601 |
| myChart1 | updateComplete | 1601 |
| legend1 | creationComplete | 1601 |
| legend1 | updateComplete | 1602 |
| hbox2 | creationComplete | 1602 |
| hbox2 | updateComplete | 1602 |
| hbox3 | creationComplete | 1602 |
| hbox3 | updateComplete | 1602 |

**Figure 4-6.** getTimer records for the initialization, creation, and laying out of the containers and components

Now that you know how to measure latency, let's go back and see how we can defer or queue the startup of containers and their components to achieve faster response times.

## Deferring and queuing component creation

Deferring or queuing container and component creation, initialization, and setup at application startup does not reduce the overall time taken to do all the operations. It only influences the distribution of the elapsed time. When you adopt an "auto" or "all" creation policy in single-view containers, you wait until the container and all its child components are set up and are available for use. When you defer the creation of some components in a container, you essentially don't create them up front. We create them later on demand. This changes the perceived elapsed time. The initial wait time is thus reduced and the application can be used even before all of it is set up.

Multiview containers, which are also called navigator containers, have such a feature of deferring component creation built into them. In other words, when a TabNavigator or an Accordion is created and initialized, only the view that is available to the users is laid out and set up in totality. The other hidden views are created only when a user navigates to the particular view. An outcome of this is less wait time up front but a slight delay later on, when accessing a new view.

Multiview containers can be forced to create all their containers and their children eagerly, if required. Setting the creationPolicy to all achieves this outcome. In a short while, you will see a sample TabNavigator, where we actually set the creation policy to all. In that example, we measure the elapsed time until the point when the applicationComplete event is dispatched. Subsequently, we compare this "application complete" elapsed time metric between the default scenario, which uses deferred or postponed creation, and the scenario where everything is created and set up up front. Here is the code for the example with all as the creation policy:

```
<?xml version="1.0"?>
<!-- TabNavigatorAllCreationPolicy.mxml. -->
<mx:Application xmlns:mx="http://www.adobe.com/2006/mxml"
    applicationComplete="getElapsedTime(event)">
<mx:Script>
    <![CDATA[
        import mx.collections.ArrayCollection;

        [Bindable]
        public var topFourIMF:ArrayCollection = new ArrayCollection([
            {Country:"United States", GDP:13843825},
            {Country:"China (PRC)", GDP:6991036},
            {Country:"Japan", GDP:4289809},
            {Country:"India", GDP:2988867}
        ]);
        [Bindable]
        public var elapsedTime:Number;

        public function getElapsedTime(evt:Event):void {
            elapsedTime = getTimer();
        }

    ]]>
</mx:Script>
    <mx:Panel title="TabNavigator" height="90%" width="90%"
        paddingTop="10"
        paddingLeft="10"
```

```
            paddingRight="10"
            paddingBottom="10">
        <mx:Label width="100%"
            text="Time elapsed till applicationComplete is➡
            {elapsedTime} milliseconds"/>
        <mx:TabNavigator id="tn1"
        width="100%"
        height="100%"
        creationPolicy="all">
            <mx:VBox label="Panel 1">
                <mx:Label text="Panel 1" />
                <mx:DataGrid dataProvider="{topFourIMF}" />
            </mx:VBox>
            <mx:VBox label="Panel 2">
                <mx:Label text="Panel 2" />
                <mx:PieChart id="myChart1"
                    dataProvider="{topFourIMF}"
                    showDataTips="true">
                    <mx:series>
                        <mx:PieSeries id="pieSeries1"
                            field="GDP"
                            nameField="Country"
                            labelPosition="callout"/>
                    </mx:series>
                </mx:PieChart>
                <mx:Legend dataProvider="{myChart1}" id="legend1"/>
            </mx:VBox>
            <mx:VBox label="Panel 3">
                <mx:Label text="Panel 3" />
                <mx:List
                dataProvider="{topFourIMF}"
                labelField="Country"
                id="list1"/>
            </mx:VBox>
        </mx:TabNavigator>
        <mx:Label width="100%"
            text="Click on the button to choose a panel."/>
        <mx:HBox>
            <mx:Button
            label="Select Tab 1"
            click="tn1.selectedIndex=0"/>
            <mx:Button
            label="Select Tab 2"
            click="tn1.selectedIndex=1"/>
            <mx:Button
            label="Select Tab 3"
            click="tn1.selectedIndex=2"/>
        </mx:HBox>
    </mx:Panel>
</mx:Application>
```

The elapsed time between the all and auto settings for this simple case is in the range of 150 milliseconds. When the application is more complex and has a large number of components, this difference is substantially larger. The elapsed time difference between setting auto and none on the TabNavigator is only 50 milliseconds. This is because the auto setting only generates the additional data grid on the default view as compared to the none setting, which creates nothing in the tab navigator.

In a single-view container, you can explicitly stop the creation of a container's children by setting its creationPolicy to none. You saw an example earlier that illustrated this behavior. Then on demand, you could call createComponentsFromDescriptors to create the components in the container. By setting the recurse value of this function to true, you traverse down the container hierarchy and create all the components within the second level and further level containers.

Setting the creationPolicy to none causes child component reference objects to be attached to the container. These children are not created or set up but are only hooked onto the container. The hooks or reference objects are called **descriptors**. Calling createComponentsFromDescriptors instantiates, initializes, and sets up the children components. Thus, the explicit call to the method controls when we create the deferred objects. Here is an example to reinforce the concept:

```
<?xml version="1.0"?>
<!-- CreateComponentsFromDescriptorsExample.mxml -->
<mx:Application xmlns:mx="http://www.adobe.com/2006/mxml" >
    <mx:Script><![CDATA[
      private function createComponents(recurseVal:Boolean):void {
          vbox1.createComponentsFromDescriptors(true);
      }
    ]]></mx:Script>
    <mx:Panel
        paddingTop="10"
        paddingLeft="10"
        paddingRight="10"
        paddingBottom="10">
        <mx:Label text="Create components from descriptors" />
        <mx:VBox id="vbox1" creationPolicy="none">
            <mx:DateChooser id="dateChooser1"/>
            <mx:DateField id="dateField1"/>
        </mx:VBox>
        <mx:Button
        label="Create components"
        click="createComponents(true)" />
    </mx:Panel>
</mx:Application>
```

Figure 4-7 shows the preceding example with the creation policy set to none. Figure 4-8 shows all the components that form the preceding example application. Components are drawn out on an explicit createComponentsFromDescriptors call. In this case, the creation of components is triggered by a button click. The button is displayed at the bottom of the interface.

**Figure 4-7.** VBox in a Panel with the creation policy set to none

**Figure 4-8.** Components drawn after an explicit call to createComponentsFromDescriptors

In a multiview container, the createComponentsFromDescriptors can be called on a specific tab so that components related to that tab are created. For example, we can have a TabNavigator as follows:

```
<mx:TabNavigator id="tn1"
width="100%"
height="100%"
creationPolicy="none">
     <mx:VBox label="Panel 1">
<!?components-->
     </mx:VBox>
     <mx:VBox label="Panel 2">
<!?components-->
     </mx:VBox>
     <mx:VBox label="Panel 3">
<!?components-->
     </mx:VBox>
</mx:TabNavigator>
```

To explicitly create all the containers and components in the second panel, labeled Panel 2, we can call

```
tn1.getChildAt(2).createComponentsFromDescriptors(true)
```

An alternative to delaying or deferring component creation is to create them progressively. Create the container shells first and then create their constituent containers one by one. This type of component creation strategy is implemented by selecting queued as the creation policy. An example that uses the queued creation policy is as follows:

```
<?xml version="1.0" encoding="utf-8"?>
<mx:Application xmlns:mx="http://www.adobe.com/2006/mxml">
<mx:Script>
   <![CDATA[
        import mx.collections.ArrayCollection;
        [Bindable]
        public var topFourIMF:ArrayCollection = new ArrayCollection([
          {Country:"United States", GDP:13843825},
```

```
                {Country:"China (PRC)", GDP:6991036},
                {Country:"Japan", GDP:4289809},
                {Country:"India", GDP:2988867}
            ]);
    ]]>
</mx:Script>
    <mx:WipeRight id="wipeRight1" duration="5000" />
    <mx:Panel id="outerPanel"
     creationPolicy="queued"
      creationIndex="2"
       creationCompleteEffect="wipeRight1">
        <mx:HBox
        creationPolicy="queued"
        creationCompleteEffect="wipeRight1">
        <mx:Panel id="innerPanel1"
        creationPolicy="queued"
        creationCompleteEffect="wipeRight1">
            <mx:HBox id="hbox1"
            creationPolicy="queued"
            creationCompleteEffect="wipeRight1">
                <mx:DateChooser id="dc1" />
                <mx:DateField id="df1" />
                <mx:List id="l1"
                dataProvider="{topFourIMF}"
                labelField="Country" />
                <mx:Panel
                id="innerPanel2"
                creationPolicy="queued"
                creationCompleteEffect="wipeRight1" >
                    <mx:HBox
                    id="hbox2"
                    creationPolicy="queued"
                    creationCompleteEffect="wipeRight1">
                        <mx:Button label="Click" />
                        <mx:Label text="Panel 3" />
                    </mx:HBox>
                </mx:Panel>
            </mx:HBox>
        </mx:Panel>
        <mx:Panel
        id="innerPanel3"
        creationPolicy="queued"
        creationIndex="3"
        creationCompleteEffect="wipeRight1">
            <mx:HBox id="hbox3"
            creationPolicy="queued"
            creationCompleteEffect="wipeRight1">
                <mx:DateChooser id="dc2" />
                <mx:DateField id="df2" />
                <mx:List id="l2"
```

```
                    dataProvider="{topFourIMF}"
                    labelField="Country" />
                    <mx:Panel
                    id="innerPanel4"
                    creationPolicy="queued"
                    creationCompleteEffect="wipeRight1" >
                        <mx:HBox
                        id="hbox4"
                        creationPolicy="queued"
                        creationCompleteEffect="wipeRight1">
                            <mx:Button label="Click" />
                            <mx:Label text="Panel 3" />
                        </mx:HBox>
                    </mx:Panel>
                </mx:HBox>
            </mx:Panel>
        </mx:HBox>
        <mx:Panel
        id="innerPanel5"
        creationPolicy="queued"
        creationIndex="1"
        creationCompleteEffect="wipeRight1">
            <mx:HBox id="hbox5">
                <mx:PieChart id="myChart1"
                    dataProvider="{topFourIMF}"
                    showDataTips="true">
                <mx:series>
                    <mx:PieSeries id="pieSeries1"
                    field="GDP"
                    nameField="Country"
                    labelPosition="callout"/>
                </mx:series>
                </mx:PieChart>
                <mx:ColumnChart id="myChart2"
                    dataProvider="{topFourIMF}" >
                <mx:horizontalAxis>
                    <mx:CategoryAxis categoryField="Country"/>
                </mx:horizontalAxis>
                <mx:series>
                    <mx:ColumnSeries id="columnSeries1"
                    yField="GDP"
                    xField="Country" />
                </mx:series>
                </mx:ColumnChart>
            <mx:Legend dataProvider="{myChart1}" id="legend1"/>
            </mx:HBox>
        </mx:Panel>
    </mx:Panel>
</mx:Application>
```

**159**

Even under progressive creation, a lightweight application like the one we just listed doesn't highlight the difference visually. To the human eye, it still appears as if everything were created at the same time. In large and complex nested container applications, the difference is visible. For the sake of demonstrating it visually, we add a `creationCompleteEffect` so that components wipe left as they get set up. Figures 4-9 and 4-10 show parts of the screen at two points during its queued creation process.

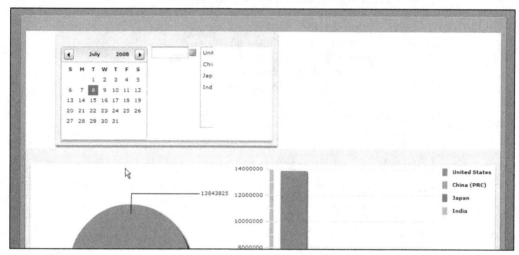

**Figure 4-9.** Queued creation in progress

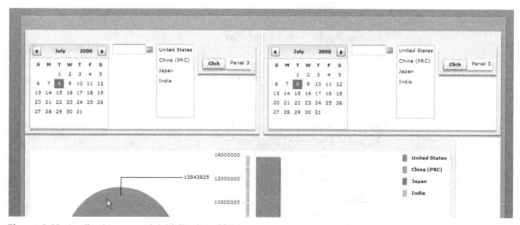

**Figure 4-10.** Application created, initialized, and laid out

Under default creation priority in a queued creation policy, components are created in the order in which they appear. Order of creation can be controlled using the `creationIndex` property, which takes numerical values. Containers with a lower value are created before those with a greater value. That is the reason why our charts in the earlier example show up before the components in the upper panels.

It's also possible to add a container with an initial creationPolicy value of none to the creation queue. The addToCreationQueue function is used to add such containers to the queue. The creation priority of such added containers is last by default. They can be added somewhere ahead in the queue by specifying the index, or priority, as the second argument of the addToCreationQueue function.

So far, I have covered the fundamentals of Flex application startup and creation policy. In this discussion, I have restricted myself to stand-alone Flex applications. Next, our focus turns to Flex applications that include other Flex applications.

## Including Flex applications within one another

It's extremely easy to include a Flex or Flash application within another Flex application. The usual method in Flex is to use the SWFLoader class to include a SWF into another SWF. Assume we have two Flex applications, named FlexApp1.swf and FlexApp2.swf. If we have to include FlexApp2.swf in FlexApp1.swf, we use the following code in FlexApp1.swf:

```
<mx:SWFLoader source="FlexApp2.swf" />
```

It will rarely be the case that we load an external Flex application into the current one and don't call the public methods of the loaded SWF. Calling methods of the loaded SWF needs no extra effort other than making sure that the SWF loader has loaded the external SWF, and the external SWF's public properties and methods are now available. SWFLoader dispatches a number of events, some of which are as follows:

- complete: Dispatched when content loading is done
- init: Dispatched when properties and methods of the loaded SWF are available
- progress: Dispatched when content is loading
- unload: Dispatched when a loaded object is removed or an old object is removed before a new version of the same object is loaded

The init method is explicitly dispatched when the properties and methods of the loaded SWF are available.

In the example that I show in a bit, we use the init event of the SWFLoader and the applicationComplete event of the loaded Application to call a method of the loaded SWF. Here is the code for FlexApp1.swf and FlexApp2.swf:

```
<?xml version="1.0" encoding="utf-8"?>
<!-- FlexApp1.mxml -->
<mx:Application xmlns:mx="http://www.adobe.com/2006/mxml" >
<mx:Script>
    <![CDATA[
        import mx.managers.SystemManager;
        import mx.events.FlexEvent;

        private var passedInParameterString:String =
        "FlexApp1 says Hello to FlexApp2";

        private function initHandlerFunction(event:Event):void {
```

```
                event.target.content.addEventListener➡
                (FlexEvent.APPLICATION_COMPLETE,
                applicationCompleteHandler);
            }

            private function applicationCompleteHandler(event:Event):void {
                event.target.application.flexApp2Function➡
                (passedInParameterString);
            }
        ]]>
    </mx:Script>
        <mx:SWFLoader
        source="FlexApp2.swf"
        init="initHandlerFunction(event)" />
    </mx:Application>

    <?xml version="1.0" encoding="utf-8"?>
    <!-- FlexApp2.mxml -->
    <mx:Application xmlns:mx="http://www.adobe.com/2006/mxml" >
    <mx:Script>
        <![CDATA[
            import mx.controls.Alert;
            public function flexApp2Function(param:String):void {
                Alert.show("Passed in param value " + param);
            }
        ]]>
    </mx:Script>
    </mx:Application>
```

When FlexApp1.swf is invoked, an output as shown in Figure 4-11 appears.

When a Flex application is loaded and run in the Flash Player, it accesses its classes and definitions within its application domain or application namespace. The application domain or application namespace is not all that important when dealing with single stand-alone Flex applications, because there is one and only one domain and a single Flex application corresponding to that domain. Things get a little more complex when we have two or more Flex applications and two or more domains in the same place. For simplicity, we will consider only two Flex applications and see the different permutations of domain relationships we can have between them. Let's first look at Figure 4-12, which summarizes the different permutations.

**Figure 4-11.** FlexApp1.swf calling FlexApp2.swf's method and passing a string argument to its method

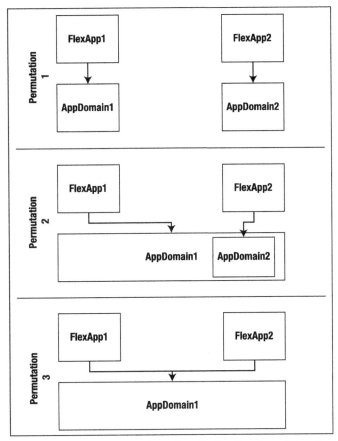

**Figure 4-12.** Possible permutations of application domains with two Flex applications, one loaded into the other

In Figure 4-12, three permutations are shown. In order of appearance, these are as follows:

- **The application domains are independent**: FlexApp1.swf and FlexApp2.swf have their own independent application domains. They don't share any classes between them. This means they obviously don't have any class conflicts.

- **The loaded application domain is a child of the application domain it is loaded into**: FlexApp2.swf's application domain is a child of FlexApp1.swf's application domain. This implies FlexApp1.swf has a preferred status as far as class loading goes. In other words, when the parent and the child application domains contain classes with the same name, it's the parent class that is loaded and not the child one. This works fine except when you intentionally override the behavior of a class in the child application domain.

- **Both applications have the same application domain**: This is the case of complete reuse. The loaded application uses the same application domain as that of the application it is loaded into. This leads to the smallest memory consumption of the three options, because there are fewer classes loaded in this case.

Use AS3 to have flexible programmatic control over how a SWF is loaded into a Flex application. The Loader class has load and loadBytes methods to load SWF files and media assets. Options for loading can be specified to a loader by setting properties on the LoaderContext. One such property controls the application domain in which the loaded SWF file resides. This property is appropriately named applicationDomain. To load a SWF into its own independent application domain, create a new ApplicationDomain and assign it as the value of the applicationDomain property before loading the SWF. This is how it can be done:

```
var loaderContext:LoaderContext;
....
loaderContext.applicationDomain = new ApplicationDomain();
```

To load the SWF into the same domain as the domain of the SWF into which it is loaded, just set the applicationDomain to the current application domain. The ApplicationDomain class has a static method named currentDomain to get hold of the current application domain. The code for loading into the same domain is as follows:

```
var loaderContext:LoaderContext;
....
loaderContext.applicationDomain = ApplicationDomain.currentDomain;
```

The third of the three combinations is to make the application domain of the loaded SWF a child of the application domain into which it is loaded. The code for doing this is as follows:

```
var loaderContext:LoaderContext;
....
loaderContext.applicationDomain =
new ApplicationDomain➡
(ApplicationDomain.currentDomain);
```

The ApplicationDomain constructor accepts a parameter that when passed in is set as the parent domain for the newly constructed application domain.

The ability to load external libraries into the main application domain of a Flex application allows for structuring applications to reuse common libraries and dynamically link to it. Libraries that can be dynamically loaded and linked to from a Flex application at run time are called run-time shared libraries or RSLs.

# Run-time shared libraries

The age-old practice of abstracting common components into libraries and reusing them across multiple applications is implemented in Flex with the help of RSLs. An RSL is a library that exists outside an application's SWF and is downloaded to a Flash Player once, when not available. Once available, it can be used across multiple applications without being downloaded again. This structure has two immediate benefits:

- The application SWF file size is reduced. This immediately boosts startup performance and enhances the user experience.
- The RSL is downloaded only once and reused as many times as required across multiple applications. This promotes an efficient application design.

An RSL is possible with Flex because the Flex compiler and the Flash Player allow for dynamic linking. The default linking type is **static linking**, where all classes required by an application are compiled into one bundle. This has advantages like quicker class loading at run time and therefore better initial response. It also has disadvantages like greater download time, because of the increased application size, and redundant inclusion of overlapping classes in multiple applications, which may share classes otherwise. **Dynamic linking** is the alternative to static linking. In dynamic linking, a set of external classes, usually bundled as a library, are linked to at run time. This has advantages like reduction of the main application SWF file size, but also has disadvantages because now the dynamic library needs to be downloaded at run time and linked to before it is ready for use.

RSL(s) themselves can be of three types:

- **Standard or regular RSLs**: Shared libraries of custom components that you use across all your applications served from a single domain.
- **Cross-domain RSLs**: Shared libraries of custom components that you use across domains. A cross-domain RSL could be thought of as a shared library with cross-domain security definition.
- **Framework RSLs**: Flex component libraries that can be dynamically linked to.

I will illustrate each of these, starting with the standard or regular RSL.

## Standard RSL

Applications that are designed in a modular fashion and involve cleanly abstracted reusable libraries are the best candidate applications for use as RSLs. In the next section, I quickly go through a few good application design principles that favor better performance. One of the simplest yet most effective of these ideas is modular application design.

There are four steps involved in using a standard RSL:

1. Create a component library.
2. Compile the Flex application to use the created component library.
3. Optimize the RSL, if required.
4. Deploy the application and the RSL.

**Create a component library** The first and essential step is to create the reusable library and package it up in such a fashion that it can be freely distributed. Flex Builder 3 includes convenient prebuilt project templates to create reusable libraries. Figures 4-13 and 4-14 show the initial two steps you follow to create a Flex library. The Flex compiler can compile a library project as a SWC file. A SWC file is an archive file that contains Flex components and media assets and usually has two necessary files in it:

- A SWF file, often called `library.swf`
- An XML manifest file, called `catalog.xml`, that contains the list of the components included in the library file

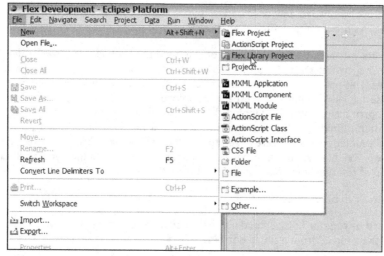

**Figure 4-13.** Dialog to create a Flex library project

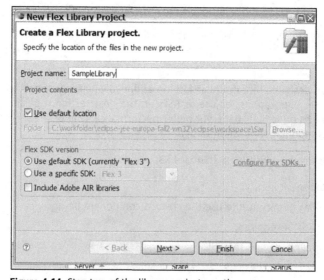

**Figure 4-14.** Step two of the library project creation process

SWC file names end with a .swc extension. Flex components can be compiled using the component compiler (compc). The component compiler can be invoked in any of the following ways:

- As a compc command-line compiler
- As a compc ant task
- Via the fcsh shell (on Unix and Mac OS)

Following is an example of using the compc command-line compiler to compile library projects:

```
compc -source-path <source-path>➡
-output <output-swc-file-name>➡
-include-classes <fully-qualified-class-name>
```

source-path specifies the path to the source file. include-classes specifies the fully qualified class name. In the preceding example, the compiled class is added to the SWC library file.

Now that you have the SWC library file available, you will see how to compile a Flex application to use it.

**Compile the Flex application to use the created component library**   Here, I outline the steps to compile a Flex application to leverage the RSL in the context of using the Flex Builder and the command-line compiler. Let's start with the command-line compiler.

A typical command to compile with a standard RSL is as follows:

```
mxmlc -runtime-shared-library-path=➡
pathTo/sharedLibrary.swc,➡
pathTo/library.swf MyApplication.mxml
```

The preceding command shows only the essential arguments that need to be passed to an application compiler. Additional parameters that allow you to specify a cross-domain policy file (relevant for a cross-domain RSL) and a failover RSL path are not shown in this example. sharedLibrary.swc is the library file that the application compiles against, and library.swf is the library component that the application downloads and links to at run time. The sharedLibrary.swc file component classes and the library.swf component classes are the same. The only difference is that library.swf is an optimized deployment-ready bundle of the RSL.

Instead of passing all arguments as command-line parameters, we can define these arguments in an external XML file and use it with the command-line compiler. The external XML configuration file could define the entries from the preceding example as follows:

```
<runtime-shared-library-path>
<path-element>pathTo/sharedLibrary.swc</path-element>
<rsl-url>pathTo/library.swf</rsl-url>
</runtime-shared-library-path>
```

Now let's see how the same things are done using the Flex Builder. First select the Flex Library path option by navigating to the project's Properties dialog box. You come to the screen shown in Figure 4-15.

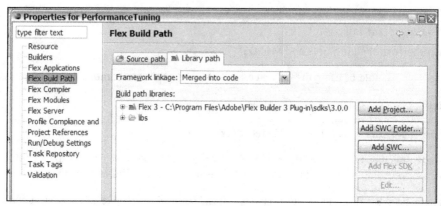

**Figure 4-15.** Flex Build Path Library path view

Then you click the Add SWC button, and you are presented with a dialog box to add a SWC file from the underlying file system. For example, you can pick up the PureMVC framework SWC and add it to the project. Part of this step is shown in Figure 4-16.

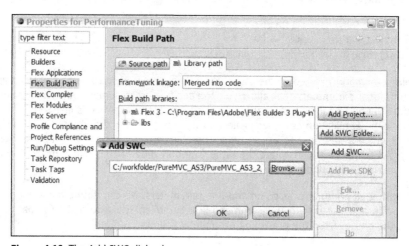

**Figure 4-16.** The Add SWC dialog box

Once the SWC is added to the library path, we change the link type to the RSL. The link type option is shown in Figure 4-17. The change to the Library Path Item Options dialog box is shown in Figure 4-18.

Since it's a standard RSL, we don't worry about defining the cross-domain policy file or choose to verify against the digest at run time. These become relevant in the other types of RSL. I will discuss digests in the context of a cross-domain RSL.

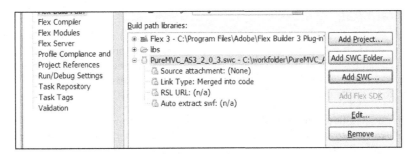

**Figure 4-17.** Display of an added SWC file

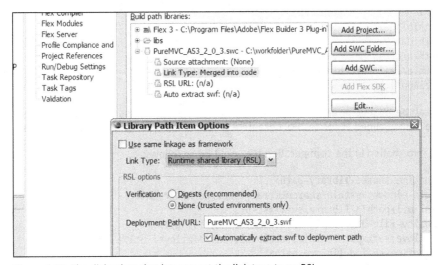

**Figure 4-18.** The dialog box that lets you set the link type to an RSL

**Optimize the RSL, if required** An RSL can be optimized with the help of an optimizer, an executable available as part of the Flex SDK. The optimizer reduces the RSL file size by removing all the debugging-related information from it. Suppose MySharedLibrary.swc is your RSL archive file. This archive file contains two files: library.swf and catalog.xml. library.swf is the component library, and catalog.xml is the supporting manifest file. The library.swf component library file contains the entire compiled source with the debug information embedded in it. When compiling applications with an RSL, the debug information is useful and required, but this debug information is an overhead when linking with the same library at run time.

Running the SWF through the optimizer can remove all the debug information. The code is as follows:

```
optimizer -input pathTo/library.swf -output pathTo/output.swf
```

You can also explicitly compile the source with debug=false to achieve the same result.

**Deploy the application and the RSL** In standard RSL deployments, the application and the RSL are on the same web server, and the deployment requires no more than uploading the two files to this web server.

## Cross-domain RSL

The cross-domain RSL, like the standard RSL, is a library of custom components. The cross-domain RSL, unlike the standard RSL, is accessible across multiple domains and subdomains. Therefore, both at application compile time and at deployment time, you need to specify a cross-domain security policy file. The creation process of the SWC is no different, except that you also create a crossdomain.xml security policy file along with the component's SWC.

At application compile time, you pass the cross-domain file location and a failover RSL location, to allow for cases where cross-domain accessibility fails. These arguments are passed as command-line parameters to the application compiler or are specified in an XML configuration file that is passed to the application compiler. The code looks as follows:

```
mxmlc -runtime-shared-library-path=
pathTo/sharedLibrary.swc,
pathTo/library.swf,
pathTo/crossdomain.xml,
pathTo/failoverLibrary.swf,
FlexApplication.mxml
```

The path can be relative or absolute, as fully qualified URLs. The crossdomain.xml file path is specified with a fully qualified absolute URL because it is meant to be accessible across domains.

This same information in the configuration file could be as follows:

```
<runtime-shared-library-path>
<path-element>pathTo/sharedLibrary.swc</path-element>
<rsl-url>pathTo/library.swf</rsl-url>
<policy-file-url>pathTo/crossdomain.xml</rsl-url>
<failover-url>pathTo/failoverLibrary.swf</failover-url>
</runtime-shared-library-path>
```

Another minor difference between a standard and a cross-domain RSL is the uploading of crossdomain.xml on the target domain.

Other than crossdomain.xml's definition and its inclusion at compile time and run time, there is no difference between standard and cross-domain RSLs.

Next, I rapidly survey the framework RSL to complete this discussion on RSLs.

## Framework RSL

The Flex framework components are available in library bundles as RSLs and can be loaded at run time as an alternative to compile-type static linking. Framework RSLs are supported only on versions of the Flash Player above version 9.0.60. The framework RSL, unlike the custom RSL, is a signed RSL. They also have a different file extension: .sgn, implying a signed RSL.

An application can be compiled with the framework RSL as follows:

```
mxmlc -runtime-shared-library-path=
pathTo/framework.swc,
framework_3.0.{build.number}.sgn,,
```

```
framework_3.0.{build.number}.swf
FlexApplication.mxml
```

The framework RSL names include the Flex SDK version number. The preceding example is for Flex 3.

The standard and cross-domain RSLs are saved in the browser cache, whereas the framework RSL is saved in the player cache.

## Disadvantages of using RSLs

The advantages of using RSLs have been implicitly listed throughout. It's understood that smaller application file size and therefore lesser initial download time enhances the user experience. Also, reuse of code across applications is a beneficial and efficient approach for application development.

Now let's take a short diversion so you understand the disadvantages of RSLs. The section brings out the message that RSLs are not suitable for every single case, and sometimes static linking may be a better option. Let's see how and when.

Say we have two applications that share a common set of components. This common set of components might seem like a candidate for an RSL. However, if the two applications use small and different parts of this RSL, it may be possible that both applications perform large downloads that hardly get used.

When we statically link to a class, only the particular class and not the entire library is compiled with the application code.

When you have a large RSL file, the first application faces the heavyweight task of downloading it. Subsequent applications that share the RSL don't have to download it again. Therefore, the advantages of RSLs become apparent when multiple applications share the components. If there are at most two applications sharing the common code, the advantages of RSLs may not be very great.

So while the benefits of RSLs are well understood, it may be wise to evaluate the use of dynamic vs. static linking in each particular case.

This chapter has covered the topic of RSLs to a fair extent, emphasizing that better application design is the hallmark of creating better-performing applications. The concept of RSLs themselves stems from the idea of modular design and clean interfaces between modules. Next, I highlight a few good application design features that tend to improve performance.

# Better application design

There are no absolute guidelines that make one application better than the other. The sheer number of approaches available makes it obvious that one size does not fit all. However, under general circumstances, a few guidelines are good practices to consider and apply. In no particular order, I list a few such principles here.

# Use containers efficiently

It's very tempting when creating Flex applications to nest containers inside each other. However, doing so can add a big performance drag to your application. Every new container involves the calculation of position, size, and style based on algorithms. If the containers dynamically adjust the relative layout as in a Panel or a Box container, then further overhead is added.

Therefore, applications also benefit when you specify the position, height, and width of components in a container. Essentially, you save some extra computation on the part of the container.

## Bindable tag vs. explicit events

When we annotate a variable as [Bindable], changes to the variable value get propagated to all its consumption points. In other words, implicit event listeners are set up at each consumption point for the change events that the variable dispatches on value change. The method is convenient and needs minimal effort.

However, not every consumption point may be interested in listening to the change, and not every change may be useful enough to be propagated. In other words, when there are a large number of variables and they are all bindable, there is an overhead on the application in terms of the numerous change events it dispatches and the numerous listeners processing it manages.

As an alternative to bindable variables, it is sometimes beneficial to dispatch explicit value change events. The consumption point of these variables can explicitly listen to these value changes and process the events. This does not work in all cases. It's a common misconception that the use of a [Bindable] tag is less efficient than explicit event dispatch. The [Bindable] metadata tag implementation uses events under the hood. When most or all changes are dispatched explicitly, there is little practical difference between the two approaches.

A simple example illustrates the two alternatives just listed. A variable can be declared bindable as follows:

```
private var myVariable:String;
public get myVariable():void {
    return myVariable;
}
[Bindable]
public set myVariable(value:String) {
    myVariable = value;
}
```

The same variable could use a getter-setter pair to explicitly dispatch an event in the setter. The code is as follows:

```
private var myVariable:String;
public get myVariable():void {
    return myVariable;
}
public set myVariable(value:String) {
    myVariable = value;
    dispatch(new Event(myVariable));
}
```

In the next section, let's take a look at an example of two data structures, one that is a raw data structure and the other a collection with many rich features.

## Array vs. ArrayCollection

In most cases, ArrayCollection has a better set of features than Array. The Array is a raw data structure that has limited methods to manipulate the data structure as effectively as an ArrayCollection. However, as far as performance goes, the Array outperforms the ArrayCollection in data manipulation tasks. The trade-off between extra features and superior performance as seen between an ArrayCollection and an Array is commonly encountered in many situations in software applications.

Doing a simple task like searching through a large collection of items or comparing the objects in a collection is much faster and lightweight with Array than with an ArrayCollection.

## Utilize lazy loading

Often loading a large amount of data eagerly can impact performance. What's more, it often turns out that you don't even use all that loaded data. So the memory and CPU time really goes to waste. Lazy loading benefits application performance and creates an efficient design.

To illustrate lazy loading, let's consider an example where we fetch average hourly, daily, and monthly temperatures for a period of 5 years and plot this data on a line chart. By default, a user views the average monthly data plotted for the 5-year period. On zooming into a selected time interval, within the 5-year period, a user can view data at the daily and subsequently at the hourly levels of granularity. Eagerly loading all the data, encompassing the three levels of granularity, may not be advisable because it's possible a user will never drill down to many portions of the hourly or even daily temperature data. Lazily loading the average daily and hourly data only when required is a better alternative.

# Memory usage, scalability, and accessibility

This section looks at the profiling options, memory usage measuring options, and the option to make applications more scalable. Let's start with the Flex Profiler, a useful feature that comes with Flex Builder 3.

## Flex Profiler

The Flex Profiler is a useful tool available as a part of Flex Builder. The Flex Profiler can help measure the following:

- Memory used for object creation and memory released on garbage collection
- Active status of the object heap
- Stack trace of objects on a continuing basis
- Stack trace of objects on a periodic basis

Invoking the Flex Profiler is easy. Use either the Profile As option from the context menu or the Profile shortcut from the menu to start the profiler.

Figure 4-19 shows the Configure Profiler dialog box that lets you choose what you want to profile. A memory snapshot of any application can be taken using the Flex Profiler. To check for memory leaks, you could take two memory snapshots within an interval and then check for loitering objects. This gives a clue to memory leaks as it shows the objects that were not properly garbage collected.

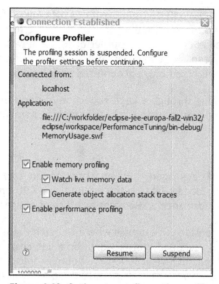

**Figure 4-19.** Options to configure the profiler

Similarly, you could also take performance snapshots at different points in time. Details of the method call can be drilled down into and detailed metrics about it can be gathered.

Although the Flex Profiler is a great tool, it's available only from within Flex Builder. Most Flex developers use Flex Builder, but I don't want to exclude the others from using some technique to measure memory usage. The next section gives a simple method to measure memory. It's not completely reliable, as it can be influenced by external factors. However, such issues exist with all performance-related tools.

## Memory usage

An intuitive and easy way to measure memory allocated to the Flash Player is to record the memory by using the following System property:

```
flash.system.System.totalMemory
```

This property measures the amount of memory allocated to the Flash Player. It's not a measure of the amount of memory used by the application at that point in time. It's possible the amount of memory an application uses is less than the amount allocated to the Flash Player.

Also, remember to minimize the amount of external influence so that the memory measurements are as accurate as possible. Doing the following is beneficial:

- Stop other heavy processes on your machine.
- Avoid using debug on the Flash Player.
- Switch the trace and logging options off.
- Switch any hardware or operating system–level factors that affect memory allocation to the Flash Player.

Following is some sample code that you could use to measure memory periodically:

```
<?xml version="1.0"?>
<!-- optimize/ShowTotalMemory.mxml -->
<mx:Application
xmlns:mx="http://www.adobe.com/2006/mxml"
initialize="initTimer()">
<mx:Script><![CDATA[
    import mx.collections.ArrayCollection;
    import flash.utils.Timer;
    import flash.events.TimerEvent;

    [Bindable]
    public var time:Number = 0;

    [Bindable]
    public var totmem:Number = 0;

    [Bindable]
    public var memoryRecording:ArrayCollection = new ArrayCollection();
    public function initTimer():void {

        var myTimer:Timer = new Timer(1000, 0);
        myTimer.addEventListener("timer", timerHandler);
        myTimer.start();
    }

    public function timerHandler(event:TimerEvent):void {
        time = getTimer()
        totmem = flash.system.System.totalMemory;
        memoryRecording.addItem({totalMemory:totmem,timePoint:time});
    }
]]></mx:Script>
<mx:Form>
<mx:FormItem label="Time:">
<mx:Label text="{time} ms"/>
</mx:FormItem>
```

```
<mx:FormItem label="Total Memory:">
<mx:Label text="{totmem} bytes"/>
</mx:FormItem>
</mx:Form>
<mx:Panel title="Line Chart">
<mx:LineChart dataProvider="{memoryRecording}" showDataTips="true" >
<mx:series>
<mx:LineSeries
yField="totalMemory"
xField="timePoint"
displayName="Memory Usage"/>
</mx:series>
</mx:LineChart>
</mx:Panel>
</mx:Application>
```

A snapshot of the output of this code is shown in Figure 4-20. These measurements are specific to my machine. The same code when run on your machine may produce a different output.

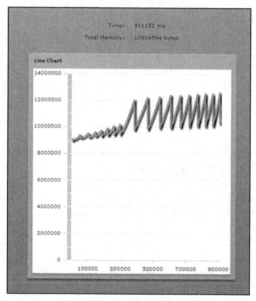

**Figure 4-20.** Memory usage measurements summary

# Load testing

Mercury Interactive's (now HP's) QuickTest Professional testing product suite includes support for testing Flex applications. These automated testing robots can mimic a user request and run the request as many times as you desire. One of the fundamental load-testing mechanisms is to create a large number of virtual users using automated robots and then run the application. This way the application's performance under a large number of users and heavy load is tested.

Flex Builder 3 incorporates an API to create your own custom load-testing agent. This API is available through three SWC library files: automation.swc, automation_dmv.swc, and automation_agent.swc. automation_agent.swc is the library that facilitates Flex application testing. Agents like QTP are built on top of this agent. automation_dmv.swc provides support for additional features like Charts and Advanced Data Grid.

Make sure to include an ID for all objects created in the application. Also, try and keep the ID strings as meaningful as possible. The testing tool is going to log activities and measures against objects using these IDs. A good naming system helps identify the components and their methods and therefore helps parse the test results gainfully.

Also, most often wrapper SWFs are created that load the SWF to be tested using the SWFLoader. The Flex applications should compile with the required automation SWC libraries by passing them as include-libraries arguments in the Flex compiler.

If you have access to an automation tool like HP QuickTest Professional (https://h10078.www1.hp.com/cda/hpms/display/main/hpms_content.jsp?zn=bto&cp=1-11-127-24^1352_4000_100) or Borland SilkTest (http://www.borland.com/us/products/silk/silktest/index.html), then you can run such an automation tool and test the applications. Flex automation APIs define agents, which stand between Flex applications and the automation tool and control communication between them. You can create your own custom testing agents.

The automation framework defines an API that has two parts:

- **Component API**: Components implement these to support automation
- **Agent API**: Agents use this API to communicate with the components

The general structure of the automation framework is summarized in Figure 4-21. The System Manager, which is at the core of a Flex application, is responsible for creating the automation manager, agent, and delegate classes. The automation class is a singleton class that extends the EventDispatcher class. This creates a delegate for each display object. The automation manager listens to events that are dispatched when display objects are added.

The automation class is a static class that maintains a map of all delegates to its corresponding components. The delegates themselves are the objects that provide hooks to the Flex components.

The agent class, as mentioned before, facilitates the communication between the Flex application and the automation tools. It listens to RECORD events and defines the automation context or environment to specify what methods, properties, and events are recorded.

The automation manager, automation classes, delegates, and agents are all mix-in classes. The init method in these classes is called by the SystemManager class.

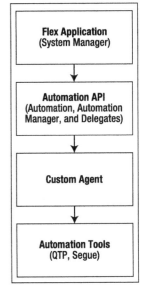

**Figure 4-21.** Automation framework overview

## Accessibility and distribution

Making components accessible allows Flex components to be available to special devices, screen readers, and other such tools that, in turn, make applications more accessible. Although traditionally not seen as a performance criterion, accessibility is an important criterion as more and more critical applications are built using Flex and related technologies.

Flex has over 28 components with built-in support for accessibility. They provide support for text equivalents, labeling controls, and keyboard access.

To enable accessibility for all Flex applications, set the accessible property to true in the flex-config.xml file. This can be done using Flex Builder or by passing in arguments on the command line to the Flex compiler.

# Summary

This chapter provides a quick introduction to performance. Performance has many facets, and so the chapter includes many topics that don't necessarily depend on each other. In no way is the treatment of the subject exhaustive here. The chapter serves only as a primer to help you focus your energies on the tuning aspects. Using the tools frequently and analyzing the collected results on an ongoing basis is the best way to master the discipline of performance tuning.

When applications are small in scope and have limited functionality, tuning efforts sometimes don't make a lot of difference. Even then, it's advisable to follow good programming and design practices, as this allows applications to be easily extended and made scalable if the need should arise.

Not all tuning aspects should be dealt with at the same time. For example, managing memory and trying to decrease startup time simultaneously is not a good approach. Often good practices have good impact in more than one way. However, as a developer or an architect, it should be your endeavor to isolate each criterion and measure and tune it while keeping the other criteria constant. This is a typical experimental approach, of the kind you'll be right at home with if you are a scientist.

Lastly, when you get down to performance tuning, never start tuning from the word go. Wait to gather enough information and analyze the problem at hand. Understanding the problem and thinking of possible solutions and side effects is more important than jumping to trying out the possible tuning concepts. Once the problem is understood, then fine-tune the application iteratively, measuring and improving, through each iteration.

## Chapter 5

# FLEX AND AIR:
# TAKING APPLICATIONS TO THE DESKTOP

By Jack Herrington

Adobe Integrated Runtime (AIR) technology provides an amazing opportunity for you to bring your Flex application into a whole new domain, the desktop. The API provides access to almost every nook and cranny you could want: the file system, native windows, native menus, and more. It also includes an embedded local database that you can use for offline storage. And it's all portable between Mac, Windows, and Linux. With these tools in hand, it's hard to think of any desktop application that you can't write with AIR.

In this chapter, I'll show several complete examples that work the limits of the AIR API. You are free to use these as templates for your own applications.

## AIR basics

If you haven't built an AIR application before, not to worry, the process is very similar to building a new Flex browser application. It starts with selecting File ➤ New and choosing Flex Project. From there you select Desktop application instead of Web application. Flex Builder 3 then takes care of building the AIR application XML file, the starting MXML application file, and so on. It also takes care of launching your application using the "adl" test launcher.

Flex Builder 3 will also help you put together the shipping version of your AIR application through a special version of the Export Release Build dialog under the Project menu. This dialog will build the .air file that your customer will download. To create the `.air` file, you will need to sign the executable by creating a digital certificate and then attaching that to the file. To create the certificate, click the Create button in the Export Release Build wizard to display the Create Self-Signed Digital Certificate dialog shown in Figure 5-1.

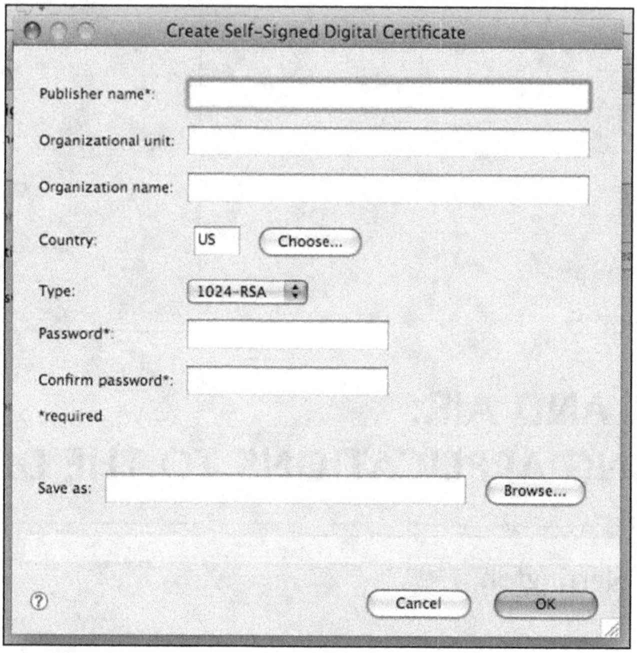

**Figure 5-1.** The Create Self-Signed Digital Certificate dialog

With this dialog, you can create a self-signed digital certificate and store it for later use. It ensures that it's password protected so that you, and only you, can sign the application.

Once you have the `.air` file created, you can upload it to your web server. From there your customers can download it (after having installed the AIR runtime) and run your application on their desktops.

# Building a browser

AIR comes with a built-in native web browser that you can use within your Flex application. It works just like any other Flash sprite. Shown here is a simple example AIR application that uses the web browser control to display any web page you wish:

```
<?xml version="1.0" encoding="utf-8"?>
<mx:WindowedApplication xmlns:mx=http://www.adobe.com/2006/mxml
  layout="absolute"
    creationComplete="onStartup()" resize="onResize(event)">
<mx:Script>
<![CDATA[
import mx.core.UIComponent;
```

```
    private var htmlPage:HTMLLoader = null;

    private function onStartup() : void {
      var ref:UIComponent = new UIComponent();
      ref.setStyle('top', 50);

      htmlPage = new HTMLLoader();
      htmlPage.width = 600;
      htmlPage.height = 600;
      ref.addChild( htmlPage );

      addChild( ref );
    }
    private function onResize( event:Event ) : void {
      if ( htmlPage ) {
        htmlPage.height = height - 50;
        htmlPage.width = width;
      }
    }
    private function onKeyDown( event:KeyboardEvent ) : void {
      if ( event.keyCode == Keyboard.ENTER )
        htmlPage.load( new URLRequest( txtUrl.text ) );
    }
  ]]>
  </mx:Script>
  <mx:Form width="100%">
  <mx:FormItem label="Url" width="100%">
  <mx:TextInput id="txtUrl" width="100%" text="http://adobe.com"
    keyDown="onKeyDown(event)" />
  </mx:FormItem>
  </mx:Form>
</mx:WindowedApplication>
```

The code for this example is pretty simple. When the application receives the creation complete event, it builds a new HTMLLoader object. Because the HTMLLoader is based on a sprite, it needs to be wrapped in a Flex UIComponent object. The code then responds to the resize event by resizing the HTML page control to match the new frame size. It also looks at the key-down event on the URL text to see when the user presses the Enter or Return key to start browsing to that location.

When I run this AIR application from Flex Builder 3, I get something that looks like Figure 5-2.

This example shows just a portion of what you can do with the browser control. You can get access to the browsing history as well as inject JavaScript objects into the runtime space of the page.

Another common use case is the viewing of a PDF file within the application. You could use a PDF to store documentation or to present the licensing agreement for the software.

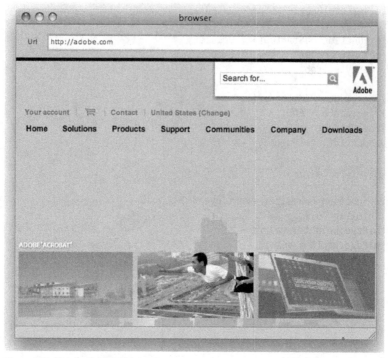

**Figure 5-2.** The built-in web browser

AIR has special support for PDF built right in. It's just as easy to look at a PDF page as it is any web page as shown in the following example code:

```
<?xml version="1.0" encoding="utf-8"?>
<mx:WindowedApplication xmlns:mx="http://www.adobe.com/2006/mxml"
  layout="absolute"
  creationComplete="onStartup()" resize="onResize()"
  title="PDF Viewer">
<mx:Script>
<![CDATA[
import mx.core.UIComponent;
private var htmlWin:HTMLLoader;
private function onResize() : void {
  if ( htmlWin ) {
    htmlWin.width = width;
    htmlWin.height = height;
  }
}
private function onStartup() : void {
  var ref:UIComponent = new UIComponent();
```

```
        htmlWin = new HTMLLoader();
        htmlWin.width = width;
        htmlWin.height = height;
        ref.addChild( htmlWin );

        addChild( ref );

        htmlWin.load( new URLRequest( '/Megan.pdf' ) );
    }
]]>
</mx:Script>
</mx:WindowedApplication>
```

In this example, I'm loading a local PDF file called Megan.pdf, which is in the AIR project locally. Just as with the original HTML reader application, the code watches for the resize event and adjusts the size of the HTML viewer to match the current window size.

When I bring this example up in Flex Builder 3, it looks like Figure 5-3.

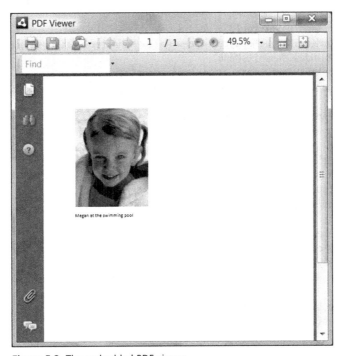

**Figure 5-3.** The embedded PDF viewer

Having PDF support (if the reader is installed on the user's computer) can be very helpful when it comes to embedding help support in your application.

# Native menus

Menus are important when it comes to creating a native user experience. Java Swing, for example, puts menus on the window regardless of how the native operating system does it. That makes for an awkward user experience on Macintosh. AIR, on the other hand, gives you real native menus and makes them easy to use.

Have a look at the following code, which creates a very simple menu, to see how easy it is to create menus:

```
<?xml version="1.0" encoding="utf-8"?>
<mx:WindowedApplication xmlns:mx="http://www.adobe.com/2006/mxml"
  layout="vertical"
  width="400" height="500" creationComplete="onStartup();">
<mx:Script>
<![CDATA[
private var itemDS:NativeMenuItem = new NativeMenuItem(
  "Drop Shadow" );
private var itemBlur:NativeMenuItem = new NativeMenuItem( "Blur" );

private function onStartup() : void {
  var filterMenu:NativeMenuItem = new NativeMenuItem("Filters");
  if(NativeWindow.supportsMenu) {
    stage.nativeWindow.menu = new NativeMenu();
    stage.nativeWindow.menu.addItem(filterMenu);
  }
  if(NativeApplication.supportsMenu)
    NativeApplication.nativeApplication.menu.addItem(filterMenu);

  var filterSubMenu:NativeMenu = new NativeMenu();

  itemBlur.addEventListener(Event.SELECT,onMenuSelect);
  itemDS.addEventListener(Event.SELECT,onMenuSelect);

  filterSubMenu.addItem( itemBlur  );
  filterSubMenu.addItem( itemDS );
  filterMenu.submenu = filterSubMenu;
}

private function onMenuSelect( event:Event ) : void {
  var mi:NativeMenuItem = event.target as NativeMenuItem;
  mi.checked = !mi.checked;
  var filters:Array = [];
  if ( itemDS.checked ) filters.push( new DropShadowFilter() );
  if ( itemBlur.checked ) filters.push( new BlurFilter() );
  myImg.filters = filters;
}
]]>
</mx:Script>
```

```
<mx:Image source="@Embed('megan.jpg')" id="myImg" />
</mx:WindowedApplication>
```

The application starts by creating a new Filter menu item. Then it adds that to the main application or window menu. From there it adds two submenu items: one for Blur and another for Drop Shadow. It also adds an event listener to these items to watch for the SELECT message that is sent when the user selects the menu item. From there the onMenuSelect method applies the selected filters to the image.

When I run this AIR application from Flex Builder 3, I first see an image with no filters as shown in Figure 5-4.

From there I can switch the filters on and off selectively and have the image instantly updated to match. For example, if I choose Drop Shadow, I get the result shown in Figure 5-5.

**Figure 5-4.** The image with no filters applied

**Figure 5-5.** The picture with the Drop Shadow filter applied

You can create menu separators, sub-submenus, and so on to give your application all of the menu options that an operating system native application would have.

# Building a photo browser

Now that you have a sense of how Flex integrates with native operating system elements such as menus, let's have a look at how to do some other things. This next example, a simple photo browser, will use native drag-and-drop, a native subwindow to display the full image, native menus, the native directory chooser, and the native task or dock bar.

I'll start by showing the complete source code for the first version of the application, and then dig into each element step by step.

```
<?xml version="1.0" encoding="utf-8"?>
<mx:WindowedApplication xmlns:mx="http://www.adobe.com/2006/mxml"
  layout="absolute"
  nativeDragEnter="onNativeDragEnter(event);"
  nativeDragDrop="onNativeDrop(event);"
  title="Photo Viewer" creationComplete="onStartup()">
<mx:Script>
<![CDATA[
private var _images:Array = [];

private function onStartup() : void {
   if(NativeApplication.supportsMenu)
   {
      var fileMenu:NativeMenuItem = NativeApplication.nativeApplication ➥
.menu.getItemAt(1);
      fileMenu.submenu.addItemAt(new NativeMenuItem("-",true),0);
      var openDirectory:NativeMenuItem = new NativeMenuItem(
         "Open Image Directory..." );
      openDirectory.addEventListener(Event.SELECT,onOpenDirectory);
      fileMenu.submenu.addItemAt(openDirectory,0);
   }
}
private function onOpenDirectory( event:Event ) : void {
  var f:File = new flash.filesystem.File();
  f.addEventListener(Event.SELECT,openDirectoryFound);
  f.browseForDirectory( "Open Image Directory" );
}
private function openDirectoryFound( event:Event ) : void {
  var d:File = event.target as File;
  for each ( var img:File in d.getDirectoryListing() ) {
    var ext:String = img.extension.toLowerCase();
    if ( ext == 'jpg' ) _images.push( img );
  }
  dgIimageList.dataProvider = _images;
  notifyComplete();
}
private  function notifyComplete():void{
  if(NativeApplication.supportsDockIcon){
     var dock:DockIcon = NativeApplication.nativeApplication.icon as ➥
DockIcon;
     dock.bounce(NotificationType.CRITICAL);
  } else if (NativeApplication.supportsSystemTrayIcon){
     stage.nativeWindow.notifyUser(NotificationType.CRITICAL);
  }
}
private function onNativeDragEnter( event:NativeDragEvent ) : void {
 if(event.clipboard.hasFormat(ClipboardFormats.FILE_LIST_FORMAT)) {
    var files:Array = event.clipboard.getData(
  ClipboardFormats.FILE_LIST_FORMAT) as Array;
```

```
      if( files.length > 0 ) NativeDragManager.acceptDragDrop(this);
    }
  }
  private function onNativeDrop( event:NativeDragEvent ) : void {
    for each ( var f:File in event.clipboard.getData(
    ClipboardFormats.FILE_LIST_FORMAT) as Array )
      _images.push(f);
    dgIimageList.dataProvider = _images;
    notifyComplete();
  }
]]>
</mx:Script>
    <mx:TileList id="dgIimageList" width="100%" height="100%"
    itemRenderer="thumbnail">
    </mx:TileList>
</mx:WindowedApplication>
```

The application handles the startup event by creating a new Open Image Directory menu item and adding it to the File menu. This new menu item is handled by the onOpenDirectory method. This method launches a native directory chooser by using the browseForDirectory method on the File object. Once the user selects a directory, the openDirectoryFound method is invoked.

The openDirectoryFound method uses the getDirectoryListing method on the File object associated with the directory to get all of the files in the directory. If files are found with the extension .jpg, we add them to the file list. If you wanted, you could easily do a recursive directory descent here to get all of the images in the directory or any of its subdirectories.

The openDirectoryFound method also uses the notifyComplete method, which bounces the icon on the dock bar, or an icon on the task bar on Windows. This lets the user know when long-running processes are finished.

The application also handles native drag-and-drop by registering the onNativeDragEnter and onNativeDragDrop methods with the WindowedApplication object. The onNativeDragEnter is called when the user first drags a file, or a set of files, over our application window. It's the operating system's way of saying, "Do you want to handle this?" We say yes if the clipboard contains a list of files.

The onNativeDragDrop is called when the user actually drops the files on the application. This method follows a process very similar to the menu item handler's. It goes through each file and adds it to the image list, and then calls the notifyComplete method to tell the user we are done.

The display of the image thumbnails in the main window is handled by the TileList object at the bottom of the application code. This TileList uses an itemRenderer to render each of the thumbnails. The code for the renderer is shown here:

```
<?xml version="1.0" encoding="utf-8"?>
<mx:HBox xmlns:mx="http://www.adobe.com/2006/mxml"
  paddingBottom="5" paddingLeft="5" paddingRight="5" paddingTop="5">
<mx:Script>
<![CDATA[
import mx.events.*;
```

```
    private function onPhotoClick( event:Event ):void {
      var newWin:photo = new photo();
      newWin.data = data;
      newWin.open();
    }
]]>
</mx:Script>
  <mx:Image horizontalAlign="center" verticalAlign="middle"
      source="{data.url}" height="100" width="100"
      doubleClick="onPhotoClick(event);" doubleClickEnabled="true">
  <mx:rollOverEffect>
      <mx:Glow blurXFrom="0" blurXTo="10" blurYFrom="0" blurYTo="10" />
  </mx:rollOverEffect>
  </mx:Image>
</mx:HBox>
```

This MXML component is based on HBox. It displays the image referenced by the File object, which is given to the component in the data parameter. It also handles a double-click on the image by running the onPhotoClick method, which launches a native subwindow to display the full image.

The code for the native subwindow is as follows:

```
<?xml version="1.0" encoding="utf-8"?>
<mx:Window xmlns:mx="http://www.adobe.com/2006/mxml"
  layout="absolute" width="100" height="100" title="{data.name}">
<mx:Script>
<![CDATA[
private function loaded() : void {
  if ( theImg.content != null && theImg.content.width > 0 ) {
    stage.nativeWindow.width = theImg.content.width + 20;
    stage.nativeWindow.height = theImg.content.height + 40;
  }
}
]]>
</mx:Script>
  <mx:Image id="theImg" source="{data.url}" httpStatus="loaded();" />
</mx:Window>
```

This MXML component is based on the Window class. This is a new class that comes with the AIR framework. It makes it very easy to build a native window that contains Flex controls.

In this case, the window contains a single image. The code then resizes the window to fit the entire image once the complete image is successfully loaded and the image size is known.

When I first launch this from Flex Builder 3, I see an empty window. I can then drag a few images over it as shown in Figure 5-6.

**190**

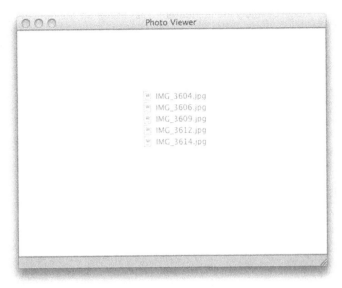

**Figure 5-6.** The image drag-and-drop in process

If everything is working, the cursor will present a little green plus sign to the user, which indicates that she can drop her files onto this window.

Once I've dropped the files, the list of images is updated and given to the TileList, which then displays the thumbnails as shown in Figure 5-7.

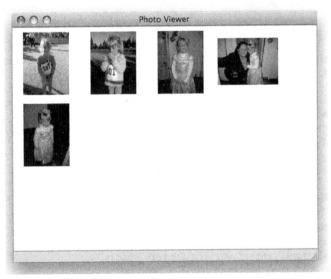

**Figure 5-7.** The thumbnail images

I can also use the Open Image Directory file menu item. That brings up the directory chooser, which is shown in Figure 5-8.

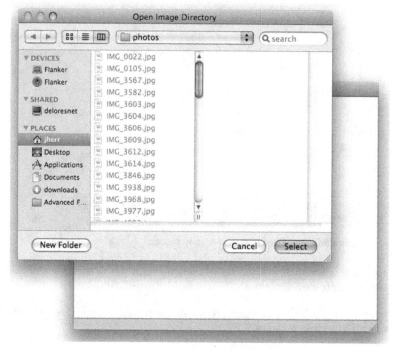

**Figure 5-8.** The Open Image Directory dialog

This is the best way to bring in masses of images quickly.

Once I have the image list set up, I can get a full-sized version of the image by double-clicking it as shown in Figure 5-9.

That's fairly cool, but what I really want, especially for photos, is to view the image in a full-screen **lightbox**. This means that the image comes up in the center of the screen, full size, and that all of the content around the rest of the area is dimmed. I can accomplish this effect by playing around a little with the photo.mxml window component.

The new code for the photo.mxml component is shown here:

```
<?xml version="1.0" encoding="utf-8"?>
<mx:Window xmlns:mx="http://www.adobe.com/2006/mxml"
  layout="absolute" title=""
  transparent="true" creationComplete="onStartup()"
  horizontalAlign="center" verticalCenter="middle"
  systemChrome="none" backgroundColor="#000000"
  backgroundAlpha="0.9" click="onClose()">
<mx:Script>
<![CDATA[
```

```
private function onClose() : void {
  stage.nativeWindow.close();
}
private function onStartup() : void {
  stage.displayState = StageDisplayState.FULL_SCREEN_INTERACTIVE;
  x = -10;
  y = -30;
  width = stage.fullScreenWidth + 20;
  height = stage.fullScreenHeight + 60;
}
private function onLoaded() : void {
  theImg.setStyle('top', ( stage.fullScreenHeight / 2 ) - ➥
  ( theImg.content.height / 2 ) );
  theImg.setStyle('left', ( stage.fullScreenWidth / 2 ) - ➥
  ( theImg.content.width / 2 ) );
}
]]>
</mx:Script>
  <mx:Image id="theImg" source="{data.url}" httpStatus="onLoaded()" />
</mx:Window>
```

**Figure 5-9.** A full-size version of the image in a native subwindow

This new version of the code sets the background color of the window to black, and then sets a strong alpha of 0.9. It also sets the transparent attribute to true, and the system chrome to none, which is required to support the transparent attribute. The onLoaded for the image now centers the image within the window. And a new startup handler sets the size of the window to the full screen with a little extra and sets the displayState of the stage to full screen.

Now when I double-click the image, I see something like Figure 5-10.

**Figure 5-10.** The full-screen lightbox effect

The entire screen is turned black with the exception of the image, which is centered in the middle of the frame. To get out of the display, I click anywhere on the screen or press the Esc key.

# Offline data entry

The next example emphasizes the use of a local database. The AIR framework comes with an SQLite database built in. You can choose to use it just for the single session of the application run. Or you can store the database locally and reuse it each time the application is run. In this example, I'll keep a database stored locally. The local database will synchronize with a remote web server to maintain a list of contacts (i.e., first name, last name, e-mail, and description).

When the AIR application first starts up, it will connect with the contacts server (written in Rails) to get the most recent contacts. This is shown graphically in Figure 5-11.

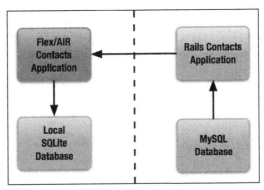

**Figure 5-11.** The local Flex/AIR application syncing from the remote Contacts application

The Rails application requests the data from the MySQL production database. It then sends that, as XML, back to the AIR application, which updates the local database to match the remote database.

From there the Flex/AIR application is offline. Any new records added to the contacts database will be stored locally and pushed to the Rails application only when the application goes back online. This push is shown in Figure 5-12.

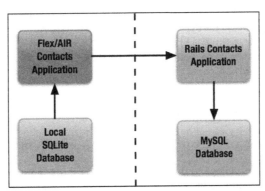

**Figure 5-12.** Pushing the new records to the Rails contacts database

Building the system starts with the Rails code for the contacts system. If you aren't familiar with Ruby on Rails, you should go to the Ruby on Rails home page (http://rubyonrails.org) to find out more. Once you have built a web application using Ruby on Rails, you will never want to use any other technology.

To start with I build a new Rails application called "Contacts" and create the MySQL database to hold the tables. I then set up the DB migration code as shown here:

```
class CreateContacts < ActiveRecord::Migration
  def self.up
    create_table :contacts do |t|
      t.column "first", :string, :default => "", :null => false
      t.column "last", :string, :default => "", :null => false
      t.column "email", :string, :default => "", :null => false
      t.column "description", :text, :default => ""
    end
  end

  def self.down
    drop_table :contacts
  end
end
```

There are four fields for each contact: first, last, email, and description. There is also an integer ID, which is automatically maintained by ActiveRecord. ActiveRecord is a Ruby on Rails class that handles all of the SQL database access for you. All you need to do is point it at a table, and it takes care of all of the rest of the work to query, insert, update, and delete records.

Once the table has been successfully created, I generate a new controller called contact, which contains this code:

```
class ContactController < ApplicationController
  scaffold :contact
  def add
    newContact = Contact.create( { :first => params[:first],
      :last => params[:last],
      :email => params[:email],
      :description => params[:description] } )
    render( :xml => newContact.to_xml )
  end
  def xml
    render( :xml => Contact.find(:all).to_xml )
  end
end
```

I use the standard Ruby "scaffolding" to put a web front end on the table. Then I add two new methods: add and xml. The add method adds a record to the database and returns the XML for the record. The xml method returns all of the contacts as XML. I let Rails handle all of the XML creation for me using the to_xml method.

With this tiny amount of code, the Rails portion of the example is complete. It's now on to building the Flex/AIR code for the offline contacts viewer. This code is shown here:

```
<?xml version="1.0" encoding="utf-8"?>
<mx:WindowedApplication xmlns:mx="http://www.adobe.com/2006/mxml"
  layout="vertical"
  creationComplete="onStartup()"
  title="Contact Viewer">
<mx:Script>
<![CDATA[
import mx.rpc.events.ResultEvent;
import flash.data.*;

private var db:SQLConnection = new SQLConnection();

private function onStartup() : void {
  db.open( File.applicationStorageDirectory.resolvePath(
  "contacts.db" ) );

  var sth:SQLStatement = new SQLStatement();
  sth.sqlConnection = db;
  sth.text = "CREATE TABLE IF NOT EXISTS contacts ( id int, ➥
first text, last text, email text, description text )";
  sth.execute();

  reqContacts.send();

  updateContactList();
}
private function onReqContacts( event:ResultEvent ) : void {
  for each( var elContact:XML in event.result..contact ) {
    var id:int = parseInt( elContact.id );

    var idFetch:SQLStatement = new SQLStatement();
    idFetch.sqlConnection = db;
    idFetch.text = "SELECT * FROM contacts WHERE id=:id";
    idFetch.parameters[ ':id' ] = id;
    idFetch.execute();
    var fetchRes:SQLResult = idFetch.getResult();
    if ( fetchRes.data == null || fetchRes.data.length == 0 )
    {
      var insFetch:SQLStatement = new SQLStatement();
      insFetch.sqlConnection = db;
      insFetch.text = "INSERT INTO contacts VALUES( :id, :first,
  :last, :email, :description )";
      insFetch.parameters[ ':id' ] = id;
      insFetch.parameters[ ':first' ] = elContact.first.toString();
      insFetch.parameters[ ':last' ] = elContact.last.toString();
      insFetch.parameters[ ':email' ] = elContact.email.toString();
```

```
                  insFetch.parameters[ ':description' ] = ➡
        elContact.description.toString();
                  insFetch.execute();
            }
          }
          updateContactList();
        }
        private function updateContactList() : void {
          var dgFetch:SQLStatement = new SQLStatement();
          dgFetch.sqlConnection = db;
          dgFetch.text = "SELECT * FROM contacts";
          dgFetch.execute();

          var resData:Array = dgFetch.getResult().data;
          dgContactList.dataProvider = resData;

          var bHasUnsent:Boolean = false;
          for each( var row:Object in resData ) {
            if ( row.id == 0 )
              bHasUnsent = true;
          }

          btnSend.visible = bHasUnsent;
        }
        private function onAddResult( event:ResultEvent ) : void {
          var email:String = event.result..email;
          var id:int = parseInt( event.result..id );

          var idUpdate:SQLStatement = new SQLStatement();
          idUpdate.sqlConnection = db;
          idUpdate.text = "UPDATE contacts SET id=:id WHERE email=:email";
          idUpdate.parameters[ ':id' ] = id;
          idUpdate.parameters[ ':email' ] = email;
          idUpdate.execute();

          updateContactList();

          if ( btnSend.visible )
            onSendToServer();
        }
        private function onSendToServer() : void {
          var dgFetch:SQLStatement = new SQLStatement();
          dgFetch.sqlConnection = db;
          dgFetch.text = "SELECT * FROM contacts WHERE id=0";
          dgFetch.execute();

          var resData:Array = dgFetch.getResult().data;
          if ( resData != null && resData.length > 0 ) {
            var url:String = "http://<Your Server>/contact/add";
```

```
      url += "?first="+escape(resData[0].first);
      url += "&last="+escape(resData[0].last);
      url += "&email="+escape(resData[0].email);
      url += "&description="+escape(resData[0].description);

      var addHS:HTTPService = new HTTPService();
      addHS.url = url;
      addHS.resultFormat = 'e4x';
      addHS.addEventListener(ResultEvent.RESULT,onAddResult);
      addHS.send();
    }
  }
private function onNewContact( event:Event ) : void {
  var nc:newcontact = event.target as newcontact;

  var insFetch:SQLStatement = new SQLStatement();
  insFetch.sqlConnection = db;
  insFetch.text = "INSERT INTO contacts VALUES( :id, :first,
  :last, :email, :description )";
  insFetch.parameters[ ':id' ] = 0;
  insFetch.parameters[ ':first' ] = nc.txtFirst.text;
  insFetch.parameters[ ':last' ] = nc.txtLast.text;
  insFetch.parameters[ ':email' ] = nc.txtEmail.text;
  insFetch.parameters[ ':description' ] = nc.txtDescription.text;
  insFetch.execute();

  updateContactList();
}
private function onNew() : void {
  var nc:newcontact = new newcontact();
  nc.addEventListener(Event.COMPLETE, onNewContact);
  nc.open();
}
]]>
</mx:Script>
<mx:HTTPService id="reqContacts" url="http://<Your server>/contact/xml"
  result="onReqContacts(event);" resultFormat="e4x" />
<mx:DataGrid id="dgContactList" width="100%" height="100%">
<mx:columns>
  <mx:DataGridColumn dataField="first" headerText="Name">
    <mx:itemRenderer>
      <mx:Component>
        <mx:Label text="{data.first} {data.last}" />
      </mx:Component>
    </mx:itemRenderer>
  </mx:DataGridColumn>
  <mx:DataGridColumn dataField="email" headerText="Email">
  </mx:DataGridColumn>
</mx:columns>
```

```
  </mx:DataGrid>
  <mx:Button label="New Contact" click="onNew()" />
  <mx:Button label="Send To Server" click="onSendToServer()"
    visible="false" id="btnSend" />
</mx:WindowedApplication>
```

It's a lot of code, but it's all fairly simple. When the creationComplete event is fired, the onStartup method is called. This onStartup method creates the local database and adds the contacts table to it. It then requests the contacts from the server using the xml method defined by Rails. The onReqContacts method is called when that request is finished, and it parses the XML returned from the server. When new records are found on the server, a local version is added. The DataGrid control is then updated with the data from the local database.

The onNew method is called when the user clicks the New Contact button. It brings up a subwindow defined by the following MXML component:

```
<?xml version="1.0" encoding="utf-8"?>
<mx:Window xmlns="*" xmlns:mx="http://www.adobe.com/2006/mxml"
  width="300" height="230" title="New Contact">
<mx:Script>
<![CDATA[
private function onAdd() : void {
  dispatchEvent(new Event(Event.COMPLETE));
  stage.nativeWindow.close();
}
private function onCancel() : void {
  stage.nativeWindow.close();
}
]]>
</mx:Script>
  <mx:Form>
    <mx:FormItem label="First">
      <mx:TextInput id="txtFirst" />
    </mx:FormItem>
    <mx:FormItem label="Last">
      <mx:TextInput id="txtLast" />
    </mx:FormItem>
    <mx:FormItem label="Email">
      <mx:TextInput id="txtEmail" />
    </mx:FormItem>
    <mx:FormItem label="Description">
      <mx:TextInput id="txtDescription" />
    </mx:FormItem>
    <mx:FormItem>
      <mx:Button label="Add" click="onAdd()" />
      <mx:Button label="Cancel" click="onCancel()" />
    </mx:FormItem>
  </mx:Form>
</mx:Window>
```

This is just a form that has text fields for the first, last, email, and description values. When the user clicks Add, the onAdd method is called, which tells anyone listening that the form has been completed.

The Contacts application listens for that notification and calls the onNewContact method, which stores the data in the local database. The ID of the new record is set to zero to indicate that this data is only stored locally.

The onSendToServer method is called when the user clicks the Send To Server button, which is shown only when there are records in the local database that are not present on the remote server. The onSendToServer method does a query to find all of the records with an ID of 0, and then calls the add method on the server to add each record, one by one, to the remote database.

The onAddResult method is called when the add method returns the XML for the record in the database. This method then uses the e-mail address to update the ID in the local database of the record with the ID from the remote server.

This is a fairly simple example of local/remote data synchronization. If you have a more complex table system, then you won't be able to use the simple ID=0 trick that I used here. You could use a Boolean field in the database to indicate whether the record has been sent to the server or not, and update the IDs after the server has returned the official record ID.

When I bring up the application in Flex Builder 3, I first see something like Figure 5-13.

**Figure 5-13.** The user interface after the initial synchronization

I've put a couple of contacts in there just to demonstrate. I can then create a new contact using the new contact subwindow form, as shown in Figure 5-14.

This contact will be stored locally and then sent to the database when I click the Send To Server button. That button is only made visible when there are contacts in the local database with the ID of zero, which indicates that they haven't been sent to the remote server yet.

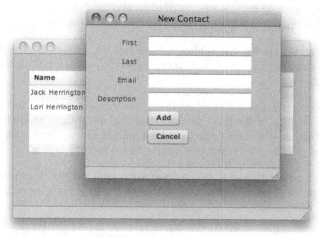

**Figure 5-14.** The new contact form

# Self-updating with AIR

One of the features that customers have come to expect from desktop applications is an ability to **self-update**. The application, on startup, should look for any updates to the code, then download and install them if the user wants to. AIR supports this through the Updater class, but there is still some user interface and networking work to be done to get it all to hang together.

The first thing to do is to define a method where the server can indicate to the AIR application what the most recent version is and where the download is. To do this, I will use a simple XML file. An example of this is shown here:

```
<version>
    <latest>1.0</latest>
    <download>http://jackherrington.com/extras/updater/update.air
    </download>
</version>
```

This file contains two key elements: the version number of the most recent revision, and the URL where the most recent version can be downloaded. In this case, I specify that the most recent version is 1.0. You can define your own format for the XML as you please. Or use any format you choose for this.

The UpdateHandler Flex class uses this XML file to get the most recent version information and if necessary download the new code and update the application. The code for UpdateHandler is as follows:

```
package com.jherrington.versioning
{
  import flash.desktop.Updater;
  import flash.events.Event;
  import flash.filesystem.*;
  import flash.net.*;
```

```
import flash.utils.ByteArray;

import mx.controls.Alert;
import mx.events.CloseEvent;
import mx.rpc.events.ResultEvent;
import mx.rpc.http.HTTPService;

public class UpdateHandler
{
  private var _version:Number = 0.0;
  private var _updateUrl:String = null;
  private var _quiet:Boolean = true;
  private var _latestVers:Number;
  private var _downloadUrl:String;

  public function UpdateHandler( version:Number, updateUrl:String,
quiet:Boolean = true )
  {
    _version = version;
    _updateUrl = updateUrl;
    _quiet = quiet;

    var versReq:HTTPService = new HTTPService();
    versReq.addEventListener(ResultEvent.RESULT, onVersionReturn);
    versReq.url = updateUrl;
    versReq.resultFormat = 'object';
    versReq.send();
  }

  private function onVersionReturn( event:ResultEvent ) : void {
    if ( event.result != null && event.result.version != null &&
event.result.version.latest != null ) {
      var versionNumber:String = event.result.version.latest;
      _latestVers = parseFloat( versionNumber );
      if ( _latestVers > _version )
      {
        _downloadUrl = event.result.version.download;
        Alert.show("Download an update to this application now?",
"Application Update",
          3, null, onDownloadPromptReturn);
      }
      else
      {
        if ( _quiet == false )
          mx.controls.Alert.show(
'You are running the most recent version' );
      }
    }
  }
```

```
        private function onDownloadPromptReturn(event:CloseEvent):void {
          if ( event.detail == Alert.YES ) {
            var codeReq:URLRequest = new URLRequest( _downloadUrl );
            var codeStream:URLStream = new URLStream();
            codeStream.addEventListener(Event.COMPLETE,onCodeReturn);
            codeStream.load( codeReq );
          }
        }

        private function onCodeReturn( event:Event ) : void {
          var codeStream:URLStream = event.target as URLStream;
          var fileData:ByteArray = new ByteArray();
          codeStream.readBytes(fileData, 0, codeStream.bytesAvailable);

          var fileName:String = _downloadUrl.substr(
      _downloadUrl.lastIndexOf("/") + 1 );
          var tempDirectory:File = File.createTempDirectory();
          var tempFile:File = new File( tempDirectory.nativePath + ➥
      File.separator + fileName );

          var fileStream:FileStream = new FileStream();
          fileStream.open(tempFile, FileMode.WRITE);
          fileStream.writeBytes(fileData, 0, fileData.length);
          fileStream.close();

          var updater:Updater = new Updater();
          updater.update( tempFile, _latestVers.toString() );
        }
      }
    }
```

The constructor takes two parameters: the current version and the URL of the XML that defines the most recent version. It also takes an optional quiet parameter. If quiet is true, which it is by default, and there is no version, the user isn't notified.

The UpdateHandler constructor makes the request of the server at this URL. The onVersionReturn method is called when the XML is found. This method parses through the objects to find the version number. If the version number is greater, it prompts the user to see if he wants to download the new code. That prompt is handled by the onDownloadPromptReturn method, which starts the download of the new code if the user wants to update the application.

The onCodeReturn method is called when the download of the new code is complete. It starts off by reading all of the data into a binary array. Then it creates a temporary file that will hold all of the code. Once the data is written into the file, the AIR Updater class is called to update the code with the most recent version.

I need to build two versions of the code in release mode. The first is version 1.0, which I keep locally. And the second is version 1.1, which I put on the site. I then launch the 1.0 version locally, and I see something like Figure 5-15.

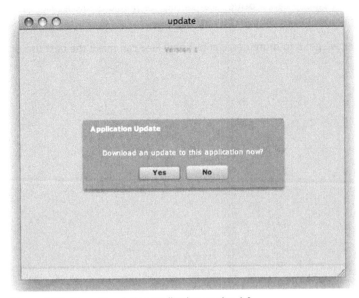

**Figure 5-15.** The self-updating application version 1.0

If I click Yes, then the code is downloaded and the application self-updates as shown in Figure 5-16.

**Figure 5-16.** The updated code

It's not a very complex example, but I think you get the point.

You should note that this will not work if the application is being run directly from Flex Builder because applications run in the test launcher ("adl") cannot self-update. You need to export the release build and run it from there.

It's important to maintain the certificate that you created when you built the release application, as the two certificates will need to be identical for the update process to work.

# Summary

I've shown you just the tip of the iceberg in this chapter when it comes to what can be done with AIR. With local file system access, you can get directly to the data from popular applications such as Excel, Word, iPhoto, or iTunes. You can provide local storage of media elements like movies or audio for offline access. The only limit is your own creativity.

In the next chapter, we get into more detail about how Flex can make the best use of Java-based web services.

# Part Two

# INTEGRATING WITH CLIENT-
# AND SERVER-SIDE TECHNOLOGIES

# Chapter 6

# INTEGRATING WITH JAVA USING SERVICES

By Shashank Tiwari

Flex and Java are complementary technologies. Flex is a leading technology for building rich, engaging interfaces, and Java is an established player on the server side. Using them together makes it possible to build enterprise-grade rich, robust, and scalable applications. Java's capability to serve as a platform for multiple languages and to integrate with multiple tools and technologies allows Flex to make remote calls to multiple languages and to reach out to diverse enterprise systems.

Adobe realized the potential benefits of this synergy and created its data services offering using Java. Data services provide a ready-made infrastructure for Flex and Java integration. The concepts behind data services and its API are explained in Chapter 7.

The integration of Flex and Java can be approached in several ways, depending on the use case and the degree of association. Let's take a look at it in terms of a couple of 2 × 2 matrices. Figure 6-1 analyzes the integration possibilities using two scales, legacy and data frequency. It indicates that if your business logic and transactional operations are in Java and you need frequent data updates, you have a case for tight integration using remoting and messaging between the two. It also recommends that if the situation is the exact opposite (little existing Java and sporadic needs to access or refresh data), you should use simple HTTP-based data interchange.

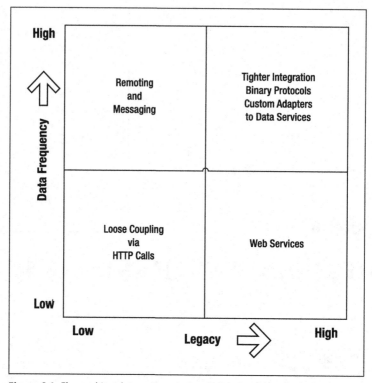

**Figure 6-1.** Flex and Java integration analyzed via a 2 × 2 matrix that measures situations on legacy and data frequency scales

Figure 6-2 analyzes the same situation using a different set of scales, namely coupling and third-party integration complexity (3PIC for short). This time all the independent factors considered earlier, such as legacy and data access frequency, along with a few others, such as application performance and response expectations, data volume, and transactional complexity, are combined into a single parameter called **coupling**. This scale is juxtaposed against the scale that measures the 3PIC parameters. So what this type of treatment suggests is that if you have sophisticated complexity requirements, for example, integration with some real-time proprietary data source feed or complicated fine-grained authentication services, and need tight coupling, you should consider using a full-blown data services infrastructure and possibly extending it with custom extension points and adapters. It also depicts the other alternatives and suggests that the best choices for the opposite case, a loosely coupled scenario with low 3PIC requirements, are simple HTTP-based communication or simple remoting.

Go ahead and take a closer look at Figures 6-1 and 6-2. The legends attempt to explain all the possible scenarios. These diagrams should give you a high-level perspective of things and might prove useful to refer back to while making initial choices.

Some of this may seem strange, but I shall be getting into the nuts and bolts soon. As soon as I walk you through the examples, everything should appear lucid and straightforward.

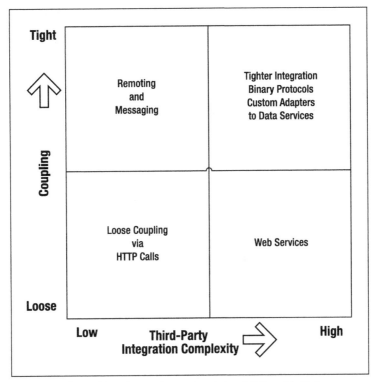

**Figure 6-2.** Flex and Java integration analyzed via a 2 × 2 matrix that measures situations on third-party integration complexity and coupling scales

# Leveraging HTTP calls and web services

Simple things first! Let's start by integrating Flex and Java using simple HTTP calls and web services. One of the well-known and often talked about benefits of open standards like HTTP and web services is interoperability and service consumption being agnostic to implementation. In other words, you fire up a web site using a URL the same way, irrespective of the language the web site makers use to implement it, and you consume a web service the same way, whether it's written using Java, .NET, or the LAMP stack. Therefore, much of what I say in this section is not specific to Java alone; it is just as applicable to PHP, Python, Ruby, C#/.NET, or any other technology on the server. The only requirement is that the technology that Flex is integrated with must support HTTP calls and the standard web services specifications. You will notice some of this conversation bubbling up again in Chapter 8, which covers PHP integration, and in Chapter 10, which discusses mashups.

# Integration based on HTTP requests

HTTP calls are simpler than web services, so let's start with them. We create a really simple Java application that uses a couple of simple classes and JSP to generate XML content. We consume this XML content from within a Flex application. The elementary Java application produces a collection of all-time top ten NBA scorers. Each entry includes the scorer's first name and last name, the total score, and his position in the top ten list. Each entry maps to a simple JavaBean class, appropriately called

Scorer.java. A collection of these entries is held in a Java class called AllTimeTop10Scorers.java. The classes Scorer.java and AllTimeTop10Scorers.java are as follows:

```java
/*Scorer.java*/

package org.advancedflex.chapter06.example;

public class Scorer implements java.io.Serializable {
    private String firstName;
    private String lastName;
    private int totalScore;
    private int position;

    public Scorer(String firstName, String lastName,
    int totalScore, int position) {
        this.firstName = firstName;
        this.lastName = lastName;
        this.totalScore = totalScore;
        this.position = position;
    }

    public String getFirstName() {
        return firstName;
    }

    public void setFirstName(String firstName) {
        this.firstName = firstName;
    }

    public String getLastName() {
        return lastName;
    }

    public void setLastName(String lastName) {
        this.lastName = lastName;
    }

    public int getTotalScore() {
        return totalScore;
    }

    public void setTotalScore(int totalScore) {
        this.totalScore = totalScore;
    }

    public int getPosition() {
        return position;
    }

    public void setPosition(int position) {
```

```
            this.position = position;
        }
    }

    /*AllTimeTop10Scorers.java*/

    package org.advancedflex.chapter06.example;

    import java.util.Vector;
    import java.util.Iterator;

    public class AllTimeTop10Scorers implements java.io.Serializable {
        private Vector top10ScorersCollection = new Vector();

        public AllTimeTop10Scorers() {
            top10ScorersCollection.addElement (new
                Scorer("Kareem", "Abdul-Jabbar", 38387, 1));
            top10ScorersCollection.addElement (new
                Scorer("Wilt", "Chamberlain", 31419, 2));
            top10ScorersCollection.addElement (new
                Scorer("Karl", "Malone", 30599, 3));
            top10ScorersCollection.addElement (new
                Scorer("Michael", "Jordan", 29277, 4));
            top10ScorersCollection.addElement (new
                Scorer("Moses", "Malone", 27409, 5));
            top10ScorersCollection.addElement (new
                Scorer("Elvin", "Hayes", 27313, 6));
            top10ScorersCollection.addElement (new
                Scorer("Oscar", "Robertson", 26710, 7));
            top10ScorersCollection.addElement (new
                Scorer("Dominique", "Wilkins", 26669, 8));
            top10ScorersCollection.addElement (new
                Scorer("John", "Havlicek", 26395, 9));
            top10ScorersCollection.addElement (new
                Scorer("Alex", "English", 25613, 10));
        }

        public Iterator getTop10ScorersCollection() {
            return top10ScorersCollection.iterator();
        }
    }
```

Now we create a really simple JSP that accesses this collection, iterates over it, and prints it out in an XML format. In real-life situations, you may have more complex middleware logic and JSP generating XML. However, Flex would be unaware of this complexity on the server side. And in case I wasn't clear earlier, Flex would interact via HTTP calls in the same manner, irrespective of the server-side technology. That's the benefit of open standards and clean abstractions.

In traditional JSP applications, you often bind these collections to some sort of an HTML view component like a table rather than casting it in XML format. When integrating such legacy code with RIA, it may be a good, quick idea to wrap existing JSP(s) to produce XML instead of HTML-rendered output, so that you can consume it easily in your RIA. Chapter 11 discusses this and more strategies for migrating Web 1.0 applications to RIA. For now, let's stick with this simple example. Here is the code for top10nbascorers.jsp:

```jsp
<%@ page contentType="text/xml" %>
<%@ page import="org.advancedflex.chapter06.example.*" %>

<%  response.setHeader ("Pragma", "no-cache");
    if (request.getProtocol().equals ("HTTP/1.1")) {
        response.setHeader ("Cache-Control", "no-cache");
    }
%>

<jsp:useBean id="collection"
class="org.advancedflex.chapter06.example.AllTimeTop10Scorers" />

<%
java.util.Iterator collectionIterator =
collection.getTop10ScorersCollection();
Scorer scorer = null;
%>


<?xml version="1.0" encoding="UTF-8"?>
<top10ScorersCollection>
    <% while (collectionIterator.hasNext()) { %>
    <% scorer = (Scorer)collectionIterator.next(); %>
    <scorer>
        <firstName><%= scorer.getFirstName() %></firstName>
        <lastName><%= scorer.getLastName() %></lastName>
        <totalScore><%= scorer.getTotalScore() %></totalScore>
        <position><%= scorer.getPosition() %></position>
    </scorer>
    <% } %>
</top10ScorersCollection>
```

The XML output that contains the top ten scorers when viewed without any defined XSL appears in Internet Explorer as shown in Figure 6-3.

This finishes the story on the server side. We now hop over to the Flex end. This data is accessible to the Flex client via a URL, and so I'll first dig a bit into how Flex interacts with URLs over HTTP in general and then come back to this specific case. The Flex framework can use a few different ways to invoke HTTP URLs and interact with them, three of which I will discuss right here:

- Using the HTTPService component
- Using URLLoader and URLVariables
- Using the Socket class

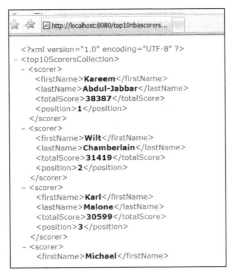

**Figure 6-3.** XML output that contains the top ten scorers when viewed without an XSL stylesheet in Internet Explorer

## HTTPService component

The HTTPService component, which is a part of the mx.rpc.http package, facilitates HTTP request/response communication. It is accessible as an MXML tag and can be imported and invoked as an ActionScript class. Any resource identifiable as a URL and accessible over HTTP or HTTPS can be invoked using this component. The URL to be invoked is bound as the value of the component's url property. A call to our JSP, top10nbascorers.jsp, using MXML looks like this:

```
<?xml version="1.0" encoding="utf-8"?>
<mx:Application xmlns:mx="http://www.adobe.com/2006/mxml">

    <mx:HTTPService id="myHTTPService" url="http://localhost:8080/➥
top10nbascorers/top10nbascorers.jsp"/>

    <mx:DataGrid dataProvider="{myHTTPService.lastResult.➥
top10ScorersCollection.scorer}" width="100%" height="100%"/>

    <mx:Button label="Invoke HTTPService"
click="myHTTPService.send()"/>

</mx:Application>
```

Notice that the send method of the HTTPService component needs to be called for the invocation to take place. For easy access and user control, we bound the call to this send method as an event handler to the click event of a button, which we labeled Invoke HTTPService. The send method could have been called from any other event handler including the creationComplete event handler, which is triggered when the creationComplete system event is fired. Once the application is set up, its child components are all created, laid out, visible, and ready to be used.

This simple example involved the default HTTP GET method call. Setting the method property value as POST would have also allowed POST method calls. Other HTTP method calls like HEAD, OPTIONS, TRACE, and DELETE can also be made using the HTTPService component, but in that case we would need to use a proxy. We will come back to this in a bit.

Once you make a request, the web server will come back with a response. If successful, it will return the desired resource or data, and if unsuccessful, it will return an error code, which can help you understand the cause of the failure. In our code, we don't do any of this. We simply bind the returned response referenced through the lastResult property of our service component to a data provider attribute. Our outcome piped to the data provider of a data grid makes the interface appear as shown in Figure 6-4.

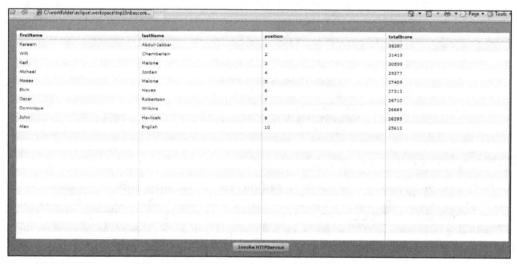

**Figure 6-4.** HTTP response displayed in a data grid

That was a useful and nice output for the minuscule amount of effort we put in so far. Now let's see how our nice example may after all not be that robust.

We haven't handled errors so far, not even budgeting for them. Not handling errors and exceptions is never good. You can experience the pain inflicted by this shortcoming by simply bringing down your web server and invoking the HTTPService one more time. This time there is no nice data grid but complaints from the Flash Player in the form of an error stack trace. Figure 6-5 shows what it looks like.

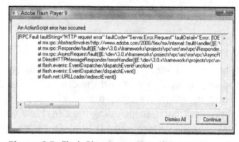

**Figure 6-5.** Flash Player error strack trace

Luckily, HTTPService, like most components and controls in Flex, defines a set of events that are trig-gered during different stages of its life cycle. In the case of HTTPService, they are result, fault, and invoke, which map to success, failure, and invocation in progress and no failure so far. As with any other event, you could define event handlers to take appropriate action. For instance, alerting the user by printing the error to the screen may be an appropriate way to handle faults. Activating this feature implies adding the following lines to our code:

```
<mx:Script>
    <![CDATA[

    import mx.controls.Alert;
    import mx.rpc.events.FaultEvent;
    private function faultHandler(event:FaultEvent):void {
        Alert.show('Oops there is a problem!....' ➥
+ event.fault.message);
    }
    ]]>
</mx:Script>
```

and modifying the <mx:HTTPService /> tag to include a fault event handler as shown here:

```
<mx:HTTPService id="myHTTPService" url="http://localhost:8080/➥
top10nbascorers/top10nbascorers.jsp"
fault="faultHandler(event)"/>
```

Now our application looks marginally better and does not crash due to the simplest of errors occur-ring during the request/response cycle.

Similarly, you can define success handlers and bind them to the result event. A **success handler**'s primary responsibility is to handle the returned data appropriately. In our example, we used the lastResult property to access the returned data and pass it on without worrying about the format in which it appears. We did nothing special; how did it still work? By default, the result set returned by the HTTP service call is available in the lastResult object and is formatted as a tree of ActionScript objects. The result set is also bindable, which implies that it gets updated as changes to the data set occur. The HTTPService component inherits from the Remote Procedure Call (RPC) executor AbstractInvoker class. The AbstractInvoker object defines the lastResult and the makeObjectsBindable properties. I mentioned a little while back that the lastResult property is of type Object and holds the result set returned by the service call. The makeObjectsBindable object is of type Boolean and is by default true. This flag determines whether the returned object should be bindable or not. In the default case, this property leads to an object type being wrapped up in an ObjectProxy and an array type being wrapped up in an ArrayCollection.

In our example, the tree of objects maps to an underlying XML. This tree of objects, which is returned as the response of the HTTP request, is assigned as the data provider of the data grid. Such an object structure is the default response data type for HTTP requests made using the Flex HTTPService object.

However, we don't always have to rely on defaults and don't have to handle returning data as an object tree. We have ample choices. We can set the resultFormat property to array, xml, flashvars, text, and e4x (ECMAScript for XML) to get data in alternative formats. For example, if we specified the resultFormat as e4x and used the corresponding syntax and expressions to access the data, our example is marginally modified as follows:

```
<TBD>
<?xml version="1.0" encoding="utf-8"?>
<mx:Application xmlns:mx="http://www.adobe.com/2006/mxml">

    <mx:HTTPService id="myHTTPService" url="http://localhost:8080/➥
top10nbascorers/top10nbascorers.jsp"/>

    <mx:DataGrid dataProvider="{myHTTPService.lastResult.➥
top10ScorersCollection.scorer}" width="100%" height="100%"/>

    <mx:Button label="Invoke HTTPService"
click="myHTTPService.send()"/>

</mx:Application>
</TBD>
```

When resultFormat is set to type e4x, the lastResult is set to type XML. In legacy ActionScript, that is, the version prior to ActionScript 3.0 (AS3), the flash.xml.XMLNode class represented an XML fragment. This is a bit clumsy considering that an XML fragment contained in a larger XML document is also XML. So the use of this class is now deprecated. However, you may still want to use it for some reason, such as backward compatibility. In such a scenario, you will need the lastResult object to be returned as an XMLNode and not an XML object. This can be achieved by setting resultFormat to xml and not e4x. Similarly, you may desire the result to be in an array or a set of name-value pairs or plain text. These results can be achieved by setting resultFormat to array, flashvars, and text, respectively.

So far, we have got almost everything done in MXML. Now we switch gears to ActionScript. This time, we recode our example using ActionScript only as follows:

```
top10nbascorers_as.mxml

<?xml version="1.0" encoding="utf-8"?>
<mx:Application xmlns:mx="http://www.adobe.com/2006/mxml" >
<mx:Script>
    <![CDATA[

    import mx.controls.Alert;
    import mx.rpc.events.FaultEvent;
    import mx.rpc.events.ResultEvent;
    import mx.collections.XMLListCollection;
    import mx.rpc.http.HTTPService;
    import mx.controls.DataGrid;


    private var myHTTPService:HTTPService;
    private var myDataGrid:DataGrid = new DataGrid();
```

```
    public function useHttpService():void {
    trace("useHttpService invoked");
    myHTTPService = new HTTPService();
        //myHTTPService.destination =
"http://localhost:8080/top10nbascorers/top10nbascorers.jsp";
        myHTTPService.url   =
"http://localhost:8080/top10nbascorers/top10nbascorers.jsp";
        myHTTPService.method = "GET";
        myHTTPService.addEventListener("result", resultHandler);
        myHTTPService.addEventListener("fault", faultHandler);
        myHTTPService.send();
    }


    public function resultHandler(event:ResultEvent):void {
    trace("resultHandler invoked");
    var result:Object = event.result;
    myDataGrid.dataProvider = result.top10ScorersCollection.scorer;
    myDataGrid.percentWidth = 100;
    myDataGrid.percentHeight = 100;
    myVBox.addChild(myDataGrid);
        //Do something with the result.
    }


    private function faultHandler(event:FaultEvent):void {
        trace("faultHandler Invoked");
        Alert.show('Oops there is a problem!....' ➥
+ event.fault.message);
    }

    ]]>
</mx:Script>

    <!-- <mx:DataGrid id="dataGrid" width="100%" height="100%"/> -->
    <mx:VBox id="myVBox" width="100%" height="100%" />

    <mx:Button label="Invoke HTTPService" click="useHttpService()"/>

</mx:Application>
```

That wasn't too different from what we did using MXML. The example is simple so things remained straightforward, even when we switched over to ActionScript.

In real-life situations, you may want to do a few other things to make your applications work:

- Make POST calls as well as GET calls.
- Send parameters down with the request.
- Invoke URL(s) that are accessible over the secure HTTPS protocol.
- Implement a notion of a user session for purposes like authentication or personalization.
- Invoke URL(s) that originate from domains that define a security policy using crossdomain.xml.
- Invoke URL(s) that originate from domains that don't define a security policy.
- Make HTTP requests that require header manipulation.

The following discussion will address these points in more detail.

## Making POST calls as well as GET calls

Making POST and GET calls is a very simple process. All you have to do is set the method property value to POST and send the request to the server.

For example, you use the following in MXML:

```
<mx:HTTPService id=" myHTTPService " method="POST" ..../>
```

and here's how you'd do this in ActionScript:

```
myHTTPService.method = "GET";
```

## Sending parameters down with the request

The first step in sending parameters with the request is to create an object of type Object, the root object in ActionScript. The next step is to create variables or attributes in this object. Variable names map to the names in the name-value parameter pairs. Next, assign the value to the corresponding variable values. Finally, pass the object as the send method call argument.

Let's walk through a quick example to see how this plays out.

Say our URL is myURL and it takes two parameters, userName and password, which can be passed to it as a part of the GET call query string like this:

```
http://myHost:myPort/myURL?userName="myName"&password="myPassword"
```

In real life, sending the password over an HTTP GET method request poses security risks. To avoid this risk, it's advisable to use either the HTTP POST method or the HTTPS secure protocol instead.

In our HTTPService request, we will do the following:

```
var params:Object = new Object();
params["userName"] = "myName";
params["password"] = "myPassword";
myHTTPService.send(params);
```

If it's a POST request, we will still take the same approach, although it would now map to hidden variable passing and not be passed as a part of the query string.

## Invoking URL(s) accessible over the secure HTTPS protocol

If a Flex application is served over HTTPS, it can make HTTP and HTTPS requests without making any special provisions. However, if the Flex application is served over HTTP and it needs to make HTTPS requests, a few extra configurations are required.

A security policy needs to be defined so that we do not violate the Flash Player security sandbox model, which restricts HTTPS requests over HTTP without such a security policy definition. Cross-domain security is defined in a file named crossdomain.xml. A simplest version of the crossdomain.xml file could be the following:

```
<cross-domain-policy>
    <allow-access-from domain="*" secure="false" />
</cross-domain-policy>
```

This is because HTTP and HTTPS are served over different ports. HTTPS usually uses port 443 and HTTP uses port 80.

A few more things need to be done beyond this cross-domain file, if a server-side proxy is in use. I am not talking about HTTPService without a server-side proxy here; therefore, we ignore the entire server-side configuration for now.

Before we progress to the next topic, one quick note: you may have read the advice to include https as the value of the protocol attribute in the HTTPService (or for that matter WebService) tag. However, this isn't applicable when there is no server-side proxy in use. With the server-side proxy, such a setting would throw an exception.

## Managing user sessions

User sessions have two use cases in HTML-based web applications:

- Maintain the conversation between the client (browser) and the server.
- Implement authentication and authorization schemes.

In Flex applications, the first of these two reasons is not relevant. However, the second situation is still valid. In data service–driven Flex applications, things can get a bit complicated, and there may be situations where the first is still valid.

Maintaining the conversation between the client (browser) and the server is important in HTML-based web applications. HTTP is a stateless protocol, and so each request is independent of all others. In order to have continuity between successive requests, you need to have a common token among them. This token, or identifier, is passed back and forth with each request. Flex is a thick client technology, because it runs within a Flash Player/VM, which can hold data in memory. Therefore, the use of sessions for the purpose of keeping the conversation going between the client and the server is redundant.

As mentioned, Flex applications may still need sessions for authentication and authorization. Whatever the purpose, the ways of implementing them are the same. We need to do the following:

1. Pass in the credentials, say username and password, as the part of the first request.
2. Generate a server-side token using the passed-in credentials. This token could be as simple as the original data or as complex as an MD5 signature. Passing the data as is would make it susceptible to hacking and is obviously not recommended.
3. Send the token back to the Flex application as a part of the response.
4. Save this token on the client. For application-wide access, save it in the SharedObject.
5. Pass in the token with all subsequent requests.

It's possible to add a session timeout feature to this process, to avoid the token being alive forever. In that case, set the session timeout when creating the token. Save the session timeout value on the server. On every request that carries the token along, verify whether the session is still valid (i.e., timeout has not been activated yet). If not, ask the user to pass the credentials one more time or keep extending the timeout with every request so that the user session is kept alive so long as the user is not inactive for the duration of the timeout. These are choices that should be made depending on the application's authentication and authorization needs.

## Invoking URLs from domains that do and don't include crossdomain.xml

If a crossdomain.xml file exists (and defines the required security credentials) at the root of the domain from where the resource is being accessed using a URL, there are no security violations and things work just fine. If crossdomain.xml is missing, the URL request would terminate with a security exception. In general, it's a good idea to understand the crossdomain.xml file, the Flash Player security model, and its significance. It's highly recommended that you read the article titled "Policy file changes in Flash Player 9" by Deneb Meketa, accessible at htp://www.adobe.com/devnet/flashplayer/articles/fplayer9_security.html.

## Manipulating HTTP headers with requests

In short, HTTPService allows custom header settings for HTTP POST method calls but does not allow them for GET method calls. In REST (Representational State Transfer) style web services, this can be a problem because things from basic HTTP authentication to content type delivery depend on it. I'll pick the topic up again in the next section when I discuss URLLoader and compare and contrast it with HTTPService.

That concludes this discussion of HTTPService. Although HTTPService can utilize server-side proxy with data services, I did not cover any of that because I have not started with data services yet. (Data services are covered in Chapter 7.) One example of where data service impacts HTTPService: HTTP methods other than GET and POST can be used, and access to sites that don't define crossdomain.xml becomes possible under proxied situations.

Let's move on to flash.net.URLLoader and its associated classes.

# URLLoader, URLRequest, and URLVariables

HTTPService is the primary class in the Flex framework that makes it possible to make HTTP requests. It supports all types of text and XML formats to get and parse text-based data. It supports the popular HTTP GET and POST methods. It allows parameter passing and provides for event-based handling of call success and failure. In the last section, you learned all of this.

Now we start exploring alternatives to HTTPService. To begin with, Flex is a framework that creates applications that run in the Flash Player. Such applications are written using ActionScript and MXML and translated to bytecode and instructions that the Flash VM understands. Prior to the existence of Flex, ActionScript alone could be used successfully to create applications that ran in the Flash Player. It's possible to do that even today. I am not suggesting you avoid the Flex framework, only pointing out that there is more to application building in the Flash Player than Flex. Also, you can use all these extra good things in your Flex applications.

One example where the Flash libraries provide features available in the Flex framework is the presence of classes to support HTTP communication. URLLoader and its associated classes, URLRequest, URLStream, URLVariables, and URLRequestMethod, can be used instead of the Flex HTTPService class to incorporate HTTP-based requests in an application. URLLoader is positioned as the class that loads networked resources, and HTTPService is positioned as the class that fetches remote data, but they do many things in common and can be interchanged in many situations. Sometimes, using URLLoader appears to be a more robust option than using HTTPService. One such case is the facility to access binary data. URLLoader is quite capable of accessing any kind of binary data, say an image file. On the other hand, HTTPService invocations to access binary data end in an error condition.

To gently get started with URLLoader and its applicability, let's reimplement our HTTPService example using URLLoader. Here is the new code, done up as an MXML application:

```
<?xml version="1.0" encoding="utf-8"?>
<mx:Application xmlns:mx="http://www.adobe.com/2006/mxml" >
    <mx:Script>
        <![CDATA[

            import XMLDataURLLoader;

            private function loadXML():void {
                var xmlDataURLLoader:XMLDataURLLoader =
new XMLDataURLLoader();
                xmlDataURLLoader.loadXMLData();
                xmlDataURLLoader.myDataGrid.percentWidth = 100;
                xmlDataURLLoader.myDataGrid.percentHeight = 100;
                myVBox.addChild(xmlDataURLLoader.myDataGrid);
            }
        ]]>
    </mx:Script>
    <mx:VBox id="myVBox" width="100%" height="100%" />

    <mx:Button label="Invoke URlLoader" click="loadXML()"/>
    </mx:Application>
```

```
XMLDataURLLoader.as

package
{
    import flash.events.Event;
    import flash.net.URLLoader;
    import flash.net.URLRequest;

    import mx.collections.XMLListCollection;
    import mx.controls.DataGrid;
    import mx.controls.dataGridClasses.DataGridColumn;

    public class XMLDataURLLoader
{
        private var URL_String:String =
"http://localhost:8080/top10nbascorers/top10nbascorers.jsp";
        private var myXMLRequest:URLRequest =
new URLRequest(URL_String);
        private var myLoader:URLLoader = new URLLoader();
         [Bindable]
        public var myDataGrid:DataGrid = new DataGrid();

        public function XMLDataURLLoader() {
            //to be implemented
        }

        private function xmlLoad(event:Event):void {
            var myXML:XML = new XML(event.target.data);
            trace("Data loaded.");
            trace(myXML);
            //trace(myXML.top10ScorersCollection.scorer);

            /*firstName DataGrid column */
            var firstNameCol:DataGridColumn = new DataGridColumn();
            firstNameCol.headerText = "firstName";
            firstNameCol.dataField = "firstName";

            /*lastName DataGrid column */
            var lastNameCol:DataGridColumn = new DataGridColumn();
            lastNameCol.headerText = "lastName";
            lastNameCol.dataField = "lastName";

            /*totalScore DataGrid column */
            var totalScoreCol:DataGridColumn = new DataGridColumn();
            totalScoreCol.headerText = "totalScore";
            totalScoreCol.dataField = "totalScore";
```

```
        /*position DataGrid column */
        var positionCol:DataGridColumn = new DataGridColumn();
        positionCol.headerText = "position";
        positionCol.dataField = "position";

        var columnArray:Array = new Array();
        columnArray.push(firstNameCol);
        columnArray.push(lastNameCol);
        columnArray.push(totalScoreCol);
        columnArray.push(positionCol);
        myDataGrid["columns"] = columnArray;
        var myXMLListCollection:XMLListCollection =
new XMLListCollection(myXML.scorer);
        trace("XMLListCollection data bound to the Data Grid.");
        trace("XMLListCollection " + XMLListCollection);
        myDataGrid.dataProvider = myXMLListCollection;
                                        myDataGrid.percentWidth = 100;
                        myDataGrid.percentHeight = 100;
    }

        public function loadXMLData():void {
        myLoader.addEventListener(Event.COMPLETE, xmlLoad);
        myLoader.load(myXMLRequest);
        }
        }
    }
```

Explaining every single line of the preceding code would be redundant, so here is a quick summary. We create the URLLoader instance and load the XML data from the JSP. The load function of URLLoader uses a URLRequest object, which defines the URL. The returned XML is wrapped up in an XMLListCollection and bound to a data grid. The DataGrid is implemented using ActionScript alone. Its columns, corresponding data fields, and header texts are explicitly defined and set on the data grid. There is a button and a VBox component in the MXML application. The data grid is added as a child of the VBox component. The Button click handler indirectly, via an intermediate method, invokes the URLLoader load method. The URLLoader class triggers a set of events as the load activity progresses. In our example, we listen to the COMPLETE event. On completion, an event handler is activated. This event handler retrieves the returned data, parses it, and binds it to the data grid. That's about it!

Although URLLoader is quite similar to HTTPService in generating the output in our example, there are a few fundamental differences:

- The events triggered differ and allow for different approaches to interacting with the HTTP request.

- Binary responses are handled differently.

- URL variables and parameters manipulation possibilities vary.

- Support for HTTP methods is not identical.

## Life-cycle events in URLLoader and HTTPService

The URLLoader class defines the following events:

- complete (flash.events.Event.COMPLETE): Dispatched when the data is decoded and assigned to the data property of the URLLoader object. This is a good time to start using the loaded resource.

- httpStatus (flash.events.HTTPStatusEvent.HTTP_STATUS): Dispatched if the load method invokes a call over HTTP. URLLoader is not restricted to making HTTP calls only, although it's a popular choice. This event is triggered on an HTTP request, not a response. This event is triggered before the COMPLETE and error events.

- ioError (flash.events.IOErrorEvent.IO_ERROR): Dispatched if the request encounters a fatal IO error and terminates the request.

- open (flash.events.Event.OPEN): Dispatched when the request starts on invocation of the load method.

- progress (flash.events.ProgressEvent.PROGRESS): Dispatched as the resource gets downloaded. This event is most relevant when the resource is large, say a huge image file, and it downloads incrementally. A progress event is fired on each chunk of bytes getting downloaded.

- securityError (flash.events.SecurityErrorEvent.SECURITY_ERROR): Dispatched if the security sandbox is violated.

whereas the HTTPService class defines the following:

- result (mx.rpc.events.ResultEvent.RESULT): Dispatched when the HTTP call returns.

- fault (mx.rpc.events.FaultEvent.FAULT): Dispatched if the call ends up in an error. Interestingly, trying to access a binary resource, say an image file, using HTTPService also ends up in an error.

- invoke (mx.rpc.events.InvokeEvent.INVOKE): Dispatched when the call is initiated and no error has shown up yet.

Therefore, there is little event-driven control to monitor progress in HTTPService. The assumption, I guess, is that fetching data is going to be quick and simple, so monitoring progress is not relevant. Error handling and HTTP status propagation is better and more fine-grained in URlLoader.

## Binary resource access

The HTTPService class is simply incapable of handling binary resources. Try out the following simple code, which attempts the task of downloading an image:

```
<?xml version="1.0" encoding="utf-8"?>
<mx:Application xmlns:mx="http://www.adobe.com/2006/mxml">
<mx:Script>
    <![CDATA[
        import mx.controls.Image;

        import mx.controls.Alert;
        import mx.rpc.events.FaultEvent;
        import mx.rpc.events.ResultEvent;
```

```
import flash.utils.describeType;

function faultHandler(event:FaultEvent):void {
    Alert.show('Oops there is a problem!....' ➥
+ event.fault.faultString);
}

function resultHandler(event:ResultEvent):void {
    trace(describeType(event.result));
    var img:Image = new Image();
    var byteLoader:Loader=new Loader();
    var byteArray:ByteArray=new ByteArray();
    byteArray.writeUTFBytes(event.result as String);
    byteLoader.loadBytes(byteArray);
    var bitMap:Bitmap=Bitmap(byteLoader.content);
    img.source = bitMap;
    myVBox.addChild(img);
    Alert.show('It Works!....' + event.result);
}
    ]]>
</mx:Script>

<mx:HTTPService id="myHTTPService"
url="http://localhost:8080/top10nbascorers/Fx.png"
fault="faultHandler(event)" result="resultHandler(event)"/>

<mx:VBox id="myVBox" width="100%" height="100%" />

<mx:Button label="Invoke HTTPService" click="myHTTPService.send()"/>

</mx:Application>
```

Instead of the image coming through, you get an error. In debug mode, you will see this:

```
[SWF] C:\workfolder\eclipse\workspace\➥
top10nbascorers\bin-debug\binaryresource.swf ➥
- 852,490 bytes after decompression
<type name="String" base="Object"
isDynamic="false" isFinal="true" isStatic="false">
  <extendsClass type="Object"/>
  <constructor>
    <parameter index="1" type="*" optional="true"/>
  </constructor>
  <accessor name="length" access="readonly"
type="int" declaredBy="String"/>
</type>
Error #2044: Unhandled IOErrorEvent:. text=➥
Error #2124: Loaded file is an unknown type.
```

Why does this happen? HTTPService is meant to handle text-based data only. Therefore, the best way of including an image using it may be one of the following:

- Get the path to the image on the server and then assign it as the source of an image control. This will display the image correctly but will not work for all binary data types. Also if you need to download the image locally using this technique, you are out of luck.

- Encode the image in Base64 format, transmit it through, decode it, and then consume it. Base64 encoding translates binary data to plain ASCII text and is defined as part of the MIME specification. It reads data in 6 bits and translates it to a character in the 64-character alphabet set. You can read more about it at http://en.wikipedia.org/wiki/Base64. Flex3 has undocumented classes to encode/decode Base64 format: mx.utils.Base64Encoder and mx.utils.Base64Decoder.

Instead of trying out these workarounds, we could use the URLLoader class, which manages binary data loading with ease and elegance. We rewrite our example that failed using HTTPService to use URLLoader, and this time it works without any problem. Here is what the rewritten code looks like:

```
<?xml version="1.0" encoding="utf-8"?>
<mx:Application xmlns:mx="http://www.adobe.com/2006/mxml">
<mx:Script>
    <![CDATA[
        import ImageURLLoader;

            private function loadImageFunction():void {
                var imageURLLoader:ImageURLLoader =
new ImageURLLoader();
                imageURLLoader.loadImage();
                myVBox.addChild(imageURLLoader.myImage);
            }
    ]]>
</mx:Script>

<mx:VBox id="myVBox" width="100%" height="100%" />

<mx:Button label="Invoke URLLoader" click="loadImageFunction()"/>

</mx:Application>
...
package
{
    import flash.display.Loader;
    import flash.events.Event;
    import flash.net.URLLoader;
    import flash.net.URLLoaderDataFormat;
    import flash.net.URLRequest;
    import flash.utils.ByteArray;
    import flash.utils.describeType;

    import mx.controls.Image;
    import flash.display.Bitmap;
```

```
import mx.core.FlexLoader;


public class ImageURLLoader
{
    private var URL_String:String =
"http://localhost:8080/top10nbascorers/Fx.png";
    private var myImageRequest:URLRequest =
new URLRequest(URL_String);
    private var myLoader:URLLoader = new URLLoader();
    private var loader:FlexLoader = new FlexLoader();

    public var myImage:Image = new Image();

    public function ImageURLLoader()
{

        //TODO: implement function
        }

    private function imageLoad(event:Event):void {
        trace("Image loaded.");
        trace(describeType(event.target.data));

        loader.loadBytes(event.target.data);
        loader.contentLoaderInfo.addEventListener➥
(Event.COMPLETE,setLoadedBytesToImage);
        }

    public function setLoadedBytesToImage(event:Event):void {
        myImage.source = loader;
    }

    public function loadImage():void {
        myLoader.dataFormat = URLLoaderDataFormat.BINARY;
        //myLoader.addEventListener(Event.OPEN, imageLoad);
        myLoader.addEventListener(Event.COMPLETE, imageLoad);
        myLoader.load(myImageRequest);
    }

}
}
```

With URLLoader, image loading is effortless. The data format could be set to binary and the image
data stream could be read in an array of bytes. When all the bytes are streamed through, they
are bound as the source of an image control. A component called FlexLoader is used in this example.
FlexLoader is part of the BSD licensed open source Yahoo! ASTRA Flash classes. The documentation is
available at http://developer.yahoo.com/flash/astra-flex/classreference/mx/core/FlexLoader.html.
FlexLoader extends flash.display.Loader and overrides the toString method to show the hierarchy

of the object in the display objects' hierarchy. Although we used FlexLoader here and it's useful to know of the Yahoo! ASTRA classes, we could easily replace FlexLoader with Loader, and things will still work fine.

The URLLoader class could actually load any binary data stream. As long as you have the encoder/decoder in place, you can use this feature without limitations. In Java web applications, a servlet could easily write binary data to an output stream. Such binary data can be consumed with ease using URLLoader.

## URL variable and parameter manipulation

It's important that URL variables and the HTTP header can be manipulated. It's common to have proprietary object attributes bind as parameters to an HTTP call in both GET and POST method scenarios. In some cases (for instance, in REST), header manipulation also adds value.

REST is an architectural style that can be loosely defined as a way of transmitting domain-specific information over HTTP without the need of additional protocol layers, as in SOAP. Central to REST is the idea of **resources**, abstractions that are accessible using URIs and components (clients and servers), which access resource representations using simple interfaces. The REST style can be implemented without HTTP or the Internet, but it has become synonymous with the GET style of simple HTTP calls that makes up most of the World Wide Web. For more on REST, read Roy Fielding's PhD thesis, "Architectural Styles and the Design of Network-based Software Architectures," which introduced the term REST and defined the way we know it today. Roy's thesis can be accessed online at http://www.ics.uci.edu/~fielding/pubs/dissertation/top.htm.

REST defines safe idempotent services and obligated services. **Safe services** are repeatable and provide a representation of the resource to the client. **Obligated services** lead to the creation of new resources or representations of a resource. Safe services involve GET method requests, and obligated services involve POST method calls. In either situation, when a representation is negotiated by the client, it is necessary that header values be set appropriately for a request. This means you would need to manipulate HTTP headers before sending the request out.

HTTPService allows any object to be sent as an argument to its send method. A call to the send method initiates a request. The passed argument object's attributes and their corresponding values form the name-value pairs, which become arguments for the HTTP methods. Any number of attributes can be defined in the object, and values can be set for these attributes. It works with both GET and POST calls. In POST calls, it's also possible to set the header values. However, things break with HTTPService when you try to set the header for a GET method call. Sometimes this is necessary, as in the case of REST, and HTTPService falls short of the requirements here.

Time to reinforce what you have learned using a simple example! The example integrates the fulfillment and checkout functionality in a Flex application using the Google Checkout XML API. The entire code is available on open source terms on Google Project and can be accessed at http://code.google.com/p/flexcheckout/. Here we focus exclusively on sending API requests with basic HTTP authentication. Basic HTTP authentication requires that HTTP request headers are set appropriately. Details about what needs to be done can be read online at http://code.google.com/apis/checkout/developer/index.html#https_auth_scheme. The part that concerns us here is the three headers that need to be set for merchant authorization and authentication. An example of the headers as shown in the Google developer manual, reproduced here, is:

```
Authorization: Basic MTIzNDU2Nzg5MDpIc1lYRm9aZkhBcXlMYONSWWVIOHFR
Content-Type: application/xml;charset=UTF-8
Accept: application/xml;charset=UTF-8
```

To set these values, we create an object, create the attributes, assign the values, and assign the object to the headers property of an HTTPService. You have seen parameter passing before, so we will skip it this time and focus on the headers alone. A snippet of the header manipulation code is shown here:

```
<! - Call to Google Checkout XML API.
Sending API Request with HTTP Basic Authentication -- >
var headerObject = new Object();
headerObject["Authorization"] =
"Basic MTIzNDU2Nzg5MDpIc1lYRm9aZkhBcXlMYONSWWVIOHFR";
headerObject["Content-Type"] = "application/xml;charset=UTF-8";
headerObject["Accept"] = "application/xml;charset=UTF-8";
<! -- HTTPService that sends Google Checkout API requests -- >
<mx:HTTPService id="myHTTPService"
url=" https://checkout.google.com/api/➥
checkout/v2/request/Merchant/MERCHANT_ID"
/*A merchant on registration with Google
checkout receives a merchant ID,
which acts as the primary identifier
for the merchant within the Google checkout application.*/
fault="faultHandler(event)" result="resultHandler(event)"
headers="{headerObject}" method="GET"  />
```

When you send this request, it does not go through successfully. HTTPService does not allow header setting for GET method calls, so this fails. Header manipulation works only with POST method calls. This is a limitation, and workarounds like using the Socket class are a way out. The next section has a detailed illustration of this workaround. For now, we evaluate URLLoader to see if it can stand up to this challenge or not.

A URL request for URLLoader is defined using the URLRequest class. URL headers can be defined in a class called URLRequestHeader and associated with a URLRequest instance. Then a URLLoader could use the instance to send the request. This seems straightforward; see it in code:

```
var loader:URLLoader = new URLLoader();

//Add event listeners to the loader

//The Base64-encoded part of the string after
the keyword Basic could be dynamically
generated and appended to
Basic before it is assigned to a URlRequestHeader instance

var header1:URLRequestHeader =
new URLRequestHeader("Authorization", "Basic➥
MTIzNDU2Nzg5MDpIc1lYRm9aZkhBcXlMYONSWWVIOHFR");
var header2:URLRequestHeader =
new URLRequestHeader➥
```

```
("Content-Type", "application/xml;charset=UTF-8");
var header3:URLRequestHeader =
new URLRequestHeader("Accept", "application/xml;charset=UTF-8");

var request:URLRequest = new URLRequest("https://checkout.google.com/➥
api/checkout/v2/request/Merchant/MERCHANT_ID");

request.data = new URLVariables("name=value");
request.method = URLRequestMethod.GET;
request.requestHeaders.push(header1);
request.requestHeaders.push(header2);
request.requestHeaders.push(header3);

// Call load() method within a
try-catch block to handle invocation time errors
loader.load(request);
```

With the exception of restricting a few keywords, like get/Get/GET, and not allowing a few header types, like Accept-Ranges and Allow, the URLRequestHeader class lets you set custom headers. Where custom header setting is required, URLLoader shines compared to HTTPService.

## Support for HTTP methods

By default and in all situations, both HTTPService and URLLoader allow the HTTP GET and POST methods. These are the two most popular methods, and so this suffices in most situations. When using a server-side proxy and specifying so by flagging useProxy="true", HTTPService is able to send HEAD, OPTIONS, PUT, TRACE, and DELETE HTTP requests as well. (If you are rusty on where and how to use these additional HTTP methods, consider referring to the online W3C documentation at http://www.w3.org/Protocols/rfc2616/rfc2616-sec9.html.) URLLoader can make requests defined in the URLRequest class. The URLRequestMethod attribute can take only POST and GET as valued values. These values are defined in URLRequestMethod.

This puts us in a fix. We can't do header manipulation in GET calls with HTTPService, and we can't make any HTTP method calls other than POST and GET in URLLoader. If we needed both simultaneously, we would have to look outside of these two options. The last option is writing things ground-up on top of the Socket class. This is what we do in the next section. For now, let's look at another issue related to HTTP methods.

WebDAV is an open community–driven standard to extend HTTP for web authoring, while keeping things interoperable. To quote a line about its goals from the WebDAV charter: "define the HTTP extensions necessary to enable distributed web authoring tools to be broadly interoperable, while supporting user needs." Information about WebDAV is available at http://www.webdav.org/. WebDAV defines a few additional HTTP methods:

- PROPFIND: Retrieves properties (stored as XML) from a resource

- PROPPATCH: Modifies multiple properties of a resource at the same time (in a single transaction)

- MKCOL: Creates directory-like collections

- COPY: Copies a resource between URI(s)

- MOVE: Moves a resource between URI(s)

- LOCK: Locks (shared or exclusive) a resource
- UNLOCK: Unlocks a resource

Neither HTTPService nor URlLoader (with URLRequest) allows HTTP method extensions and definition of new ones. Thus they offer no support for WebDAV at the time of writing.

You have seen HTTPService and URLLoader; now it is time to look at the mechanism that uses the Socket class. In this day and age, spending time on low-level details is typically shunned in the software development world. In that sense, Socket is surely the bad guy in town!

## Using Sockets

AS3 defines two types of sockets, one that can be used to transmit XML data and another that can send binary data. You specify a host and a port, and Socket can create a connection on this host and port. The connection will stay alive until explicitly closed. Therefore, a persistent channel is opened up, and the client does not need to reconnect between requests if the connection is alive. The server can also send data back to the client on this connection.

Socket implements IDataInput and IDataOutput interfaces. IDataInput and IDataOutput define the different read and write methods, respectively. To get a full list of methods available to read bytes, boolean, integer, object, float, and double types, take a look at the ASDoc (accessible through Flex 3 LiveDocs). In this manner, Socket is similar to ByteArray and URLStream.

Creating and using a socket in ActionScript is no different in mechanism from creating and using a socket in almost any programming language. The Socket class acts as the socket client. That means you will need a socket server to listen to the requests that your client will make. You can write a socket server in any language of your choice. The code for a simple socket server written in Groovy follows. Groovy was chosen because in this chapter we are talking about integration with Java, and Groovy runs in the JVM. The obvious alternative would be to use Java itself instead of Groovy. There is a simple Java server example in the Flex 3 Live Docs, so re-creating the same example, or a similar one, would be a waste of space here. Also, I wish to reinforce the idea that you can use Groovy, Jython, JRuby, or Scala instead of Java itself in the JVM. That means many Java-specific things discussed in this chapter will hold true for these other JVM languages as well.

```
server = new ServerSocket(8080)
while(true) {
    server.accept() { socket ->
        socket.withStreams { input, output ->
            w = new PrintWriter(output)
            w << "ActionScript Socket Client is Sending Some Through"
            w.flush()
            r = input.readLine()
            System.err.println
"Message received by the the server socket $r"
            w.close()
        }
    }
}
```

Now that you have the server socket, it is time to create the socket and send a message to the listening server socket. Either Socket or XMLSocket could be created. The choice depends on the type of data transmitted. Our server socket is quite elementary and is not reading for binary data, so we create a simple XMLSocket instance. The code for the XMLSocket client could be as follows:

```
package {
    import flash.display.Sprite;
    import flash.events.*;
    import flash.net.XMLSocket;

    public class MyXMLSocket extends Sprite {
        private var hostName:String = "domain.com";
        private var port:uint = 8080;
        private var socket:XMLSocket;

        public function MyXMLSocket() {
            socket = new XMLSocket();
            configureListeners(socket);
            socket.connect(hostName, port);
        }

        public function send(data:Object):void {
            socket.send(data);
        }

        private function configureListeners➥
(dispatcher:IEventDispatcher):void {
            dispatcher.addEventListener(Event.CLOSE, closeHandler);
            dispatcher.addEventListener(Event.CONNECT, connectHandler);
            dispatcher.addEventListener(DataEvent.DATA, dataHandler);
            dispatcher.addEventListener➥
(IOErrorEvent.IO_ERROR, ioErrorHandler);
            dispatcher.addEventListener➥
(ProgressEvent.PROGRESS, progressHandler);
            dispatcher.addEventListener➥
(SecurityErrorEvent.SECURITY_ERROR, securityErrorHandler);
        }

        private function closeHandler(event:Event):void {
            trace("closeHandler: " + event);
        }

        private function connectHandler(event:Event):void {
            trace("connectHandler: " + event);
        }

        private function dataHandler(event:DataEvent):void {
            trace("dataHandler: " + event);
        }
```

```
            private function ioErrorHandler(event:IOErrorEvent):void {
                trace("ioErrorHandler: " + event);
            }

            private function progressHandler(event:ProgressEvent):void {
                trace("progressHandler loaded:" ➡
     + event.bytesLoaded + " total: " + event.bytesTotal);
            }

            private function securityErrorHandler➡
        (event:SecurityErrorEvent):void {
                trace("securityErrorHandler: " + event);
            }
        }
    }
```

The assumption is that the server socket is running locally. In such an instance, the preceding code works without any extra help. In real-life deployment environments, this will rarely be the case. The server socket would run on some domain.com and would listen on some port, say 8080. Like everything else in Flash, the player security restrictions and requirements will kick in. A policy file will need to be defined so that such operations are permitted. It's possible to configure the application in such a way that the policy file is read over the same port, and then the socket connection is established and used for communication.

In this chapter, the primary inspiration is to integrate Flex and Java. Often the remote data published by Java is going to be accessible over standard protocols like HTTP. So classes like HTTPService and URLLoader would be enough to communicate in most cases. However, as seen before, both these classes have their limitations, and in some cases, it is a viable idea to use the Socket class. In such cases, the requirement may be to connect over port 80, which is usually the default HTTP port. According to the security policy, any port below 1024 when accessed through Sockets needs special permission in its policy files. So once more, we would have to ensure that the policy file has the relevant permissions and is in place.

This ends our peek into the Socket classes. However, before it's time to wrap up and move to the next topic, it is extremely important to mention a few things about Sockets:

- AS3 does not define any server Socket class. It is not expecting an application running in the Flash Player to act as one.

- Data could be sent over the persistent Socket connection, without being asked for. So, data streaming from the server to the client can be achieved quite efficiently. Such arriving data triggers the DataEvent.DATA event.

- Data upload onto the Socket channel is asynchronous, and as of now, there is no way to measure how much of it has been transmitted to the server until the entire process completes.

- If you are looking to write an HTTP client using Socket so that the limitations of HTTPService and URLLoader are eradicated, you are in luck. Do not reinvent the wheel, just go ahead and use as3httpclientlib (http://code.google.com/p/as3httpclientlib/). This library's API resembles the Apache HTTP client, simple and clean.

- Sockets can be used to build real-time systems where the server needs to stream data up to the client, but it wouldn't work if this connection has a firewall to cross.

That finishes our look at Sockets. Although there's more to the topic than what I cover here, further discussion is outside the scope of this book. Next, we jump to the second main topic of this chapter: web services.

# Integration through web services

A web service, to quote W3C, is "a software system designed to support interoperable machine-to-machine interaction over a network." Rapid adoption in the last few years has taken this standard from obscurity to ubiquity. In general, the idea is simple: service consumers look up a registry, discover a service, which exposes its public operation using a metadata file, and invoke its operations. Service producers create services that are accessible along with the metadata that defines what they are capable of, what they accept, and what they return.

Over the years, there has been much activity and debate over ways to define metadata, expose operations, encode messages, and consume them. SOAP and REST have emerged as the two most popular web service architectural styles. SOAP is a robust choice for building interoperable web services using XML messages. REST uses the basic concepts behind HTTP and the World Wide Web (see the section "URL variable and parameter manipulation" earlier in this chapter). These are not the only two. Following are some other standards linked to web services:

- JSON-RPC
- XINS
- Burlap
- GXA
- Hessian
- XML-RPC
- BEEP

Flex 3 officially supports only SOAP. You have seen in the last section how you could also manage to use REST. JSON-RPC and XML-RPC can be incorporated with the help of a few open libraries. Hessian can be used with Flex quite easily and is well supported as an alternative to sending AMF (Action Message Format) binary data.

Let's start with the stuff that's official: SOAP.

## Using SOAP-based web services

SOAP defines the protocol and messaging layer that enables XML messaging between service producers and service consumers. The most common style of interaction involves RPC between one node (the client) and another node (the server). In order to make this happen, SOAP uses a specification called Web Services Description Language (WSDL) to define network services as a set of endpoints. The set of endpoints are essentially operations that act on messages, which contain document- or procedure-oriented information. WSDL describes the service endpoints in an XML format.

In order to consume a SOAP-based web service in Flex, we first create a WebService object. WebService is the implementation class that abstracts all web service–related features in an object-oriented manner. After that, we access the associated WSDL file. Once WSDL information is read, it is used to initialize the WebService object appropriately, by setting its property values. Now we are ready to call a web service method or operation. A web service component defines a few events that map to the life cycle of a web service interaction and allows for listeners to be added for these events. Two logical outcomes are possible in a method call: success or failure. WebService dispatches events of these two types. They are called result and fault. So, we define event handlers for each of these methods and register them. Finally, we make the web service method call and consume the results.

In Flex Builder 3, there is a nifty little feature to automate the process of web service proxy generation. You could point to a WSDL file, and it generates the proxy automatically by introspecting the WSDL. We can always hand code the web service proxies and look up the allowed operations by browsing the WSDL port type section, but I will favor productivity here. If you don't use Flex Builder to build Flex applications, then you will have to go back to hand coding.

To keep our focus on SOAP web services consumption, let's look at a simple example. On the XMethods web site (http://www.xmethods.net) is a list of publicly available web services that you could use. One of the services on that list helps validate 10- and 13-digit ISBNs. An ISBN, short for International Standard Book Number, is a unique way of identifying a published and cataloged item. This web service is provided by a company called Data Access Europe BV (http://www.dataaccess.eu). To get started, we get hold of the WSDL. You can get it from http://webservices.daehosting.com/services/isbnservice.wso?WSDL.

We create a Flex project in Flex Builder. In our case, we call it ISBNValidationWebService. Now we do the following (to generate the web service proxies on the basis of WSDL):

1. Select Import Web Services from the Data menu in Flex Builder. The screen looks as shown in Figure 6-6. This brings the wizard up.

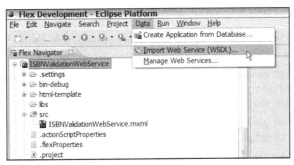

**Figure 6-6.** Select Import Web Services from the Data menu to start the process of web service proxy generation on the basis of WSDL.

2. In the wizard, specify which source folder would you like the web service proxies to reside in.

**3.** Next, point to the WSDL URI. Figure 6-7 shows how I did it. At this stage, you also have two radio button options to choose between that allow either direct client access (which requires crossdomain.xml) or proxied access (which implies going through a data service). Because we have not started with remoting yet, select Directly from the client.

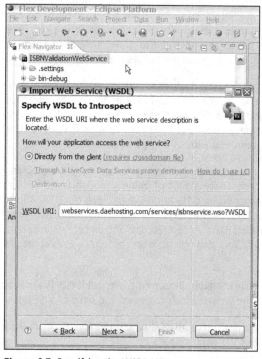

**Figure 6-7.** Specifying the WSDL URI

**4.** The tool quickly introspects the WSDL and shows the available operations in the next screen, as you can see in Figure 6-8.

**5.** Next, click Finish to generate the required ActionScript classes. It's possible to change the package structure. It's also possible to deselect services for which you do not want to generate stubs. You can also select a different service and or port.

**6.** The classes are all generated and, as specified, are in the destination source folder in the desired package structure.

It's possible to update the generated classes by adding, deleting, and modifying existing entries. This can be done using the Manage Web Services option in the Data menu. You can read more about this online in Flex 3 LiveDocs (http://livedocs.adobe.com/flex/3/html/data_4.html).

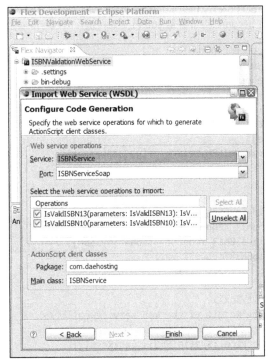

**Figure 6-8.** Web service operation endpoints as deciphered from WSDL

The automated process generates the following eight classes:

- BaseISBNService.as
- BaseISBNServiceSchema.as
- IISBNService.as
- ISBNService.as
- IsValidISBN10_request.as
- IsValidISBN10ResultEvent.as
- IsValidISBN13_request.as
- IsValidISBN13ResultEvent.as

These generated web proxies are now ready to be consumed. When we create the Flex project, the MXML application file is created. We retain the default name, so it's called ISBNValidationWebService.mxml. If you wish to name it something else, you are free to do so.

In ISBNValidationWebService.mxml, first make the web proxy classes available by attaching a namespace to it. The namespace is aliased ws for short. In our small example, we validate a 13-digit book ISBN. The argument value is set to the ISBN of this book (*AdvancED Flex 3*), which is 9781430210276. An ISBNService instance is created and an instance of IsValidISBN13_request is passed to the service instance. The application has a button and text control. The click event of the button triggers a call to the web service method (procedure), which validates the 13-digit ISBN. The result of the call is bound to the text control. Things will become clearer as you look through the code, which is included here:

```xml
<?xml version="1.0" encoding="utf-8"?>
<mx:Application xmlns:mx="http://www.adobe.com/2006/mxml"
xmlns:ws="com.daehosting.*" >
<mx:Script>
    <![CDATA[
        /* Advanced Flex3 (Apress) ISBN */
        [Bindable]
        private var myISBN:String = "9781430210276";
    ]]>
</mx:Script>

<ws:ISBNService id="myISBNWebService">
    <ws:isValidISBN13_request_var>
        <ws:IsValidISBN13_request sISBN="{myISBN}" />
    </ws:isValidISBN13_request_var>
</ws:ISBNService>

<mx:VBox id="resultVBox">
    <mx:Label text="Result of the web service call:"/>
    <mx:Text id="textOutput"
text="{myISBNWebService.isValidISBN13_lastResult}"
fontWeight="bold"/>
</mx:VBox>

<mx:Button id="myButton"
label="Call ISBN 13 validation operation"
click="myISBNWebService.isValidISBN13_send()" />
</mx:Application>
```

Although this is a simple example, you will have realized that consuming web services using the introspection tool is quite appealing. If you would like to go the traditional route, you could use the <mx:WebService /> tag. In using that tag, you need to know in advance the callable remote methods or procedures, exposed as web service endpoints. This can be done using some means of introspection or by the crude method of browsing the port type definitions in WSDL. If the WSDL exposes very few methods, there would be little problem with physically looking it up, else it could be a tedious effort. The rest of the logic, which involves service invocation and result handling, is hardly different from our previous method. As always in Flex, the service has two events that it can dispatch: result and fault. If the call goes through successfully, our result handler populates the text; otherwise it errors out. Let's morph our existing example within this style; here is how it looks:

```xml
<?xml version="1.0" encoding="utf-8"?>
<mx:Application xmlns:mx="http://www.adobe.com/2006/mxml">
<mx:Script>
    <![CDATA[
        import mx.rpc.events.ResultEvent;
        import mx.rpc.events.FaultEvent;
        import mx.rpc.soap.LoadEvent;
```

```
    import mx.controls.Alert;

    /* Advanced Flex3 (Apress) ISBN */
     [Bindable]
    private var myISBN:String = "9781430210276";
     [Bindable]
    private var resultString:String;

    private function loadHandler(event:LoadEvent):void {
        trace("WSDL Loaded");
        trace(event.wsdl.xml);
    }

    private function resultHandler(event:ResultEvent):void {
        resultString = event.result as String;
        trace(resultString);
    }

    private function faultHandler(event:FaultEvent):void {
        resultString = event.fault.faultString;
        Alert.show(resultString);
    }

    ]]>
</mx:Script>

<mx:WebService id="myISBNWebService" wsdl=
"http://webservices.daehosting.com/➥
services/isbnservice.wso?WSDL"
    load="loadHandler(event)"
    result="resultHandler(event)"
    fault="faultHandler(event)" />

<mx:VBox id="resultVBox">
    <mx:Label text="Result of the web service call:"/>
    <mx:Text id="textOutput" text="{resultString}" fontWeight="bold"/>
</mx:VBox>

<mx:Button id="myButton"
label="Call ISBN 13 validation operation"
click="myISBNWebService.IsValidISBN13(myISBN)" />
</mx:Application>
```

In our example, we call a single web service method. It's possible to call two or more methods at the same time. If a button's click event invokes two methods, say method1() and method2(), of a web service referenced by the ID myWebService, its click event looks like this:

```
click=" myWebService.method1();myWebService.method2()"
```

Doing this without making any other modifications will imply that the two methods have a common set of result and fault handlers. This may not be the desired behavior. Different methods would likely need different result handlers because the results will need to be processed appropriately. Sometimes, they may even need different fault handlers. Not to worry, it's easy to define a unique event handler for each of the methods. Just include as many <mx:operation/> compiler tags as the number of methods, for which you need unique handlers. A possible implementation may look like this:

```
<mx:WebService id="myWebService"
wsdl="http://localhost:portNumber/Simple?wsdl"
load=" myWebService.method1(); myWebService.methd2()"
fault="genericFaultHandler(event)">
<mx:operation name="method1" result="method1ResultHandler(event)"/>
<mx:operation name="method2" result="method2ResultHandler(event)"/>
</mx:WebService>
```

Fault and result handlers can be defined for each operation in a web service endpoint. If there are multiple operations and some of these do not have custom fault or result handlers, the default <mx:operation> tag-level fault and result handlers are used. The assumption is that the tag-level fault and result handlers are defined.

The information so far would get you through most SOAP web services consumption in Flex, without any problem. Remember that web services are subject to the same security constraints as HTTPService calls. This implies that a crossdomain.xml file with correct configurations will need to reside in a web service provider domain, if it's different from the one from which the Flex SWF is served.

## A REST web service in action

A fair bit of discussion and analysis of REST has already been included in the earlier sections on HTTPService and URLLoader. Let's walk through a complete simple example to reinforce what you have learned so far.

Our example application uses the Yahoo! News Search REST API to fetch news items and then display them on a Flex-built interface. To get started, register with the Yahoo! Developer Network and get an application ID. The application ID is a mandatory part of every request you make to the Yahoo! API. It's easy to get one; just go to http://developer.yahoo.com/wsregapp/index.php.

Yahoo! News Search involves simple HTTP REST calls that you can hand code fairly easily in ActionScript and consume in your Flex application. Essentially, you would create a query with all the required parameters and the headers. Use URLRequest, URLRequestHeader, and URLVariables to do this. Then pass the URLRequest instance (which contains all the arguments for the REST call) to a URLLoader instance and send a request to the service. Once the result returns, consume it and bind it to a view component.

This is exactly what I intended to do here, but then I stumbled upon the excellent client libraries implemented by Yahoo! to do this. Yahoo! has client libraries for the Search API in almost all major languages, and they package and distribute them as part of the SDK. You can download the SDK from http://developer.yahoo.com/search/ by following the link available with the section labeled

Download the SDK. These client libraries will save you from reinventing the wheel. If you plan to write a Flex/ActionScript client component for REST web service calls, use this implementation as a guideline to work with.

Once I got down to using the Yahoo! AS3 client, all I had to do was consume it in my application. This is what I did:

```
<?xml version="1.0" encoding="utf-8"?>
<mx:Application
    xmlns:mx="http://www.adobe.com/2006/mxml"
    xmlns:yahoo="com.yahoo.webapis.search.*" >

    <!-- The formatter to format the total results with commas -->
    <mx:NumberFormatter id="commaFormatter"/>

    <!-- The Service for all types of searches -->
    <yahoo:SearchService id="searchService"
applicationId="YahooDemo"
query="{criteriaTextInput.text}"
type="web"
maximumResults="50"/>

    <!-- The form for searching -->
    <mx:HBox defaultButton="{searchButton}">

        <mx:TextInput id="criteriaTextInput"/>
        <mx:Button id="searchButton"
label="search"
click="searchService.send()"/>

    </mx:HBox>

    <mx:Label
text="{commaFormatter.format(➥
searchService.numResultsAvailable)}
results" visible="{Boolean(searchService.numResultsAvailable)}"/>

    <!-- The results as a List -->
    <mx:List id="resultsList"
showDataTips="true"
dataProvider="{searchService.lastResult}"
variableRowHeight="true" width="100%" height="100%">
        <mx:itemRenderer>
            <mx:Component>
            <mx:VBox toolTip="{data.summary}"
doubleClickEnabled="true"
```

```
            doubleClick="navigateToURL(➡
            new URLRequest(data.clickURL), '_blank')">
                        <mx:HBox >
                        <mx:Label text="{data.index  + 1}" width="25"/>
                        <mx:Text text="{data.name}" fontWeight="bold"/>
                        </mx:HBox>
                        <mx:Image source="{data.thumbnail.url}" />
                </mx:VBox>
                </mx:Component>
                </mx:itemRenderer>
            </mx:List>
        </mx:Application>
```

I will not explain the Yahoo! client library itself. For that, you can peruse the ASDoc available in the SDK. Let me assure you it's intuitive and easy to understand.

With that, the REST web service example is complete. Now, let's move on to a few web service protocols beyond SOAP and REST. XML-RPC, JSON-RPC, and Hessian (from Caucho Technologies—http://www.caucho.com) seem the best alternatives beyond the big two.

# Understanding the potential of XML-RPC

XML-RPC is a simple set of specifications and software that lets distributed applications talk to each other. It is based on exchanging XML messages over HTTP. The official web site for XML-RPC is at http://www.xmlrpc.com/. Plenty of documentation and information about the vibrant XML-RPC community is available at this site.

XML-RPC is a protocol that makes remote procedure calling possible. It uses the HTTP POST method for this purpose. The XML payload is sent as the body of an HTTP POST request. Responses also come back as XML. It supports basic types like strings, numbers, and dates and also complex types like lists and records. Details about the request-and-response format can be obtained by reading the specification, available online at http://www.xmlrpc.com/spec.

There are two entities involved in an XML-RPC communication. They play the roles of the client and the server. When you integrate Flex and Java using XML-RPC, you can usually expect Flex to be the client and Java to be the server. Therefore, I present an example application here to illustrate that XML-RPC usage assumes the same roles.

Let's start with the server. To get it up and running, we do the following:

1. Create a class with a few methods. In our case, we create a very simple Java class that joins two strings and reverses a given string. Here is what the code looks like:

```
package org.advancedflex.chapter06.xmlrpc;

public class StringManipulator {

        public String joinString➡
(String firstString, String secondString) {
                return firstString + secondString;
        }
```

```
public String reverseString (Syring sourceString) {
    int i, len = sourceString.length();
    StringBuffer dest = new StringBuffer(len);

    for (i = (len - 1); i >= 0; i--)
        dest.append(sourceString.charAt(i));

    return dest.toString();
    }
}
```

**2.** Configure and set up an XML-RPC server. We won't create one here because there are many good ones available out there, and it's easy to include them in a Java web application.

**3.** Expose the methods of our class so that they could be invoked remotely over XML-RPC.

We choose the XML-RPC implementation from Apache, called Apache XML-RPC, for our example application in this chapter. Information and downloads related to the Apache XML-RPC implementation are accessible at http://ws.apache.org/xmlrpc/index.html. The Apache XML-RPC server can be effortlessly included in a Java web application (a servlet container or a Java EE application server). We use Tomcat.

The first thing we do is to download the latest stable release of the software. Get the binary version of the distribution (the file ending with extension .bin.tar.gz), unless you intend to modify the source code.

Copy the following files from the lib directory of the distribution to your WEB-INF/lib folder:

- commons-logging-1.1.jar
- ws-commons-util-1.0.2.jar
- xmlrpc-common-3.1.jar
- xmlrpc-server-3.1.jar
- xmlrpc-client-3.1.jar

The last one on this list—xmlrpc-client-3.1.jar—is not required because our client is going to reside in the Flex application, and we are not going to use a Java client. However, it may be useful to retain it for testing.

The version number I am using is 3.1 because it's the latest stable release number. Yours could vary depending on when you download this software.

The server implementation includes an object called XmlRpcServer, which receives and executes RPC calls. This server object can be embedded in a servlet container or a web server. XmlRpcServlet, which is available with the server distribution, contains an embedded instance of XmlRpcServer. The example at hand is elementary, so it's best to use this servlet, XmlRpcServlet, which can get us started very quickly.

The object containing the methods that need to be exposed over XML-RPC should be configured with XmlRpcServlet. This can be done by making an entry in the XmlRpcServlet.properties file. For our object, the entry looks like this:

```
StringManipulator=org.advancedflex.chapter06.xmlrpc.StringManipulator
```

The last thing we need to do before we are ready to use XmlRpcServlet is to configure it in web.xml. Add the following entries to the file:

```
<servlet>
        <servlet-name>XmlRpcServlet</servlet-name>
        <servlet-class>org.apache.xmlrpc.➥
webserver.XmlRpcServlet</servlet-class>
        <init-param>
            <param-name>enabledForExtensions</param-name>
            <param-value>true</param-value>
            <description>
                Sets, whether the servlet supports
vendor extensions for XML-RPC.
            </description>
        </init-param>
</servlet>
<servlet-mapping>
        <servlet-name>XmlRpcServlet</servlet-name>
        <url-pattern>/xmlrpc</url-pattern>
</servlet-mapping>
```

The XML-RPC server is now ready to be accessed over the following endpoint: http://127.0.0.1:8080/xmlrpc.

The assumption is that the server is running locally and Tomcat is listening for HTTP on port 8080.

Next, we do the following:

1. Create a client application able to communicate over XML-RPC.
2. Make the Flex client and the Java server talk to each other over XML-RPC.

To create the Flex client, the idea is again to avoid reinventing the wheel. So an obvious choice is to use an existing open source library. There is one available: as3-rpclib (http://code.google.com/p/as3-rpclib/), which seems the most robust open source library achieving this functionality for Flex, although at the time of writing it still claims to be in beta phase. The library implements HTTPService-based support for RPC over AMF0 (binary original AMF format), XML-RPC, and JSON-RPC (which I discuss next). We use it for JSON-RPC as well.

The first step is to download the library and get hold of the SWC file. Next, as with any Flex application (with Flex Builder), we create a Flex project and go with the defaults. We add the as3-rpclib.swc file to the library path. Figure 6-9 shows a snapshot while we are adding the SWC file.

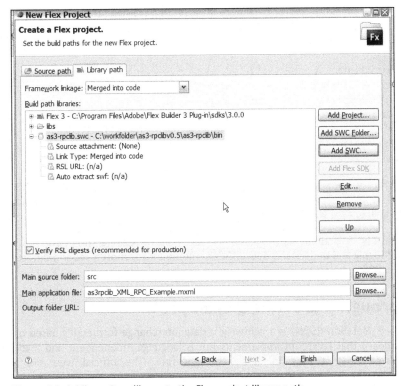

**Figure 6-9.** Adding as3-rpclib.swc to the Flex project library path

All the setup is done, and finally we create the Flex application code that uses XML-RPC to communicate with the server we created a short while back. The server exposes the two string manipulation methods over the channel, and that is what our Flex application invokes. Here is the Flex application code:

```
<mx:Application xmlns:mx="http://www.adobe.com/2006/mxml"
layout="absolute"
xmlns:as3rpclib="com.ak33m.rpc.xmlrpc.*"
creationComplete="callFunction();">
    <mx:Script>
      <![CDATA[
        import mx.controls.Alert;

        var firstString:String;
        var secondString:String;

        var output:String;

        function callFunction ()
        {
          output = xmlrpctojava.joinString(firstString,secondString);
          trace(output);
```

```
                output = xmlrpctojava.reverseString(firstString);
                trace(output);
            }
        ]]>
    </mx:Script>
    <as3rpclib:XMLRPCObject id="xmlrpctojava"
endpoint="http://127.0.0.1:8080/xmlrpc"
destination="xmlrpcendpoint"
fault="Alert.show(event.fault.faultString,event.fault.faultCode)">
    </as3rpclib:XMLRPCObject >
</mx:Application>
```

The XMLRPCObject is the key component of the as3-rpclib library that provides the XML-RPC client functionality. The XMLRPCObject indirectly inherits from mx.rpc.AbstractService, which is the base class for both WebService and RemoteObject.

This is all I will say here about XML-RPC. To use XML-RPC in real-life situations, you should study as3-rpclib thoroughly and understand how different method invocation types and different data types work with XML-RPC.

# Walking through a JSON-RPC example

JavaScript Object Notation (JSON) is a lightweight data interchange format. It's based on a subset of the ECMA standard that JavaScript implements but is language independent and involves a simple text-based format that is easy to parse and generate. The official web site for JSON is http://www.json.org.

AS3 Core Library (http://code.google.com/p/as3corelib/), an open source and well-supported library for AS3, has utility classes to serialize and parse JSON messages. If your remote Java source publishes data in JSON format and is accessible over a URL, you could get the data and consume it with the help of this library. A simple application may look like this:

```
<?xml version="1.0" encoding="utf-8"?>
<mx:Application xmlns:mx="http://www.adobe.com/2006/mxml" xmlns="*"
    creationComplete="service.send()">

    <mx:Script>
        <![CDATA[
            import mx.collections.ArrayCollection;
            import mx.rpc.events.ResultEvent;
            import com.adobe.serialization.json.JSON;

            private function onJSONLoad(event:ResultEvent):void
            {
                //get the raw JSON data and cast to String
                var rawData:String = String(event.result);

                //decode the data to ActionScript using the JSON API
                //in this case, the JSON data
                is a serialize Array of Objects.
```

```
                var arr:Array = (JSON.decode(rawData) as Array);

                //create a new ArrayCollection
passing the de-serialized Array
                //ArrayCollections work better
as DataProviders, as they can
                //be watched for changes.
                var dp:ArrayCollection = new ArrayCollection(arr);

                //pass the ArrayCollection to
the DataGrid as its dataProvider.
                grid.dataProvider = dp;


            }
        ]]>
    </mx:Script>

    <mx:HTTPService id="service" resultFormat="text"
            url="http://someurl.com/somedata.json"
            result="onJSONLoad(event)" />

    <mx:DataGrid id="grid" right="10" left="10" top="10" bottom="10">
        <mx:columns>
                <mx:DataGridColumn
headerText="Service" dataField="src"/>
                <mx:DataGridColumn
headerText="Title" dataField="title"/>
        </mx:columns>
    </mx:DataGrid>
</mx:Application>
```

JSON-RPC is a lightweight Remote Procedure Call specification that uses the simple but powerful JSON message scheme. JSON-RPC defines communication between two peers. The specification does not limit the type of protocol for communication but recommends persistent communication over TCP/IP-based socket connections. JSON-RPC could also use HTTP with a few workarounds. The peers can send two types of messages:

- Requests that are replied to with a response
- Notifications that are not replied to

A remote method call translates to sending one of these two types of messages. In each case, the message is a single object serialized using JSON.

Request objects have three properties:

- Method: Name of the method to be invoked
- Params: Array of arguments
- Id: Request identifier

Notification has the same three properties but null for Id, because notifications are not expected to get a response.

Responses to requests have three properties:

- Result: Returned object. Null if error.
- Error: Returned error object. Null of no error.
- Id: Same as the request identifier.

In order to communicate between a Flex application and a Java server using JSON-RPC, you would need to create JSON-RPC-related gateways/endpoints, serializers, and parsers at both ends.

A Java JSON-RPC server can be easily set up. jabsorb (http://jabsorb.org/), a JSON-RPC implementation for Java, can easily be set up with a web application to act as a JSON-RPC server. We will not include the details of the server setup here, but it is fairly simple and involves inclusion of jabsorb libraries, a servlet configuration, and registration with web.xml.

Assuming the JSON-RPC endpoint is accessible at http://localhost:8080/jsonrpc, we create a Flex application to consume it. Once again we use the as3-rpclib to create the Flex client. The steps to set that up in a Flex project are identical to what I explained in the section "Understanding the potential of XML-RPC." Finally, we code the application, as follows:

```
<mx:Application
xmlns:mx="http://www.adobe.com/2006/mxml"
layout="absolute" xmlns:as3rpclib="com.ak33m.rpc.jsonrpc.*"
creationComplete="callFunction();">
    <mx:Script>
        <![CDATA[
          import mx.controls.Alert;

          var firstString:String;
          var secondString:String;

          var output:String;

          function callFunction ()
          {
            output = jsonrpctojava.joinString(firstString,secondString);
            trace(output);

            output = jsonrpctojava.reverseString(firstString);
            trace(output);
          }
        ]]>
    </mx:Script>
    <as3rpclib:JSONRPCObject id="jsonrpctojava"
endpoint="http://127.0.0.1:8080/jsonrpc"
destination="jsonrpcendpoint"
fault="Alert.show(event.fault.faultString,event.fault.faultCode)">
```

```
        </as3rpclib:JSONRPCObject >
    </mx:Application>
```

The example reuses the same string manipulation class that we used in the XML-RPC example. The only difference is that we use JSON-RPC as the communication protocol instead of XML-RPC and so use a different server infrastructure. JSONRPCObject is similar to XMLRPCObject and also indirectly extends mx.rpc.AbstractService.

XML-RPC and JSON-RPC are both popular protocols for communication between disparate systems. They are based on open standards and offer alternatives to SOAP and REST web services. Although more popular in the JavaScript-driven Ajax world, they have a place in the realm of Flex applications as well. All the communication mechanisms discussed so far involve text-based messaging and have their own limitations related to latency, high volume, and complex structure transmission. Flex brings the efficiency of binary communication with AMF. In the next chapter, which covers remoting to a Java server, I focus on this and show you how the data services infrastructure provides effective integration between Flex and Java. However, before I discuss that, let's take a quick look at Hessian, a binary web services protocol developed by Caucho Technologies. Hessian can be used to combine Flex and Java, and it provides an alternative binary communication to AMF.

## Combining Hessian and Flex

Hessian is a binary web services protocol that is open sourced under the Apache 2.0 license. It has language-specific implementations for many popular languages including Java, Python, Flash/Flex, Ruby, C# .NET, and PHP. Our interest lies in the Java and Flash/Flex implementations.

For this discussion, we will skip the part on Hessian support and configuration on the Java server side. We will assume that is ready to use. It comes preconfigured in Resin, the application server from Caucho Technologies, the creators of Hessian. In others, it can be configured fairly easily.

Methods exposed on the remote service are the only piece that will be quickly discussed. Once again, we implement the same mundane yet useful service that exposes two methods, one that joins two strings and the other that reverses as String. This time we separate the server-side class into an interface and an implementation. The interface will look like this:

```
package org.advancedflex.chapter06.hessian;

    public interface StringManipulator {

        public String➥
joinString(String firstString, String secondString) ;

        public String reverseString (Syring sourceString) ;
    }
```

The corresponding implementation class would look like this:

```
package org.advancedflex.chapter06.hessian;

    public class StringManipulatorImpl
extends HessianServlet implements StringManipulator {
```

```
        public String➡
joinString(String firstString, String secondString) {
        return firstString + secondString;
    }

        public String reverseString (Syring sourceString) {
        int i, len = sourceString.length();
        StringBuffer dest = new StringBuffer(len);

        for (i = (len - 1); i >= 0; i--)
            dest.append(sourceString.charAt(i));

        return dest.toString();
    }
}
```

To use Hessian to communicate from Flex to Java, we employ the Hessian client-side library for Flash/Flex. The SWC library file is available for download from the Hessian home page (http://hessian.caucho.com/). For Flex, you need to get hessian-flex-*version_number*.swc from the binary distribution list. Links to API documentation and example applications (including server-side push using Comet) are available from this page.

The Hessian Flash/Flex client library uses mx.rpc.AbstractService and mx.rpc.AbstractOperations like the libraries for XML-RPC, JSON-RPC, WebService, and RemoteService. The service that manages RPC extends AbstractService, and the remote methods map to AbstractOperations. The primary component is abstracted as HessianService, and that is where we configure the remote Hessian destination. In MXML, this tag looks like this:

```
<hessian:HessianService xmlns:hessian="hessian.mxml.*"
    id="hessianService" destination="remoteDestination"/>
```

The destination is what points to the Hessian server endpoint or gateway. By specifying only remoteDestination, we are implying a relative path from the SWF application path. Therefore, a SWF application at a path of the type http://domain:port/approot/MyApp.swf, wanting to access the Hessian endpoint at http://domain:port/approot/remoteDestination, would specify the destination as remoteDestination. Fully qualified URLs can also be assigned as values to the destination property. If the domain of the Hessian endpoint and the SWF are different, the Flash security restrictions apply; do not forget to put a crossdomain.xml file at the remote server root, appropriately configured as needed.

In our Flex application code, we will invoke the remote methods with the configured HessianService handle. So a call to joinString would look somewhat like this:

```
hessianService.joinString.send(firstStringParam, secondStringParam);
```

A call to the Hessian service is asynchronous, where the send method maps to mx.rpc.AbstractOperation.send(), so we need to use the AsyncToken and a callback handler to get the response. The callback handler could be any class that implements the mx.rpc.IResponder interface. The IResponder interface defines two methods, result and fault. On a successful result, the result callback method is invoked, and on error, the fault callback method is invoked.

Very simplistically we could do this:

```
var token:AsyncToken =
hessianService.joinString(firstStringParam, secondStringParam);
token.addResponder(IResponderImplClass);
```

Now when the response comes back, we will receive it in the result(event:Object) method. In the IResponderImpl we would take event.result and get the response concatenated string from it.

Our example has been simple to help you stay focused on understanding the main ideas instead of getting lost in the details.

This is where I end the discussion on web services.

# Summary

This chapter started with loose coupling using HTTP and finished with different styles of web service–based integration. I also mentioned that AMF-based integration provides for tighter integration than anything seen so far.

At this time we step back a bit and view the Flex and Java integration options by first illustrating it at a high level and then progressively drilling down to a detailed perspective.

Using 30,000-foot analogy, the integration can be viewed as pull-only vs. pull-and-push type integration. This is summarized in Figure 6-10.

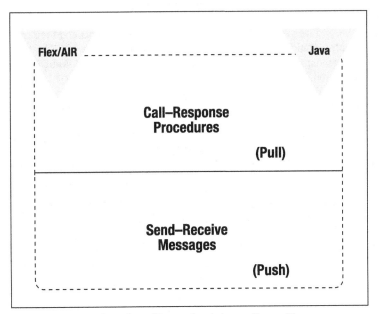

**Figure 6-10.** 30,000-foot view of integration between Flex and Java

Drilling down a bit further, and reaching 10,000 feet, the situation seems divided between the ideas and components that facilitate RPCs vs. ideas that enable messaging. Figure 6-11 shows the 10,000-foot view.

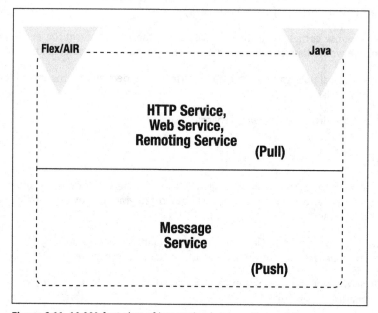

**Figure 6-11.** 10,000-foot view of integration between Flex and Java

One more level down, and we get into the realm of individual components and their roles. Figure 6-12 is a self-explanatory representation of this level, which has been titled as the 1,000-foot view. The diagram lists a few data services, namely LCDS, BlazeDS, GraniteDS, OpenAMF, and WebORB. The next chapter provides more information on these data services.

This chapter has shown a fair bit of these viewpoints in practice, and the following chapter builds on them. Learning from these should be applicable to languages beyond Java and situations more complex than the ones illustrated. Service-Oriented Architecture (SOA) is transforming legacy and driving new applications to create a loosely coupled scalable server-side infrastructure. Flex-rich interfaces can be integrated with such an SOA infrastructure using the methodologies you learned in this chapter.

Next we move on to the subject of tighter integration between Flex and Java over AMF-based data services and media servers. That is the topic for the next chapter.

Finally, at close enough levels, like 100 feet, the details of the wiring and the interaction model comes to light. Figure 6-13 shows this level.

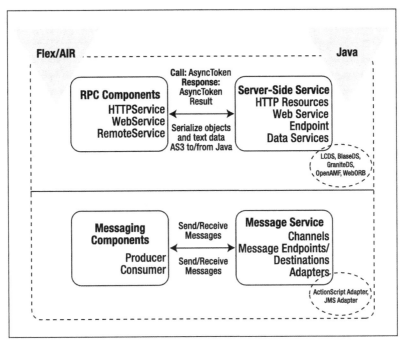

**Figure 6-12.** 1,000-foot view of integration between Flex and Java

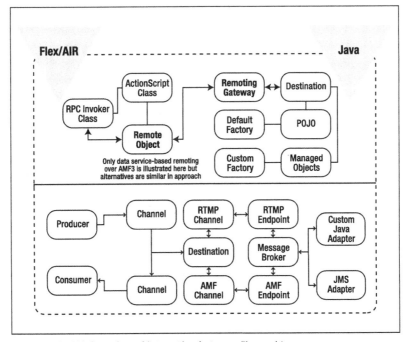

**Figure 6-13.** 100-foot view of integration between Flex and Java

Chapter 7

# INTEGRATING VIA DATA AND MEDIA SERVICES

By Shashank Tiwari

So far, you know how to combine Flex and Java using HTTP and web services. The last chapter surveyed a bunch of alternative mechanisms to achieve this. Most of these mechanisms involve loosely coupled text-based data interchange. Most of them interact by pulling data. Only one of them, Hessian, transmits binary data. Only one, Hessian again (with additional infrastructure powered by the new Java IO), allows data push.

Now, we delve into more tightly coupled scenarios and efficient binary data transmission using AMF (Action Message Format). The AMF specification can be accessed online at http://opensource.adobe.com. This chapter looks at both pull- and push-based interactions—using data services and media servers. Adobe offers two alternatives for data services—the commercial LifeCycle Data Services (LCDS) and the open source BlazeDS—and it offers a suite of products for media servers: Flash Media Server (FMS) products. There are a few open source alternatives to these as well.

In this chapter, I will analyze these products in the context of their applicability to rich, engaging enterprise-grade applications. Functionally they can be divided into the following three topics:

- Remoting and RPC
- Messaging and data push
- Media streaming

At this point of the book, remoting and RPC should be familiar territory, so let's start there.

# Remoting and RPC

Flex applications can access the Java server side using data services. They can access Java objects and invoke remote methods on them. The Flex framework includes a client-side component called RemoteObject. This object acts as a proxy for a data service destination on the server. When configured properly, this object handle can be used to invoke RPCs. Before we get into the nitty-gritty of this object and destination configuration, let's step back and look at the data services architecture.

## Data services architecture

Figure 7-1 is a pictorial summary of the data services architecture. The view is biased to highlight the functional elements. It includes technical aspects but skips the internal details in many places. As you look deeper into the nuts and bolts in this chapter, many of these details will emerge.

As Figure 7-1 depicts, data services includes the following:

- Gateway to intercept server-bound calls
- Parser to make sense of AMF messages
- Serializer and deserializer to transform objects between ActionScript 3.0 (AS3) and Java
- Manager to coordinate with and delegate responsibility to server-side objects
- Messaging service provider to send and receive messages

By data services, I mean a class of products that enable remoting and messaging over AMF and protocols like Real Time Messaging Protocol (RTMP). RTMP is a proprietary protocol developed by Adobe Systems for streaming audio, video, and data over the Internet. More information on RTMP can be found on Wikipedia at http://en.wikipedia.org/wiki/Real_Time_Messaging_Protocol and at http://osflash.org/documentation/rtmp.

As mentioned, there are two data services implementations from Adobe and a few open source alternatives. Following are the most popular ones:

- **LifeCycle Data Services (Adobe)**: http://www.adobe.com/products/livecycle/dataservices/
- **BlazeDS (open source from Adobe)**: http://opensource.adobe.com/wiki/display/blazeds/
- **Granite Data Services (GDS)**: http://www.graniteds.org/
- **WebORB for Java**: http://www.themidnightcoders.com/weborb/java/
- **OpenAMF**: http://sourceforge.net/projects/openamf/

OpenAMF is not a very active project at the time of writing. The last release dates back to 2006. This project's mission was to port AMFPHP to Java. AMF was a closed specification back then, and AMFPHP was a reverse-engineered open source option for PHP servers. OpenAMF is closer to Flash remoting than data services.

This chapter sticks mostly to LCDS and BlazeDS, but the same concepts apply to the alternatives. LCDS and BlazeDS are quite similar in form and structure and share the same codebase. BlazeDS can be thought of as a marginally scaled-down version of LCDS.

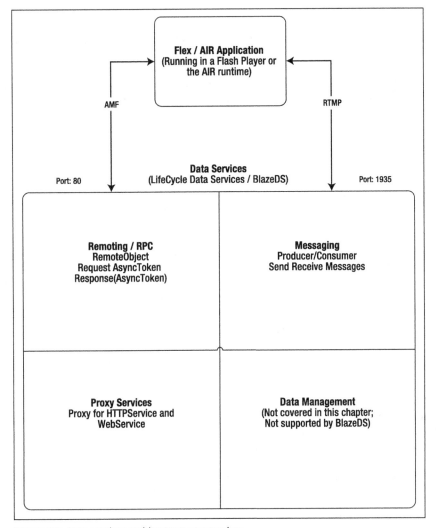

**Figure 7-1.** Data services architecture: an overview

Data services uses AMF3 (Action Message Format version 3) to transmit binary data between Flex and Java. The genesis of this product lies in the Flash remoting server, which used to support AMF0 as the binary protocol. Flash remoting still exists, in many forms, but data services replaces it as a better alternative.

Whichever data service we choose, it is a web application from a Java server perspective. Let's dig a bit deeper to see what this means. (Of course, we are talking only about data services for Java. There are remoting servers for other technologies, but that is beyond the scope of this book.)

# It's a web application

**Web applications** are applications built on the technology that powers the Web. The HTTP protocol and the associated programming paradigm are a prominent part of this technology set. In Java, the raw low-level HTTP and related infrastructure is abstracted out as a higher-level API and managed components. At the heart of this abstraction is the Servlet specification, which wraps HTTP methods and HTTP protocol handling in objects. Web applications written in Java are packaged with all assets, associated libraries, class files, and any other resources into a special archive file format: a web application archive (WAR). These WAR files are deployed on a servlet container or an application server (which contains a servlet container).

Most data services, especially LCDS and BlazeDS, are web applications and exist as WAR files. The remoting gateway is a servlet, and data service elements are web components. A little later, in the section "Downloading and deploying the web application," you will see how deploying LCDS or BlazeDS is identical to deploying any other web application distributed in a WAR file format.

In both BlazeDS and LCDS, the primary communication responsibilities are handled by a message broker, which is created on startup by a servlet called the `MessageBrokerServlet`. The application server's standard class loader loads it like any other servlet. This message broker is extremely flexible, and all types of available services and endpoints can be configured for it fairly easily. All such configurations reside in an XML configuration file, which I talk about later in the section "Configuring data services."

# Protocols, channels, destinations, and endpoints

One of the primary advantages of data services is their use of AMF to transmit data between Flex and Java. AMF is a binary protocol, and the Flash Player natively supports it. Therefore, transmission using AMF is fast and efficient. AMF is a high-level (application layer) protocol that uses HTTP for communication. Almost all data services dialog happens over HTTP or its secure alternative, HTTPS. AMF specification is now available under the open source license and is accessible for download at `http://download.macromedia.com/pub/labs/amf/amf3_spec_121207.pdf`. When remoting, AMF is marshaled and unmarshaled at both ends (Java and Flex) for the data interchange to work.

The data services messaging module and media server use RTMP. LCDS and FMS support RTMP, but BlazeDS does not. BlazeDS uses HTTP tunneling and AMF long pooling to achieve a push-based model. Red5 (`http://osflash.org/red5`), an open source alternative to Flash Media Server, partially reverse-engineers RTMP and provides streaming capabilities over this derived protocol.

Apart from AMF over HTTP and RTMP, the Flash Player also supports Transmission Control Protocol (TCP) over Sockets. TCP is a protocol from the Internet protocol suite that facilitates reliable ordered delivery of byte streams. Secure versions of the protocol, such as AMF and HTTP over Secure Sockets Layer (SSL) and RTMP over Transport Layer Security (TLS), can be used as well. Both SSL and TLS are cryptographic protocols that facilitate secure communication over the Internet. TLS is a newer generation protocol compared to SSL. Although similar, SSL and TLS are not interchangeable. TLS 1.0 is a standard that emerged after SSL 3.0. These protocols involve endpoint authentication, message integrity, and key-based encryption. Both protocols support a bunch of cryptographic algorithms including RSA. RSA is a popular cryptographic algorithm for public key cryptography, which involves two different keys, one to encrypt a message and another to decrypt it.

The Flash Player does not support the entire repertoire of protocols and even misses the ubiquitous User Datagram Protocol (UDP), which is very useful for multicasting. **Multicasting** is a method of information delivery to multiple destinations simultaneously whereby messages are delivered over each link of the network only once. Copies of the message are created only if the links to the destinations bifurcate.

You will not be able to take advantage of protocols like UDP with data services.

Protocols help make effective and efficient communication possible, but higher-level abstractions increase the usability of these protocols. These higher-level abstractions help you focus on business logic and reduce the burden of dealing with low-level communication handling. One such useful higher-level construct in Flex is called **destination**.

Destinations are one of the key abstractions available in the Flex framework and data services. Server-side entities are mapped to logical names and configured to be invoked using these logical names. These configured server-side elements, or destinations, have a handle (logical name) and expose server-side functionality to remote clients. Many Flex client components, especially those that facilitate remoting—for example RemoteObject—map to a destination. The section "Configuring data services," which comes a little later, illustrates the configuration files. In that section, you will learn how to define, configure, and use a destination. Then, in the section "Extending data services for advanced remoting use cases," you will see how to use custom extensions as destinations. In data services, almost all server-side elements that facilitate remoting and messaging are configured as destinations.

HTTPService and WebService, when routed through a data service proxy, also map to a destination.

When you interact with a server-side service via a destination, you use a messaging channel to communicate back and forth. A **messaging channel** is a bundle that defines a protocol and an endpoint set. An endpoint set means a URI, a listening port number, and an endpoint type definition. For example, an AMF channel could be established with the help of the AMF channel implementation class (mx.messaging.channels.AMFChannel) and an endpoint definition, which could be a combination of an endpoint type (flex.messaging.endpoints.AmfEndpoint) and its availability via a URI (say /sampleapp/messagebroker/amf) over a certain listening port (which by default for AMF is 8100).

Sometimes, services need special adapters to communicate with server-side elements. These adapters may translate the message and act as the classical conduit that helps different programming interfaces communicate and interact with each other. (An **adapter** by definition is something that modifies an API to make it adapt to the required integration scenario.) Data services define a set of built-in adapters and provide an API to create your own.

That is enough theory; time now to roll our sleeves up and see data services in action. We first install data services and then quickly create a small example application to see how it works.

# Installing a data service

The last section claimed data services to be a Java web application. You will see that claim reinforced by deploying a data service like any other Java web application in a Java application server (with a servlet container). Once we have deployed it successfully, we will go ahead and configure it so that we are ready to build an example application.

## Downloading and deploying the web application

For the purposes of illustration, we will pick BlazeDS as the data service and choose JBoss Application Server (AS) as the Java application server. If the data service is LCDS and the application server is any other, such as Apache Tomcat, BEA WebLogic, IBM WebSphere, Apache Geronimo, Caucho Resin, or GlassFish, the situation is not very different. Each of these application servers has its own directory structure and styles of deployment. Deploying BlazeDS or LCDS involves the same level of complexity as deploying any other Java web application packaged as a WAR. Adobe Labs has published some notes on the specific installation instructions for a few of the popular application servers. These notes are online at http://labs.adobe.com/wiki/index.php/BlazeDS:Release_Notes#Installing_BlazeDS.

The first step is to get all the required software and to install it.

**Getting the software and installing it** BlazeDS is available under the open source GNU LGPL license. Go to http://opensource.adobe.com/wiki/display/blazeds/BlazeDS and download the latest stable release build. You will have a choice to download the binary or the source versions. The binary version is what you should choose unless you intend to make modifications to the code. The distribution is available as a ZIP file. When you unzip the archive file, you will find a file called blazeds.war. This is the WAR file that has everything in it needed to use BlazeDS. In addition, you may find the following files:

- blazeds-samples.war: A set of sample applications
- blazeds-console.war: Monitoring application for BlazeDS deployments

If this is the first time you are deploying BlazeDS, it's recommended you deploy blazeds-samples.war and verify that the sample applications run without a problem.

The other piece of the puzzle is the Java application server. I will assume that you have downloaded and installed one for your use. In this example, we download the latest stable release of JBoss AS from the community download page accessible at http://www.jboss.org/projects/download/. At the time of writing, version 4.2.2.GA is the latest stable release. This may differ depending on when you download it. The JBoss AS download is an archive file that is ready to use as soon as it's expanded in the file system. (It may at most require a few environment variable settings.) On the PC, we just unzip it within a directory on the main partition.

The JBoss AS directory server appears as shown in Figure 7-2.

BlazeDS runs with any Java application server that supports JDK 1.4.2+ or JDK 5. Most current versions of application servers support these JDK versions.

**Deploying the WAR file** Deploying a web application in JBoss is as elementary as traversing down the server ➤ default ➤ deploy folders and copying the WAR files there. Once this is done, start up the server. Go to the bin directory and start the server with the "run" script. To verify deployment, fire up your browser and request the samples application. In our case, JBoss is bound to

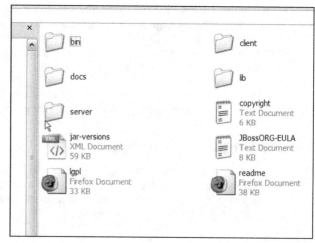

**Figure 7-2.** JBoss AS directory structured after unzipping it on a PC

port 8080 for HTTP requests, and so the URL for samples looks like this: http://localhost:8080/blazeds-samples/. If you are able to access the samples application, you are ready to move to the next step of configuring data service.

With LCDS, the deployment is no different. The WAR file in LCDS has a different name—flex.war as opposed to blazeds.war—and it has a few extra features compared to BlazeDS, but from a deployment standpoint things don't change.

GDS, the open source alternative to LCDS, has a slightly different approach to software distribution. GDS is distributed as multiple bundles, each integrating with one Java server-side technology. Also, GDS is distributed as source and not binary, which means you need to set up the development environment to build the software. If you are a Java developer who also writes Flex applications, you may already have the development environment set up. The required pieces of software are

- Eclipse 3.2+ (with JDK 5+)
- Flex 3 SDK (If you use Flex Builder, you already have it.)
- Flex 3 Ant tasks (http://labs.adobe.com/wiki/index.php/Flex_Ant_Tasks)

Once the environment is set up, you could get hold of one of these bundles:

- graniteds-ejb3-1.0.0.zip: Hooks to EJB
- graniteds-seam-1.0.0.zip: Integrates with Seam (stateful web beans)
- graniteds-spring-ejb3-1.0.0.zip: Provides Spring services
- graniteds-guice-1.0.0.zip: Provides services for Google Guice
- granite-pojo-1.0.0.zip: Interfaces with plain Java
- granite-chat-1.0.0.zip: Includes Java New I/O (NIO) and Comet-based data push

The choice of bundle depends on your requirements. Also, the bundle version numbers could vary depending on when you download the files. As of now, the release version is 1.0.0. Each of these bundles is an Eclipse project. Once you get the bundle you need, unzip it and import it into Eclipse. Subsequently, you build it using Ant tasks.

## Configuring data services

In BlazeDS and LCDS, there is more to configure than code. In both these cases, a message broker servlet is the central manager of all communication and service invocations. Configuring data services is equivalent to configuring this message broker. In the web.xml file where you set up this servlet, you define the configuration file it should read. The portion of web.xml where you define this is as follows:

```
<servlet>
    <servlet-name>MessageBrokerServlet</servlet-name>
    <display-name>MessageBrokerServlet</display-name>
    <servlet-class>flex.messaging.MessageBrokerServlet</servlet-class>
    <init-param>
        <param-name>services.configuration.file</param-name>
        <param-value>/WEB-INF/flex/services-config.xml</param-value>
    </init-param>
    <load-on-startup>1</load-on-startup>
</servlet>
```

You may notice that the value for the services.configuration.file is /WEB-INF/flex/ services-config.xml. This is the default configuration, and most often there is no need to change it. However, if you need the configuration file to be at a different location or have a different name, you know where to make the modifications so that the new values are picked up.

All service and endpoint configurations are specified in this configuration file, which by default is called services-config.xml. From a functional standpoint, a data service tries to accomplish the following:

- Facilitate remote procedure calls to Java objects on the server and transmit data between AS3 and Java classes.

- Provide proxy services, especially for HTTPService and WebService, where security restrictions (the lack of a cross-domain definition via crossdomain.xml) disallow these services otherwise.

- Send/Receive messages between Flex and Java and between two different Flex clients.

- Manage data for the application. This topic is not discussed in this book at all. BlazeDS does not provide this off the shelf, but LCDS does.

Therefore, Adobe partitions the configuration file into four different pieces, each corresponding to one of the functional responsibilities just listed. Each of these pieces resides in a separate file, and all are included in the original configuration file by reference. The default names for these four files, in the same order in which they correspond to the functional areas listed previously, are

- remoting-config.xml
- proxy-config.xml
- messaging-config.xml
- data-management-config.xml

The portion of services-config.xml at /flex/WEB-INF from our BlazeDS installation, where three of these four files are included (BlazeDS does not have data management features), is as shown here:

```
<?xml version="1.0" encoding="UTF-8"?>
<services-config>
    <services>
        <service-include file-path="remoting-config.xml" />
        <service-include file-path="proxy-config.xml" />
        <service-include file-path="messaging-config.xml" />
    </services>
```

A few aspects like logging, security, and channel definitions are cross-cutting concerns and are used across services, so these are defined in services-config.xml itself. All other service configurations and definitions typically fall in one of the four files (or three if we are using BlazeDS) I spoke about.

In this chapter, there is no intent to cover every single aspect of configuration. Only a few important ones are sampled and explained. For an exhaustive syntax-level account of each allowed configuration, it's advisable to refer to the LiveDocs. For BlazeDS, you could refer specifically to a LiveDocs section titled "About service configuration files," which can be found online at http:// livedocs.adobe.com/blazeds/1/blazeds_devguide/help.html?content=services_config_2.html.

Let's survey a few configuration options to get a flavor of things.

**Common configuration** Let's start with logging. BlazeDS and LCDS use log4j for logging. Logging-related configurations reside in services-config.xml itself. The most important aspect of configuration is the logging level. The permissible values and their respective meanings are as follows:

- ALL: Logs every single message.
- DEBUG: Includes internal Flex activities. This is an appropriate level during development and troubleshooting, and is an incremental expansion beyond INFO. Therefore, all errors, warnings and information messages are included.
- INFO: Logs additional information that may be pertinent to developers or administrators. This level builds on top of the WARN level.
- WARN: Includes warnings as well as errors.
- ERROR: Logs only errors that cause service disruption.
- NONE: Logs nothing.

If you are familiar with log4j logging levels, then you have seen this before.

Next come channel definitions. In terms of importance, this rates above the logging-level definitions. Channels are the vital protocol and endpoint combination that make communication possible between the Flex client and the server. In BlazeDS, the default AMF channel configurations look like this:

```
<channels>
    <channel-definition id="my-amf" class=➥
"mx.messaging.channels.AMFChannel">
        <endpoint url="http://{server.name}:{server.port}/➥
{context.root}/messagebroker/amf"
class="flex.messaging.endpoints.AMFEndpoint"/>
    </channel-definition>

    <channel-definition id="my-secure-amf"
class="mx.messaging.channels.SecureAMFChannel">
        <endpoint url="https://{server.name}:{server.port}/➥
{context.root}/messagebroker/amfsecure"
class="flex.messaging.endpoints.SecureAMFEndpoint"/>
        <properties>
            <add-no-cache-headers>false</add-no-cache-headers>
        </properties>
    </channel-definition>

    <channel-definition id="my-polling-amf"
class="mx.messaging.channels.AMFChannel">
        <endpoint url="http://{server.name}:{server.port}/➥
{context.root}/messagebroker/amfpolling"
class="flex.messaging.endpoints.AMFEndpoint"/>
        <properties>
            <polling-enabled>true</polling-enabled>
            <polling-interval-seconds>4</polling-interval-seconds>
        </properties>
    </channel-definition>
</channels>
```

Three different AMF channels are defined using the preceding configuration. In each case, a fully qualified class name specifies the class that implements the channel. The channel is accessible via a configured endpoint. The endpoints include a set of tokens, namely server.name, server.port, and context.root. When a SWF is loaded in a browser, as happens with all Flex applications, these tokens are replaced with the correct values, and the endpoints are configured properly. In AIR and even with RTMP channels (in RTMP, server.port needs a specific port number definition), these tokens are not resolved automatically, and so channels don't work as expected, if configured using tokens.

To test a channel, it may a good idea to try and access the endpoint URL with the browser and see whether you get a success message, such as 200 OK, or not. Where required, channels could accept additional properties. As an example, a polling AMF channel defines the polling interval using properties. An interesting fact is that property settings can create entirely different channels. AMF and polling AMF channels have the same class for implementing the channels, but they have different sets of properties and therefore different behavior.

Using services-config.xml, the channel configurations are done at compile time. It's also possible to configure channels and associate them with destinations at run time. More information about configuration at run time is covered in the section "Configuring at run time" later in this chapter.

The third important common configuration pertains to security. Exhaustive and complex security definitions are possible with data services, but we will go with the defaults for now. We shall deal with security configurations in data services in the section "Additional useful data services tips" later in this chapter.

Although this chapter has not exhaustively covered the configuration options, you know the basics of configuration by now. You will learn more about configuration as you explore the other topics that relate to data services.

Our new focus is to get data services into action. The three configuration files, remoting-config.xml, proxy-config.xml, and messaging-config.xml, configure services, so we will look at these in the next few sections as we implement such services using BlazeDS or LCDS.

# Calling remote methods and serializing objects

You know AMF is an efficient binary protocol and a data service lets you exchange data between Flex and Java. Let's dig deeper so you can see what you need to do to leverage this mechanism in your Flex application. Because "seeing is believing" and, like pictures, working code speaks louder than words, we will first create a simple example application that will establish RPC over AMF using a data service. In this example, our data service is BlazeDS.

## A simple example in action

The example application is fairly simple. It displays a list of people and the country they come from. A person is identified by an ID, first name, and last name. A country is identified by a name. The initial list is populated from an XML data file that has four names in it. A user is allowed to add names to the list and delete existing ones.

To demonstrate data services and remoting, the list and the methods to manipulate the list are kept on the server. These remote Java objects and their methods are accessed from a Flex client.

We create this example using Flex Builder 3, but we could also do without it and compile directly using mxmlc, the command-line compiler, or use Flex Ant tasks, available from within Eclipse. The command-line compiler and the Flex Ant tasks are available free of charge. The command-line compiler comes bundled with the free Flex 3 SDK. The Flex Ant tasks software bundle can be downloaded from http://labs.adobe.com/wiki/index.php/Flex_Ant_Tasks.

As a first step, we create a new Flex project, choose Web application as the application type and J2EE as the server technology. We name this project VerySimpleRemotingExample. Figure 7-3 shows these settings in the New Flex Project dialog.

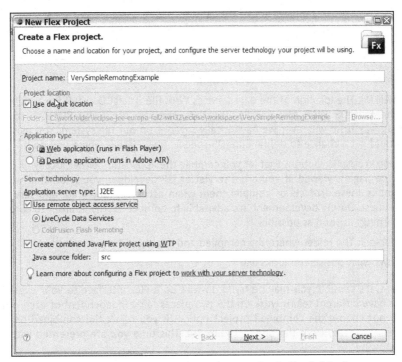

**Figure 7-3.** The initial screen for new Flex project creation in Flex Builder 3

You will see that Flex Builder offers only two choices for a data service, namely LifeCycle Data Services and ColdFusion Flash Remoting. At first, this often causes confusion among developers, when using BlazeDS. Choose LifeCycle Data Services as the option in the current dialog box when using BlazeDS. In the next dialog box, you will have an opportunity to point to either the BlazeDS WAR or the BlazeDS directories, deployed on your application server.

In the very first screen, a choice is offered to create a combined Java/Flex project using WTP. WTP, which stands for Web Tools Platform, is the set of tools available within Eclipse to create Java web applications. The WTP project is hosted at http://www.eclipse.org/webtools/. You can go to the project page to get more information on WTP.

The "data services" software available for the Flex framework consists of web applications that run in a web container. Any custom logic you write with the data services either will be part of a web application or will be accessed from a web application. Therefore, if you are starting from scratch, choosing to create a joint project is often useful. If your Java-side application already exists, as in the case of integration with existing systems, do not choose this option. Depending on the choice at this stage, the next screen varies.

If you choose the option to create the combined project, the screen lets you define the following:

- Target runtime: The application server on which you wish to deploy the data services application. Eclipse allows you to configure the application server run time. A JBoss AS instance is configured for the purpose. The details of JBoss AS configuration are out of the scope of this chapter. However, a quick search on the Web or a look at the JBoss AS documentation (available online at `http://www.jboss.org/jbossas/docs/`) could help you configure a JBoss AS successfully.

- Context root: The root of the web application, usually the same as the application name.

- Content folder: The folder for the source files.

- Flex WAR file: The location of the data services WAR file. The LCDS WAR file is called `flex.war`, and the BlazeDS WAR file is called `blazeds.war`. We are using BlazeDS, so we choose `blazeds.war` from wherever we have locally saved it on our file system. You may recall I said you would get a chance to define BlazeDS-specific files. Here is where you do it.

- Compilation options: Options that let you compile the application either locally or on the server when the page is viewed. If you are a servlet or JSP developer, you know that you can either precompile these artifacts or compile them when accessed, initialized, and served based on user request. During development, it's advisable to compile locally in order to catch any errors and warnings as soon as possible.

- Output folder: The folder where the compiled and packaged files are saved.

Figure 7-4 shows what this screen looks like.

As I said before, it's possible you may be trying to wire up a Flex interface to your existing Java web application or have different teams work on the two pieces fairly independent of each other. In such cases, you do not choose the combined project option. If you reject the combined project option, your next screen will vary from the one in Figure 7-4. This time you are presented with a dialog to specify the following:

- Root folder: This is the folder where the existing web application is deployed. Make sure this folder contains a `WEB-INF/flex` folder.

- Root URL: This is the URL of the web application. In our case, we configure JBoss AS to listen for HTTP requests on port 8080, and we run it on the same machine from which we access the Flex interface via a browser, so the value is `http://localhost:8080/MyWebApplication`.

- Context root: The root of the web application, typically the same as its name.

- Compilation options: Already explained, in the context of the joint Java/Flex application.

- Output folder: The folder where the compiled and packaged files are saved.

Figure 7-5 shows this alternative screen, which was captured before any choices were made. This is intentional. Flex comes with an integrated JRun Java application server. You can choose to use it or ignore it in favor of any other Java application server. We ignored it and chose JBoss. However, if you decided to choose JRun, you have the advantage of Flex Builder's default configurations coinciding with what JRun wants. In Figure 7-5, you see these choices grayed out because the Use default location for LifeCycle Data Services server option is selected.

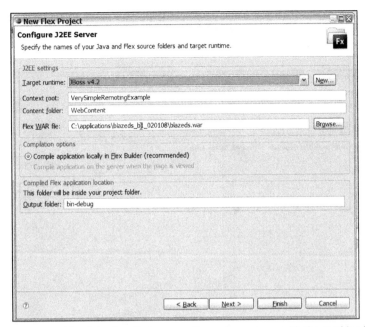

**Figure 7-4.** The dialog box that appears if you choose to go with the combined Java/Flex project using the WTP option

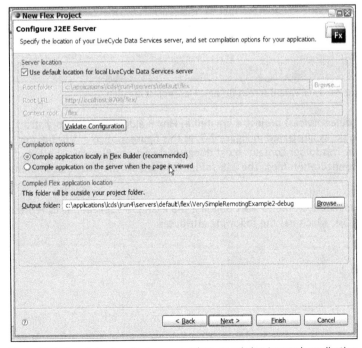

**Figure 7-5.** The dialog box that appears when an existing Java web application is referenced as the target for the data services application

In either of the two cases, once you make your selections, you move to the next screen, shown in Figure 7-6, which lets you add any external library files to the project and asks you to confirm the project creation. When you click the Finish button, the project is created.

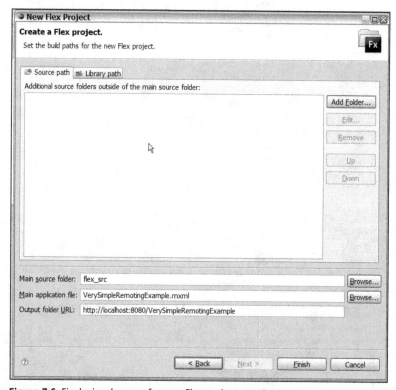

**Figure 7-6.** Final wizard screen for new Flex project creation

A new Flex (with data services) project is created in Flex Builder. The directory structure of our newly created project looks as illustrated in Figure 7-7. In this figure, notice a WEB-INF folder appears in the WebContent folder. This folder contains most things pertaining to BlazeDS. The flex folder in WEB-INF contains all the configuration files. The lib folder contains all the JARs that implement the BlazeDS functionality.

Now we are set up, and it's time to start building the example application. To represent the data, we define a Person class, which has the following attributes:

- id
- firstName
- lastName
- country

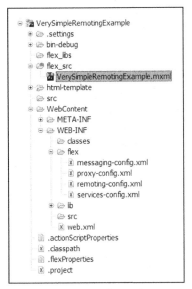

**Figure 7-7.** The new Flex project,
VerySimpleRemotingExample, in Flex Builder 3

We also define a collection of persons that we call PeopleCollection. PeopleCollection contains Person objects. The object to represent these abstractions is created both in Java and AS3. Here is what the Java class looks like:

```java
package advancedflex3.ch07.remoting;
public class Person
{
    private int id;
    private String firstName;
    private String lastName;
    private String country;

    public int getId() {
        return id;
    }

    public void setId(int id) {
        this.id = id;
    }

    public String getFirstName() {
        return firstName;
    }

    public void setFirstName(String firstName) {
        this.firstName = firstName;
    }
```

```
        public String getLastName() {
            return lastName;
        }

        public void setLastName(String lastName) {
            this.lastName = lastName;
        }

        public String getCountry() {
            return country;
        }

        public void setCountry(String country) {
            this.country = country;
        }
    }
```

If you are a Java developer, you will quickly recognize this class as a JavaBean type of class. It has a set of properties and set of accessor methods to get and set the attribute values. We create a similar structure in AS3. Again, we will have a set of attributes and a set of accessors to get/set those attributes. The attribute names in the Java class and the AS3 class are identical because that is how the fields are matched. This is what the AS3 class looks like:

```
    package advancedflex3.ch07.remoting
    {
        [RemoteClass(alias="advancedflex3.ch07.remoting.Person")]
        [Managed]
        public class Person
        {
            public var id:int;
            public var firstName:String;
            public var lastName:String;
            public var country:String;


        }
    }
```

Looking at the code, you may wonder where the accessor methods are. In AS3, a class with public variables has implicit accessor methods. Therefore, the lack of explicit get and set method pairs is not a problem in this situation, and things will still work. If the properties (attributes) were private, explicit getters and setters would be required. Also, notice that the RemoteClass metadata links the AS3 class to its Java counterpart by specifying the fully qualified class name of the Java class as a value of the alias parameter. Further, you see this class annotated with another metadata element: Managed. Annotating a class with the Managed metadata tag is another way of implementing the mx.data. IManaged interface. The IManaged interface extends the IPropertyChangeNotifier interface. IPropertyChangeNotifier is a marker interface, which defines a contract such that all implementing classes dispatch a property change event for all properties of the class and any nested class exposed publicly as properties. As a result, as changes occur, the remote server class and the local class are kept in sync.

By explicitly defining a counterpart to our server-side Java class, we establish a typed association. Therefore, on data interchange, the deserialization of the serialized Java class involves mapping of the data elements into this ActionScript class. If we did not define such a class on the ActionScript side, the deserialization would still happen successfully, except that this time the ActionScript class would be dynamically created. From a performance and optimization perspective, typed associations are preferred over dynamic creation.

Next, we create a collection class that holds the set of Person objects on both sides of the wire, and define properties and accessor methods on it. Again, we keep the names and definitions consistent on both sides.

Our collection class on the Java server side is called PeopleCollection.java, and this is how it looks:

```java
package advancedflex3.ch07.remoting;

import java.io.*;
import java.net.URLDecoder;

import javax.xml.parsers.*;
import org.w3c.dom.*;
import java.util.List;
import java.util.ArrayList;

public class PeopleCollection
{
    public PeopleCollection() {

    }

    public List getPersons() {

        List list = new ArrayList();

        try {
            String filePath = URLDecoder.decode(getClass().➥
getClassLoader().getResource➥
("advancedflex3/ch07/PeopleCollection.xml").➥
getFile(), "UTF-8");;
            DocumentBuilderFactory factory =
DocumentBuilderFactory.newInstance();
            factory.setValidating(false);
            Document doc =
factory.newDocumentBuilder().➥
parse(new File(filePath));
            NodeList personNodes = doc.getElementsByTagName("person");
            int length = personNodes.getLength();
            Person person;
            Node personNode;
            for (int i=0; i<length; i++) {
                personNode = personNodes.item(i);
```

```
                    person = new Person();
                    person.setId(getIntegerValue(personNode, "id"));
                    person.setFirstName(getStringValue➡
        (personNode, "firstName"));
                    person.setLastName(getStringValue➡
        (personNode, "lastName"));
                    person.setCountry(getStringValue➡
        (personNode, "country"));
                }
            } catch (Exception e) {
                e.printStackTrace();
            }

            return list;
        }

        private String getStringValue(Node node, String name) {
            return ((Element) node).getElementsByTagName➡
        (name).item(0).getFirstChild().getNodeValue();
        }

        private int getIntegerValue(Node node, String name) {
            return Integer.parseInt(getStringValue(node, name) );
        }
    }
```

You will notice that this class reads the data from an XML file called PeopleCollection.xml. This XML file contains four records, each of which corresponds to an attribute of the Person class. Here are the entries in that file:

```
<peopleCollection>
    <person>
        <id>1</id>
        <firstName>John</firstName>
        <lastName>Smith</lastName>
        <country>United States</country>
    </person>
    <person>
        <id>2</id>
        <firstName>Amit</firstName>
        <lastName>Sharma</lastName>
        <country>India</country>
    </person>
    <person>
        <id>3</id>
        <firstName>Alex</firstName>
        <lastName>Smirnov</lastName>
        <country>Russia</country>
    </person>
```

```
        <person>
            <id>4</id>
            <firstName>Ying</firstName>
            <lastName>Chen</lastName>
            <country>China</country>
        </person>
    </peopleCollection>
```

That takes care of the data on the server side. Let's now configure these classes with data services. Once we have done that successfully, we will move on to consuming this remote data by calling remote methods from the Flex client.

We get into the WEB-INF/flex directory and open remoting-config.xml. You already know that remoting-config.xml is one of the constituent files of services-config.xml, which configures the message broker servlet and allows data services to deliver the expected functionality.

We configure the PeopleCollection object as a remoting destination so that it becomes accessible from the Flex client. Here is the snippet from remoting-config.xml:

```
<service id="remoting-service"
    class="flex.messaging.services.RemotingService">
    <adapters>
        <adapter-definition id="java-object"
class="flex.messaging.services.➦
remoting.adapters.JavaAdapter"
default="true"/>
    </adapters>

    <default-channels>
        <channel ref="my-amf"/>
    </default-channels>

    <destination id="peopleCollection">
        <properties>
            <source>advancedflex3.ch07.remoting.➦
PeopleCollection</source>
        </properties>
    </destination>
</service>
```

The adapters and default channels we use here were preconfigured with the BlazeDS distribution. It's possible to configure additional adapters and modify the default channels. The piece we add to this configuration file is the one that defines the destination. That configuration maps a logical name (handle) to the class, identified by the fully qualified class name, which holds the collection of persons. In Flex, the logical name will be referenced from within RemoteObject to invoke methods on this class. If you are familiar with any distributed computing technology like web services, EJB, COM, CORBA, or any other RPC-supporting technology, you will find this extremely familiar in approach and style.

A destination allows many more property settings beyond the essential source property determination. One of these is the scope property, which takes three valid values: Application, Session, and

Request. Application-scoped remote objects get bound to the ServletContext and are available to the entire web application. Session-scoped objects are bound to a FlexSession instance, which abstracts the session of the current conversation. Request-scoped objects are instantiated on each invocation. Other properties commonly used are the attribute-id and the factory properties. Object instances are bound to the name specified as the value of the attribute-id property. The factory property specifies the factory that creates the object. In the case of managed components, this property plays a major role. Later in the chapter, in the section "Creating custom factories," you will see this being used.

On the Java server side we are done, except for compiling the code and copying the class files over in the proper directory structure, which maps to the package structure, to WEB-INF/classes. This is how BlazeDS would be able to load these classes. It is a standard Java web application requirement to have the compiled Java classes available either in the WEB-INF/classes folder or as a packaged archive in the WEB-INF/lib folder for it to be available to the web application.

The last part of this example is the Flex application code, which calls the remote methods, gets the data across the wire, and populates a data grid with that data. For now, all of this is put in a single MXML file. The source of that MXML file is as follows:

```
<?xml version="1.0" encoding="utf-8"?>
<mx:Application
xmlns:mx="http://www.adobe.com/2006/mxml"
layout="absolute"
creationComplete="initApp()">
<mx:Script>
    <![CDATA[
        import advancedflex3.ch07.remoting.Person;
        import mx.rpc.events.ResultEvent;
        import mx.collections.ArrayCollection;
        import mx.controls.Alert;

        [Bindable]
        private var items:ArrayCollection;

        private function initApp():void
        {
            ro.getPersons();

        }

        private function resultHandler(event:ResultEvent):void
        {
            items = event.result as ArrayCollection;
            var length:int = items.length;

        }
    ]]>
</mx:Script>
    <mx: RemoteObject
id="ro"
```

```
        destination="peopleCollection"
        result="resultHandler(event)"/>
            <mx:DataGrid dataProvider="{items}" />
        </mx:Application>
```

RemoteObject maps to the PeopleCollection Java class via a destination, which we configured in remoting-config.xml. In the preceding MXML file, we could call the getPersons method of the PeopleCollection class using the remote object handle. If we wanted to manipulate the data further and manipulate the items in this collection, we could do that, because each of the items in the collection is a Person object that has a type association in AS3. In the interest of keeping our focus on the basic mechanics of remoting, I will avoid discussing any details of such business logic. However, the code for the application contains an implementation for updating the collection, adding new items and deleting existing ones, and sorting items in the collection. You can peruse the source code to understand how it's implemented.

Now that you have seen a basic remoting example, the next section builds on this knowledge to cover two important related topics:

- Java to/from AS3 serialization/deserialization
- Asynchronous communication

We will start with serialization and deserialization.

## Java to Flex serialization basics

The simplest of our examples established that objects get serialized and deserialized between Java and AS3, across the wire. To analyze this subject further, it is appropriate to compare and contrast the available data types in the two languages and see how they map to each other. Table 7-1 presents this comparison tersely.

**Table 7-1.** Juxtaposing AS3 and Java Data Types

| AS3 | Java |
| --- | --- |
| int/uint | Integer |
| Number | Double |
| Object | Map |
| String | String |
| Boolean | Boolean |
| Date | java.util.Date |
| Array (dense) | List |
| Array (sparse) | Map |
| XML | org.w3c.dom.Document |
| flash.utils.ByteArray | byte[] |
| undefined | null |

This table is not exhaustive but should serve as an introductory guide. Here are a few notes to help you understand the mappings:

- Java `float`, `long`, `BigDecimal`, and `BigInteger` convert to AS3 Number.

- `Date`, `Time`, and `Timestamp` (from the `java.sql` package) and `java.util.Calendar` map to AS3 `Date`.

- In AS3, "true" and "false" strings can also represent a Boolean value.

- Dense arrays are those that have no holes. As an example, if an array has four elements and I put the fifth element at position 9, then in a sparse array (the opposite of a dense array) there will be no values, what I call holes, in position 4 to 8. ActionScript sparse arrays tally with `java.util.Map` to avoid sending null values across.

- Depending on the interface type at the Java end, a dense ActionScript array maps to an implementation type. For example, `List` and `Collection` become `ArrayList`, `Set` becomes `HashSet`, and `SortedSet` becomes `TreeSet`.

- Typed associations can be established between custom types with the help of corresponding bean type classes on each side and the `[RemoteClass]` metadata tag. Our simple example uses such a mapping.

In the case of custom type associations, it's possible to include extra properties in the bean type object as far as the existing ones on the source (i.e., the server) match the other properties in the ActionScript type. For example, you may have an object represent an order with a single line item. In such an object, you may want the serializable object to contain the unit price of the item and the quantity of the item, but not the total value (which is essentially a product of the other two properties). You may want the AS3 type to have a third property to hold the total value, which you could calculate by multiplying the other two property values. If you did this and made this AS3 object the associated counterpart of the Java object (which effectively has one property less), nothing would break; everything will still work fine. It's advisable to follow this technique and reduce the serialization overhead, especially when derived and calculated values are involved.

Serialization and deserialization with transmission over AMF is a very efficient process and beats almost all other transmission alternatives.

I mentioned earlier on that I would be covering two more special topics related to remoting. This section dealt with one, and now we will move on to the other—asynchronous communication, the only style that Flex adopts.

## Asynchronous communication

All types of communication in the Flex framework are asynchronous. This has its advantages but also poses some challenges. To list a few, some advantages are as follows:

- Calls are nonblocking and therefore resources are not held up.

- Asynchronous communication and events go well together and help create loosely coupled systems.

- This type of communication allows clean separation of duties: the call invoker and the response receiver could be different entities.

- The sequence in which calls are issued, or their linearity, have little significance, and so there is usually no need to queue calls.

No choice has advantages without disadvantages. The disadvantages of asynchronous communication are often caused by the same things that make it advantageous. A few common challenges of asynchronous communication are as follows:

- Transaction management is not trivial because we are not talking about call and response in the same cycle. To roll back, it's important to have a common token to relate back to the event.

- Flows that need calls in a linear order need to be managed externally.

- In many cases, the invoker has little control over the response, i.e., when it arrives and how it is handled.

A common established way to manage asynchronous communication is to espouse the Asynchronous Completion Token (ACT) pattern, which originated at the Department of Computer Science and Engineering at Washington University in St. Louis. This pattern's universal applicability in the area of asynchronous communication caused it to become popular rather quickly. You can find a description and an explanation of the pattern online at http://www.cs.wustl.edu/~schmidt/PDF/ACT.pdf.

The Flex framework adopts ACT ideas natively in its framework constructs. Almost all asynchronous communication in Flex follows this pattern:

- A call is made and an asynchronous token is returned.

- Every response dispatches events, indicating either success or failure.

- Event listeners are registered with the object that is capable of receiving the response. Sometimes the implementation of a marker interface makes a class eligible to receive responses.

- When a response arrives, events are dispatched. The response comes back with the asynchronous token. Call and response are correlated using this token.

- The appropriate handler gets the response. On receipt, it processes the response.

By default, a call is dispatched as soon as it's made, and there is never any certainty about when the response will come. Let's take a simple example of an editable collection in a data grid, where this behavior could make our life difficult. Say we have a few rows of data. Now we select one of the rows of data and edit the values, and then we do the same with another row. When we are editing the second row, we realize our first row modification wasn't accurate, and so we need to revisit it. Under normal circumstances, the first row modification call has already been dispatched by now, and rolling back the modification is cumbersome. This situation can get more complex if our operation deletes a row and we need to recover it, or if we make two modifications to the same data element and the first modification completes after the second one. In general, to take care of these types of complexities, we need to allow the following:

- Sequencing of calls in some order

- Batching of calls into a logical bundle

- Locking of data elements, where applicable

- Definition of transactional boundaries to facilitate commit and rollback

In LCDS, the data management module takes care of these complicated scenarios, but in most other cases you need to take care of this yourself.

# Extending data services for advanced remoting use cases

You have seen the basics of remoting to simple Java classes, which a few years back were given the interesting name of Plain Old Java Objects (POJOs). Now let's look at a couple of advanced use cases.

## Supporting additional data types

Although AS3 and Java are strikingly similar in programming style, static type system, and syntax, the mapping between AS3 and Java objects is far from optimal. One of the key reasons for this is the lack of AS3 parallels for many Java data types, a glaring example of which can be seen in the two languages' collection types. Java has many advanced collection data types, whereas AS3 has very few. For example, there is no equivalent of a SortedSet in AS3. Even if such data types were added to AS3, how could they be mapped to the existing Java data types? There is no way of translating automatically between the two. For instance, a strongly typed enumerated type can be created in AS3 to resemble a Java 5 Enum, but it's by no means easy to ensure that serialization and deserialization happen between the two smoothly.

Adding support for additional data types is possible but not trivial. In order to understand the path to this addition, it's important to understand the PropertyProxy interface. PropertyProxy in the flex.messaging.io package allows customized serialization and deserialization of complex objects. It has access to each of the steps in the serialization and the deserialization process. During serialization, a PropertyProxy is asked to provide the class name, its properties, and its peculiarities. During deserialization, a PropertyProxy instantiates an object instance and sets the property values. PropertyProxy is a higher-order interface that has been implemented for many different data types. In the BlazeDS Javadocs, you will see the following classes implementing the PropertyProxy interface:

- AbstractProxy
- BeanProxy
- DictionaryProxy
- MapProxy
- PageableRowSetProxy
- SerializationProxy
- StatusInfoProxy
- ThrowableProxy

When adding support for a specific new data type, you could start by either implementing the PropertyProxy for that type or extending one of its available implementations.

## Creating custom factories

Data services (both LCDS and BlazeDS) can load and instantiate simple Java classes without a problem. However, they don't work without modification if the remote object is a managed object like an EJB or a Spring bean. This is only natural, because these data services cannot automatically instantiate these objects. Managed objects are instantiated, maintained, and garbage collected within the managed environment or container they reside in. If these objects need to be consumed within data services, they warrant a factory mechanism, which can get hold of a managed object instance and make it accessible within a data service namespace.

The custom factory varies depending on how the managed object is accessed. Both LCDS and BlazeDS include a so-called factory mechanism to include objects that reside in other namespaces. Theoretically, the idea is simple and goes like this:

1. Implement a common interface, which defines a method to create a factory.

2. Configure this factory creator so that it can be instantiated and used when needed.

3. Pass the name of this configured factory creator to a destination (which points to the managed object), so that it knows which factory to use to get hold of an object instance.

4. Use the factory to look up an instance of the managed object. Though called a factory, this factory is not really creating anything. It's looking up an instance from a different namespace.

5. Use the object as you would use any other simple Java class. In other words, once bound to a destination and configured, it is ready for RPC.

Practically, most work goes into implementing the lookup method. Start with a custom class and have that custom class implement the FlexFactory interface. Implement the three most important methods, namely

- initialize: To get the factory instance configured and ready

- createFactoryInstance: To create a FactoryInstance

- lookup: To return a handle of the object the factory is meant to get hold of

Then configure the factory in services-config.xml like this:

```
<factories>
    <factory
id="ejbFactory"
class="flex.samples.factories.EJBFactory"/>
</factories>
```

We configure an EJB factory here. Now we can refer to this factory from within a destination setting. A possible case could be the following:

```
<destination id="MyEJBPoweredService">
    <properties>
        <factory>ejbFactory</factory>
        <source>MyUsefulBean</source>
    </properties>
</destination>
```

We have successfully created a custom factory and it's ready for use. Once again, I show only the logic that helps you learn the topic at hand—namely, creating custom factories.

This chapter has covered a fair bit on remoting, although it has merely scratched the surface. Next, I give you a look at the second most important feature of BlazeDS: messaging.

# Messaging and real-time updates

Flex reconfirms the supremacy of event-driven systems. It thrives on asynchronous communication, and it defines the loosely coupled robustness that excites all of us to create fascinating applications using it. A concept that goes hand in hand with events and asynchronous communication is message-driven communication. Flex includes it in its repertoire of core features.

Messaging in Flex, with its adapters and channels, makes it possible to push data up from a server or a client to another client. Although today data push can be done in Java using the Java NIO Comet technique, the BlazeDS messaging-based data push provides an easy option to create rich, engaging, real-time event-driven systems. More information on Java NIO and Comet can be obtained from the following links:

- http://en.wikipedia.org/wiki/New_I/O
- http://en.wikipedia.org/wiki/Comet_(programming)

## Essential messaging and pushing data

To understand messaging in Flex, we will dive into a sample application first and then explore the different aspects of the model in the light of the application. The application is a collaborative form that is filled in by two users at the same time. Changes on either side are propagated to the other one. A possible use case could be travel booking by a customer in association with an agent, where the agent assists in real time by validating the data and adding expertise to find the best deal.

There are two main roles in the world of messaging: message producer and message consumer. A **message producer**, as the name suggests, produces messages, and a **message consumer** consumes messages. Our collaborative application acts as both a producer and a consumer. As a producer, it sends all updates out as messages. Subscribed consumers receive these messages and process them. The collaborative application is used by two users, although in its current shape the application itself doesn't restrict the number of users collaborating simultaneously. Each instance of the application acts as both consumer and producer, so an instance acting as a consumer receives its own messages, sent in the capacity of a producer. Updates, when applied to the producing instance, have no impact because the data is already present there; after all, it's the source of the updates.

In a real-life situation, you may want to bind these roles to specific parts of the form and have logic to skip and apply updates, but here we adopt the most elementary approach. You can get hold of the code and extend it to include any or all of these features.

Our collaborative application is in a single MXML file, which appears as shown here:

```
<?xml version="1.0" encoding="utf-8"?>
<mx:Application
xmlns:mx="http://www.adobe.com/2006/mxml"
creationComplete="initApp()">
    <mx:Script>
        <![CDATA[
            import mx.messaging.messages.*;
            import mx.messaging.events.*;

            private function processUserFormInput➡
```

```
(uName:String, uRequest:String):void {
            /* Set first message parameter to */
/* identify the message sender: a user or an agent */
            sendMessage("user",uName, uRequest);
        }

        private function processAgentFormInput➡
(aName:String, aComments:String):void {
            sendMessage("agent",aName, aComments);
        }

        private function initApp():void {
            consumer.subscribe();
        }

        private function messageHandler(event: MessageEvent):void {
            var paramArray:Array = (event.message.body).split(":");
            if(paramArray[0] == "user") {
                userName = paramArray[1];
                userRequest = paramArray[2];
            }else if(paramArray[0] == "agent") {
                agentName = paramArray[1];
                agentComments = paramArray[2];
            }

        }

        private function sendMessage➡
(param0:String,param1:String, param2:String):void {
            var message: AsyncMessage = new AsyncMessage();
            message.body = param0 + ":" + param1 + ": " + param2;
            producer.send(message);
        }
    ]]>
</mx:Script>

<mx:Producer id="producer" destination="CollaborationTopic"/>
<mx:Consumer id="consumer"
destination="CollaborationTopic"
message="messageHandler(event)"/>

<mx:Form id="collaborativeForm1" defaultButton="{updateUserInput}">
    <mx:FormItem label="User Name">
        <mx:TextInput id="userName"/>
    </mx:FormItem>
    <mx:FormItem label="User Request">
        <mx:TextInput id="userRequest"/>
    </mx:FormItem>
    <mx:FormItem>
```

```
                    <mx:Button label="Update User Inputs" id="updateUserInput"
                        click="processUserFormInput➡
(userName.text, userRequest.text);"/>
            </mx:FormItem>
        </mx:Form>
        <mx:Form
id="collaborativeForm2"
defaultButton="{updateAgentInput}">
            <mx:FormItem label="Agent Name">
                <mx:TextInput id="agentName"/>
            </mx:FormItem>
            <mx:FormItem label="Agent Comments">
                <mx:TextInput id="agentComments"/>
            </mx:FormItem>
            <mx:FormItem>
                <mx:Button label="Update Agent Input" id="updateAgentInput"
                    click="processAgentFormInput➡
(agentName.text, agentComments.text);"/>
            </mx:FormItem>
        </mx:Form>
</mx:Application>
```

The most interesting new controls in the preceding code are those that relate to a producer and a consumer. The Producer and the Consumer point to a server-side destination, which (as you will have noticed) have the same value. Data services provide messaging services, which are accessible through destinations like the remoting services. Most data services support the two main messaging domains: point-to-point and publish-and-subscribe. Point-to-point messaging is about sending messages from one queue to the other. Publish-and-subscribe messaging is a way of distributing information where topics act as the central conduit. Consumers subscribe to a topic, and producers send messages to it. All subscribed consumers receive all the messages.

Although the concept of messaging domains and the related roles are fairly universal, each programming language or platform has its own set of frameworks and tools to handle them. In Java, messaging is defined by a specification called Java Message Service (JMS). BlazeDS has the ability to plug in adapters to process messages using custom parsers, formatters, and message handlers. By default, it includes adapters for AS3 and JMS. This example does not involve any communication with JMS or Java, but it is restricted to two or more Flex clients, and so utilizes the ActionScript adapter. Here is the configuration snippet from messaging-config.xml, which may explain things a bit further:

```
<service id="message-service"
    class="flex.messaging.services.MessageService"
    messageTypes="flex.messaging.messages.AsyncMessage">
    <adapters>
        <adapter-definition id="actionscript"
        class="flex.messaging.services.messaging.
            adapters.ActionScriptAdapter" default="true"/>
        <adapter-definition id="jms"
            class="flex.messaging.services.➡
messaging.adapters.JMSAdapter"/>
    </adapters>
```

```
<destination id=" CollaborationTopic">

<adapter ref="actionscript"/>
<properties>
    <server>
        <max-cache-size>1000</max-cache-size>
        <message-time-to-live>0</message-time-to-live>
        <durable>true</durable>
        <durable-store-manager>
            flex.messaging.durability.FileStoreManager
        </durable-store-manager>
    </server>
    <network>
        <session-timeout>0</session-timeout>
        <throttle-inbound policy="ERROR" max-frequency="50"/>
        <throttle-outbound policy="REPLACE" max-frequency="500"/>
    </network>
</properties>

<channels>
    <channel ref="samples-rtmp"/>
    <channel ref="samples-amf-polling"/>
</channels>
</destination>
</service>
```

This configuration file is divided into three parts to make it easier for you to understand the details part by part and not get consumed in the complexity of a large configuration file. The three parts are as follows:

- Adapters
- Channels
- Destinations

Configuring a message service is not very different from configuring any other service, such as remoting or data management.

Two types of adapters are defined in this configuration. One is for ActionScript and the other is for JMS. The collaborative form destination uses the ActionScript adapter. Destinations use the channels to communicate, and send and receive messages. Channels are abstractions that bundle a protocol and an endpoint. Besides these, a destination can take a few properties to define its behavior. The preceding snippet has settings for the following properties:

- Server: Parameters affecting the storage of messages can be defined here. Maximum cache size, file size, file store root, and durability are typical parameters.
- Network: Timeout and inbound and outbound throttle policies can be set here.

This quick example should have established the elegant message features available with data services. Different data services implement message push differently. Protocols vary. LCDS uses RTMP to stream

**285**

messages, BlazeDS relies on AMF polling, and GDS uses Java NIO Comet. In all cases, the feature itself is very useful. We built a trivial example, but sophisticated real-time applications can be built on the basis of a reliable message infrastructure.

Before we close this discussion on messaging, we will look at integration with JMS and highlight the performance criteria that may be of paramount importance in production applications. You will also learn how to write a custom message adapter.

**Messaging and JMS** We will now take our last example, the collaborative form, and transform it into a real-time negotiation application. The negotiation involves two parties, a buyer and a seller. A buyer makes a bid and specifies the preferred price and quantity. A seller makes a bid by stating the desired price and the quantity. The matchmaking part of the negotiation is not included here. It's assumed the two parties go back and forth with a few bids and offers and finally close on a price and quantity that is acceptable to both. To keep the negotiation process neutral and unbiased, information about the last price at which somebody else traded is displayed in real time. We assume the system that collates and emits the last trade price is a Java application and is capable of sending these prices out as JMS messages. In the current context, how we consume this external data within our application is the main agenda. The Flex application consumes JMS messages with the help of data services, which rely on the JMS adapter to receive and send messages to JMS.

The application interface is simple and could look like Figure 7-8 on startup. We are assuming the JMS subscription triggers on creation being complete, and so we have fetched some data already.

**Figure 7-8.** A view of the negotiation application at startup

The code behind this application is equally simple, and its structure is as follows:

```
<?xml version="1.0" encoding="utf-8"?>
<mx:Application
xmlns:mx="http://www.adobe.com/2006/mxml"
creationComplete="initApp()" >
    <mx:Script>
        <![CDATA[
            import mx.messaging.events.MessageEvent;
```

```
            private function processBid(zip:String, pn:String):void {
                // Process the Bid ?
                //match it with the average last trade and the ask
            }

            private function processAsk(zip:String, pn:String):void {
                // Process the Ask ?
                //match it with the average last trade and the bid
            }

            [Bindable]
            var lastTradeValue:String = "USD 99.99";

            private function messageHandler(event:MessageEvent):void {
                // Get the message and process it
                // set the value of lastTradeValue
                //based on the received message
            }

            private function initApp():void {
                //consumer.subscribe();
            }
        ]]>
    </mx:Script>

    <!-- <mx:Consumer id="consumer"
destination="lastTradePrice"
message="messageHandler(event)" /> -->
    <mx:Panel horizontalAlign="center">

    <mx:Form id="buyerBid" defaultButton="{submitBid}">
        <mx:FormItem label="Bid Quantity">
            <mx:TextInput id="bidQuantity"/>
        </mx:FormItem>
        <mx:FormItem label="Bid Price">
            <mx:TextInput id="bidPrice"/>
        </mx:FormItem>
        <mx:FormItem>
            <mx:Button label="Submit Bid" id="submitBid"
                click="processBid(bidQuantity.text, bidPrice.text);"/>
        </mx:FormItem>
    </mx:Form>

    <mx:Form id="sellerAsk" defaultButton="{submitAsk}">
        <mx:FormItem label="Ask Quantity">
            <mx:TextInput id="askQuantity"/>
        </mx:FormItem>
        <mx:FormItem label="Ask Price">
            <mx:TextInput id="askPrice"/>
```

```
        </mx:FormItem>
        <mx:FormItem>
            <mx:Button label="Submit Ask" id="submitAsk"
                click="processAsk(askQuantity.text, askPrice.text);"/>
        </mx:FormItem>
    </mx:Form>
    <mx:Label
text="Last Trade Price: {lastTradeValue}"
textAlign="center"
fontWeight="bold" />
    </mx:Panel>
</mx:Application>
```

The highlight of this example isn't the application functionality but the integration with JMS, so we jump to the configuration file to see how that was made to work smoothly. Here is the snippet of messaging-config.xml:

```
<?xml version="1.0" encoding="UTF-8"?>
<service
id="message-service"
class="flex.messaging.services.MessageService">
    <adapters>
        <adapter-definition
id="actionscript"
class="flex.messaging.services.messaging.➡
adapters.ActionScriptAdapter"
default="true" />
        <adapter-definition
id="jms"
class="flex.messaging.services.➡
messaging.adapters.JMSAdapter"/>

</adapters>
    <default-channels>
<channel ref="my-streaming-amf"/>
<channel ref="my-polling-amf"/>
    </default-channels>
 <destination id="dashboard_chat">
 <properties>
   <server>
<durable>false</durable>
   </server>
   <jms>
     <destination-type>Topic</destination-type>
<message-type>javax.jms.TextMessage</message-type>
<connection-factory>ConnectionFactory</connection-factory>
<destination-jndi-name>topic/testTopic</destination-jndi-name>
<delivery-mode>NON_PERSISTENT</delivery-mode>
```

```
<message-priority>DEFAULT_PRIORITY</message-priority>
<acknowledge-mode>AUTO_ACKNOWLEDGE</acknowledge-mode>
<transacted-sessions>false</transacted-sessions>
  </jms>
 </properties>

<channels>
    <channel ref="my-polling-amf"/>
 </channels>
 <adapter ref="jms"/>
 </destination>

</service>
```

JMS defines extensive possibilities for message durability, acknowledgements, and message filtering. Data services extend most of those features to Flex. The default JMS adapter in BlazeDS and LCDS supports these features.

In the preceding example, we send text messages, but it's also possible to send object messages. Data services remoting works in association with messaging to serialize and deserialize between Java and ActionScript.

JMS in Flex started out by supporting only publish-and-subscribe messaging, but point-to-point communication has now been included. The Flex framework also includes filters and subtopics to allow fine-grained and rule-based message filtering. The Consumer control has a selector property to filter messages, which takes a string value. SQL expressions can also be defined to filter messages. For example, to filter messages based on headerProp, a header property, you could have a criterion like this:

```
headerProp > someNumericalValue
```

Message headers are accessible via a message handle. They are stored as an associative array and can be modified as required. It's also possible to add newer members to this hash. For example:

```
var message:AsyncMessage = new AsyncMessage();
message.headers = new Array();
message.headers["newProp"] = newValue;
```

This was just a part of the code but it confirms that arbitrary numbers of header manipulations are possible with messages. Selector tags operate only on the headers and not on the message body.

An alternative to using selectors is to use subtopics. Whereas a selector evaluates every message through an expression, a subtopic creates subcategories within a destination. The subcategories can be created using specific names. Before sending a message out, a producer sets the subtopic. A small code snippet might look like this:

```
var message:AsyncMessage = new AsyncMessage();
producer.subtopic = "subTopicLevel1.subTopicLevel2.subTopicLevel3 ";
producer.send(message);
```

A consumer sets the subtopic at the time of subscription. A subtopic is set before the subscribe method is called. Following is an example code snippet that does this:

```
consumer.destination = "ConfiguredDestination";
consumer.subtopic = " subTopicLevel1.subTopicLevel2.subTopicLevel3";
consumer.subscribe();
```

It's possible to use wildcards with subtopics. For example, there may be multiple subtopics at level 2, and you may want to receive messages that fall in all those subcategories. In that case, instead of subscribing to each of them individually, you could subscribe to subTopicLevel1.* and get the same effect.

By now, you know the message service is a useful feature and provides fairly sophisticated ways to build complex applications. You are also familiar with the built-in adapters that work behind the scenes to create robust integration points. Despite these features, the variety of messaging styles and infrastructure requires the ability to write custom adapters to work with scenarios beyond ActionScript and JMS.

The good news is that BlazeDS and LCDS provide a clean and simple API to write custom adapters.

# Writing custom message adapters

Writing a custom message adapter involves the following steps:

1. Use the BlazeDS (or LCDS) API to write a custom message adapter.
2. Configure the adapter in services-config.xml so that destinations can use it.
3. Refer to this custom adapter in a message destination.
4. Create producers and consumers and send and receive messages using this custom adapter.

I will focus on the first two of these four steps. Also, when I talk about writing the adapter, I will focus on the API and the requirements and not delve into implementation of any specific behavior.

All message adapters in BlazeDS extend directly or indirectly from flex.messaging.services. ServiceAdapter. MessagingAdapter is the base class for publish-and-subscribe messaging, and it inherits directly from the ServiceAdapter. Depending on the desired behavior, and therefore potential reusability of MessagingAdapter implementation, you can choose to start with either the ServiceAdapter or the MessagingAdapter.

All adapters are required to implement the invoke method, which is invoked on receipt of a message. The invoke method is expected to take a Message object and return an Object type. It's common to use the AsyncMessage class as the class that implements the Message interface.

In the ActionScript adapter, the invoke method sends the message out to all subscribers by calling the pushMessageToClients method. This is the custom behavior that you need to implement depending on what you expect from the adapter.

The MessagingAdapter class also defines a few other methods, including those that help initialize it, allow subtopics, and set security constraints. The initialize method takes two arguments: a string ID and a ConfigMap object. What you define in the services-config.xml or its associated configuration files becomes available via the ConfigMap object. You have seen JMS adapter–specific property settings in the last example. You can similarly set properties to your custom adapter. For example, you may call your custom adapter customAdapter and have its properties within the <customAdapter> </customAdapter> XML tags. The initialize method will be able to get all the properties from such an XML node and will be able to initialize the adapter as you instruct it to.

Writing a custom adapter is a large topic and could fill up an entire chapter, if not a small book; however, I have walked you through the essentials and will stop at that. Before moving on, I would like to mention an open source initiative called dsadapters that I launched a few months back to provide adapters for many common messaging situations and platforms. The project is online at http://code.google.com/p/dsadapters/. You might find your desired custom adapter in this project and thus save yourself some time and energy.

# Advanced issues in messaging

This section picks up an assortment of topics that pertain to advanced messaging concepts. In none of these do I get under the hood. The text only briefly surveys the topics and gives you a preview of some ideas that lie ahead.

## Pushing over sockets

As discussed in the last chapter, it's possible to create socket connections over TCP/IP to an external host and port as long as the security restrictions are satisfied. If the messaging entities (i.e., producers and consumers) are available over a unique network address, creating the connection would be effortless. Socket connections can be of two types: those that transmit text and XML data, and those that transmit binary data. It may be possible to use sockets with binary data to push data efficiently. However, there are drawbacks to this approach, namely the following:

- Non-HTTP ports could have restrictions across a firewall.
- The scalability is seriously suspect, as each logical connection maps to a physical connection.

Therefore, though sockets may be a possibility, it is probably wiser to stick with data services.

## Connection scalability

LCDS uses RTMP to push data, whereas BlazeDS uses AMF polling to send the data through to the client. In AMF polling, data push, though possible, is not scalable. It has limitations because of inefficiencies in the mechanism. BlazeDS does not have RTMP and probably never will, unless RTMP becomes open source.

In the meanwhile, you could use Comet-style persistent connections to push data. The Servlet 3.0 specification is trying to come up with a uniform standard to create HTTP 1.1–style persistent connections for data push using the NIO-based framework Comet. However, even before the specification is ready and accepted, the Apache foundation has already implemented a way to do this in Apache Tomcat. The Jetty team has achieved similar success.

For BlazeDS to use this scalable option, the message broker servlet needs to be modified to listen to Comet events. That way a blocked long-polling connection can be created with no threads being utilized on the server. Such connections can easily scale and have up to 30,000 or more connections on a single 64-bit machine.

## Transactions

Message-based systems can support transactions and allow for explicit commit and rollback. With JMS, it's possible to have transactions in a messaging session or have more robust arrangements with the help of the Java Transaction API (JTA). In data services such as LCDS and BlazeDS, it's possible to use a JMS **transacted session**. A transacted session supports transactions within a session. Therefore, a rollback in a transacted session will roll back all the sends and receives in that session. However, it will have no impact on transactions that are outside of the session. In other words, if the JMS messages interacting with Flex also affect a transaction in another enterprise application or the database, a rollback will only impact the JMS session and not these external systems.

Turning this feature on is as simple as setting the `transacted-sessions` value in the configuration file to true. This is what it looks like:

```
<jms>
....
    <transacted-sessions>true</transacted-sessions>
....
</jms>
```

# Using server-side proxies

HTTPService and WebService were covered in enough detail in the last chapter. There we emphasized that these services promote loose coupling and can be used to access data in a Flash Player independent of a server infrastructure. The only mandatory requirement was that the external host provide a cross-domain security policy definition. This requirement was never a concern if the host already had a `crossdomain.xml` file allowing access or if it was possible to request the host maintainers to put one in place. However, in the vast expanse of the World Wide Web, it's not always possible for such a good arrangement to be in place. In situations where we are unable to access data from an external host due to security restrictions, it's viable to fetch it via data services. In this role, data services provide the proxy service for HTTPService and WebService components.

The server-side configurations for proxy settings are made in the `proxy-config.xml` file. This file is included by reference in `services-config.xml`. The HTTPService sends HTTP requests down to the proxy, and the WebService sends SOAP web service calls down to the proxy. In either case, we need a service adapter to take these requests and translate them into the final call. For example, an HTTP request needs to end up with a URL invocation. You saw messaging service adapters in the context of messaging. The service adapters for HTTP and web service proxies implement a similar set of classes to create a service adapter. Default HTTP proxy and SOAP web service proxy adapters are available in BlazeDS.

For HTTPService, you can define a URL for the proxy setting or set up a set of dynamic URL(s) that are resolved to the appropriate URL based on the URL value set in the client-side HTTP call. For web services, you define either the WSDL URL or the SOAP endpoint URL pattern. These URL configurations are done with destination configuration. It's also possible, especially with HTTPService, to define a default destination and have a set of dynamic URLs with it. Then every HTTPService call via data services is routed through this destination to the HTTP proxy adapter.

The proxy service itself can be configured with a number of properties. We present a sample of the configuration file available in the distribution and in the documentation and explain the properties in context. Here is the sample configuration:

```
<service
id="proxy-service"
class="flex.messaging.services.HTTPProxyService">
    <properties>
        <connection-manager>
            <max-total-connections>100</max-total-connections>
            <default-max-connections-per-host>
2</default-max-connections-per-host>
</connection-manager>
<!-- Allow self-signed certificates;
should not be used in production -->
        <allow-lax-ssl>true</allow-lax-ssl>
        <external-proxy>
            <server>10.10.10.10</server>
            <port>3128</port>
            <nt-domain>mycompany</nt-domain>
            <username>flex</username>
            <password>flex</password>
            </external-proxy>
    </properties>
    </service>
```

The HTTP proxy adapter in BlazeDS uses the Apache HttpClient as the user agent. The configuration max-total-connections translates to the use of a multithreaded concurrent connections manager for HttpClient. max-connections-per-host sets the default number of connections if the host supports hardware clustering. The allow-lax-ssl true value means self-signed certificates will work. If the connection to the host is made through an external proxy, the external proxy can be specified in the configuration file as well. Authentication credentials like the password can be passed to the external proxy.

# Additional useful data services tips

Data services are useful and extensible pieces of software. You have seen how they can be extended to support additional features with the help of custom factories and custom service adapters. What I discuss next are the interesting features around run-time configuration and application security that data services offer.

## Configuring at run time

So far, almost all the configurations I have spoken about have related to compile-time configuration, where the entries are made in the configuration files. However, it's also possible to make many of these configurations and settings at run time. Run-time configuration makes systems more flexible and amenable to tweaking at the time of use. At run time, you can define channels, create consumers, set up subscriptions, and affect destination configurations. However, I only show you one of these possibilities here: channel definitions.

**Defining channels at run time** At run time, channels can be created on the client with the help of a ChannelSet object, which may contain one or more Channel objects. Essentially, the process is first to create a ChannelSet object and then dynamically create channels and add channels to it. After this, the channel set is associated with the channelSet property of the RemoteObject. This is what a sample piece of code may look like:

```
var cs:ChannelSet = new ChannelSet();
var newChannel:Channel = new AMFChannel("my-amf", endpointUrl);
cs.addChannel(newChannel);
remoteObject.channelSet = cs;
```

The endpoint URL can be defined dynamically at run time. ChannelSet has the ability to search among the set of configured channels. Each channel can define a failover URL.

# Application security

In many cases, especially in enterprise scenarios, you may need to restrict access to server-side destinations. It's possible to define a secure destination without much trouble. Data service configurations allow definitions for both authentication and authorization. **Authentication** means confirming one's identity, and **authorization** relates to the server-side resources that an authenticated user can access.

Security is configured using security constraints. These constraints can be defined at multiple levels, namely the following:

- **Global**: One set of definitions for all destinations. Usually such configuration would reside in the common configuration area: within services-config.xml itself.

- **Destination specific**: Security constraints for a destination. You can define such constraints inline within the destination configuration tags.

- **Fine-grained**: For remoting destinations, you could create an include list by using multiple include-method tags (or using the exclude-method tag). Such lists will ensure that only the included methods are callable on the remote destinations. Calling any other method would cause an error.

Authentication mechanisms can be custom or basic. This implies that you could leverage your existing authentication systems using the custom route.

Following is an example of a destination-level configuration that uses custom authentication:

```
<destination id="ro">
    <security>
        <security-constraint>
            <auth-method>Custom</auth-method>
            <roles>
                <role>roUser</role>
            </roles>
        </security-constraint>
    </security>
</destination>
```

HTTPService, WebService, and RemoteObject support passing and invalidation of login credentials using the setCredentials and the logout methods, respectively. You can also pass credentials to remote services using setRemoteCredentials.

A simple example of setCredentials with RemoteObject is as follows:

```
var myRemoteObject:RemoteObject = new RemoteObject();
myRemoteObject.destination = "SecureDestination";
myRemoteObject.setCredentials("userName", "myPassword");
myRemoteObject.send({param1: 'param1Value'});
```

Implementing custom security and setting up fine-grained access control can be tedious, but with BlazeDS you can utilize such constructs without adding any additional overhead.

# Leveraging the media server

So far, it's been all about data services. Data pull and push are critical for most modern applications. Equally important and becoming ever more popular is the availability of information as media assets, audio and video. The Flash Media Server suite of products is a solution for large-volume on-demand media streaming. In this section, I introduce you to the fundamentals of this product and whet your appetite to seek more information.

Flash Media Server (FMS) is a licensed product, but a free developer edition can be downloaded from the Adobe web site. The latest stable release version at the time of writing is version 3. Red5 is an open source alternative to this product.

Although FMS can be accessed from multiple venues—the Web (using the Flash Player), desktops (within AIR), and mobile devices (using FlashLite)—we will focus on getting it from the Web. An application deployed in the Flash Player (i.e., as a SWF) and built using Flex or Flash can use FMS to stream media, such as a long, high-quality video, within its context. Before we put such an arrangement to the test, it's logical to question the importance and need for such an infrastructure. Videos can be played and downloaded from Flash applications without using FMS. Video player components and controls within Flex can help load, run, and display video content with ease and elegance. Videos can be dropped into a web server and accessed via a Flex application without any problem. Why then should you use FMS?

The question is valid and the answer lies in understanding the different approaches to media delivery to a Flash Player over the Internet. The situations talked about so far are all related to the type of media delivery known as progressive download. In **progressive download**, the media file itself is external to the SWF. (Only for really small media files may it make sense to embed the media file. The SWF would be terribly bloated if large media files were embedded, and your application would take forever to download and start up.)

When the media file, say a video, is accessed, it is downloaded locally to the user agent machine, and when it buffers up a sufficient amount, it is played back. The media resource is transmitted over the regular HTTP channel on port 80, just like any web page or other web resource. In contrast to this download and playback model, there is also the model of streaming bits through a persistent connection and playing it as soon as it comes through. This type of model is called **streaming**. Files are kept external to the SWF in this case as well, so the advantages of this are available with streaming just as with progressive download. In addition, streaming provides a few additional benefits, namely the following:

- Adjustment of transmission bitrate depending on network bandwidth availability
- Fast start as you don't have to wait for the download to complete
- Advanced control over the media portions and playback
- Ability to seek and navigate to a portion of the media
- Capture and play live as events occur
- Include interactive features
- Enhance security and enforce digital media rights

FMS makes streaming possible and uses it as the de facto mechanism to deliver media. This should answer the question why you should consider using FMS.

To achieve streaming, FMS uses RTMP as the underlying protocol. LCDS uses the same protocol for data push as part of the messaging infrastructure. RTMP is replaced with AMF polling in BlazeDS for data push because RTMP is a proprietary protocol and BlazeDS is an open source product.

FMS supports a variety of variations of the RTMP protocol, as summarized in Table 7-2.

**Table 7-2.** RTMP Flavors in Flash Media Server

| Protocol Name | Description | Port Used |
| --- | --- | --- |
| RTMP | Default RTMP | 1935 (default, then 443, 80) |
| RTMPT | Tunneled over HTTP | 80 |
| RTMPS | RTMP over SSL | 443 |
| RTMPE | Encrypted RTMP (better than SSL) | 1935 (then 443, 80) |
| RTMPTE | Encrypted RTMP tunneled over HTTP | 80 |

FMS supports a lot of different media formats, but I am not going to list them here. On the Flash Player, FLV is the most popular and best supported media format for videos. You can use FLV in FMS.

Now that we have this supercharged infrastructure, let's see how we could use it with a Flex application. A Flex application is delivered as a SWF to a client machine user agent (a browser). This SWF file has the ability to connect to an external FMS, running on an external host, using RTMP. FMS is accessed pretty much the way Flex applications access external data from other hosts. Unlike regular data access, the protocol isn't HTTP, and the connections are persistent in the case of FMS.

A simple example is included to demonstrate the following:

1. Connect from Flex to FMS.
2. Make a remote method call over a net connection.
3. Get a video stream input.

The assumption is that you have the Flash Media Server installed and running. If not—if you just want to play with it—you can download a developer edition of the Flash Media Server and install it.

The first thing to do to interact with FMS from Flex is to connect to it. When you connect to an FMS3 server, you connect to an instance of the server. Therefore, the connection URL will point to such an instance. This is what the connection code might look like:

```
var nc:NetConnection = new NetConnection();
nc.addEventListener(NetStatusEvent.NET_STATUS, netStatus);
nc.addEventListener(SecurityErrorEvent.➥
SECURITY_ERROR, netSecurityError);
nc.connect("rtmp://localhost/MyApplication");
```

NetConnection is the primary class used to connect to FMS. When connecting from Flex, you use the AS3 version of the class, which adopts the event-driven model like the connection classes you have seen before.

Now that the connection is established, we will make a remote call to a server resource. This server resource is the media resource that we will be streamed across to our Flex application. We use the NetStream class to consume it and display it in our Flex application.

I will ignore most of the manipulation code on the Flex side here and just show small pieces of the call and the NetStream code, the intent being to simply introduce FMS.

Typically, a call to the server is made like this:

```
nc.call("serverMethod", MyResponder, "MethodParameter");
```

If the call returns a video stream, we can read the stream using the NetStream class. Then we can bind the video to a UIComponent, which we can add to the stage.

Programming FMS with Flex does not involve fundamentally different paradigms. It's all ActionScript programming of the kind you do with your other applications. The only new element is the API, with which you'll want to familiarize yourself. As with all Adobe products, the Flash Media Server 3 developer guide (LiveDocs) is the best place to go to get that information. It's available online at http://livedocs.adobe.com/flashmediaserver/3.0/hpdocs/help.html?content=Book_Part_31_deving_1.html.

# Summary

This chapter rapidly covered a fair number of topics related to data services and the media server, with the focus more on the former. The introduction to media server was meant to be a high-level overview.

The chapter started with an overview of the data services architecture. Then you explored the steps involved in installing data services and configuring it. Subsequently you built an example application and saw data services in action.

The review of the features of data services topics included Java to Flex serialization, asynchronous communication, support for additional data types, custom adapters, connection scalability, data push over sockets, and transactions. Server-side proxy and its usage for HTTP-based calls as well as web services were also illustrated.

Both data services and media servers position the Adobe Flex and AIR technologies as viable choices for some serious applications for the present and the future. In the age of event-driven, real-time, responsive rich systems, where the Web is transforming itself into a read-write media network, technologies as these are bound to shine.

In the next chapter, we deal with Flex and PHP integration. Although PHP does not offer the same type of data services as Java does, the remoting possibilities from Flex to PHP are many. Fundamental concepts that relate to RPC and the media server, which you learned in this chapter, will be useful when dealing with analogous concepts in the world of PHP as well.

# Chapter 8

# PHP AND FLEX

By Jack Herrington

Wait! If you are thinking to yourself, "I don't use PHP so this chapter isn't for me," think again. The first example in this chapter demonstrates a helpful proxy for Flex that will be valuable to anyone, regardless of whether you use PHP in your application or not. Of course, if you are a PHP user already, then just dig in.

PHP and Flex make a good team. Flex is capable of using data in almost any format, and PHP is capable of delivering data in almost any format and it's available everywhere. Flex can make use of text, XHTML, XML, JSON, or AMF data directly. Or it can go directly to the port level and connect any service it wants using any format. PHP can deliver text, HTML, XHTML, and JSON natively, and there is an extension to provide AMF services to Flash applications.

In this chapter, I'll demonstrate a variety of data transport techniques you can use to connect your Flex application to your PHP application quickly and easily. The PHP code I present works for both PHP 4 and PHP 5.

## A Flex proxy

Connecting a Flex application to your server is easy. First, the server needs to export some format that you can read in your application. Second, you write the application to connect to the server, get the data, parse and display it, and so on. Unfortunately, that first part isn't always so easy. Because of the security restrictions on the Flash

Player, you can't directly connect to just any server. You can connect to one in the same domain. But you are restricted from connecting to any server that doesn't have a crossdomain.xml file on it.

A crossdomain.xml file sits in the root directory of any domain that supports Flash application access. Following is an example crossdomain.xml file:

```
<?xml version="1.0"?>
<!DOCTYPE cross-domain-policy SYSTEM ➥
"http://www.macromedia.com/xml/dtds/cross-domain-policy.dtd">
<cross-domain-policy>
    <allow-access-from domain="*" />
</cross-domain-policy>
```

If you want to specify a different location for the crossdomain.xml file, you can use the System. security.loadPolicyFile API provided by the Flash Player to specify your own URL.

You can set all kinds of policies and things on this, but the one I've shown here just allows access from anywhere, which is probably what you want in most cases. For example, if you're going to make a Flex widget to connect to your application, that widget will sit on any page in any domain, so you are not going to want to restrict what domains have access to your web application.

The crossdomain.xml file is the first thing that I upload to all of my web applications, since it allows for both Flash and Silverlight to access the services directly.

So let's take an example scenario. You have downloaded Flex Builder on your own, played around a bit, gotten excited by what it can do, and now you want to connect it to your work application and see if it can make use of that data. But unfortunately, your work application server doesn't have the crossdomain.xml file. So either you need to convince your systems administrator to put that file on the server or you need a way around that restriction. That's where a proxy comes in.

A **proxy** is a small piece of server code that sits in a domain that you do have access to and requests data from a domain that you do not have access to. Some proxies go further and rewrite the code coming through, but we don't need anything that fancy.

Figure 8-1 shows the data request flow from the Flash application on your machine to a server under your control that has a proxy installed on your machine. The proxy makes a request to the machine you do not control, and returns the data to you.

Our proxy is so small it takes just three lines of PHP code.

```
<?php
$ch = curl_init($_REQUEST['url']);
curl_exec($ch);
curl_close($ch);
?>
```

This PHP code uses the CURL library, which is built into most PHP installations. If you do not have access to CURL, you will need to reinstall PHP from scratch with the CURL library installed.

This code will run almost anywhere. If you have a Macintosh, you can drop it into the /Library/WebServer/Documents directory. If you have a Windows machine, you first have to install PHP, which you can download from http://php.net, and then install this script in a document directory of the PHP or Apache installation. For Windows, you can also use the XAMPP installer (http://www.apachefriends.org/en/xampp.html) to get PHP, MySQL, Apache, and more all in one shot.

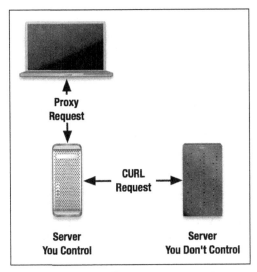

**Figure 8-1.** The proxy flow

The script takes one argument, the URL to get. It then uses CURL to request the data from the specified URL and returns it as the body of the response. For example, if I were to install this on the localhost, and then make this request:

    http://localhost/proxy.php?url=http://slashdot.net

it would return the Slashdot homepage.

I should mention that this proxy is not something that you should install on any production sites. It's far too insecure for production, as it allows anyone to use your site to make web requests to anywhere.

To demonstrate the use of the proxy, I'll show a Flex application that requests an HTML page through the proxy, parses the returned HTML, and then displays the data in the data grid. This will show you two things: how to use the proxy, and how to use regular expressions to parse HTML code.

Let's imagine that your web application is some game, and you have a list of high scorers on the homepage. Now you want to be able to show those high scorers in your Flex application. Here's a sample of what the HTML code might look like:

```
<html><body>
<p>Here are the most recent scores
<table width=100%>
<tr><td>Joe</td><td>10,000</td></tr>
<tr><td>Dan</td><td>9,000</td></tr>
<tr><td>Ted</td><td>8,500</td></tr>
</table>
```

This code will display correctly in a browser, but you can't read it using an XML parser, even though it has tags. That's because the tags are unbalanced. Notice on the second line the <p> is not terminated properly—there's no </p> following it. That's fine by web standards but doesn't work for XML. So we need to read this back as text and then use regular expressions to extract the data from the <table> tag.

Just for the sake of demonstration, I've uploaded this HTML to my localhost server and called it testdata.html. The Flex code that will make the request of the proxy, parse the data, and then display it in a data grid is shown here:

```
<?xml version="1.0" encoding="utf-8"?>
<mx:Application xmlns:mx="http://www.adobe.com/2006/mxml"
  layout="vertical"
  creationComplete="onStartup(event);">
<mx:Script>
<![CDATA[
import mx.rpc.events.ResultEvent;
import mx.rpc.http.HTTPService;

private function onStartup( event:Event ) : void {
  var proxyUrl:String = "http://localhost/proxy.php?url=";
  var dataUrl:String = "http://localhost/testdata.html";

  var proxyGet:HTTPService = new HTTPService();
  proxyGet.url = proxyUrl + dataUrl;
  proxyGet.method = 'GET';
  proxyGet.resultFormat = "text";
  proxyGet.addEventListener(ResultEvent.RESULT,onHttpResult);
  proxyGet.send();
}

private function onHttpResult( event:ResultEvent ) : void {
  var scoreData:Array = new Array();

  var foundRows:Array = event.result.toString().match(
  /\<tr\>(.*?)\<\/tr\>/g );
  for each( var row:String in foundRows ) {
    var cells:Array = row.match( /\<td\>(.*?)\<\/td\>/g );
    var name:String = cells[0];
    name = name.replace( /\<.*?\>/g, '' );
    var score:String = cells[1];
    score = score.replace( /\<.*?\>/g, '' );
    score = score.replace( /,/g, '' );

    scoreData.push( { name: name, score: score } );
  }
  dgScores.dataProvider = scoreData;
}
]]>
</mx:Script>
```

```
<mx:DataGrid id="dgScores" width="100%" height="100%" />
</mx:Application>
```

There are two big sections in this code. The first is the onStartup method, which makes the HTTPService request to the proxy code on my local server. And the second is the onHttpResult method, which takes the returned HTML as text, runs some regular expressions against it, creates a data set, and then sets the data provider in the DataGrid.

The onStartup method is pretty straightforward. First, we define the two URLs, one for the proxy, and the other the destination URL where the data is located. Then the script creates a new HTTPService object, sets the URL, sets the method, and then sets the result format. The result format has to be text because the HTML returned from this page is invalid XML. If you don't set the result format, onHttpResult will never get called. A fault event will happen instead because by default HTTPService is looking to get XML back.

The onHttpResult method is a little more complicated simply because it uses a lot of regular expressions. It would've been nice to be able to use ActionScript's outstanding E4X syntax to read the data, but unfortunately the HTML is invalid as XML. And since we don't have control of the server, there is nothing we can do about that.

The first thing the method does is to find all the <tr> tags in the result. For each of the rows, it then finds the <td> tags as an array—the first tag having the name of the player, and the second tag having a score. The code then uses some regular expressions to clean off the tags and strip away the commas.

At the end of the method, the code sets the dataProvider attribute on the DataGrid Flex control, which is smart enough to create the correct columns and display the data.

When I run this on my browser, I see something like Figure 8-2.

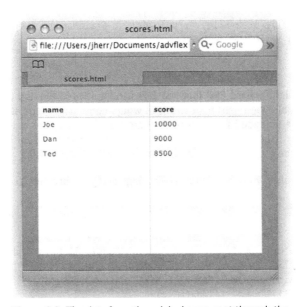

**Figure 8-2.** The data from the original page, sent through the proxy and displayed

So now you can see that the Flex application has made a request to the proxy, which in turn made another request, got the data back, and sent it back to Flex. The Flex code then parsed the HTML, found the data it needed, and displayed it.

Now clearly this is not optimal. If the application server had had a crossdomain.xml file on it, I could have made the request directly. And if the application server returned the scores in XML, I wouldn't have had to parse through the HTML to get to the data. In fact, it's the parsing of the HTML that is the weakest link in this entire example. That's because if the format of the HTML changes for whatever reason, for example, if another table is added, the code will break.

This type of proxy system is best used when you want to create a prototype Flex application all on your own with data from the server, without having to get anyone to change the server. That's really handy if you want to do "skunk works" development.

# Uploading media with AIR

Rich Internet media, audio and especially video, has ruled the Web 2.0 revolution. It's pretty easy to create a PHP application to display HTML pages that link to audio or video. But it can be painful for your users to get that audio or video to your application. What I'll demonstrate here is the use of Adobe Integrated Runtime (AIR) technology to create a very simple uploader application that sits on the desktop. Your user can simply drag and drop a file onto the application and have it sent to the server.

First, let's take a look at the PHP code on the server.

```
<html>
<?php
$tempFile = $_FILES['Filedata']['tmp_name'];
$fileName = $_FILES['Filedata']['name'];
move_uploaded_file($tempFile, "./uploads/" . $fileName);
echo "Uploaded $fileName";
?>
</html>
```

This is some pretty straightforward PHP that just takes the uploaded file and puts it into an uploads directory. The only trouble you might have with this would come from permissions on the temporary directory that holds the uploaded files before they are transferred to the uploads directory. Or you might have permissions issues on the uploads directory. Or sometimes your files are too large and you'll need to change the maximum upload size setting in your PHP.ini file.

To make sure all that's okay, you can use this HTML page and your browser to test uploading a file to the server:

```
<html>
<body>
<form enctype="multipart/form-data" action="basicFileUpload.php"
  method="post">
<input type="hidden" name="MAX_FILE_SIZE" value="2000000" />
<input type="file" name="Filedata" />
<input type="submit" value="Upload" />
```

```
    </form>
  </body>
</html>
```

If this page works properly, and you see the uploaded file on the server, then you know the Flex code should work.

The next step is to create an AIR application project using Flex Builder 3. For this example, I'm calling it "upload." The first code for the application is shown here:

```
<?xml version="1.0" encoding="utf-8"?>
<mx:WindowedApplication xmlns:mx="http://www.adobe.com/2006/mxml"
  layout="vertical"
  width="400" height="300" creationComplete="onStartup(event);">
<mx:Script>
<![CDATA[
import flash.desktop.*;
import flash.filesystem.*;

private var _files:Array = [];

private function onStartup(event:Event): void {
  addEventListener(NativeDragEvent.NATIVE_DRAG_ENTER, onDragIn);
  addEventListener(NativeDragEvent.NATIVE_DRAG_DROP, onDrop);
}
private function onDragIn(event:NativeDragEvent):void {
  if(event.clipboard.hasFormat(ClipboardFormats.FILE_LIST_FORMAT)) {
    var files:Array = event.clipboard.getData(
  ClipboardFormats.FILE_LIST_FORMAT) as Array;
    if( files.length > 0 ) NativeDragManager.acceptDragDrop(this);
  }
}
private function onDrop(event:NativeDragEvent) : void {
  for each ( var f:File in event.clipboard.getData(
  ClipboardFormats.FILE_LIST_FORMAT) as Array )
    _files.push(f);
  uploadNextFile();
}
private function uploadNextFile(event:Event=null) : void {
  if ( _files.length > 0 ) {
    var f1:File = _files.pop() as File;
    f1.addEventListener(DataEvent.UPLOAD_COMPLETE_DATA,uploadNextFile);
    f1.upload( new URLRequest(
  'http://localhost/basicFileUpload.php' ), 'Filedata' );

    txtStatus.text = "Uploading "+f1.name;
  } else {
    txtStatus.text = "Drop your files here";
  }
}
```

```
        ]]>
        </mx:Script>
            <mx:Label id="txtStatus" text="Drop your files here" />
        </mx:WindowedApplication>
```

There isn't much to the user interface of this Flex application. When you start it up, all you see is an empty box that says "Drop your files here". The important parts are in the ActionScript code. The onStartup method registers the application with the native drag-and-drop manager. That's a new class that comes along with the rest of the AIR API.

The onDragIn method is called when the user drags a file or group of files over the application. In this case, it just looks to make sure that there is at least one file in a drag group, and if so it says that the application will accept the drop.

The onDrop method is called when the user actually drops the file or files onto the application. It adds all the files to an array of files to be uploaded, and then calls uploadNextFile. The uploadNextFile method is the one that actually does the work. It pops the first file off the list of files and then calls the upload method on it. It also adds an event listener that will get called after the upload is complete. And that event listener just calls back to itself. Once the list of files is exhausted, it sets the static text back to "Drop your files here".

The vast majority of the work here is done in the upload method on the file class provided by AIR. All it requires to upload a file is the URL of the form handler to take the upload and the name of the POST variable associated with the file. How cool is that?

Of course, in production you'll probably want to add some user authentication, and so on, but to keep the sample short, I've kept it to just the file upload.

When I start this application, I see something like Figure 8-3.

**Figure 8-3.** The drag-and-drop AIR application

I can then pick up a file off the desktop and move it over the application, as shown in Figure 8-4.

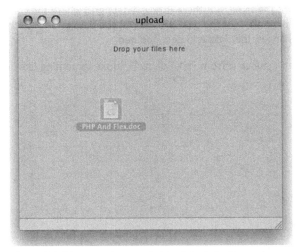

**Figure 8-4.** Moving a document over the application

And then drop a file, and it's uploaded to the server through the PHP script.

Of course the interface isn't all that interesting, or helpful, so we can make a slight tweak to the application and user data grid to show the files are queued up for upload. This new code is shown here:

```
<?xml version="1.0" encoding="utf-8"?>
<mx:WindowedApplication xmlns:mx="http://www.adobe.com/2006/mxml"
  layout="vertical"
  width="400" height="300" creationComplete="onStartup(event);">
<mx:Script>
<![CDATA[
// ...
private function uploadNextFile(event:Event=null) : void {
  if ( _files.length > 0 ) {
    var f1:File = _files.pop() as File;
    f1.addEventListener(DataEvent.UPLOAD_COMPLETE_DATA,uploadNextFile);
    f1.upload( new URLRequest(
  'http://localhost/basicFileUpload.php' ), 'Filedata' );
  }
  dgFileList.dataProvider = _files;
}
]]>
</mx:Script>
    <mx:DataGrid id="dgFileList" width="100%" height="100%">
      <mx:columns>
        <mx:DataGridColumn dataField="name"/>
      </mx:columns>
    </mx:DataGrid>
</mx:WindowedApplication>
```

Most of the code remains the same, but there is now a data grid where the static text used to be. And in the uploadNextFile method, I set the data provider of the data grid to be the list of files. That way each time the file list changes, the data grid gets updated.

This new interface, when I launch it from Flex Builder 3, looks something like Figure 8-5.

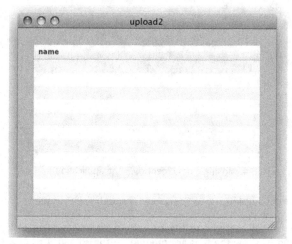

**Figure 8-5.** The upgraded drag-and-drop interface

Now when I drop a group of files on the application, I will see the list in the data grid. As each file is uploaded, the list will get smaller and smaller until all of the files have been uploaded.

Of course, Flex being Flex, it wouldn't be right not to show images if we are uploading. And that is pretty easy to do as well. All we need to do is change the DataGrid to a HorizontalList and put in an itemRenderer that displays the images. That code update is shown here:

```
<mx:HorizontalList id="dgFileList" width="100%" height="100%">
  <mx:itemRenderer>
    <mx:Component>
      <mx:Image source="{data.url}" height="240" width="200" />
    </mx:Component>
  </mx:itemRenderer>
</mx:HorizontalList>
```

When I run that AIR application from Flex Builder 3 and drag a few images onto it, I see something like Figure 8-6.

To make the example complete, you should add a progress indicator on the status of the upload. The upload method on the AIR File class also provides for a status callback so that you can show the user how the upload is proceeding. This is particularly useful on slow connections.

**Figure 8-6.** The image uploader in action

# AMFPHP

Flex and Flash applications support a remote procedure standard called **Remote Objects**. The upside of Remote Objects are that it's ridiculously easy for Flex applications to invoke methods on the server. The downside is that the process uses a proprietary AMF binary standard to do the communication. Not to fear though; where there is a will, there is a way, and so was born AMFPHP (http://amfphp.org/). This open source extension to PHP allows your PHP server to very easily provide new services to Flex or Flash applications as Remote Objects. AMF has been open sourced as part of the BlazeDS (http://opensource.adobe.com) project.

To demonstrate this, I'll create a service that returns the names and years of all of the Mars missions. It's a data set that I used for a lecture at NASA Ames. The data is stored in a MySQL database called nasa. Following is the code to create the database:

```
DROP TABLE IF EXISTS mission;

CREATE TABLE mission (
     name TEXT,
     year TEXT
);

INSERT INTO mission VALUES ( "Marsnik 1 (Mars 1960A)","1960" );
INSERT INTO mission VALUES ( "Marsnik 2 (Mars 1960B)","1960" );
...
```

I've left off the rest of the missions to keep the code sample short. I'm sure you get the point though.

Now to create an AMF service I first need to download the latest version of AMFPHP from `http://amfphp.org` and place the amfphp file in my web server's root directory. From there I can use my web browser to navigate to the browser Flex application that comes with the code (see Figure 8-7).

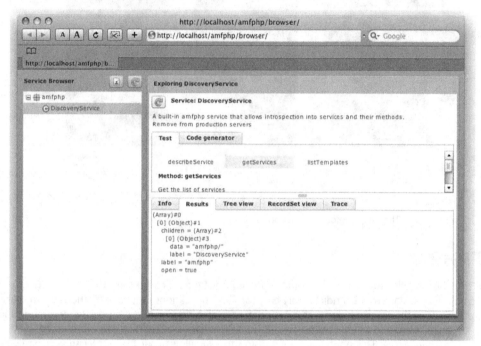

**Figure 8-7.** The remote services browser

This shows that there is one service installed on the server. It's called amfphp, and its job is to report on what services are provided by the server. Next, click getServices and then click the call button, and you will see the reply with the object shown.

So, great, at this point we know the PHP server is working, that AMFPHP is working properly, and that Flex can connect to it. The next step is to create our own nasa service to return the list of Mars flights.

I create a directory called nasa underneath services in the AMFPHP directory. From there, I create a new file called NasaService.php with the following code:

```php
<?php
require_once("MDB2.php");
include_once(AMFPHP_BASE . "shared/util/MethodTable.php");
class NasaService
{
  function getMissions()
  {
        $dsn = 'mysql://root@localhost/nasa';
        $mdb2 =& MDB2::factory($dsn);
        $sth =& $mdb2->prepare( "SELECT * FROM mission" );
        $res = $sth->execute( );
```

```
        $missions = array();
        while ($row = $res->fetchRow(MDB2_FETCHMODE_ASSOC)) {
    $missions []= $row; }
        return $missions;
    }
}
```

This script uses the portable database library MDB2 to run a query on the database to return the list of Mars flights. MDB2 is now a standard part of PHP installations. It's a library that provides access to every different type of database server through a single API. With earlier versions of PHP, you needed to use the MySQL API to access MySQL, the Oracle API to access Oracle, and so on. With MDB2, you get to use one API for any database.

It first opens the connection, prepares a SELECT query, then executes it and loads all of the data into the $missions array. From there, it simply returns the $missions array. AMFPHP does all the work of converting the data from a PHP array into an AMF array.

With the exception of the include_once for the AMFPHP code at the top, there is nothing AMF specific about this class at all. You could use this class in your PHP application as is, as well as using it with Flex and Flash through AMF. That is so cool!

To check that the service is running, I go back to the browser Flex application again (see Figure 8-8).

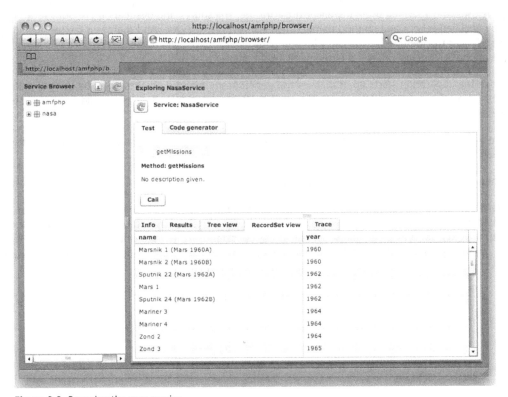

**Figure 8-8.** Browsing the nasa service

As you can see, the AMFPHP system has detected the module automatically, and I can run the getMissions method and get back all of the missions as an array. The browser interface is even helpful enough to throw a DataGrid display on it so that we can see the data more clearly.

Now all that remains is to invoke this in a Flex application. To do that, I'll use the DataGrid control just like the browser does to display the data. The code is shown here:

```
<?xml version="1.0" encoding="utf-8"?>
<mx:Application xmlns:mx=http://www.adobe.com/2006/mxml
  layout="vertical"
  creationComplete="nasaRO.getMissions.send();">
<mx:RemoteObject id="nasaRO"
  endpoint="http://localhost/amfphp/gateway.php"
  source="nasa.NasaService" destination="nasa.NasaService"
  showBusyCursor="true">
<mx:method name="getMissions" />
</mx:RemoteObject>
<mx:DataGrid width="100%" height="100%"
  dataProvider="{nasaRO.getMissions.lastResult}">
</mx:DataGrid>
</mx:Application>
```

The majority of the Flex code is in the definition of the RemoteObject tag. It needs to point to the server, which is specified using the endpoint attribute. The source and destination are both set to the fully qualified service and method name, which is nasa.NasaService. And there is a <mx:method> tag that defines the method we can call with the name getMissions. Of course, a service can have multiple methods, and you can specify arguments to the methods as well.

When the application starts up, it invokes the getMissions method on the server by using the send method on the nasaRO.getMissions object. If there were parameters, those would go in the send message.

The DataGrid monitors the lastResult on the RemoteObject's getMissions value and updates itself when there is new data.

When I bring this up in my browser, it looks like Figure 8-9.

Were it not for the fact that AMF is a binary standard that is somewhat coupled to Flex and Flash, it would be hands-down the easiest way to do web services. Certainly if you have a project where Flex is your only web services client, you should definitely consider using Remote Objects over AMF. AMF can be used by JavaScript. Check out the Flex-Ajax Bridge project (http://labs.adobe.com/wiki/index.php/Flex_Framework:FABridge) for more information.

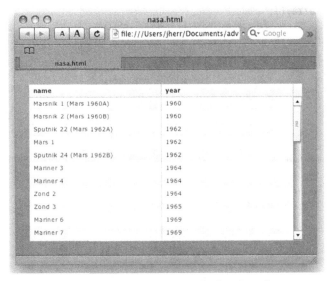

**Figure 8-9.** The DataGrid with the returned values from the server

# Flex and JSON

Because of the popularity of JavaScript web widgets, JavaScript Object Notation (JSON)–based web services have become very popular. JSON is just encoded JavaScript objects. It's easy for web clients to parse JSON because all they need to do is "eval" it to get the data (though this can have some security ramifications).

AS3 doesn't have eval, but it can read JSON data using the JSONDecoder class in the AS3 Core Library (as3corelib). You can download the core library from Google Code at http://code.google.com/p/as3corelib/.

Once you have downloaded it, drag the src directory from the download into a new project. This is shown in Figure 8-10.

From here, we need a JSON service to connect to the Flex application. I'll use the NASA Mars missions as an example. To prepare for the example, I follow the same steps as I did preparing the database in the AMFPHP example.

The code to export this with JavaScript is shown here:

```php
<?php
require_once("MDB2.php");
$dsn = 'mysql://root@localhost/nasa';
$mdb2 =& MDB2::factory($dsn);
$sth =& $mdb2->prepare( "SELECT * FROM mission" );
$res = $sth->execute( );
```

```
$missions = array();
while ($row = $res->fetchRow(MDB2_FETCHMODE_ASSOC)) {
  $missions []= $row; }
print json_encode( $missions);
?>
```

**Figure 8-10.** The JSONDecoder in the AS3 Core Library

This is the same query as in the AMFPHP example, but this time I use the PHP built-in json_encode function to turn it into JSON objects.

When I upload this to the web server root directory and bring it up in my browser, I see something like Figure 8-11.

That looks about right; the json_encode function turned the PHP array of objects into a JavaScript array of objects.

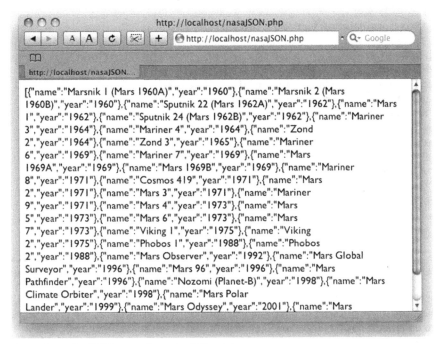

**Figure 8-11.** The JSON export from the PHP script

Next, we need a Flex application that uses the JSONDecoder class to turn the data from the server into ActionScript objects that we can use directly. That Flex application is as follows:

```
<?xml version="1.0" encoding="utf-8"?>
<mx:Application xmlns:mx="http://www.adobe.com/2006/mxml"
  layout="vertical"
      creationComplete="nasaData.send()">
<mx:Script>
<![CDATA[
import com.adobe.serialization.json.JSONDecoder;
import mx.rpc.events.ResultEvent;

private var missions:Array;

private function onNasaResult(event:ResultEvent) : void {
  var jsd:JSONDecoder = new JSONDecoder(event.result.toString());
  missions = jsd.getValue();
  onYearChange();
}
private function onYearChange() : void {
  var filteredMissions:Array = new Array();
  for each ( var mission:Object in missions ) {
    if ( mission.year >= hsYear.value )
      filteredMissions.push( mission );
```

**317**

```
        }
      dgMissions.dataProvider = filteredMissions;
    }
]]>
</mx:Script>
<mx:HTTPService id="nasaData" resultFormat="text"
  url="http://localhost/nasaJSON.php"
  result="onNasaResult(event);"/>
<mx:HBox>
<mx:Label text="After year" />
<mx:HSlider id="hsYear" minimum="1960" maximum="2008"
  value="2000" change="onYearChange()"
  liveDragging="true" snapInterval="1" />
</mx:HBox>
<mx:DataGrid id="dgMissions" width="100%" height="100%"  />
</mx:Application>
```

This code starts by running the send method on the nasaData HTTPService. That service is set up to request data from the JSON PHP script as text, and then send it on to the onNasaResult event handler.

The onNasaResult event handler then uses the JSONDecoder class from the AS3 Core Library to decode the JSON string into a set of basic ActionScript 3 objects. From there I use the onYearChange() method to update the DataGrid to show the missions that the user has requested.

When I run this in Flex Builder 3, it looks like Figure 8-12.

Now I can use the slider to filter the list based on year. Because liveDragging is set to true, the table is updated with each click of the slider.

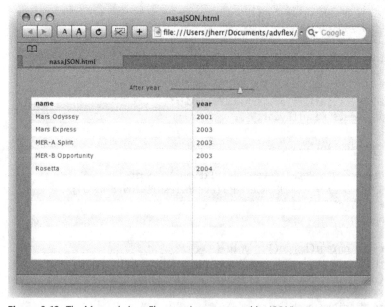

**Figure 8-12.** The Mars missions Flex app (now powered by JSON)

# Flex for chat

To demonstrate using XML with PHP and ActionScript, I'll put together a simple chat application. This starts with building a database to hold all of the messages. The MySQL code to create the table for the messages is shown here:

```
DROP TABLE IF EXISTS messages;

CREATE TABLE messages (
    message_id INTEGER NOT NULL AUTO_INCREMENT,
    username VARCHAR(255) NOT NULL,
    message TEXT,
    PRIMARY KEY ( message_id )
);
```

You can use this code to build the table by using either the phpMyAdmin interface to run the SQL after creating the database, or by using the command-line mysql interface.

It's a pretty simple table with three columns containing the following: a unique ascending message ID integer, the username, and the message.

We also need a PHP script that adds a message to the database. I'll call that add.php. The code for it is shown here:

```php
<?php
require_once("MDB2.php");

$dsn = 'mysql://root@localhost/aschat';

$mdb2 =& MDB2::factory($dsn);
if (PEAR::isError($mdb2)) { die($mdb2->getMessage()); }

$sth = $mdb2->prepare( "INSERT INTO messages VALUES ( null, ?, ? )");
$sth->execute( array( $_REQUEST['user'], $_REQUEST['message'] ) );
?>
```

This script uses the database-independent MDB2 library to connect to the MySQL database. It then prepares an INSERT statement and executes it with two values taken from the request: the username, and the message.

The final script for the server is messages.php. This script returns all of the messages in the table. The code is shown here:

```php
<?php
require_once("MDB2.php");

header( 'Content-type: text/xml' );

$dsn = 'mysql://root@localhost/aschat';

$mdb2 =& MDB2::factory($dsn);
```

**319**

```
?>
<messages>
<?php
$sth =& $mdb2->prepare( "SELECT * FROM messages" );
$res = $sth->execute();
while ($row = $res->fetchRow()) {
?>
<message user="<?php echo($row[1]) ?>">
<?php echo($row[2]) ?>
</message>
<?php
}
$res->free();
$mdb2->disconnect();
?>
</messages>
```

The output from this is XML. There is a root <messages> tag and within that a set of <message> tags, one for each message.

Now with the server component done, it's time to put together the Flex application for the front end. Here's the code for the Flex chat application:

```
<?xml version="1.0" encoding="utf-8"?>
<mx:Application xmlns:mx="http://www.adobe.com/2006/mxml"
  layout="vertical"
      creationComplete="checkMessages();">
<mx:Script>
<![CDATA[
import mx.rpc.events.ResultEvent;
import mx.rpc.http.HTTPService;

private function checkMessages( event:Event = null ) : void {
  var url:String = "http://localhost/aschat/messages.php?t="+➥
((new Date()).valueOf());
  var htMessages:HTTPService = new HTTPService();
  htMessages.url = url;
  htMessages.resultFormat = 'e4x';
  htMessages.addEventListener(ResultEvent.RESULT, onMessages);
  htMessages.send();
}
private function onMessages( event:ResultEvent ) : void {
  var messages:Array = [];
  for each( var msg:XML in event.result..message ) {
    messages.push( { user: msg.@user, message: msg.valueOf() } );
  }
  dgMessages.dataProvider = messages;

  var t:Timer = new Timer( 1000, 1 );
```

```
            t.addEventListener(TimerEvent.TIMER,checkMessages);
            t.start();
        }
        private function onKeyDown( event:KeyboardEvent ) : void {
            if ( event.keyCode == Keyboard.ENTER ) {
                var url:String = "http://localhost/aschat/add.php";
                url += "?user="+escape(user.text)+"&message="+escape(msg.text);
                var htMessages:HTTPService = new HTTPService();
                htMessages.url = url;
                htMessages.send();
                msg.text = '';
            }
        }
    }
    ]]>
    </mx:Script>
    <mx:DataGrid id="dgMessages" width="100%" height="100%">
      <mx:columns>
        <mx:DataGridColumn width="100" dataField="user" headerText="" />
        <mx:DataGridColumn dataField="message" headerText="" />
      </mx:columns>
    </mx:DataGrid>
    <mx:Form width="100%">
      <mx:FormItem label="User name" width="100%">
        <mx:TextInput id="user" width="100%" text="Jack" />
      </mx:FormItem>
      <mx:FormItem label="Message" width="100%">
        <mx:TextInput id="msg" width="100%" keyDown="onKeyDown(event);" />
      </mx:FormItem>
    </mx:Form>
    </mx:Application>
```

The ActionScript code to get and send messages is at the top of the file, and the user interface for the application is located at the bottom. As the application starts up, it calls checkMessages to start a request for the message list from the server. To ensure that we always make a fresh request, the checkMessages method adds the current time value to the URL. That way each request is unique and will not be cached. The checkMessages function sets the onMessages method as the callback for the messages request.

The onMessages function parses the XML using the E4X syntax and creates a simple messages list for the dgMessages DataGrid. It then sets a timer for 1000 milliseconds (one second) to start the process over again.

The onKeyDown method is called when the user presses any key in the message field located at the bottom of the application. When the user presses the Enter or Return key, the message is posted to the add.php script on the server.

When I launch this from Flex Builder 3, I see something like Figure 8-13.

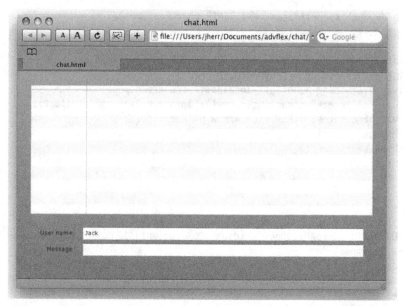

**Figure 8-13.** The empty chat window

I can then type in a chat message and press Return. That posts the message to the add.php script. After a short delay, the messages.php script is requested again, and the message will appear as shown in Figure 8-14.

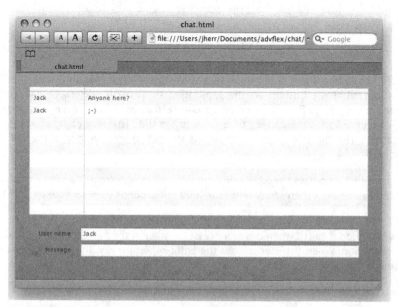

**Figure 8-14.** The chat system with a few messages in it

It's a simple system, to be sure. And it does have the downside that it can have performance problems when hundreds of clients are all polling the same server.

The only problem is that with each message the returned XML gets larger and larger. To optimize this, the messages.php script should return the IDs of each of the messages in the XML. It should also take an ID as an argument and only return messages with a greater ID than the one specified. This would mean that most of the time the server would respond with an empty <messages> tag, indicating that there were no new messages.

The updated code for messages.php is as follows:

```php
<?php
require_once("MDB2.php");

header( 'Content-type: text/xml' );

$id = 0;
if ( array_key_exists( 'id', $_GET ) ) { $id = $_GET['id']; }

$dsn = 'mysql://root@localhost/aschat';

$mdb2 =& MDB2::factory($dsn);
?>
<messages>
<?php
$sth =& $mdb2->prepare(
    "SELECT * FROM messages WHERE message_id > ?" );
$res = $sth->execute( array( $id ) );
while ($row = $res->fetchRow()) {
?>
<message id="<?php echo($row[0]) ?>" user="<?php echo($row[1]) ?>">
<?php echo($row[2]) ?>
</message>
<?php
}
$res->free();
$mdb2->disconnect();
?>
</messages>
```

This new code looks for an ID in the request arguments. If none is provided, it uses 0. It also adds a conditional WHERE clause to the query to get only messages with IDs higher than the one specified.

The updates to the Flex code to support this are shown here:

```xml
<?xml version="1.0" encoding="utf-8"?>
<mx:Application xmlns:mx="http://www.adobe.com/2006/mxml"
  layout="vertical"
      creationComplete="checkMessages();">
<mx:Script>
<![CDATA[
import mx.rpc.events.ResultEvent;
import mx.rpc.http.HTTPService;
```

```
private var lastID:int = 0;

private function checkMessages( event:Event = null ) : void {
  var url:String = "http://localhost/aschat/messages.php?id="+lastID;
  url += "&t="+((new Date()).valueOf());
  var htMessages:HTTPService = new HTTPService();
  htMessages.url = url;
  htMessages.resultFormat = 'e4x';
  htMessages.addEventListener(ResultEvent.RESULT, onMessages);
  htMessages.send();
}
private function onMessages( event:ResultEvent ) : void {
  var messages:Array = [];
  for each( var msg:XML in event.result..message ) {
    lastID = parseInt( msg.@id );
    messages.push( { user: msg.@user, message: msg.valueOf() } );
  }
  dgMessages.dataProvider = messages;

  var t:Timer = new Timer( 1000, 1 );
  t.addEventListener(TimerEvent.TIMER,checkMessages);
  t.start();
}
...
]]>
</mx:Script>
...
</mx:Application>
```

The user interface doesn't change at all. The only changes are the addition of a lastID variable that tracks the ID of the last message seen and the ID parameter to the URL on the request.

Although this new code is more efficient, it would be interesting to see just how much easier it would be to implement with Remote Objects.

# Chatting on AMFPHP

After setting up the AMFPHP server as we did earlier in this chapter the next step is to create a service for the chat system. To do that, we create a directory under services called chat and add the code for the ChatService, shown here:

```php
<?php
require_once("MDB2.php");
include_once(AMFPHP_BASE . "shared/util/MethodTable.php");
class ChatService
{
  function getMessages( $id )
  {
        $dsn = 'mysql://root@localhost/aschat';
        $mdb2 =& MDB2::factory($dsn);
        $sth =& $mdb2->prepare(
  "SELECT * FROM messages WHERE message_id > ?" );
        $res = $sth->execute( $id );
                $messages = array();
        while ($row = $res->fetchRow(MDB2_FETCHMODE_ASSOC)) {
  $messages []= $row;    }
        return $messages;
  }
  function addMessage($user,$message)
  {
        $dsn = 'mysql://root@localhost/aschat';
        $mdb2 =& MDB2::factory($dsn);
        $sth =& $mdb2->prepare( "INSERT INTO messages VALUE (0,?,?)" );
        $sth->execute( array( $user, $message ) );
  }
}
?>
```

We only need the two functions, one to get the messages after a certain ID, and the other to add a message given the username and the message.

With the service code installed, I can go to the service browser as shown in Figure 8-15 and have a look for myself.

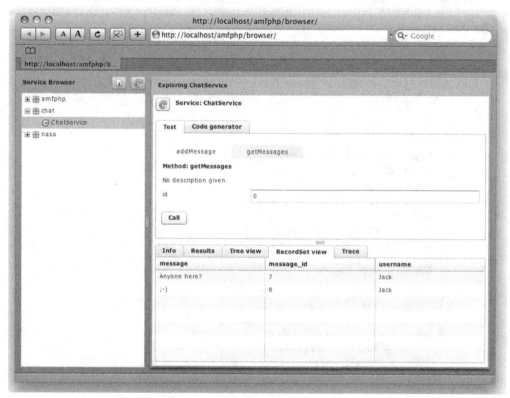

**Figure 8-15.** The AMFPHP service browser showing the chat service

All right, everything looks good with getting the messages from the AMFPHP service. Now it's time to retool Flex to use Remote Objects instead of XML. The updated code for the chat interface is shown in the following listing:

```
<?xml version="1.0" encoding="utf-8"?>
<mx:Application xmlns:mx="http://www.adobe.com/2006/mxml"
  layout="vertical"
      creationComplete="checkMessages();">
<mx:RemoteObject id="chatRO"
  endpoint="http://localhost/amfphp/gateway.php"
  source="chat.ChatService" destination="chat.ChatService"
  showBusyCursor="true">
<mx:method name="getMessages" result="onMessages()" />
<mx:method name="addMessage">
<mx:arguments>
  <mx:Array>
```

```
        <user>{user.text}</user>
        <message>{msg.text}</message>
    </mx:Array>
  </mx:arguments>
  </mx:method>
</mx:RemoteObject>
<mx:Script>
<![CDATA[
import mx.rpc.events.ResultEvent;
import mx.rpc.http.HTTPService;

private var lastID:int = 0;
private var messages:Array = [];

private function checkMessages( event:Event = null ) : void {
  chatRO.getMessages.send( lastID );
}
private function onMessages() : void {
  for each ( var msg:Object in chatRO.getMessages.lastResult ) {
    lastID = msg.message_id;
    messages.push( msg );
  }
  dgMessages.dataProvider = messages;
  var t:Timer = new Timer( 1000, 1 );
  t.addEventListener(TimerEvent.TIMER,checkMessages);
  t.start();
}
private function onKeyDown( event:KeyboardEvent ) : void {
  if ( event.keyCode == Keyboard.ENTER ) {
    chatRO.addMessage.send();
    msg.text = '';
  }
}
}
]]>
</mx:Script>
  ...
</mx:Application>
```

The user interface portion at the end doesn't change at all, so I've left that part of the listing out. But the rest of the ActionScript code has gone through some reworking. The top of the file now has a definition for the Remote Objects provided by the AMFPHP server.

The getMessage definition is pretty simple. But the addMessage is cool because it binds directly to the text fields from the form. That means that when sending a message, all I have to do is run the send() method on the addMessage operation. You can see that code in the onKeyDown handler.

The checkMessages function is now greatly simplified; it just calls the getMessages Remote Objects operation.

The onMessages function now takes the result, which is just the set of new messages since the last check, and appends it to the existing list of messages. It then restarts the timer to request the messages again in another second.

Not only is the server code cleaner in this example, but so is the user interface code. Moreover the binary transport mode used by AMF is a whole lot more efficient than going over XML.

If you are serious about using Flex for chat, you should check out the XIFF library (http://osflash.org/xiff) for Flex that allows you to connect your Flex application to Jabber servers. Not only is this a good way to implement chat, but also XMPP, the Jabber standard, is extensible enough to allow for peer-to-peer or group data interaction with any data types.

# Summary

As you can see from the examples I've provided, Flex and PHP work very well together. PHP helps draw out the power of Flex by providing a robust, easy to implement and maintain back end for the Flex interface. And Flex has enough horsepower to connect with PHP no matter what language it's speaking. The question for you is, what will you do with Flex and PHP?

In the next chapter, we dig into how to more thoroughly integrate Flex applications into the web browser environment using JavaScript.

**Chapter 9**

# TALKING WITH JAVASCRIPT AND HTML: WEB PAGE INTEGRATION

By Jack Herrington

Opinions vary, but what I think made YouTube the success that it has become is the ability for customers to embed videos from YouTube in their own sites and blogs. In short, it was the widgets. Flex 1 and 2 should have made building widgets easy, but until Flex 3, the file sizes of the Flash applications built by Flex were too large to make for good widgets. Now that we have the ability to cache the framework in the Flash Player using remote shared libraries (RSLs), the size of an individual Flash application can be much smaller. So now, we can truly make widgets and integrate our applications fully into the page.

This chapter will cover two topics related to creating widgets. The first is JavaScript integration—both in the sense of JavaScript getting called by your Flex application and having the JavaScript on the page call the Flex application code. I'll also cover using the RSL technology in Flash 9 and Flex to build Flash applications small enough to be widgets.

## Hacking the Flex Builder page template

Since a lot of the work we will be doing in this chapter involves JavaScript, we are going to be messing around with the HTML of the page. Flex Builder 3 maintains an HTML template for your application in the html-template directory. This file is shown in Figure 9-1.

**Figure 9-1.** The HTML page template

To edit the file, right-click it and select Open as Text. Don't edit the index.html file in bin-debug or bin-release. That file is written over each time the application is compiled, so all of your changes will be lost.

# Flex calling JavaScript

The first type of connection between Flex and JavaScript that I want to explore is a Flex application calling out to a JavaScript function. This is handy when you want to integrate some interactive component within the Flex application with another element on the web page. For example, if you use a Flex widget to do navigation and you want the JavaScript on the page to use Ajax to dynamically load a section of content, you will want that Flex widget to tell you whenever customers have selected that they wish to see some content.

My first example is a fairly arbitrary one. There is a List control with a set of values, and when the customer double-clicks a value, the JavaScript function itemSelected is called. This code is shown here:

```
<?xml version="1.0" encoding="utf-8"?>
<mx:Application xmlns:mx="http://www.adobe.com/2006/mxml"
  layout="horizontal">
<mx:Script>
<![CDATA[
private function onDoubleClick( event:Event ) : void {
  ExternalInterface.call('itemSelected', theList.selectedItem );
}
]]>
</mx:Script>
<mx:List id="theList" width="300" doubleClick="onDoubleClick(event);"
  doubleClickEnabled="true">
  <mx:dataProvider>
    <mx:Array>
      <mx:String>Apples</mx:String>
```

```
        <mx:String>Oranges</mx:String>
        <mx:String>Bananas</mx:String>
      </mx:Array>
    </mx:dataProvider>
  </mx:List>
</mx:Application>
```

The magic is performed by the Flash Player API's ExternalInterface class, which does the work of connecting to JavaScript and registering methods that can be called by JavaScript. In this case, I use the call method on the ExternalInterface class to call a JavaScript method with the currently selected item's text.

The JavaScript code that responds to this is as follows:

```
<script>
function itemSelected( itemName ) {
    alert( itemName );
}
</script>
```

If you were to stop and run the example at this point, you would get a security violation from the player. To get JavaScript and Flash to talk together, you have to change every location in the index.template.html file that references allowScriptAccess to always. Here's an example portion:

```
<object classid="clsid:D27CDB6E-AE6D-11cf-96B8-444553540000"
    id="${application}" width="${width}" height="${height}"
    codebase="http://fpdownload.macromedia.com/get/flashplayer/➥
current/swflash.cab">
    <param name="movie" value="${swf}.swf" />
    <param name="quality" value="high" />
    <param name="bgcolor" value="${bgcolor}" />
    <param name="allowScriptAccess" value="always" />
    <embed src="${swf}.swf" quality="high" bgcolor="${bgcolor}"
      width="${width}" height="${height}" name="${application}"
      align="middle"
      play="true"
      loop="false"
      quality="high"
      allowScriptAccess="always"
      type="application/x-shockwave-flash"
      pluginspage="http://www.adobe.com/go/getflashplayer">
    </embed>
  </object>
```

This means that you are allowing the Flash Player to connect with the JavaScript layer, and vice versa.

Now when I run this from Flex Builder 3, I see something like Figure 9-2.

**Figure 9-2.** The Flex application on the page

I then double-click an item and see Figure 9-3.

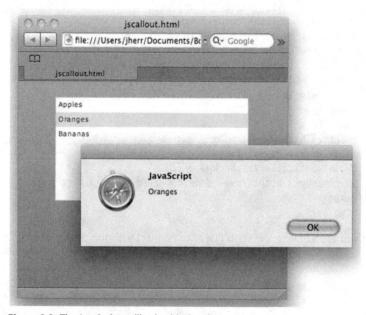

**Figure 9-3.** The JavaScript callback with the alert

Excellent. My Flex applications can now talk to the JavaScript layer. But what if I want the JavaScript layer to be able to specify the name of the function to call? Well, in that case, I can specify a parameter to the SWF for the application. That Flex code is shown here:

```
<?xml version="1.0" encoding="utf-8"?>
<mx:Application xmlns:mx="http://www.adobe.com/2006/mxml"
  layout="horizontal"
  creationComplete="onStartup()">
<mx:Script>
<![CDATA[
private var _callbackName:String = '';
private function onStartup() : void {
  _callbackName = ( parameters['callback'] != null ) ? ➥
parameters['callback'] : 'itemSelected';
}
private function onDoubleClick( event:Event ) : void {
  ExternalInterface.call(_callbackName, theList.selectedItem );
}
]]>
</mx:Script>
<mx:List id="theList" width="300" doubleClick="onDoubleClick(event);"
  doubleClickEnabled="true">
  <mx:dataProvider>
    <mx:Array>
      <mx:String>Apples</mx:String>
      <mx:String>Oranges</mx:String>
      <mx:String>Bananas</mx:String>
    </mx:Array>
  </mx:dataProvider>
</mx:List>
</mx:Application>
```

Now if I pass a different value for callback, the new value will be used as the name of the JavaScript function to get the callback message.

I also need to change the index.template.html page to create the Flash with the parameter. This change is shown here:

```
AC_FL_RunContent(
    "src", "${swf}?callback=myCallback",
    "width", "${width}",
    "height", "${height}",
    "align", "middle",
    "id", "${application}",
    "quality", "high",
    "bgcolor", "${bgcolor}",
    "name", "${application}",
    "allowScriptAccess","always",
    "type", "application/x-shockwave-flash",
    "pluginspage", "http://www.adobe.com/go/getflashplayer"
);
```

**335**

And I need to change the JavaScript function to match the one I specified to the SWF application.

```
<script>
function myCallback( item ) { alert( item ); }
</script>
```

After making all these changes, I can run the example again in Flex Builder 3, and it should look and work exactly the same.

Having shown this connection, two questions arise: how many arguments can I send over, and how complex can they be? The answer to the first is as many as you like. As for the second, primitive values (strings, numbers, etc.) all work, as do arrays. Variables of type Object can go across as JavaScript associative arrays.

To demonstrate this, I'll show one further refinement on the original example. This new code is shown here:

```
<?xml version="1.0" encoding="utf-8"?>
<mx:Application xmlns:mx="http://www.adobe.com/2006/mxml"
  layout="horizontal">
<mx:Script>
<![CDATA[
private var _items:Array = [ 'Apples', 'Oranges', 'Bananas' ];
private function onDoubleClick( event:Event ) : void {
  ExternalInterface.call('itemSelected', theList.selectedIndex,
  _items );
}
]]>
</mx:Script>
<mx:List id="theList" width="300" doubleClick="onDoubleClick(event);"
  doubleClickEnabled="true"
  dataProvider="{_items}">
</mx:List>
</mx:Application>
```

In this case, I send over the index of the selected item and the list of items as an array.

The JavaScript code on the other side looks like this:

```
<script>
function itemSelected( index, data ) {
  alert( [ index, data ] );
}
</script>
```

It takes the two arguments, and then puts up an alert with the index and the data.

When I run this from Flex Builder 3 and double-click an item, I see something like Figure 9-4.

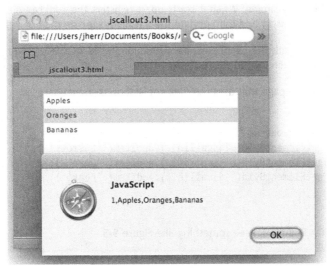

**Figure 9-4.** The more complex Javascript callback

So as you can see, integers, strings, and arrays come over just fine.

# Calling from JavaScript into Flex

Now that you know how to call from Flex into JavaScript, you need to learn how to go the other way. To demonstrate, I'll allow the JavaScript on the page to dynamically add items to a Flex control using an addItem method that I will export through the ExternalInterface.

Following is the code for this JavaScript-driven Flex application:

```
<?xml version="1.0" encoding="utf-8"?>
<mx:Application xmlns:mx="http://www.adobe.com/2006/mxml"
  layout="horizontal"
  creationComplete="onStartup()">
<mx:Script>
<![CDATA[
private var _itemsList:Array = [];
private function onStartup() : void {
  ExternalInterface.addCallback( "addItem", ➥
function( str:String ) : void {
    _itemsList.push( str );
    theList.dataProvider = _itemsList;
  } );
  ExternalInterface.call( 'jscallinLoaded' );
}
]]>
</mx:Script>
<mx:List id="theList" width="200" height="250" />
</mx:Application>
```

The Flex application is fairly simple. When it starts up, it registers the addItem method as a function that will add an item to an array and then update the dataProvider on the list with the new array.

The Flex application then calls the jscallinLoaded function in the JavaScript code to let it know that the Flash application has been loaded successfully.

The JavaScript code on the page that uses this Flex application is shown here:

```
<script>
function jscallinLoaded() {
  document.getElementById( 'jscallin' ).addItem( 'Carrots' );
  document.getElementById( 'jscallin' ).addItem( 'Corn' );
  document.getElementById( 'jscallin' ).addItem( 'Peas' );
}
</script>
```

When I run this in Flex Builder 3, I see something like Figure 9-5.

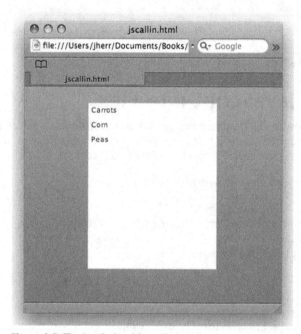

**Figure 9-5.** The JavaScript-driven Flex application

You might be asking yourself, why call out to JavaScript only to have it call back? Can't the JavaScript call in directly? It could, if the Flex application were loaded. But the loading sequence can vary from browser to browser and between operating systems. I have found that the most predictable way to know that a Flash application has been loaded is for it to call back into the JavaScript layer.

# Flex for widgets

Flex applications built without RSLs are too big to be widgets; 250 kilobytes is too much to download to put an RSS reader on a page. But with RSLs, the application size can decrease to the 60-to-90 kilobyte range. That's very acceptable.

To get started with RSL, open up the Project dialog and navigate to the Library Path section of the Flex Build Path tab. This is shown in Figure 9-6.

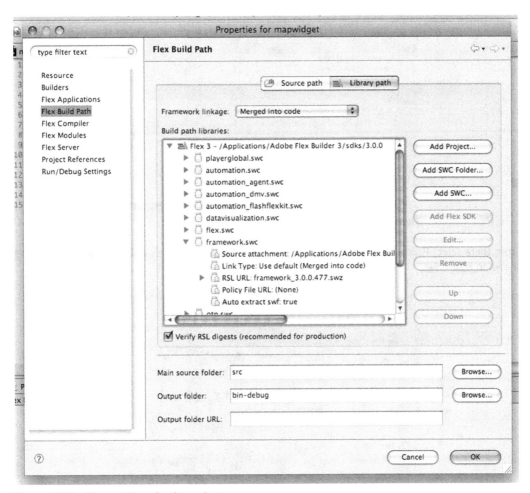

**Figure 9-6.** The library settings for the project

Next, click the `framework.swc` library and click the Edit button. This will take you to the dialog shown in Figure 9-7.

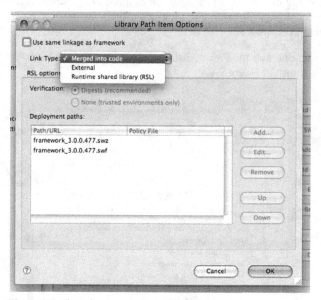

**Figure 9-7.** The selection of RSL for the framework

From there select Runtime Shared Library and click the Add button, which will take you to the dialog shown in Figure 9-8.

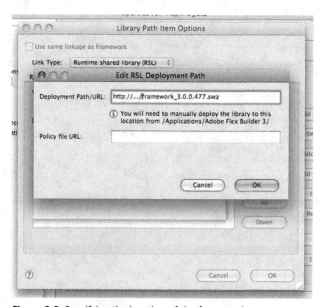

**Figure 9-8.** Specifying the location of the framework

This dialog allows you to specify the URL where the framework is located on **your** web site. That means you have to copy this file from the Flex Builder 3 library to your web site in the location you specified.

To experiment with this, I'm going to create a little Yahoo! Maps widget using their Flash library. You can download that Flash library from Yahoo (http://developer.yahoo.com/flash/maps/) and install it in your project's lib directory.

From there, I can create a Flex application that references the library, as shown in the following code:

```
<?xml version="1.0" encoding="utf-8"?>
<mx:Application
  xmlns:mx="http://www.adobe.com/2006/mxml"
  layout="absolute"
  creationComplete="handleCreationComplete();">
<mx:UIComponent id="mapContainer" width="100%" height="100%"/>
<mx:Script>
<![CDATA[
import mx.events.ResizeEvent;
import com.yahoo.maps.api.YahooMap;
import com.yahoo.maps.api.YahooMapEvent;
import com.yahoo.maps.api.core.location.Address;
import com.yahoo.maps.webservices.geocoder.GeocoderResult;
import com.yahoo.maps.webservices.geocoder.events.GeocoderEvent;

private var _yahooMap:YahooMap;
private var _address:Address = new Address(
    "1 market, san francisco, ca");
private var _bFirst:Boolean = true;

private function handleCreationComplete() : void {
  ExternalInterface.addCallback( "gotoAddress",
  function( add:String ) : void {
  _address = new Address( add );
    _address.addEventListener(GeocoderEvent.GEOCODER_SUCCESS,
  handleGeocodeSuccess);
    _address.geocode();
  } );

  var appid:String = Application.application.parameters.appid;
  _yahooMap = new YahooMap();
  _yahooMap.addEventListener(YahooMapEvent.MAP_INITIALIZE,
  handleMapInitialize);
  _yahooMap.init(appid,mapContainer.width,mapContainer.height);

  mapContainer.addChild(_yahooMap);
  mapContainer.addEventListener(ResizeEvent.RESIZE,
  handleContainerResize);
```

```
  _yahooMap.addPanControl();
  _yahooMap.addZoomWidget();
  _yahooMap.addTypeWidget();
}

private function handleMapInitialize(event:YahooMapEvent):void
{
  _address.addEventListener(GeocoderEvent.GEOCODER_SUCCESS,
  handleGeocodeSuccess);
  _address.geocode();
}

private function handleGeocodeSuccess(event:GeocoderEvent):void {
  var result:GeocoderResult = _address.geocoderResultSet.firstResult;
  _yahooMap.zoomLevel = result.zoomLevel;
  _yahooMap.centerLatLon = result.latlon;
  if ( bFirst ) {
    ExternalInterface.call( "mapComplete" );
    bFirst = false;
  }
}

private function handleContainerResize(event:ResizeEvent):void {
  _yahooMap.setSize(mapContainer.width,mapContainer.height);
}
]]>
</mx:Script>
</mx:Application>
```

There are two important elements here. The first is in handleCreationComplete where I add a new external method called gotoAddress. This will allow the JavaScript on the page to navigate the map to any address it wishes. The second important piece is in handleGeocodeSuccess where the Flex application calls the mapComplete function in the JavaScript code when the map is ready for action.

I then create a JavaScript wrapper around this Flex application called mapwidget.js. The code for this is shown here:

```
var _gotoLocation = '';

function mapComplete() {
  document.getElementById('mapwidget').gotoAddress( _gotoLocation );
}

function putMapWidget( gotoLocation )
{
```

```
        _gotoLocation = gotoLocation;
       AC_FL_RunContent(
         "src", "mapwidget",
         "width", "100%",
         "height", "100%",
         "align", "middle",
         "id", "mapwidget",
         "quality", "high",
         "allowScriptAccess","always",
         "type", "application/x-shockwave-flash",
         "pluginspage", "http://www.adobe.com/go/getflashplayer"
       );
     }
```

This script defines a new function called putMapWidget that my customers can use to put a mapping widget on their pages. This function takes one parameter, an address. This address is used by the mapComplete function to set the map to the specified address using the exposed gotoAddress method.

I then replace the entire index.template.html page with the contents shown here:

```
<html lang="en">
<head>
<script src="AC_OETags.js" language="javascript"></script>
<script src="mapWidget.js" language="javascript"></script>
</head>

<body>
<div style="width:200px;height:300px;">
<script language="JavaScript" type="text/javascript">
putMapWidget( '357 Riverview Rd., Swarthmore PA, 19081' );
</script>
</div>
</body>
</html>
```

This template represents how customers might use the widget on their page. They first include the standard AC_OETags.js JavaScript file, and then the mapwidgets.js file, and finally they invoke the putMapWidget function wherever they want a map.

**343**

Figure 9-9 shows the resulting widget page.

**Figure 9-9.** The mapping widget centered on Swarthmore

From here the customer can scroll around, change mapping modes, zoom in and out, and so on.

But what if the customer wants to have a code copy function in the widget, so that anyone who wants the map on his page can click the button and get the JavaScript code that he should use to put the map on their own page?

The updated code, which has a code copy button, is shown here:

```
<?xml version="1.0" encoding="utf-8"?>
<mx:Application
  xmlns:mx="http://www.adobe.com/2006/mxml"
  layout="absolute"
  creationComplete="handleCreationComplete();">
<mx:UIComponent id="mapContainer" width="100%" height="100%"/>
<mx:HBox width="100%" horizontalAlign="right" paddingTop="50"
  paddingRight="10">
<mx:Button click="onCopyCode()" label="&lt; &gt;" />
</mx:HBox>
<mx:Script>
<![CDATA[
import mx.controls.TextArea;
import mx.events.ResizeEvent;
import com.yahoo.maps.api.YahooMap;
```

```
import com.yahoo.maps.api.YahooMapEvent;
import com.yahoo.maps.api.core.location.Address;
import com.yahoo.maps.webservices.geocoder.GeocoderResult;
import com.yahoo.maps.webservices.geocoder.events.GeocoderEvent;

private var _yahooMap:YahooMap;
private var _location:String = "1 market, san francisco, ca";
private var _address:Address;

private function onCopyCode() : void {
  var html:String = '';
  html += '<script src="AC_OETags.js" language="javascript">➥
</script>'+"\n";
  html += '<script src="mapWidget.js" language="javascript">➥
</script>'+"\n";
  html += '<script language="JavaScript" type="text/javascript">'+"\n";
  html += 'putMapWidget( "'+_location+'" );'+"\n";
  html += '</script>'+"\n";
  System.setClipboard( html );
}

private function handleCreationComplete() : void {
  ExternalInterface.addCallback( "gotoAddress",
  function( add:String ) : void {
    _location = add;
    _address = new Address( _location );
    _address.addEventListener(GeocoderEvent.GEOCODER_SUCCESS,
    handleGeocodeSuccess);
    _address.geocode();
  } );
...
}

private function handleMapInitialize(event:YahooMapEvent):void
{
  _address = new Address( _location );
  _address.addEventListener(GeocoderEvent.GEOCODER_SUCCESS,
  handleGeocodeSuccess);
  _address.geocode();
}
...
]]>
</mx:Script>
</mx:Application>
```

Most of the code remains the same. But now there is a button that the customer can use to get the JavaScript code required to place the widget on any page.

When I bring this version up from Flex Builder 3, I see the widget as shown in Figure 9-10.

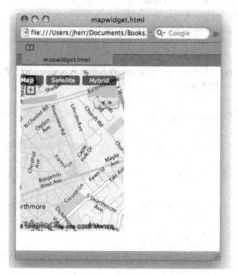

**Figure 9-10.** The widget with the code copy button

From there, I click the copy button and paste the JavaScript code into a TextEdit window. This is shown in Figure 9-11.

**Figure 9-11.** The pasted code

Not bad. It even has my custom location in the address field. That way my customer will look at whatever I am looking at.

# Summary

The big advantage of using Flash and Flex for widgets is that the code will run the same everywhere. The Flash runtime is extremely consistent, unlike JavaScript support, which can vary greatly between the different browsers.

With the addition of RSLs to the Flex framework, the doors have been opened to put your Flex application almost anywhere. And who knows, with Open Screen you might really be able to put your Flex application on almost any device.

In the next chapter, you will learn how to create amazing Flex applications using a selection of APIs you can get off the shelf. These mashup examples make for excellent widgets, so you can leverage your RSL experience right away.

Part Three

# GAINING REAL ADVANTAGE
# IN THE NEW WEB

## Chapter 10

# FLEX MASHUPS

By Elad Elrom

In this chapter, I am going to explain one of the most talked-about concepts on the Web today: mashups. What is a mashup? And what is all the buzz about?

The word "mashup" was originally used in the pop and hip hop music industry back in the mid 1990s to describe a song created out of two or more songs mixed together.

> An **application mashup** combines at least two data sources to create a new application.

For instance, consider mixing Google search results with a snapshot of a web page, YouTube videos, and a link to Google Maps. The result is SearchMash (http://www.searchmash.com), a web site operated by Google, as shown in Figure 10-1.

**Figure 10-1.** Mashup example source: SearchMash

> As a metaphor for a mashup, take this example from real life: a client hires a detective agency. As a result of the client's request for an investigation, a salesperson (mashup) assigns a few detectives to handle the case. The detectives check all sorts of clues (data sources) found on the Internet, in public records, at the scene itself, etc. All of these clues are processed, filtered, and formed to determine an answer. At that point, the salesperson responds to the client with the findings of the investigation.

In recent years, the Web has been going through a transformation into what many call **Web 2.0**, a term first used by O'Reilly to describe the transformation of the Web into a sharing and collaborative vehicle. To learn more, visit http://www.oreillynet.com/pub/a/oreilly/tim/news/2005/09/30/what-is-web-20.html.

Today, an increasing number of components, web services, data sources, and of course cloud computing services are available. These services allow developers to create new and exciting applications by simply mixing them together.

> *Cloud computing is an architecture consisting of a large network of servers that are running parallel to each other. Companies such as Amazon (through its EC2) provide cloud computing on a per-usage basis through a web service or RESTful connection. Using cloud servers allows high performance and ensures stability while keeping cost per usage low.*

Currently, Flex is not one of the most common technologies used for writing mashups. I believe the reason is that Flex is still relatively new. Additionally, the Flash Player requires remote networks to install a crossdomain.xml file. Unfortunately, most services do not upload crossdomain.xml, or they upload it with a restricted policy, which adds extra work in order to overcome the security restriction and makes Flex a less common platform to develop mashups. However, the fact that Flex mashups are not so common actually gives you a tremendous opportunity to develop exciting new applications with little effort.

Each mashup should add value to an existing service. Building a Flex Rich Internet Application (RIA) mashup creates an additional value. Not only can you add value by stitching different pieces together, but you can also create an easy-to-use user interface (UI) that will transform an existing data source, such as Craigslist, Google search results, or others, into a cool stateful application that allows the client to view changes without having to refresh his browser.

Now, let's look at an example of a Flex application mashup. In this example, you can submit an address, and the application searches for a product on eBay, Google Base, and Amazon. It then returns back to the client a list of the available products, as well as a map showing where each product is located.

Here's what is going on behind the scenes. A client submits a request for a product and an address. The Flex application sends the request to Yahoo! Pipes, a mashup platform, which sends requests to all of the services (eBay, Google Base, and Amazon). The services form a response based on results from the data sources and send the response back to Yahoo! Pipes. The results are processed and filtered. Yahoo! Pipes then generates a web feed as a response. The Flex application receives the web feeds response, updates the model, and displays the results in a custom List component along with a map. Figure 10-2 visually illustrates this process.

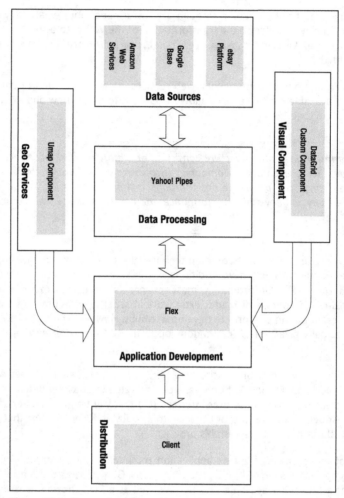

**Figure 10-2.** Flex application mashup example block diagram

# Accessing data sources

The core of building a Flex mashup is accessing data and distributing it into your application. When connecting to services across the Web, many technologies are being used such as SOAP, web services, RSS feeds, REST, JSON, Atom, and more. I will cover the different types of data connections that are available in this section. In addition, I will show you how to interconnect the data to create a data object that can be easily used across your application.

*Representational State Transfer (REST) is an architecture style used by the Internet. Services that follow REST architecture are described as RESTful.*

The Flash Player can connect to different types of remote networks; the connections are made using a Remote Procedure Call (RPC). Using the Flash Player, you have two ways to connect to a remote network. One way is to connect directly to the remote network (see Figure 10-3).

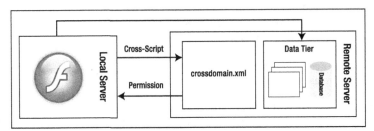

**Figure 10-3.** Connecting to a remote server through crossdomain.xml

When an RPC is being made, the Flash Player accesses the network and downloads the crossdomain.xml policy file. The crossdomain.xml file includes a set of permission instructions for connecting the player to the network. After permission is given, the Flash Player creates the connection, and you are able to retrieve data and media.

Otherwise, in the scenario where the crossdomain.xml file is not available on the remote network or the policy restricts the Flash Player from accessing the data, you will need to create a proxy interface between your application and the remote network to overcome the crossdomain.xml limitation.

The proxy is a server-side script that will be able to access the information and make the information available to the Flash Player (see Figure 10-4). Since the server-side script does not have the same restriction as the Flash Player, it is able to access the file. The Flash Player is able to connect to the proxy since it is located on the same domain.

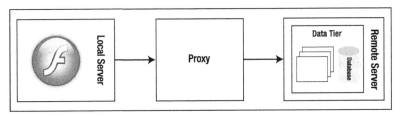

**Figure 10-4.** Connecting to a remote server through a proxy

The crossdomain.xml file is necessary to connect directly to a service on a remote network. It is beneficial to understand how to read and create a crossdomain.xml file so you can figure out at an early stage whether you are able to connect directly to a service or need to use a proxy.

# Creating the crossdomain.xml policy file

The Flash Player requires that a `crossdomain.xml` file be uploaded to the root of the server. The file gives instructions to the Flash Player whether to allow a remote SWF to access the server.

Placing the following `crossdomain.xml` file in the root of a server will allow the Flash Player to connect to the server from any domain. In the line of code `allow-access-from domain="*"` the star indicates that Flash Player can connect on any domain.

```
<?xml version="1.0 "?>
<!DOCTYPE cross-domain-policy SYSTEM ➥
"http://www.macromedia.com/xml/dtds/cross-domain-policy.dtd">
<cross-domain-policy>
        <allow-access-from domain="*"/>
</cross-domain-policy>
```

The XML file structure is always the same, and the only things that really change are the tags inside `<cross-domain-policy>`. For instance, to restrict the connection to a particular site, use the following tags inside the `crossdomain.xml` node:

```
<allow-access-from domain="www.site1.com"/>
<allow-access-from domain="site2.com"/>
```

Another example is to create a `crossdomain.xml` file that allows a secure server connection. You would use `secure="true"`.

```
<allow-access-from domain="www.site3.com" secure="true" />
```

You can also restrict access to a specific port or ports. For instance, to allow any remote server to connect to ports 80 and 110, use the following tags:

```
<allow-access-from domain="*" to-ports="21,80"/>
```

You can connect to a lower TCP socket through the Socket and XMLSocket APIs. Flash Player version 9.0.115.0 changed the security on how the socket policy files work. The new policy increases security and blocks unauthorized connections.

Here's an example of a valid socket connection policy for Flash Player version 9.0.115.0:

```
<site-control permitted-cross-domain-policies="master-only"/>
<allow-access-from domain="mysite.com" to-ports="999,8 080-8082"/>
```

These ports represent access to different services on the server; each service is assigned to a specific port. Here are some of the ports most often used:

| Service | Port |
|---------|------|
| FTP | Port 21 |
| SSH | Port 22 |
| Telnet | Port 23 |
| SMTP | Port 25 |
| Web | Port 80 |
| Pop 3 | Port 110 |
| IMAP | Port 143 |

You can allow access to every server that ends with a certain name by using an asterisk (*), as shown here:

```
<allow-access-from domain="*.yahoo.com" />
```

You can allow access to a specific IP address:

```
<allow-access-from domain="66.500.0.20" />
```

Since the crossdomain.xml is uploaded to the root directory of the server, such as http://www.WebSite.com/crossdomain.xml, it is easy to find out whether the crossdomain.xml file is installed by navigating to the address of that file.

For instance, checking Yahoo! Maps service (http://maps.yahoo.com) reveals a crossdomain.xml file installed when navigating via a browser to http://maps.yahoo.com/crossdomain.xml, as shown in Figure 10-5. Remember that the file can also be written this way: CrossDomain.xml.

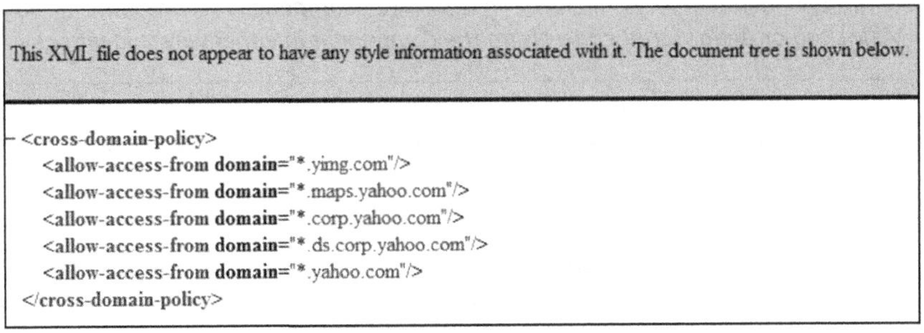

**Figure 10-5.** Connecting to a remote network through crossdomain.xml

Most services you will be using in your Flex mashup that have the crossdomain.xml file installed and unrestricted will allow you to make an RPC. There are three types of RPC components available in Flex: HTTPService, WebService, and RemoteObject.

In terms of performance, HTTPService and RemoteObject connections are faster than WebService connections. In small applications with very little data being transferred and few calls, it does not really matter what you choose, but as you increase the number of calls and amount of data, even a mere 100ms difference per call can become noticeable.

The HTTPService component is a powerful method and the most common way to retrieve data. HTTPService allows you to send GET and POST requests. After making the request, you receive a data response. Mashups often use the HTTPService component to access web syndication.

**Web syndication** is a term used to describe web feeds. A link to a web feed can be recognized by the web syndication icon (see Figure 10-6).

**Figure 10-6.** Web syndication icon

# Connecting to a RESTful data source

Although Adobe describes the HTTPService component as equivalent to a RESTful service, you can only use the GET and PUT methods with this method; you cannot use any other methods such as HEAD, OPTIONS, PUT, TRACE, or DELETE.

If you need to use any methods other than GET or POST, you can use either the BlazeDS component or a proxy.

So what's the most common usage for the HTTPService Component?

- HTTPService is often used to load web syndication.

- HTTPService also provides a common connection to retrieve information through a server-side proxy such as PHP, JSP, or ASP.

- HTTPService is often used to communicate with a local database through a proxy.

> *There are two identical ways to create* HTTPService *component service calls: through an MXML tag or ActionScript code. Using the component in either way is identical.*

We will be using the following XML file, src/assets/xml/employees.xml, in the examples in this chapter:

```
<employees>
    <employee>
        <name>John Do</name>
        <phone>212-222-2222</phone>
        <age>20</age>
        <email>john@youremail.com</email>
    </employee>
        <employee>
        <name>Jane Smith</name>
        <phone>212-333-3333</phone>
        <age>21</age>
        <email>jane@youremail.com</email>
```

```
        </employee>
    </employees>
```

Here is an example of creating an HTTPService call using an MXML tag:

```
<mx:HTTPService
  url="assets/xml/employees.xml"
  resultFormat="e4x"
  result="resultHandler(event);"
  fault="faultHandler(event);"/>
```

Using ActionScript 3.0 code, the same HTTPService call would look as follows. Notice that the HTTPService component has a property called resultFormat, which allows you to specify how you would like Flex to format the data response.

```
private var service:HTTPService = new HTTPService();
private function setService():void
{
    service.url = "assets/xml/employees.xml";
    service.resultFormat = "e4x"
    service.addEventListener(ResultEvent.RESULT, resultHandler);
    service.addEventListener(FaultEvent.FAULT, faultHandler);
    service.send();
}
```

After you make a request, the response will be handled either by the result or fault methods, depending on whether the request was successful or not.

Here's the implementation of the results and fault methods:

```
private var dataProvider:ArrayCollection = new ArrayCollection();
private function resultHandler(event:ResultEvent):void
{
    service.removeEventListener(ResultEvent.RESULT, resultHandler);
    for each (var property:XML in event.result.employees.employee)
    {
        dataProvider.addItem({name:property.name, ➥
        phone:property.phone, email:property.email});
    }
}

private function faultHandler(event:FaultEvent):void
{
    service.removeEventListener(FaultEvent.FAULT, faultHandler);
    Alert.show(event.fault.message, "Error connecting");
}
```

HTTPService allows you to format the data results you receive. Here are your options:

- e4x returns XML that can be accessed through ECMAScript for XML (E4X) expressions.
- flashvars returns an object with name-value pairs separated by ampersands.
- Object returns an object parsed as an AS tree.
- text returns a regular string.
- xml returns a flash.xml.XMLNode instance.

The format you should be using depends on the results you expect to get from the request. For instance, if the service returns a success or fail string message, you can just use the text result format. However, most services return an XML result, so you will be using either the xml or e4x format.

E4X is preferred over regular XML when dealing with XML responses, since you can access the results easily and can perform expressions to filter the results. E4X is a language in its own right, and it has been incorporated into ActionScript 3.0. Many claim E4X to be a simple and easy way to access XML; however, it is not as easy as people make it out to be. To underscore this point, let's take a look at E4X syntax.

I will use the same employees.xml file I mentioned before to walk through some examples on how to work with E4X.

The following example demonstrates E4X object style capabilities. The variables results1 through results4 are going to give the exact same output, that is, the complete list of employees. The asterisk notation can be used anywhere and gives you powerful control in cases where the node name is different.

```
import mx.rpc.events.ResultEvent;
private function resultHandler(event:ResultEvent):void
{
    var employeesList:XML = event.result as XML;
    var results1:XMLList  = employeesList.employees.employee;
    var results2:XMLList  = employeesList.employees.child("*");
    var results3:XMLList  = employeesList.employees.*;
    var results4:XMLList  = employeesList..employee;
}
```

You can also use the object style to check the number of items on each node by using the length property:

```
var len:int = employeesList.employees.employee.length();
```

Use the XML type to retrieve an item as follows:

```
var filter1:XML = employeesList.employees.employee[0];
```

The following examples demonstrate using expressions in E4X:

```
var filter2:XMLList = employeesList.employees ➡
.employee.(phone == '212-333-3333');
```

```
        var filter3:XMLList = employeesList.employees ➡
.*.(age >= 19 || age == 18);
```

The complete working example of E4X code follows. When testing, insert a line break-point and use the Eclipse variable window to examine the results:

```
<?xml version="1.0" encoding="utf-8"?>
<mx:Application xmlns:mx="http://www.adobe.com/2006/mxml"
  layout="absolute"
  initialize="httpService.send();">

  <mx:Script>
    <![CDATA[

        import mx.controls.Alert;
        import mx.rpc.events.FaultEvent;
        import mx.rpc.events.ResultEvent;

        private function resultHandler(event:ResultEvent):void
        {
            var employeesList:XML = event.result as XML;
            var len:int = employeesList.employees.employee.length();
            var results1:XMLList = employeesList.employees.employee;
            var results2:XMLList = employeesList.employees.child("*");
            var results3:XMLList = employeesList.employees.*;
            var results4:XMLList = employeesList..employee;
            var filter1:XML = employeesList.employees.employee[0];
            var filter2:XMLList = employeesList.employees.employee. ➡
 (phone == '212-333-3333');
            var filter3:XMLList = employeesList.employees. ➡
*.(age >= 19 || age == 18);
        }

        private function faultHandler(event:FaultEvent):void
        {
        httpService.removeEventListener(FaultEvent.FAULT, ➡
faultHandler);
        Alert.show("Error connecting");
        }

    ]]>
  </mx:Script>

  <mx:HTTPService id="httpService"
    url="assets/xml/employees.xml"
    resultFormat="e4x"
    result="resultHandler(event);"
    fault="faultHandler(event);"/>

</mx:Application>
```

Flex HTTPService is often used for RESTful services. HTTPService emulates HTTP protocols; however, as mentioned before, it is restricted to GET and POST requests.

Google Base has deprecated SOAP services and is now available through RESTful services. Let's access Google Base using Flash's HTTPService component.

> *Google Base* is an online database that allows any user to add content easily. Once the content is added, it can be accessed through RESTful services. Google Base is still in beta version.

To view search results from Google Base, you can send a request with the parameter bq=keywords. You will need to pass the variable through the HTTP protocol in the HTTPService component. You do so by placing a request tag inside the HTTPService MXML tag like so:

```
<mx:request>
<bq>digital+camera</bq>
</mx:request>
```

It is recommended that keywords be bindable. Attaching a bindable variable allows us to reassign different keywords in order to do a new search, with no need to refresh the browser, keeping our application stateful.

```
<bq>{keywords}</bq>
```

You can also pass the variable by sending it directly through the send method as follows:

```
httpService.send({bp:digital+camera});
```

You can also invoke the RESTful service by attaching the query at the end of the URL as shown here: http://www.google.com/base/feeds/snippets?bq=digital+camera.

The results from the query of the feeds are shown in Figure 10-7. Google Base is using the Atom namespace. I will discuss namespaces and Atom in more detail in the next section, "Working with web feeds and namespaces," so if you don't understand namespaces now, don't worry.

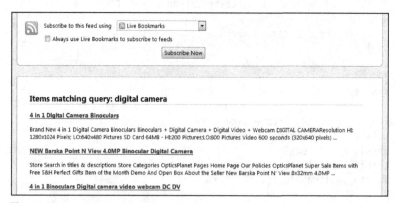

**Figure 10-7.** Google Base feeds results

In order to access elements and properties in the XML that was returned from the Google Base service, we need to define the Atom namespace:

```
private namespace atom = "http://www.w3.org/2005/Atom";
use namespace atom;
```

Here is the complete code of the application for sending a request to Google Base and receiving a response with the results:

```
<?xml version="1.0" encoding="utf-8"?>
<mx:Application xmlns:mx="http://www.adobe.com/2006/mxml"
    layout="absolute"
    initialize="service.send()">

    <mx:Script>
    <![CDATA[

        import mx.controls.Alert;
        import mx.rpc.http.HTTPService;
        import mx.rpc.events.ResultEvent;
        import mx.rpc.events.FaultEvent;

        [Bindable]
        private var keywords:String = "digital+camera";

        // Define and use atom namespace.
        private namespace atom = "http://www.w3.org/2005/Atom";
        use namespace atom;

        // Handle results event
        private function resultHandler(event:ResultEvent):void
        {
            var feeds:XML = event.result as XML;
            service.removeEventListener(ResultEvent.RESULT, ➡
resultHandler);
            trace(feeds.entry[0].title);
        }

        // Handle faults event
        private function faultHandler(event:FaultEvent):void
        {
            service.removeEventListener(FaultEvent.FAULT, faultHandler);
            Alert.show("Error connecting");
        }

    ]]>
    </mx:Script>

    <mx:HTTPService id="service"
        url="http://www.google.com/base/feeds/snippets"
```

```
            resultFormat="e4x"
            result="resultHandler(event);"
            fault="faultHandler(event);">

        <mx:request>
        <bq>{keywords}</bq>
        </mx:request>

    </mx:HTTPService>

</mx:Application>
```

# Connecting to a SOAP data source

Another common connection, SOAP, is often used by APIs to send and receive XML messages through HTTP protocols.

SOAP is explained in detail in Chapters 6 and 7. Since SOAP is heavy across the wire and requires higher client-side memory and processing, many web services, such as Google SOAP Search API, are moving away from SOAP to RESTful services such as web feeds.

Keep in mind that SOAP is still very common and has its own advantages, especially when the communication is done behind proxies or firewalls, or the protocol is utilizing other application layer protocols such as SMTP.

One service that uses SOAP is Amazon API. Amazon Web Services, which are often used in mashup applications, include the following:

- **Alexa services**: Provides information regarding web pages
- **Amazon Clouds**: Includes services such as storage, database, and queue services
- **Amazon Associates**: Allows developers to earn referral fees for every purchase made by your referral

In the following example, we will be using SOAP to connect to the Amazon Associates service.

To connect to SOAP service, use the <mx:WebService> tag and set the WSDL property.

```
<mx:WebService id="AmazonService
    wsdl=http://webservices.amazon.com/AWSECommerceService/➥
AWSECommerceService.wsdl
/>
```

In this example, we make two calls to two operations (methods). The first operation is to retrieve the list of music based on keywords. We first define the operation:

```
<mx:operation name="ItemSearch" resultFormat="object"
    fault="faultHandler(event)"
    result="searchResultHandler(event)">
      <mx:request>
        <AWSAccessKeyId>{DEVELOPER_KEY}</AWSAccessKeyId>
```

```
            <Shared>
                <Keywords>beatles</Keywords>
                <SearchIndex>Music</SearchIndex>
                <Count>10</Count>
            </Shared>
        </mx:request>
    </mx:operation>
```

Notice that DEVELOPER_KEY is defined as a static member, so we will be able to assign it to the XML in the operation.

```
    [Bindable]
    private static var DEVELOPER_KEY:String;
```

In order to get an Amazon access key ID, apply at https://aws-portal.amazon.com/gp/aws/developer/registration/index.html.

In the second operation, we follow the same logic; first you need to define the operation and the methods that will handle the result. Notice that we are using the same handler to handle the fault response, since we will handle the fault response the same way, by displaying an error message.

```
    <mx:operation name="ItemLookup"
        resultFormat="object"
        fault="faultHandler(event)"
        result="itemResultHandler(event)">
```

The second XML request will pass the detail of the title found in the first operation; notice the ItemID is bindable, so we will be able to pass asin, which is an Amazon unique primary key needed to retrieve information regarding a product.

```
    <mx:request>
        <AWSAccessKeyId>{DEVELOPER_KEY}</AWSAccessKeyId>
            <Shared>
                <ItemId>{asin}</ItemId>
                <ResponseGroup>ItemAttributes,Images</ResponseGroup>
            </Shared>
    </mx:request>
```

Following is the complete working code. Notice that you need to replace the DEVELOPER_KEY string with your developer key, in order to run this example.

```
    <?xml version="1.0" encoding="utf-8"?>
    <mx:Application
        xmlns:mx="http://www.adobe.com/2006/mxml"
        layout="absolute"
        initialize="AmazonService.ItemSearch.send();">

        <mx:Script>
            <![CDATA[
                import mx.rpc.events.FaultEvent;
```

**365**

```
                import mx.controls.Alert;
                import mx.rpc.events.ResultEvent;

                [Bindable]
                private var asin:String;

                // Replace with Amazon Access Key ID:
                [Bindable]
                private static var DEVELOPER_KEY:String = "**********";

                // search results handler
                private function searchResultHandler(event:ResultEvent):void
                {
                    var object:Object = event.result.Items.Item;
                    asin = object[0].ASIN;
                    AmazonService.ItemLookup.send();
                }

                // item results handler
                private function itemResultHandler(event:ResultEvent):void
                {
                    trace(event.result.Items.Item[0].SmallImage.URL);
                }

                private function faultHandler(event:FaultEvent):void
                {
                    Alert.show("Error connecting"+event.fault.faultString);
                }

            ]]>
        </mx:Script>

    <mx:WebService id="AmazonService"
        wsdl="http://webservices.amazon.com/AWSECommerceService/ ➥
    AWSECommerceService.wsdl"
        showBusyCursor="true"
        fault="Alert.show(event.fault.faultString)">

        <!-- itemSearch method -->
        <mx:operation name="ItemSearch"
          resultFormat="object"
          fault="faultHandler(event)"
          result="searchResultHandler(event)">
          <mx:request>
            <AWSAccessKeyId>{DEVELOPER_KEY}</AWSAccessKeyId>
            <Shared>
              <Keywords>beatles</Keywords>
              <SearchIndex>Music</SearchIndex>
              <Count>10</Count>
```

```
        </Shared>
      </mx:request>
    </mx:operation>

    <!-- itemLookup method -->
    <mx:operation name="ItemLookup"
      resultFormat="object"
      fault="faultHandler(event)"
      result="itemResultHandler(event)">
      <mx:request>
        <AWSAccessKeyId>{DEVELOPER_KEY}</AWSAccessKeyId>
        <Shared>
          <ItemId>{asin}</ItemId>
          <ResponseGroup>ItemAttributes,Images</ResponseGroup>
        </Shared>
      </mx:request>
    </mx:operation>

  </mx:WebService>

</mx:Application>
```

# Connecting to a data source using AMF

Action Message Format (AMF) is a data format created by Macromedia with the release of Flash Player 6. AMF is now open source and part of BlazeDS, available to download here: http://opensource.adobe.com.

> There are many types of AMF connections, but they all share the same basic principles of serializing (encoding) into a binary format and deserializing (decoding) once the data is returned to Flex.

AMF uses code data types such as Byte (8 bit), Int (16 bit), and many others. With the release of ActionScript 3.0, Adobe updated AMF: it is now called AMF3 (the older version now being referred to as AMF0), and it supports more data types.

Working with unformatted binary data has significant advantages: the speed of communication across the wire is much faster, it needs less memory from the client computer, and it reduces processing time over HTTPService or WebService.

Although connecting to AMF services is usually not provided through APIs, you may use it to retrieve data from your own local database or server as part of your data sources to your mashup. Flash provides built-in AMF-based APIs such as the following:

- **RemoteObject**: ActionScript 3.0 API that allows access to Java objects
- **Socket Connection**: ActionScript 3.0 API that allows connection through sockets
- **NetConnection**: API used to initiate commands on a remote server and play streaming video

Additionally, there are many open source and commercial AMF implementations that provide a gateway between the Flash Player and the implementation. Here are some of the popular ones:

- **AMFPHP** and **SabreAMF**: Allows access to PHP
- **RubyAMF**: Allows access to Ruby
- **AMF.NET**: Allows access to .NET
- **BlazeDS**: Allows access to data in real time

RemoteObject encoding uses AMF and allows you to access Java objects or ColdFusion (which consists of Java objects internally) methods. RemoteObject still connects using the HTTP or HTTPS protocol; however, the data is serialized into a binary format and then deserialized once the data is returned to the Flash Player.

Following is an example of invoking methods on ColdFusion. First, the RemoteObject is declared with the destination driver and the source ColdFusion file.

```
<mx:RemoteObject
    id="CFService"
    showBusyCursor="true"
    destination="ColdFusion"
    source="cf.ReadFile"
    result="dataHandler(event)" />
```

To invoke the RemoteObject component, you need to call the method inside the ColdFusion file and pass any needed arguments:

```
CFService.getQuery("1");
```

Now let's create the content of cf.ReadFile.cf:

```
<cfcomponent>
    <cffunction name="getQuery" access="remote" returntype="query">
    <cfargument name="State" required="true">
        <cfset var qRead="">
        <cfquery name="qRead" datasource="data_source_name"
            SELECT * FROM 'tableName' WHERE
            PrimaryKey=<cfqueryparam
            value="#arguments.key#"
            cfsqltype="CF_SQL_STRING">
        </cfquery>
        <cfreturn qRead>
    </cffunction>
</cfcomponent>
```

The result can be handled with the dataHandler method, which casts the object to an ArrayCollection.

```
private function dataHandler(event:ResultEvent): void
{
    DataResult = event.result as ArrayCollection;
}
```

# Working with web feeds and namespaces

Many XML web feeds have elements and attributes that are associated by a namespace. In order to be able to use namespaces, you will need to open the namespaces so you can access and use the elements and attributes on your feeds.

Many different namespace formats exist, and it would be difficult to cover all of them; however, once you master the principles, you will be able to handle any namespace that you come across.

When working with XML files, I recommend installing an open source plug-in for Eclipse called XMLBuddy. It allows you to work with XML easily and efficiently since it has built-in features such as the following:

- Validating
- Coloring
- Dynamic code assist
- Updated outline (tree) view

To install XMLBuddy, follow these directions:

1. Download the plug-in from http://www.xmlbuddy.com.
2. Unzip the plug-in and place it in your Eclipse plug-ins directory: C:\eclipse\plugins\, or in Mac, eclipse > plugins.
3. Restart Eclipse, and make sure the shortcut has a target argument –refresh, in order for Eclipse to recognize the new plug-in.
4. To ensure XMLBuddy was installed correctly, create an XML file: select File ➤ New ➤ Other ➤ XML ➤ Next. Enter NewFile.xml, and click Finish.

With XMLBuddy equipped, you can now add elements and attributes as well as namespaces by right-clicking the document. Now that you have XMLBuddy in your toolkit, we are ready to explore some of the most popular namespaces.

## SPARQL namespace

SPARQL is a query language for the Resource Definition Framework (RDF), and it is often used to express SQL queries across various data sources.

RDF is a framework used for describing and interchanging metadata. RDF can be anything with a URI associated to it. For more information visit http://www.w3.org/RDF/.

Here is an example of XML formatted in SPARQL:

```
<?xml version="1.0" encoding="utf-8"?>
<sparql xmlns="http://www.w3.org/2005/sparql-results#">

    <head>
        <variable name="x"/>
        <variable name="hpage"/>
    </head>
```

**369**

```
    <results>
        <result>
            <binding name="x">
                <bnode>r2</bnode>
            </binding>
            <binding name="hpage">
                <uri>http://work.example.org/bob/</uri>
            </binding>
            <binding name="name">
                <literal xml:lang="en">Bob</literal>
            </binding>
            <binding name="age">
                <literal datatype=➡
"http://www.w3.org/2001/XMLSchema#integer">
                    30
                </literal>
            </binding>
            <binding name="mbox">
                <uri>mailto:bob@work.example.org</uri>
            </binding>
        </result>
    </results>

</sparql>
```

Define the SPARQL namespace and set it to the SPARQL URL. Then, include the use statement for that namespace. Without the definition, you do not have access to the contents of the loaded XML document.

```
private namespace sparql="http://www.w3.org/2005/sparql-results#";
use namespace sparql;
```

Once the namespace is defined and is in use, you can access the attributes and elements. Using XMLBuddy and E4X, you can easily set the elements you need (see Figure 10-8).

```
feeds.results.result[0].binding.uri.
```

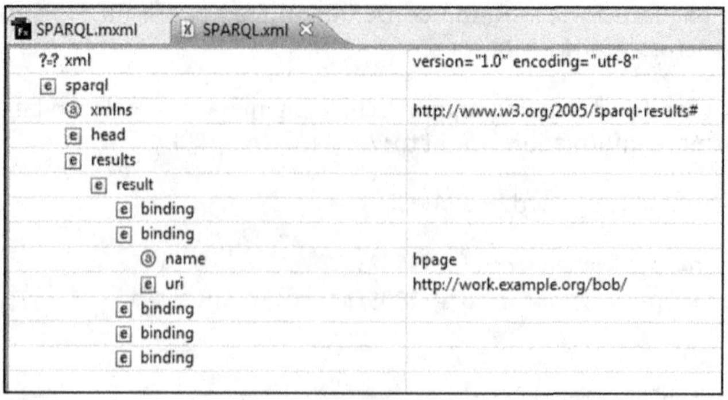

**Figure 10-8.** SPARQL.xml tree view

Here is the complete code for the example that accesses elements and attributes on the SPARQL XML file:

```
<?xml version="1.0" encoding="utf-8"?>
<mx:Application xmlns:mx="http://www.adobe.com/2006/mxml"
    layout="absolute"
    initialize="service.send();">

    <mx:Script>
        <![CDATA[
            import mx.controls.Alert;
            import mx.rpc.http.HTTPService;
            import mx.rpc.events.ResultEvent;
            import mx.rpc.events.FaultEvent;

            // Define and use SPARQL namespace. ➥
private namespace sparql = ➥
"http://www.w3.org/2005/sparql-results#";
            use namespace sparql;

            private function resultHandler(event:ResultEvent):void
            {
                var feeds:XML = event.result as XML;
                trace(feeds.results.result[0].binding.uri);
            }

            private function faultHandler(event:FaultEvent):void
            {
                service.removeEventListener(FaultEvent.FAULT, ➥
                faultHandler);
                Alert.show(event.fault.message, "Error connecting");
            }
        ]]>
    </mx:Script>

    <mx:HTTPService id="service"
    url="assets/xml/SPARQL.xml"
    resultFormat="e4x"
    result="resultHandler(event);"
    fault="faultHandler(event);"/>

</mx:Application>
```

## Atom namespace

Atom syndication format is an XML language that is used for web feeds, intended to improve RSS feeds. The primary usage of Atom feeds is syndication of different types of web content, such as that found on weblogs or news sites, to web sites or directly to users. To learn more, visit Atom's official site: http://www.atomenabled.org.

**371**

To access Atom attributes, the first step is to define and use Atom's namespace:

```
private namespace atom="http://www.w3.org/2005/Atom";
use namespace atom;
```

Now we can access the elements and attributes of this namespace. For instance, let's say you want to access the following XML:

```
<?xml version="1.0" encoding="utf-8"?>
<feed xmlns="http://www.w3.org/2005/Atom">
    <title>Example Feed</title>
    <link href="http://example.org/"/>
    <updated>2003-12-13T18:30:02Z</updated>
    <author>
        <name>John Doe</name>
    </author>
    <id>urn:uuid:60a76c80</id>

    <entry>
        <title>Atom-Powered Robots Run Amok</title>
        <link href="http://example.org/2003/12/13/atom03"/>
        <id>urn:uuid:1225c695</id>
        <updated>2003-12-13T18:30:02Z</updated>
        <summary>Some text.</summary>
    </entry>
</feed>
```

Again, using E4X and XMLBuddy, we can easily access the attribute feeds.entry[0].title (see Figure 10-9).

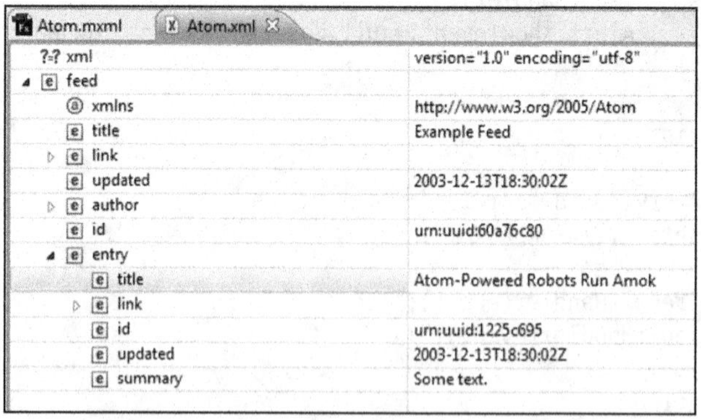

**Figure 10-9.** Atom.xml tree view

Here's the complete code:

```
<?xml version="1.0" encoding="utf-8"?>
<mx:Application
    xmlns:mx="http://www.adobe.com/2006/mxml"
```

```
            layout="absolute"
            initialize="service.send();">

      <mx:Script>
          <![CDATA[

              import mx.controls.Alert;
              import mx.rpc.http.HTTPService;
              import mx.rpc.events.ResultEvent;
              import mx.rpc.events.FaultEvent;

              // Define and use Atom namespace.
              private namespace atom="http://www.w3.org/2005/Atom";
              use namespace atom;

              private function resultHandler(event:ResultEvent):void
              {
                  var feeds:XML = event.result as XML;
                  trace(feeds.entry[0].title);
              }

              private function faultHandler(event:FaultEvent):void
              {
                  service.removeEventListener(FaultEvent.FAULT, ➥
faultHandler);
                  Alert.show(event.fault.message, "Could not load XML");
              }

          ]]>
      </mx:Script>

      <mx:HTTPService id="service"
          url="assets/xml/Atom.xml"
          resultFormat="e4x"
          result="resultHandler(event);"
          fault="faultHandler(event);"/>

</mx:Application>
```

## GeoRSS namespace

GeoRSS is a lightweight format that is often used in feeds to map locations by adding basic geometries such as point, line, and box. To learn more about GeoRSS, visit its official site at http://georss.org/.

Let's look at an example of a GeoRSS XML:

```
<rss version="2.0" xmlns:georss="http://www.georss.org/georss">
<item>
    <georss:point>37.75988 -122.43739</georss:point>
```

```
        </item>
    </rss>
```

To extract the longitude and latitude point values, you first need to set a namespace just as we did before:

```
var georss:Namespace = new Namespace("http://www.georss.org/georss");
```

Then you can pull the XML using the E4X standard object type format:

```
var geoResults:String = event.result.item.georss::point;
```

Following is the complete code for the GeoRSS example:

```
<?xml version="1.0" encoding="utf-8"?>
<mx:Application
    xmlns:mx="http://www.adobe.com/2006/mxml"
    layout="absolute"
    initialize="service.send();">

    <mx:Script>
        <![CDATA[

            import mx.controls.Alert;
            import mx.rpc.http.HTTPService;
            import mx.rpc.events.ResultEvent;
            import mx.rpc.events.FaultEvent;

            private function resultHandler(event:ResultEvent):void
            {
                var georss:Namespace = new ➥
Namespace("http://www.georss.org/georss");
                trace(event.result.item.georss::point);
            }

            private function faultHandler(event:FaultEvent):void
            {
                service.removeEventListener(FaultEvent.FAULT, ➥
faultHandler);
                Alert.show("Error connecting");
            }
        ]]>
    </mx:Script>

    <mx:HTTPService id="service"
        url="assets/xml/GeoRSS.xml"
        resultFormat="e4x"
        result="resultHandler(event);"
        fault="faultHandler(event);"/>

</mx:Application>
```

Run the application and place a line breakpoint in the `resultHandler` handler. As shown in Figure 10-10, we retrieved longitude and latitude point values.

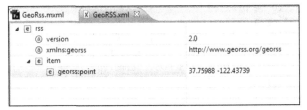

**Figure 10-10.** GeoRSS.xml tree view

# Creating a proxy

The lack of `crossdomain.xml` can create a scenario where your Flex application works fine on your local machine but not on your server. The solution for the lack of a `crossdomain.xml` file is to use a proxy to connect to the data source and have Flash connect to the proxy instead of the data source directly. There are a few ways to use proxies; one is to create a server-side script to connect to the data source.

Following are three open source examples of proxies that can be used for RESTful POST and GET methods, as well as for downloading binary data such as SWF files from a remote server. The proxy scripts will be available for download from the friendsofED site (`http://friendsofed.com`) as part of the example files that accompany this book.

## PHP proxy

When using a server with PHP, you can use a lightweight open source PHP proxy script that handles two types of data: RESTful methods of GET and PUT and binary data such as SWF files or images. Keep in mind that PHP supports the CURL method in order for this script to work.

The following example loads XML/text:

```
http://yourserver.com/proxy.php?url= ➡
http://yourserver.com/blog/index.xml
```

This example loads a SWF (binary data) file:

```
http://yourserver.com/proxy.php?url= ➡
http://yourserver.com/files/some.swf& ➡
mimeType=application/x-shockwave-flash
```

Here's the complete code:

```php
<?php
// PHP Proxy
// Responds to both HTTP GET and POST requests
//
// Author: Abdul Qabiz
```

```php
// March 31, 2006
//

// Get the URL to be proxied
// Is it a POST or a GET?
$url = ($_POST['url']) ? $_POST['url'] : $_GET['url'];
$headers = ($_POST['headers'])?$_POST['headers']:$_GET['headers'];
$mimeType =($_POST['mimeType'])?$_POST['mimeType']: ➥
$_GET['mimeType'];

//Start the CURL session
$session = curl_init($url);

// If it's a POST, put the POST data in the body
if ($_POST['url']) {
    $postvars = '';
    while ($element = current($_POST)) {
        $postvars .= key($_POST).'='.$element.'&';
        next($_POST);
    }
    curl_setopt ($session, CURLOPT_POST, true);
    curl_setopt ($session, CURLOPT_POSTFIELDS, $postvars);
}

// Don't return HTTP headers. Do return the contents of the call
curl_setopt($session,CURLOPT_HEADER,($headers=="true")?true:false);

curl_setopt($session, CURLOPT_FOLLOWLOCATION, true);
//curl_setopt($ch, CURLOPT_TIMEOUT, 4);
curl_setopt($session, CURLOPT_RETURNTRANSFER, true);

// Make the call
$response = curl_exec($session);

if ($mimeType != "")
{
    // The web service returns XML.
    // Set the Content-Type appropriately
    header("Content-Type: ".$mimeType);
}

echo $response;

curl_close($session);

?>
```

## ASP proxy

When using a server with ASP technology, you can use a lightweight open source ASP proxy script. This proxy can be used for RESTful services as well as binary data.

Usage:

```
http://yourserver.com/proxy.asp?url=<url_encoded_destination_url> ➡
[&mimeType=<mimeType>]
```

Example of using the ASP proxy to download binary data: http://yourserver.com/proxy. asp?url=http://someserver/1.jpg &mimeType=image/jpg

Following is an open source script for a server that supports ASP:

```
<%
set objHttp = Server.CreateObject("Msxml2.ServerXMLHTTP")
strURL = Request("url")"
objHttp.open "GET", strURL, False
objHttp.Send

If objHttp.status = 200 Then
    Response.Expires = 90
    Response.ContentType = Request("mimeType")
    Response.BinaryWrite objHttp.responseBody
    set objHttp = Nothing
End If
%>
```

## JSP proxy

Following is an open source script for a server that supports JSP:

```
<%@ page language="java" contentType="text/html; charset=utf-8"
pageEncoding="utf-8"
import="java.io.BufferedReader,
java.io.InputStreamReader,
java.io.IOException,
java.io.InputStream,
java.net.MalformedURLException,
java.net.URL,
java.net.URLConnection"

private String contentURL;
public static final String CONTENT_URL_NAME = "contentURL";

// get the URL through the request:
If (contentURL == null) {
    contentURL = (String)request.getAttribute(CONTENT_URL_NAME);

    if (contentURL == null) {
```

```
            contentURL=(String)request.getParameter(CONTENT_URL_NAME);
        }
    }

    if (contentURL == null) {
        throw new ServletException("A content URL must be provided, ➥
as a"'" + CONTENT_URL_NAME + ➥
"'" request attribute or request parameter.");
        URL url = null;
    }

    try {
        // get a connection to the content:
        url = new URL(contentURL);
        URLConnection urlConn = url.openConnection();

        // show the client the content type:
        String contentType = urlConn.getContentType();
        response.setContentType(contentType);

        // get the input stream
        InputStream in = urlConn.getInputStream();
        BufferedReader br = new BufferedReader(➥
new InputStreamReader(in));
        char[] buffer = new char[1024];
        String contentString = "";
        String tmp = br.readLine();

        do
          {
              contentString += tmp + "\n";
              tmp = br.readLine();
          }

        while (tmp != null);
        out.flush();
        out.close();
    }

    catch (MalformedURLException me)  {
        // on new URL:
        throw new ServletException("URL:'"+contentURL+"' ➥
is malformed.");
    }

    catch (IOException ioe)  {
        // on open connection:
        throw new ServletException("Exception while ➥
opening '" +
```

```
        contentURL + "': " + ioe.getMessage());
}

catch (Exception e) {
    // on reading input:
     throw new ServletException
        ("Exception during proxy request: "+ ➥
e.getMessage());
}

%>
```

# Utilizing mashup platforms as proxies

You can also utilize a mashup platform to be your proxy when a proxy is needed. Such mashup platforms as Yahoo! Pipes, Google Mashup Editor, and Microsoft Popfly encourage users to create mashups using visual editors. These tools allow users to create a complete application and publish it on their cloud without any programming knowledge at all.

Many of these platforms have a `crossdomain.xml` policy installed already, which allows you to utilize these platforms as your proxy, saving you time and reducing your server resources since you don't need to create a server-side proxy. In addition, these platforms can reduce bandwidth on your server, and they include modules to combine many feeds together, and to filter as well as format results, saving some of the interconnectivity work.

I recommend using Yahoo! Pipes, since it is a Flash-friendly platform and it has a nonrestrictive `crossdomain.xml` policy. To view Yahoo! Pipes' `crossdomain.xml` file, visit http://pipes. yahooapis.com/crossdomain.xml.

These services can help you, the Flex developer, create XML feeds that you will be able import into your application, saving you hours of coding; it's also ideal in cases where you are trying to create proof of concept (POC) and need to limit the amount of hours spent on development. As an example, you can create logic by mixing a few feeds together, and then publish the pipe as a service and import it into a Flex application.

Yahoo! Pipes allows you to create a data source, publish it, and access it in different formats such as RSS or JSON output. As an exercise, let's create a service that will show Rolex watches available for sale in ZIP code 10005 from Google Base, Craigslist, and Yahoo! Local. We will generate three feeds in Yahoo! Pipes and add a "union" item to combine them into one feed, making the feeds from these three sites ready to import into Flex Builder.

Go to Yahoo! Pipes at http://www.pipes.yahoo.com and create an account. Then choose to create a pipe.

First we'll add the data sources using the drag-and-drop toolbar on the left (see Figure 10-11):

1. Drag and drop a Fetch Feed module and enter the Craigslist feed URL.
2. Drag and drop a Google Base module and set the ZIP code in keywords.

**Figure 10-11.**
Yahoo! Pipes toolbar

**3.** Drag and drop a Yahoo! Local module and set the keyword and ZIP code.

Next, choose Operators and then drag and drop a Union module in order to combine these three data sources into one feed.

Finally, connect the Yahoo! Pipe Output to the Union module and test. You should have a pipe that looks like the one in Figure 10-12.

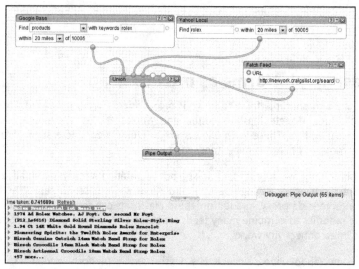

**Figure 10-12.** Complete Yahoo! pipes

Once the pipe is ready, you can run the pipe and publish it. You can see the results on a map (see Figure 10-13). You have options to access the results in different formats. I will show you how to access the results as RSS feeds and JSON.

**Figure 10-13.** Published Yahoo! pipe

We can access the information as RSS feeds using E4X. Choose More Options, and then choose RSS feeds in the published pipe. You can see the results in Figure 10-14.

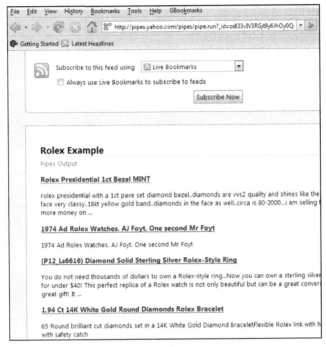

**Figure 10-14.** Yahoo! pipe RSS feeds

The following code retrieves the RSS feeds using E4X:

```
<?xml version="1.0" encoding="utf-8"?>
<mx:Application
    xmlns:mx="http://www.adobe.com/2006/mxml"
    layout="absolute"
    initialize="service.send();">

    <mx:Script>
        <![CDATA[

            import mx.rpc.events.ResultEvent;

            [Bindable]
            private var urlLocation:String =
                    "http://pipes.yahoo.com/pipes/pipe.run?_id= ➥
zs833vIV3RGjt9y6JhOyOQ&_render=rss";

            private function handleResults(event:ResultEvent):void
            {
                var list:XML = event.result as XML;
```

```
                }

            ]]>
        </mx:Script>

        <mx:HTTPService id="service"
                url="{urlLocation}"
                resultFormat="e4x"
                result="handleResults(event)"/>

    </mx:Application>
```

Another format we can use is JSON. Make sure that as3corelib.swc is added to your libs directory before running this script:

```
<?xml version="1.0" encoding="utf-8"?>
<mx:Application xmlns:mx="http://www.adobe.com/2006/mxml"
    layout="absolute"
    initialize="service.send();">

<mx:Script>
    <![CDATA[

        import mx.rpc.events.ResultEvent;

        [Bindable]
        private var urlLocation:String =
            "http://pipes.yahoo.com/pipes/pipe.run?_id= ➥
zs833vIV3RGjt9y6JhOyoQ&_render=json";

        private function managerJSON(event:ResultEvent):void
        {
            var list:XML = event.result as XML;
        }

    ]]>
</mx:Script>

    <mx:HTTPService id="service"
        url="{urlLocation}"
        resultFormat="e4x"
        result="managerJSON(event)">
    </mx:HTTPService>

</mx:Application>
```

Let's create another Yahoo! pipe. In this example, we will create a pipe that allows the user to enter information. It's more complex than the previous example, but it will give you an idea how you can maximize your use of pipes.

We will use some RSS feeds from Indeed.com, a job search service. The RSS service expects three parameters: q, l, and radius.

- q: (Stands for query) Allows you to sort results based on keywords
- l: (Stands for location) Accepts an address or a ZIP code
- radius: Accepts a number and represents the distance in miles to retrieve results

For instance, `http://rss.indeed.com/rss?q=flex+developer&l=10005&radius=25` will provide RSS results for Flex developer positions within the ZIP code 10005 and a radius of 25 miles. Please keep in mind that Indeed.com can change their parameters at any time, and you will have to adjust your application accordingly.

We will be using a URL Builder module, which allows us to connect an input box module. Let's drag and drop a URL Builder module under the URL tool. We will place the base URL, `http://rss.indeed.com/rss`, in the base input box, and then create three query parameters for each one of the queries: q, l, and radius.

Next, drag and drop a User Input module and connect it to the query parameters in the URL Builder.

We then add a Fetch Feed module and connect it to the URL Builder module.

Now, we need to extract and format geographic information. Indeed, RSS has a geo namespace, and we can save work in Flex Builder by using a particular Yahoo! Pipes module: Location Extractor analyzes the feeds looking for location and will format in a latitude and longitude subelement.

The last step is to connect Fetch Feed to Pipe Output (see Figure 10-15), and run and publish the pipe. You can see the final Yahoo! pipe results in Figure 10-16.

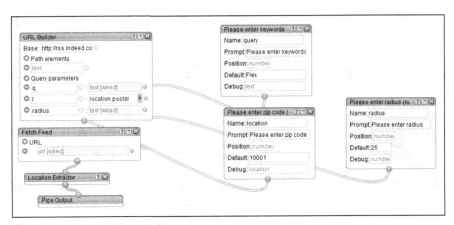

**Figure 10-15.** Yahoo! pipe RSS diagram

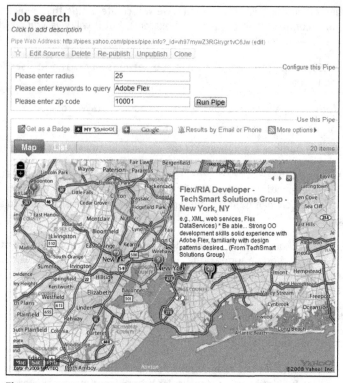

**Figure 10-16.** Yahoo! pipe published page

# Data interconnectivity

Now that we have connected to data sources to send and retrieve data, the next step is **interconnectivity**. This is the process of placing the data into a data model, preparing the data for display, and attaching the data into a user interface.

When building a mashup, you retrieve information through a UI from the user. You then may need to validate the information, format it, create a data model, and send the request to a data source (see Figure 10-17).

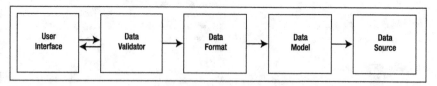

**Figure 10-17.** Reading data, interconnectivity, and sending results to a UI

Similarly, once you retrieve information from a data source, you may need to validate the information, format it, create a data model, and display the results back in a UI (see Figure 10-18).

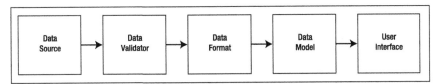

**Figure 10-18.** Getting information from the user, interconnectivity, and sending results to a data source

Keep in mind that following all these steps is not always necessary, since there may be times when you don't need to validate or format the information.

## Data model

A **data model** is an abstract model that describes data properties and how to access that data.

The three most popular ways to generate a data model is to create a data model using the data model tag in MXML, create a data model object that can be used in an MVC (Model-View-Controller) architecture such as Cairngorm, or place a data model into a data provider such as the ArrayCollection data type or DataProvider tag.

Advantages of creating data modes objects:

- A data model object contains properties for storing data and optional helpers' methods for additional functionality.
- Creating a data model allows you to bind user interface data to a data model, or you can bind data from a service directly to a data model.

You can define a simple data model in an MXML tag. When you need to manipulate your data model, use an ActionScript 3.0 value object (VO).

Let's create two data models: one using the MXML tag and the other as a VO.

You create a data model tag as follows. Notice how the properties are bindable to the UI component.

```
<mx:Model id="infoVO">
    <infoVOistration>
        <fullName >{Name.text}</fullName>
            <email>{email.text}</email>
            <phone>{phone.text}</phone>
            <zip>{zip.text}</zip>
        </infoVOistration>
</mx:Model>
```

Here is the same data model as an object class, often used in MVC architectures.

```
package vo {

    [Bindable]
    public class InfoVO
    {
```

**385**

```
        public function InfoVO()
        {
            public var fullName:String;
            public var email:String;
            public var phone:uint;
            public var zip:String;
        }
    }
}
```

Here is how you would set the properties of the VO:

```
var infoVO:InfoVO = new InfoVO();
infoVO.fullName = "John Do";
```

You can also create a collection to hold the information such as XML using the E4X format:

```
<mx:XML id="information" format="e4x">
        <registration>
                <fullName>{fullName}</fullName>
                <email>{email}</email>
                <phone>{phone}</phone>
                <zip>{zip}</zip>
                <ssn>{ssn}</ssn>
        </registration>
</mx:XML>
```

# Data validation

**Data validation** is the process of ensuring data meets your requirements before sending or display-ing the data. Data validation is often used as part of building any Flex application in general, but is also an important step to creating a successful Flash mashup. You will often need to validate UI forms before sending the information through an RPC component.

ActionScript 3.0 has a Validator API as part of the framework and allows you to evaluate formats from different data types such as the following:

- CreditCardValidator: Class used to validate credit card length and prefix, and passes a card type algorithm

- CurrencyValidator: Class used to validate currency expression

- DateValidator: Class used to validate proper dates and format

- EmailValidator: Class used to validate e-mail address format such as inclusion of an @ sign and other requirements

- NumberValidator: Class used to ensure a string is a valid number

- PhoneNumberValidator: Class used to validate that a string is in a valid phone number format

- RegExpValidator: Class used with a custom validator that allows you to use a regular expres-sion to validate a field

- SocialSecurityValidator: Class used to ensure a string is a valid United States Social Security number
- StringValidator: Class used to validate a string is between certain lengths
- ZipCodeValidator: Class used to validate proper length and format

In addition, to verify format and other properties, the Validator class can set a field as required.

We will be using the same model object as before.

```
<mx:Model id="infoVO">
    <infoVOistration>
        <email>{email.text}</email>
        <phone>{phone.text}</phone>
        <zip>{zip.text}</zip>
    </infoVOistration>
</mx:Model>
```

To create a code that uses the EmailValidator component to validate the format of a data model, we first need to create the validator MXML:

```
<mx:EmailValidator source="{infoVO}" property="email"
    trigger="{submit}" triggerEvent="click" listener="{email}"/>
```

We need to validate more properties upon submitting the form. The listener is bindable to the UI component, and it controls both the border color of the component as well as the tooltip error message.

```
<mx:PhoneNumberValidator source="{infoVO}" property="phone"
    trigger="{submit}" triggerEvent="click" listener="{phone}"/>
```

Here's the complete working code:

```
<?xml version="1.0" encoding="utf-8"?>
<mx:Application
    xmlns:mx="http://www.adobe.com/2006/mxml"
    layout="absolute">

    <mx:Model id="infoVO">
        <infoVOistration>
            <email>{email.text}</email>
            <phone>{phone.text}</phone>
            <zip>{zip.text}</zip>
        </infoVOistration>
    </mx:Model>

    <mx:EmailValidator source="{infoVO}" property="email"
        trigger="{submit}" triggerEvent="click" listener="{email}"/>
    <mx:PhoneNumberValidator source="{infoVO}" property="phone"
        trigger="{submit}" triggerEvent="click" listener="{phone}"/>
    <mx:ZipCodeValidator source="{infoVO}"
```

```
                property="zip" trigger="{submit}"
                triggerEvent="click" listener="{zip}"/>


        <!-- Form contains user input controls. -->
        <mx:Form>
            <mx:FormItem label="Email" required="true">
                <mx:TextInput id="email" width="200"/>
            </mx:FormItem>
            <mx:FormItem label="Phone" required="true">
                <mx:TextInput id="phone" width="200"/>
            </mx:FormItem>
            <mx:FormItem label="Zip" required="true">
                <mx:TextInput id="zip" width="60"/>
            </mx:FormItem>
            <mx:FormItem>

                <mx:Button id="submit" label="Validate"/>
            </mx:FormItem>
        </mx:Form>

    </mx:Application>
```

# Data format

When sending an RPC request to a service as part of your mashup or when receiving a response from a service, you often need to format some fields before displaying them in a UI or submitting them to a service.

Many services require that you format the date or other fields according to their requirements. In addition, many services will return a result in a format that is common in the native service language, and you will need to format the value before displaying the results in a UI.

Data-formatting components let you format data into a customized string. Different types of data-formatting components are available such as the following:

- CurrencyFormatter: Class used for formatting a number, plus adding the currency symbol
- DateFormatter: Class used for formatting the date and time in many different combinations
- NumberFormatter: Class used for formatting a numeric data
- PhoneFormatter: Class used for formatting a phone number
- ZipCodeFormatter: Class used for formatting United States and Canadian ZIP codes

To format a date, start by declaring a DateFormatter component with an MM/DD/YYYY date format. Next, bind the formatted version of a Date object that is returned from a web service to the text property of a TextInput component. Here is an example:

```
<?xml version="1.0" encoding="utf-8"?>
<mx:Application xmlns:mx="http://www.adobe.com/2006/mxml"
```

```
    layout="absolute">

    <mx:PhoneFormatter id="phoneFormatter"
        areaCode="212" formatString=" ###-####" />
    <mx:DateFormatter id="dateFormatter"
        formatString="month: MM, day: DD, year: YYYY"/>

    <mx:VBox>
        <mx:Label text="Enter your Manhattan 7 digit phone number:"/>
        <mx:TextInput id="phone" change="if (phone.text.length == 7)
            { phone.text = phoneFormatter.format(phone.text) } "/>
        <mx:Label text="Enter date (mm/dd/yyyy):"/>
        <mx:TextInput id="date" change="if (date.text.length == 10)
            { date.text = dateFormatter.format(date.text); } "/>
    </mx:VBox>

</mx:Application>
```

Each data formatting component includes event handling for invalid values and invalid formats. The error message is placed in a public variable called error. If an error occurs, the formatting component will return an empty string.

See the same example with an error message:

```
<?xml version="1.0" encoding="utf-8"?>

<mx:Application
    xmlns:mx="http://www.adobe.com/2006/mxml"
    layout="absolute">
<mx:PhoneFormatter id="phoneFormatter"
    areaCode="212" formatString=" ###-####" />
<mx:DateFormatter id="dateFormatter"
    formatString="month: MM, day: DD, year: YYYY"/>

<mx:VBox>
    <mx:Label text="Enter your Manhattan 7 digit phone number:"/>
    <mx:TextInput id="phone" change="if (phone.text.length == 7) ➡
        { phone.text = phoneFormatter.format(phone.text);
        error.text = phoneFormatter.error } "/>
    <mx:Label text="Enter date (mm/dd/yyyy):"/>
    <mx:TextInput id="date" change="if (date.text.length == 10) ➡
        { date.text = dateFormatter.format(date.text);
        error.text = dateFormatter.error } "/>
    <mx:Label text="Errors:"/>
    <mx:TextInput id="error" />
</mx:VBox>

</mx:Application>
```

# Attaching data to a UI component

After the data is returned, validated, and formatted, the last part of data interconnection is *attaching the data to a UI component*. You can use any UI component that is part of the framework shipped with Flex, or you can use a custom component.

List type components such as the following will be suitable for many results:

- dataGrid
- List
- TileList

Common to these types of components is their acceptance of all ArrayCollection data types as data feeds. Once you retrieve information from an RPC, you can format the information and then place it into an ArrayCollection and easily attach it to a component. Once you attach the information to a component, you can use a repeater or a renderer to style and format the results.

We will create code to search for product results in Google Base. The application will look as shown in Figure 10-19.

**Figure 10-19.** Google Base search results attached to a UI component

Define a bindable variable to hold the keywords and an ArrayCollection to hold the results.

```
[Bindable]
private var keywords:String = "rolex";

[Bindable]
private var dataProvider:ArrayCollection = new ArrayCollection();
```

Navigate to Google Base: http://www.google.com/base/feeds/snippets?bq=[keyword].

Download a sample XML and place it in Eclipse. You can then view the document structure using XMLBuddy (see Figure 10-20).

**Figure 10-20.** Variable window result object

Looking at the elements tree, it appears that each entry has detail nodes under <g:element>. We need to add the namespace to be able to access all the xmlns:gnamespace elements. Looking at the header of the feeds, we can determine the URL that needs to be used to open the xmlns:g namespace: http://base.google.com/ns/1.0.

Define the Atom and g namespacing:

```
private namespace atom = "http://www.w3.org/2005/Atom";
use namespace atom;
private namespace g = "http://base.google.com/ns/1.0 ";
use namespace g;
```

Create the HTTPService component and set the request and response handlers:

```
<mx:HTTPService id="service"
    url="http://www.google.com/base/feeds/snippets"
    resultFormat="e4x"
    result="resultHandler(event); "
    fault="faultHandler(event); ">
```

Handle the response for a successful connection:

```
private function resultHandler(event:ResultEvent): void
{
    var title:String;
    var publish:String;
    var content:String;
    var author:String;
    var image:String;
    var price:String;

    for each (var property:XML in event.result.entry)
    {
        title = property.title;
        publish = property.published;
        content = property.content;
        author = property.author.name;
        image = property.image_link;
        price = property.price;

        dataProvider.addItem({label: title, publish: publish,
        content: content, author: author, icon: image, price: price});
    }
}
```

Attach the results to a UI component. Notice that the item will be formatted as renderers. TileListItemRenderer, a common practice when dealing with List type components.

```
<mx:TileList id="CameraSelection" height="250" width="500"
    itemRenderer="renderers.T ileListItemRenderer"
    maxColumns="5" rowHeight="120" columnWidth="125"
    dataProvider="{dataProvider}" />
```

The item renderer is located here: renderers/TileListItemRenderer. The parameter data is assigned to automatically hold the item DataProvider.

```
<?xml version="1.0 " encoding="utf-8"?>
<mx:VBox xmlns:mx="http://www.adobe.com/2006/mxml"
    verticalAlign="middle" horizontalAlign="center"
    horizontalScrollPolicy="off" verticalScrollPolicy="off"
    width="100%" height="100%">

    <mx:Image source="{data.icon}" />
    <mx:Label text="{data.label}"
        truncateToFit="true" width="100" height="14"/>
    <mx:Label text="{data.price}"
        truncateToFit="true" width="100" />

</mx:V Box>
```

Following is the complete code:

```
<?xml version="1.0" encoding="utf-8"?>
<mx:Application
    xmlns:mx="http://www.adobe.com/2006/mxml"
    layout="absolute"
                initialize="service.send();">

    <mx:Script>
        <![CDATA[
        import mx.collections.ArrayCollection;

        import mx.controls.Alert;
        import mx.rpc.http.HTTPService;
        import mx.rpc.events.ResultEvent;
        import mx.rpc.events.FaultEvent;

        [Bindable]
        private var keywords:String = "rolex";

        [Bindable]
        private var dataProvider:ArrayCollection = ➥
new ArrayCollection();

        // Define and use atom & gnamespace.
        private namespace atom = "http://www.w3.org/2005/Atom";
        use namespace atom;
        private namespace g = "http://base.google.com/ns/1.0";
        use namespace g;

        private function resultHandler(event:ResultEvent):void
        {

          var title:String;
          var publish:String;
          var content:String;
          var author:String;
          var image:String;
          var price:String;

          for each (var property:XML in event.result.entry)
          {
            title = property.title;
            publish = property.published;
            content = property.content;
            author = property.author.name;
            image = property.image_link;
            price = property.price;
```

```
                    dataProvider.addItem({label: title, publish: publish, ➡
                        content: content, author: author, icon: image, ➡
                        price: price});
                }
            }

            private function faultHandler(event:FaultEvent):void
            {
                service.removeEventListener(FaultEvent.FAULT, ➡
                faultHandler);
                Alert.show("Error connecting");
            }

        ]]>
    </mx:Script>

        <mx:HTTPService id="service"
            url="http://www.google.com/base/feeds/snippets"
            resultFormat="e4x"
            result="resultHandler(event);"
            fault="faultHandler(event);">

            <mx:request>
                <bq>{keywords}</bq>
            </mx:request>
    </mx:HTTPService>

        <mx:TileList id="CameraSelection"
            height="250" width="500"
            itemRenderer="renderers.TileListItemRenderer"
            maxColumns="5" rowHeight="120" columnWidth="125"
            dataProvider="{dataProvider}" />

    </mx:Application>
```

# Mixing additional resources

Mashups are not only about mixing data sources. Enormous numbers of open source resources and commercial resources are available for you to mix and integrate, saving you time. These additional resources can be scripts, libraries, skins custom components, and other elements.

Before building your mashup, it is recommended you spend time designing your application and figuring out what components and services are necessary. Then, research to find out if there are any resources you can utilize that will help you and also save you time. There is no need to reinvent the wheel if someone already spent hours creating libraries or classes you can use. Many of these resources are open source, and you can find them in blogs, dedicated web sites, and search engines. In many cases, it would be beneficial to use these open source resources. Once you create your own APIs and components, feel free to share your work with others; that's what open source is all about!

# Additional libraries

Additional libraries consist of classes that add to the Flex framework. These libraries are offered as open source and can be used in accordance with the license agreement provided with them. In the past, Adobe used to host these projects, but many of them have moved to Google Code. Here are some popular libraries:

- **as3youtubelib**: The YouTube library provides an interface to search videos from YouTube.
- **as3flickrlib**: The Flickr library provides classes to access the entire Flickr online photo-sharing API.
- **Tweener**: The Tweener library provides classes to help create tweenings and transitions.
- **CoreLib**: The CoreLib library provides classes for working with MD5, SHA 1 hashing, image encoders, JSON serialization, and data APIs.
- **Degrafa**: This framework provides components that can be used as MXML tags to draw shapes.

# Custom components

Years ago, I was stubborn and insisted on always creating my own components. Since then, I learned that whatever I need, there is a good chance someone else already created it and is sharing or selling it.

There are many open source and commercial custom components that can be used as part of your mashup. These components should be used in accordance with their copyright licenses. Adding a pre-built custom component can quickly enhance your UI. Of course, there are times when you have to write your own custom component. But before doing so, check whether someone already built the exact same component and shared it as open source or with a commercial license.

Here are some Flex component directories you want to visit before starting to code your own components:

- http://flexbox.mrinalwadhwa.com/
- http://flex.org/components/
- http://www.afcomponents.com/components/

# Skins and templates

Part of building a mashup application is manipulating CSS to create your UI. The number of open source skins and templates available keeps increasing. Making a mashup application is all about building an application quickly and mixing existing resources and data sources. Why not take advantage of open source skins and templates already available? Here are two sites that offer free downloading of templates and skins:

- http://fleksray.org/Flex_skin.html
- http://www.scalenine.com

Some of these skins and templates may not be exactly what you need, but they can provide you with a starting point; and you can adjust the code and make them work with what you need, saving time in design and development. Using these skins and templates can also be a great option while building a POC.

# Connections to popular APIs

There are thousands of different APIs to choose from to use in your mashups. Many of the mashups you will be developing will be based on maps. Yahoo! has a clear advantage over other map providers since it can be integrated with Flex.

## Yahoo! Maps API

Yahoo! Maps recently updated its SWC file to work with ActionScript 3.0. Using Yahoo! Maps is relatively easy; however, it doesn't offer full integration as does ASTRA. We will be building a simple application to look for businesses in a particular ZIP code, as shown in Figure 10-21.

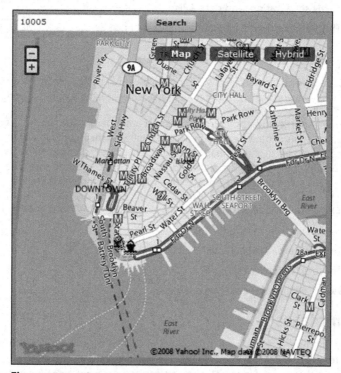

**Figure 10-21.** Yahoo! Maps mashup

> A **SWC file** is an archive file often used to package Flex components and other assets.

Create variables to hold the YahooMap component, an Address class for the geo location, and a LocalSearch class to access Yahoo! data sources of local businesses.

```
private var yahooMap:YahooMap;
private var address:Address;
private var localSearch:LocalSearch;
```

The user interface contains the input box, button, and an empty container to hold the YahooMap component, as well as a submit button.

```
<mx:Button x="178" y="10" label="Search"
    click="searchYahooMap(inputBox.text);
    setMarker(inputBox.text)" />
<mx:TextInput id="inputBox" x="10" y="10" text="10005"/>
<mx:UIComponent id="map" width="400" height="400" x="10" y="40" />
```

Once the map application is loaded, we can attach the YahooMap component to the empty container map and controllers on the map.

```
private function handleCreationComplete():void
{
    yahooMap = new YahooMap();
    yahooMap.addEventListener(YahooMapEvent.MAP_INITIALIZE, ➥
        handleMapInitialize);
    yahooMap.init("appid",map.width,map.height);

    map.addChild(yahooMap);

    yahooMap.addPanControl();
    yahooMap.addZoomWidget();
    yahooMap.addTypeWidget();
}
```

When the map is uploaded, we can resize it.

```
private function handleContainerResize(event:ResizeEvent): void {
    yahooMap.setSize(map.width,map.height);
}
```

Upon click of the search button, we create an instance of the Address class to attach results and do a search. Results will be handled at handlerGeocodeSuccess.

```
private function searchYahooMap(searchAddress:String): void
{
    address = new Address(searchAddress);
    address.addEventListener(GeocoderEvent.GEOCODER_SUCCESS, ➥
handleGeocodeSuccess);
    address.geocode();
}

private function handleGeocodeSuccess(event:GeocoderEvent): void
{
    var result:GeocoderResult = address.geocoderResultSet.firstResult;

    yahooMap.zoomLevel = result.zoomLevel;
    yahooMap.centerLatLon = result.latlon;

}
```

**397**

Once we have the results back, we can set markers on the map.

```
private function setMarker(address:String): void
{
    var marker:Marker = new SimpleMarker();

    marker.address = new Address(address);
    yahooMap.markerManager.addMarker(marker);
}
```

The complete code is shown here:

```
<?xml version="1.0" encoding="utf-8"?>
<mx:Application
    xmlns:mx="http://www.adobe.com/2006/mxml"
    layout="absolute"
    creationComplete="handleCreationComplete();">

 <mx:Script>
  <![CDATA[

    import com.yahoo.maps.webservices.local.LocalSearch;
    import com.yahoo.maps.api.markers.SearchMarker;
    import com.yahoo.maps.webservices.local.LocalSearchResults;
    import com.yahoo.maps.webservices.local.LocalSearchItem;
    import com.yahoo.maps.api.managers.MarkerManager;
    import com.yahoo.maps.webservices.local.events.LocalSearchEvent;
    import com.yahoo.maps.api.markers.SimpleMarker;
    import com.yahoo.maps.api.markers.Marker;

    import mx.events.ResizeEvent;
    import com.yahoo.maps.api.YahooMap;
    import com.yahoo.maps.api.YahooMapEvent;
    import com.yahoo.maps.webservices.geocoder.GeocoderResult;
    import com.yahoo.maps.webservices.geocoder.events.GeocoderEvent;
    import com.yahoo.maps.api.core.location.Address;


    private var yahooMap:YahooMap;
    private var address:Address;
    private var localSearch:LocalSearch;

    private function handleCreationComplete():void
    {
        yahooMap = new YahooMap();
        yahooMap.addEventListener(YahooMapEvent.MAP_INITIALIZE, ➥
handleMapInitialize);
        yahooMap.init("appid",map.width,map.height);

        map.addChild(yahooMap);
```

```
        yahooMap.addPanControl();
        yahooMap.addZoomWidget();
        yahooMap.addTypeWidget();
    }

    private function handleMapInitialize(event:YahooMapEvent):void
    {
        searchYahooMap(inputBox.text);
    }

    private function searchYahooMap(searchAddress:String):void
    {
        address = new Address(searchAddress);
        address.addEventListener(GeocoderEvent.GEOCODER_SUCCESS, ➥
handleGeocodeSuccess);
        address.geocode();
    }

    private function handleGeocodeSuccess(event:GeocoderEvent):void
    {
        var result:GeocoderResult = ➥
address.geocoderResultSet.firstResult;

        yahooMap.zoomLevel = result.zoomLevel;
        yahooMap.centerLatLon = result.latlon;

    }

    private function handleContainerResize(event:ResizeEvent):void {
        yahooMap.setSize(map.width,map.height);
    }

    private function setMarker(address:String):void
    {
        var marker:Marker = new SimpleMarker();

        marker.address = new Address(address);
        yahooMap.markerManager.addMarker(marker);
    }

    ]]>
</mx:Script>

    <mx:Button x="178" y="10" label="Search"
        click="searchYahooMap(inputBox.text);
        setMarker(inputBox.text)"/>
    <mx:TextInput id="inputBox" x="10" y="10"
        text="10005"/>
    <mx:UIComponent id="map" width="400" height="400"
```

```
                x="10" y="40" />

    </mx:Application>
```

Although the Yahoo! Maps API is a great API for using simple maps, it is limited in functionality. When you require more features, such as creating markers that display information or custom overlays, it is preferable to use the Yahoo! ASTRA API.

To view more tutorials visit `http://developer.yahoo.com/flash/tutorials/index.html`.

## ASTRA API

The Yahoo! ASTRA API is a library that allows you to access Yahoo! public APIs.

We will create an application that retrieves job search results from Indeed.com (`http://www.indeed.com`), and then we will be using the Yahoo! pipes that we created previously. These pipes will behave as the proxy since the Indeed.com service does not have the `crossdomain.xml` policy installed on its remote server. After the results are retrieved, we will display them on a Yahoo! Maps component (see Figure 10-22).

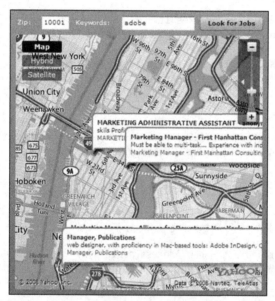

**Figure 10-22.** Indeed.com search results displayed on Yahoo! Maps

Download the ASTRA API from here: `http://developer.yahoo.com/flash/astra-webapis/`. Next, add the `AstraWebAPIs.swc` file to the `lib` folder. You can also paste in the complete library, which will allow you to look at the code.

The Map API in ASTRA is different from the Yahoo! Maps API; it utilizes a map through a SWF file.

First, we need to set the parameters we will be using in our application. We can set a static member called SWF_DOM_ID, which must match the same name as the MXML file name.

```
private static var SWF_DOM_ID:String = "YahooAstra";
```

Define YAHOO_API_KEY, which will contain the Yahoo! API key.

```
private static var YAHOO_API_KEY:String = " ****************";
```

You can get a Yahoo! API key from here: http://www.developer.yahoo.com/wsregapp/.

Also create variables to hold the URL location of the map, which was provided with the ASTRA library folder. Define overlays to display markers and the map controllers.

```
private static var MAP_SWF:String="assets/swf/as2map.swf";
private var overlays:Overlays;
private var mapController:MapController;
private var latLonController:LatLonController;
```

A user interface will include the YahooMap component, input boxes for the ZIP code, and the keywords to search and input the submit button.

```
<yahoo:YahooMapService id="as2Map"
        UUID="{getTimer()}"
        swfDomId="SWF_DOM_ID"
        apiId="YAHOO_API_KEY"
        mapURL="MAP_SWF"
        width="400" height="400"
        scaleContent="false"
        x="10" y="40"/>

<mx:TextInput id="location" x="51" y="10"
        width="46" text="10005" maxChars="5"
        restrict="0-9"/>

<mx:TextInput id="keywords" x="182" y="10"
        width="118" text="Adobe Flex"/>

<mx:Button id="findhouse"
        x="308" y="10"
        label="Look for Jobs"
        click="displayResults()"/>
```

Once YahooMap is loaded, we can add controllers.

```
private function initEvents():void {
    as2Map.addEventListener('onMapLoad',
            onMapLoadedHandler);
    as2Map.addEventListener('onMapError',
            function():void { Alert.show("Error loading!" );  } );
}
```

**401**

```
private function onMapLoadedHandler(event:O bject): void {
    var panTools:PanTool = new PanTool(as2Map);
    panTools.setPanTool(true);

    var widgets:Widgets = new Widgets(as2Map);
    widgets.showNavigatorWidget();
    widgets.showSatelliteControlWidget();

    overlays = new Overlays(as2Map);
    mapController = new MapController(as2Map);
    latLonController = new LatLonController(as2Map);

}
```

When a user submits the results, we can use a method called ShowGeoRssOverlay, which takes RSS feeds and displays them on a map. It expects to get results in the following format:

```
<?xml version="1.0"?>
<rss version="2.0"
    xmlns:geo="http://www.w3.org/2003/01/geo/wgs84_pos#">
    <channel>
        <item>
            <title></title>
            <link></link>
            <description><description>
            <geo:lat></geo:lat>
            <geo:long></geo:long>
        </item>
    </channel>
</rss>
```

The submit button will initiate displayResults, which will set the ShowGeoRssOverlay method.

```
public function displayResults():void {
    var pipeURL:String = "http://pipes.yahoo.com/pipes/pipe.run?_ ➡
id=vh97mywZ3RGlrygr1vC6Jw&_render=rss&location= ➡
"+location.text+"&query="+keywords.text;

    overlays.removeGeoRssOverlay();
    overlays.showGeoRssOverlay(pipeURL);

    mapController.setCenterByAddressAndZoom(location.text, 6);
}
```

The complete code is shown here:

```
<?xml version="1.0" encoding="utf-8"?>
<mx:Application
        xmlns:mx="http://www.adobe.com/2006/mxml"
        xmlns:yahoo="com.yahoo.webapis.maps.*"
```

```
            creationComplete="initEvents()" layout="absolute">

    <mx:Script>
      <![CDATA[

        import flash.utils.getTimer;
        import mx.controls.Alert;
        import flash.utils.setTimeout;
        import com.yahoo.webapis.maps.methodgroups.*;
        import com.yahoo.webapis.maps.events.*;

        // This static member should match this MXML file name
        private static var SWF_DOM_ID:String = "YahooAstra";
        // Apply to a Yahoo! API Key
        private static var YAHOO_API_KEY:String = " ****************";
        // location of as2map.swf
        private static var MAP_SWF:String = "assets/swf/as2map.swf";

        private var overlays:Overlays;
        private var mapController:MapController;
        private var latLonController:LatLonController;

        private function initEvents():void {
            as2Map.addEventListener('onMapLoad', onMapLoadedHandler);
            as2Map.addEventListener('onMapError', ➥
            function():void { Alert.show("Error loading!"); } );
        }

        private function onMapLoadedHandler(event:Object):void {
            var panTools:PanTool = new PanTool(as2Map);
            panTools.setPanTool(true);

            var widgets:Widgets = new Widgets(as2Map);
            widgets.showNavigatorWidget();
            widgets.showSatelliteControlWidget();

            overlays = new Overlays(as2Map);
            mapController = new MapController(as2Map);
            latLonController = new LatLonController(as2Map);

        }

        public function displayResults():void {
            var pipeURL:String = ➥
"http://pipes.yahoo.com/pipes/pipe.run?_id=vh97mywZ3RGlrygr1vC6Jw& ➥
_render=rss&location="+location.text+"&query="+keywords.text;

            overlays.removeGeoRssOverlay();
            overlays.showGeoRssOverlay(pipeURL);
```

```
                    mapController.setCenterByAddressAndZoom(location.text, 6);
            }

        ]]>
    </mx:Script>

    <yahoo:YahooMapService id="as2Map" UUID="{getTimer()}"
            swfDomId="SWF_DOM_ID"
            apiId="YAHOO_API_KEY"
            mapURL="MAP_SWF"
            width="400" height="400"
            scaleContent="false"
            x="10" y="40"/>

    <mx:Label x="10" y="12" text="Zip: " color="white"/>
    <mx:TextInput id="location" x="51" y="10"
        width="46" text="10005" maxChars="5" restrict="0-9"/>
    <mx:Label x="105" y="12" text="Keywords: " color="white"/>
    <mx:TextInput id="keywords" x="182" y="10" width="118"
        text="Adobe Flex"/>
    <mx:Button id="findhouse" x="308" y="10"
        label="Look for Jobs" click="displayResults()" />

</mx:Application>
```

## UMap

Another choice for displaying results on a map is UMap, which stands for Universal Mapping. UMAP integrates with OpenStreetMap and Microsoft Virtual Earth map data to display map results.

Here's an example for a UMAP custom component:

```
<?xml version="1.0" encoding="utf-8"?>
<mx:Panel xmlns:mx="http://www.adobe.com/2006/mxml"
    width="400" height="400"
    horizontalScrollPolicy="off" verticalScrollPolicy="off"
    creationComplete="onCreationComplete(event)">

    <mx:Script>
        <![CDATA[

            import mx.controls.scrollClasses.ScrollBar;
            import com.afcomponents.umap.styles.MarkerStyle;
            import com.afcomponents.umap.styles.Style;
            import com.afcomponents.umap.overlays.Marker;
            import com.afcomponents.umap.types.LatLngBounds;
            import mx.collections.ArrayCollection;
            import com.afcomponents.umap.display.InfoWindow;
            import events.MapEvents;
```

```
import com.afcomponents.umap.types.LatLng;
import mx.core.UIComponent;
import com.afcomponents.umap.gui.*;
import com.afcomponents.umap.core.UMap;
import com.afcomponents.umap.types.LatLng;
import com.afcomponents.umap.styles.InfoWindowStyle;
import com.afcomponents.umap.styles.TextStyle;
import com.afcomponents.umap.display.InfoWindow;
import com.afcomponents.umap.types.Size;
import com.afcomponents.umap.styles.DropShadowStyle;

[Event(name="mapCreationComplete", ➡
type="events.MapEvents")]
private var map:UMap;

private var myWindow:InfoWindow;
private var infoWindowOpenFlag:Boolean = false;
public var mapReadyFlag:Boolean = false;

public function onCreationComplete(event:Event) : void
{
    var ref:UIComponent = new UIComponent();
    map = new UMap();
    map.setSize(this.width-15, this.height-30);
    ref.addChild(map);
    mapCanvas.addChild(ref);
    ref.focusManager.deactivate();
    map.addControl(new MapTypeControl());
    map.addControl(new ZoomControl());
    map.addControl(new PositionControl());
    this.dispatchEvent( new MapEvents➡
("mapCreationComplete") );
    mapReadyFlag = true;
}

public function setCenter(latLng:LatLng):void
{
    map.setCenter(latLng);
}

public function zoomMap(times:int):void
{
    for (var i:int=0; i<times; i++)
    map.zoomIn();
}

public function openInfo(latLng:LatLng, title:String, ➡
description:String):void {
    if (infoWindowOpenFlag)
```

```
            map.closeInfoWindow();

        // define info window style
        var infoStyle:InfoWindowStyle = new InfoWindowStyle();
        infoStyle.fill = "rgb";
        infoStyle.fillRGB = 0x000000;
        infoStyle.fillAlpha = .65;
        infoStyle.strokeRGB = 0xFF66CC;
        infoStyle.strokeAlpha = .6;
        infoStyle.closeRGB = 0x6699FF;
        infoStyle.closeAlpha = .6;
        infoStyle.radius = 3;

        //Sets Scroll Bar in Info Window
        InfoWindow.setScrollBarClass(ScrollBar);
        infoStyle.scroll = true;
        infoStyle.maxSize = new Size(300, 150);
        infoStyle.autoSize = InfoWindowStyle.AUTO_SIZE_SIDE;

        //Style Title in Info Window
        var infoTitleStyle:TextStyle = new TextStyle();
        infoTitleStyle.textFormat.bold = true;
        infoTitleStyle.textFormat.color = 0xFFFFFF;
        infoTitleStyle.textFormat.font = "verdana";
        infoTitleStyle.textFormat.size = 14;
        infoStyle.titleStyle = infoTitleStyle;

        //Turn on HTML, use a style sheet to style content text
        infoStyle.contentStyle.html = true;
        infoStyle.contentStyle.styleSheet = new StyleSheet();
        infoStyle.contentStyle.styleSheet.setStyle("html", ➥
{fontFamily:"arial", fontSize:12, color:"#CCCCCC"});

        //Style Drop Shadow
        var shadowStyle:DropShadowStyle = ➥
new DropShadowStyle();
        shadowStyle.blurX = 5;
        shadowStyle.blurY = 5;
        shadowStyle.alpha = .5;
        shadowStyle.angle = 20;
        shadowStyle.color = 0xFF6699;
        shadowStyle.distance = .5;
        infoStyle.shadowStyle = shadowStyle;

        //Define the Parameters of our Info Window
        var param:Object = new Object();
        param.title = title;
        param.content = description;
        param.position = latLng;
```

```
                    param.autoClose = false;
                    map.openInfoWindow(param, infoStyle);
                    infoWindowOpenFlag = true;
                }

                public function setMarkersLocations(dp:ArrayCollection): ➥
        void
                {
                    // create new MarkerStyle
                    var style:MarkerStyle = new MarkerStyle();
                    style.fill = "rgb";
                    style.fillAlpha = 0.9;
                    style.strokeRGB = 0x0;
                    style.strokeAlpha = 1.0;
                    var pos:LatLng;
                    var geoArray:Array;
                    var bounds:LatLngBounds = map.getBoundsLatLng();
                    var marker:Marker;

                    // create Markers
                    for (var i:int = 0; i < dp.length; i++) {
                    style.fillRGB = Math.random() * 0xFFFFFF;
                    geoArray = new Array();
                    geoArray = String(dp.getItemAt(i).geo).split(" ");

                    //trace(geoArray[0]+","+geoArray[1]);
                    pos = new LatLng(geoArray[0], geoArray[1]);
                    marker = new Marker({autoInfo: false, ➥
        draggable:false});
                    marker.index = String.fromCharCode(65 + i);
                    marker.position = pos;
                    marker.setStyle(style);
                    map.addOverlay(marker);
                }
            ]]>
        </mx:Script>
        <mx:Canvas id="mapCanvas" backgroundColor="#352D69"
                x="0" y="0"
                horizontalScrollPolicy="off" verticalScrollPolicy="off"
                width="{this.width}" height="{this.height}"/>
    </mx:Panel>
```

# Flickr

A common integration in mashups is photos. Flickr is an online photo management and sharing application. Flickr is a good choice for mashups since it has the crossdomain.xml policy file installed on its remote server. We will be using an open source library that was developed by Adobe and can handle all the integration with Flickr.

We will create a Flickr mashup that allows you to search by tags or usernames. It then displays the results in two components, and images can be dragged to a wish list. Once an image is dragged, the component will reorganize itself, as shown in Figure 10-23.

**Figure 10-23.** Flickr mashup

To access Flickr, we will be using an Adobe open source API. The following script connects to Flickr and retrieves results:

```
<?xml version="1.0" encoding="utf-8"?>
<mx:Application xmlns:mx="http://www.adobe.com/2006/mxml"
    layout="absolute"
    initialize="initApp();
    searchFlickr('flower');">
  <mx:Script>
    <![CDATA[

    import com.adobe.flickr.SearchCriteria;
    import mx.collections.ArrayCollection;
    import mx.controls.Alert;
    import com.adobe.flickr.events.FlickrEvent;
    import com.adobe.flickr.Flickr;
    private var flickr:Flickr = new Flickr();

    private function initApp() : void
    {
        flickr.addEventListener( FlickrEvent.SEARCH_COMPLETE_EVENT, ➥
searchCompleteEventHandler );
        flickr.addEventListener( FlickrEvent. ➥
CONNECTION_FAILED_EVENT, function(event:FlickrEvent):void {
Alert.show( event.failMsg, "Connection Failure" ) } );
        flickr.addEventListener( FlickrEvent.PHOTO_INFO_EVENT, ➥
```

```
photoInfoEventHandler );
    }

    private function searchFlickr(tags:String):void
    {
        var numPerPage:Number = 50;
        var searchCriteria:SearchCriteria = new SearchCriteria();
        searchCriteria.tags = tags;
        flickr.photoSearch(numPerPage,searchCriteria);
    }

    private function searchCompleteEventHandler(event:FlickrEvent):void
    {
        var data:Object = event.data;
        var dp:ArrayCollection = (data.photo as ArrayCollection);
        flickr.getPhotoInfo(dp.getItemAt(0).id, ➡
dp.getItemAt(0).secret);
    }

    private function photoInfoEventHandler(event:FlickrEvent):void
    {
        var result:Object = event.data;
    }
    ]]>
  </mx:Script>

</mx:Application>
```

Next, we are going to include a custom open source component that was built by Ely Greenfield. You can download the component from here: http://demo.quietlyscheming.com/DragTile/ DragDrop.html. This component is an animated DragTile component in which the container reorganizes itself once you drag and drop an item.

```
package qs.event
{
    import flash.events.Event;

    public class DragTitleEvent extends Event
    {
        // Public constructor.
        public function DragTitleEvent(type:String, ➡
selectedImage:String)  {
                super(type);
                this.selectedImage = selectedImage;
        }

        // Define static constant.
        public static const SELECTED_IMAGE_CHANGED:String= ➡
"selectedImageChanged";
```

```
            // Define public variable to hold state of the enable property.
            public var selectedImage:String;

            // Override the inherited clone()method.
            override public function clone():Event {
                return new DragTitleEvent(type,  selectedImage);
            }
        }
    }
```

We will be adding a custom event to dragDrop(e:DragEvent) at qs.controls.DragTile so we can
display the image that was dragged in a larger format.

```
    // custom event to pass image changed
     var event:DragTitleEvent = new DragTitleEvent ➥
    ("selectedImageChanged", this.dataProvider[_dragTargetIdx]);
    this.dispatchEvent(event);
```

Here is the complete code:

```
    <?xml version="1.0" encoding="utf-8"?>
    <mx:Application
        xmlns:mx="http://www.adobe.com/2006/mxml"
        layout="absolute"
        initialize="initApp();
        searchFlickr('flower');">

        <mx:Script>
         <![CDATA[
           import com.adobe.flickr.SearchCriteria;
           import mx.collections.ArrayCollection;
           import mx.controls.Alert;
           import com.adobe.flickr.events.FlickrEvent;
           import com.adobe.flickr.Flickr;

           private var flickr:Flickr = new Flickr();

           private function initApp() : void
           {
                flickr.addEventListener ➥
    (FlickrEvent.SEARCH_COMPLETE_EVENT, searchCompleteEventHandler);
                flickr.addEventListener ➥
    (FlickrEvent.CONNECTION_FAILED_EVENT, ➥
    function(event:FlickrEvent):void ➥
    { Alert.show( event.failMsg, "Connection Failure" ) });
                flickr.addEventListener(FlickrEvent.PHOTO_INFO_EVENT, ➥
    photoInfoEventHandler);
           }
```

```
        private function searchFlickr(tags:String):void
        {
           var numPerPage:Number = 50;
           var searchCriteria:SearchCriteria = new SearchCriteria();
           searchCriteria.tags = tags;
           flickr.photoSearch(numPerPage,searchCriteria);
        }

        private function searchCompleteEventHandler ➡
    (event:FlickrEvent):void
        {
           var data:Object = event.data;
           var dp:ArrayCollection = (data.photo as ArrayCollection);
           flickr.getPhotoInfo(dp.getItemAt(0).id, ➡
    dp.getItemAt(0).secret);
        }

        private function photoInfoEventHandler(event:FlickrEvent):void
        {
           var result:Object = event.data;
        }

     ]]>
     </mx:Script>

</mx:Application>
```

# Creating your own Flex mashup

Now that you know about data access, interconnectivity, and mixing additional scripts, you are ready to create your own Flex mashup. But where do you start?

I suggest splitting the process of creating mashups into four steps:

1. **Pick a subject**: Picking a subject is the base for every Flex mashup. Your subject should add value, although Flex has an advantage as a starting point, since the Flex stateful user interface already adds value. Many times you will add a service or data source to an existing application so the subject is already known. A good place to start is to get familiar with all the available APIs, and a good resource to find all the APIs that are available is http://www.programmableweb.com/apis.

2. **Choose services**: Now that you know the subject of your mashup application, the next step is to decide which service or services you will use. Many times you have available more than one API that provides the same or similar functionality, so you need to decide which one to use or whether to combine a few together.

   I personally prefer using services that are part of a cloud. You can rely on a service that sits on a cloud server's infrastructure rather than a small web site hosted by a shared hosting plan. The following companies have a massive network of servers: Google, Yahoo!, Amazon, and Salesforce.

Once you select all the APIs and services you will be using in your mashup, sign up for or download the APIs needed. Many APIs provide a key or a unique ID number. Some APIs are being sold on a license basis or given away as open source. Once you select the APIs you will be using, spend some time checking out the manuals, the reliability of service, and the performance.

For example, you may find a few services that offer the same functionality, but one may have a better performance because it is based on REST rather than SOAP. Although you will be able to switch and change your application later, it is better to check the service or API before you get started.

3. **Design**: Follow the same patterns you use when developing any Flex application such as creating a UML diagram, design document, or any other process you use. In addition to your regular process, it is recommended you figure out the design of the services you will be using. By this, I mean you create a block diagram covering all the services, APIs, and any other additional resources you will be using up front.

Microsoft Visio is a good tool to create block diagrams, but feel free to use any other software you are comfortable with. To create a block diagram in MS Visio, follow these instructions:

   **a.** Choose File on the top menu, point to New, select the General folder, and choose Block Diagram.

   **b.** Drag shapes onto the drawing page.

   **c.** Right-click a shape, and then select Fill to change the default color.

   **d.** Double-click a shape to add text.

   **e.** Ctrl-click corners to resize the drawing page.

   For an example of a Visio 2007 block diagram, see Figure 10-2 earlier in the chapter.

4. **Start coding**: Once your block diagram and any other support documents such as UML diagram, wire frames, and design documents are ready, you can start coding.

   I recommend creating a connection to any API or services following best practices such as using loosely coupled components, so you can reuse a component and publish it as open source for the benefit of others.

# Summary

In this chapter, I covered all the basics you need to know in order to build a successful mashup. As the Web is undergoing transformation into sharing and collaboration, and an increasing number of services are available, developers can now create new and exciting applications by simply mixing these services together.

You learned how to read and create the crossdomain.xml file policy and how to overcome restricted or lack of crossdomain.xml policy by creating a proxy. You also saw how to utilize mashup frameworks to act as your proxies, reducing resources on your server. You learned how to deal with different types of namespaces that you can encounter using web feeds. You then explored some of the best practices of interconnectivity involving such factors as valuators, format, data model, and attaching data to a UI. You also explored how to utilize the Web and the enormous amount of resources available today, such as APIs, libraries, custom components, and skins.

To help you get started, I showed you how to build some exciting mashups using some of the most popular APIs such as Yahoo!, Amazon, Flickr, and UMap, as well as giving you tips and tricks on how to start building your own mashup application.

Mashup applications include some of the most visited and interesting sites available on the Web today. Flex mashups offer a Flex stateful paradigm where you can keep changing your application, without refreshing your browser, giving additional value for every mashup application.

Have fun creating exciting mashup applications.

## Chapter 11

# MIGRATING WEB 1.0 INTERFACES TO RIA

By Shashank Tiwari

Many enterprises and organizations are heavily invested in legacy web technologies, ranging from first-generation applets to recent HTML-based server-side user interfaces. Therefore, even if the organizations have a compelling need to adopt today's rich and engaging platforms, writing off all that investment and starting from scratch is not an option for them. Often, the preferred course is to reuse as much as possible and add bits of the newer technologies incrementally, thus gaining some benefits without disrupting existing systems that continue to work effectively.

A few purists argue against such reuse, but the possibilities of substantial and quick benefits from incremental adoption are immense, and it would be imprudent for you to ignore them. Moreover, your development team members may not be ready to discard their faithful old technologies and tools completely and move on with the newer options. So for now, we will leave the purists aside and find solutions to our quest of adopting RIA gradually, while keeping parts of the legacy intact.

We do not argue that creating RIA from scratch is necessarily a bad idea. We are only suggesting that reality may not allow you to start from scratch in many cases. This chapter will help further the cause of incremental RIA adoption and will provide a path to achieving success in this pursuit.

The chapter starts by talking about minor refactoring and restructuring to plug in RIA on top of existing systems and moves on to providing ideas for substantial replacements of existing modules, where necessary.

# Weighing up the status quo

Let's first survey the current landscape and understand our starting context.

Our target is the Rich Internet Application (RIA), so our starting point could be any platform that has some characteristics of RIA or benefits from the features that RIA supports. This brings us to the obvious question: what is RIA? A comprehensive literal definition is easy enough to give. RIA is

- **Rich**: Highly interactive and engaging, desktop-like in a traditional sense
- **Internet**: Networked and accessible worldwide and across devices
- **Application**: An implementation of a required (business) solution

With this definition, we could consider both desktop and web applications as our starting point.

Currently, with only a few exceptions, the desktop and web technologies are disparate and are viewed as alternative paradigms for application deployment and distribution. Also, they are seen as satisfying completely different requirements. Desktop applications are suitable where high performance "fat clients" are desired, and web technologies are suitable where the application needs to be accessible to a large audience and flexible enough to be modified easily to keep up with changing requirements.

Desktop applications are usually built using C, C++, Java, or the Microsoft alternatives (including C# .NET). They usually implement the two-tier client-server communication model. They often make use of native calls to the operating system and its hardware drivers. Although sometimes viewed as legacies, they thrive as heavy-duty office and enterprise applications. In the last few years, desktop applications have started leveraging the Internet and often connect to networks using the Internet protocols. Instant messaging clients and soft-phones are examples of such applications.

Web applications, on the other hand, are built using a number of different technologies, programming paradigms, programming languages, and frameworks. However, they could be classified under two categories:

- HTML-based web applications
- Virtual machine (VM) based web applications

HTML technologies–based web applications create user interfaces that are interpreted and rendered within the browser. This means the output is HTML markup, with JavaScript elements. These user interfaces are generated mostly on the server and only sometimes have large client-centric manipulations. JSP and PHP applications fall in this category.

VM-based web applications live and run within a virtual machine. The virtual machines themselves are housed within the browser, but applications existing in a virtual machine don't interact with the browser directly. The virtual machines exist as plug-ins in the browser, which help interpret the specific code implementation in a browser-independent manner. Applications built using Java applets, Flex, and Silverlight are VM-based web applications.

Our RIA is Flex-based, so migrating to RIA implies moving from any of these web technologies to Flex. Desktop applications also have a few features in common with RIA. So porting them over to Flex and AIR is also a possibility, though the topic is out of scope for this chapter. The focus here is on web applications only.

The next couple of sections dig deeper into web applications, the source applications that we intend to port over to Flex.

# HTML web technologies

As mentioned, HTML technologies can be further classified as server centric or client centric. I will illustrate HTML technologies using this classification.

## Server-centric approaches

A large number of web user interfaces leverage server-side platforms to generate HTML outputs. Sometimes they supplement these HTML outputs with dynamic JavaScript (which manipulates the HTML Document Object Model at run time) based decorations that add richer functionality. The server-side platforms are varied and diverse, but they are often written in Java, PHP, ColdFusion, Python, or Ruby. Irrespective of the programming languages and framework used to generate the user interface, these server-side options generate HTML and JavaScript outputs. Figure 11-1 shows this in a diagram.

Let's first see some simple JSP and PHP applications so you can understand how they work. Later, we will morph these simple applications to work with Flex. If you don't use either of these technologies, you will still find the discussion useful. The idea of these examples is not to teach you to write web applications using any of these server-side technologies, but to show how they can be migrated from their current forms to a new form that includes a Flex user interface. You will be able to apply what you learn to your own server-centric web environment, which may be Ruby, Python, Perl, ColdFusion, or anything else.

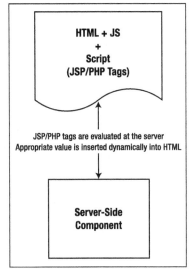

**Figure 11-1.** HTML generation in typical server-centric web applications

Our simple JSP example displays a list of stock prices in an HTML table. The example is crude because it uses direct database connection and includes all the code together. In a real-life situation, you will distribute the code into three separate tiers: database, middle tier (with database access and business logic), and web layer. The code for this example is as follows:

```
<%@ page import="java.sql.*"%>
<%@ page import="java.util.*"%>
<%
List stockList = new ArrayList();
Class.forName("sun.jdbc.odbc.JdbcOdbcDriver");
Connection conn =
DriverManager.getConnection➡
(//pass the connection credentials);
Statement stmt = conn.createStatement();
ResultSet rs =
stmt.executeQuery➡
("select id,symbol, name, price from Stocks");
while(rs.next()){
Map stock = new HashMap();
```

```
stock.put("id",rs.getInt(1));
stock.put("Symbol",rs.getString(2));
stock.put("name",rs.getString(3));
stock.put("price",rs.getString(4));
stockList.add(stock);
}
rs.close();
stmt.close();
conn.close();
%>
<html><head>
<title>Stocks</title>
</head>
<body>
<h1>Stocks</h1>
<table border="1">
<%
for(int i=0;i<stockList.size();i++){
Map stock = (Map)stockList.get(i);
%>
<tr>
<td align="right"><%=stock.get("id")%></td>
<td><%=emp.get("symbol")%></td>
<td><%=emp.get("name")%></td>
<td><%=emp.get("price")%></td>
</tr>
<%
}
%>
</table>
</body></html>
```

In this simple example, we bind the result set of our database queries to an HTML table. This is a typical case where data is dynamically accessed and presented as HTML. Later in this chapter, you will see how XML could be generated (instead of HTML) and consumed in a Flex interface.

Our next example, a PHP web application, is another that is trivial from a real-life point of view. It shows a simple form that has a button to submit the input data. All the code is in a single file that mixes HTML with PHP script. Here is what the code looks like:

```
<html>
<head>
<title>Login Form</title>
</head>
<body>
<form method="post" action="<?php echo $PHP_SELF;?>">
User Name:<input type="text"
size="12"
maxlength="36"
name="username">:<br />
```

```
Password:<input type="text"
size="12"
maxlength="15"
name="password">:<br />
Role::<br />
Administrator:<input type="radio" value="Admin" name="role">:<br />
Super User:<input type="radio" value="SuperUser" name="role">:<br />
Regular User:<input type="radio"
value="RegularUser"
name="role">:<br />
Please choose your preferences::<br />
Remember Password:<input type="checkbox"
value="RememberPassword"
name="preferences[]">:<br />
Expire session only on logout:<input type="checkbox"
value="ExpireOnLogout"
name="preferences[]">:<br />
<textarea
rows="5"
cols="20"
name="quote"
wrap="physical">
Leave a message for the administrator if required
</textarea>:<br />
Select your department:<br />
<select name="department">
<option value="InformationSystems">Information Systems</option>
<option value="Sales">Sales</option>
<option value="Operations">Operations</option></select>:<br />
</body>
</html>
```

In this PHP example, there isn't much server-side data access. The example has user interface components. These are plain HTML elements with PHP code that adds the processing conveniences and the additional rendering and validation features. When porting such applications to Flex, you would use only the data access and business logic parts and discard the user interface elements. Figure 11-2 shows a screenshot of the PHP example.

Although web applications are almost always more complicated than these two examples, they are often built using similar concepts. A little later we will inspect these, and a few other examples, to see how to modify them and convert them to Flex applications.

## Client-centric alternatives

Although server-side HTML technologies are popular and widespread, rich JavaScript-based client-centric manipulations are now commonly becoming part of web applications. This client-centric asynchronous interaction approach is popularly known as Ajax. With Ajax, JavaScript and DHTML are becoming

**Figure 11-2.** The simple PHP example

**419**

more than mere animation decorations. In some cases, Ajax clients are able to provide some of the rich functionality that VM-based options provide. From a Flex perspective, interacting with JavaScript is easy. You can read Chapter 9 to understand how to connect JavaScript and Flex. When replacing JavaScript user interfaces with Flex alternatives, the same remoting infrastructure can be reused, but often the user interface components themselves overlap with what Flex provides and need to be completely discarded. I will discuss a few bits of this in the context of our solutions later in this chapter.

Next, let's take a quick look at the VM-based web applications.

# Virtual machines in the browsers

Unlike HTML-based web applications, VM-based web applications run in a managed VM environment. A managed VM environment provides a uniform run-time platform across browsers and keeps the code shielded from the difficulties arising due to browser differences. Applets have existed since the mid-1990s, whereas Silverlight is only a little over a year old. Flex is also a VM-based RIA framework. Most often migrating from another VM environment to Flex implies re-creating the entire UI. The only portions that are reused are the services that the UI interacts with.

In practice, almost all popular HTML-based web applications, whether built for consumers or enterprises, use frameworks under the hood. In complex scenarios, frameworks manage all the basic plumbing. The next section lists a few of these frameworks.

# Frameworks behind the scenes

There are innumerable numbers of frameworks out there to build web applications. Every language has a few popular ones.

Popular web frameworks written in PHP include the following:

- **symfony**: http://www.symfony-project.org/
- **CakePHP**: http://cakephp.org/

Then there are full-stack, pluggable, module-based frameworks like Drupal (http://drupal.org/), which are especially popular for content management.

Ruby has an extremely popular web framework offering in Rails (http://www.rubyonrails.org/). Python has a framework similar to Rails called Django (http://www.djangoproject.com/). Groovy's Grails (http://grails.org/) is a web framework that falls in the same category as Rails and Django.

Some newer languages like Scala (http://www.scala-lang.org/) also offer web frameworks; Scala's is called Lift (http://liftweb.net/index.php/Main_Page).

Java has uncountable web frameworks. Apache Struts (http://struts.apache.org/) historically has been the most popular of them all. Newer web frameworks include JBoss Seam (http://seamframework.org/), Spring MVC and Web Flow (http://www.springframework.org/), Tapestry (http://tapestry.apache.org/), Wicket (http://wicket.apache.org/), Struts 2 (http://struts.apache.org/2.x/index.html), and Stripes (http://www.stripesframework.org/display/stripes/Home). There are many other frameworks apart from the ones just listed. Most frameworks have their own unique proposition. Some enable Ajax, some simplify and enhance Java Server Faces (JSF), a few provide deeper integration with the server side, and a few offer a set of user interface components.

I could spend a lot of time and fill up a lot of pages listing web frameworks, but I will stop right here. What you need to understand here is how to migrate applications built using these frameworks to leverage Flex. Because each framework has its own complexity, there is no universal porting strategy that will work for all.

Therefore, I will pick two important frameworks from this list and see how applications built using them can be refactored to use Flex. The two frameworks of choice are

- Apache Struts
- Ruby on Rails

Discussions about migrating applications built using these two frameworks are included in the sections where I talk about migration strategies. The specific section that deals with porting framework applications is entitled "Strategies to port framework-based applications."

Coverage of only two frameworks is not comprehensive, but what you will learn in their context will help you create your own strategy for your framework, outside this list.

Now let's start with some recommendations and recipes for migration.

# Migration strategies

This chapter does not provide an exhaustive list of migration strategies and techniques. It only analyzes a few very important ones. Most of the recommendations apply to HTML technologies–based web applications, but don't hold good for applications that run in the browser plug-ins.

## Generating XML

As a first step, we need to explore replacing the HTML in web applications with a Flex user interface and reusing everything up to the point where HTML generation starts. Most often the embedded script tags in HTML, which are interpreted on the server, are dynamically replaced with HTML elements. These embedded script tags could be JSP or PHP tags. This is how dynamic data is incorporated, while the output remains plain HTML.

Although Flex applications can be made to consume HTML as text—and possibly you could write a parser to cull the data from it—this technique is both inefficient and ugly. An elegant modification would be to generate XML instead of HTML. Then you could apply an XSLT (http://www.w3.org/TR/xslt) stylesheet to transform the XML output to an XHTML output. That way we still generate HTML (or more accurately XHTML) while creating XML as an intermediate output. Flex applications can consume the intermediate XML. So an old application gets refactored to work simultaneously with both HTML and Flex. Figure 11-3 summarizes this technique in a diagram.

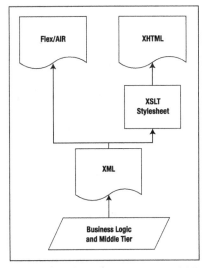

**Figure 11-3.** Generate XML. Consume XML in Flex and transform it to XHTML using an XSLT stylesheet.

**421**

Let's take our earlier JSP example and make it generate XML. Here is the modified code:

```
<?xml version="1.0" encoding="ISO-8859-1"?>
<%@ page contentType="text/xml;charset=ISO-8859-1" %>
<%@ page import="java.sql.*"%>
<%@ page import="java.util.*"%>
<%
List stockList = new ArrayList();
Class.forName("sun.jdbc.odbc.JdbcOdbcDriver");
Connection conn =
DriverManager.getConnection➡
(//pass the connection credentials);
Statement stmt = conn.createStatement();
ResultSet rs =
stmt.executeQuery➡
("select id,symbol, name, price from Stocks");
while(rs.next()){
Map stock = new HashMap();
stock.put("id",rs.getInt(1));
stock.put("Symbol",rs.getString(2));
stock.put("name",rs.getString(3));
stock.put("price",rs.getString(4));
stockList.add(stock);
}
rs.close();
stmt.close();
conn.close();
%>
<%
for(int i=0;i<stockList.size();i++){
Map stock = (Map)stockList.get(i);
%>
<Stocks>
<stock><%=stock.get("id")%></stock>
<symbol><%=emp.get("symbol")%></symbol>
<name><%=emp.get("name")%></name>
<price><%=emp.get("price")%></price>
</Stocks>
<%
}
%>
```

The HTML elements are taken out and XML tags, including the XML declaration tag, are introduced into the code. This JSP creates XML. An XSLT stylesheet can be applied to the XML to generate XHTML. I won't go into how that happens, because it's not relevant to our purpose here.

Assuming this JSP is accessible via a URL, say http://localhost:8080/generateXML.jsp, it can be consumed in Flex using the HTTPService component. Flex has rich capabilities for XML parsing. Its

XML capabilities can be utilized to bind the data effectively to the desired interfaces. The HTTPService code in MXML could be as follows:

```
<mx:HTTPService
id="xmlFromJSP"
url="http://localhost:8080/generateXML.jsp"
useProxy="false"
method="GET"
resultFormat="e4x" />
```

This code assumes no usage of a server-side proxy and the presence of required security definitions in a crossdomain.xml file. The cross-domain policy file is discussed in Part 2 of this book.

The trick of generating XML instead of HTML is very simple and straightforward, but it comes with its limitations. Such a transformation assumes that you still keep all the logic and state in the server. This is not the best way of using Flex. Flex is capable of managing state and interaction logic on the client. This capability is a big driver for rich and engaging experiences. In the next case, you'll see how a server-side service orientation could be an improvement over plain XML data access.

## Service-orienting legacy

Existing web applications could be restructured according to the business functions they achieve. Each function would be encapsulated in an independent service. Service outcomes could be controlled using passed-in parameters. In short, an application could be reengineered using Service-Oriented Architecture (SOA) concepts.

Although it all sounds fairly logical and simple, converting traditional web applications to service-oriented forms is neither easy nor quick. Also, migrating applications implies smoothly converting over from one form to the other, without seriously affecting the users. This can be a challenging requirement.

A few modern web applications already include service-oriented features. Such applications are great candidates for migration to Flex. The next few paragraphs examine such a case and scrutinize the details of the migration.

We take the Pentaho Dashboard as the subject of our case study. Pentaho is a commercial open source business intelligence suite, details of which can be seen at http://www.pentaho.com. The Dashboard tool is a part of the product suite, which comes with a sample example to demonstrate the features of the desktop.

We use the Pentaho Dashboard sample application as our source application and remaster it to utilize a Flex front end. In the original version, the user interface is built using Java EE (especially JSP). The sample application accesses data via service-oriented calls. So when we remaster the application, we don't touch any of the parts behind these services. We just consume the services through a new interface.

Because we reuse much of the sample application, it makes sense for you to download and install it first. Instructions for this are on the Pentaho web site. The sample application is installed within a servlet container, such as Apache Tomcat. Once you have installed the application, the services are available via URLs.

The original dashboard application is as shown in Figure 11-4.

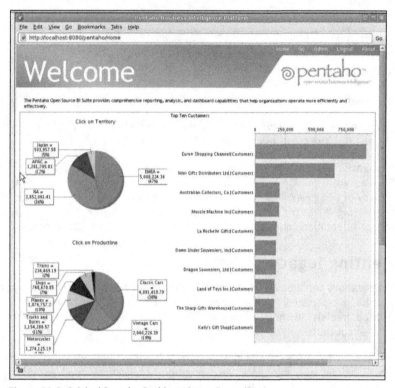

**Figure 11-4.** Original Pentaho Dashboard sample application

The new Flex interface is shown in Figure 11-5. The Flex interface primarily includes components from the charting library and defines a few click events on the charts to add interactivity. I will skip the explanation for all of that, though you will soon see the entire source code.

The most interesting part is how we hook into the services and consume the data. We use the Flex HTTPService components to do that because the services are exposed as RESTful web services via HTTP GET calls. For example, the Sales by Territory data is exposed via a URL as follows:
http://localhost:8080/pentaho/ServiceAction?solution=samples&path=steel-wheels/homeDashboard&action=Sales_by_Territory.xaction.

This assumes the sample application is running on the localhost, and the application server is listening for HTTP calls on port 8080. This URL, when invoked using the HTTPService components, is as follows:

```
<mx:HTTPService
id="tSrv"
url="http://localhost:8080/pentaho/ServiceAction?solution=➡
samples&path=steel-wheels/homeDashboard&action=➡
Sales_by_Territory.xaction"
result="handleTResult(event)"/>
```

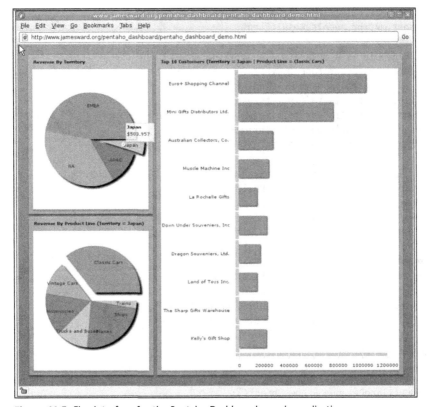

**Figure 11-5.** Flex interface for the Pentaho Dashboard sample application

handleTResult is the method that is invoked on return of a successful result set. That function is responsible for transforming the data we received into the form that the Charts need. Whether we are using Charts or other components like the DataGrid, we might have to tweak the function a bit to make it work with the particular components.

The entire Flex application that provides the new front end to the Pentaho Dashboard sample application is in a single MXML file and is as follows:

```
<?xml version="1.0" encoding="utf-8"?>
<mx:Application
xmlns:mx="http://www.adobe.com/2006/mxml"
creationComplete="initApp()"
layout="horizontal">
  <mx:Script>
<![CDATA[
// import classes used in ActionScript and not used in the MXML
// ActionScript is code generated from MXML
//by the free Flex SDK's mxmlc compiler
// The generated ActionScript can be viewed if you
//pass mxmlc the -compiler.keep-generated-actionscript argument
import mx.charts.HitData;
```

**425**

```
import mx.collections.ArrayCollection;
import mx.rpc.events.ResultEvent;

// Bindable is a metadata / annotation which
//generates event code so that the variable
// can be used in an MXML Binding Expression,
//i.e. dataProvider="{territoryRevenue}"
[Bindable] public var territoryRevenue:ArrayCollection;
[Bindable] public var productlineRevenue:Object;
[Bindable] public var topTenCustomersRevenue:Object;

 // Variables in ActionScript have namespaces like in Java.
 //You can use the typical public,
// private, and protected namespaces as
//well as create your own namespaces
// Object types are specified with a colon
//character and are optional but recommended.
private var _selectedTerritory:String = "*";
private var _selectedProductLine:String = "*";

// the initApp function is called when the
//Application's creationComplete event is
//Fired (see the mx:Application tag above)
private function initApp():void
{
// initializes our data caches
productlineRevenue = new Object();
topTenCustomersRevenue = new Object();

// initiates the request to the server
//to get the Sales by Territory data
// tSrv is defined in MXML below.
//It could also have been defined in
//ActionScript but would have been
//slightly more verbose tSrv.send();

// Since the Sales by Product Line and
//Top Ten Customer Sales depend on the selected territory
// we make a call to the functions that
//will fetch the data based on
//the selected territory (or pull it from cache)
// in this case the selected territory is "*" or
//our indicator for all.  When the user selects a new territory
// these methods will be called again but
//the selected territory will be different
updateProductLineRevenue();
updateTopTenCustomersRevenue();
```

```
}

// Setter method that causes the data stores for
//the Sales by Product Line and Top Ten Customer Sales
// to be updated and the charts to be updated accordingly
public function set selectedTerritory(territory:String):void
{
// update the private backing variable
_selectedTerritory = territory;

updateProductLineRevenue();
updateTopTenCustomersRevenue();
}

// Getter method that returns the selected Territory
// This method has the Bindable metadata /
//annotation on it so that
//the selectedTerritory property can
// be used in a binding expression
[Bindable] public function get selectedTerritory():String
{
return _selectedTerritory;
}

// Setter method similar to selectedTerritory
// but for the selected product line
public function set selectedProductLine(productLine:String):void
{
_selectedProductLine = productLine;

updateTopTenCustomersRevenue();
}

[Bindable] public function get selectedProductLine():String
{
return _selectedProductLine;
}

// If the data is in cache, then just directly
//update the chart based on the selected territory.
// If the data is not in cache, then assemble
//the name-value pairs that are needed by the
// web service request, then make the request.
private function updateProductLineRevenue():void
{
if (productlineRevenue[_selectedTerritory] == undefined)
```

```
{
productlineRevenue[_selectedTerritory] = new ArrayCollection();

var p:Object = new Object();

if (_selectedTerritory != "*")
{
p.territory = _selectedTerritory;
}

plSrv.send(p);
}
else
{
plPie.dataProvider = productlineRevenue[_selectedTerritory];
}
}

// Similar to updateProductLineRevenue
//except that both the selected territory and
// the selected product line determine the data set.
private function updateTopTenCustomersRevenue():void
{
if (topTenCustomersRevenue➡
[_selectedTerritory + '_' + _selectedProductLine] == undefined)
{
topTenCustomersRevenue➡
[_selectedTerritory + '_' + _selectedProductLine] = ➡
new ArrayCollection();

var p:Object = new Object();

if (_selectedTerritory != "*")
{
p.territory = _selectedTerritory;
}

if (_selectedProductLine != "*")
{
p.productline = _selectedProductLine;
}

ttcSrv.send(p);
}
else
{
ttcBar.dataProvider =
```

```
topTenCustomersRevenue➥
[_selectedTerritory + '_' + _selectedProductLine];
  }
  }

 // This function handles a response from
 //the server to get the Sales by territory.
 //It reorganizes that data
 // into a format that the chart wants it in.
 //The tPie chart notices
//changes to the underlying ArrayCollection
 // that happen inside the for each loop.
 //When it sees changes it updates its view of the data.
 private function handleTResult(event:ResultEvent):void
 {
 territoryRevenue = new ArrayCollection();
 tPie.dataProvider = territoryRevenue;

 var hdr:ArrayCollection =
event.result.Envelope.Body.ExecuteActivityResponse.➥
swresult['COLUMN-HDR-ROW']['COLUMN-HDR-ITEM'];
 for each (var pl:Object in event.result.Envelope.Body.➥
ExecuteActivityResponse.swresult['DATA-ROW'])
 {
 var spl:Object = new Object();
 spl[hdr[0]] = pl['DATA-ITEM'][0];
 spl[hdr[1]] = pl['DATA-ITEM'][1];
 territoryRevenue.addItem(spl);
 }
 }

 // Similar to handleTResult except that it
 //handles the data for Sales by Product Line
 private function handlePLResult(event:ResultEvent):void
 {
 var hdr:ArrayCollection =
event.result.Envelope.Body.ExecuteActivityResponse.➥
swresult['COLUMN-HDR-ROW']['COLUMN-HDR-ITEM'];

 for each (var pl:Object in event.result.Envelope.Body.➥
ExecuteActivityResponse.swresult['DATA-ROW'])
 {
 var spl:Object = new Object();
 spl[hdr[0]] = pl['DATA-ITEM'][0];
 spl[hdr[1]] = pl['DATA-ITEM'][1];
 productlineRevenue[_selectedTerritory].addItem(spl);
 }
```

```
    plPie.dataProvider = productlineRevenue[_selectedTerritory];
    }

    // Similar to handleTResult except that it
    //handles the data for Top Ten Customer Sales
    private function handleTTCResult(event:ResultEvent):void
    {
    var hdr:ArrayCollection =
    event.result.Envelope.Body.ExecuteActivityResponse.➡
    swresult['ROW-HDR-ROW'];
    var pl:ArrayCollection =
    event.result.Envelope.Body.ExecuteActivityResponse.➡
    swresult['DATA-ROW'];

    for (var i:int = 0; i < pl.length; i++)
    {
    var spl:Object = new Object();
    spl.name = hdr[i]['ROW-HDR-ITEM'][0];
    spl.sales = pl[i]['DATA-ITEM'];
    topTenCustomersRevenue➡
    [_selectedTerritory + '_' + _selectedProductLine].➡
    addItemAt(spl,0);
    }

    ttcBar.dataProvider =
    topTenCustomersRevenue➡
    [_selectedTerritory + '_' + _selectedProductLine];
    }

    // This function is called to format
    //the dataToolTips on the tPie chart.
    private function formatTPieDataTip(hitdata:HitData):String
    {
    return "<b>" + hitdata.item.TERRITORY +
    "</b><br>" +
    cf.format(hitdata.item.SOLD_PRICE);
    }
    ]]>
    </mx:Script>

    <!-- These HTTP Services communicate via HTTP to a server -->
    <mx:HTTPService
    id="tSrv"
    url="http://localhost:8080/pentaho/ServiceAction?solution=➡
    samples&path=steel-wheels/homeDashboard&action=➡
    Sales_by_Territory.xaction"
    result="handleTResult(event)"/>
```

```
  <mx:HTTPService
id="plSrv"
url="http://localhost:8080/pentaho/➡
ServiceAction?solution=samples&path=➡
steel-wheels/homeDashboard&action=➡
Sales_by_Productline.xaction"
result="handlePLResult(event)"/>
  <mx:HTTPService
id="ttcSrv"
url="http://localhost:8080/pentaho/➡
ServiceAction?solution=samples&path=➡
steel-wheels/homeDashboard&action=➡
topnmdxquery.xaction"
result="handleTTCResult(event)"/>
  <!-- Non-visual component to format currencies correctly.
Used in the formatTPieDataTip function -->
 <mx:CurrencyFormatter id="cf" precision="0"/>

 <!-- Effects used to make the charts more interactive -->
 <mx:SeriesInterpolate id="plEffect"/>
 <mx:SeriesSlide id="ttcSlide" direction="right"/>

 <!-- Stacked vertical layout container -->
 <mx:VBox height="100%" width="40%">
 <!-- Nice box with optional drop shadows,
title bars, and control bars -->
 <mx:Panel width="100%" height="100%" title="Revenue By Territory">
 <!-- Pie Chart -->
 <mx:PieChart
id="tPie"
width="100%"
height="100%"
showDataTips="true"
dataTipFunction="formatTPieDataTip">
 <!-- Sets the itemClick property on the PieChart
to the embedded ActionScript code.
We could have also called a function defined above. -->
 <mx:itemClick>
 // calls the appropriate setter method
 selectedTerritory = event.hitData.item.TERRITORY;

 // tells the pie chart to explode the pie wedge the user clicks on
 var explodeData:Array = [];
 explodeData[territoryRevenue.getItemIndex(event.hitData.item)] = 0.15;
 tPie.series[0].perWedgeExplodeRadius = explodeData;
 </mx:itemClick>
```

```
<!-- Sets the series property on the Pie Chart. -->
<mx:series>
<!-- The Pie Series defines how the Pie Chart displays its data. -->
<mx:PieSeries
nameField="TERRITORY"
field="SOLD_PRICE"
labelPosition="insideWithCallout"
labelField="TERRITORY"/>
</mx:series>
</mx:PieChart>
</mx:Panel>

<!-- A Binding Expression in the title bar of
the Panel uses the Bindable getter
for the selectedTerritory property -->
<mx:Panel
width="100%"
height="100%"
title="Revenue By Product Line ➡
(Territory = {selectedTerritory})">
<mx:PieChart
id="plPie"
width="100%"
height="100%"
showDataTips="true">
<mx:itemClick>
selectedProductLine = event.hitData.item.PRODUCTLINE;

var explodeData:Array = [];
explodeData[productlineRevenue➡
[_selectedTerritory].getItemIndex➡
(event.hitData.item)] = 0.15;
plPie.series[0].perWedgeExplodeRadius = explodeData;
</mx:itemClick>
<mx:series>
<!-- The showDataEffect on the Series uses
Binding to (re)use an effect defined above -->
<mx:PieSeries
nameField="PRODUCTLINE"
field="REVENUE"
labelPosition="insideWithCallout"
showDataEffect="{plEffect}"
labelField="PRODUCTLINE"/>
</mx:series>
</mx:PieChart>
</mx:Panel>
</mx:VBox>
```

```
    <mx:Panel
width="100%"
height="100%"
title="Top 10 Customers ➡
(Territory = {selectedTerritory} | ➡
Product Line = {selectedProductLine})">
 <mx:BarChart
id="ttcBar"
width="100%"
height="100%"
showDataTips="true">
 <mx:series>
 <mx:BarSeries xField="sales" showDataEffect="{ttcSlide}"/>
 </mx:series>
 <mx:verticalAxis>
 <mx:CategoryAxis categoryField="name"/>
 </mx:verticalAxis>
 </mx:BarChart>
 </mx:Panel>
 </mx:Application>
```

The preceding code has comments and annotations explaining the implementation. This was a good example of a service-oriented legacy web application that can be easily transformed to become rich and interactive. The modifications were deliberately kept simple. Advanced behavior and better interaction can be added to the Flex version of this user interface.

## Resolving state management complexity

In the previous couple of cases, we read data. In real-life situations you will also create, update, and delete data. The moment such manipulations come into play, you need to decide where you want to hold the data state and where you wish to manipulate the data. In Flex applications, the recommendation is to hold the state at the client and manipulate the data right there before it's committed.

The legacy web applications are of two types, HTML based and VM based. HTML-based applications typically perform state maintenance on the server. These applications keep a conversation going between a client and the server using some shared token, most often a session. VM-based applications hold state on the client.

When we are talking migration or porting, we are primarily talking about moving HTML web technologies over to Flex, because moving VM-based technologies is closer to starting from scratch in most cases.

So the big question to answer while remastering HTML web applications is this: where should you keep the state? The right answer in a new project is to keep state on the client and leverage the rich, interactive, and engaging model. However, this may imply completely trashing the current infrastructure and rendering it useless when migrating over (i.e., when not starting from scratch).

In general, it's advisable to put some effort into getting rid of session management and the complications around it, and abstract the create, read, delete, and update (CRUD) operations into services. Keep the services fine-grained to allow flexibility but also have coarse-grained aggregations of these services. For most read calls, use the coarse-grained calls. Maintain application state on the client and be sure to switch off auto-commits to avoid excessive back-and-forth traffic. Demarcate your CRUD, especially create, update, and delete operations, using transactions, as you do in traditional client-server operations. On every transaction milestone, invoke the fine-grained service calls to complete the operation. For example, you may be manipulating a related set of rows in a data grid and may want to commit the changes only after all the modifications to the related set of rows are made and not when each constituent change occurs.

Flex has server-side remoting counterparts. Such server-side software is available for Java, PHP, Python, .NET, and Ruby. These server-side frameworks leverage HTTP endpoints as gateways and have the capability to create and maintain sessions between the Flex client and the server side. In some cases, it may be useful to use this facility.

A related problem that needs to be tackled is that of the frequency of round-trips from the client to the server and back.

## Optimizing the frequency of round-trips

In traditional client-server applications, the number of calls between the client and the server is drastically reduced. The client is thick, so it holds the data and the logic and interacts with the server only to share the updates or save the commits back to the database.

In web applications, this problem is not as straightforward. The immediacy of the Web, combined with the concurrency requirements of such applications, pose the age-old complications around dirty and phantom reads. Let's take a small diversion and recap what these problems are.

The problems of dirty and phantom reads are defined under the larger umbrella of isolation and concurrency. Typically, isolation levels are defined under the following four categories:

- **Read uncommitted**: One transaction may see uncommitted changes made by another transaction. Dirty reads may occur in this case.

- **Read committed**: Data records retrieved by one transaction are not protected from being modified by another transaction. Nonrepeatable reads may occur.

- **Repeatable read**: All retrieved data cannot be changed by another process because it is locked by the transaction that retrieves it. Phantom reads can occur though as range locks are not established. In other words, the where clause of a select statement may have candidate rows that have newly appeared since the select was made, but these new rows will not show up.

- **Serializable**: Everything is isolated and no transactional problems occur.

The question is, which isolation level is best when creating a Flex interface with a legacy server side? A naïve recommendation is to use the serializable level to avoid all problems, but this is usually not practical, as the impact on performance and scalability would be unacceptable. What then is the right level?

Also, is it advisable to lock pessimistically every time, or to use optimistic locking in most cases? Pessimistic locking means you expect conflicts to occur often and so lock every time you initiate an operation, whereas optimistic locking means you lock only in exceptional cases, because you don't expect conflicts to occur often.

As with state management, the choice is neither universal nor easy. In most cases, optimistic locking and maintaining repeatable reads is advisable. Setting up explicit transactional boundaries to avoid unnecessary round-trips is a good idea, too.

Next, we consider a completely different scenario. This is a case where the application is database driven, and the screens act as windows to the underlying tables.

## Generating database-driven applications

Database-driven applications are built using all types of web development technologies. With either HTML or VM technologies, if the application is largely database driven, it may be beneficial to re-create the application when building it using Flex. Flex Builder 3 Professional Edition has a nifty little feature for generating database-driven applications that you could try. In this case, reinvention is faster and better than incremental adoption. The only things that are reused are the database schema and the data.

We create a Flex, PHP, and MySQL database application to delve deeper into how the database creation utility in Flex Builder 3 Professional Edition can be leveraged.

We do the following to create this sample application:

1. Install MySQL 5.1 Server (Community Edition), Apache HTTP Server 2.2, and PHP Version 5.2.6 on a personal computer running the Windows XP operating system. (If you are not a Windows XP user, then set up these pieces of software on a platform of your choice; the rest of the steps will still work.)

2. Configure MySQL, PHP, and Apache to work together. (Look up respective documentation to get this done. The details are out of the scope of this chapter.)

3. Create a database called saventech and a table called books within this database in the MySQL instance. (In a real-life case, the table would exist beforehand. Remember, we are modifying an existing application to use Flex.)

4. Use Flex Builder 3 Professional Edition's database-driven application creation wizard to generate a CRUD application that can be used to view, update, delete, and insert into the records from the books table.

Next, we walk through the details of the Flex Builder 3 Professional Edition Create Application from Database Wizard.

The first step is to create a Flex project that supports a PHP application server. Figures 11-6 and 11-7 show snapshots of the New Flex Project Creation Wizard. We call our project DatabaseDrivenSampleApplication. Figure 11-7 shows how the web root and root URL for the PHP application are specified. It's possible to validate this configuration before moving forward. Validation can be done with a single click of the button labeled Validate Configuration. Errors will be thrown if the web server configurations are not correct.

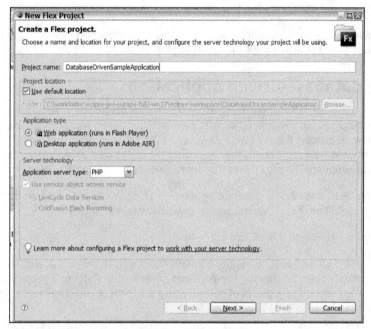

**Figure 11-6.** New Flex Project Creation Wizard, initial screen

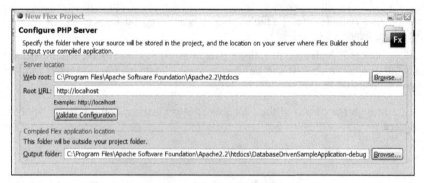

**Figure 11-7.** New Flex Project Creation Wizard, second screen

This newly created Flex project will be the target for our database-driven application. To invoke the wizard to create an application from a database, we choose Data ➤ Create Application from Database as shown in Figure 11-8.

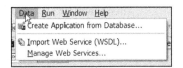

**Figure 11-8.** Choose Create Application from Database from the Data menu.

On the next screen, our wizard lets us choose the database, the table in the database, and the primary key column. We can choose any column as the primary key column as long as the values uniquely identify the data. In the MySQL table books, we do not specify any primary key. Figure 11-9 shows the wizard screen that lets you specify the database details, and Figure 11-10 shows the output of the `describe table` command run on the MySQL command-line client. Figure 11-10 confirms that no primary key is specified at the database level.

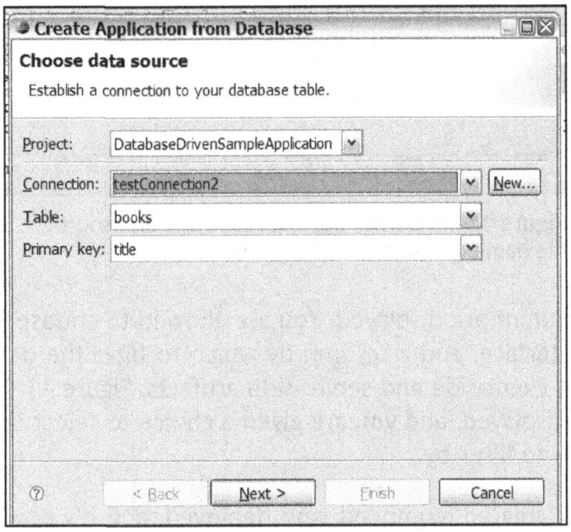


**Figure 11-9.** Database credentials passed to the wizard

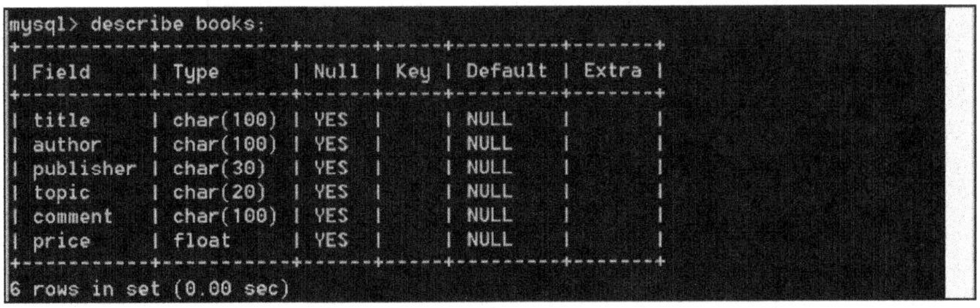

```
mysql> describe books;
+-----------+-----------+------+-----+---------+-------+
| Field     | Type      | Null | Key | Default | Extra |
+-----------+-----------+------+-----+---------+-------+
| title     | char(100) | YES  |     | NULL    |       |
| author    | char(100) | YES  |     | NULL    |       |
| publisher | char(30)  | YES  |     | NULL    |       |
| topic     | char(20)  | YES  |     | NULL    |       |
| comment   | char(100) | YES  |     | NULL    |       |
| price     | float     | YES  |     | NULL    |       |
+-----------+-----------+------+-----+---------+-------+
6 rows in set (0.00 sec)
```

**Figure 11-10.** Table description for the table named books

Figure 11-9 shows a connection named testConnection2. You can define a new connection or modify existing connections. To create a new connection, you must specify database access and login credentials.

Then the wizard lets you specify the server-side source folder and the file name that it creates. Figure 11-11 depicts this screen.

**Figure 11-11.** Server-side source folder and source file name specification

Next the database table columns are displayed. You are allowed to choose the columns that you want to be visible on the Flex interface, and a column by which to filter the data. After this, the wizard is ready to generate both the client-side and server-side artifacts. Figure 11-12 shows the screen where the database columns are displayed, and you are given a choice to select the columns to show on the Flex screen and the column to filter by.

That's it! The application is created, compiled, and deployed, and it's now ready for access. We first see the output in Figure 11-13 and then peek into the directory of generated files in Figure 11-14.

**Figure 11-12.** Selecting the database columns and the columns to filter by

| title | author | publisher | topic | comment | price |
|---|---|---|---|---|---|
| My Life | Mickey Mouse | Disney | Biography | What can I say? | 9 |
| The Essential Guide to Flex 3 | Charles E Brown | friends of ED (APress) | Flex 3 | | 54.99 |
| Creating Mashups with Adobe Flex a | John Crosby, David Hassoun, Chris l | friends of ED (APress) | Flex 3, AIR | ria mashups | 42.99 |
| AdvancED AIR Applications | Marco Casario, Koen De Weggheleir | friends of ED (APress) | AIR | | 49.99 |
| AdvancED ActionScript 3.0 Animation | Keith Peters | friends of ED (APress) | AS3 | | 39.99 |

Search by title

**Figure 11-13.** The Flex user interface that is created based on the books table

This generated application lets you search for records, filter records by title, add new line items to the records, and delete existing items. So to add a book's details to our books table, we could simply click the add item icon (button) and add the details in the screen that is presented to us. The add item screen (see Figure 11-15) presents a form to add data.

The preceding paragraphs showed how easy it is to generate Flex applications based on database tables. So it's always prudent to create applications from scratch when the primary purpose is to create a user interface for a table data.

Continuing the quest of presenting the aspects involved and the techniques available to migrate from Web 1.0 applications to RIA, the next section evaluates ways to preserve the middle tier.

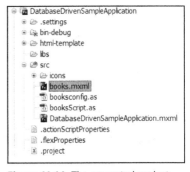

**Figure 11-14.** The generated project directory structure

# Reusing the middle tier

Everything lying between the database and the user interface is termed the middle tier. So choosing a single strategy to preserve this varied set of software artifacts would be overambitious. To make it more specific, let's separately consider the middle tier in two contrasting environments: Java EE and PHP.

## Java EE middle tier

In Java EE, the data access and business logic objects constitute the middle tier. These objects can be Plain Old Java Objects (POJOs) or managed objects like Enterprise Java Beans (EJBs) and Spring beans. POJOs run in

**Figure 11-15.** The add item screen generated by the Create Application from Database Wizard in Flex Builder 3 Professional Edition

**439**

the JVM and have simple getters and setters to access and manipulate their member variables. Managed objects live in a container and have special characteristics depending on their type. For example, EJBs can be data persistence objects, stateless business logic components, or stateful business logic entities. Spring beans, objects that live within the Spring Framework, can have dependencies injected into them at initialization.

The Flex and Java EE environments can be integrated in many ways. (Chapters 6 and 7 give details of how Flex and Java can be integrated.) Both POJOs and managed objects can be invoked and accessed via the Remote Procedure Call (RPC) mechanism.

Therefore, when migrating, you could reuse your middle-tier Java EE objects and access and invoke them from your new Flex interface.

Next, let's quickly review a typical PHP middle tier.

### PHP middle tier

PHP objects and scripts are less governed by specification than Java EE objects. Therefore, the form in which a PHP middle tier exists could be quite varied. It could be within a container, like the Zend engine, or it could live as objects on a PHP-enabled web server. The PHP code may be procedural or object oriented.

Flex to PHP remoting options like the AMFPHP remoting library can be used to facilitate RPCs. However, there is one possible obstacle to direct usage of the middle-tier methods. Not all PHP applications cleanly demarcate between presentation logic and behavior, so directly consuming the data returned by PHP methods in Flex may require additional parsing on the Flex side. In such situations, you may benefit from following the preceding advice on making PHP generate XML or service-orienting the existing application.

# Strategies to port framework-based applications

As mentioned earlier, we pick two frameworks, Apache Struts and Ruby on Rails, and port them over to use a Flex user interface. If you are planning to port applications of either of these two types, then this section will give you a starting point in your endeavor. If your framework is not one of these two, then you will still benefit indirectly, as the examples will give you some insight into the migration options at your disposal.

Let's rework an Apache Struts 1.*x* application to include a Flex user interface.

## Apache Struts 1.*x* and Flex

First, take a look at Figure 11-16, which pictorially describes Apache Struts. Requests to an Apache Struts–powered web application are intercepted by its front controller. The front controller routes requests to appropriate action classes. The framework configuration and the request URL to action mapping are accessed from the struts-config.xml file and the action mapping class instance. Action classes access the middle-tier objects and the underlying data and then forward the output to a JSP. Alternatively, Apache Tiles can be used to construct the views.

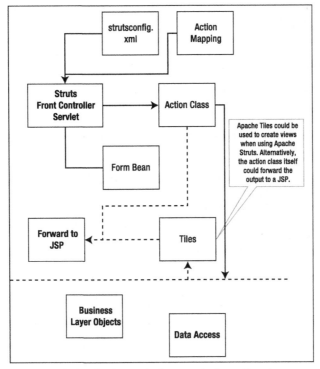

**Figure 11-16.** Apache Struts—its front controller, action classes, action mapping, configuration, and form bean

The preceding description is true for Apache Struts 1.x. Apache Struts 2.0 is a drastic overhaul of the framework and is out of the scope of the current discussion.

A possible migration path from Apache Struts 1.x to Flex is to replace the View part of the Apache Struts Model-View-Controller (MVC) structure. (Refer to Chapter 1 for details on MVC.) In order to migrate smoothly, we need to make the following modifications:

- Create a new Flex user interface.

- Invoke Apache Struts actions based on requests from Flex.

- Forward the output to a JSP that does not display the data but forwards the data in a format that can be consumed by the Flex interface.

- Forward the error messages to a JSP that does not display the error messages but forwards the data in a format that can be consumed by the Flex interface.

The Model and Controller parts can be kept as they are.

Data can be exchanged between the Flex user interface and the Apache Struts application either in a text-based format like XML or in an object format streamed over the binary Action Message Format (AMF) protocol. When using XML, the Flex HTTPService object can be used to invoke the Apache Struts action URLs. For example, a current Apache Struts action may be accessed using a URL string as

**441**

follows: http://hostname:port/SomeAction.do. Such a URL can be invoked using the Flex HTTPService object as well.

When using object streams and AMF, you need to write a component on the Apache Struts side that can marshal and unmarshal between the AS3 and Java objects.

Although you can write all the artifacts required to migrate an Apache Struts 1.*x* application to Flex, you can also leverage open source implementations that already do part or all of this job. One such package to look at is FxStruts. FxStruts is an open source set of components and libraries that facilitates the migration from Apache Struts 1.*x* to Flex. FxStruts is hosted on Google Code and can be accessed at http://code.google.com/p/fxstruts.

FxStruts implements the JSPs and tag libraries that route output and error messages to a Flex user interface. It also implements a Flex component that extends the HTTPService component and enables HTTP requests that send and receive data over the binary AMF protocol. A component to marshal and unmarshal between AS3 and Java is also included in the package. The distribution comes as a couple of JAR files and a Flex SWC library file. The JAR files are deployed with the Apache Struts application, and the SWC file is referenced from within the Flex project.

Apache Struts provides a tag library to include in the JSPs. These tag libraries implement the features that write the output and the error messages as well. For example, the bean:write tag facilitates the writing of Java objects to display elements on the JSP. FxStruts implements a tag library that uses a similar nomenclature and includes an fx:write tag that behind the scenes facilitates the writing of a JavaBean to a Flex interface, on the way converting the Java object to AS3 and turning it into a format that the Flex interface understands.

FxStruts comes with documentation and includes a sample application. I suggest that you refer to the documentation available online from Google Code to learn the details. Although the fundamental concepts illustrated are explained, the details are intentionally left out because duplicating publicly available information in this book would be redundant.

The information given so far will get you ready to refactor your Apache Struts 1.*x* application to utilize a Flex interface. This knowledge will also help you improvise on the techniques to successfully migrate Apache Struts applications that use Apache Tiles to generate views.

Next, we look at using Ruby on Rails and Flex together.

# Ruby on Rails and Flex

**Rails** is an agile web application development framework that is built using the dynamic Ruby language. If you don't know Ruby, then you may want to start by downloading and installing it from http://ruby-lang.org. Exhaustive documentation on Ruby and Rails is available from the following online resources:

- Extracts from *Programming Ruby: The Pragmatic Programmer's Guide*: http://www.rubycentral.com/book
- *Why's (poignant) Guide to Ruby* (free book): http://www.poignantguide.net/ruby
- Ruby on Rails Wiki: http://wiki.rubyonrails.com/rails
- Rails API: http://api.rubyonrails.org

Here, I assume you know the basics of both Ruby and Rails.

For the purpose of adding a Flex interface to a Ruby on Rails application, let's revisit the example application presented in the section "Generating database-driven applications." That example application showed how a Flex interface facilitated CRUD operations on a table that maintained a list of books. Ruby on Rails is very capable of generating CRUD applications based on database tables, and so the example fits in well to demonstrate how Rails and Flex can be combined effectively.

The Rails framework provides an MVC implementation, in which the model, view, and controller classes are generated based on the configuration and the underlying database. When we use Flex and Rails together, we keep the model and the controller within Rails and create a Flex view to work with the Rails model and controller.

If you worked through the example earlier, you have the MySQL table called books within the saventech database. If not, create the table and populate it with data as instructed earlier in the chapter.

Now go to the directory where you would like to create your Rails application and enter rails book_list on the command-line interface. This will create a rails project called "book_list" for you. Remember that the command-line interface will vary according to your operating system. (Moreover, I am assuming that you have Rails installed and configured.)

At this stage, the Rails framework generates the essential artifacts, which will be used to generate the model, view, and controller. Now get inside the project directory, book_list, and enter the command to generate the model and the controller.

To create the model, you enter the following command:

```
ruby script/generate model book
```

Similarly, to create the controller, you enter the following command:

```
ruby script/generate controller books
```

So far the model and controller classes are generated to support CRUD operations on the books table.

The database credentials can be specified in the database configuration file, called database.yml, that resides in the Rails project folder. This will help the Rails application connect to the database.

By default, a Rails application will not generate the view output in a format that a Flex application can use. As in the case of Apache Struts, we can do one of the following:

- Exchange data in XML format and use the standard Flex HTTPService component to call the Ruby methods.
- Exchange data in object format streamed over the binary AMF protocol and use a custom component on the Flex side to facilitate the HTTP-based calls.

XML data exchange is simpler, and we will choose that for our current example. The only required modification is to output the data from the controller in XML format. On the other hand, using object-based data exchange requires us to implement a component that can marshal and unmarshal between Ruby and AS3 objects on both ends of the wire. Also, it's necessary to extend the HTTPService component to make HTTP requests and consume object streams over AMF.

**443**

To make the controller return XML data for all the CRUD operations, we only need to modify the generated books_controller.rb Ruby source file. You will find this file in the book_list/app/controllers folder.

Add the following code to the books_controller.rb file:

```
def create
    @book = Book.new(params[:book])
    @book.save
    render :xml => @book.to_xml
end

def list
    @books = Book.find :all
    render :xml => @books.to_xml
end

def update
    @book = Book.find(params[:book])
    @book.update_attributes(params[:book])
    render :xml => @book.to_xml
end

def delete
    @book = Book.find(params[:id])
    @book.destroy
    render :xml => @book.to_xml
end
```

The methods create, list, update, and delete map to the CRUD features create, read, update, and delete, respectively. A Rails application exposes these methods over REST-style HTTP GET URLs. Assuming you set this Rails application with the default web server, WEBrick, and used the default port 3000 on a host called "hostname," the following URLs would be chosen for these operations:

- Create: http://hostname:3000/books/create
- Read: http://hostname:3000/books/list
- Update: http://hostname:3000/books/update
- Delete: http://hostname:3000/books/delete

These URL requests can be made to the server from a Flex interface using the HTTPService component. I will not show the Flex interface here.

This completes our brief example of migrating a regular Ruby on Rails application to a Flex user interface.

On the basis of the two examples I have shown, you should now be able to refactor applications built using other frameworks as well. In all cases, remember to keep the model and controller within the framework, and use Flex as the view.

# Summary

This chapter surveyed a few topics that arise when you migrate a legacy HTML-based web application to RIA. First, you learned about possible migration candidates. Then you saw the challenges and benefits of different techniques that come into play. You also looked at a couple of framework-based applications refactored to utilize a Flex interface.

A few things to keep in mind:

- Migrating a VM-based web application to Flex implies rewriting it.
- HTML-based web applications can be refactored to use a Flex interface.
- There are many ways to make a web application talk to a Flex interface. XML and object-based data exchange are the most common options.
- Most web applications are built using a framework. Migrating a framework-based application to Flex can be thought of as using Flex as the view within the framework's MVC structure.

Adopting RIA gradually can be beneficial; you have many ways to follow an incremental adoption path.

## Chapter 12

# SCULPTING INTERACTIVE BUSINESS INTELLIGENCE INTERFACES

By Shashank Tiwari

The power of rich interactive applications is often well realized in solutions that present data in interactive and engaging ways and allow users to manipulate the data to cull out deductions and inferences for better decision making. Business intelligence (BI) is usually defined as the collection, integration, analysis, and presentation of business information. The intent of such an exercise is to facilitate better decision making so that the business performs better and stays ahead of competition.

When I talk about BI interfaces in this chapter, I focus on the analysis and presentation aspects of the definition. So, the agenda here is to illustrate the tools and techniques available in Flex 3 to create highly interactive interfaces to present business information, so that you and your users can benefit from such creations that help analyze information effectively for superior decision making.

Visually appealing representations of data are often easy for human beings to understand. Therefore, charts are the starting point in this Flex and BI discussion.

# Charts and graphs

Charts and graphs represent complex data in visually appealing formats. With annotations, labels, and color coding, they become effective tools for knowledge acquisition and dissemination. Let's consider a couple of examples to support this statement. The first example plots the four largest economies, rated on the basis of purchasing power parity (PPP), a comparative economic measure, using a column chart. The units are measured in US dollars (USD), and the example relies on records from the International Monetary Fund (IMF) and *The 2007 World Factbook* published by the CIA. Figure 12-1 shows the output. The relative position of each nation is easily determined by looking at the relative height of the bars.

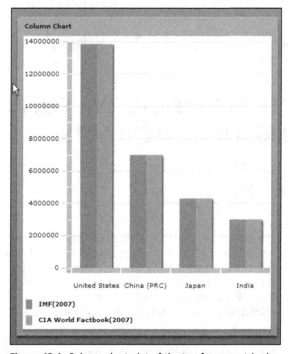

**Figure 12-1.** Column chart plot of the top four countries by GDP (PPP)

It's clearly evident that the third largest economy, Japan, is less than half the size of the largest economy, United States. Also, the chart shows that the IMF and *The 2007 World Factbook* data are in agreement as far as the top four economies go.

The source that's generating this column chart is as follows:

```
<?xml version="1.0"?>
<!-- FourLargestEconomiesByPPP.mxml -->
<mx:Application xmlns:mx="http://www.adobe.com/2006/mxml">
  <mx:Script><![CDATA[
      import mx.collections.ArrayCollection;
      [Bindable]
      public var topFourIMF:ArrayCollection = new ArrayCollection([
          {Country:"United States", GDP:13843825},
          {Country:"China (PRC)", GDP:6991036},
          {Country:"Japan", GDP:4289809},
          {Country:"India", GDP:2988867}
      ]);
      [Bindable]
      public var topFourCIAWorldFactbook:ArrayCollection =
new ArrayCollection([
          {Country:"United States", GDP:13840000},
          {Country:"China (PRC)", GDP:6991000},
          {Country:"Japan", GDP:4290000},
          {Country:"India", GDP:2989000}
      ]);
  ]]></mx:Script>
  <mx:Panel title="Column Chart">
      <mx:ColumnChart
id="myChart"
dataProvider="{topFourIMF}"
showDataTips="true">
          <mx:horizontalAxis>
             <mx:CategoryAxis categoryField="Country"/>
          </mx:horizontalAxis>
          <mx:series>
             <mx:ColumnSeries
                 dataProvider="{topFourIMF}"
                 yField="GDP"
                 xField="Country"
                 displayName="IMF(2007)"/>
             <mx:ColumnSeries
                 dataProvider="{topFourCIAWorldFactbook}"
                 yField="GDP"
                 xField="Country"
                 displayName="CIA World Factbook(2007)"/>
          </mx:series>
      </mx:ColumnChart>
      <mx:Legend dataProvider="{myChart}"/>
  </mx:Panel>
</mx:Application>
```

The second example plots the four largest economies, ranked by gross domestic product (GDP) measured in terms of PPP, along with the rest of the total global economy in a pie chart. This time, the example only uses the IMF data set. Figure 12-2 shows the output of the second example.

Because the rest of the world segment is larger than half the "pie," we can conclude that the top four economies combined make up less than half of the global economy.

Here is the source that creates this pie chart:

```
<?xml version="1.0"?>
<!-- FourLargestEconomiesPie.mxml -->
<mx:Application xmlns:mx="http://www.adobe.com/2006/mxml">
  <mx:Script><![CDATA[
      import mx.collections.ArrayCollection;
      [Bindable]
      public var topFourIMF:ArrayCollection = new ArrayCollection([
          {Country:"United States", GDP:13843825},
          {Country:"China (PRC)", GDP:6991036},
          {Country:"Japan", GDP:4289809},
          {Country:"India", GDP:2988867},
          {Country:"Rest of the World", GDP:36789726}
      ]);
  ]]></mx:Script>
  <mx:Panel title="Pie Chart">
    <mx:PieChart id="myChart"
        dataProvider="{topFourIMF}"
        showDataTips="true"
    >
        <mx:series>
           <mx:PieSeries
                field="GDP"
                nameField="Country"
                labelPosition="callout"
           />
        </mx:series>
    </mx:PieChart>
    <mx:Legend dataProvider="{myChart}"/>
  </mx:Panel>
</mx:Application>
```

These two quick examples have hopefully interested you in the question of creating productive BI interfaces. There are plenty of possibilities with charts and advanced data representations, and my coauthors and I will illustrate many of the available features related to these two throughout this book. Let's get deeper into graphs and charts.

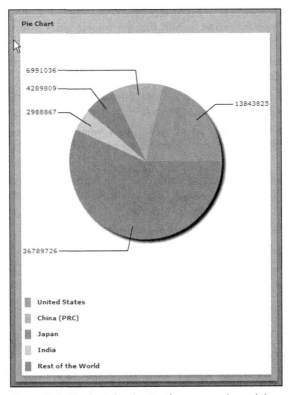

**Figure 12-2.** Pie chart showing top four economies and the economy for the rest of the world

# Charting components in Flex 3

Flex Builder 3 Professional Edition includes a set of prebuilt graph and chart components. All these components lie in the flex.charts.* package hierarchy. Each chart could be divided into two parts:

- The pictorial representation
- A set of points or data behind the representation

In the charts package, there are two classes for each chart, corresponding to the pictorial representation and the underlying data, respectively. For example, a column chart has two associated classes, ColumnChart and ColumnSeries. ColumnChart is the class for the visual representation, and ColumnSeries defines the underlying set of data points. Go back to the earlier example where we plot the top four economies in a column chart and you will see these two classes in action.

The built-in charts package in the Flex framework defines visual control and series classes for the following types of charts:

- **Area**: Represents data as an area bounded by a line connecting the data points. Multiple elements can be stacked in an area chart. The boundary lines of an area chart are similar to a line chart.

- **Bar**: Represents data as a set of horizontal bars, where the bar length corresponds to the data value. Similar to a column chart, except that the column chart is vertical and the bar chart is horizontal.

- **Bubble**: Represents data as bubbles on a two-dimensional plane. The size of the bubbles corresponds to the data values.

- **Candlestick**: Popular in the world of finance, these charts represent the opening, closing, high, and low values in the shape of a candlestick. HLOC charts can also represent such data.

- **Column**: Represents data as a set of vertical bars, where the bar length corresponds to the data value. Similar to a bar chart, except that the bar chart is horizontal while the column chart is vertical.

- **HighLowOpenClose (HLOC)**: Popular in the world of finance, these charts represent the opening, closing, high, and low values. Candlestick charts can also represent this type of financial data.

- **Line**: Represents a set of data values as a continuous line.

- **Pie**: Represents data in a circular pie. Sector sizes correspond to the data values.

- **Plot**: Plots data values on a two-dimensional plane. Similar to the bubble chart, except that data point marker sizes do not correspond to data values in a plot chart.

Each of these chart types is supported by two classes, a visual representation class and a data set or series class. The names of the chart and the series classes for a particular chart type is the name of the chart type suffixed with "Chart" and "Series," respectively. For example, the plot chart has two associated classes, PlotChart and PlotSeries, managing the representation and the data set, respectively. With the exception of the pie chart, all of the charts just listed represent data on Cartesian or rectangular coordinates. Pie charts represent data on polar coordinates. All charts extend from the ChartBase class. ChartBase has two immediate subclasses, called CartesianChart and PolarChart, which are the base classes for charts, represented using rectangular and polar coordinates, respectively. Therefore, a pie chart extends from PolarChart, and the rest of them extend from CartesianChart.

Charting features in Flex could be classified into the following four categories:

- **View**: The visual representation itself, with the ability to change the look and feel and representation formats.

- **Data mapper**: Series that maps data sources onto charts and chart elements, for example, mapping a particular data field to an axis.

- **Data provider**: The source of the data set. Data could be defined locally or accessed from remote destinations.

- **Interaction controller**: The component that helps interact with a user. This includes the events and effects that support the interactions.

These features work together to create rich interactive experiences. However, for the sake of lucidity, this text illustrates the rich charting features using the preceding classification. That way we can focus on one aspect at a time.

## View

The look and feel of all types of charts can be altered as desired. Charts can be styled like any other Flex component. If you are rusty about styling concepts, you may benefit from reading the section "Styles and skins" in Chapter 2.

Let's modify the default styles of a column chart and get a flavor of the possibilities. We reuse the earlier example that shows the top four economies, rated on the basis of GDP measured on PPP terms. The first set of style changes we apply are as follows:

- Modify the fill colors.
- Change the font type.
- Change the font size.
- Change the font color.

We use CSS to apply the style. You learned in Chapter 2 that CSS can be used to define styles for Flex components. You also learned that CSS can be defined inline or in an external file, and it can be applied either statically or dynamically at run time. All these concepts apply to styling in charts as well. In the example that follows, we use static inline CSS-based styling using the MXML Style tag. Here is the source code:

```
<?xml version="1.0"?>
<!-- FourLargestEconomiesChartWithStyle.mxml -->
<mx:Application xmlns:mx="http://www.adobe.com/2006/mxml">
  <mx:Style>
      ColumnChart {
          fontFamily:Georgia;
          fontSize:18;
          color: #0000FF;
          chartSeriesStyles: PCCSeries1, PCCSeries2;
      }
      .PCCSeries1 {
         fill: #D2691E;
      }
      .PCCSeries2 {
         fill: #0000CD;
      }
  </mx:Style>
  <mx:Script><![CDATA[
      import mx.collections.ArrayCollection;
      [Bindable]
      public var topFourIMF:ArrayCollection = new ArrayCollection([
          {Country:"United States", GDP:13843825},
          {Country:"China (PRC)", GDP:6991036},
          {Country:"Japan", GDP:4289809},
          {Country:"India", GDP:2988867}
      ]);
      [Bindable]
      public var topFourCIAWorldFactbook:ArrayCollection =
```

```
            new ArrayCollection([
                    {Country:"United States", GDP:13840000},
                    {Country:"China (PRC)", GDP:6991000},
                    {Country:"Japan", GDP:4290000},
                    {Country:"India", GDP:2989000}
                ]);
            ]]></mx:Script>
        <mx:Panel title="Column Chart">
            <mx:ColumnChart
id="myChart"
dataProvider="{topFourIMF}"
showDataTips="true">
                <mx:horizontalAxis>
                    <mx:CategoryAxis categoryField="Country"/>
                </mx:horizontalAxis>
                <mx:series>
                    <mx:ColumnSeries
                        dataProvider="{topFourIMF}"
                        yField="GDP"
                        xField="Country"
                        displayName="IMF(2007)"
                    />
                    <mx:ColumnSeries
                        dataProvider="{topFourCIAWorldFactbook}"
                        yField="GDP"
                        xField="Country"
                        displayName="CIA World Factbook(2007)"
                    />
                </mx:series>
            </mx:ColumnChart>
            <mx:Legend dataProvider="{myChart}"/>
        </mx:Panel>
    </mx:Application>
```

The modified chart now uses Georgia size 18 font in blue. It has its columns filled with chocolate and medium blue colors. Figure 12-3 shows the modified chart.

You can define these styles inline as well. The font style setting on the column chart when done inline looks as follows:

```
<mx:ColumnChart
id="myChart"
dataProvider="{topFourIMF}"
showDataTips="true"
        fontFamily="Georgia" fontSize="18" color="#0000FF" >
```

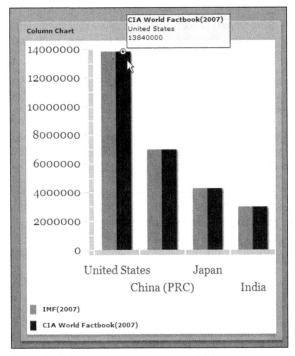

**Figure 12-3.** Column chart with custom styling

Styles can also be defined using class selectors. You could define a class named customStyle in the CSS as follows:

```
.customStyle {
fontFamily:Georgia;
        fontSize:18;
        color: #0000FF;
}
```

and then assign it as the value of the styleName property for the ColumnChart. Doing so will set the font style to Georgia size 18 in the color blue. This is how the styleName assignment could be done:

```
<mx:ColumnChart
id="myChart"
dataProvider="{topFourIMF}"
showDataTips="true"
        styleName="customStyle">
```

In two-dimensional rectangular charts, the horizontal and the vertical axes are the two defining structures. Flex predefines style class selectors for these two axes. For the horizontal and vertical axes, respectively, these are

- horizontalAxisStyleName
- verticalAxisStyleName

**455**

Styles can be defined and assigned to these predefined selectors to style the axes. Each of these axes is rendered in the charts using an AxisRenderer. It's possible explicitly to define an AxisRenderer and bind it to an axis. In such situations, one easy way to style the coordinates would be to assign the custom style class to the styleName property of the AxisRenderer.

The styling examples covered so far are only indicative of the possibilities. You may want to play with the various style properties and style alternatives to get comfortable with the styling features. Your current knowledge is adequate to get you started.

**Useful decorations on the charts** The examples you saw so far include no decorations in the data representation. Sometimes adding annotations, background images, or grid lines can help highlight certain display areas, leading to better information representation.

Our next example adds grid lines and a background image to our chart that displays the top four economies. This time, for variety, we display the data in a bar chart. Figure 12-4 displays the output. A company's logo is set as the background image, and its alpha is set to 0.4, which is why the image is showing up so prominently. It's a JPEG file. Any JPEG, GIF, PNG, or SVG file could be set as the background. Also we align it vertically in the middle of the container. The second set of decorations is the blue horizontal grid lines that we add to the bar chart. The code is as follows:

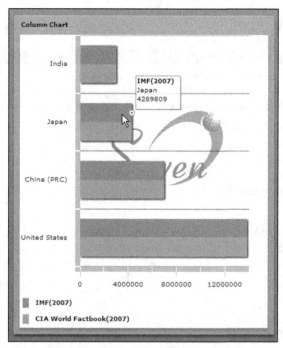

**Figure 12-4.** Top four economies displayed in a bar chart with background image and grid lines

```
<?xml version="1.0"?>
<!-- FourLargestEconomiesBarChart.mxml -->
<mx:Application xmlns:mx="http://www.adobe.com/2006/mxml">
```

```
  <mx:Script><![CDATA[
    import mx.collections.ArrayCollection;
    [Bindable]
    public var topFourIMF:ArrayCollection = new ArrayCollection([
       {Country:"United States", GDP:13843825},
       {Country:"China (PRC)", GDP:6991036},
       {Country:"Japan", GDP:4289809},
       {Country:"India", GDP:2988867}
    ]);
    [Bindable]
    public var topFourCIAWorldFactbook:ArrayCollection =
new ArrayCollection([
       {Country:"United States", GDP:13840000},
       {Country:"China (PRC)", GDP:6991000},
       {Country:"Japan", GDP:4290000},
       {Country:"India", GDP:2989000}
    ]);
  ]]></mx:Script>
  <mx:Panel title="Column Chart">
    <mx:BarChart
id="myChart"
dataProvider="{topFourIMF}"
showDataTips="true">
       <mx:verticalAxis>
          <mx:CategoryAxis categoryField="Country"/>
       </mx:verticalAxis>
       <mx:series>
          <mx:BarSeries
              dataProvider="{topFourIMF}"
              xField="GDP"
              yField="Country"
              displayName="IMF(2007)" />
          <mx:BarSeries
              dataProvider="{topFourCIAWorldFactbook}"
              xField="GDP"
              yField="Country"
              displayName="CIA World Factbook(2007)" />
       </mx:series>
       <mx:annotationElements>
          <mx:GridLines>
           <mx:horizontalStroke>
               <mx:Stroke
                   color="#0000FF"
                   weight="2"
                   alpha=".3" />
           </mx:horizontalStroke>
          </mx:GridLines>
       </mx:annotationElements>
       <mx:backgroundElements>
```

**457**

```
            <mx:Image
                verticalAlign="middle"
                source="@Embed('../assets/saven_logo.jpg')"
                alpha=".4" />
        </mx:backgroundElements>
    </mx:BarChart>
    <mx:Legend dataProvider="{myChart}"/>
</mx:Panel>
</mx:Application>
```

We used the Stroke class to control the property of the grid lines. The Stroke class has three properties: color, width, and alpha, to control the line color, thickness, and transparency, respectively. This class also comes in handy when drawing axis renderers, tick strokes, or custom arbitrary line drawings on the data canvas. In the case of a line chart, it could be used not only for the annotations just mentioned, but also to control the rendering of the chart lines themselves. Again, we re-create the example that shows the top four economies and this time use a line chart to display it. The line properties of the chart are controlled using the Stroke class. Here is the code:

```
<?xml version="1.0"?>
<!-- FourLargestEconomiesLineChart.mxml -->
<mx:Application xmlns:mx="http://www.adobe.com/2006/mxml">
  <mx:Script><![CDATA[
      import mx.collections.ArrayCollection;
      [Bindable]
      public var topFourIMF:ArrayCollection = new ArrayCollection([
          {Country:"United States", GDP:13843825},
          {Country:"China (PRC)", GDP:6991036},
          {Country:"Japan", GDP:4289809},
          {Country:"India", GDP:2988867}
      ]);
  ]]></mx:Script>
  <mx:Panel title="Line Chart">
    <mx:LineChart dataProvider="{topFourIMF}"
        id="myChart"
        showDataTips="true" >
      <mx:horizontalAxis>
        <mx:CategoryAxis
            categoryField="Country"/>
      </mx:horizontalAxis>
      <mx:series>
        <mx:LineSeries
          yField="GDP"
          displayName="GDP">
          <mx:lineStroke>
              <mx:Stroke
                  color="#FFD700"
                  weight="5"
                  alpha=".8"/>
          </mx:lineStroke>
```

```
            </mx:LineSeries>
          </mx:series>
      </mx:LineChart>
      <mx:Legend dataProvider="{myChart}"/>
    </mx:Panel>
  </mx:Application>
```

This line chart that uses the Stroke class to draw its chart lines is shown in Figure 12-5. Sometimes, information is better represented when custom drawing is used on top of the charts. For example, a line could be drawn between two data points to highlight them or to show the difference in level between them. Toward the beginning of this chapter, when I first introduced the example graphically displaying the four largest economies, I mentioned that it was easy to spot that the Japanese economy is less than half the size of the American economy. Now this is an important observation, and we may want highlight it by drawing a line from the middle of the column that represents the American economy to the middle of the column that represents the Japanese economy, as shown in Figure 12-6. The modified code is as follows:

```
<?xml version="1.0"?>
<!-- FourLargestEconomiesWithDrawing.mxml -->
<mx:Application xmlns:mx="http://www.adobe.com/2006/mxml">
  <mx:Script><![CDATA[
    import mx.collections.ArrayCollection;
    import mx.charts.series.items.ColumnSeriesItem;
    import mx.charts.ChartItem;

    [Bindable]
    public var topFourIMF:ArrayCollection = new ArrayCollection([
      {Country:"United States", GDP:13843825},
      {Country:"China (PRC)", GDP:6991036},
      {Country:"Japan", GDP:4289809},
      {Country:"India", GDP:2988867}
    ]);
    private function connectUSToJapan(country1:String,
      value1:Number,
      country2:String,
      value2:Number
    ):void {
      canvas.clear();
      canvas.lineStyle(4,
        0xCC99FF,
        .75,
        true,
        LineScaleMode.NORMAL,
        CapsStyle.ROUND,
        JointStyle.MITER,
        2
      );
      canvas.moveTo(country1, value1);
      canvas.lineTo(country2, value2);
```

**459**

```
        }
    ]]></mx:Script>
    <mx:Panel title="Column Chart">
        <mx:ColumnChart
creationComplete="connectUSToJapan➥
('United States',13843825,'Japan',4289809)"
            id="myChart"
            showDataTips="true"
            dataProvider="{topFourIMF}"
            selectionMode="single">
            <mx:annotationElements>
                <mx:CartesianDataCanvas
id="canvas"
includeInRanges="true"/>
            </mx:annotationElements>
            <mx:horizontalAxis>
                <mx:CategoryAxis
                    dataProvider="{topFourIMF}"
                    categoryField="Country />
            </mx:horizontalAxis>
            <mx:series>
                <mx:ColumnSeries
                    id="series1"
                    xField="Country"
                    yField="GDP"
                    displayName="GDP"
                    selectable="true"/>
            </mx:series>
        </mx:ColumnChart>
        <mx:Legend dataProvider="{myChart}"/>
    </mx:Panel>
</mx:Application>
```

Lines are not the only shapes that you can draw on the data canvas. You can draw all geometrical shapes, including circles, triangles, squares, rectangles, and ellipses. You may have noticed that we used the moveTo and the lineTo method to draw our line, which used the data points as the parameters. We did not draw the line using X and Y coordinates as you do on a sprite display canvas. This is extremely convenient and flexible for positioning drawings close to specific data points.

There are two types of two-dimensional charts in Flex, those that map to the Cartesian or rectangular coordinates and those that map to the polar coordinates. Therefore, Flex has data canvases of two types that correspondingly match to each of these coordinate types. CartesianDataCanvas maps to the Cartesian or rectangular coordinates, and PolarDataCanvas maps to the polar coordinates. Through methods like moveTo and lineTo, these data canvases allow you to draw on the basis of the data points and avoid using X and Y positions. The data canvas includes a rich set of methods to draw all geometrical shapes, including convenience methods like drawRect and drawEllipse to draw rectangles and ellipses. Because the data canvas is also a display component, you can add any UIComponent class as a child to it. addChild and addChildAt methods can be used to add child components, and removeChild and removeChildAt can be used to remove child components. The clear method can be called to make the data canvas invisible.

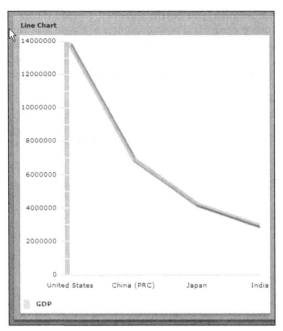

**Figure 12-5.** Line chart with Stroke class to draw the chart lines

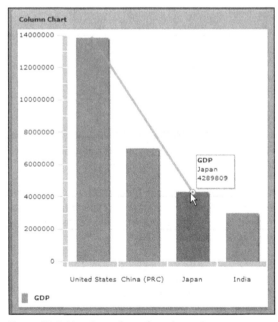

**Figure 12-6.** Line drawn from the column that represents the United States to the column that represents Japan

The types of view-level manipulations you can do with chart controls is unlimited because not only are all the typical Flex component design and styling features available, but we can also create our own custom charts and custom renderers to create displays as desired. Our next topic is data mapping from the source to the charts. However, before we go there, let me show you one smaller styling feature to reinforce that with Flex, it's easy to leverage the view manipulations to effectively present information.

This time, we use color gradients to fill our chart columns. Color gradients can be very effective in expressing concentration points, trends, or points of interest. This example merely uses the idea to show you how it works. The color gradient is applied to the background of a column chart. Figure 12-7 displays the chart with the color gradients.

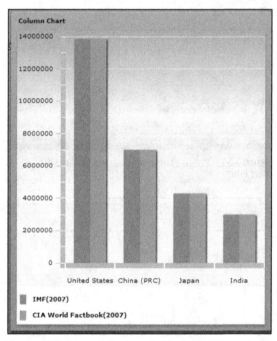

**Figure 12-7.** Color gradient applied to the background of a column chart

The color gradient used here is of LinearGradient type, which starts at the boundary of a component. Individual gradient elements that make up the gradient are encapsulated in a GradientEntry class. It's also possible to have a gradient that emanates out from the center. The RadialGradient class implements such a transition. Here is our example code:

```
<?xml version="1.0"?>
<!-- FourLargestEconomiesWithColorGradient.mxml -->
<mx:Application xmlns:mx="http://www.adobe.com/2006/mxml">
  <mx:Script><![CDATA[
    import mx.collections.ArrayCollection;
    [Bindable]
    public var topFourIMF:ArrayCollection = new ArrayCollection([
```

```
                {Country:"United States", GDP:13843825},
                {Country:"China (PRC)", GDP:6991036},
                {Country:"Japan", GDP:4289809},
                {Country:"India", GDP:2988867}
        ]);
        [Bindable]
        public var topFourCIAWorldFactbook:ArrayCollection =
new ArrayCollection([
                {Country:"United States", GDP:13840000},
                {Country:"China (PRC)", GDP:6991000},
                {Country:"Japan", GDP:4290000},
                {Country:"India", GDP:2989000}
        ]);
    ]]></mx:Script>
    <mx:Panel title="Column Chart">
        <mx:ColumnChart
        id="myChart"
        dataProvider="{topFourIMF}"
        showDataTips="true">
            <mx:horizontalAxis>
                <mx:CategoryAxis categoryField="Country"/>
            </mx:horizontalAxis>
             <mx:fill>
                    <mx:LinearGradient angle="90">
                        <mx:entries>
                            <mx:GradientEntry
                                color="0xC5C551"
                                ratio="0"
                                alpha="1" />
                            <mx:GradientEntry
                                color="0xFEFE24"
                                ratio=".33"
                                alpha="1" />
                            <mx:GradientEntry
                                color="0xECEC21"
                                ratio=".66"
                                alpha=".2" />
                        </mx:entries>
                    </mx:LinearGradient>
            </mx:fill>
        <mx:series>
            <mx:ColumnSeries
                dataProvider="{topFourIMF}"
                yField="GDP"
                xField="Country"
                displayName="IMF(2007)"/>
            <mx:ColumnSeries
                dataProvider="{topFourCIAWorldFactbook}"
                yField="GDP"
```

```
                    xField="Country"
                    displayName="CIA World Factbook(2007)"/>
                </mx:series>
            </mx:ColumnChart>
            <mx:Legend dataProvider="{myChart}"/>
        </mx:Panel>
    </mx:Application>
```

Now we are ready to move to the next topic, which concerns data mapping.

## Data mapper

We know that the chart components in Flex have a <ChartType>Chart and a <ChartType>Series class for each chart type. The series class in each of these cases is the data mapper. Sources of data whether present locally or at remote locations need to be tied to the chart control. The Series class takes on the responsibility of maintaining this mapping. Mapping through an intermediary is beneficial for the following reasons:

- The source of the data and the chart control are loosely coupled. Sources can be changed provided the definitions as per the series still hold true and the new source can continue to provide data in the required format.

- The source of data may contain many fields that have no significance to the chart control. The series acts as the filter, mapping only the required fields and ignoring everything else.

- Series allow for fine-grained control of field mapping to the coordinate axes, labels, and legends.

- Series also allow for inclusion of presentation modifications and stylings, including specification of fill types, color gradients, axis renderers, and drawing elements.

Each series type corresponds to a chart type. Be careful not to use an incorrect series type with a particular chart type. You have already seen the series components in action in this chapter's examples. Now you will see one more. This time, it's a BubbleSeries with a BubbleChart. Once again, the data is the list of top four economies as measured by GDP. The bubble size for each country corresponds to its GDP size. The code is as follows:

```
<?xml version="1.0"?>
<!-- FourLargestEconomiesBubble.mxml -->
<mx:Application xmlns:mx="http://www.adobe.com/2006/mxml">
    <mx:Script>
        <![CDATA[
        import mx.collections.ArrayCollection;
    [Bindable]
    public var topFourIMF:ArrayCollection = new ArrayCollection([
        {Rank:1, Country:"United States", GDP:13843825},
        {Rank:2, Country:"China (PRC)", GDP:6991036},
        {Rank:3, Country:"Japan", GDP:4289809},
        {Rank:4, Country:"India", GDP:2988867}
    ]);
    ]]>
```

```
        </mx:Script>
        <!-- Define custom color and line style for the bubbles. -->
        <mx:SolidColor id="scId" color="yellow" alpha=".3"/>
        <mx:Stroke id="strokeId" color="yellow" weight="4"/>
         <mx:Panel title="BubbleChart">
            <mx:BubbleChart id="myChart" showDataTips="true">
                <mx:series>
                    <mx:BubbleSeries
                        dataProvider="{topFourIMF}"
                        displayName="GDP"
                        xField="Rank"
                        yField="GDP"
                        radiusField="GDP"
                        fill="{scId}"
                        stroke="{strokeId}" />
                </mx:series>
            </mx:BubbleChart>
            <mx:Legend dataProvider="{myChart}"/>
        </mx:Panel>
    </mx:Application>
```

The series in this case specifies custom values for the `fill` and `stroke` properties. Series therefore acts not just as the data mapper, but also the agent that maps all the other custom transitions and styles that customize the presentation. Figure 12-8 shows the bubble chart we just created.

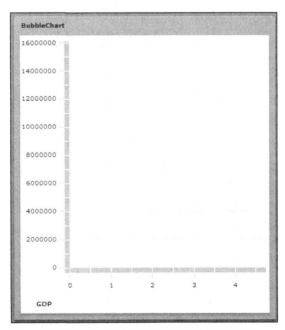

**Figure 12-8.** Bubble chart that shows the four largest economies

465

The data itself can be configured to a series or to the control that uses the series. Like all Flex components, the dataProvider property holds a reference to the data. The real data may reside inline in a Model tag or in a data structure, say a Collection, or it may be accessed from an external service. The next section lists the alternative ways of accessing and binding data.

Keeping things consistent, Flex has the same mechanism for data binding and access with charts as with any other component.

## Data provider

You can supply data to the charts from any of the following sources:

- Data structures created in ActionScript, residing in external files or in local Script blocks
- External files, in formats ranging from XML to plain text
- Objects in remote destinations, accessed via RemoteObject
- Web services
- Services accessed via HTTP calls
- MXML model blocks

The chart dataProvider and the series dataProvider accept Collection objects, arrays, and XML lists as sources of data. Therefore, data after being accessed from the source needs to be transformed to one of these objects. Also, it's advisable to make these data objects bindable, so that charts consuming them can receive updates as their value changes. This is no different from data consumption in a nonchart Flex component, say a DataGrid or a Tree. There is no point explaining the data provider concepts again because you already know them. However, for completeness, let's look at three examples of specifying data to charts. You have seen Collection objects, specifically ArrayCollection, being used throughout the examples so far. So our next two examples show array and XML sources being bound to chart controls. Our third example highlights real-time data consumption as the data itself evolves.

In the first example, data in an array is bound to a column chart. We take our example of the top four economies and replace the ArrayCollection data structure with a corresponding Array data structure, and things work just fine.

Our original ArrayCollection declaration and definition was as follows:

```
import mx.collections.ArrayCollection;
    [Bindable]
    public var topFourIMF:ArrayCollection = new ArrayCollection([
        {Country:"United States", GDP:13843825},
        {Country:"China (PRC)", GDP:6991036},
        {Country:"Japan", GDP:4289809},
        {Country:"India", GDP:2988867}
    ]);
    [Bindable]
    public var topFourCIAWorldFactbook:ArrayCollection =
```

```
new ArrayCollection([
        {Country:"United States", GDP:13840000},
        {Country:"China (PRC)", GDP:6991000},
        {Country:"Japan", GDP:4290000},
        {Country:"India", GDP:2989000}
    ]);
```

When we use an Array instead, the code is modified as follows:

```
[Bindable]
    public var topFourIMF:Array = [
        {Country:"United States", GDP:13843825},
        {Country:"China (PRC)", GDP:6991036},
        {Country:"Japan", GDP:4289809},
        {Country:"India", GDP:2988867}
    ];
    [Bindable]
    public var topFourCIAWorldFactbook:Array = [
        {Country:"United States", GDP:13840000},
        {Country:"China (PRC)", GDP:6991000},
        {Country:"Japan", GDP:4290000},
        {Country:"India", GDP:2989000}
    ];
```

Everything else remains just the same, and the display is generated as it was in our first example. The output is shown in Figure 12-1 earlier.

Our second example uses XML data to bind to a chart component. This time, we take the same example and cull out the IMF-provided GDP data to an XML file. We name the external XML file Top4EconomiesByGDP.xml and save it a directory called data in our Flex project. Following is the content of Top4EconomiesByGDP.xml:

```
<data>
    <dataitem>
        <Country>United States</Country>
        <GDP>13843825</GDP>
    </dataitem>
    <dataitem>
        <Country>China (PRC)</Country>
        <GDP>6991036</GDP>
    </dataitem>
    <dataitem>
        <Country>Japan</Country>
        <GDP>4289809</GDP>
    </dataitem>
    <dataitem>
        <Country>India</Country>
        <GDP>2988867</GDP>
    </dataitem>
</data>
```

**467**

Now we modify our code to consume data from this external XML file. Here is the modified source:

```
<?xml version="1.0"?>
<!-- FourLargestEconomiesWithXMLData.mxml -->
<mx:Application xmlns:mx="http://www.adobe.com/2006/mxml">
  <mx:Model id="topFourIMF" source="../data/Top4EconomiesByGDP.xml"/>
    <mx:Panel title="Column Chart">
        <mx:ColumnChart
        id="myChart"
        dataProvider="{topFourIMF.dataitem}"
        showDataTips="true">
            <mx:horizontalAxis>
                <mx:CategoryAxis categoryField="Country"/>
            </mx:horizontalAxis>
            <mx:series>
                <mx:ColumnSeries
                    dataProvider="{topFourIMF.dataitem}"
                    yField="GDP"
                    xField="Country"
                    displayName="IMF(2007)" />
            </mx:series>
        </mx:ColumnChart>
        <mx:Legend dataProvider="{myChart}"/>
    </mx:Panel>
</mx:Application>
```

When run, this application is as shown in Figure 12-9.

The last of the examples is about charts getting updated in real time as the data itself evolves. Showing this in practice requires dynamic display, not static pictures. Unfortunately, I can't do that in this book. So I will show you the underlying source and two snapshots of the interface as it evolves to explain the concept. This time, we plot a single stock price using a line chart and simulate a few random values so that the price keeps changing. Here is the code for it:

```
<?xml version="1.0"?>
<!-- DataUpdateInRealTime.mxml -->
<mx:Application
xmlns:mx="http://www.adobe.com/2006/mxml"
initialize="initTimer()">
  <mx:Script><![CDATA[
  import flash.utils.Timer;
  import flash.events.TimerEvent;
  import mx.collections.ArrayCollection;
  [Bindable]
  public var stockPriceDataSeries:ArrayCollection =
new ArrayCollection();

  public function initTimer():void {
        var myTimer:Timer = new Timer(1000, 0);
        myTimer.addEventListener("timer", timerHandler);
```

```
         myTimer.start();
    }

    public function timerHandler(event:TimerEvent):void {
        var obj:Object = new Object();
        obj.time = getTimer();
        obj.stockPrice = 40.39 + Math.random()*2;
        stockPriceDataSeries.addItem(obj);
    }
    ]]></mx:Script>

    <mx:LineChart id="chart" dataProvider="{stockPriceDataSeries}"
        showDataTips="true">
        <mx:horizontalAxis>
            <mx:LinearAxis/>
        </mx:horizontalAxis>
        <mx:verticalAxis>
            <mx:LinearAxis minimum="35"/>
        </mx:verticalAxis>
        <mx:series>
            <mx:LineSeries yField="stockPrice"/>
        </mx:series>
    </mx:LineChart>
</mx:Application>
```

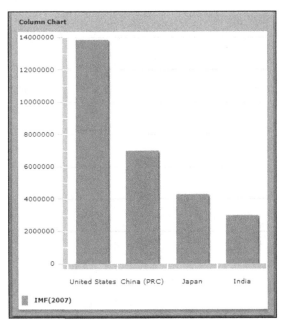

**Figure 12-9.** Column chart created with data accessed from
an external XML file

The output is a dynamic and evolving display, which you can see in two snapshots of the interface as it evolves. Figure 12-10 shows the output at the 15th time interval, and Figure 12-11 shows the output at the 38th time interval.

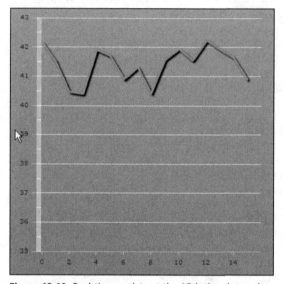

**Figure 12-10.** Real-time update at the 15th time interval

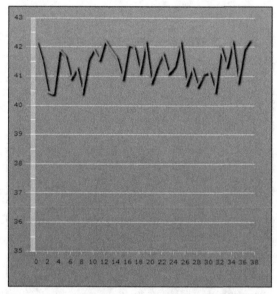

**Figure 12-11.** Real-time update at the 38th time interval

That is all as far as the discussion on data providers goes. Next, let's pick up the last of the aspects related to charts. It's about the events and effects that make the charts interactive.

## Interaction controller

Interactivity is the critical tool that enables a business user to glean actionable information from data. In Flex charts, the rich engaging interactivity is made feasible with support for events and effects. Let's start exploring the features through examples.

Our first example focuses on chart events. Chart events are ones that the chart as an entity triggers. Chart components support the entire range of MouseEvent types, such as mouseIn, mouseOut, mouseUp, and mouseDown, that all classes inheriting from the UIComponent support. Apart from that, the base class of all Flex 3 charts, ChartBase, supports two additional event types:

- ChartEvent: Triggered when a user clicks the chart, but outside of any chart data element
- ChartItemEvent: Triggered when a user clicks a chart data item

In our first example, we use ChartEvent types to capture single and double mouse clicks on a chart. On event, we bring up an Alert box and show the type of click as the message string. We stick to our old example of top four countries by GDP, measured in terms of PPP. Here is the code:

```
<?xml version="1.0"?>
<!-- SingleDoubleClickChartEvents.mxml -->
<mx:Application xmlns:mx="http://www.adobe.com/2006/mxml">
  <mx:Script><![CDATA[
      import mx.collections.ArrayCollection;
      import mx.charts.events.ChartEvent;
      import mx.controls.Alert;

      [Bindable]
      public var topFourIMF:ArrayCollection = new ArrayCollection([
         {Country:"United States", GDP:13843825},
         {Country:"China (PRC)", GDP:6991036},
         {Country:"Japan", GDP:4289809},
         {Country:"India", GDP:2988867}
      ]);
      [Bindable]
      public var topFourCIAWorldFactbook:ArrayCollection =
new ArrayCollection([
         {Country:"United States", GDP:13840000},
         {Country:"China (PRC)", GDP:6991000},
         {Country:"Japan", GDP:4290000},
         {Country:"India", GDP:2989000}
      ]);
      private function chartEventHandler(event:ChartEvent):void {
         Alert.show("Event of type: " + ➥
event.type,"ChartEvent",Alert.OK);
      }

   ]]></mx:Script>
   <mx:Panel title="Column Chart">
      <mx:ColumnChart
      id="myChart"
      dataProvider="{topFourIMF}"
```

**471**

```
            showDataTips="true"
                chartClick="chartEventHandler(event)"
                chartDoubleClick="chartEventHandler(event)">
            <mx:horizontalAxis>
                <mx:CategoryAxis categoryField="Country"/>
            </mx:horizontalAxis>
            <mx:series>
                <mx:ColumnSeries
                    dataProvider="{topFourIMF}"
                    yField="GDP"
                    xField="Country"
                    displayName="IMF(2007)" />
                <mx:ColumnSeries
                    dataProvider="{topFourCIAWorldFactbook}"
                    yField="GDP"
                    xField="Country"
                    displayName="CIA World Factbook(2007)" />
            </mx:series>
        </mx:ColumnChart>
        <mx:Legend dataProvider="{myChart}"/>
    </mx:Panel>
</mx:Application>
```

When clicking the chart outside the sensitive range of any chart data item, we see an alert box with the message telling us of the chart event type that was triggered. Figure 12-12 shows the alert box appearing on a single click in an area that has no data items.

Now we take the same example and modify it further to define event listeners for chart data item events. Chart data item events are triggered when a data item is interacted with, as when a mouse is hovered over a data item or when a data item is clicked. Figure 12-13 shows what the screen looks like on clicking over a column, which represents a data item in a column chart.

Data item events are unique to charts. They are the primary drivers of interactivity in charts because often a user wants to work with a chart data item and not the chart as a whole. To get our data event item example to work, we add the following lines to the previous example Script block:

```
import mx.charts.events.ChartItemEvent;
private function chartDataEventHandler(event:ChartItemEvent):void {
        Alert.show("Data Event of type: " + ➥
event.type,"ChartDataEvent",Alert.OK);
}
```

and modify the ColumnChart MXML tag to assign the newly added function as the event listener of an itemClick event. Here is a snippet of the code:

```
<mx:ColumnChart
id="myChart"
dataProvider="{topFourIMF}"
showDataTips="true"
        chartClick="chartEventHandler(event)"
        chartDoubleClick="chartEventHandler(event)"
        itemClick="chartDataEventHandler(event)">
```

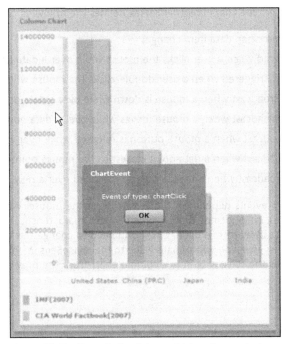

**Figure 12-12.** Chart single-click event triggering an alert

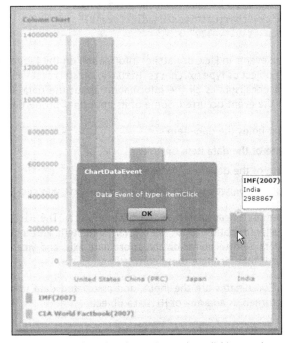

**Figure 12-13.** Chart data item triggered on clicking a column of a ColumnChart

All data item events are of type ChartItemEvent. Flex defines the following chart item event types:

- change: Dispatched when data item changes
- itemClick: Triggered when a user clicks the mouse while over a data item
- itemDoubleClick: Triggered when a user double-clicks the mouse while over a data item
- itemMouseDown: Broadcast when a mouse is down while over a data point
- itemMouseMove: Broadcast when a mouse moves while over a data point
- itemMouseUp: Broadcast when a mouse button is released while over a data point
- itemRollOut: Broadcast when a data point closest to the mouse pointer changes
- itemRollOver: Broadcast when a mouse pointer is moved over a new data point

Most of these chart item events depend on the sensitivity of the mouse. Whether a particular data item is within the mouse's range or not is determined by this characteristic. In default situations, the sensitivity is up to 3 pixels away from a data item. If you need to change this and set a different value for your specific case, then assign an appropriate value to the mouseSensitivity property of the chart object. To set 20 pixels as the sensitivity in our column chart from the previous example, we modify the code as follows:

```
<mx:ColumnChart
id="myChart"
dataProvider="{topFourIMF}"
showDataTips="true"
        chartClick="chartEventHandler(event)"
        chartDoubleClick="chartEventHandler(event)"
        itemClick="chartDataEventHandler(event)"
        mouseSensitivity="20" >
```

A ChartItemEvent, like all events in Flex, dispatches information on the target and the event type. In addition, it dispatches an object of type mx.charts.HitData, which is accessible via the hitData property. The HitData object encapsulates all the information about the data item that was within the mouse's sensitivity when the event occurred. Some of its important properties are as follows:

- Item: Property that holds the data item
- x: The X coordinate of the data item on screen
- y: The Y coordinate of the data item on screen
- distance: The distance between the point where the mouse was clicked and where the data is

Data points on the screen are encapsulated in ChartItem objects. The HitData object accesses the ChartItem object to get all information about the relevant data item. Flex includes a few convenience methods to translate a data item to points on the coordinate axis, and vice versa. Following are the three convenience methods that facilitate these conversions:

- findDataPoints: Coordinates are the input, and associated data points are the output. The data points are returned as an array of HitData objects.

- localToData: Coordinates are the input, and associated data points are the output. The data points are returned as an array of flash.geom.Point objects.
- dataToLocal: Data point is the input, and coordinates are the output.

"Coordinates" implies different things depending on the type of the underlying coordinate system. It means the X and Y axes for charts that map to Cartesian or rectangular coordinates, and it translates to an angle and a distance from the center for charts that map to polar coordinates. Therefore, dataToLocal on a column chart data item will return the X and Y values, whereas dataToLocal on a pie chart data item will return the angle and the radial distance values.

Events with these convenience methods can be used effectively to support interactivity in charts. Display can be altered or new data can be shown based on user events. One such important use case involves drilling down on charts. The previous examples have shown the top four economies in various chart formats. Say you wanted to know the main sectors that make up the huge American economy. Would it not be convenient to allow clicking the American economy data point, a column in a column chart, and explode it to show a new chart with all the constituent sectors that make up the American economy?

You will see how this works in a short while. Before we get to that though, I will explain effects and transitions in charts. Chapter 2 briefly reviewed the topic of effects for Flex components. I said that effects were analogous to events and were fired at the same trigger points. I defined effect handlers that applied specific behavioral modifications to the UI components. Then I explained transitions in the context of these behavioral modifications.

Similar effects and behaviors are applicable to charts as well. On top of these, there are newer types of effects that are specific to charts and applicable to data series that bind to the chart. Once you understand effects, we will come back to our drill-down example and use events and effects together so you can see how to create an effective interactive experience.

**Effects in charts** Chart components support the typical Flex effects like Zoom, Blur, Fade, and WipeDown. These apply to the chart component as a whole. All chart components extend ChartBase, which in turn extends UIComponent. Therefore, it's not surprising that all charts support the effects that UI components in Flex do.

Although useful, like chart events, these don't impact data items alone. In charts, standard effects cause the structures beyond the data items (i.e., axis, labels, legend, or annotations) to also undergo the behavioral modifications. This may not be desired in many situations. Series effects come to your rescue in such situations.

Flex defines three types of Series effects. These are as follows:

- SeriesInterpolate: First moves the existing data and then applies the transition to the newly added data set. The other two effects cause the behavioral modification to be applied to the old and new data set.
- SeriesSlide: Slides a data series into and out of the chart boundaries. The direction of the slide (i.e., right, left, up, or down) is determined by the direction property.
- SeriesZoom: Implodes and explodes the chart data from the point of focus.

These are triggered by the showDataEffect and hideDataEffect effects. Remember that these effects are related to the chart data and impacted by the change in the data set. So during all these effects, there are two types of data: the old one before the change and the new one after the change. hideDataEffect is triggered when the old data is about to change. showDataEffect is triggered when the new data is applied. This three-step process is summarized in Figure 12-14.

To see Series effects in action, let's look at an example of an application that uses the SeriesInterpolate effect. The stock price real update example you saw earlier is modified to update the prices at a slower rate, and each price point is shown as a column in a column chart. Here is the code:

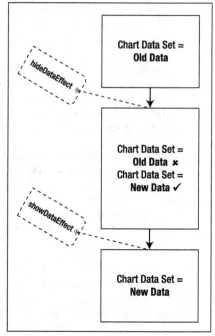

**Figure 12-14.** The data Series effects triggered in chart components

```
<?xml version="1.0"?>
<!-- DataUpdateInRealTimeSeriesInterpolate.mxml
-->
<mx:Application
xmlns:mx="http://www.adobe.com/2006/mxml"
initialize="initTimer()">
  <mx:Script><![CDATA[
  import flash.utils.Timer;
  import flash.events.TimerEvent;
  import mx.collections.ArrayCollection;

  [Bindable]
  public var stockPriceDataSeries:ArrayCollection =
new ArrayCollection();
  public function initTimer():void {
        var myTimer:Timer = new Timer(5000, 0);
        myTimer.addEventListener("timer", timerHandler);
        myTimer.start();
  }
  public function timerHandler(event:TimerEvent):void {
    var obj:Object = new Object();
    obj.time = getTimer();
    obj.stockPrice = 40.39 + Math.random()*2;
    stockPriceDataSeries.addItem(obj);
  }
]]></mx:Script>
<mx:SeriesInterpolate id="redrawSeries"
    duration="1500"
    minimumElementDuration="200"
    elementOffset="0"/>
<mx:ColumnChart id="chart" dataProvider="{stockPriceDataSeries}"
    showDataTips="true">
    <mx:horizontalAxis>
        <mx:LinearAxis/>
```

```
        </mx:horizontalAxis>
        <mx:verticalAxis>
            <mx:LinearAxis minimum="40"/>
        </mx:verticalAxis>
        <mx:series>
            <mx:ColumnSeries
             yField="stockPrice"
             showDataEffect="redrawSeries"/>
        </mx:series>
    </mx:ColumnChart>
</mx:Application>
```

We apply the series interpolate effect on the chart. As it is dynamic, it's difficult to depict the transition on paper. The best I can do is to show snapshots at two different times. Figure 12-15 and Figure 12-16 show the chart at the 14th and the 18th update, respectively. If you run the application, you may see something entirely different because the data is being generated randomly.

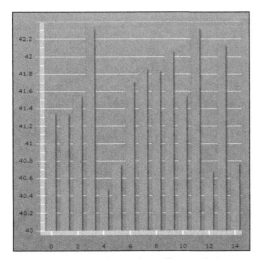

**Figure 12-15.** Series interpolate effect applied to real-time chart; snapshot at the 14th update

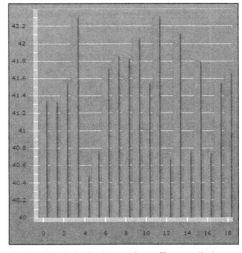

**Figure 12-16.** Series interpolate effect applied to real time chart; snapshot at the 18th update

Now we are ready to come back and look at drill-down features in charts. Let's create some fictitious data to break the American GDP value into subparts. GDP is measured as the sum of consumption, gross investment, government spending, and net of imports and exports. The American economy in real life has more imports than exports, and so the net of imports and exports is negative. We cook up a few numbers in line with the trend that real GDP numbers follow. So we divide the American GDP as follows:

- **Total**: 100%, or 13,843,825
- **Consumption (C)**: 75.5%, or 10,452,087.88
- **Gross investment (I)**: 15.1%, or 2,090,417.575
- **Government spending (G)**: 18.9%, or 2,616,482.925
- **Net of imports and exports (X-M)**: –9.5%, or –1,315,163.375

**477**

Now we re-create our pie chart, but this time we allow users to drill down into the sector that depicts the United States economy. On drill down, users are presented with a new pie chart that shows the constituents of the United States economy. Because showing negative values in a pie chart doesn't make much sense, we only show the positive constituents of the economy.

Our example is extremely simple so it does not take care of transitions back from the drill down to the aggregated level and does not include any effects to smoothen the drill-down transitions. The only check it implements is that the drill down is activated only if the user selects the sector that corresponds to "United States." This is useful because if you want to see the constituents of the American economy, drilling down into the Japanese economy doesn't seem to help. The verification is done by checking that the selected item corresponds to United States. Flex charts allow selection of chart data items. You can specify single or multiple selection possibilities by setting the selectionMode property value on the chart object. Selections can be made with the help of mouse clicks, keyboard presses, or programmatically. Here we implement selection using mouse clicks. We use single selection because it suffices for our needs. Here is the code for the implementation:

```
<?xml version="1.0"?>
<!-- FourLargestEconomyPieWithDrillDown.mxml -->
<mx:Application xmlns:mx="http://www.adobe.com/2006/mxml">
  <mx:Script><![CDATA[
    import mx.collections.ArrayCollection;
    import mx.charts.events.ChartItemEvent;

    [Bindable]
    public var topFourIMF:ArrayCollection = new ArrayCollection([
        {Country:"United States", GDP:13843825},
        {Country:"China (PRC)", GDP:6991036},
        {Country:"Japan", GDP:4289809},
        {Country:"India", GDP:2988867},
        {Country:"Rest of the World", GDP:36789726}
    ]);
    [Bindable]
    public var americanGDP:ArrayCollection = new ArrayCollection([
        {Category:"Consumption(C)", GDPContribution:10452087.88},
        {Category:"Gross Investment(I)", GDPContribution:2090417.575},
        {Category:"Government spending(G)", ➥
GDPContribution:2616482.925}
        /*{Category:"Exports-Imports(X-M)", ➥
GDPContribution:-1315163.375 }*/
    ]);

    private function itemClickHandler(e:ChartItemEvent):void {
        var selectedIndx:int = e.currentTarget.series.selectedIndex;
        trace("selectedIndx: " + selectedIndx);
        if(selectedIndx==0) {
            myChart.dataProvider = americanGDP;
            ps1.field="GDPContribution";
            ps1.nameField="Category";
        }

    }
  ]]></mx:Script>
```

```
<mx:Panel title="Pie Chart">
    <mx:PieChart id="myChart"
        dataProvider="{topFourIMF}"
        showDataTips="true"
        itemClick="itemClickHandler(event)"
        selectionMode="single" >
        <mx:series>
            <mx:PieSeries
                id="ps1"
                field="GDP"
                nameField="Country"
                labelPosition="callout"
                selectable="true" />
        </mx:series>
    </mx:PieChart>
    <mx:Legend dataProvider="{myChart}"/>
</mx:Panel>
</mx:Application>
```

Our initial Pie chart looks the same as in Figure 12-2, shown earlier. On clicking the sector that corresponds to "United States," we see a new pie chart that replaces the original one. Figure 12-17 shows what it looks like.

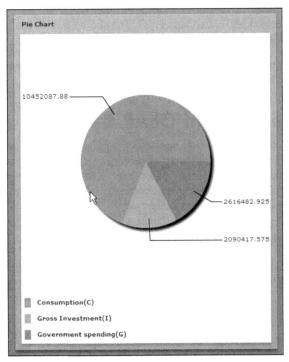

**Figure 12-17.** The pie chart that appears on drill down and shows the United States economy constituents

I could extend this discussion of interactivity and effects, because you can combine the features available to produce a large number of compositions. But I shall leave that part of the discovery process to you. Hopefully, the content so far has whetted your appetite and inspired you to try the features out.

## 3D charts and domain-specific charts

We have traversed Flex's charting features. All the features illustrated deal with charts in two dimensions (2D). Charts can also be created in three dimensions (3D). Sometimes 3D charts can be more appropriate for data representation. For example, in business intelligence scenarios, the classic data cube represents data in three dimensions, thus getting simultaneous data comparisons on six rectangular coordinates, along the surfaces of the cube. Chapter 15 explains how to construct 3D Flex applications. Once you have learned these techniques, you can create your own 3D charts.

However, a few commercial versions of 3D charts are freely available today. You may want to look at ILOG's Elixir charting component set. More information about this can be obtained at http://www.ilog.com/products/ilogelixir/.

The charting features available off the shelf in Flex Builder 3 Professional Edition are exhaustive, and you can create charts of any type you desire. Sometimes it makes sense to extend the standard controls and create charts for a specific domain. Financial services seem to be one area where such custom sets of charts fit in very well. Out of box, Flex includes a couple charts like candlestick and HighLowOpenClose charts that have relevance to the financial services industry. However, this is just a starting point, and many more charts need to be created. The company I work for created such a bundle called Saven Flex Charts for the financial services industry. Details about it can be obtained at http://www.saventech.com/flex/Flex-Charts.pdf. This should inspire you to think in terms of custom extensions for specific domains and industry verticals.

Now we are ready to move on to the next important aspect of BI, which involves manipulating large amounts of data and representing data relationships.

# AdvancedDataGrid and OLAP data grid

So far, you have seen rich graphical representations of data used for information expression and dissemination. Now we turn to a more traditional yet powerful technique: portraying information in data tables and grids. From basic products like Microsoft Excel to advanced tools from BI suite vendors like Oracle and IBM, the data matrix prevails. In this section, I walk you through some of the advanced manipulations possible with such structures in Flex.

## AdvancedDataGrid

The DataGrid in Flex is the most basic control that is used to show data in a grid or tabular format. Let's look at a quick example to see how the DataGrid works. Here is the code:

```
<?xml version="1.0" encoding="utf-8"?>
<!-- GrocerySalesDataGrid.xml -->
<mx:Application xmlns:mx="http://www.adobe.com/2006/mxml"
    width="600" height="300" >
<mx:Script>
    <![CDATA[
```

```
        import mx.collections.ArrayCollection;
        [Bindable]
        private var grocerySalesData:ArrayCollection =
new ArrayCollection([
        {Grocer:"Grocer A", Category:"Fruits", ➡
Item:"Apple", Q1:15000, Q2:10000},
        {Grocer:"Grocer A", Category:"Fruits", ➡
Item:"Banana", Q1:25000, Q2:15000},
        {Grocer:"Grocer A", Category:"Meats", ➡
Item:"Chicken", Q1:35000, Q2:42000},
        {Grocer:"Grocer A", Category:"Meats", ➡
Item:"Beef", Q1:42000, Q2:35000},
        {Grocer:"Grocer B", Category:"Fruits", ➡
Item:"Apple", Q1:17000, Q2:12000},
        {Grocer:"Grocer B", Category:"Fruits", ➡
Item:"Pineapple", Q1:17000, Q2:15000},
        {Grocer:"Grocer B", Category:"Meats", ➡
Item:"Pork", Q1:43000, Q2:43000}
        ]);
    ]]>
</mx:Script>
    <mx:DataGrid dataProvider="{grocerySalesData}"
        width="100%" height="100%" />
</mx:Application>
```

The data in this example is of two fictitious grocers' sales across the categories they stock. The data is for the first two quarters of 2008. It is intentionally kept simple and will be reused for most of the examples in this section. The data is bound to a simple data grid. Figure 12-18 shows what the output looks like.

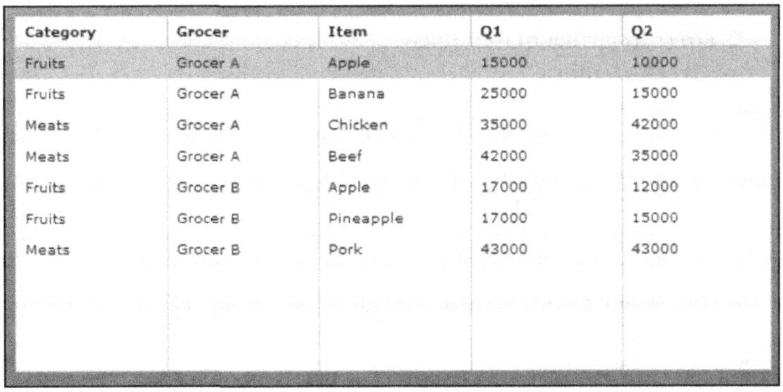

| Category | Grocer | Item | Q1 | Q2 |
|---|---|---|---|---|
| Fruits | Grocer A | Apple | 15000 | 10000 |
| Fruits | Grocer A | Banana | 25000 | 15000 |
| Meats | Grocer A | Chicken | 35000 | 42000 |
| Meats | Grocer A | Beef | 42000 | 35000 |
| Fruits | Grocer B | Apple | 17000 | 12000 |
| Fruits | Grocer B | Pineapple | 17000 | 15000 |
| Meats | Grocer B | Pork | 43000 | 43000 |

**Figure 12-18.** DataGrid with hierarchical sales data

The DataGrid has some very useful features. For example, it allows you to sort by column, select a row of data, edit the data cells, and define custom item renderers and formatters to show data appropriately. BI tools usually need all of these features and also often need to manage hierarchical and grouped data effectively. As a good example, the current display could be far more effective if it showed data in a hierarchical tree grid structure so that we could understand the data better. Creating

**481**

hierarchical displays with the DataGrid is possible, but it entails customization of data manipulation logic or modification of the underlying data structure. It also needs custom components with a customized item renderer to display hierarchical data. This is what you had to do if you wanted to treat hierarchical and grouped data well with Flex 2. Luckily, with Flex 3 we have a set of new controls that make things simple. Let's re-create our example using the AdvancedDataGrid control. Here is the new code:

```
<?xml version="1.0" encoding="utf-8"?>
<!-- GrocerySalesAdvancedDataGrid.mxml -->
<mx:Application xmlns:mx="http://www.adobe.com/2006/mxml"
    width="600" height="300" >
<mx:Script>
    <![CDATA[
        import mx.collections.ArrayCollection;
        [Bindable]
        private var grocerySalesData:ArrayCollection =
new ArrayCollection([
        //same as in the earlier example
        ]);
    ]]>
</mx:Script>
    <mx:AdvancedDataGrid id="myAdvancedDG"
        width="100%" height="100%"
        defaultLeafIcon="{null}"
        initialize="gc.refresh();">
        <mx:dataProvider>
            <mx:GroupingCollection id="gc" source="{grocerySalesData}">
                <mx:Grouping>
                    <mx:GroupingField name="Grocer"/>
                    <mx:GroupingField name="Category"/>
                </mx:Grouping>
            </mx:GroupingCollection>
        </mx:dataProvider>
        <mx:columns>
            <mx:AdvancedDataGridColumn dataField="GroupLabel"
                headerText="Grocer/Category"/>
            <mx:AdvancedDataGridColumn dataField="Item"
                headerText="Product(Item)"/>
            <mx:AdvancedDataGridColumn dataField="Q1"/>
            <mx:AdvancedDataGridColumn dataField="Q2"/>
        </mx:columns>
    </mx:AdvancedDataGrid>
</mx:Application>
```

The data set, grocerySalesData ArrayCollection, is taken out of the source listing this time. Please refer to the earlier example to see the details of the data structure. The output of this code is shown in Figure 12-19.

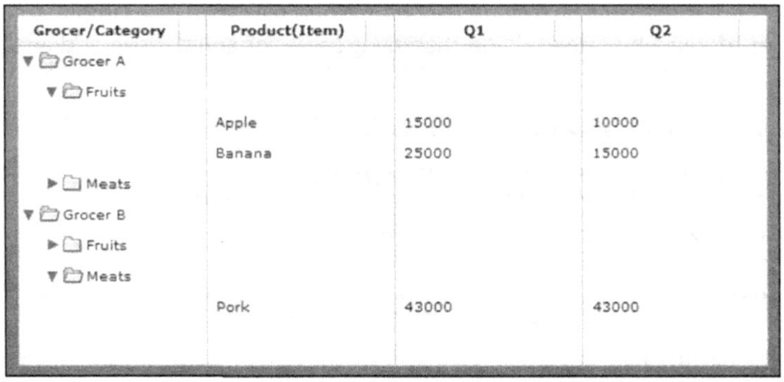

**Figure 12-19**. AdvancedDataGrid with hierarchical sales data

The AdvancedDataGrid makes the representation substantially more useful than the DataGrid. The underlying data is flat, so we use the GroupingCollection class to group and bind the data to the AdvancedDataGrid. We define the grouping criteria by specifying the group by data fields. Data fields are bound to the columns. The first column just stores the grouping information and avoids redundancy in data display. If you compare the preceding two data grids, you will see that the grouped data grid has fewer columns than the flat matrix. The grouping column can have a label of its own defined by setting the value of the dataField as GroupLabel and specifying the display label as the value of the headerText.

The grouping is first by grocer and then by category. We can easily reverse the order—that is, group by category first and then grocer. The code needs only a small change as follows:

```
<mx:Grouping>
    <mx:GroupingField name="Category"/>
    <mx:GroupingField name="Grocer"/>
</mx:Grouping>
```

If you compare this with the previous code listing, you will notice that all we have done is to flip the order in which the grouping fields occur. The changes in the UI due to this change are shown in Figure 12-20.

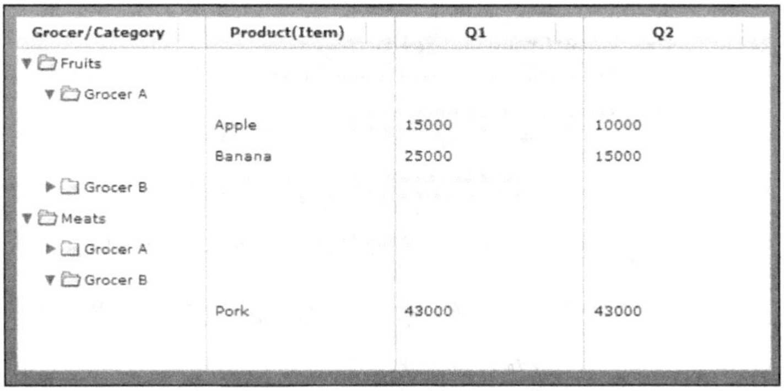

**Figure 12-20.** Grouping data first by category and then by grocer

**483**

Often summarization of data goes hand in hand with grouping data. For example, it may be useful to see the total sales of items by category and then by grocers for comparison and analysis. Here is the code for it:

```
<?xml version="1.0" encoding="utf-8"?>
<!-- GrocerySalesAdvancedDataGridWithSummary.mxml -->
<mx:Application xmlns:mx="http://www.adobe.com/2006/mxml"
    width="600" height="300" >
<mx:Script>
    <![CDATA[
        import mx.collections.ArrayCollection;
        [Bindable]
        private var grocerySalesData:ArrayCollection =
new ArrayCollection([
        //Same as the code above
        ]);
    ]]>
</mx:Script>
    <mx:AdvancedDataGrid id="myAdvancedDG"
        width="100%" height="100%"
        defaultLeafIcon="{null}"
        initialize="gc.refresh();">
        <mx:dataProvider>
            <mx:GroupingCollection id="gc" source="{grocerySalesData}">
                <mx:Grouping>
                    <mx:GroupingField name="Grocer">
                    <mx:summaries>
                        <mx:SummaryRow summaryPlacement="group">
                          <mx:fields>
                            <mx:SummaryField dataField="Q1"
                                label="Q1 Total" operation="SUM"/>
                            <mx:SummaryField dataField="Q2"
                                label="Q2 Total" operation="SUM"/>
                          </mx:fields>
                        </mx:SummaryRow>
                    </mx:summaries>
                    </mx:GroupingField>
                    <mx:GroupingField name="Category">
                    <mx:summaries>
                        <mx:SummaryRow summaryPlacement="group">
                          <mx:fields>
                            <mx:SummaryField dataField="Q1"
                                label="Q1 Total" operation="SUM"/>
                            <mx:SummaryField dataField="Q2"
                                label="Q2 Total" operation="SUM"/>
                          </mx:fields>
                        </mx:SummaryRow>
                    </mx:summaries>
                    </mx:GroupingField>
```

```
                                </mx:Grouping>
                        </mx:GroupingCollection>
                </mx:dataProvider>
                <mx:columns>
                        <mx:AdvancedDataGridColumn dataField="GroupLabel"
                                headerText="Grocer/Category"/>
                        <mx:AdvancedDataGridColumn dataField="Item"
                                headerText="Product(Item)"/>
                        <mx:AdvancedDataGridColumn dataField="Q1"/>
                        <mx:AdvancedDataGridColumn dataField="Q2"/>
                        <mx:AdvancedDataGridColumn dataField="Q1 Total"/>
                        <mx:AdvancedDataGridColumn dataField="Q2 Total"/>
                </mx:columns>
        </mx:AdvancedDataGrid>
</mx:Application>
```

The summary rows are added at the group level. This is because we set the summaryPlacement property to group. The alternatives are to set it to first or last, which causes the summary-level information to appear as the first row and the last row of the grouping sets, respectively. Also, the summary in our example is a SUM of the values. The other operations available off the shelf are

- MIN: Minimum value of the group
- MAX: Maximum value of the group
- AVG: Average value of the group
- COUNT: Number of elements or members in the group

If you need summary operations beyond these, you can write one of your own. Flex defines two properties that take callback methods as values to facilitate implementation of custom summary functions. These properties are

- SummaryRow.summaryObjectFunction: This property can take a callback function as a value. The callback function should return a SummaryObject. The SummaryObject affects what is displayed on the summary row.
- SummaryField.summaryFunction: This property can take a callback function as a value. The callback function should return a result of type Number. This is the function that implements the custom operation.

Summaries are attached to the grouping field. The summary data becomes somewhat like a virtual row of your underlying data and can be displayed by binding it to an AdvancedDataGridColumn. Figure 12-21 shows our data with summaries.

| Grocer/C... | Product(... | Q1 | Q2 | Q1 Total | Q2 Total |
|---|---|---|---|---|---|
| ▼ 🗀 Grocer A | | | | 117000 | 102000 |
| ▼ 🗀 Fruits | | | | 40000 | 25000 |
| | Apple | 15000 | 10000 | | |
| | Banana | 25000 | 15000 | | |
| ▶ 🗀 Meats | | | | 77000 | 77000 |
| ▼ 🗀 Grocer B | | | | 77000 | 70000 |
| ▼ 🗀 Fruits | | | | 34000 | 27000 |
| | Apple | 17000 | 12000 | | |
| | Pineapple | 17000 | 15000 | | |
| ▶ 🗀 Meats | | | | 43000 | 43000 |

**Figure 12-21.** AdvancedDataGrid with summary information

Grouping columns may add further value to this data, by making it easy to recognize the data set. Q1 and Q2 column numbers are related and are on similar lines, so it may be valuable to combine the two columns together in a single bundle. Similarly, it may be pragmatic to group Q1 Total and Q2 Total columns. Figure 12-22 shows such a grouping of columns.

| Grocer/C... | Product(... | Quarters | | Quarter Totals | |
|---|---|---|---|---|---|
| | | Q1 | Q2 | Q1 Total | Q2 Total |
| ▼ 🗀 Grocer A | | | | 117000 | 102000 |
| ▶ 🗀 Fruits | | | | 40000 | 25000 |
| ▶ 🗀 Meats | | | | 77000 | 77000 |
| ▼ 🗀 Grocer B | | | | 77000 | 70000 |
| ▼ 🗀 Fruits | | | | 34000 | 27000 |
| | Apple | 17000 | 12000 | | |
| | Pineapple | 17000 | 15000 | | |
| ▶ 🗀 Meats | | | | 43000 | 43000 |

**Figure 12-22.** AdvancedDataGrid with summary and column groups

The code variation for generating column groups is minimal. All we do is flip in <mx:groupedColumns> for <mx:columns> and put the columns that need to grouped within the tags of an AdvancedDataGridColumnGroup. A snippet of the code that implements the grouping is follows:

```
<mx:groupedColumns>
        <mx:AdvancedDataGridColumn dataField="GroupLabel"
            headerText="Grocer/Category"/>
        <mx:AdvancedDataGridColumn dataField="Item"
            headerText="Product(Item)"/>
        <mx:AdvancedDataGridColumnGroup headerText="Quarters">
            <mx:AdvancedDataGridColumn dataField="Q1"/>
            <mx:AdvancedDataGridColumn dataField="Q2"/>
        </mx:AdvancedDataGridColumnGroup>
        <mx:AdvancedDataGridColumnGroup
headerText="Quarter Totals">
            <mx:AdvancedDataGridColumn dataField="Q1 Total"/>
```

```
            <mx:AdvancedDataGridColumn dataField="Q2 Total"/>
        </mx:AdvancedDataGridColumnGroup>
    </mx:groupedColumns>
```

Now we go back to our data and mutate it from a flat structure to a hierarchy. The data in its new shape is as follows:

```
private var grocerySalesData:ArrayCollection = new ArrayCollection([
    {Grocer:"Grocer A", childMembers:[
        {Category:"Fruits", childMembers: [
            {Item:"Apple", Q1:15000, Q2:10000},
            {Item:"Banana", Q1:25000, Q2:15000}]},
        {Category:"Meats", childMembers: [
            {Item:"Chicken", Q1:35000, Q2:42000},
            {Item:"Beef", Q1:42000, Q2:35000}]}
    ]},
    {Grocer:"Grocer B", childMembers: [
        {Category:"Fruits", childMembers: [
            {Item:"Apple", Q1:17000, Q2:12000},
            {Item:"Pineapple", Q1:17000, Q2:15000}]},
        {Category:"Meats", childMembers: [
            {Item:"Pork", Q1:43000, Q2:43000}]}
    ]}
]);
```

Next, we use this data in an AdvancedDataGrid. Let's start by looking at the output in Figure 12-23.

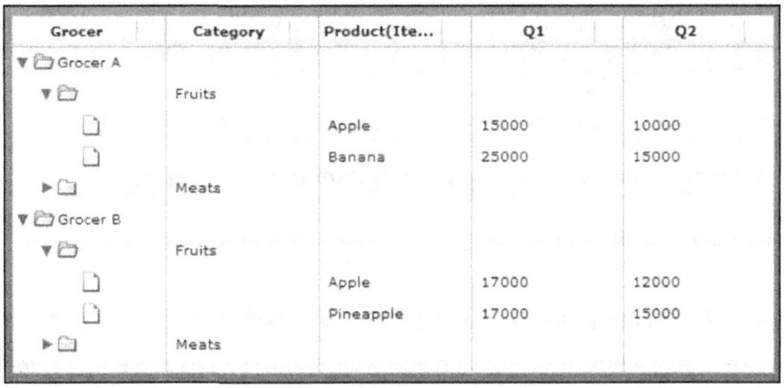

**Figure 12-23.** AdvancedDataGrid with hierarchical data

The code that creates the UI in Figure 12-23 is as follows:

```
<?xml version="1.0" encoding="utf-8"?>
<!-- GrocerySalesADGWithHierarchicalData.mxml -->
<mx:Application xmlns:mx="http://www.adobe.com/2006/mxml"
    width="600" height="300" >
<mx:Script>
    <![CDATA[
```

```
            import mx.collections.ArrayCollection;
            [Bindable]
            private var grocerySalesData:ArrayCollection =
    new ArrayCollection([
            //we showed it a few lines back so we avoid repeating it here
        ]]>
    </mx:Script>
        <mx:AdvancedDataGrid id="myAdvancedDG"
            width="100%" height="100%" >
            <mx:dataProvider>
                <mx:HierarchicalData source="{grocerySalesData}"
                    childrenField="childMembers"/>
            </mx:dataProvider>
            <mx:columns>
                <mx:AdvancedDataGridColumn dataField="Grocer"/>
                <mx:AdvancedDataGridColumn dataField="Category"/>
                <mx:AdvancedDataGridColumn dataField="Item"
                    headerText="Product(Item)"/>
                <mx:AdvancedDataGridColumn dataField="Q1"/>
                <mx:AdvancedDataGridColumn dataField="Q2"/>
            </mx:columns>
        </mx:AdvancedDataGrid>
    </mx:Application>
```

One big change from what you have seen so far is that we use a HierarchicalData object instead of a GroupingCollection object to bind the data. This is because now the underlying data itself has an inherent hierarchy. This also implies that you cannot group and summarize data as you could with the flat structure. It's an important aspect to remember while creating BI interfaces. If you use an underlying BI engine to generate the hierarchy and create the grouping, then use the HierarchicalData object to bind that data to the AdvancedDataGrid.

With this, I am getting ready to wrap up this discussion on AdvancedDataGrid and move on to the OLAP data grid. I want to make a couple of passing but important remarks before going there though:

- Styles can be applied to AdvancedDataGrid rows and columns.

- Formatters can be used with AdvancedDataGrid.

- Custom item renderers can be used with AdvancedDataGrid. A common custom item renderer can be used across columns, or multiple item renderers can be used in a single column.

- Multiple contiguous and noncontiguous cells can be selected. Remember the DataGrid selected rows instead of cells.

- Data can be sorted on multiple columns at the same time by setting the sortExpertMode property of AdvancedDataGrid to true.

Next and last of all, as far as this chapter goes, is the OLAP data grid.

# OLAP data grid

Online Analytical Processing (OLAP) is an approach to creating and presenting multidimensional analytical queries and results. Along with data mining, it forms an important part of BI. Flex 3 provides a set of components and controls to simplify OLAP implementation using the technology.

In general, OLAP does not deal with data collection. It is assumed that transactional systems collect data, and OLAP uses that data for dimensional analytical processing. It's normal for transactional data to be recorded in a flat structure because data itself is captured in that form, and the point of capture is typically neither aware nor concerned with the various possible summarizations and aggregations of the data.

The Flex OLAP components were created to support manipulation of flat data into dimensional structures, before displaying it in multidimensional formats. In order to understand this better, we go back to our grocery example and flatten the data out further. The completely flattened data for Grocer A is as follows:

```
private var flatGrocerySalesData:ArrayCollection = ➡
        new ArrayCollection([
        {Grocer:"Grocer A", Category:"Fruits", ➡
Item:"Apple", Quarter:"Q1",Sales:15000, Year:2008},
        {Grocer:"Grocer A", Category:"Fruits", ➡
Item:"Apple", Quarter:"Q2",Sales:10000, Year:2008},
        {Grocer:"Grocer A", Category:"Fruits", ➡
Item:"Apple", Quarter:"Q3",Sales:25000, Year:2007},
        {Grocer:"Grocer A", Category:"Fruits", ➡
Item:"Apple", Quarter:"Q4",Sales:25000, Year:2007},
        {Grocer:"Grocer A", Category:"Fruits", ➡
Item:"Banana",Quarter:"Q1",Sales:25000, Year:2008},
        {Grocer:"Grocer A", Category:"Fruits", ➡
Item:"Banana",Quarter:"Q2",Sales:15000, Year:2008},
        {Grocer:"Grocer A", Category:"Fruits", ➡
Item:"Banana",Quarter:"Q3",Sales:23000, Year:2007},
        {Grocer:"Grocer A", Category:"Fruits", ➡
Item:"Banana",Quarter:"Q4",Sales:21000, Year:2007},
        {Grocer:"Grocer A", Category:"Meats", ➡
Item:"Chicken",Quarter:"Q1",Sales:35000, Year:2008},
        {Grocer:"Grocer A", Category:"Meats", ➡
Item:"Chicken",Quarter:"Q2",Sales:42000, Year:2008},
        {Grocer:"Grocer A", Category:"Meats", ➡
Item:"Chicken",Quarter:"Q3",Sales:35000, Year:2007},
        {Grocer:"Grocer A", Category:"Meats", ➡
Item:"Chicken",Quarter:"Q4",Sales:45000, Year:2007},
        {Grocer:"Grocer A", Category:"Meats", ➡
Item:"Beef", Quarter:"Q1",Sales:42000, Year:2008},
        {Grocer:"Grocer A", Category:"Meats", ➡
Item:"Beef", Quarter:"Q2",Sales:35000, Year:2008},
        {Grocer:"Grocer A", Category:"Meats", ➡
Item:"Beef", Quarter:"Q3",Sales:43000, Year:2007},
        {Grocer:"Grocer A", Category:"Meats", ➡
```

```
Item:"Beef", Quarter:"Q4",Sales:43000, Year:2007},
    // Grocer B data in the same format
]);
```

Additional fields including a year field have been added to the data set. Also, data for two additional quarters is added so that you can better appreciate the power of OLAP. Now we create an OLAP report or output so that quarters roll up to a year and items roll up to a category. Let's see the report first, which is shown in Figure 12-24.

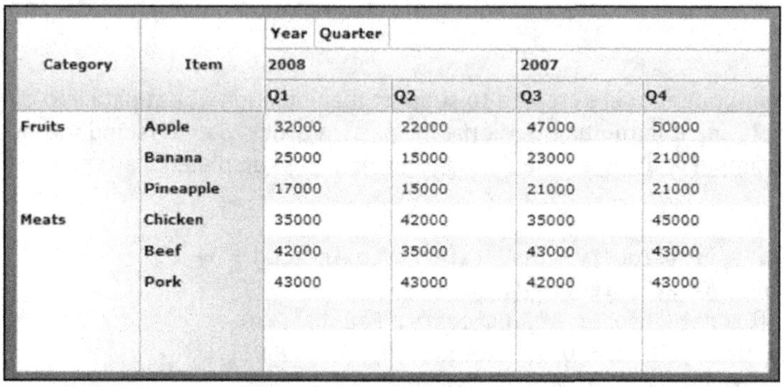

| Category | Item | Year | Quarter | | |
|---|---|---|---|---|---|
| | | 2008 | | 2007 | |
| | | Q1 | Q2 | Q3 | Q4 |
| Fruits | Apple | 32000 | 22000 | 47000 | 50000 |
| | Banana | 25000 | 15000 | 23000 | 21000 |
| | Pineapple | 17000 | 15000 | 21000 | 21000 |
| Meats | Chicken | 35000 | 42000 | 35000 | 45000 |
| | Beef | 42000 | 35000 | 43000 | 43000 |
| | Pork | 43000 | 43000 | 42000 | 43000 |

**Figure 12-24.** Grocery sales data in an OLAP data grid

The code that powers what you see in Figure 12-24 is as follows:

```
<?xml version="1.0"?>
<!-- GrocerySalesOLAPDataGrid.mxml -->
<mx:Application xmlns:mx="http://www.adobe.com/2006/mxml"
        creationComplete="creationCompleteHandler();"
        width="600" height="300" >
    <mx:Script>
      <![CDATA[
        import mx.rpc.AsyncResponder;
        import mx.rpc.AsyncToken;
        import  mx.messaging.messages.ErrorMessage;
        import mx.olap.OLAPQuery;
        import mx.olap.OLAPSet;
        import mx.olap.IOLAPQuery;
        import mx.olap.IOLAPQueryAxis;
        import mx.olap.IOLAPCube;
        import mx.olap.OLAPResult;
        import mx.events.CubeEvent;
        import mx.controls.Alert;
        import mx.collections.ArrayCollection;
        [Bindable]
        private var flatGrocerySalesData:ArrayCollection =
new ArrayCollection([
//Data same as shown above
        ]);
```

```
        private function creationCompleteHandler():void {
            myMXMLCube.refresh();
        }

        private function getQuery(cube:IOLAPCube):IOLAPQuery {
            var query:OLAPQuery = new OLAPQuery;

            var rowQueryAxis:IOLAPQueryAxis =
                query.getAxis(OLAPQuery.ROW_AXIS);
            var categorySet:OLAPSet = new OLAPSet;
            categorySet.addElements(
                cube.findDimension("ProductDim").➥
findAttribute("Category").children);
            var itemSet:OLAPSet = new OLAPSet;
            itemSet.addElements(
                cube.findDimension("ProductDim").➥
findAttribute("Item").children);
            rowQueryAxis.addSet(categorySet.crossJoin(itemSet));

          var colQueryAxis:IOLAPQueryAxis =
                query.getAxis(OLAPQuery.COLUMN_AXIS);
            var yearSet:OLAPSet= new OLAPSet;
            yearSet.addElements(
                cube.findDimension("TimeDim").findAttribute➥
("Year").children);
            var quarterSet:OLAPSet= new OLAPSet;
            quarterSet.addElements(
                cube.findDimension("TimeDim").findAttribute➥
("Quarter").children);
            colQueryAxis.addSet(yearSet.crossJoin(quarterSet));

            return query;
        }

        private function runQuery(event:CubeEvent):void {
            var cube:IOLAPCube = IOLAPCube(event.currentTarget);
            var query:IOLAPQuery = getQuery(cube);
            var token:AsyncToken = cube.execute(query);
            token.addResponder(new AsyncResponder➥
(showResult, showFault));
        }

        private function showFault(error:ErrorMessage, ➥
token:Object):void {
            Alert.show(error.faultString);
        }

        private function showResult(result:Object, token:Object):void {
            if (!result) {
```

```
                    Alert.show("No results from query.");
                    return;
                }
                myOLAPDG.dataProvider= result as OLAPResult;
            }
        ]]>
    </mx:Script>

    <mx:OLAPCube name="FlatSchemaCube"
        dataProvider="{flatGrocerySalesData}"
        id="myMXMLCube"
        complete="runQuery(event);">
      <mx:OLAPDimension name="GrocerDim">
            <mx:OLAPAttribute name="Grocer" dataField="Grocer"/>
            <mx:OLAPHierarchy name="GrocerHierarchy" hasAll="true">
                <mx:OLAPLevel attributeName="Grocer"/>
            </mx:OLAPHierarchy>
        </mx:OLAPDimension>
        <mx:OLAPDimension name="ProductDim">
            <mx:OLAPAttribute name="Category" dataField="Category"/>
            <mx:OLAPAttribute name="Item" dataField="Item"/>
            <mx:OLAPHierarchy name="Product-Type"
                hasAll="true">
                <mx:OLAPLevel attributeName="Category"/>
                <mx:OLAPLevel attributeName="Item"/>
            </mx:OLAPHierarchy>
        </mx:OLAPDimension>
        <mx:OLAPDimension name="TimeDim">
            <mx:OLAPAttribute name="Year" dataField="Year"/>
            <mx:OLAPAttribute name="Quarter" dataField="Quarter"/>
            <mx:OLAPHierarchy name="Time-Period"
                hasAll="true">
                <mx:OLAPLevel attributeName="Year"/>
                <mx:OLAPLevel attributeName="Quarter"/>
            </mx:OLAPHierarchy>
        </mx:OLAPDimension>
        <mx:OLAPMeasure name="Sales"
            dataField="Sales" />
    </mx:OLAPCube>
    <mx:OLAPDataGrid id="myOLAPDataGrid" width="100%" height="100%"/>
</mx:Application>
```

To understand the preceding code and illustrate the different pieces in the OLAP data grid, let's dissect it into two parts: the OLAP schema and the OLAP query.

## OLAP schema

In the previous example, the flat data is converted or attached along multiple dimensions. This is all defined in the OLAPCube object. OLAP dimensions are defined in an OLAPDimension object. Attributes of the underlying data are first associated with a dimension. Where relevant, a hierarchy is also associated with the attributes. For example, the Item is the child of a Category so items show up a level lower in the hierarchy than categories.

An OLAP cube is a multidimensional structure, which (in spite of its name) can have as many dimensions as you choose. In the case of three dimensions, it has six two-dimensional surfaces. Usually each axis has discrete data points so we can simplify from all points in the surface to all cells where the discrete axes intersect. So each cell on the six surfaces represents a data point, either present in the native form or calculated as a result of the operations. Such data points in OLAP jargon are called measures. You can have any number of measures you want because you can define as many operations on the data as you please. Out of the box, aggregate operations like SUM, MIN, MAX, AVG, and COUNT are supported. So apart from dimensions, you also define measure in an OLAPCube.

Those are the main things that you absolutely need to know about the OLAP schema in order to do the simplest things with the OLAP data grid. Next, we quickly survey the part where we build the OLAP query.

## OLAP query

When we talk about displaying data using the Flex OLAP data grid, we are talking about two-dimensional rectangular axis displays. Therefore, we have two axes that represent the row and the column of the data grid. The OLAP data grid supports a third axis, called the slice axis, to deal with multiple dimensions.

In this example, we have only the row and column axes. We add the dimensions and the hierarchy that we need to display to a set and add that to an axis.

The last thing we need to do to get the results is to run the query. We invoke the query on the cube and get back an AsyncToken. Later we display the results on a success event. This asynchronous mechanism is standard throughout Flex.

Although there is a lot more to be said about OLAP and the OLAP data grid, we will stop here after showing one last example, where we set the aggregator property of our OLAPMeasure to SUM and show categories as the finest level of drill down on the row axis.

The modifications to the earlier code are minimal in this example. We need to change the data set we bind to the row axis and alter the measure properties to sum up the data. The new row axis–related code is as follows:

```
rowQueryAxis.addSet(categorySet);
```

All the code that adds the Item dimension to the row axis is removed.

The new measure tag is as follows:

```
<mx:OLAPMeasure name="Sales"
        dataField="Sales"
        aggregator="SUM" />
```

With this example, we come to the end of the chapter.

# Summary

By now, you know most of the techniques available in Flex to represent, aggregate, and manipulate data effectively for BI scenarios. You learned all about charts, and you saw a fair bit about the AdvancedDataGrid and the OLAP data grid. The best way to gain mastery of these tools and extend and utilize them in creative ways is to get hands-on with it. Many fascinating pictorial representations and 3D renderings are also possible with Flex and the Flash Platform. Although 2D is the officially supported set of dimensions, there is plenty of aid available from the open source community to help you get to 3D.

So the tools are plentiful, but like wise programmers, don't chase the tools for their own sake; just use whatever you need to solve the problem at hand. Always start by understanding your data source and the desired output, and then use the correct combination of charts, data grids, and other tools to get the job done. Most often the data can be accessed via web services or remoting from external sources. Use your knowledge from Part 2 of this book to effectively access and bind with data. Finally, you can always customize Flex components and controls as desired. (Refer to Chapter 2 for more information on creating custom Flex components.) Never hesitate to express your creativity.

**Chapter 13**

# WORKING WITH WEB 2.0 APIS

By Jack Herrington

Web 2.0 is a huge change from Web 1.0 for two main reasons: the emphasis on community and the emphasis on services. Successful sites like YouTube, Twitter, Salesforce, and others emphasize both of these. They use the Web to build communities around content, and then use services to distribute the content outside of the walls of their sites.

In this chapter, I'll use Flex in combination with these sites and services to show you how to connect and interact with them at the API level.

## Twitter

The first example I'll show is an AIR/Flex application that allows the customer to update her Twitter (http://twitter.com) status. If you aren't familiar with Twitter, it's an application where you can update what you are doing on a moment-to-moment basis. Think of an instant message version of a blog but with snippet-sized updates instead of long rambling soliloquies.

To get started, you will need a free account on Twitter. Then you need to download the Twitter Flex library (http://youxylo.com/projects/twitter/).

After downloading the Twitter library, create a new AIR project and add the ActionScript source for the library to it. You then need to modify the endpoint.php script with your login and password and install it on your local server.

With the script installed, use the following code to create the Twitter desktop application:

```
<?xml version="1.0" encoding="utf-8"?>
<mx:WindowedApplication xmlns:mx="http://www.adobe.com/2006/mxml"
  layout="horizontal"
  creationComplete="onStartup()" width="400" height="100"
  title="Twitter Updater">
<mx:Script>
<![CDATA[
import twitter.api.Twitter;

private var _twitter:twitter.api.Twitter = new twitter.api.Twitter();

private function onStartup() : void {
  _twitter.setProxy( 'http://localhost/endpoint.php' );
  _twitter.setAuth( 'your account', 'your password' );
}
private function updateStatus() : void {
  _twitter.setStatus( 'Playing around' );
}
]]>
</mx:Script>
<mx:TextInput id="txtStatus" text="Playing around" width="100%" />
<mx:Button click="updateStatus()" label="Update" />
</mx:WindowedApplication>
```

The Flex API for Twitter is really easy. You just give it your authentication details and the location of the proxy, and then set your status to whatever you choose. In this case, I use a text box to allow the customer to enter his status as text, as shown in Figure 13-1.

**Figure 13-1.** The simple Twitter Updater interface

Once I click the Update button, I can go to the Twitter site and see for myself that the status has been updated, as in Figure 13-2.

But you could put any user interface you want on it. You could set the status using a set of preloaded buttons or read the status from a local application. The idea is to get as close to the customer as possible.

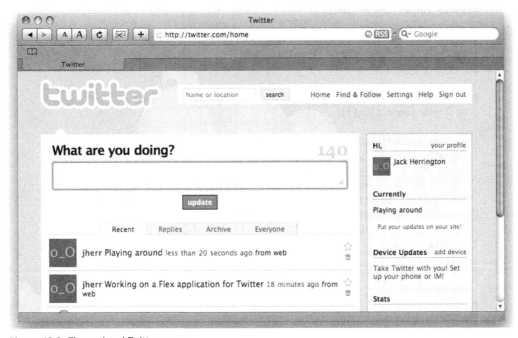

**Figure 13-2.** The updated Twitter page

# Integrating with Salesforce

Salesforce (http://salesforce.com) might not be sexy, but it's definitely Web 2.0. Sales and service people can collaborate around their customer bases, using not only the standard Salesforce applications, but also additional web applications built on the AppExchange protocol (http://www.salesforce.com/developer/). Salesforce excels at putting its services in the hands of engineers as well. Both of these are hallmarks of a good Web 2.0 application.

To demonstrate Salesforce's Flex API, I'll first create an application that shows the contact details of the customers in my Salesforce development database. To get started, you need to sign up for a Salesforce developer account. Once you have that, you can download the Flex Salesforce developer API and install either the source or SWC libraries in your project.

The code for the contact-viewing application is shown here:

```
<?xml version="1.0" encoding="utf-8"?>
<mx:WindowedApplication xmlns:mx="http://www.adobe.com/2006/mxml"
  layout="vertical"
  creationComplete="onStartup()" title="Salesforce contacts">
<mx:Script>
<![CDATA[
import com.salesforce.results.QueryResult;
import com.salesforce.objects.LoginRequest;
import com.salesforce.Connection;
import com.salesforce.AsyncResponder;
```

```
      private var ac:Connection;

      private function onQueryResult( event:QueryResult ) : void {
        dgContacts.dataProvider = event.records;
      }

      private function onStartup() : void {
        ac = new Connection();

        var login:LoginRequest = new LoginRequest();
        login.username = 'your email';
        login.password = 'your password';
        login.callback = new AsyncResponder( function (result:Object):void {
          ac.query( "Select FirstName, LastName, Phone, Email, Title From ➥
Contact Where AccountID=''", new AsyncResponder( onQueryResult ) );
        }, function (info:Object) :void {
          trace( info );
        } );

        ac.login(login);
      }
    ]]>
    </mx:Script>
    <mx:DataGrid width="100%" height="100%" id="dgContacts">
    <mx:columns>
      <mx:DataGridColumn headerText="Name" dataField="LastName">
        <mx:itemRenderer>
          <mx:Component>
            <mx:Text text="{data.FirstName} {data.LastName}" />
          </mx:Component>
        </mx:itemRenderer>
      </mx:DataGridColumn>
      <mx:DataGridColumn headerText="Title" dataField="Title" />
      <mx:DataGridColumn headerText="Email" dataField="Email" />
      <mx:DataGridColumn headerText="Phone" dataField="Phone" />
    </mx:columns>
    </mx:DataGrid>
    </mx:WindowedApplication>
```

Much like the Twitter application, the code first creates a connection to the service by providing your login credentials. However, in the case of Salesforce, you will need to add your secret key to the end of your password to get the service to respond to your requests. If you don't know your secret key, just request a new password, and Salesforce will send you an e-mail with your new secret key and instructions on how to use it.

Once a connection has been established, the application will run a query for all of the contacts against the Salesforce database. Salesforce's API is a lot like SQL. When the query result is returned, the application sets the dataProvider on a DataGrid control to show the contacts.

When I run this in Flex Builder 3, I see something like Figure 13-3.

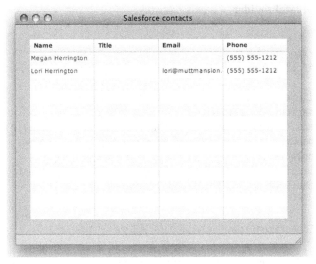

**Figure 13-3.** My Salesforce contacts

If that works, you know you can connect to the Salesforce database properly. If not, you will likely need to check your password, add the secret key value, or add your current IP address to the list of secure addresses in your Salesforce accounts administration page.

When that's all working, the next step is to write data to Salesforce. In this case, I'll allow the customer to add a contact from a VCard file. That means adding a menu item and parsing the contents of the VCard file, which I will do using the VCard parse in the AS3 Core Library at http://as3corelib.googlecode.com.

Here's the new code for the Salesforce Contacts application:

```
<?xml version="1.0" encoding="utf-8"?>
<mx:WindowedApplication xmlns:mx="http://www.adobe.com/2006/mxml"
  layout="vertical"
  creationComplete="onStartup()" title="Salesforce contacts">
<mx:Script>
<![CDATA[
import com.adobe.fileformats.vcard.Phone;
import com.adobe.fileformats.vcard.Email;
import com.salesforce.objects.SObject;
import com.adobe.fileformats.vcard.VCardParser;
import com.adobe.fileformats.vcard.VCard;
import com.salesforce.results.QueryResult;
import com.salesforce.objects.LoginRequest;
import com.salesforce.Connection;
import com.salesforce.AsyncResponder;

private var ac:Connection;

private function onQueryResult( event:QueryResult ) : void {
```

```
    dgContacts.dataProvider = event.records;
}

private function onStartup() : void {
  if(NativeApplication.supportsMenu)
  {
      var fileMenu:NativeMenuItem = NativeApplication.➥
nativeApplication.menu.getItemAt(1);
      fileMenu.submenu.addItemAt(new NativeMenuItem("-",true),0);
      var openDirectory:NativeMenuItem = new NativeMenuItem➥
( "Import Contact..." );
      openDirectory.addEventListener(Event.SELECT,onImportContact);
      fileMenu.submenu.addItemAt(openDirectory,0);
  }

  ac = new Connection();

  var login:LoginRequest = new LoginRequest();
  login.username = 'your email';
  login.password = 'your password';
  login.callback = new AsyncResponder( function (result:Object):void {
    updateContactList();
  }, function (info:Object) :void {
    trace( info );
  } );

  ac.login(login);
}
private function updateContactList() : void {
  ac.query( "SELECT FirstName, LastName, Phone, Email, Title FROM ➥
Contact WHERE AccountID=''", new AsyncResponder( onQueryResult ) );
}
private function onImportContact( event:Event ) : void {
  var f:File = File.desktopDirectory;
  f.addEventListener(Event.SELECT, fileSelected);
  f.browseForOpen( "Import Contact" );
}
private function fileSelected( event:Event ) : void
{
  var fs:FileStream = new FileStream();
  fs.open( event.target as File, FileMode.READ );
  var contents:String = fs.readUTFBytes( fs.bytesAvailable );
  fs.close();

  var ncon:SObject = new SObject( "contact" );
  for each( var line:String in contents.split( /\n/ ) ) {
    var nameFound:Array = line.match( /^N:(.*);/ );
    if ( nameFound != null && nameFound.length > 1 ) {
        var nameElems:Array = nameFound[1].split( /;/ );
        ncon.LastName = nameElems[0];
```

**502**

```
            ncon.FirstName = nameElems[1];
            break;
        }
    }

    var vcp:Array = VCardParser.parse( contents );
    var vcard:VCard = vcp[0] as VCard;
    for each ( var email:Email in vcard.emails ) {
      if ( email.type == 'work' )
        ncon.Email = email.address;
    }
    for each ( var phone:Phone in vcard.phones ) {
      if ( phone.type == 'work' )
        ncon.Phone = phone.number;
    }

    ac.create( [ ncon ],
      new AsyncResponder( function( result:Object ) : void {
      updateContactList();
    } ) );
}
]]>
</mx:Script>
<mx:DataGrid width="100%" height="100%" id="dgContacts">
<mx:columns>
   <mx:DataGridColumn headerText="Name" dataField="LastName">
     <mx:itemRenderer>
       <mx:Component>
         <mx:Text text="{data.FirstName} {data.LastName}" />
       </mx:Component>
     </mx:itemRenderer>
   </mx:DataGridColumn>
   <mx:DataGridColumn headerText="Title" dataField="Title" />
   <mx:DataGridColumn headerText="Email" dataField="Email" />
   <mx:DataGridColumn headerText="Phone" dataField="Phone" />
</mx:columns>
</mx:DataGrid>
</mx:WindowedApplication>
```

In the startup function, I now add a menu item to the File menu in addition to creating the Salesforce connection. When the customer selects the menu item, the application runs the browseForOpen method on the desktop directory to get the file. The fileSelected method then parses the file that the customer has selected using a combination of a regular expression to get the first and last name, and the VCard parser to get the e-mail addresses and phone numbers. From there, the application creates a new contact object and adds it to the database using the create method on the Salesforce connection.

When Salesforce responds that the contact has been created, the application once again queries the contact table in Salesforce and updates the DataGrid with the new records.

**503**

When I bring this up in Flex Builder 3 and select the Import Contact menu item, I see something like Figure 13-4.

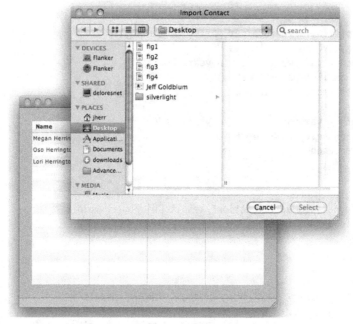

**Figure 13-4.** Adding a VCard to the Salesforce account

I then select the Jeff Goldblum contact file and click Select. This launches the file parser, which then creates a contact in the Salesforce database. The result is shown in Figure 13-5.

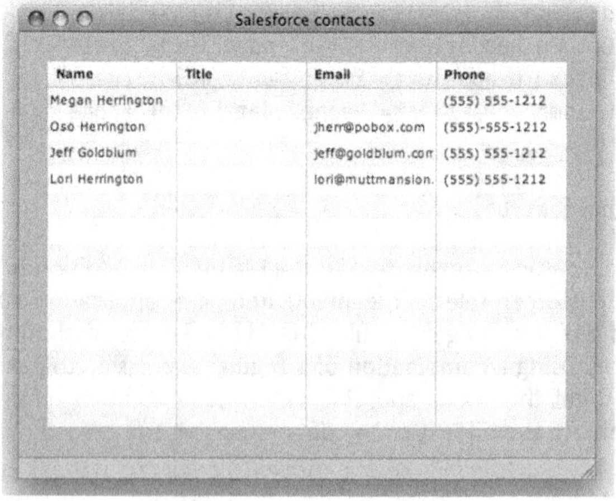

| Name | Title | Email | Phone |
|---|---|---|---|
| Megan Herrington | | | (555) 555-1212 |
| Oso Herrington | | jherr@pobox.com | (555)-555-1212 |
| Jeff Goldblum | | jeff@goldblum.com | (555) 555-1212 |
| Lori Herrington | | lori@muttmansion. | (555) 555-1212 |

**Figure 13-5.** The updated Salesforce contacts

You can get access to every element of your Salesforce application through this extensive Flex API. Salesforce, the company, has entered into a strategic partnership with Adobe around Flex, so it is committed to the resulting Flex/Salesforce API.

# Using Amazon S3 for file sharing

An important part of collaboration is sharing resources like documents, images, and other files. To make that easy, Amazon has created a set of services for Web 2.0 applications, including one called S3, which is a distributed storage service. For a small monthly fee, you can store any type of data you want on S3 and access it from anywhere.

To get started, you need to sign up for the S3 service. You do that by going to the Amazon Web Services site (http://www.amazonaws.com), creating an Amazon account (if you don't have one already), and adding the S3 service to it. This is shown in Figure 13-6.

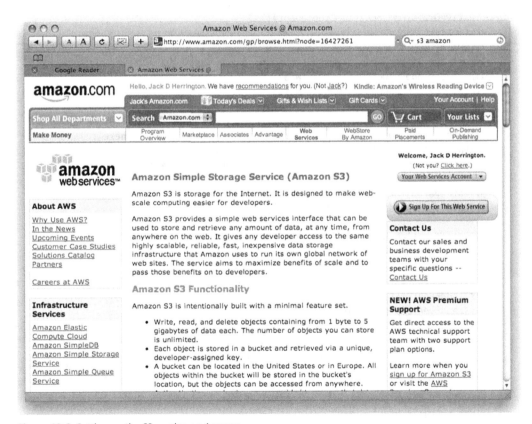

**Figure 13-6.** Setting up the S3 service on Amazon

From here, you will get a public key and a secret key to the S3 service. You will need both of these to read and write data to S3.

As an example, I'm going to build a drag-and-drop repository for images, where the images them-selves are hosted on S3. To create it easily, I'm going to use the excellent Amazon Web API for Flex library (http://code.google.com/p/as3awss3lib/). This library also requires the AS3 Crypto library (http://crypto.hurlant.com/), and the AS3 Core Library (http://code.google.com/p/as3corelib/).

To start, I create a new AIR application and add the necessary AS3 libraries to the project. I then add the following code to the application:

```
<?xml version="1.0" encoding="utf-8"?>
<mx:WindowedApplication xmlns:mx="http://www.adobe.com/2006/mxml"
  layout="vertical"
  creationComplete="onStartup()" height="600" width="800"
  title="S3 Image Store"
  paddingBottom="5" paddingLeft="5" paddingRight="5"
  paddingTop="5" nativeDragEnter="onNativeDragEnter(event);"
  nativeDragDrop="onNativeDrop(event);">
<mx:Script>
<![CDATA[
import com.adobe.webapis.awss3.S3Object;
import com.adobe.webapis.awss3.AWSS3Event;
import com.adobe.webapis.awss3.AWSS3;
import flash.filesystem.*;

private static const PUBLIC_KEY:String = 'Put your public key here';
private static const SECRET_KEY:String = 'Put your secret key here';
private static const BUCKET_NAME:String = 'Your bucket name';

private var s3:AWSS3;
private var uplodingImages:Array = [];

private function onStartup() : void {
  s3 = new AWSS3(PUBLIC_KEY,SECRET_KEY);
  s3.addEventListener(AWSS3Event.BUCKET_CREATED,onBucketCreatedReturn);
  s3.addEventListener(AWSS3Event.OBJECT_SAVED,onObjectSavedReturn);
  s3.addEventListener(AWSS3Event.LIST_OBJECTS,onObjectListReturn);
  s3.addEventListener(AWSS3Event.OBJECT_RETRIEVED,onObjectGet);
  s3.createNewBucket(BUCKET_NAME);

  s3images.dataProvider = File.applicationStorageDirectory.➥
getDirectoryListing();
}
private function onObjectGet( event:AWSS3Event ) : void {
  var s3obj:S3Object = event.data as S3Object;

  if ( File.applicationStorageDirectory.exists == false )
    File.applicationStorageDirectory.createDirectory();
```

```
   var f:File = new File( File.applicationStorageDirectory.nativePath + ➥
File.separator + s3obj.key );
  var fs:FileStream = new FileStream();
  fs.open( f, FileMode.WRITE );
  fs.writeBytes( s3obj.bytes, 0, s3obj.size );
  fs.close();

  s3images.dataProvider = File.applicationStorageDirectory.➥
getDirectoryListing();
}
private function onObjectSavedReturn( event:AWSS3Event ) : void {
  s3.listObjects(BUCKET_NAME);
  s3images.dataProvider = File.applicationStorageDirectory.➥
getDirectoryListing();
  uploadImage();
}
private function onObjectListReturn( event:AWSS3Event ) : void {
   for each ( var s3obj:S3Object in event.data ) {
      var f:File = new File( File.applicationStorageDirectory.➥
nativePath + File.separator + s3obj.key );
      if ( f.exists == false )
        s3.getObject(BUCKET_NAME,s3obj.key);
   }
}
private function onBucketCreatedReturn( event:AWSS3Event ) : void {
  s3.listObjects(BUCKET_NAME);
}
private function uploadImage() : void {
  if ( uplodingImages.length > 0 ) {
    var f:File = uplodingImages.pop();
    s3.saveObject(BUCKET_NAME,f.name,'image/jpeg',f);
    s3upload.dataProvider = uplodingImages;
  }
}
private function onNativeDragEnter( event:NativeDragEvent ) : void {
 if(event.clipboard.hasFormat(ClipboardFormats.FILE_LIST_FORMAT)) {
    var files:Array = event.clipboard.getData(ClipboardFormats.➥
FILE_LIST_FORMAT) as Array;
    if( files.length > 0 ) NativeDragManager.acceptDragDrop(this);
  }
}
private function onNativeDrop( event:NativeDragEvent ) : void {
  for each ( var f:File in event.clipboard.getData(
  ClipboardFormats.FILE_LIST_FORMAT) as Array )
    uplodingImages.push(f);
  s3upload.dataProvider = uplodingImages;
  uploadImage();
}
]]>
```

```
    </mx:Script>
    <mx:VDividedBox width="100%" height="100%">
    <mx:Panel title="S3 Images" width="100%" height="60%">
      <mx:TileList id="s3images" width="100%" height="100%" >
        <mx:itemRenderer>
          <mx:Component>
            <mx:HBox paddingBottom="5" paddingLeft="5" paddingRight="5"
              paddingTop="5">
              <mx:Image source="{data.url}" height="150" width="150"
                horizontalAlign="center" verticalAlign="middle" />
            </mx:HBox>
          </mx:Component>
        </mx:itemRenderer>
      </mx:TileList>
    </mx:Panel>
    <mx:Panel title="Uploading Files" width="100%" height="40%">
      <mx:TileList id="s3upload" width="100%" height="100%">
        <mx:itemRenderer>
          <mx:Component>
            <mx:HBox paddingBottom="5" paddingLeft="5" paddingRight="5"
              paddingTop="5">
              <mx:Image source="{data.url}" height="150" width="150"
                horizontalAlign="center" verticalAlign="middle" />
            </mx:HBox>
          </mx:Component>
        </mx:itemRenderer>
      </mx:TileList>
    </mx:Panel>
    </mx:VDividedBox>
    </mx:WindowedApplication>
```

It may look complex, but it really isn't. The code starts in the onStartup method, which connects to S3. It then creates the bucket for the images if there isn't one already. (**Bucket** is S3 parlance for a folder.) You can give your bucket any name you choose, but it must be unique across the entire S3 service.

From there, the application gets the contents of the bucket by calling listObjects on the S3 connection. That method calls back to onObjectListReturn, which in turn calls getObject for any file that has not been previously downloaded. The getObject method calls back to onObjectGet, which stores the image locally for fast access. Each time the local store is updated, the dataProvider is set on the list of images in the user interface, which is updated to show the thumbnails of the local images.

To facilitate the drag and drop, I include two event handlers, onNativeDragEnter and onNativeDrop. The onNativeDragEnter method is called whenever a customer drags something over the window. The code checks to see whether it's a list of files, and if so, it says it can handle the drop. The onNativeDrop method is called if the customer does indeed drop the files onto the application. It uses the uploadImage method to add the images to S3 one by one.

When I bring this application up in Flex Builder 3 and drag a few images onto it, I see something like Figure 13-7.

**Figure 13-7.** The shared S3 image store application

Anyone I give this application to can then use it to add their files to a central repository of images. And since all of the files are downloaded locally, we can all share all of the files as a community.

Of course, you can use this code to manage any types of files, not just images.

## Hacking YouTube

If there is one service that typifies Web 2.0, it's YouTube. Something that has always frustrated me about YouTube is that it's bound to the online nature of the network. There is no offline access mode. To fix that, I built a small AIR application that uses YouTube's feeds to find videos, and then downloads and caches the videos for later playback offline.

This application requires the AS3 Core Library (http://code.google.com/p/as3corelib/). This library provides a JSON interpreter that's used to parse the video details from YouTube's HTML page. With these details, the code can get direct access to the raw FLV file that contains the video.

The code for this application is shown here:

```
<?xml version="1.0" encoding="utf-8"?>
<mx:WindowedApplication xmlns:mx="http://www.adobe.com/2006/mxml"
    layout="horizontal"
```

**509**

```
   width="800" height="600" paddingBottom="5" paddingLeft="5"
   paddingRight="5" paddingTop="5"
   creationComplete="updateLocalVideoList()">
<mx:Script>
<![CDATA[
import com.adobe.serialization.json.JSONDecoder;
import mx.rpc.events.ResultEvent;

namespace atom = "http://www.w3.org/2005/Atom";
namespace media = "http://search.yahoo.com/mrss/";

private function onSearch(  ) : void {
  srchYoutube.send();
}

private function onSearchResult( event:ResultEvent ) : void {
  use namespace atom;
  use namespace media;
  var movieList:Array = [];
  for each( var entry:XML in event.result..entry ) {
    var group:XML = entry.group[0];
    movieList.push( {
      id:group.player.@url.toString(),
      description:entry.content.toString(),
      thumbnail:group.thumbnail[0].@url.toString() } );
  }
  srchFound.dataProvider = movieList;
}

private function onThumbComplete( movieData:Object,
   event:Event ) : void {
  var stream:URLStream = event.target as URLStream;
  var movieID:String = movieData.id.split( /=/ )[1];

  var byteLength:int = stream.bytesAvailable;
  var bytes:ByteArray = new ByteArray();
  stream.readBytes( bytes, 0, byteLength );
  stream.close();

  if ( File.applicationStorageDirectory.exists == false )
     File.applicationStorageDirectory.createDirectory();

  var f:File = new File( File.applicationStorageDirectory.nativePath + ➥
File.separator + movieID + '.jpg' );
  var fs:FileStream = new FileStream();
  fs.open( f, FileMode.WRITE );
  fs.writeBytes( bytes, 0, byteLength );
  fs.close();
```

```
    updateLocalVideoList();
}

private function onVideoComplete( movieData:Object,
 event:Event ) : void {
  var stream:URLStream = event.target as URLStream;
  var movieID:String = movieData.id.split( /=/ )[1];

  var byteLength:int = stream.bytesAvailable;
  var bytes:ByteArray = new ByteArray();
  stream.readBytes( bytes, 0, byteLength );
  stream.close();

  if ( File.applicationStorageDirectory.exists == false )
     File.applicationStorageDirectory.createDirectory();

  var f:File = new File( File.applicationStorageDirectory.nativePath + ➥
File.separator + movieID + '.flv' );
  var fs:FileStream = new FileStream();
  fs.open( f, FileMode.WRITE );
  fs.writeBytes( bytes, 0, byteLength );
  fs.close();

  updateLocalVideoList();
}

private function onHTMLReturn( movieData:Object,
  event:ResultEvent ) : void {
  var youTubeHTML:String = event.result.toString();

  var found:Array = youTubeHTML.match( /var swfArgs =(.*?);/ );
  var argsJS:JSONDecoder = new JSONDecoder( found[1] );
  var args:Object = argsJS.getValue();

  var tmpURL:String = 'http://youtube.com/get_video.php';
  var first:Boolean = true;
  for( var k:String in args ) {
    if ( args[k] != null && args[k].toString().length > 0 ) {
      tmpURL += first ? '?' : '&';
      first = false;
      tmpURL += k+'='+escape(args[k]);
    }
  }

  var thumbReq:URLRequest = new URLRequest( movieData.thumbnail );
  var thumbLoader:URLStream = new URLStream();
  thumbLoader.addEventListener(Event.COMPLETE, function ( event:Event )
  : void { onThumbComplete( movieData, event ); } );
  thumbLoader.load( thumbReq );
```

```
    var flvReq:URLRequest = new URLRequest( tmpURL );
    var flvLoader:URLStream = new URLStream();
    flvLoader.addEventListener(Event.COMPLETE, function ( event:Event ) :
    void { onVideoComplete( movieData, event ); } );
    flvLoader.load( flvReq );
}

private function downloadVideo() : void {
  var htmlGet:HTTPService = new HTTPService();
  htmlGet.resultFormat = 'text';
  htmlGet.url = srchFound.selectedItem.id;
  htmlGet.addEventListener(ResultEvent.RESULT, function(
   event:ResultEvent ) : void
   { onHTMLReturn( srchFound.selectedItem, event ); } );
  htmlGet.send();
}

private function playVideo() : void {
  movieDisplay.source = localList.selectedItem.movie.url;
  movieDisplay.play();
}

private function updateLocalVideoList() : void {
    var fileNames:Object = new Object();
    for each ( var file:File in File.applicationStorageDirectory.➥
getDirectoryListing() ) {
        var fName:String = file.name.split( /[.]/ )[0];
        fileNames[ fName ] = true;
    }
    var movieList:Array = [];
    for( var fileKey:String in fileNames ) {
        var thumb:File = new File( File.applicationStorageDirectory.➥
nativePath + File.separator + fileKey + '.jpg' );
        var movie:File = new File( File.applicationStorageDirectory.➥
nativePath + File.separator + fileKey + '.flv' );
        if ( thumb.exists && movie.exists )
            movieList.push( { thumbnail: thumb, movie: movie } );
    }
    localList.dataProvider = movieList;
}
]]>
</mx:Script>
<mx:HTTPService id="srchYoutube"
  url="http://gdata.youtube.com/feeds/api/videos/?vq=➥
{escape(txtSearch.text)}&amp;orderby=updated"
  resultFormat="e4x" result="onSearchResult( event );" />
<mx:HDividedBox width="100%" height="100%">

<mx:Panel width="40%" title="Search" height="100%"
```

```
                  paddingBottom="5" paddingLeft="5" paddingRight="5" paddingTop="5">
    <mx:HBox width="100%">
    <mx:TextInput id="txtSearch" text="Al Gore" width="100%" />
    <mx:Button label="Search" click="onSearch()" />
    </mx:HBox>
    <mx:TileList id="srchFound" width="100%" height="100%"
      doubleClickEnabled="true"
      doubleClick="downloadVideo()">
      <mx:itemRenderer>
        <mx:Component>
          <mx:HBox paddingBottom="5" paddingLeft="5" paddingRight="5"
           paddingTop="5">
          <mx:Image source="{data.thumbnail}" toolTip="{data.description}"
            height="100" width="130">
          </mx:Image>
          </mx:HBox>
        </mx:Component>
      </mx:itemRenderer>
    </mx:TileList>
    </mx:Panel>
    <mx:Panel width="60%" height="100%" title="Offline Videos"
      paddingBottom="5" paddingLeft="5" paddingRight="5" paddingTop="5">
    <mx:HorizontalList id="localList" width="100%"
      doubleClickEnabled="true"
      doubleClick="playVideo()">
      <mx:itemRenderer>
        <mx:Component>
          <mx:HBox paddingBottom="5" paddingLeft="5" paddingRight="5"
           paddingTop="5">
          <mx:Image source="{data.thumbnail.url}" height="100" width="130">
          </mx:Image>
          </mx:HBox>
        </mx:Component>
      </mx:itemRenderer>
    </mx:HorizontalList>
    <mx:HBox width="100%" height="100%" verticalAlign="middle"
      horizontalAlign="center">
    <mx:VideoDisplay id="movieDisplay" width="400" height="300" />
    </mx:HBox>
    </mx:Panel>

    </mx:HDividedBox>
    </mx:WindowedApplication>
```

Much like the user interface shown in Figure 13-8, the code for this application is really broken into two parts. The first is the search portion, on the left of the display, which uses YouTube's feed system to run searches for video and to present thumbnails. The right side of the display shows the current videos that are stored locally and starts playback if the customer double-clicks a video.

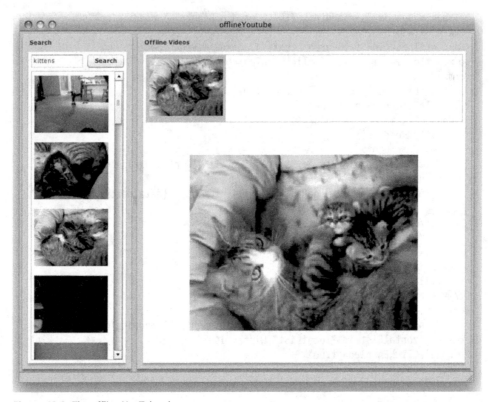

**Figure 13-8.** The offline YouTube viewer

The search code starts with the onSearch method, which sends a request to the YouTube search service. The XML returned from the service is parsed in the onSearchResult method. That method sets the dataProvider on the List object to show the thumbnails of the videos that were found.

The downloads start when the user double-clicks an item in the search list. From there, the downloadVideo method is called. This method gets the HTML page for the requested video and finds the JavaScript portion that contains the details necessary for the request to get_video.php. This information is parsed out in the onHTMLReturn method.

The onHTMLReturn method makes a request for the thumbnail and the video, which are both stored in the local directory. Once the downloads are complete, the updateVideoList is called. That method looks at the local directory to see what videos are available and updates the list of thumbnails on the right-hand panel of the display.

When the user double-clicks a local video, the VideoDisplay object is given the URL of the local file, and playback begins.

## Summary

Flash and Flex are already key components of successful Web 2.0 applications. The ability to view video, reliably connect to services, and work across platforms and even on the desktop is indispensable to Web 2.0 developers. Hopefully this chapter has given you a taste of the types of things that Flex can be used for in this context. I can't wait to see where you take it from here.

In the next chapter, you'll move from working with images to the fascinating world of audio and video streaming with Flex.

## Chapter 14

# FACILITATING AUDIO AND VIDEO STREAMING

By Elad Elrom

Adobe Flash Video has become the standard in delivering video over the Web, and it is being used on sites such as YouTube, Google Video, Yahoo! Video, and many others.

> The term **Flash Video** is used to describe an FLV file format. FLV is a compressed video format that can be viewed using the Flash Player.

The next major step in Flash Video is here. With the release of Flash Player 9.0.115.0, Adobe has pushed the envelope and included support for other formats such as H.264 (MPEG-4) video as well as the High Efficiency AAC (HE-AAC) audio codec.

In this chapter, I will show you how to develop an exciting high-definition (HD) quality video player application similar in basic functionality to YouTube (see Figure 14-1). The application will be developed using enterprise-level software and applying best practices, as it is intended to support a large number of concurrent users.

Combine an HD Flash Video application with today's increasing bandwidth, and you have a video player application capable of delivering hardware-scaled, HD content to fill the entire screen with video files quickly downloadable from the Web.

**Figure 14-1.** VideoList application

Since this chapter is mostly hands on, I decided to split the development of the application into parts. You can visit http://www.friendsofed.com to download the project files.

Notice that the project includes seven steps. Each time a step is completed, I will tell you so you will be able to compare your project with mine and ensure we are on the same page. Additionally, I tried to keep it as simple as possible without assigning too many CSS styles or extra code. I kept the application "bare bones" so that you will be able to change it to meet your requirements as well as easily understand it and how it was built.

# Planning phase

Our video application will store information such as user information, videos, tags, and categories.

As you recall from Chapter 3, I spoke about stateful client-server architecture. Before we build our application, we need to decide the technologies we will be using in our remote server (see Figure 14-2).

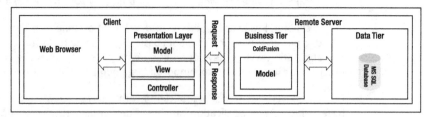

**Figure 14-2.** Client, remote server diagram

## Presentation layer

For the presentation layer, we will be using Cairngorm as the framework, which was introduced in Chapter 1.

## Why Cairngorm?

Cairngorm is not the ideal solution for all Flex applications. In software development, simplicity is key when developing applications. For instance, small user interfaces requiring little user interaction will be much simpler and easier to read and understand without the use of Cairngorm.

Our case is a good candidate for using Cairngorm since we are developing an enterprise application that will often be using many services to update the model between the server and the client.

Our application is also intended to call many **user gestures** (think of each gesture as a user interaction). Our goal is to be able to easily maintain and scale the codebase since there is a good chance that an application of this size is going to be written by more than one developer, meaning a few developers may be working on the same codebase at the same time.

## Business layer

For the business layer, we will be using ColdFusion for all of our services. The reason we choose ColdFusion is that Adobe has created the ColdFusion/Flex Application Wizard to generate the services, client model, server model, and CRUD operations easily. We will be able to take advantage of this wizard's ability to generate our code quickly, and even the most anti-ColdFusion developer will be impressed. Additionally, ColdFusion has an advantage in that it allows you to easily switch to a different data layer with almost no change to your code.

## Data layer

We will use Microsoft SQL Server (MS SQL Server) database to store our information. Additionally, I will show you how to switch your data layer to MySQL. I picked MS SQL Server since MS SQL Server has proven in benchmark studies to be a good solution when performance and scalability are important; however, you can use any database you feel comfortable with. ColdFusion allows connection to any data source as long as you have the appropriate Java driver.

# Setting up your environment and configuring the application

Now that you know the technologies we will be using, you can install all the necessary software as well as tools that will make life easier. For development, we will be using our local machine to act as the remote server, so we will be able to test our application easily. Once we are done testing, we can easily upload the application to a live server.

> Visit http://www.friendsofed.com/ to download the project. This section is going to be under the VideoList/Step1 directory.

# ColdFusion 8 Developer Edition

You can download ColdFusion developer edition for free from Adobe: https://www.adobe.com/cfusion/tdrc/index.cfm?product=coldfusion.

During installation, choose the default settings and make the following selections:

- Select Developer Edition when asked for a serial number. Select Server configuration when asked for the type of server.
- Select Built-in web server for the web server type.

Once installation is complete, go to the following URL to ensure ColdFusion was successfully installed as well as to finalize your installation: http://livedocs.adobe.com/coldfusion/8/htmldocs/help.html?content=othertechnologies_11.html.

# Installing ColdFusion extensions for Eclipse

You will need to have the ColdFusion extensions for Eclipse installed. If they are not already installed on your system, instructions on how to install the extensions can be found here: http://localhost:8500/CFIDE/administrator/index.cfm.

# Installing the CFEclipse plug-in

The CFEclipse plug-in for Eclipse is not necessary, but because we will be changing ColdFusion scripts as well as looking at components in tree view, having this plug-in may prove helpful. You can view instructions and download the plug-in from here: http://www.cfeclipse.org/download.cfm/.

# Installing Microsoft SQL Server 2005 Express

> *I will show you how to use a MySQL database, so there is no need to install Microsoft SQL 2005 or SQL Server Management Studio if you decide to use a different data layer. In this case, skip all sections related to installing and setting up MS SQL Server.*

Microsoft provides a free version of its MS SQL Server called SQL Server 2005 Express, which has reduced functionality and limited user capabilities, at the following site: http://www.microsoft.com/sql/editions/express/default.mspx.

# Installing SQL Server Management Studio Express

This tool will enable you to manage the MS SQL Server. You can download it from the same site you use to download MS SQL Server.

During installation, choose the default settings, and for username and password, select Windows Authentication.

After installation is complete, ensure the database was installed correctly by navigating to Program Files ➤ Microsoft SQL Server 2005 ➤ SQL Server Management Studio Express. Log in using your Windows Authentication username and password (see Figure 14-3).

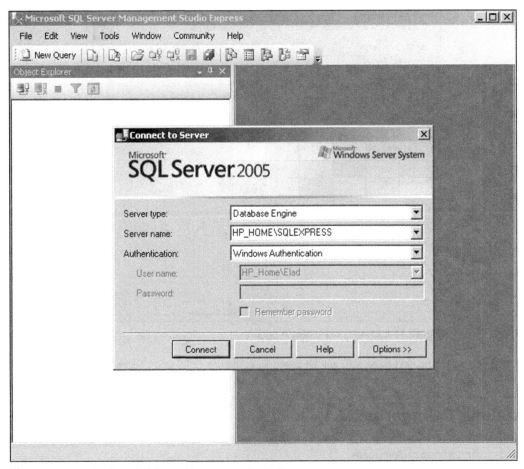

**Figure 14-3.** Logging in to SQL Server Management Studio Express

# Setting the project workbench in Eclipse

Open Eclipse and set your workbench to your ColdFusion location. The default location of ColdFusion is C:\ColdFusion8\wwwroot.

The reason we will be using the ColdFusion directory as our work area is that we want our application to be able to run the ColdFusion services when we compile the application without changing the default settings. By default, localhost is mapped to point to the ColdFusion directory.

Create a new Flex project by selecting File ➤ New ➤ Flex Project. Call the project VideoList. Select ColdFusion for the server technology (see Figure 14-4).

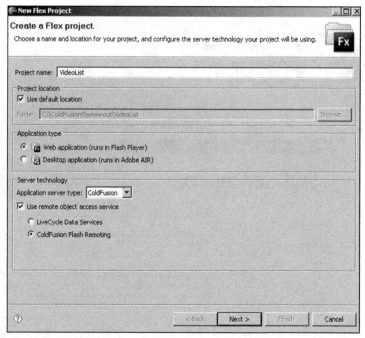

**Figure 14-4.** Creating our VideoList project

Once you go to the next page, you will be asked to configure ColdFusion Server. Choose the default settings, and click Finish once done.

## Installing Cairngorm 2.2.1

Next, download the latest Cairngorm framework from here: http://labs.adobe.com/wiki/index.php/Cairngorm:Downloads.

- Be sure to download both binary (SWC) and source ZIP files.
- Create the directory structure and place the source directory here: VideoList/src/com/Cairngorm.
- Place the SWC here: VideoList/src/com/Cairngorm.

The reason we are using both the binary and the source is that it allows us to "step into" the code and view the classes; however, if changes are made to the code by mistake, it will not affect our code.

Right-click the project and select Project Properties ➤ Flex Build Path and click the Library path tab. Then click Edit to edit the folder path under Source attachment (see Figure 14-5). Paste in the location of Cairngorm: com/adobe/cairngorm.

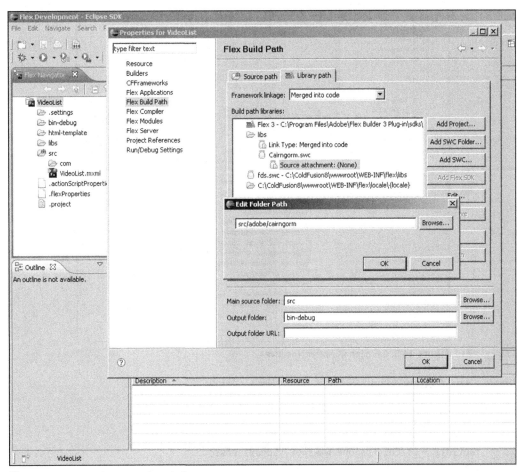

**Figure 14-5.** VideoList Properties window

# Installing the Cairngen tool

Cairngen is a small Ant utility script that allows automatic generation of many common classes needed for Cairngorm (see Figure 14-6). Download Cairngen from here: http://code.google.com/p/cairngen/.

**Figure 14-6.** Cairngen in Ant perspective

Create a new directory called tools and unzip Cairngen into it.

Edit the file tools/project.properties by setting the following:

```
project.name = VideoList
root.dir = C:/ColdFusion8/wwwroot/VideoList/src
com.dir = com
domain.dir = elromdesign
project.dir = VideoList
```

Every class that is generated by Cairngen will have a custom comment header. Place your own header message here: tools/build/templates/file-header-copy.tpl.

# Configuring Cairngen

Open the Ant perspective by selecting Window Show ➤ View ➤ Other ➤ Ant and clicking OK. Drag and drop tools/build/build.xml into the Ant perspective.

First we want to create the Cairngorm directory structure. We can use Cairngen to generate the directories for us. Click `create-cairngorm-directories` in the Ant perspective. Refresh your project, and you will see the directories under the `src/com` directory. Next, click create-cairngorm-project, which will generate your `FrontController`, `ModelLocator`, and `Services` classes.

If you refresh your project in Flex Navigation view, you will be able to see the Cairngorm directories as well as the classes that were added.

We are ready to get started with the development of our project, now that you have all of the necessary software and tools installed. In the next sections, we will create the remote server data layer and the business layer. You can download this section, which includes the progress we have made so far, from `http://www.friendsofed.com`. The project is under the directory VideoList/Step1.

# Creating the server data layer

The first step in designing and creating our database is to understand the business needs, which entails identifying all the business rules we need to apply to the application. Understanding the business rules is an important step in creating any database. Based on these rules, we will be able to design our database. Many developers make the mistake of dealing with the business rules in the presentation layer. At that point, it's too late and you can easily add overhead to your application.

Here are the business rules we need to keep in mind:

- Users can sign up and log in.
- Users will be able to upload videos with different file formats.
- Each video will be related to a user.
- A user cannot be removed once videos are attached to that user's account.
- Users can be in an active or inactive status.
- Each video will be assigned to a subcategory.
- Each subcategory is related to a main category.
- Users can tag videos with many keywords.
- Users can view statistical information regarding a video.
- Users can set and view ratings regarding a video.

Based on these business rules, we can now design our database (see Figure 14-7). Let's identify the different entities and their properties:

- Users: Will store all the users accounts and users' personal information
- Videos: Will store the video information
- UsersVideosINT: Will store the videos that each user uploads
- VideoCategory: Will store a list of categories and subcategories
- VideoCategoriesINT: Will store a list of all the categories each video belongs to
- VideoTag: Will store a list of keywords
- VideoTagsINT: Will store a list of videos and the tag IDs associated with each video

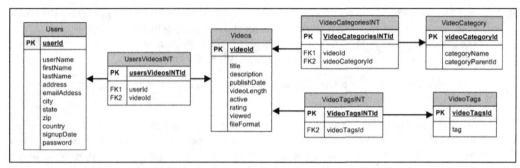

**Figure 14-7.** UML database entities diagram for our VideoList application

Based on our UML design, we can create the database.

1. Open Microsoft SQL Server Management Studio Express. Right-click Database and select New Database. For the database name, type VideoList and click OK. You will see VideoList under the available databases since you created it previously.

2. Right-click VideoList and select New Query. Copy the content of MSSQLDumpFile.sql, which is available with the project, or listed below, paste the complete SQL command into the query window, and click Execute to run the script. In the messages window, you should see a confirmation of success: Command(s) completed successfully.

> *I will not go into detail about how the following SQL command was generated. You can of course write it on your own if you are familiar with the SQL language. Otherwise, convert your database design into a Microsoft Access database following the same entity relationship and properties structure as in Figure 14-7. Then you can generate an ODBC connection or use third-party software to upload the database into MS SQL Server.*

```
USE [VideoList]
SET ANSI_NULLS ON
SET QUOTED_IDENTIFIER ON
SET ANSI_PADDING ON

CREATE TABLE [dbo].[Videos](
            [videoId] [int] IDENTITY(1,1) NOT NULL,
            [title] [varchar](255) NULL,
            [description] [text] NULL,
            [publishDate] [datetime] NULL,
            [videoLength] [int] NULL,
            [active] [bit] NULL DEFAULT ((0)),
            [rating] [int] NULL DEFAULT ((0)),
            [viewed] [int] NULL DEFAULT ((1)),
            [fileFormat] [varchar](50) NULL,
 CONSTRAINT [PK_Videos] PRIMARY KEY CLUSTERED
(
            [videoId] ASC
```

```
)WITH (PAD_INDEX  = OFF, STATISTICS_NORECOMPUTE  = ➡
OFF, IGNORE_DUP_KEY = OFF, ALLOW_ROW_LOCKS  = ➡
ON, ALLOW_PAGE_LOCKS  = ON) ON [PRIMARY] ➡
) ON [PRIMARY] TEXTIMAGE_ON [PRIMARY]

CREATE TABLE [dbo].[Users](
                [userId] [int] IDENTITY(1,1) NOT NULL,
                [userName] [varchar](100) NULL,
                [firstName] [varchar](100) NULL,
                [lastName] [varchar](100) NULL,
                [address] [varchar](255) NULL,
                [emailAddress] [varchar](255) NULL,
                [city] [varchar](100) NULL,
                [state] [varchar](50) NULL,
                [signupDate] [datetime] NULL,
                [password] [varchar](255) NULL,
 CONSTRAINT [PK_Users] PRIMARY KEY CLUSTERED
(
                [userId] ASC
)WITH (PAD_INDEX  = OFF, STATISTICS_NORECOMPUTE  = ➡
OFF, IGNORE_DUP_KEY = OFF, ALLOW_ROW_LOCKS  = ON, ➡
ALLOW_PAGE_LOCKS  = ON) ON [PRIMARY] ➡
) ON [PRIMARY]

CREATE TABLE [dbo].[VideoTags](
                [videoTagsId] [int] IDENTITY(1,1) NOT NULL,
                [tag] [int] NULL,
 CONSTRAINT [PK_VideoTags] PRIMARY KEY CLUSTERED
(
                [videoTagsId] ASC
)WITH (PAD_INDEX  = OFF, STATISTICS_NORECOMPUTE  = ➡
OFF, IGNORE_DUP_KEY = OFF, ALLOW_ROW_LOCKS  = ON, ➡
ALLOW_PAGE_LOCKS  = ON) ON [PRIMARY] ➡
) ON [PRIMARY]

CREATE TABLE [dbo].[UsersVideosINT](
                [usersVideosINTId] [int] IDENTITY(1,1) NOT NULL,
                [userId] [int] NULL,
                [videoId] [int] NULL,
 CONSTRAINT [PK_UsersVideosINT] PRIMARY KEY CLUSTERED
(
                [usersVideosINTId] ASC
)WITH (PAD_INDEX  = OFF, STATISTICS_NORECOMPUTE  = ➡
OFF, IGNORE_DUP_KEY = OFF, ALLOW_ROW_LOCKS  = ON, ➡
ALLOW_PAGE_LOCKS  = ON) ON [PRIMARY] ➡
) ON [PRIMARY]

CREATE TABLE [dbo].[VideoCategory](
                [videoCategoryId] [int] IDENTITY(1,1) NOT NULL,
```

**527**

```
                 [categoryName] [varchar](255) NULL,
                 [categoryParentId] [int] NULL,
 CONSTRAINT [PK_VideoCategory] PRIMARY KEY CLUSTERED
(
                 [videoCategoryId] ASC
)WITH (PAD_INDEX  = OFF, STATISTICS_NORECOMPUTE  = ➥
OFF, IGNORE_DUP_KEY = OFF, ALLOW_ROW_LOCKS  = ON, ➥
ALLOW_PAGE_LOCKS  = ON) ON [PRIMARY] ➥
) ON [PRIMARY]

CREATE TABLE [dbo].[VideoCategoriesINT](
                 [VideoCategoriesINTId] [int] IDENTITY(1,1) NOT NULL,
                 [videoId] [int] NULL,
                 [videoCategoryId] [int] NULL,
 CONSTRAINT [PK_VideoCategoriesINT] PRIMARY KEY CLUSTERED
(
                 [VideoCategoriesINTId] ASC
)WITH (PAD_INDEX  = OFF, STATISTICS_NORECOMPUTE  = ➥
OFF, IGNORE_DUP_KEY = OFF, ALLOW_ROW_LOCKS  = ON, ➥
ALLOW_PAGE_LOCKS  = ON) ON [PRIMARY] ➥
) ON [PRIMARY]

CREATE TABLE [dbo].[VideoTagsINT](
                 [VideoTagsINTId] [int] IDENTITY(1,1) NOT NULL,
                 [videoId] [int] NULL,
                 [videoTagsId] [int] NULL,
 CONSTRAINT [PK_VideoTagsINT] PRIMARY KEY CLUSTERED
(
                 [VideoTagsINTId] ASC
)WITH (PAD_INDEX  = OFF, STATISTICS_NORECOMPUTE  = ➥
OFF, IGNORE_DUP_KEY = OFF, ALLOW_ROW_LOCKS  = ON, ➥
ALLOW_PAGE_LOCKS  = ON) ON [PRIMARY] ➥
) ON [PRIMARY]

ALTER TABLE [dbo].[VideoCategoriesINT]  WITH ➥
CHECK ADD  CONSTRAINT ➥
[FK_VideoCategoriesINT_VideoCategory] ➥
FOREIGN KEY([videoCategoryId])
REFERENCES [dbo].[VideoCategory] ([videoCategoryId])
ALTER TABLE [dbo].[VideoCategoriesINT] ➥
CHECK CONSTRAINT ➥
[FK_VideoCategoriesINT_VideoCategory] ➥
ALTER TABLE [dbo].[VideoCategoriesINT]  WITH ➥
CHECK ADD  CONSTRAINT [FK_VideoCategoriesINT_Videos] ➥
FOREIGN KEY([videoId])
REFERENCES [dbo].[Videos] ([videoId])
ALTER TABLE [dbo].[VideoCategoriesINT] CHECK ➥
CONSTRAINT [FK_VideoCategoriesINT_Videos]
ALTER TABLE [dbo].[UsersVideosINT]  WITH CHECK ADD ➥
```

```
CONSTRAINT [FK_UsersVideosINT_Users] FOREIGN KEY([userId]) ➡
REFERENCES [dbo].[Users] ([userId])
ALTER TABLE [dbo].[UsersVideosINT] CHECK ➡
CONSTRAINT [FK_UsersVideosINT_Users]
ALTER TABLE [dbo].[UsersVideosINT]  WITH CHECK ➡
ADD  CONSTRAINT [FK_UsersVideosINT_Videos] ➡
FOREIGN KEY([videoId])
REFERENCES [dbo].[Videos] ([videoId])
ALTER TABLE [dbo].[UsersVideosINT] CHECK CONSTRAINT ➡
[FK_UsersVideosINT_Videos]
IF  EXISTS (SELECT * FROM sys.foreign_keys ➡
WHERE object_id = OBJECT_ID(N'[dbo].[FK_VideoTagsINT_Videos]') ➡
AND parent_object_id = OBJECT_ID(N'[dbo].[VideoTagsINT]'))
ALTER TABLE [dbo].[VideoTagsINT] DROP ➡
CONSTRAINT [FK_VideoTagsINT_Videos]
IF  EXISTS (SELECT * FROM sys.foreign_keys WHERE ➡
object_id = OBJECT_ID(N'[dbo].[FK_VideoTagsINT_VideoTags]') ➡
AND parent_object_id = OBJECT_ID(N'[dbo].[VideoTagsINT]'))
ALTER TABLE [dbo].[VideoTagsINT] DROP ➡
CONSTRAINT [FK_VideoTagsINT_VideoTags]

GO
```

**3.** Once the SQL command is executed, refresh the screen, and you will be able to view the entities, insert information, change entities, and much more (see Figure 14-8).

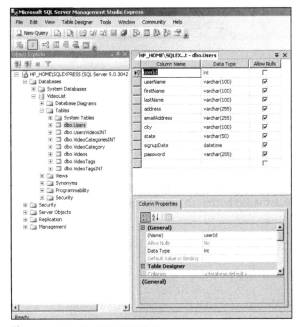

**Figure 14-8.** VideoList MS SQL Server

You can also use MySQL as your data layer using the following process.

Install XAMPP for PC (http://www.apachefriends.org/en/xampp.html) or MAMP for Mac (http://www.mamp.info/en/index.php). For tutorials and notes on how to install these tools, visit Chapter 3.

Open phpMyAdmin, located on your local machine:

    http://localhost/phpmyadmin/index.php.

Select Create new database and type in VideoList as your database name (see Figure 14-9).

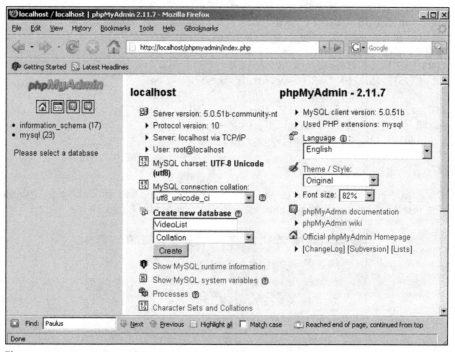

**Figure 14-9.** Creating the VideoList database

After the database is created, you will be able to see and navigate to the database (see Figure 14-10). Select the SQL tab near the top of the window and either enter the SQL command that follows or download the SQL command from http://www.friendsofed.com and paste it in (the file is called MySQLDumpFile.sql). Click the Go button to execute the SQL command.

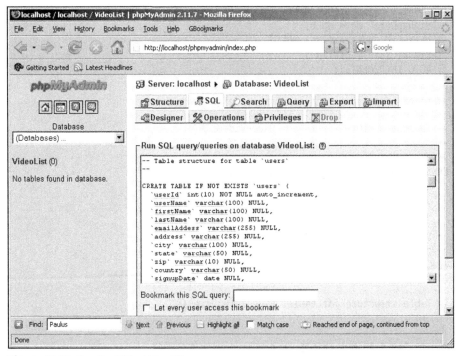

**Figure 14-10.** Creating VideoList entities

```
-- phpMyAdmin SQL Dump
-- PHP Version: 5.2.6

SET SQL_MODE="NO_AUTO_VALUE_ON_ZERO";


--
-- Database: `VideoList`
--

-- --------------------------------------------------------
--
-- Table structure for table `users`
--

CREATE TABLE IF NOT EXISTS `users` (
  `userId` int(10) NOT NULL auto_increment,
  `userName` varchar(100) NULL,
  `firstName` varchar(100) NULL,
  `lastName` varchar(100) NULL,
  `emailAddess` varchar(255) NULL,
  `address` varchar(255) NULL,
  `city` varchar(100) NULL,
  `state` varchar(50) NULL,
  `zip` varchar(10) NULL,
```

```
  `country` varchar(50) NULL,
  `signupDate` date NULL,
  `password` varchar(255) NULL,
  PRIMARY KEY  (`userId`)
) AUTO_INCREMENT=1;


-- --------------------------------------------------------
--
-- Table structure for table `UsersVideosINT`
--

CREATE TABLE IF NOT EXISTS `UsersVideosINT` (
  `usersVideosINTId` int(10) NOT NULL auto_increment,
  `userId` int(10) NOT NULL,
  `videoId` int(10) NOT NULL,
  PRIMARY KEY  (`usersVideosINTId`)
) AUTO_INCREMENT=1;


-- --------------------------------------------------------
--
-- Table structure for table `VideoCategoriesINT`
--

CREATE TABLE IF NOT EXISTS `VideoCategoriesINT` (
  `VideoCategoriesINTId` int(10) NOT NULL auto_increment,
  `videoId` int(10) NOT NULL,
  `videoCategoryId` int(10) NOT NULL,
  PRIMARY KEY  (`VideoCategoriesINTId`)
) AUTO_INCREMENT=1;



-- --------------------------------------------------------
--
-- Table structure for table `VideoCategory`
--

CREATE TABLE IF NOT EXISTS `VideoCategory` (
  `videoCategoryId` int(10) NOT NULL auto_increment,
  `categoryName` varchar(255) NOT NULL,
  `categoryParentId` int(10) NOT NULL,
  PRIMARY KEY  (`videoCategoryId`)
) AUTO_INCREMENT=1;



-- --------------------------------------------------------
--
-- Table structure for table `Videos`
--
```

```
CREATE TABLE IF NOT EXISTS `Videos` (
  `videoId` int(10) NOT NULL auto_increment,
  `title` varchar(255) NULL,
  `description` text NULL,
  `publishDate` date NULL,
  `videoLength` int(10) NULL,
  `active` tinyint(1) NULL default '0',
  `rating` int(10) NULL default '0',
  `viewed` varchar(1) default '0',
  `fileFormat` varchar(50) default NULL,
  PRIMARY KEY (`videoId`)
) AUTO_INCREMENT=1;



-- ---------------------------------------------------------
--
-- Table structure for table `VideoStatistic`
--

CREATE TABLE IF NOT EXISTS `VideoStatistic` (
  `videoStatisticId` int(10) NOT NULL auto_increment,
  `videoId` int(10) NULL,
  `rates` decimal(10,0) NULL,
  `views` int(10) NULL,
  PRIMARY KEY (`videoStatisticId`)
) AUTO_INCREMENT=1;

-- ---------------------------------------------------------
--
-- Table structure for table `VideoTags`
--

CREATE TABLE IF NOT EXISTS `VideoTags` (
  `videoTagsId` int(10) NOT NULL auto_increment,
  `tag` varchar(255) NULL,
  PRIMARY KEY (`videoTagsId`)
) AUTO_INCREMENT=1;

-- ---------------------------------------------------------
--
-- Table structure for table `VideotagsINT`
--

CREATE TABLE IF NOT EXISTS `VideotagsINT` (
  `VideoTagsINTId` int(10) NOT NULL auto_increment,
  `videoId` int(10) NULL,
  `videoTagsId` int(10) NULL,
  PRIMARY KEY (`VideoTagsINTId`)
) AUTO_INCREMENT=1;
```

At this point, you will get a message indicating the success of the operation, and you will be able to view the database. Using phpMyAdmin, you will be able to administrate the database, insert values, and much more. To learn more about phpMyAdmin, visit http://www.phpmyadmin.net/home_page/index.php.

# Creating the business layer

We created our data layer corresponding to our business rules. Our next step is to create the business layer, which will consist of the services that let us update the model on the client and the server.

As mentioned before, we will be using ColdFusion. Recall that in Chapter 4 you created a CMS system utilizing the ColdFusion wizards. We can do the same here so we will be able to view, edit, and update our application without needing to use the SQL Server Management Studio Express tool.

## Configuring ColdFusion data sources

ColdFusion allows us to manage our Data Source Names (DSNs) and access different types of data layers. ColdFusion is shipped with different types of drivers for different data sources. It also provides us the option to connect to additional data sources as long as we have the appropriate drivers.

## Configuring MS SQL Server TCP/IP settings

MS SQL Server needs to be configured in order for ColdFusion to be able to access the database. If you choose to connect to a MySQL database, you can skip this section.

1. Open Microsoft SQL Server Management Studio, and then click the register server icon to open up the Register Servers window.
2. Right-click the local instance server [*computer name*]/sqlexpress and select SQL Server Configuration Manager.
3. Right-click TCP/IP, select Enable, and double-click TCP/IP. Select IP Addresses, click Enable, and set the IP to1433 for every IP type (see Figure 14-11).

We also need a user account in order for ColdFusion to be able to access the MS SQL Server. I personally like to use the built-in system administrator username, sa, for the development environment since all the permissions are already set for that user. Keep in mind that once you switch to a production environment, you should create a fixed server role user just for ColdFusion so you can monitor its usage.

1. Set the sa password by opening Object Explorer, right-clicking the server, and selecting Security ➤ Logins. Double-click sa and set the password (see Figure 14-12).
2. Restart the SQL service for the changes to go into effect by navigating to Control Panel ➤ Administrative Tools ➤ services.lnk and finding SQL Server (SQLEXPRESS). Then right-click and select Restart.

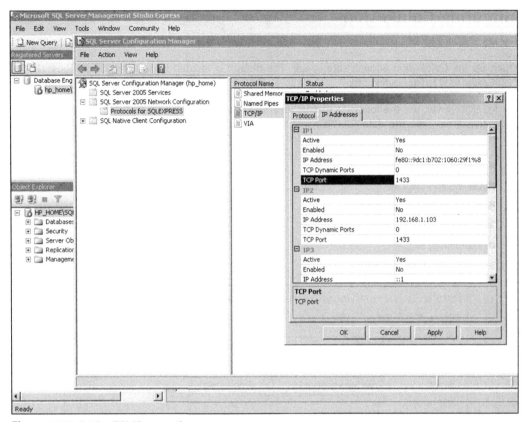

**Figure 14-11.** Setting TCP/IP properties

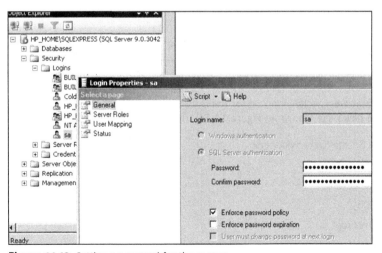

**Figure 14-12.** Setting a password for the sa user

# Configuring ColdFusion

For MS SQL and MySQL databases, you can use ColdFusion's built-in drivers to easily create a DSN.

Open up the ColdFusion administrator page. The default is located here: http://localhost:8500/ CFIDE/administrator/index.cfm.

For MS SQL Server, use the following instructions. Select Data & Services ➤ Data Sources from the left navigation area. Type the data source name, in our case VideoList, select the driver Microsoft SQL Server, click Add, and in the page that appears (shown in Figure 14-13), fill the following information:

- CF Data Source Name: VideoList
- Database: VideoList
- Server: [*Your server name*]
- Port: 1433
- User name: sa
- Password: [*Your password*]

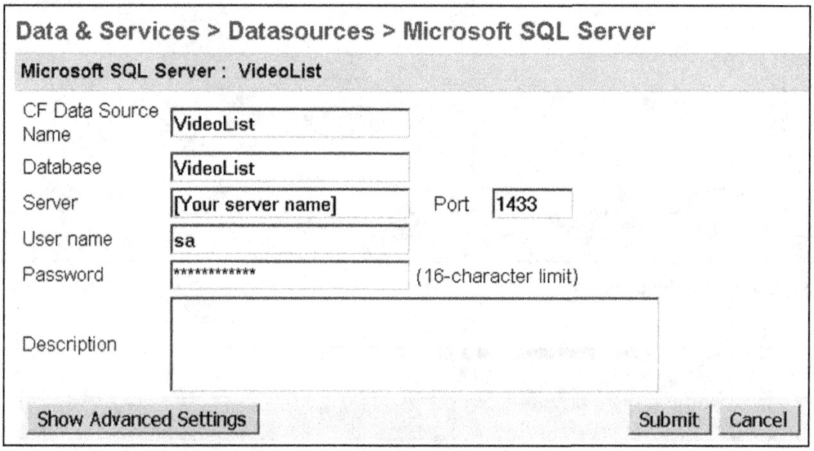

**Figure 14-13.** Setting the ColdFusion DSN for MS SQL Server

For a MySQL database, specify VideoList for the Data Source Name, choose the driver MySQL (4/5), click Add, and in the new page (shown in Figure 14-14), fill in the following information:

- CF Data Source Name: VideoList
- Database: VideoList
- Server: localhost
- Port: 3306
- User name: root
- Password: [*root has no password unless you set one*]

Click Submit once done.

Data & Services > Datasources > MySQL (4/5)

**MySQL (4/5) : VideoList1**

| | |
|---|---|
| CF Data Source Name | VideoList |
| Database | VideoList |
| Server | localhost       Port  3306 |
| Username | root |
| Password | (16-character limit) |
| Description | |

Show Advanced Settings        Submit   Cancel

**Figure 14-14.** Setting the ColdFusion DSN for MySQL

To ensure ColdFusion is connected successfully and has access to all the entities in the database, open up Eclipse and select Window ➤ Show View ➤ Other ➤ ColdFusion ➤ RDS Dataview.

This will open the RDS Dataview perspective, which will enable you to view the database. Using the RDS password that you specified during installation of ColdFusion, you will be able to expand the databases available as well as view the entities and properties (see Figure 14-15).

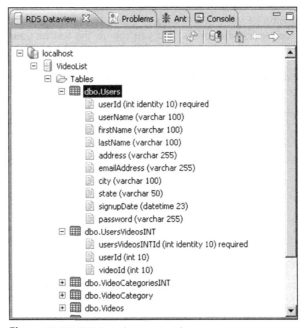

**Figure 14-15.** RDS Dataview perspective

**537**

# Creating server services

We can now create the services we will be using in our application. We will place all of our services in our project directory.

Create the directory structure shown in Figure 14-16 under components/cf.

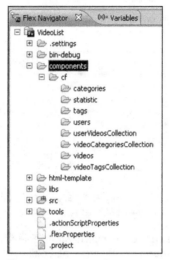

**Figure 14-16.** ColdFusion
components directory structure

We will be using ColdFusion's Create CFC Wizard to generate the services automatically. I will show you how to generate one service, dbo.Users, and you can do the rest on your own by following the same process.

1. In the RDS Dataview perspective, expand localhost and Tables. Select dbo.Users. Right-click and select ColdFusion Wizards ➤ Create CFC, as shown in Figure 14-17.

**Figure 14-17.** Selecting a ColdFusion wizard from the RDS Dataview

2. The CFC Value Object Wizard opens up. You can set the CFC directory and package to the directory structure you created: VideoList/components/cf/users. Additionally, you can generate the client VO automatically. Following are the settings shown in Figure 14-18:

- Set the AS folder to VideoList/src/com/elromdesign/VideoList/vo.

- Set the AS3 package name to src.com.elromdesign.VideoList.vo.

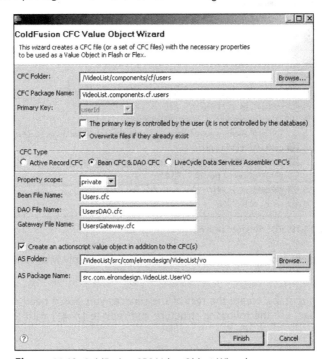

**Figure 14-18.** ColdFusion CFC Value Object Wizard

> *The* CFC Package Name *text input box is filled in automatically once you insert the CFC folder information. However, make sure it follows the same structure; otherwise, ColdFusion will not be able to map to the correct component, and you will get an error message.*

Four classes were created automatically for us: Users.cfc, UsersDAO.cfc, UsersGateway.cfc, and UserVO.

3. Open the Services browser by selecting Window ➤ Show View ➤ Other ➤ ColdFusion ➤ Services Browser. In this perspective, you can view the content of each class easily (see Figure 14-19).

- UsersDAO.cfc: Includes a DAO (Data Access Object) similar to a Java DAO and includes the CRUD components.

- UsersGateway.cfc: Includes all the methods you will be using to submit CRUD SQL commands.

- Users.cfc: Represents the server model. All of the work of serializing was automatically done for us.

- UserVO: Represents the client model, which ColdFusion generated for us here: src/com/ elromdesign/VideoList/User.

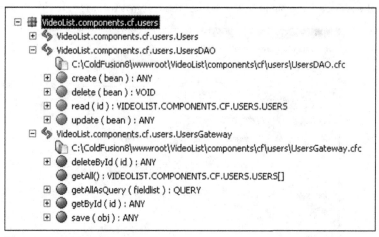

**Figure 14-19.** RDS Services browser

**4.** Refactor the client model name Users to UserInfoVO to comply with Cairngorm's naming conventions.

Following the preceding steps, create the rest of the services you would need on your own. For the CFC folder and package, use the following structure and replace [*name*] with the appropriate name from Table 14-1:

- /VideoList/components/cf/[*name*]
- VideoList.components.cf.[*name*]

**Table 14-1.** Create Services Information

| DBO | CFC Folder and Package | Refactor |
| --- | --- | --- |
| Users | users | UserInfoVO |
| UsersVideosINT | userVideosCollection | UserVideosCollectionVO |
| VideoCategoriesINT | videoCategoriesCollection | VideoCategoriesCollectionVO |
| VideoCategory | categories | VideoCategoriesVO |
| Videos | videos | VideoVO |
| VideoStatistic | statistic | VideoStatisticVO |
| VideoTags | tags | VideoTagsVO |
| VideoTagsINT | videoTagsCollection | VideoTagsCollectionVO |

Open one of the client VO classes, such as UserVO. Notice that each class points to the service class, for instance:

```
[RemoteClass(alias="VideoList.components.cf.users.Users")]
```

Even if you are not a big fan of ColdFusion, you must admit that what you accomplished in about 30 minutes to an hour with ColdFusion could have taken you at least two full days of work otherwise. A version of the project that shows the progress we have made so far can be downloaded from http://www.friendsofed.com. The project is under the directory VideoList/Step2.

# Creating the presentation layer

At this point, we have our remote server ready with its database and services, and we can start building the presentation layer—the front end of our application. The application will have four main elements:

- Signup and login page
- Page to let users upload their videos
- List component to display video thumbnails
- High-definition video component

## Creating the signup and login component

The signup and login forms will be combined into one component so that the user will be able to toggle between the forms as needed.

### Creating signup and login sequences

Before we create the UI components themselves, let's create the sequences we need, which will include the events, commands, delegates, and services necessary for the signup and login components.

We will need the following sequences:

- SetUserInfo: The sequence will receive a UserInfoVO and pass the information to the delegate.
- GetUserInfo: The sequence will search for a user based on e-mail address and password.

Both of these commands will share the same delegate since they will be using the same service component.

Let's take a step back and look at Figure 14-20 so you can understand the process. The user submits a form with his information. SetUserInfoEvent is dispatched, which passes the data to the front controller (VideoListController), and the call is assigned to the SetUserInfoCommand command. Once the command is executed, a UserDelegate delegate is assigned to handle the service request. This delegate sends the request to the service (Services.mxml), and then returns the results back to the SetUserInfoCommand command. Once the results get back to this command, UserInfoVO is stored at the model locator and displayed at the user interface.

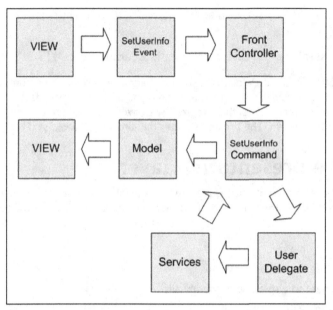

**Figure 14-20.** SetUserInfo sequence

To create the sequences, we will be using the Cairngen tool, which you installed earlier. To use this tool, we just need to set the sequence name we want to use and run a command. Cairngen will generate the classes automatically.

Set the sequence name by opening tools/project.properties and specifying the following:

```
sequence.name = SetUserInfo, GetUserInfo
```

Now run the command by dragging and dropping the tools/build.xml script into the Ant perspective and double-clicking create-multiple-sequences-exclude-delegates, as you can see in Figure 14-21.

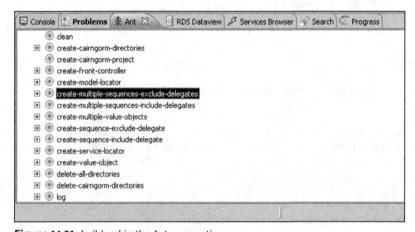

**Figure 14-21.** build.xml in the Ant perspective

Refresh your project, and you will see that the following files were added to the project under the directory VideoList/src/com/elromdesign/VideoList:

- commands/GetUserInfoCommand.as
- commands/SetUserInfoCommand.as
- events/GetUserInfoCommand.as
- events/SetUserInfoCommand.as

Also if you open your front controller, VideoListController, you will see that the following commands were added automatically:

- this.addCommand( SetUserInfoEvent.SETUSERINFO_EVENT, SetUserInfoCommand );
- this.addCommand( GetUserInfoEvent.GETUSERINFO_EVENT, GetUserInfoCommand );

The front controller enlists all the commands and will be able to map each event to the related command in that sequence.

When the event is dispatched, we need to pass the information from the model to the delegate, which will invoke the service.

To pass the data from the model to the delegate, create the following members in GetUserInfoEvent:

- public var emailAddress:String;
- public var password:String;

Also, change the default constructor to receive these parameters so it will be able to create an instance of the event and include the necessary parameters:

```
public function GetUserInfoEvent(emailAddress:String, password:String)
{
  this.emailAddress = emailAddress;
  this.password = password;
  super( GETUSERINFO_EVENT );
}
```

Setting SetUserInfoEvent, we need to pass the user information (UserInfoVO) from the model to the delegate, which will save the data. Create the following member in SetUserInfoEvent:

```
public var userInfo:UserInfoVO;
```

Next, set the default constructor:

```
public function SetUserInfoEvent(userInfo:UserInfoVO)
{
    this.userInfo = userInfo;
    super( SETUSERINFO_EVENT );
}
```

Now that the events are ready, we need to create our service and delegate classes. Open business/Services.mxml, which was generated automatically by Cairngen.

Each service will have its own service component and a constant for convenience in assigning the service we need.

```
<?xml version="1.0" encoding="utf-8"?>
<cairngorm:ServiceLocator xmlns:mx="http://www.adobe.com/2006/mxml"
          xmlns:cairngorm="com.adobe.cairngorm.business.*" >

    <mx:Script>
        <![CDATA[

            //todo: implement service constants
            public static const USER_INFORMATION:String ➥
= "userInformation";

        ]]>
    </mx:Script>

    <mx:RemoteObject id="userInformation" destination="ColdFusion"
        source="VideoList.components.cf.users.UsersGateway">
        <mx:method name=" getByEmailAndPassword " />
        <mx:method name="save" />
    </mx:RemoteObject>

</cairngorm:ServiceLocator>
```

Notice that RemoteObject will be using two methods: getByEmailAndPassword and save. These correspond with ColdFusion methods that we will be using for this service. The save method is already defined by the ColdFusion wizard. However, getByEmailAndPassword is a custom request and was not generated automatically for us by the wizard, so we will have to create it ourselves.

The getByEmailAndPassword method will allow us to search the database based on an e-mail address and a password. This service will essentially authenticate our user.

Open VideoList/components/cf/users/UsersDAO.cfc and add the following method:

```
<cffunction name="readByEmailPassword"
output="false" access="public"
returntype="VideoList.components.cf.users.Users">
    <cfargument name="emailAddess" required="true">
    <cfargument name="password" required="true">
    <cfset var qRead="">
    <cfset var obj="">

    <cfquery name="qRead" datasource="VideoList">
        select userId, userName, firstName,
        lastName, address, emailAddress,
        city, state, signupDate, password
```

```
            from dbo.Users
            where emailAddress =
<cfqueryparam cfsqltype="CF_SQL_VARCHAR" ➥
value="#arguments.emailAddess#" />
AND password =
<cfqueryparam cfsqltype="CF_SQL_VARCHAR" ➥
value="#arguments.password#" />
      </cfquery>

      <cfscript>
            obj = createObject("component", "VideoList. ➥
components.cf.users.Users").init();
            obj.setuserId(qRead.userId);
            obj.setuserName(qRead.userName);
            obj.setfirstName(qRead.firstName);
            obj.setlastName(qRead.lastName);
            obj.setaddress(qRead.address);
            obj.setemailAddress(qRead.emailAddress);
            obj.setcity(qRead.city);
            obj.setstate(qRead.state);
            obj.setsignupDate(qRead.signupDate);
            obj.setpassword(qRead.password);
            return obj;
      </cfscript>
</cffunction>
```

We also need to add a method in VideoList/components/cf/users/UsersDAO/UsersGateway.cfc:

```
<cffunction name="getByEmailAndPassword"
output="false" access="remote">
      <cfargument name="emailAddress" required="true" />
      <cfargument name="password" required="true" />
      <cfreturn createObject("component", "UsersDAO"). ➥
readByEmailPassword(arguments.emailAddress, ➥
arguments.password)>
</cffunction>
```

Next, we need to create our delegate. UserDelegate has to include the two methods for the purposes of this project; however, keep in mind that in the future if you need more methods related to the user information service, you can just add them to the same delegate.

Each method will represent a service call.

```
public function save(userInfo:UserInfoVO):void {
   var call:Object = service.save(userInfo);
   call.addResponder( responder );
}

public function getByEmailAndPassword(emailAddress:String, ➥
password:String):void {
```

**545**

```
    var call:Object = service.getByEmailAndPassword ➥
(emailAddress, password);
    call.addResponder( responder );
}
```

Here's the complete code:

```
package com.elromdesign.VideoList.business
{
    import com.adobe.cairngorm.business.ServiceLocator;
    import mx.rpc.IResponder;


    public final class UserDelegate
    {
        private var responder:IResponder;

        private var service:Object;

        public function UserDelegate(responder:IResponder)
        {
            service =  ServiceLocator.getInstance(). ➥
getRemoteObject(Services.USER_INFORMATION);
            this.responder = responder;
        }

        public function save(userInfo:UserInfoVO):void {
            var call:Object = service.save(userInfo);
            call.addResponder( responder );
        }

        public function getByEmailAndPassword ➥
(emailAddress:String, password:String):void {
            var call:Object = service.getByEmailAndPassword ➥
(emailAddress, password);
            call.addResponder( responder );
        }


    }
}
```

Lastly, we need to modify our commands so they can get an instance of the UserDelegate delegate and we can initiate the methods needed for each command. Once the delegate is initialized, we can pass a RemoteObject RPC request to ColdFusion in order to read and update the database.

In the GetUserInfoCommand class, replace the execute method with the following method to make the service request:

```
public function execute(event:CairngormEvent) : void
{
    var evt:GetUserInfoEvent = event as GetUserInfoEvent;
```

```
    var delegate:UserDelegate = new UserDelegate( this );
    delegate.getByEmailAndPassword(evt.emailAddress, evt.password);
}
```

We also need methods to handle successful responses. We can use explicit data binding to cast our data from the RemoteObject to UserInfoVO:

```
public function result(data:Object) : void
{
    var result:ResultEvent = data as ResultEvent;
    var userInfo:UserInfoVO = result.result as UserInfoVO;
}
```

Additionally, we want to store the user information as global information. To store the information across the application, we will be adding the VO to the model locator. Open ModelLocator.as and add userInfo. Notice we don't create a new instance of UserInfoVO so that we will be able to know when the user has logged in, since userInfo will stay null otherwise.

```
public var userInfo:UserInfoVO;
```

Now that we added the VO, we can update the model locator (ModelLocator.as) in the GetUserInfoCommand class:

```
private var model:ModelLocator = ModelLocator.getInstance();

public function result(data:Object) : void
{
    var result:ResultEvent = data as ResultEvent;
    var userInfo:UserInfoVO = result.result as UserInfoVO;

    if (userInfo.userId > 0)
    {
        model.userInfo = userInfo;
        model.signupRegistrationViewState = ➥
SignupRegistrationStates.SUCCESS_STATE;
    }
    else
    {
        Alert.show("User name or password are incorrect");
    }
}
```

We are trying to keep the code simple, so we are using an Alert box if the user doesn't exist or the password is incorrect. However, you can handle this in a more elegant way by creating another state on the view to handle fault requests.

To get SetUserInfoCommand to call the delegate, open VideoList/commands/SetUserInfoCommand.as and replace the execute method as well as add a result handler:

```
public function execute(event:CairngormEvent) : void
{
```

```
        var evt:SetUserInfoEvent = event as SetUserInfoEvent;
        var delegate:UserDelegate = new UserDelegate( this );
        delegate.save(evt.userInfo);
    }

    public function result(data:Object) : void
    {
        var result:ResultEvent = data as ResultEvent;
        var userInfo:UserInfoVO = result.result as UserInfoVO;

        model.userInfo = userInfo;
    }
```

The ColdFusion service component will respond by sending back the same object we submitted upon success so that we can set the client model to the user info data.

Make sure to add a failure handler for requests that fail. Add the following method to SetUserInfoCommand.as:

```
    public function fault(info:Object) : void
    {
        var fault:FaultEvent = info as FaultEvent;
        Alert.show(fault.toString());
    }
```

This section appears in the version of the project located in the VideoList/Step3 directory of the files you downloaded from the friends of ED site.

## Creating the view

Now that the model and controller classes are ready, we can create the UI (view) components to log in and register a new user. Create a new MXML component with a name of SignupRegistrationView.mxml and place it in the com.elromdesign.view package.

The SignupRegistrationView component will have three states:

**1.** Login

**2.** Registration

**3.** Success

We will bind the SignupRegistrationView component to a member in the model called registrationState. This class will allow us to change the state of the component without really changing anything in the component itself, keeping our code clean and easy to maintain.

Create a static enum class named VideoList.model.SignupRegistrationStates.as:

```
    package com.elromdesign.VideoList.model
    {
        public final class SignupRegistrationStates
        {
```

```
        public static const LOGIN_STATE:String = '';
        public static const REGISTRATION_STATE:String = 'Register';
        public static const SUCCESS_STATE:String = 'Success';
    }
}
```

Add the state property to the ModelLocator.as so we can store the state globally:

```
public var signupRegistrationViewState:String = '';
```

Notice that the state is set as equal to no string, which will point to the first state. You can achieve the same thing by setting the state property to the enum state:

```
public var signupRegistrationViewState:String = ➥
SignupRegistrationStates.LOGIN_STATE;
```

Once we make changes to the model, the view changes accordingly. We will set the model to be bindable to the view so that once the user signs up or registers, the state changes automatically.

To achieve this, we need to create a sequence so we can dispatch an event and change the model. Call the sequence setSignupRegistrationViewState, and use the Cairngen command create-sequence-exclude-delegate in the Ant perspective.

With this design, we are creating a stateful application that will change without the user refreshing his browser.

Once the Cairngen command is done, two classes are added for us: SetSignupRegistrationViewStateEvent and SetSignupRegistrationViewStateCommand. The event should pass the state and the command should update the model.

Open com.elromdesign.VideoList.SetSignupRegistrationViewStateEvent.as and add the state member:

```
public var state:String;
```

Next, change the default constructor:

```
public function SetSignupRegistrationViewStateEvent(state:String)
{
    this.state = state;
    super( SETSIGNUPREGISTRATIONVIEWSTATE_EVENT );
}
```

In the command class com.elromdesign.VideoList.SetSignupRegistrationViewStateCommand.as, update the model.

```
public function execute(event:CairngormEvent) : void
{
        var evt:SetSignupRegistrationViewStateEvent = ➥
event as SetSignupRegistrationViewStateEvent;
        model.signupRegistrationViewState = evt.state;
}
```

**549**

The sequence is now ready, and we will be able to update the state using SetSignupRegistrationViewStateEvent.

For the UI, create a new class named com.view.SignupRegistrationView.mxml. This class will have the three states and methods to invoke the commands. We didn't include validators or formatting since we wanted to keep it simple, but feel free and add them yourself (refer to Chapter 3 to learn more on how to add validators and formatting).

Set the current state to be bindable to the model so that we will be able to change the state by changing the model property:

```
<?xml version="1.0" encoding="utf-8"?>
<mx:Panel xmlns:mx="http://www.adobe.com/2006/mxml"
    width="386" height="232"
    currentState="{model.signupRegistrationViewState}">
```

Set a model property so we will be able to access the model locator and the login and submitForm methods to call the events we created earlier. We also add a method called getUserInfoVO, which will create a new instance of UserInfoVO and get the data from the form:

```
[Bindable]
private var model:ModelLocator = ModelLocator.getInstance();

// called once user submits registration information.
private function submitForm():void
{
    var userInfo:UserInfoVO = getUserInfoVO();

    new SetUserInfoEvent(userInfo).dispatch();
}

// called once user submits login information.
private function login():void
{
    new GetUserInfoEvent(loginEmailAdderss.text, ➥
loginPassword.text).dispatch();
}

// Create UserInfoVO based on information
// from the registration form.
private function getUserInfoVO():UserInfoVO
{
    var userInfo:UserInfoVO = new UserInfoVO();

    userInfo.userName = userName.text;
    userInfo.firstName = firstName.text;
    userInfo.lastName = lastName.text;
    userInfo.address = address.text;
    userInfo.city = city.text;
    userInfo.state = state.text;
```

```
    userInfo.emailAddress = emailAddress.text;
    userInfo.password = password.text;
    userInfo.signupDate = new Date();

    return userInfo;
}

// Change component state
private function changeState(state:String):void
{
    new SetSignupRegistrationViewStateEvent(state). ➥
dispatch();
}
```

Our default state is the login state:

```
<mx:HBox id="hbox1">
    <mx:Label text="Login Form"  x="10" y="10" id="label1"/>
</mx:HBox>

<mx:Form id="form1"
    width="292" height="110"
    x="10" y="36"
    horizontalScrollPolicy="off" verticalScrollPolicy="off">
    <mx:FormItem label="Email Address:" required="true">
        <mx:TextInput id="loginEmailAdderss"/>
    </mx:FormItem>
    <mx:FormItem label="Password" required="true">
        <mx:TextInput id="loginPassword"/>
    </mx:FormItem>
</mx:Form>
```

We need to add a button so we can switch between the login and the signup states:

```
<mx:ControlBar id="controlbar1">
    <mx:LinkButton id="registerLink"  label="Need to Register?"
        click="changeState(SignupRegistrationStates. ➥
REGISTRATION_STATE)"/>
    <mx:Spacer width="100%" />
    <mx:Button label="Submit" click="login()" id="button1"/>
</mx:ControlBar>
```

Next, create the registration and success states. To do that, we will be using the MXML states tags, and we can place the state tag inside as follows:

```
<mx:states>
        <mx:State name="Register" />
        <mx:State name="Success" />
</mx:states>
```

The registration state needs a form that includes all the properties with the user information:

```
<mx:State name="Register">

    <mx:SetProperty name="height" value="396"/>
    <mx:RemoveChild target="{form1}"/>

    <mx:AddChild relativeTo="{controlbar1}" position="before">
     <mx:Form width="292" height="270"
         horizontalScrollPolicy="off"
         verticalScrollPolicy="off">
       <mx:FormItem label="User Name:" required="true">
         <mx:TextInput id="userName"/>
       </mx:FormItem>
       <mx:FormItem label="First Name" required="true">
         <mx:TextInput id="firstName"/>
       </mx:FormItem>
       <mx:FormItem label="Last Name" required="true">
         <mx:TextInput id="lastName"/>
       </mx:FormItem>
       <mx:FormItem label="Address" required="true">
         <mx:TextInput id="address"/>
       </mx:FormItem>
       <mx:FormItem label="Email Address" required="true">
         <mx:TextInput id="emailAddress"/>
       </mx:FormItem>
       <mx:FormItem label="City" required="true">
         <mx:TextInput id="city"/>
       </mx:FormItem>
       <mx:FormItem label="State" required="true">
         <mx:TextInput id="state"/>
       </mx:FormItem>
       <mx:FormItem label="Password" required="true">
         <mx:TextInput id="password"/>
       </mx:FormItem>
     </mx:Form>
    </mx:AddChild>

    <mx:SetProperty target="{registerLink}" name="label"
        value="Already a member, login!"/>
    <mx:SetEventHandler target="{registerLink}" name="click"
        handler="changeState(SignupRegistrationStates.LOGIN_STATE)"/>
    <mx:SetProperty target="{label1}" name="text"
        value="Register"/>
    <mx:SetEventHandler target="{button1}"
        name="click" handler="submitForm()"/>
</mx:State>
```

The success state binds to the model `model.userInfo.firstName` and will display a welcome message:

```
<mx:State name="Success">
    <mx:RemoveChild target="{form1}"/>
    <mx:RemoveChild target="{label1}"/>
    <mx:RemoveChild target="{hbox1}"/>
    <mx:RemoveChild target="{registerLink}"/>
    <mx:RemoveChild target="{button1}"/>
    <mx:AddChild relativeTo="{controlbar1}" position="before">

    <mx:VBox height="100%" width="371">
        <mx:Spacer height="20" />
        <mx:Label text="Welcome {model.userInfo.firstName}, ➥
you are now signin."
            width="369" color="#FFFFFF"
            fontWeight="bold" fontSize="13"
            height="81"/>
</mx:VBox>
    </mx:AddChild>
</mx:State>
```

To run the application, we would need to attach this UI to our entry point: `VideoList.mxml`. Our entry point needs to have a reference to the front controller and the services; otherwise, our events will not be directed to the correct command, and the services will not be able to use the RPC component. Add the following components to `VideoList.mxml`:

```
<business:Services/>
<control:VideoListController />
```

We will be using the TabNavigator component to store different pages. Here's the complete code:

```
<?xml version="1.0" encoding="utf-8"?>
<mx:Application xmlns:mx="http://www.adobe.com/2006/mxml"
    layout="absolute"
    xmlns:business="com.elromdesign.VideoList.business.*"
    xmlns:control="com.elromdesign. ➥
VideoList.control.*"
    xmlns:view="com.elromdesign.VideoList.view.*">

    <business:Services/>
    <control:VideoListController />

    <mx:TabNavigator x="10" y="10" width="774" height="616">
        <mx:Canvas label="Videos" width="100%" height="100%">
        </mx:Canvas>

        <mx:Canvas label="Login/Registration" width="100%" height="100%">
            <view:SignupRegistrationView  x="50" y="50"/>
        </mx:Canvas>
        <mx:Canvas label="Upload Videos" width="100%" height="100%">
```

```
        </mx:Canvas>
    </mx:TabNavigator>

</mx:Application>
```

Run the application and try to register as well as log in. You can also place a line breakpoint in the different events and commands to get a better understanding of the application cycle.

To add a little twist, we will be using some open source templates to make our application look more appealing. Recall that I spoke about skins in Chapter 10, when I explained mashups. Here, we will be using a skin template that makes the application look like iTunes. Download the CSS styles and images from here: http://www.scalenine.com/themes/itunes7/itunes7.zip.

You can also choose different skins from here and see how your application changes: http://www.scalenine.com/gallery/index.php.

Unzip the folder and place the files here: VideoList/src/assets/css. Then place a reference in the entry point VideoList.mxml.

```
<mx:Style source="assets/css/jukebox.css" />
```

Compile and run the application (see Figure 14-22).

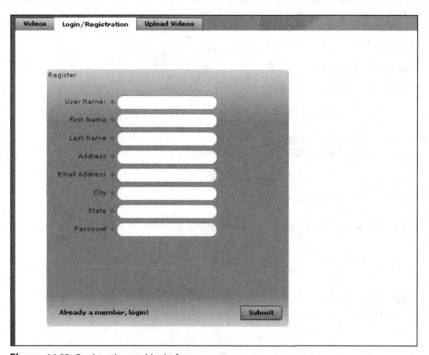

**Figure 14-22.** Registration and login forms

Everything we have done so far in our application appears in the version of the project located in the VideoList/Step4 directory of the files you downloaded from the friends of ED site.

# Uploading videos to the server

Our next task is to create a component so the user will be able to upload videos to the server. We will start by creating all the sequences we will need.

In tools/project.properties, set the sequence name and run the Ant command create-sequence-exclude-delegate:

```
sequence.name  = SetUserVideo, GetUserVideo, ➡
SetVideoInformation, SetFileUploadState
```

The command will generate the following classes:

- GetUserVideosCollection: Retrieves user and video information from the server
- SetUserVideosCollection: Saves a collection of users and videos
- SetFileUploadState: Changes the state of the video upload page

## Uploading files to the server sequences

In order to upload the video files to the server, we need to create a ColdFusion proxy that will handle the process of uploading the files. The client will pass the video ID and the file extension to the ColdFusion proxy, which will upload the video file and assign the concatenated video ID and extension as the file name. Using the VideoId as the file name is a way of ensuring that we don't have any duplicates since VideoId is a unique primary key in the Videos entity.

Create VideoFile.as in the following package: VideoList.utils. The class has one method to handle uploading files names, uploadFile, and event listeners to handle error messages.

```
package com.elromdesign.VideoList.utils
{
    import com.elromdesign.VideoList.events.SetFileUploadStateEvent;
    import com.elromdesign.VideoList.model.FileUploadState;
    import flash.events.Event;
    import flash.events.HTTPStatusEvent;
    import flash.events.IOErrorEvent;
    import flash.events.ProgressEvent;
    import flash.events.SecurityErrorEvent;
    import flash.net.FileReference;
    import flash.net.URLRequest;
    import flash.net.URLVariables;
    import mx.controls.Alert;

    public final class VideoFile
    {

        public function uploadFile(file:FileReference, videoId:int):void
        {
            var uploadURL:URLRequest = new URLRequest;
            var postVars:URLVariables = new ➡
URLVariables("videoId="+String(videoId)+"&fileType="+file.type);
```

```
        uploadURL.url = "http://localhost:8500/VideoList/ ➥
components/cf/utils/upload.cfm";
        uploadURL.method = "GET";
        uploadURL.data = postVars;
        uploadURL.contentType = "multipart/form-data";

        file.addEventListener(ProgressEvent.PROGRESS, ➥
progressHandler);
        file.addEventListener(Event.COMPLETE, completeHandler);
        file.addEventListener(Event.OPEN, openHandler);
        file.addEventListener(SecurityErrorEvent.SECURITY_ERROR, ➥
securityErrorHandler);
        file.addEventListener(IOErrorEvent.IO_ERROR,ioErrorHandler);
        file.addEventListener(HTTPStatusEvent.HTTP_STATUS, ➥
httpStatusHandler);
        file.upload(uploadURL);
    }

    private function completeHandler(event:Event):void
    {
        new SetFileUploadStateEvent(FileUploadState. ➥
UPLOAD_COMPLETED_STATE).dispatch();
    }

    private function openHandler(event:Event):void
    {
    }

    private function ioErrorHandler(event:IOErrorEvent):void
    {
        Alert.show(String(event),"ioError",0);
    }

    private function securityErrorHandler ➥
(event:SecurityErrorEvent):void
    {
        Alert.show(String(event),"Security Error",0);
    }

    private function httpStatusHandler(event:HTTPStatusEvent):void
    {
        if (event.status != 200)
        {
            Alert.show(String(event),"Error",0);
        }
    }

    private function progressHandler(event:ProgressEvent):void
    {
```

```
        trace(event.bytesLoaded,event.bytesTotal);
    }

  }
}
```

We also would need to create the ColdFusion proxy, VideoList/components/cf/utils/upload.cfm:

```
<!---
Upload file to server handler
--->

<cftry>

    <cffile action="upload"
            filefield="filedata"
            destination="#ExpandPath('\')#VideoList\src\assets\ ➥
usersVideos\#videoId##fileType#"
            nameconflict="makeunique"
            accept="application/octet-stream"/>

<!---
Any errors will be placed into an output pdf file.
--->
    <cfcatch type="any">
        <cfdocument format="PDF" overwrite="yes" ➥
filename="errordebug.pdf">
            <cfdump var="#cfcatch#"/>
        </cfdocument>
    </cfcatch>
</cftry>
```

As you can see from the script, the files that the proxy will generate will be placed in the src/assets/usersVideos directory. If this server causes any problems, a PDF file will be generated and placed in the output directory VideoList/bin-debug so we can debug any issues in ColdFusion.

Add the services we are using to the services class, VideoList/business/Services.mxml:

```
<?xml version="1.0" encoding="utf-8"?>
<cairngorm:ServiceLocator
        xmlns:mx="http://www.adobe.com/2006/mxml"
        xmlns:cairngorm="com.adobe.cairngorm.business.*">

    <mx:Script>
        <![CDATA[

            //todo: implement service constants
            public static const USER_INFORMATION: ➥
String = "userInformation";
            public static const VIDEO_INFORMATION: ➥
```

```
String = "videoInformation";
        public static const USER_VIDEO_COLLECTION:String = ➥
"userVideosCollection";

    ]]>
</mx:Script>

<mx:RemoteObject id="userInformation" destination="ColdFusion"
    source="VideoList.components.cf.users.UsersGateway">
    <mx:method name="getByEmailAndPassword" />
    <mx:method name="save" />
</mx:RemoteObject>

<mx:RemoteObject id="videoInformation" destination="ColdFusion"
    source="VideoList.components.cf.videos.VideosGateway">
    <mx:method name="getById" />
    <mx:method name="save" />
</mx:RemoteObject>

<mx:RemoteObject id="userVideosCollection" destination="ColdFusion"
    source="VideoList.components.cf.userVideosCollection. ➥
UsersVideosINTGateway">
    <mx:method name="getAllAsQuery" />
    <mx:method name="save" />
</mx:RemoteObject>

</cairngorm:ServiceLocator>
```

Add two delegates to handle the service, the first being UserVideosCollectionDelegate.as:

```
public function UserVideosCollectionDelegate(responder:IResponder)
{
    service = ServiceLocator.getInstance(). ➥
getRemoteObject(Services.USER_VIDEO_COLLECTION);
    this.responder = responder;
}

public function save(userVideosCollection: ➥
UserVideosCollectionVO):void {
            var call:Object = service.save(userVideosCollection);
            call.addResponder( responder );
}

public function getAllVideoByUser(userId:int):void {
            var call:Object = service.getAllAsQuery(userId);
            call.addResponder( responder );
}
```

And the second, VideoInformationDelegate.as:

```
public function VideoInformationDelegate(responder:IResponder)
{
    service = ServiceLocator.getInstance(). ➡
getRemoteObject(Services.VIDEO_INFORMATION);
    this.responder = responder;
}

public function save(videoInfo:VideoVO):void {
    var call:Object = service.save(videoInfo);
    call.addResponder( responder );
}

public function getAll():void {
    var call:Object = service.getAll();
    call.addResponder( responder );
}
```

Now we can create the events and commands to tie everything together.

SetVideoInformationEvent will receive the file to be uploaded and the VideoVO object to submit to the database.

```
public var videoInfo:VideoVO;
public var file:FileReference;

public function SetVideoInformationEvent(videoInfo:VideoVO, ➡
file:FileReference)
{
    this.videoInfo = videoInfo;
    this.file = file;
    super( SETVIDEOINFORMATION_EVENT );
}
```

And in the command SetVideoInformationCommand, we need to create a reference to the model and a variable to store the file.

```
private var model:ModelLocator = ModelLocator.getInstance();
private var file:FileReference;
```

The process is as follows. We first update the Videos entity in the database and get the primary key, videoId. Then we rename the file and upload the video to the server. Recall that the videoId property has a unique auto-increment primary key so that when the database is empty, the primary key will be 1, then 2, 3, 4, and so on. The user will submit a file, let's say movie.mp4. We will concatenate the primary key of the video with the file extension and upload it to the server. For instance, for primary key 1, we will store the file as 1.mp4.

Once the command is executed, we will pass the videoVO to the delegate, which will make the RPC service call:

```
public function execute(event:CairngormEvent) : void
{
    var evt:SetVideoInformationEvent =➡
event as SetVideoInformationEvent;
    var delegate:VideoInformationDelegate =➡
new VideoInformationDelegate( this );

    file = evt.file;
    delegate.save(evt.videoInfo);
}
```

When the service returns a successful response, we can extract the videoId and call the methods to upload the video. We also need to make another service call to insert the information into the UsersVideosINT entity in the database, so the video will be associated with the user, and we will be able to retrieve all the videos a user has uploaded. For that call, we will be using SetUserVideosCollectionCommand:

```
public function result(data:Object) : void
{
    var result:ResultEvent = data as ResultEvent;
    var video:VideoVO = result.result as VideoVO;

    uploadVideoToServer(video.videoId);

    setAsUserVideo(video.videoId);

    model.videosCollection.addItem(video);
}
```

Notice that we add the video to a collection on the model when the service responds. We want to keep the client model in sync with the server model so that we end up with a collection list of all the users' videos.

Remember to add a member on the ModelLocator:

```
public var videosCollection:ArrayCollection = new ArrayCollection();
```

Going back to SetVideoInformationCommand, we need to add a method to upload the video uploadVideoToServer to the server. We are calling a utility class to upload the video, and passing the file and the primary key.

```
private function uploadVideoToServer(videoId:int):void
{
    var videoFile:VideoFile = new VideoFile();
    videoFile.uploadFile(file, videoId);
}
```

Next let's create the setAsUserVideo method. setAsUserVideo is called from the result method and in turn calls the delegate:

```
private function setAsUserVideo(videoId:int):void
{
    var userVideosCollection:UserVideosCollectionVO = ➡
new UserVideosCollectionVO();

    userVideosCollection.userId = model.userInfo.userId;
    userVideosCollection.videoId = videoId;

    new SetUserVideosCollectionCommand().execute( new ➡
SetUserVideosCollectionEvent(userVideosCollection) );
}
```

Notice that we are calling the command and not the event, since we are already in the SetVideoInformationCommand command, so there is no need to go through the front controller again.

In SetUserVideosCollectionCommand, we will make a call to the service in order to save the information in the database:

```
public function execute(event:CairngormEvent) : void
{
    var evt:SetUserVideosCollectionEvent = ➡
event as SetUserVideosCollectionEvent;
    var delegate:UserVideosCollectionDelegate = ➡
new UserVideosCollectionDelegate( this );
    delegate.save(evt.userVideosCollection);
}
```

In SetUserVideosCollectionCommand, we need to create a result method so we can assign the results to the model. Once the model has a list of the videos users have uploaded, we can create a user interface that displays all the videos uploaded by each user.

```
public function result(data:Object) : void
{
    var result:ResultEvent = data as ResultEvent;
    var userVideosCollection:UserVideosCollectionVO = ➡
result.result as UserVideosCollectionVO;

}
```

## The uploading videos view

The uploading videos view will have two states: one for uploading a video and another that will give the user a message once the video has been successfully uploaded to the server (see Figure 14-23).

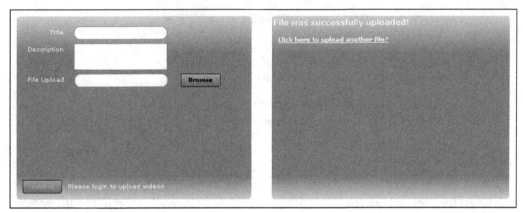

**Figure 14-23.** Upload file user interface

First, create a new MXML component, FileUploadForm, and place it in the view package.

As you can see from Figure 14-23, the component has two states: upload completed state and upload file state. Once a user uploads a video successfully, we use the upload completed state:

```
<mx:states>
    <mx:State name="UploadCompleted">
        <mx:RemoveChild target="{button1}"/>
        <mx:RemoveChild target="{formitem1}"/>
        <mx:RemoveChild target="{formitem2}"/>
        <mx:RemoveChild target="{formitem3}"/>
        <mx:RemoveChild target="{button2}"/>
        <mx:RemoveChild target="{formitem4}"/>
        <mx:RemoveChild target="{hbox1}"/>
        <mx:RemoveChild target="{form1}"/>
        <mx:AddChild relativeTo="{controlbar1}" position="before">
            <mx:Label text="File was successfully uploaded!"
                color="#FFFFFF"
                fontWeight="bold" fontSize="13"/>
        </mx:AddChild>
        <mx:AddChild relativeTo="{controlbar1}" position="before">
        <mx:LinkButton label="Click here to upload another file?"
            color="#FEFEFE" textDecoration="underline"
            click="new SetFileUploadStateEvent ➥
(FileUploadState.UPLOAD_FILE_STATE).dispatch();"/>
        </mx:AddChild>
    </mx:State>
</mx:states>
```

The default state is the upload file state:

```
<mx:Form width="388" height="263" id="form1">
    <mx:FormItem label="Title" id="formitem1" color="#FFFFFF">
        <mx:TextInput id="videoTitle" />
    </mx:FormItem>
    <mx:FormItem label="Description" id="formitem2" color="#FFFFFF">
        <mx:TextArea id="description" />
    </mx:FormItem>
    <mx:HBox id="hbox1">
        <mx:FormItem label="File Upload"
            id="formitem3" color="#FFFFFF">
            <mx:TextInput id="uploadFileURL" editable="false"/>
        </mx:FormItem>
        <mx:FormItem id="formitem4">
            <mx:Button label="Browse" click="browseFiles()"
                buttonMode="true"  id="button2"/>
        </mx:FormItem>
    </mx:HBox>
</mx:Form>
<mx:ControlBar id="controlbar1">
    <mx:Button label="Submit" click="submit()"
        buttonMode="true"  id="button1"
        enabled="{model.userInfo == null ? false : true }"/>
    <mx:Label text="Please login to upload videos"
        width="209" color="#FFFFFF"
        visible="{model.userInfo == null ? true : false }"/>
</mx:ControlBar>
```

Notice that we insert a bindable reference to the model userInfo:

```
{model.userInfo == null ? false : true }
```

We want to enforce a condition that the user can upload a video only after logging in.

Next, we need to create the methods to handle the browse operation, to upload a video file, and to submit the results.

To browse for a file, we use the FileReference class, which opens a browser window. We only want to look for files that the Flash Player can play; recall that the new Flash Player can handle files with the extensions .mp4, .flv, .mov, and .3gp, so we will be using the FileFilter class to filter the files we can select:

```
public var videoTypes:FileFilter = new FileFilter
("Flash Video Files (*.flv; *.mp4; *.mov; *.3gp)", ➥
"*.flv;  *.mp4; *.mov; *.3gp");
```

The complete methods are as follows:

```
private var fileref:FileReferenceList = new FileReferenceList();
public var videoTypes:FileFilter = new FileFilter("Flash Video Files ➥
(*.flv; *.mp4; *.mov; *.3gp)","*.flv;  *.mp4; *.mov; *.3gp");

private var filefilter:Array = new Array(videoTypes);
private var file:FileReference = new FileReference;

[Bindable]
private var model:ModelLocator = ModelLocator.getInstance();

private function browseFiles():void
{
    fileref.addEventListener(Event.SELECT, ➥
selectFileEventHandler);
    fileref.browse(filefilter);
}

private function selectFileEventHandler(event:Event):void {
    file = FileReference(event.currentTarget.fileList[0]);
    uploadFileURL.text = event.currentTarget.fileList[0].name;
}

private function submit():void
{
    new SetVideoInformationEvent(getVideoVO(), file).dispatch();
}

private function getVideoVO():VideoVO
{
    var video:VideoVO = new VideoVO();
    video.active = 1;
    video.description = description.text;
    video.title = videoTitle.text;
    video.publishDate = new Date();

    return video;
}
```

We should also create a static class to hold the different states, just as we did with the signup/ registration components, so that we will be able to change the state by updating the model.

```
package com.elromdesign.VideoList.model
{
    public final class FileUploadState
    {
```

```
        public static const UPLOAD_FILE_STATE:String = '';
        public static const UPLOAD_COMPLETED_STATE: ➥
    String = 'UploadCompleted';
        }
    }
```

Assign a string to store the state in the model locator com.elromdesign.VideoList.model: ModelLocator:

```
    public var fileUploadState:String = '';
```

Also assign the current state as a bindable reference from the model in the FileUploadForm.mxml view. What will happen is that changes in the model will change the state of the view component automatically:

```
    <mx:Panel xmlns:mx="http://www.adobe.com/2006/mxml"
            width="400" height="300"
            currentState="{model.fileUploadState}">
```

Create a sequence so you will be able to update the model state. Call the sequence SetFileUploadState.

Once the classes are created, implement the execute method in the SetFileUploadStateCommand command:

```
    public function execute(event:CairngormEvent) : void
    {
        var evt:SetFileUploadStateEvent = event as ➥
    SetFileUploadStateEvent;
        model.fileUploadState = evt.fileUploadState;
    }
```

The event, of course, will pass the state SetFileUploadStateEvent:

```
    public var fileUploadState:String;

    public function SetFileUploadStateEvent(fileUploadState:String)
    {
        this.fileUploadState = fileUploadState;
        super( SETFILEUPLOADSTATE_EVENT );
    }
```

Run the application, and you will be able to upload a video after you log in to your account (see Figure 14-24). The complete code for the project up to this point is located under the VideoList/Step5 directory.

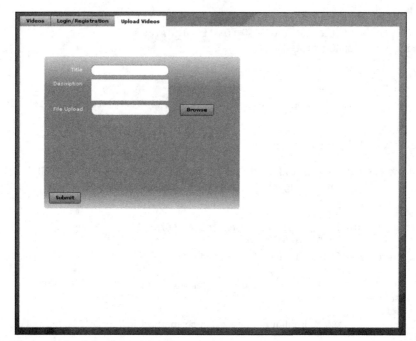

**Figure 14-24.** Uploading a video file

# Displaying videos in a List component

Now that the user can create an account, upload videos, and insert information about each video, we want to create a component that will display all the videos that are available. To achieve this, we will create a list component that holds thumbnails. Once the user clicks a thumbnail for a particular video, that video will play automatically.

## Displaying video list sequence

We first need to create a sequence that will return collections of all the videos in the database. Name the sequence getAllVideos. After the code is generated, we are ready to implement the command.

```
public function execute(event:CairngormEvent) : void
{
    var evt:getAllVideosEvent = event as getAllVideosEvent;
    var delegate:VideoInformationDelegate = ➥
new VideoInformationDelegate( this );
    delegate.getAll();
}

public function result(data:Object) : void
{
              var result:ResultEvent = data as ResultEvent;
}
```

Next, let's call the event from our entry point VideoList.mxml and place it in the Application tag of the view. So once you run the application, the videos will be uploaded at startup:

```
preinitialize="new getAllVideosEvent().dispatch()"
```

The complete Application tag is shown here:

```
<mx:Application xmlns:mx="http://www.adobe.com/2006/mxml"
    layout="absolute"
    xmlns:business="com.elromdesign.VideoList.business.*"
    xmlns:control="com.elromdesign.VideoList.control.*"
    xmlns:view="com.elromdesign.VideoList.view.*"
    preinitialize="new GetAllVideosEvent().dispatch()">
```

Then place a debug line breakpoint in the result method so we can watch the results we are getting back from the server.

Debug the application, and you will be able to view the results in the Variable view, as you can see in Figure 14-25.

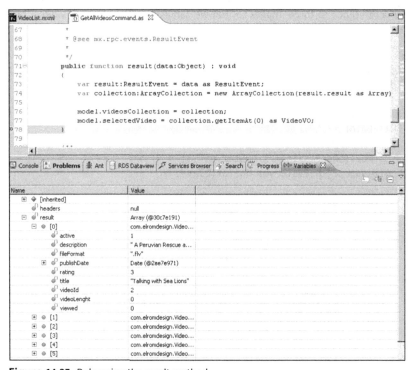

**Figure 14-25.** Debugging the result method

As you can see from Figure 14-25, result is an object collection that contains all the videos in the database, where each video is a videoVO. We can use the results just the way they are and cast them as an ArrayCollection and then assign them to the model, as shown here:

```
private var model:ModelLocator = ModelLocator.getInstance();

public function result(data:Object) : void
{
    var result:ResultEvent = data as ResultEvent;
    model.videosCollection = result.result as ArrayCollection;
}
```

## Creating the view

For the view, we will be using a data grid component. The results will be rendered by VideoRatingRenderer.mxml, which will be using VideoRatingStar.mxml to draw the stars for the rating.

- VideoRatingStar.mxml: Component that will be used by VideoRatingRenderer to display stars

- VideosDataGrid.mxml: Component that includes a DataGrid component to display the videos

- VideoRatingRenderer.mxml: Component that will render the columns of the DataGrid component

Let's start by creating the VideoRatingStar.mxml component. Create an MXML file. Name it VideoRatingStar.mxml, and place it in the com.elromdesign.VideoList.view package. The component will have a reference to three images so that we can assign a star to each video. The component also has three states that will set the image:

```
<?xml version="1.0" encoding="utf-8"?>
<mx:Canvas xmlns:mx="http://www.adobe.com/2006/mxml"
    width="20" height="20" currentState="noStar">

    <mx:Script>
      <![CDATA[

        [Embed("assets/images/noStar.gif")]
        [Bindable] private var noStar:Class;

        [Embed("assets/images/halfStar.gif")]
        [Bindable] private var halfStar:Class;

        [Embed("assets/images/fullStar.gif")]
        [Bindable] private var fullStar:Class;

        // states types
        public static const NO_STAR:String = "noStar";
        public static const HALF_STAR:String = "halfStar";
        public static const FULL_STAR:String = "fullStar";

      ]]>
    </mx:Script>

    <mx:Image id="starImage" height="20" width="20" />

    <mx:states>
      <mx:State name="noStar">
```

```
        <mx:SetProperty target="{starImage}"
            name="source" value="{noStar}" />
    </mx:State>
    <mx:State name="halfStar">
        <mx:SetProperty target="{starImage}"
            name="source" value="{halfStar}" />
    </mx:State>
    <mx:State name="fullStar">
        <mx:SetProperty target="{starImage}"
            name="source" value="{fullStar}" />
    </mx:State>
</mx:states>


</mx:Canvas>
```

Next, we create the VideosDataGrid.mxml component. The component will be used by the grid to render columns with VideoRatingRenderer. Create an MXML file. Name it VideosDataGrid.mxml, and place it in the com.elromdesign.VideoList.view package.

We will use the mx:DataGrid component. Bind the data provider to the model dataProvider="{model.videosCollection}" to include all the videos from all the users; binding the model will ensure that any changes to the collection will be displayed.

```
<mx:DataGrid width="330" height="536" x="0" y="0"
    dataProvider="{model.videosCollection}"
    selectedIndex="0">
    <mx:columns>
        <mx:DataGridColumn headerText="Video" >
            <mx:itemRenderer>
                <mx:Component>
                    <mx:VBox verticalGap="2" paddingLeft="5"
                        horizontalScrollPolicy="off"
                        verticalScrollPolicy="off">

                        <mx:Canvas>
                            <mx:VideoDisplay
                                source="{'assets/usersVideos/'+data. ➥
videoId+data.fileFormat}"
                                width="100" height="100" autoPlay="true"
                                playheadUpdate="event.target.stop();" />
                        </mx:Canvas>

                        <mx:Label text="{data.title}" />
                    </mx:VBox>
                </mx:Component>
            </mx:itemRenderer>
        </mx:DataGridColumn>

        <mx:DataGridColumn headerText="Rating" width="125"
            itemRenderer="com.elromdesign.VideoList.view. ➥
```

```
    VideoRatingRenderer"/>

    </mx:columns>
</mx:DataGrid>
```

Notice that in one of the columns, we use a VideoDisplay component so users can see the available videos.

The data provider is videosCollection, which includes a collection of VideoVOs. We will use the information to generate the URL of the location of the videos:

```
source="{'assets/usersVideos/'+data.videoId+data.fileFormat}"
```

Our next view component is VideoRatingRenderer.mxml. We will be using this component to set the rating and generate the star. The component consists of a setter and getter as well as a switch conditional to check the stars left to display:

```
<?xml version="1.0" encoding="utf-8"?>
<mx:HBox xmlns:mx="http://www.adobe.com/2006/mxml"
    horizontalGap="2"
    width="100%" height="100%"
    horizontalAlign="center"
    verticalAlign="middle">

    <mx:Script>
      <![CDATA[

          private var _data:Object;

        override public function set data(value:Object):void
        {
           var rating:Number = Number(value.rating);
           var videoStar:VideoRatingStar;
           var starState:String;

           _data = value;
           this.removeAllChildren();

           for(var i:int = 0; i<5; i++)
           {
              starState = VideoRatingStar.NO_STAR;
              videoStar = new VideoRatingStar();

              if (rating >= 1)
              {
                 starState = VideoRatingStar.FULL_STAR;
                 rating -= 1;
              }
              else if (rating <= 0.5 && rating > 0)
              {
```

```
            starState = VideoRatingStar.HALF_STAR;
            rating -= 0.5;
         }

         videoStar.currentState = starState;
         this.addChild(videoStar);
      }
   }

   override public function get data():Object
   {
      return _data;
   }
}

]]>
</mx:Script>


</mx:HBox>
```

Since we haven't built the UI to vote for videos or enter ratings, we can upload videos and edit the entries directly in the database using Microsoft SQL Server Management Studio Express (see Figure 14-26) or using phpMyAdmin if you used a MySQL database.

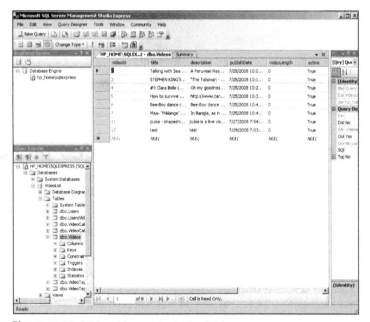

**Figure 14-26.** Editing video entries in the database

Compile and run the application, and you can see the results in Figure 14-27. The complete code we just built is under the VideoList/Step6 directory.

**Figure 14-27.** DataGrid component result

# Creating an H.264 high-definition video player

As mentioned at the start of this chapter, the Flash Player supports the H.264 video format (also known as MPEG-4). This makes use of the H.264 encoding, which is next-generation video compression technology.

MPEG-4 is an industry standard for video and includes HD capability. It is used for HD content online, on 3G mobile devices, and on HD broadcast technologies such as Blu-ray.

Flash Player 9 Update 3 also supports a new audio format called Advanced Audio Coding (AAC), which is a higher-quality audio file format designed to replace the MP3 format. We are not building a music player so we will not be using this file format, but it's worth mentioning that AAC is the standard audio format defined in MPEG-4.

Flash Player 9 Update 3 supports HE-AAC version 2. This is an extension of AAC that uses spectral band replication (SBR) as well as parametric stereo (PS) techniques to increase coding efficiency while keeping low bit rates.

*AAC is a high-efficiency (HE) and high-fidelity (hi-fi) low-bandwidth audio codec used today in devices such as Apple's iPod and Sony's PlayStation 3. AAC is also used in Adobe's editing tools for audio and video such as Adobe Premiere Pro, Adobe After Effects, Adobe Soundbooth, and Adobe Audition, so you can start leveraging these tools with Flex.*

In order to start using these new file formats, we can either use the VideoDisplay component, which is shipped with Flex, or we can create our own custom component. Our application allows using the MPEG-4 file format so we can already upload MP4 videos and play them.

In the previous section, we created a DataGrid component. Once the user clicks the component, we want to display the selected video. Let's start by creating a sequence called setSelectedVideo. This sequence will update the ModelLocator once the user selects a video.

In the event setSelectedVideoEvent, add a property called video to store the video that was selected in the DataGrid component.

```
public var video:VideoVO;
```

And change the default constructor:

```
public function setSelectedVideoIdEvent(video:VideoVO)
{
   this.video = video;
   super( SETSELECTEDVIDEOID_EVENT );
}
```

The command setSelectedVideoCommand will update the model:

```
public function execute(event:CairngormEvent) : void
{
   var evt:setSelectedVideoEvent = event as setSelectedVideoEvent;
   model.selectedVideo = evt.video;
}
```

Of course, add the member to the ModelLocator:

```
public var selectedVideo:VideoVO;
```

Once the application first starts, we want to assign the first video, so change the GetAllVideosCommand:result method:

```
model.selectedVideo = collection.getItemAt(0) as VideoVO;
```

Now we just need to make changes to the view, VideoDataGrid.mxml. Once a thumbnail is selected, the setSelectedVideoEvent event will be dispatched:

In VideoDataGrid.mxml, add a change event:

```
<mx:DataGrid width="330" height="536" x="0" y="0"
      dataProvider="{model.videosCollection}"
      selectedIndex="0" change="itemClicked(event)" >
```

Now in VideoDataGrid.mxml, create a method to handle click events, which will use the event we created.

```
    private function itemClicked(event:Event):void
    {
        var listData:Object = event as Object;
        var index:int = listData.rowIndex;
        var video:VideoVO = model.videosCollection. ➥
    getItemAt(index) as VideoVO;

        new setSelectedVideoEvent(video).dispatch();
    }
```

In the VideoList.src.com.elromdesign.VideoList.view package, create a new MXML component for the video component and name it VideoPlayerView.mxml.

Add a VideoDisplay component with a reference to the model to play the video:

```
    <?xml version="1.0" encoding="utf-8"?>
    <mx:Canvas xmlns:mx="http://www.adobe.com/2006/mxml"
        width="400" height="520">

        <mx:Script>
            <![CDATA[
                import com.elromdesign.VideoList.model.ModelLocator;

                [Bindable]
                private var model:ModelLocator = ModelLocator.getInstance();

            ]]>
        </mx:Script>

        <mx:VideoDisplay x="10" y="10" width="370" height="225"
            source="{'assets/usersVideos/'+ ➥
    String(model.selectedVideo.videoId)+ ➥
    model.selectedVideo.fileFormat}"
            autoPlay="true"/>

        <mx:VBox x="10" y="250" width="370" borderStyle="solid">
            <mx:Label text="{model.selectedVideo.title}" />
            <mx:TextArea text="{model.selectedVideo.description}"
                width="368" borderThickness="0"/>
        </mx:VBox>

    </mx:Canvas>
```

Run the application, and you will be able to view the first video as well as select other videos, as shown in Figure 14-28.

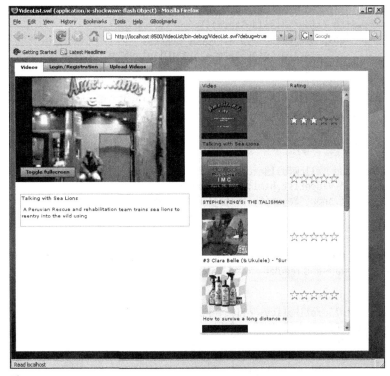

**Figure 14-28.** Video component

Since we can use MPEG-4 HD videos, we should add a small feature to enhance the user experience: a full-screen toggle button so the user can view the video in full-screen mode.

To display in full-screen mode, we use StageDisplayState:

```
import mx.core.Application;
stage.displayState = StageDisplayState.FULL_SCREEN;
```

We can also set the size and the location of the full screen by creating a rectangle and using video properties. The stage.fullScreenSourceRect method will use the VideoDisplay component size and location when users toggle to full screen so they can see only video on the screen.

```
var screenRectangle:Rectangle = new Rectangle ➡
(video.x, video.y, video.width, video.height);
stage.fullScreenSourceRect = screenRectangle;
```

Here's the complete method:

```
private function toggleFullScreen():void {

    var screenRectangle:Rectangle = ➡
new Rectangle(video.x, video.y, video.width, video.height);
    stage.fullScreenSourceRect = screenRectangle;
```

```
        try {
            switch (stage.displayState) {
                case StageDisplayState.FULL_SCREEN:
                    stage.displayState = StageDisplayState.NORMAL;
                    break;
                default:
                    stage.displayState = StageDisplayState.FULL_SCREEN;
                    break;
            }
        } catch (err:SecurityError)
        {
            // add "allowfullscreen", "true"
            // in VideoList.html:AC_FL_RunContent
            Alert.show("SecurityError: Full screen mode is not allowed.");
        }
    }
```

We need to replace the VideoDisplay tag with the following script, which adds a button to toggle between full-screen state and regular-screen state:

```
<mx:Canvas id="video"
    horizontalScrollPolicy="off" verticalScrollPolicy="off">
    <mx:VideoDisplay width="370" height="225"
        source="{'assets/usersVideos/' ➥
+String(model.selectedVideo.videoId) ➥
+model.selectedVideo.fileFormat}"
        autoPlay="true"/>
    <mx:Button label="Toggle fullscreen"
        click="toggleFullScreen()"
        y="193" x="10"/>
</mx:Canvas>
```

If you try to run the script and toggle to full mode, you will get an error message. The reason is that you need to add a parameter in the HTML wrapper. Open VideoList/bin-debug/VideoList.html and change the Flash object to include allowfullscreen:

```
AC_FL_RunContent(
    "src", "VideoList",
    "width", "100%",
    "height", "100%",
    "align", "middle",
    "id", "VideoList",
    "quality", "high",
    "bgcolor", "#869ca7",
    "name", "VideoList",
    "allowfullscreen", "true"
    "allowScriptAccess","sameDomain",
    "type", "application/x-shockwave-flash",
    "pluginspage", "http://www.adobe.com/go/getflashplayer"
);
```

Make sure that you stop the application from creating an HTML wrapper; otherwise, it will overwrite the file, and you will have to add allowfullscreen each time you clean and compile your project.

Right-click the project and select Properties ➤ Flex compiler. Uncheck the Generate HTML wrapper file option.

Compile and run the application to toggle between full-screen and regular-screen mode. The complete code is listed under the VideoList/Step7 directory.

# Summary

In this chapter, I showed you hands-on techniques for creating a Flex HD video application. Using Cairngorm to build a large enterprise application with many user interactions as well as many services at first glance seems to require more effort but actually yields better maintainability and scalability.

I showed you how to create a complete application, building both the client and the remote server components, and in the process gave you the knowledge to develop complete, large-scale Flex applications.

I covered the data layer by designing, configuring, and creating a Microsoft SQL database as well as a MySQL database. I also demonstrated configuring MS SQL Server to "talk" to ColdFusion so the model can be updated easily and quickly through an AMF connection.

You learned to use best practices in ColdFusion to generate services as well as create custom components to fit the exact needs of the project.

Building the application presentation layer, you saw how to create the view component for the application to display a list of videos, the upload page, and the video component.

Finally, you explored the new features Flash Video has to offer with new file formats and HD capabilities. If you like, continue working on the application, using more services and building new presentation components to add and extend more exciting features. Have fun with it!

## Chapter 15

# USING 3D IN FLEX

By Joshua Mostafa

3D in Flex is an exciting field to be working in at the moment. It's moving very fast: there are several major 3D APIs to choose from, most of which are themselves moving rapidly forward; and developments in the Flash platform itself promise advancements. This does, however, make it a bit tricky to keep up!

## 3D on the Web

Until the release of Flash Player 10, 3D rendering in Flex was all handled by software. The move to AVM2 (the interpreter for bytecode generated from AS3, as opposed to AVM1, which is for AS2) delivered some significant performance gains.

But it is still many times less powerful than the hardware-accelerated 3D to which we have become accustomed in games for the PC and for consoles. There, the number crunching is handled by the graphics processor, which is optimized to handle these kinds of operations (that's why graphics cards are sold as "3D" cards).

### Knowing your (VM's) limitations

When everything is done in software, it's a different story. The calculations required for 3D rendering and animation have to compete for CPU cycles with all the other things your Flex app may be doing. You can't re-create a full Halo 3– or even Quake-style game in a Flex app and expect the Flash Player to handle the number of polygons involved. Results vary depending on processor speed and the 3D library you choose, but don't expect the Flash Player to handle more than a few thousand polygons without getting sluggish and unresponsive.

Things are set to change somewhat with the forthcoming release of Flash Player 10. Certain basic 3D properties can be set *natively* on sprites and manipulated at runtime: rotations in 3D space, for instance, and shading. This means that the rendering math is taken care of by hardware, which does a much better job of it, leaving the Flash Player free to handle all the other things your Flex app requires.

The 3D capabilities of Flash Player 10, though, are likely to be pretty basic. Don't expect a fully immersive world, with cameras, z-index management, and so on. You will need to look at one of the software libraries such as Papervision3D to manage that. However, it may be that all your Flex app needs is little touches of 3D to jazz up its look and feel. If so, the native capabilities of Flash Player 10 are likely to be the best option for you.

## Choosing the right tools for the job

At the other end of the scale, you may be looking to give your users a full-fledged, immersive 3D experience with highly detailed textures and lots of visual complexity. Some use cases for this would be a first-person shooter game, or a Second Life–style virtual world. I would not really recommend the Flash Player (and thus Flex) as the most appropriate platform for this; it just isn't up to it. You could consider writing for the Unity3D platform; although it has the disadvantage of requiring users to install a browser plug-in that they are unlikely to have already, it does mean that they are getting a "real" 3D experience, powered by OpenGL hardware acceleration.

Where the AS3 3D libraries come into their own is the space between these two extremes: creative use of 3D, perhaps in combination with 2D elements, to enable an experience that, while not trying to compete with PlayStation, engages the user and provides new graphical possibilities.

# 3D and HID

As in much software development, the issues in system design coalesce not so much around what is *possible* but what is *desirable*. The kinds of human interface you can create using 3D are almost unlimited. However, you should be guided by exactly the same usability principles as apply to a 2D human interface.

In most cases, that means keeping the controls simple, intuitive, and familiar. There are of course edge cases. If you're building a specialized application that demands sophisticated control from the user—software for building SketchUp models, for instance—you might need a fully immersive 3D world, and consider bundling it with specialized hardware such as the "WiiMote" controller for Nintendo's Wii game console, which can be used as an input to a Flex app thanks to the open source WiiFlash project, and allows tracking of movements in 3D space. But in the context of a web site or a web application, it doesn't make sense to disorient the user. 3D—like any other UI tool at your disposal—should be the means, not the end in itself.

This may seem like an obvious point, but the fact is that working in 3D is a lot of fun for the developer and has a certain "wow" factor that makes it very tempting to throw it in gratuitously. Resist that temptation! Use it where it really makes sense.

# 3D and AS3

One of the most mature APIs (relatively—there is no such thing as a really mature 3D API in AS3) is Papervision3D. It's open source, and has a fairly stable 1.0 version. At the time of writing, the 2.0 version is officially an alpha release, and changes are being made rapidly. This is known informally as the "Great White" branch. (There is also an "Effects" branch that for a while contained some of the most interesting features, such as separate render layers that can have filters and effects applied to them—but most of the functionality from there is currently being ported to Great White.)

The Away3D library was originally a branch of Papervision3D; it split away some time ago to pursue a slightly different set of development objectives. In specific, the handling of z-order (which object should appear "in front" of another) was a problem in Papervision3D at the time of the fork. The two libraries still share a lot of architecture and syntax. They have also ported improvements from each other's codebase over time. Other libraries include Alternativa3D, Sandy, and Five3D (this last one does not provide a full 3D environment; it's a specialist library for easily drawing vector shapes in 3D space and has utilities for working with 3D typography).

## The 3D world

Before starting to build our example app, it's worthwhile establishing some basic 3D concepts. These should apply regardless of which library you opt for.

The **3D coordinates** are represented by X, Y, and Z: the distances, along each axis, are measured from a hypothetical 0,0,0 point in 3D space. The Y axis is easy to remember: it's the same as in 2D space (up-and-down). The X axis is also similar to its corresponding 2D axis (left-and-right). The new one to consider is the Z axis (forward-and-backward). Right, up, and forward are positive (greater than zero); left, down, and backward are negative (less than zero).

## 3D animation

Your 3D environment won't be very engaging unless something in it moves, whether that's the 3D sprites themselves or the user's viewpoint. In fact, it's only by movement that we can create the illusion of 3D. Otherwise, users could assume they are looking at a prerendered bitmap image.

My own favorite is the TweenLite family of classes, an open source AS3 animation API. There are three variants of this, of which TweenLite is, as the name suggests, the most lightweight, and TweenMax the most feature-rich (TweenFilterLite is the median between the two). I tend to use TweenMax; it offers sophisticated controls like Bezier curves for the tween paths (you can use this on the camera object of a 3D scene to create dramatic sweeps of viewpoint). In my opinion these features are worth the weight, and I'll be using TweenMax in these examples. You can find all three at GreenSock (http://greensock.com).

## Content creation

There are some very sophisticated tools out there to create 3D models and shapes. Although some 3D AS3 libraries (notably Papervision3D) have made considerable effort to parse a variety of formats, don't assume that your favorite tool's default format is supported. In my experience, the process of importing 3D models is still pretty hit-and-miss. The Collada format is the most extensively supported; in fact, the ASCollada project, used by Papervision3D, is actually a separate project that just concentrates on using the Collada format in AS3.

# The brief

Here is our hypothetical brief (based on a real brief for a project developed for a client, albeit in a simplified form).

The good people at Client X want to create a web site to show off their stock of high-tech gadgets, with 3D elements to engage the user and make their site stand out. They don't want to make the whole web site 3D, because they feel (rightly) that this would compromise usability; most of the actual content, such as the catalog of products, will be delivered in traditional 2D panels.

But neither do they want to make the 3D element just an intro (of the notorious Flash "skip intro" style of fluff). So they want the navigation between the various sections to be where the 3D comes in. The user zooms through 3D space, and arrives at a panel which then becomes the normal 2D display of the information. To make things easier, there is a menu that always stays onscreen with the various parts of the site (product catalog, company information, contact form, etc.).

# Papervision3D and Flex

For this example, we'll be using the Papervision3D API but not because it's necessarily the best. Each of the alternative systems has its own advantages and disadvantages: for instance, Away3D began life as a fork of the Papervision3D codebase, in part to provide a more accurate z-ordering of objects (i.e., which objects appear in front of others), and it still has the edge in that aspect. But Papervision3D has a far bigger user base than any of the alternatives, and although documentation is still quite basic, there are plenty of tutorials online: especially important if, like me, you're not a 3D expert to begin with. Also, it has a broad API with a lot of the features we'll need for an immersive 3D user experience.

You will immediately hit upon a problem when you try to put a Viewport3D object (i.e., the "window" into 3D space) into a Flex app. Since it does not implement IUIComponent, it cannot be added directly using addChild(). You will find the same problem with the BasicView class, a class that includes viewport, camera, and render engine all together as a convenience.

Help is at hand with the use of the CanvasView3D class, originally developed by "Xero" Harrison of the.fontvir.us (http://the.fontvir.us). This class wraps BasicView, and it *does* implement IUIComponent. You can add it to the canvas much as you would any other Flex component, with addChild().

## Shapes in space

Papervision3D comes with some prebuilt shapes to make your life easier: Plane, Cone, Cylinder, Cube, Sphere, etc. These classes can be found in the org.papervision3d.objects.primitives package. They allow someone (such as myself) who has little understanding of 3D geometry to quickly create some 3D shapes and add them to the scene. (You can also create your own complex shapes using TriangleMesh3D—if you want to get really creative.) All these classes extend the basic DisplayObject3D class.

To start with, let's create a red square and put it in our 3D space. I assume you have already added your CanvasView3D component and given it an ID of view3d. Add an attribute plane with type Plane to your application, and then have this code execute sometime after adding your scene:

```
var redMaterial:ColorMaterial = new ColorMaterial(0xffffff);
redMaterial.doubleSided = true;
plane = new Plane(redMaterial, 50, 50, 3, 3);
view3d.scene.addChild(plane);
```

Let's look at that line by line. First we set up a material—what Papervision3D uses to fill in the shape. A ColorMaterial is a very simple material that shows a block color: just use the hex value of the color you want as the constructor argument. There are many other materials you can use here: MovieMaterial, which uses the bitmap data from a (2D) DisplayObject as the fill; VideoStreamMaterial, which uses video data; and various "shader" materials that allow for lighting effects. You'll find the material classes in the org.papervision3d.materials package.

On the next line, we tell Papervision3D that we want the material to show up on whichever side we look at (otherwise our square will disappear if we rotate it too far).

Then we create the square itself, using the Plane class. The first argument determines the material to use. The next two tell it the dimensions of the square (width and height). The final two represent the number of segments to use to build the square. These numbers are important because they give you control over the trade-off between performance and quality. Too few segments and you might see unnatural-looking artifacts (uneven edges, for instance) when the Plane object is rendered. Too many—at least if you have many Plane objects, or objects of other DisplayObject3D-derived classes, all with too many segments—means that Papervision3D has to work harder to render, which will result in sluggish performance. So keep these figures as few as you can get away with, without visible quality degradation.

Finally, you add the Plane object to the scene. Note that you don't add it to the CanvasView3D object itself; you use the scene attribute. This addChild() method takes an argument of type DisplayObject3D, rather than IUIComponent.

You might not be able to see your red square immediately. Move your camera backward a little to make sure that you haven't put your Plane object in the same spot as the camera:

```
view3d.camera.z = -500;
```

Remember that Z is the forward-and-backward axis in 3D space; the extra dimension we add to the familiar X and Y. So -500 means to move back by 500.

So we have a red square. Great. But it looks pretty similar to a 2D square at the moment. Let's animate it to prove to ourselves that our square "lives" in the 3D world. Make your app listen to Event.ENTER_FRAME events with this handler method:

```
private function handleEnterFrame(event:Event):void {
plane.rotationZ += 2;
plane.rotationX += 3;
plane.rotationY += 4;
}
```

Movement! Makes all the difference. Try commenting out all but each of the lines in turn to get a feel for what each type of rotation looks like. I remember which of these is which by imagining a line along, say, the Y axis (up-and-down), and the 3D object attached to it like part of a child's hanging collage, or a single wind chime. The object can rotate only *around* the line. The same goes for the X and Z axes.

# Inside the sphere

Back to our hypothetical project brief. Let's say that the graphic design concept given to us by the designer consists of the inside of a sphere, with many small squares arranged along the surface of the sphere. Some of these squares are used for the site navigation, some are merely decoration. There is also a 2D menu bar along the top of the screen to make it easy to access the different elements, so that the impatient user can ignore the 3D elements and still get to the content.

First we need to generate the coordinates for each piece of our sphere. Because the viewpoint is intended to be within the sphere, we can leave our camera at the zero point (0,0,0) and arrange the squares around it.

Here we need to get into a bit of 3D geometry to find out the locations of the squares. If, like me, you have only hazy memories of math at school, don't worry! There are plenty of resources on the Web where you can find the equations you need—you don't need to understand them fully, you just need to know where to apply them. Wikipedia is a good place to start, especially for the math novice. If, on the other hand, geometry comes naturally to you—well, you're lucky.

The calculations we need, to locate a given square at a radius distance $r$ from the center of the sphere, are these:

```
x = Math.cos(theta) *Math.sin(phi)r
y = Math.sin(theta) * Math.sin(phi)r
z = Math.cos(phi)* r
```

We can arrive at the values theta and phi using these functions, given the total number of points we are calculating (i.e., how many squares we are going to attach to our square) and the index of the particular square we are dealing with at present:

```
private function getPhi(index:Number, total:Number):Number {
return Math.acos(-1 + (2 * index - 1) / total);
}

private function getTheta(phi:Number, total:Number):Number {
return Math.sqrt(total * Math.PI) * phi;
}
```

So, to create our sphere nav, we don't really need to use Papervision3D's Sphere primitive; we can just add the squares at the right positions and the sphere shape will be suggested. Just make sure you get all the squares to point in toward the center (where the camera is); you can use the lookAt() method to achieve this.

# Interactivity: Getting the user involved

Now, we have our user's viewpoint inside the sphere, but he needs to be able to look around to see all sides. Let's say we're using the camera type FreeCamera3D, which allows you to move the camera around exactly like any other 3D object. (Another option is the Camera3D class, which can be used to track a specific object and "hover" around it, reacting to the movement of the mouse. It's a great effect, but not exactly what we want here—the elements need to stay equidistant from the camera.)

As the user moves the mouse, the camera should turn up or down (rotations around the X axis: rotationX) or left or right (rotations around the Y axis: rotationY) depending on what edge of the screen the mouse is nearest. The movement should be quite subtle for most of the screen; only when the user is near the edge should it move quickly. We don't want to disorient him.

Try calling this method each frame—use the argument to make a stronger or a softer motion.

```
protected function adjustCameraByMouse(speed:Number):void {
    var camera:FreeCamera3D = view3d.camera;
  camera.rotationX += (stage.mouseX / stage.stageWidth - .5) * speed;
  camera.rotationY += (stage.mouseY / stage.stageHeight - .5) * speed;
}
```

You will also need to trap the user's clicks of the squares. When the user clicks one of the squares that act as navigation, your app needs to know about it.

It's a very similar technique to what you're used to in Flex; just the event type is different. For each of your squares, listen for events thus:

```
plane.addEventHandler(InteractiveScene3DEvent.OBJECT_PRESS,
    handlePlanePress);
```

There are other event types too in the InteractiveScene3DEvent class: OBJECT_RELEASE, OBJECT_OVER, OBJECT_OUT, and so on.

The main thing we want to do, once the user has clicked one of the squares, is to "fly" the camera up to that square and close up on it. At the same time, we will have a 2D element (this can be a normal Flex component) that starts off the same color as the square that appears over the top of it; then its contents (other components, text, whatever is required for that section of the web site) can alpha-fade up. This sleight-of-hand allows us to transition smoothly from 3D to 2D.

To make this happen, we'll need to animate the camera to just in front of the square, so it's close. Now, what does "just in front" mean? Considering that our camera starts off at the zero position—and the center of the sphere—it means that we will be somewhere along the (imaginary) radius line between the center of the sphere and the square.

That's a good thing! It means we can use the same math we used earlier to work out where to put the squares: getPhi(), getTheta(), and so on. We'll use a slightly shorter radius than the radius of the circle, and the index of the square itself (i.e., how far along the for loop that we used to populate the sphere with squares)—it might be a good idea to save the index when we populate, for ease of reference. There's a handy little attribute called extra you can use to store arbitrary data on any DisplayObject3D.

Use a Number3D object (which just houses the three coordinates used to represent a point in 3D space) to store the coordinates you calculate. Let's call it cameraDestination. Then just animate the camera:

```
TweenMax.to(view3d.camera, 2, {
    x : cameraDestination.x,
    y : cameraDestination.y,
    z : cameraDestination.z
    ease : Regular.easeInOut
});
```

**585**

## Lighting and shading

Papervision3D lets you set up a light source and use it to apply shading to your 3D objects—provided they are using the appropriate kind of material (such as FlatShaderMaterial or PhongMaterial).

To create the light source, just create a LightObject3D, add it to the scene, and position it:

```
var lightSource:LightObject3D = new LightObject3D();
view3d.scene.addChild(lightSource);
lightSource.y = 800;
```

Then, modify the code where the squares are set up. Instead of a ColorMaterial, use a FlatShadeMaterial. And use the light source object you set up previously as its first constructor argument:

```
var material:FlatShadeMaterial = new FlatShadeMaterial(
lightSource, 0xeeeeee, 0x666666);
```

The two hex numbers represent the lightest possible and darkest possible colors. Which of them, or what proportions of both are used to create the shade, depends on the angle of the shape containing the material, in relation to the light source.

# Summary

In this chapter, we've taken a high-level look at the available tools for 3D in Flex; then we've zoomed in on the basic techniques you need to get to grips with the 3D space, populate with some objects, and manipulate them.

3D in Flex is an exciting and fast-moving field. New experiments and techniques are pioneered almost daily: just sign up to the mailing lists of Papervision3D or Away3D to keep track of progress. The concepts in this chapter, though, should stand you in good stead to embark on your own 3D projects. Unless you're doing this purely for fun, though, remember the needs of the client. Sometimes less is more—use your imagination, just don't let it run away with you!

# INDEX

# D

**607**

# friendsofed.com/forums

Join the friends of ED forums to find out more about our books, discover useful technology tips and tricks, or get a helping hand on a challenging project. *Designer to Designer*™ is what it's all about—our community sharing ideas and inspiring each other. In the friends of ED forums, you'll find a wide range of topics to discuss, so look around, find a forum, and dive right in!

- **Books and Information**

  Chat about friends of ED books, gossip about the community, or even tell us some bad jokes!

- **Flash**

  Discuss design issues, ActionScript, dynamic content, and video and sound.

- **Web Design**

  From front-end frustrations to back-end blight, share your problems and your knowledge here.

- **Site Check**

  Show off your work or get new ideas.

- **Digital Imagery**

  Create eye candy with Photoshop, Fireworks, Illustrator, and FreeHand.

- **ArchivED**

  Browse through an archive of old questions and answers.

---

### HOW TO PARTICIPATE

Go to the friends of ED forums at **www.friendsofed.com/forums**.

---

Visit **www.friendsofed.com** to get the latest on our books, find out what's going on in the community, and discover some of the slickest sites online today!

friendsof ED™

DESIGNER TO DESIGNER™

*an Apress® company*